Mayflower Marriages

George Ernest Bowman, ca. 1897

Mayflower Marriages

FROM THE FILES OF GEORGE ERNEST BOWMAN
At the Massachusetts Society of Mayflower Descendants

by
Susan E. Roser

Genealogical Publishing Co., Inc.

Contents

Preface

George Ernest Bowman (1860-1941) is a well known and respected name in the field of Mayflower research. In 1896 he founded the Massachusetts Society of Mayflower Descendants and served as Secretary, Genealogist and Editor for 45 years, until 1941. He was the Editor of the **Mayflower Descendant,** a quarterly genealogical magazine specializing in primary source material, published between 1899 and 1937. In his book, **Plymouth Colony, Its History & People 1620-1691,** Eugene A. Stratton, FASG, former Historian General of the General Society of Mayflower Descendants, pays tribute to Bowman:

> *The greatest genealogical scholar of Plymouth Colony was George Ernest Bowman . . . He left a living legacy in the Mayflower Descendant, a timeless and unsurpassed collection of original records of the people of colonial Plymouth. Moreover, he left a methodology for precision in acquiring data that has been all too little appreciated in the past, but has been gaining recognition with time.*

Mr. Bowman was a dedicated and disciplined genealogist whose goal was to trace the ancestry of each Mayflower family right up to present-day descendants. Either he did not fully appreciate the enormity of the research involved or he had extremely high expectations of himself (probably the latter), in any case, his goal was never realized although he spent almost half a century trying. Referring to his work as The Mayflower Genealogies, he did manage to accumulate approximately 20,600 pages containing probate, court, church and bible records, cemetery inscriptions, wills, charts, lineages and documentation. The Massachusetts Society admits some of his work "has been superseded by research done since 1941, but the collection remains the largest documented manuscript resource on Mayflower genealogy."

In 1983 the Society filmed the collection on microfiche. The Bowman Files, as it is now referred to, consists of 229 microfiche cards, grouped by family name, with each card containing approximately 96 handwritten and typed pages.

Mayflower Marriages is a compilation of marriages extracted and transcribed from these Files. It is hoped that by printing Mr. Bowman's research it will be more accessible to researchers and therefore provide assistance in the advancement of Mayflower research; after all, wasn't that Mr. Bowman's lifelong objective?

Introduction

Bowman's **Mayflower Marriages** contains upwards of 10,000 entries and spans five centuries. The format used is easy to follow and is compatible with the Bowman Files themselves. Within each family, microfiche numbers are given to indicate where the marriages can be found; if additional research on a family is desired, refer to the microfiche number in the Files. Wherever possible, data has been transcribed in the order found to ensure easier reference.

The majority of the Mayflower marriages are accompanied by line of descent as found in the Files, thus enabling the reader to trace a genealogy through marriage. A name which is accompanied by a name in brackets can be followed back to the first generation. Simply backtrack to find the entries for each preceding bracketed name. Third generation names will not be accompanied by a bracketed name because they are listed under a second generation heading. Line of descent for a non-Mayflower name is shown back to the *first* generation in certain cases where the surname could be confused with a similar Mayflower descent surname (e.g. p. 242, Barnabas Winslow was descended not from Edward Winslow but his brother Kenelm, therefore Barnabas is not of Mayflower descent). Inter-marriage among Mayflower descendants is shown with the descent of the partner back to the *second* generation. A name that does not include Mayflower line of descent does not necessarily mean that the person in question does not have Mayflower descent, only that it is not shown as so in the Files.

Although chapter titles read, for example, "Stephen Hopkins Descendants," not all names found in this chapter are descendants of Stephen Hopkins. When researching vital records Bowman quite often copied all entries with similar surnames, possibly for future reference. (For example, Hopkins fiche #12 contains a list of 65 Hopkins marriages in Boston.)

Guidelines were used in deciding what data would be transcribed from the Files. With a few exceptions, a name was not extracted if the husband's surname or wife's maiden name was not known, unless the woman was a widow (e.g. Sarah ( ) Alden is used but not Sarah ( )). In an effort to provide as much genealogical data as possible, marriage partners are given with an approximate date, or without a date if one was not available. In the tracing of ancestry the confirmation of a marriage between two people is vital in compiling a lineage and should not be omitted because the date is unknown. Partners are also included who were not married but had a child together. Some might say these particular cases have no place in a book of marriages, but the fact that no marriage record would ever be found by even the most zealous ancestor hunter is proof that they should be included.

Several points should be mentioned in order to assist the less experienced genealogist. First is the variation in name spellings. Names were recorded the way they sounded; the correct spelling was not a high priority (e.g. Haward/Howard/Hayward). Surnames were often altered from generation to generation (e.g. Thompson-Thomson-Tomson). Christian names are not spared either; Zerviah and Zeruiah are often confused, and Aphelia could turn up as Nephele. In addition, name spellings within the Files are sometimes inconsistent; a name may vary from one page to the next with no explanation given. Keeping these facts in mind, be sure to check all possible variations when searching for a particular name. The terms "Mrs." and "Jr." or "Sr." were not always used in the same context as they are today. As well as referring to father and son, Jr. and Sr. were used in order to distinguish between two unrelated men of the same name. The term Mrs. not only applied to married women but single women of high standing. If a woman is shown in the Files as Mrs. Mary Brown, with no indication as to which is the case, it should be remembered that she could be either Mary (   ) Brown, widow or Mary Brown, single.

Abbreviated source listings are given as found, and in some cases, particularly family genealogies, the exact source is not detailed (e.g. "White Genealogy"—further elaboration as to which White Genealogy is not given. Microfiche #2 of the White file lists 15 different White Genealogies). If more detail is required in identifying vital records or genealogies it is suggested the reader refer to the microfiche file number in question for possible clues. Where an approximate date is given (c1697; pre 9 May 1736, etc.) an accompanying source refers to the determination of said date through the death of a previous spouse, birth of a first child, etc., and is not necessarily a confirmation of the name of the marriage partner.

Mayflower genealogical research increases both in volume and worth with each passing year. In the past 50 years facts have been uncovered that eluded Bowman. Two such examples must be mentioned here as the errors are repeated throughout the Files in the lines of descent. First is the Alden Family where it is shown that **Mary Alden** married Thomas Delano. It is now known that it was not Mary but Rebecca Alden who married Delano. In extracting the marriages, the line of descent for the Delano line has been changed to accommodate this correction although in the Files the line is shown to be through Mary. The second significant case is in the **Cooke Family** with the children of Jane Cooke and Experience Mitchell. While Bowman attributes all eight Mitchell children to Jane, further research has uncovered the probability that only two, Thomas and Elizabeth, were Jane's children. Descendants of the remainder of the Mitchell children appear frequently throughout the Files as they very often married a Mayflower descendant, so the line of descent, while still included here, has been amended to show non-Mayflower descent from Experience Mitchell, not Jane Cooke. In addition to the suggested reading on p. 152, the reader may wish to consult Robert S. Wakefield, "Not All the Children of Experience Mitchell are Mayflower Descendants," TAG 59:28 and Merton T. Goodrich, "Gaining Experience—A Problem in the Mitchell Family," TAG 12:193.

It is necessary to take many things into consideration when transcribing hand-written research. The handwriting of Bowman and his assistants must sometimes be closely scrutinized. If a name was difficult to ascertain it is shown here as Lydia Seurs/Leurs, Hannah Scales(sp), etc. The use of a pencil versus a pen is an issue that must not be ignored. According to the Massachusetts Society, Bowman used a pencil if he was unsure of his data. While this does indeed appear to be true, quite often it is obvious that he did not discriminate between the pen and pencil. Penciled data on one page appears in pen on the following page; entire lists of vital records, deeds, probate data, etc., were copied in pencil as well as pen. If a chart is sparse with data and contains only a penciled spouse, then the assumption must be made that a great deal of research had not been done on this family; and the possibility exists that the data was not prop-erly verified by Bowman. Instead of omitting the data, it would be of more benefit to include it with the word "poss . . ." so the researcher would have a clue as to what could very possibly be the correct information. At the same time, if a chart is filled with both pen and penciled data, including all or most vital dates, with sources, then one must assume research has been done on this family, so there is no reason to question penciled data unless Bowman himself has raised the question. (Quite often the data is verified elsewhere in the Files.) If he has suggested the data is questionable, or used a question mark with the entry, it is included here (e.g. Rebecca (Keen?) Thacher) or discussed in footnotes. In both cases, whether the use of "poss . . ." or "?", keep in mind the data is not necessarily incorrect, but at the time it was found to be inconclu-sive, with further research needed.

As with any undertaking of such immense proportions, the Bowman Files are not without error, and although Bowman was, and still is, a recognized expert in the area of Mayflower research, he was not infallible. For this reason, the Files, as well as this book, cannot be cited for documentation to gain acceptance into the General Society of Mayflower Descendants. However, sources cited within each may be used.

Susan E. Roser

I wish to acknowledge the Massachusetts Society of Mayflower Descendants for their kindness in allowing the Bowman Files to be transcribed, and, in particular, Alicia C. Williams, State Historian and Editor of the **Mayflower Descendant** for her interest and helpful suggestions. And for his unequivocal support—thanks to my hus-band Hugh.

JOHN ALDEN DESCENDANTS

Daniel ALDEN^4 (Jos.$^{3-2}$) and 2nd Mrs. Rebecca CANTICE, 30 Mar. 1762, Stafford CT

Zephaniah ALDEN and 2nd Hannah FOSTER, 19 July 1750, Stafford CT

Zephaniah ALDEN and 3rd Mrs. Ann(a) DIMMOCK, 8 Apr. 1778, Stafford CT

Ezra ALDEN^5 (Eleazer^4, Jos.$^{3-2}$) and 1st Miriam RICHARDSON, 16 Oct. 1760, Stafford

Ezra ALDEN^5 (Eleazer^4) and 2nd Sarah (RUGGLES) Harwood

Rev. Abishai ALDEN^6 (Jos.^{5}, Dan.^{4}, Jos.$^{3-2}$) and Mrs. Eliza PARKER, 16 Aug. 1782,
Wilmington CT

Fear ALDEN^6 (--, John^3, Jos.^{2}) and David GLAZIER, 18 Sept. 1794, Wilmington CT

Irene ALDEN and Joseph MERICK, 21 Oct. 1796, Wilmington CT

Sarah ALDEN^2 and Alexander STANDISH^2

David ALDEN^2 (John^1)

David ALDEN^2 and Mary SOUTHWORTH

Alice ALDEN^3 and Judah PADDOCK, 5 Dec. 1706, Duxbury (MD 9:108)

Rebecca PADDOCK^4 (Alice Alden^3) and Thomas SPOONER, 10 June 1742

Samuel PADDOCK^4 (Alice Alden^3) and Thankful HOWES, 1744

Grace PADDOCK^4 (Alice Alden^3) and John SEARS, Int. 15 Feb. 1733/34, Harwich (MD 19:55)

David SEARS^5 (Grace Paddock^4) and Phebe TAYLOR^6 (John^5, Abigail Hopkins^4, Joshua^3,
Gyles^2), 8 Apr. 1773, Eastham

Rebecca SEARS and Robert WHEELER, 12 Oct. 1797 (Int.- Hampden ME VR 1:323)

Catharine S. WHEELER and Josiah BABCOCK, 7 Nov. 1853, ME

Rebecca S. WHEELER and Isaac WILKINS, 26 Aug. 1852, ME

Mary Ann WHEELER and John Francis STILSON, 23 Apr. 1854, ME

Emma WHEELER and Manly HARDY, 24 Dec. 1862, ME

Capt. Williard WHEELER and Bethiah FREEMAN, 16 Feb. 1830 (Int.- Hampden ME VR 2:318)

Rhoda SEARS^5 (Grace Paddock^4) and Stevens ATWOOD, 12 July 1772, Boston (Rcd.Com.30:432)

Mary PADDOCK^4 (Alice Alden^3) and Judah SEARS

Benjamin ALDEN^3 and Hannah BREWSTER^4 (Wrestling^3, Love^2), betw. 3 Oct. 1707 -
1 Jan. 1709/10 (MD 10:185, 20:115)

Bezaleel ALDEN^4 (Ben.^{3}) and Lydia BARTLETT, 22 Dec. 1748, Duxbury (VR:211,217)

Elizabeth ALDEN^3 and John SEABURY, 9 Dec. 1697, Duxbury (MD 9:108)

Sarah SEABURY and William MORGAN, 24 Sept. 1747, Groton CT (VR1:116)

David SEABURY^4 (Eliz. Alden^3) and Abigail SEABURY^4 (Sam.$^{3-2}$, John^1), 3 Jan. 1726/27,
    Duxbury (MD 11:240)

Abigail SEABURY^5 (David^4) and 1st John MASON, 14 Feb. 1761 (N. Yarmouth ME VR)

Patience MASON^6 (Abigail Seabury^5) and John OAKES, 16 Jan. 1781 (N. Yarmouth ME VR)

Abigail OAKES^7 (Patience Mason^6) and Nathaniel STAPLES, c1800-1805

Micro #2 of 16

Nathaniel King STAPLES^8 (Abigail Oakes^7) and Susan Staples CONANT, poss. Temple ME

Rachael Hoyt STAPLES^9 (Nath.^{8}) and George Washington MOORE, 29 Aug. 1868, Temple (VR)

George Albert MOORE^{10} (Rachael Staples^9) and Grace Briston HARRINGTON, 8 Oct. 1902

Patience SEABURY^4 (Eliz. Alden^3) and Joseph LATHAM, 28 Nov. 1722, Groton CT (VR 1:124)

Priscilla ALDEN^3 and Samuel CHEESBOROUGH, 4 Jan. 1699, Duxbury (MD 9:109)

Amos CHEESBOROUGH^4 (Prisc. Alden^3) and Desire WILLIAMS, 2 Dec. 1729, Stonington CT
    (VR 1:129)

Priscilla CHEESBOROUGH^4 (Prisc. Alden^3) and 1st Jabez CHEESBOROUGH, 26 Dec. 1723,
    Stonington CT (VR 2:19)

Priscilla CHEESBOROUGH^4 and 2nd Thomas PALMER, aft. 13 June 1731

Prudence CHEESBOROUGH^4 (Prisc. Alden^3) and John STANTON, 27 Feb. 1736/37, Groton CT
    (VR 1:181)

Ruth ALDEN^3 and Samuel SPRAGUE, 29 Nov. 1694, Duxbury (MD 9:25)

Ruth SPRAGUE^4 (Ruth Alden^3) and Israel HAMMOND, Int. 24 Mar. 1732/33, Rochester
    (VR 2:153, 290)$^{<1>}$

Elizabeth SPRAGUE^4 (Ruth Alden^3) and Isaac CHAPMAN, 20 May 1720, Rochester (VR 2:71)

Micah SPRAGUE^4 (Ruth Alden^3) and Elizabeth TURNER, 22 Aug. 1731, Rochester (VR)

Ruth SPRAGUE^5 (Micah^4) and Benjamin BUMPAS, 15 Jan. 1756, Rochester (Bailey's Plym.
    Co. Mgs.:188)

Nathaniel SPRAGUE^5 (Nath.^{4}, Ruth Alden^3) and 1st Mary BASSETT, 28 May 1769, Rochester

Nathaniel SPRAGUE^5 and 2nd Elizabeth HAMMOND, Int. 10 Dec. 1772, Rochester

Noah SPRAGUE^4 (Ruth Alden^3) and Sarah HAMMOND, 26 Apr. 1722, Rochester (VR)

Noah SPRAGUE^5 (Noah^4) and Mercy DEXTER, Int. 20 Nov. 1756, Rochester (VR 2:163)

Priscilla SPRAGUE^4 (Ruth Alden^3) and 1st Benjamin HAMMOND, 12 Nov. 1730, Rochester

Priscilla SPRAGUE^4 and 2nd Rev. Thomas WEST, 30 Nov. 1763, Rochester (VR)

Samuel SPRAGUE^4 (Ruth Alden^3) and Anna BARLOW $^{<2>}$

Anna BARLOW and 2nd Samuel WING, 1 Jan. 1728/29, Rochester (VR)

Samuel ALDEN^3 and Sarah SPRAGUE, 26 Feb. 1727/28, Duxbury (MD 11:80)

Alethea ALDEN^4 (Sam.^{3}) and William LORING (MD 20:76)

Rebecca ALDEN^4 (Sam.^{3}) and Thomas FRAZIER, 27 Nov. 1760, Duxbury (VR)

Elizabeth ALDEN^2 (John^1)

Elizabeth ALDEN^2 and William PABODIE, 26 Dec. 1644, Duxbury (MD 8:231)

Elizabeth PABODIE^3 and John ROGERS^3 (John^2), Nov. 1666, Duxbury (MD 8:232)

Hannah PABODIE^3 and 1st Samuel BARTLETT^4 (Ben.^{3}, Mary Warren^2), 2 Aug. 1683
    Duxbury (MD 8:232)

Hannah PABODIE^3 and 2nd Sergt. John CHURCHILL, 4 Mar. 1715, Plymouth (MD 14:37)

Lydia PABODIE^3 and Daniel GRINELL, c1683 (MD 6:130)

Sarah GRINELL^4 (Lydia Pabodie^3) and John BROOKS, 29 Apr. 1717, Saybrook CT (VR2:410)

George GRINELL^4 (Lydia Pabodie^3) and Mary BULL, 31 Jan. 1725/26, Saybrook CT

Lydia GRINNELL^4 (Lydia Pabodie^3) and Joseph CLARK, 25 Sept. 1712, Saybrook CT (VR2:540)

Jospeh CLARK^5 (Lydia Grinnell^4) and Lydia (   ), 9 Nov. 1749, Haddam (LR 5:276)

Mary GRINNELL^4 (Lydia Pabodie^3) and Robert LAY, 12 Dec. 1703, Saybrook CT (VR2:168)

Jerusha LAY and Robert ELY, 28 Apr. 1768, Saybrook CT (VR 2:225)

Priscilla GRINNELL^4 (Lydia Pabodie^3) and Theophilus REDFIELD, 24 Dec. 1706, Killings-
    worth CT

Martha PABODIE^3 and 1st Samuel SEABURY^2 (John^1), 4 Apr. 1677, Duxbury (MD 8:232)

Martha PABODIE^3 and 2nd William FOBES, c1682 (MD 6:131)

Elizabeth SEABURY^3 (Sam.^{2}, John^1) and 1st Joseph CHILDS, c1690 (MD 6:19)

Elizabeth SEABURY^3 and 2nd Laurance CRANE, 31 July 1718, Marshfield (MD 7:133)

Priscilla CHILDS and Shubael TINKHAM, 17 Dec. 1718, Marshfield (MD 7:131)

Richard CHILDS and Elizabeth CROCKER, c1678 (MD 4:120)

Samuel SEABURY^2 (John^1) and 1st Patience KEMP, 16 Nov. 1660, Duxbury (MD 8:232)

Samuel SEABURY^3 (Sam.^{2}, John^1) and Abigail ALLEN, 13 Dec. 1688, Duxbury (MD 9:24)

Samuel SEABURY^4 (Sam.$^{3-2}$, John^1) and Deborah WISWALL^4 (Priscilla Pabodie^3), 21 Oct. 1717,
    Duxbury (MD 11:25)

Barnabas SEABURY^4 (Sam.$^{3-2}$, John^1) and 1st Mary JOHNSON, c1722 (MD 15:91)

Joseph SEABURY^4 (Martha Pabodie^3) and 1st Phebe SMITH, 25 Sept. 1701, Little Compton (VR)

Elizabeth SEABURY^5 (Jos.^{4}, Martha Pabodie^3) and Daniel ALLEN, 16 Oct. 1751, Dartmouth
    (VR 2:435)

Humphrey ALLEN^6 (Eliz. Seabury^5) and Phebe BURGES, 17 July 1775, Dartmouth (VR2:612)

Humphrey ALLEN^6 (Eliz. Seabury^5) and Phebe BURGES, 17 July 1775, Dartmouth (VR2:612)

Martha SEABURY^4 (Martha Pabodie^3) and Josiah SAWYER, 20 Dec. 1705, Little Compton (VR1:3)

Constant FOBES^4 (Martha Pabodie^3) and John LITTLE^4 (Ephraim^3, Anna Warren^2),

    8 Apr. 1708, Little Compton

Elizabeth FOBES^4 (Martha Pabodie^3) and William BRIGGS, 10 June 1708, Little Compton (VR)

<u>Micro #4 of 16</u>

Isaac SIMMONS^4 (Mercy Pabodie^3) and Martha CHANDLER, c1695 (MD 8:178, 12:108)

Isaac SIMMONS^4 and 2nd Elizabeth SAMS/SAMMS, 11 May 1737, Duxbury (Gen. Adv. 1:108)

Isaac SIMMONS^5 (Isaac^4) and Lydia CUSHMAN, 24 Oct. 1732, Duxbury (MD 11:81)

Jehiel SIMMONS^6 (Isaac^5) and Rhoda STETSON, 10 Apr. 1764, Scituate (MD 1:234)

Levi SIMMONS^6 (Isaac^5) and Lydia SEARS/LEURS(sp), 10 Oct. 1765, Marshfield (VR)

John SIMMONS^4 (Mercy Pabodie^3) and Susanna TRACY, 4 Nov. 1715, Duxbury (MD 11:24)

Joseph SIMMONS^4 (Mercy Pabodie^3) and Mary WESTON, 8 Feb. 1709/10, Duxbury (MD11:23)

Rebecca SIMMONS^5 (Jos.^{4}) and Reuben PETERSON^4 (Jonathan^3, Mary Soule^2),

    6 July 1732, Duxbury (MD 11:80)

Jedediah SIMMONS^5 (Jos.^{4}) and Lydia SOULE^5 (John^4, Joshua^3, John^2), 23 Aug. 1750,

    Duxbury (VR)

Nathaniel SIMMONS^5 (Jos.^{4}) and Mercy SIMMONS^5 (Moses^4, Mercy Pabodie^3), 12 June 1739,

    Duxbury (MD 11:82)

Joseph SIMMONS^6 (Nathaniel^5) and Elizabeth CHAMBERLIN^6 (Job^5, Mary Soule^4, Aaron^3,

    John^2)

Nancy RICHARDS^6 (Hannah^5, Ben. Simmons^4, Mercy Pabodie^3) and George James YATES

Rizpah RICHARDS^6 (Hannah^5) and John MITCHELL^5 (Lydia Hatch^4, Sam.^{3}, Mary Doty^2)

William RICHARDS^6 (Hannah^5) and Ruth BRYANT

Joshua SIMMONS^4 (Mercy Pabodie^3) and Sarah DELANO^4 (Eliz. Standish^3, Alexander^2),

    4 Apr. 1728, Duxbury (MD 11:80)

Martha SIMMONS^4 (Mercy Pabodie^3) and 1st Ebenezer DELANO^3 (Philip$^{2-1}$), 29 Dec. 1699,

    Duxbury (MD 9:109)

Martha SIMMONS^4 and 2nd Samuel WEST, 20 June 1709, Duxbury (MD 9:26)

Joshua DELANO^5 (Martha Simmons^4) and Hopestill PETERSON^4 (Jonathan^3, Mary Soule^2),

    c1722 (MD 10:185)

Hopestill DELANO^6 (Joshua^5) and Abigail EVERSON

Joshua DELANO^6 (Joshua^5) and Mary CHANDLER

Moses SIMMONS^4 (Mercy Pabodie^3) and Rachel SAMSON^3 (Caleb^2), 26 Mar. 1718,

    Duxbury (MD 11:25)

Mary FOBES[4] (Martha Pabodie[3]) and Edward SOUTHWORTH[4] (Rebecca Pabodie[3])

Mary PABODIE[3] and Edward SOUTHWORTH[3] (Constant[2]), 16 Nov. 1671, Duxbury (MD 8:232)

Mercy SOUTHWORTH[4] (Mary Pabodie[3]) and Moses SOULE[3] (John[2]) (MD 8:246)

Benjamin SOUTHWORTH[4] (Mary Pabodie[3]) and Rebecca DELANO[4] (Eliz. Standish[3], Alexander[2])
    4 Aug. 1715, Duxbury (MD 11:24)

Hannah SOUTHWORTH[5] (Ben.[4]) and Hezekiah HERRINGTON, 1 Mar. 1738/39, Duxbury (MD 11:82)

Thomas SOUTHWORTH[5] (Ben.[4]) and Anna HATCH, 26 Nov. 1761, Scituate (MD 1:167)

Constant SOUTHWORTH[4] (Mary Pabodie[3]) and Rebecca SIMMONS[4] (Mercy Pabodie[3]), 10 Feb. 1715,
    Duxbury (MD 11:24)

Mercy SOUTHWORTH[5] (Constant[4]) and Micah SOULE[4] (Josiah[3], John[2]), 31 May 1740,
    Duxbury (MD 11:81)

Mary SOUTHWORTH[5] (Constant[4]) and Thomas WESTON

Thomas WESTON and 2nd Martha (   ), 15 Jan. 1767, Duxbury

Elizabeth SOUTHWORTH[4] (Mary Pabodie[3]) and Samuel WESTON, 14 Mar. 1716/17, Duxbury
    (MD 11:24)

Elnathan WESTON[5] (Eliz. Southworth[4]) and Jemima BISBEE, 8 Nov. 1750, Duxbury (VR:220,329)

Thomas SOUTHWORTH[4] (Mary Pabodie[3]) and Sarah ALDEN[3] (Jonathan[2]), c1701 (MD 9:231)

Jedediah SOUTHWORTH[5] (Tho.[4]) and Hannah SCALES(sp), c1728 (MD 12:29)

James SOUTHWORTH[6] (Jedediah[5]) and Sarah DREW, 28 Nov. 1762, Duxbury (VR)

Mary SOUTHWORTH[5] (Tho.[4]) and Thomas LORING, 3 Feb. 1723/24, Duxbury (MD 11:240)

Perez LORING[6] (Mary Southworth[5]) and Sarah FREEMAN, 23 Feb. 1758, Duxbury (VR:274,256)

Braddock LORING[7] (Perez[6]) and Mary/Polly MATHERS, 13 Aug. 1783, Duxbury (VR:274,277)

Perez LORING[8] (Braddock[7]) and 1st Elizabeth SMALLEDGE, 5 Oct. 1806, Boston

Perez LORING[8] and 2nd Isabel W. RUSS, aft. 1858

Mercy PABODIE[3] and John SIMMONS, 16 Nov. 1669, Duxbury (MD 8:232)

Benjamin SIMMONS[4] (Mercy Pabodie[3]) and 1st Lorah SAMSON, 3 Jan. 1705/06, Duxbury
    (MD 9:108)

Benjamin SIMMONS[4] and 2nd Priscilla DELANO[4] (Eliz. Standish[3], Alexander[2]),
    7 July 1715, Duxbury (MD 11:24) [3]

Aaron SIMMONS[5] (Ben.[4]) and Sarah HOLMES, 14 Jan. 1749, Marshfield (VR 2:160)

Benjamin SIMMONS[5] (Ben.[4]) and Fear SAMSON[5] (Nathaniel[4], Lorah Standish[3], Alexander[2]),
    26 Oct. 1731, Duxbury (Gen.Adv.1:40)

Hannah SIMMONS[5] (Ben.[4]) and William RICHARDS, 7 Sept. 1738, Pembroke (VR:337, 346)

Ruth RICHARDS and Josiah FARROW, 21 Feb. 1785, Bristol

Erastus RICHARDS[6] (Hannah[5]) and Betty Doty SHERMAN[5] (Mary Oakman[4], Eliz. Doty[3],

Edward^2), 16 May 1765, Marshfield (VR 2:150)

Deborah RICHARDS and Story THOMPSON, Int. 13 Sept. 1791, Bristol ME (VR)

Zachariah SIMMONS^5 (Ben.^{4}) and Deborah BISHOP, 27 May 1731, Pembroke (Gen. Adv. 1:110)

Ichabod SIMMONS^5 (Moses^4, Mercy Pabodie^3) and 1st Lydia SOULE^4 (Josiah^3, John^2,
 George^1), 8 Dec. 1743, Duxbury (Gen. Adv. 2:83)

Ichabod SIMMONS^5 and 2nd Mercy (   ) SPRAGUE, Aug. 1781

Consider SIMMONS^6 (Ichabod^5) and Aphelia/Nephela SOULE^5 (Micah^4, Josiah^3, John^2,
 25 Feb. 1763, Duxbury (Ch.rcds.1:256)

Ichabod SIMMONS^6 (Ichabod^5) and Urainy(sp) HOLMES, 16 Jan. 1783, Duxbury

Lemuel SIMMONS^6 (Ichabod^5) and Abigail PIERCE, 15 Mar. 1769/70

Nathaniel SIMMONS^6 (Ichabod^5) and Lydia SPRAGUE, 7 Dec. 1780, Duxbury (VR:308, 315)

Noah SIMMONS^6 (Ichabod^5) and Sylvia SOUTHWORTH, 2 July 1769, Duxbury (VR:308, 314)

Lydia SIMMONS^5 (Moses^4) and Judah DELANO, c1743 (MD 12:29)

William SIMMONS^4 (Mercy Pabodie^3) and Abigail CHURCH^4 (Joseph^3, Eliz. Warren^2)
 c1696 (MD 22:23-25)

Joseph SIMMONS^5 (Wm.^{4}, Mercy Pabodie^3) and Rebecca WOOD, 28 Mar. 1726, Little Compton RI

Edward SIMMONS^6 (Jos.^{5}) and 1st Mary ROBINSON, 10 May 1753, Newport (VR)

Jonathan SIMMONS^7 (Edward^6) and Elizabeth (SMITH?), c1778

Edward SIMMONS^8 (Jonathan^7) and Sally FREEBORN, 18 June 1799, Newport RI (VR 12:30)

John SIMMONS^6 (Joseph^5) and Lydia GRINNELL

Benoni SIMMONS^7 and Nancy BAILEY

Priscilla PABODIE^3 and Rev. Ichabod WISWALL, 2 Dec. 16( ), Duxbury (MD 8:232)[4]

Deborah WISWALL^4 (Prisc. Pabodie^3) and Samuel SEABURY^4 (Sam.$^{3-2}$, John^1), 21 Oct. 1717,
 Duxbury (MD 11:25)

Hannah WISWALL^4 (Prisc. Pabodie^3) and Rev. John ROBINSON, 31 Jan./June 1705

Alethea ROBINSON^5 (Hannah Wiswall^4) and Abel STILES

Elizabeth ROBINSON^5 (Hannah Wiswall^4) and Rev. Jacob ELIOT, 4 May 1732, Duxbury (MD11:241)

Faith ROBINSON^5 (Hannah Wiswall^4) and Jonathan TRUMBLE, 9 Dec. 1735, Duxbury (MD11:241)

Hannah ROBINSON^5 (Hannah Wiswall^4) and Nathaniel THOMAS Jr., 1 Sept. 1729, Duxbury
 (MD 11:240)

Ichabod ROBINSON^5 (Hannah Wiswall^4) and Lydia BROWN

John ROBINSON^5 (Hannah Wiswall^4) and Thankful HINCKLEY, 17 Jan. 1743, Lebanon

Mercy WISWALL^4 (Prisc. Pabodie^3) and John WADSWORTH, 25 Jan. 1704/05, Duxbury (MD 9:108)

John WADSWORTH and 2nd Mary (   ) VERDIE, 4 Apr. 1718, Boston (MD 11:24)[5]

Dorothy WADSWORTH^5 (Mercy Wiswall^4) and Joseph BARTLETT^5 (Ichabod^4, Ben.^{3}, Mary Warren^2)

Ichabod WADSWORTH^5 (Mercy Wiswall^4) and Anne HUNT, 25 Nov. 1736, Duxbury (MD 11:241)

Rhoda WADSWORTH^6 (Ichabod^5) and Perez CHANDLER, 11 Dec. 1755, Duxbury (ch. rcds.1:256)

Wadsworth CHANDLER^7 (Rhoda Wadsworth^6) and Mercy CHANDLER, 27 Nov. 1800, Duxbury (VR)

Asenath CHANDLER^7 (Rhoda Wadsworth^6) and Nathaniel HOLMES^7 (Ephraim$^{6-5}$, Mary
    Brewster^4, Wrestling^3, Love^2), 25 Dec. 1798

Benjamin CHANDLER^7 (Rhoda Wadsworth^6) and 1st Wealthy BENSON

Benjamin CHANDLER^7 and 2nd Sarah BARKER

Stephen HOLMES^8 (Asenath Chandler^7) and Mahala BARTLETT

Betty CHANDLER^7 (Rhoda Wadsworth^6) and 1st Joseph DARLING, 21 Nov. or Dec. 1780

Betty CHANDLER^7 and 2nd Sceva CHANDLER, Mar. 1798, Duxbury (VR)

Sceva CHANDLER and 1st Edith SAMPSON, 20 June 1782, Duxbury (VR)

John WADSWORTH^5 (Mercy Wiswall^4) and Mary ALDEN^4 (Ben.^{3}, David^2)

Peleg WADSWORTH^5 (Mercy Wiswall^4) and Lusanna SAMSON^4 (John^3, Stephen^2), c1741

Peleg WISWALL^4 (Prisc. Pabodie^3) and Elizabeth ROGERS, Int. 25 Nov. 1719, Boston
    (Rcd. Comm.28:98)

Priscilla WISWALL^4 (Prisc. Pabodie^3) and Gershom BRADFORD^4 (Sam.^{3}, Wm.^{2}), 23 Oct.
    1716, Plymouth (MD 14:38)

Rebecca PABODIE^3 and William SOUTHWORTH

Elizabeth SOUTHWORTH^4 (Rebecca Pabodie^3) and David LITTLE^4 (Ephraim^3, Anna Warren^2)

Micro #7 of 16

Alice SOUTHWORTH^4 (Rebecca Pabodie^3) and John COOK, 25 May 1709, Little Compton RI

Stephen SOUTHWORTH^4 (Reb. Pabodie^3) and Lydia WARREN^5 (Rebeca Church^4, Caleb^3, Eliz.
    Warren^2), 27 Jan. 1725/26

Thomas SOUTHWORTH^5 (Stephen^4) and Sarah WARD, 13 Nov. 1753

Ruth PABODIE^3 and Benjamin BARTLETT^4 (Ben.^{3}, Mary Warren^2), Dec. 1676 or 1678,
    Duxbury (MD 8:232)

Sarah PABODIE^3 and John COE, 10 Nov. 1681, Duxbury (MD 8:232)

Elizabeth COE^4 (Sarah Pabodie^3) and Edward BURGESS, 27 July/Oct. 1720, Little Compton RI

John COE^4 (Sarah Pabodie^3) and Rebecca TAYLOR, 10 Dec. 1741, Little Compton RI (VR)

Lydia COE^4 (Sarah Pabodie^3) and John BAILEY, 11 Jan. 1710, Little Compton RI (VR)

Samuel COE^4 (Sarah Pabodie^3) and 1st Mary CHADWICK, 18 Apr. 1716, Little Compton (VR)

Samuel COE^4 and 2nd Elizabeth PECKHAM, 21 July 1746, Little Compton RI (VR)

Sarah COE^4 (Sarah Pabodie^3) and Samuel TOMPKINS, 24 Jan. 1712, Little Compton RI
    (VR 4:6:21)

William PABODIE[3] and 1st Judith (   )

William PABODIE[3] and 2nd Elizabeth (   )

William Pabodie[3] and 3rd Mary (MORGAN) Starr, aft. 1747

Priscilla PABODIE[4] (Wm.[3]) and William WILCOX, 14 Oct. 1733

Mary PABODIE[4] (Wm.[3]) and Nathaniel FISH, 28 Nov. 1736, poss. Stonington CT

Margaret FISH and Ichabod FORD, 11 Nov. 1767, Norwich CT (VR 5:55)

Joseph FISH and Abigail LOTHROP, 4 July 1776, Norwich CT (VR 5:56)

Bettey FISH and Oliver CLARKE, 15 Apr. 1778, Norwich CT (VR 5:56)

William FISH and Elisabeth HAUGHTON, 10 Feb. 1761, Norwich CT (VR 2:272)

William FISH and Deborah BACKUS, 25 Mar. 1772, Norwich CT (VR 3:176)

Andrew LOTHROP and 1st Deborah WOODWORTH, 15 Oct. 1755, Norwich CT (VR 2:181)

Andrew LOTHROP and 2nd Abigail FISH, 14 Sept. 1763, Norwich CT (VR 2:348)

John ALDEN[2] (John[1])

John ALDEN[2] and 1st Elizabeth (   )

John ALDEN[2] and 2nd Elizabeth (PHILLIPS) Everill, 1 Apr. 1660, poss. Boston

Elizabeth PHILLIPS and 1st Abiel EVERILL, 6 July 1655, Boston (Rcd. Com.9:52)

Abigail ALDEN and James DALTON, 24 Jan. 1740, Boston (Rcd. Com.28:332)

Peter ALDEN and Lydia BROWN/BOWEN, 18 May 1739, Boston (Rcd. Com.28:330)

Lydia ALDEN and John CUMBER/CHAMBER, 3 Jan. 1743, Boston (Rcd. Com.28:240)

Elizabeth ALDEN[3] and 1st John WALLEY, c1683

Elizabeth ALDEN[3] and 2nd Simon WILLARD, 30 Apr. 1702, Boston (Rcd. Com.28:6)

Elizabeth WALLEY[4] (Eliz. Alden[3]) and Joseph RUSSELL, 12 July 1716, Boston

Elizabeth ALDEN[4] (Zachariah[3]) and Timothy GREEN, 12 Jan. 1726, Boston (Rcd. Com.28:132)

Mary ALDEN[4] (Zachariah[3]) and Samuel KNEELAND, 8 Feb. 1721, Boston (Rcd. Com.28:101)

Abigail WILLARD[4] (Eliz. Alden[3]) and Joseph BRIDGHAM, 18 Oct. 1722, Boston(Rcd.Com.28:104)

John BRIDGHAM[5] (Abigail Willard[4]) and Joanna COOMER, 28 Feb. 1754, Plympton (VR:268,294)

John BRIDGHAM[6] (John[5]) and Sibilla SHAW, 11 June 1778, Plympton

John BRIDGHAM[7] (John[6]) and Elizabeth GREENWOOD

Joseph BRIDGHAM[5] (Abigail Willard[4]) and Martha BRICKLIN(sp)

Charlotte BRIDGHAM and Cyrus MARTIN, Int. 19 Feb. 1785, Rehoboth (VR:430, 474)

Katherine WILLARD[4] (Eliz. Alden[3]) and Rev. Othniel CAMPBELL, c1734

Rev. Othniel CAMPBELL and 2nd Deborah TORREY, 22 Nov. 1737, Boston (Gen. Reg. 42:251)

Katharine CAMPBELL[5] (Katherine Willard[4]) and Samuel ELLIS, c1766

John ALDEN^3 and 1st Elizabeth (   ), c1687

John ALDEN^3 and 2nd Susanna WINSLOW^4 (Edw.^{3}, Mary Chilton^2), 22 Nov. 1722
    Boston (Rcd. Com.28:104)

Hannah ALDEN^4 (John^3) and John JONES, 4 Aug. 1726, Boston (Rcd. Com.28:133)

John ALDEN^4 (John^3) and Anna BRAME, 1 May 1718, Boston (Rcd. Com.28:73)

Anna BRAME and 2nd Henry BURCHSTED, 20 May 1728, Boston (Rcd. Com.28:141)

Anna ALDEN^5 (John^4) and Samuel BURRILL

Elizabeth BURRILL^6 (Anna^5) and Samuel GRAVES

Eunice BURRILL^6 (Anna Alden^5) and Joseph HART, 11 Nov. 1766, Lynn

Anna HART^7 (Eunice Burrill^6) and Joseph LYE, Jr., c1737

Nathaniel ALDEN^4 (John^3) and Mary SMITH, c1729

Mary ALDEN and Richard BLAKE, Int. 19 Dec. 1750, Boston (Rcd. Com.28:296)

Elizabeth ALDEN^5 (Nathaniel^4) and Anthony JONES, 9 Feb. 1747, Hopkinton (VR:215,308)

Elijah JONES and Mehitable HAYNES, 18 Mar. 1800, Sudbury (VR:214, 225)

John JONES^6 (Eliz. Alden^5) and Hannah HOLMES

John H. JONES^7 (John^6) and Sally Sears BALLARD

Samuel JONES^6 (Eliz. Alden^5) and Rachel HAYNES, 12 Feb. 1778, Sudbury (VR:226, 214)

Samuel JONES and Hepzebath JONES, 25 Apr. 1771, Concord (VR:232)

Asa JONES^7 (Sam.^{6}) and Rebecca HOWE

Sarah JONES^6 (Eliz. Alden^5) and Aaron BUTTER

Hannah ALDEN^5 (Nathaniel^4) and Michael HOMER, 15 Oct. 1767, Boston (Rcd. Com.30:52)

Thomas ALDEN^4 (John^3) and Jane WHIPPE, Int. 12 Dec. 1726, Boston (Rcd. Com.28:163)

Jane WHIPPE and 2nd Peter HEAIRO, 20 Sept. 1739, Boston (Rcd. Com.28:330)

Nathaniel ALDEN^3 and Hephzibah MOUNTJOY, 1 Oct. 1691, Boston (Rcd. Com.9:198)

Hephzibah MOUNTJOY and 2nd John MORTEMORE, 8 June 1703, Boston (MD 10:78)

Hephzibah ALDEN^4 (Nathaniel^3) and Nathaniel HAYWOOD, 28 Apr. 1718, Boston (Rcd. Com.28:76)

Mary ALDEN^4 (Nathaniel^3) and Joseph BRIGHTMAN, 3 Oct. 1714, Boston (Rcd. Com.28:49)

William ALDEN^3 and Mary DRURY, 21 May 1691, Boston (Rcd. Com.9:198)

Elizabeth ALDEN^4 (Wm.^{3}) and Thomas BETTERLY, 26 July 1720, Boston (Rcd. Com.28:86)

Lydia ALDEN^4 (Wm.^{3}) and Peter BRITTON, 12 Nov. 1722, Boston (Rcd. Com.28:104)

Mary ALDEN^4 (Wm.^{3}) and Joseph GALE, 29 Apr. 1736, Boston (Rcd. Com.28:196)

Zachariah ALDEN^3 and Mary VIAL, 13 Jan. 1700, Boston (Rcd. Com.28:1)

Zachariah ALDEN^4 (Zach.^{3}) and 1st Jemima HALL, Int. 2 Dec. 1724, Boston (Rcd. Com.28:161)

Zachariah ALDEN^4 and 2nd Lydia CRANE, 17 Nov. 1728, Boston (Rcd. Com.28:141)

Jonathan ALDEN[2] (John[1])

Jonathan ALDEN[2] and Abigail HALLET, 10 Dec. 1672, Duxbury (MD 10:232)

Pelatiah WEST and Elizabeth (ALDEN[3]) Chandler, 12 July 1722, Duxbury (VR)

Andrew ALDEN[3] and Lydia STANFORD, 4 Feb. 1713/14, Duxbury (MD 11:24)

Prince ALDEN[4] (Andrew[3]) and Mary FITCH, c1746

Anna ALDEN[3] and Josiah SNELL, 21 Dec. 1699, Duxbury (MD 9:109)

Josiah SNELL[4] (Anna Alden[3]) and Abigail FOBES, 23 Jan. 1728, Bridgewater

Anna SNELL[5] (Josiah[4]) and Edmund HAYWARD, 22 Aug. 1751, Bridgewater

Waldo HAYWARD[6] (Anna Snell[5]) and Lucy BARTLETT, 5 or 15 Dec. 1781, Bridgewater

Ira HAYWARD[7] (Waldo[6]) and Sarah EDSON, 3 Apr. 1806 or 1807, Bridgewater

Ambrose HAYWARD[8] (Ira[7]) and Hannah HOWLAND[7] (Jabez[6], Ansel[5], Jabez[4], Shubael[3], John[2])
      11 Apr. 1833, Barnstable

Albert Francis HAYWARD[9] (Ambrose[8]) and Louisa Miranda BELDEN, 9 Dec. 1873

Carle Reed HAYWARD[10] (Albert[9]) and Mary Gordon MURRAY, 29 June 1915, Quincy

Elizabeth ALDEN[3] and 1st Edmund CHANDLER, pre 2 July 1711

Elizabeth ALDEN[3] and 2nd Pelatiah WEST (above)

John ALDEN[3] and Hannah BRIGGS, 12 Jan. 1709/10, Scituate (VR 1:2:18)

Samuel ALDEN[4] (John[3]) and Edith (   ) WILLIAMS

Abigail ALDEN[4] (John[3]) and Anthony THOMAS[5] (Lydia Waterman[4], Sarah Snow[3], Abigail
      Warren[2]), 23 Jan. 1745/46

Anna ALDEN[4] (John[3]) and Benjamin LORING, 8 Feb. 1739 (Hist. Duxbury:217)

Samuel LORING[5] (Anna Alden[4]) and Prudence CHAPMAN

Briggs ALDEN[4] (John[3]) and Mercy WADSWORTH, 19 Nov. 1741, Duxbury (MD 11:81)

Hannah ALDEN and John GRAY, Int. 11 Dec. 1766, Boston (Rcd. Com.30:426)

Judah ALDEN[4] (John[3]) and Abigail ROE, 30 Dec. 1739, Boston (Rcd. Com.28:331)

Jonathan ALDEN[3] and Elizabeth ARNOLD[5] (Eliz. Gray[4], Mary Winslow[3], Mary Chilton[2]),
      17 Jan. 1717/18, Marshfield (MD 8:43)

Elizabeth ARNOLD[5] and 1st Anthony WATERMAN[4], (Sarah Snow[3], Abigail Warren[2])

Austin ALDEN[4] (Jonathan[3]) and Salome LOMBARD, 25 Nov. 1756, Gorham ME

Elizabeth ALDEN[5] (Austin[4]) and Jesse HARDING, 27 Mar. 1777, Gorham ME

Austin HARDING[6] (Eliz. Alden[5]) and Polly MURCH, poss. c1808, Hampden ME

Hannah HARDING[7] (Austin[6]) and Enoch HOLBROOK

Seth ALDEN[4] (Jonathan[3]) and Lydia ALDEN

Sarah ALDEN^3 and Thomas SOUTHWORTH^4 (Mary Pabodie^3, Eliz. Alden^2), c1701 (MD 9:231)

Joseph ALDEN^2 (John^1)

Joseph ALDEN^2 and Mary SIMMONS (MD 31:60)

Elizabeth ALDEN^3 and Benjamin SNOW^3 (Rebecca Brown^2)

Hopestill ALDEN^3 and Joseph SNOW^3 (Rebecca Brown^2), c1689 (MD 14:208)

Isaac ALDEN^3 and Mehitable ALLEN, 2 Dec. 1685, Bridgewater (MD 3:9)

Ebenezer ALDEN^4 (Isaac^3) and Anna KEITH, 16 Apr. 1717, Bridgewater (MD 16:191)

Jephtha BYRAM and Susanna WASHBURN, 19 Feb. 1761

Nathan ALDEN^5 (Ebenezer^4) and 1st Mary HUDSON, 1750

Nathan ALDEN^5 and 2nd Lydia RICHARDS

Nathan ALDEN^6 (Nathan^5) and Sarah BARRELL^7 (Wm.$^{6-5}$, Lydia Turner^4, Mary Brewster^3),
     24 Jan. 1776

Nathan ALDEN^6 and 2nd Joanna (   ) SOULE, 1819

Susanna ALDEN^5 (Ebenezer^4) and Ephraim CAREY

Abigail ALDEN^5 (Ebenezer^4) and Ebenezer BYRAM, 22 Nov. 1738

Ezra ALDEN^5 (Ebenezer^4) and Rebecca KEITH

Rebecca KEITH and 2nd John BISBEE, Int. 14 Nov. 1771, Bridgewater (VR 21:53)

Abigail ALDEN^6 (Ezra^5) and George VINING, 27 July 1778, Bridgewater

Jemima ALDEN^4 (Isaac^3) and Thomas WHITMAN, 22 Nov. 1727, Bridgewater (MD 16:45)

Thomas WHITMAN and 2nd Rebecca (RICKARD) Allen, 1767

Jemima WHITMAN^5 (Jemima Alden^4) and David KEITH, 1754

David KEITH and 2nd Charity (KINGMAN) Brett, 1773

Lewis L. KEITH^7 (Calvin^6, Jemima Whitman^5) and Asaba CHURCHILL^8 (Cynthia Packard^7,
     Solomon^6, Susanna Kingman^5, Mary Mitchell^4, Jacob^3, Experience), 22 Sept. 1819,
     East Bridgewater (VR 2:81:214)

Samuel G. ALDEN and Harriet L. KEITH, 20 May 1838, E. Bridgewater (ch. rcds.)

Amos WHITMAN^5 (Jemima Alden^4) and Anna WASHBURN^7 (Eleazer^6, Noah^5, Sam.^{4}, Eliz.
     Mitchell^3, Jane Cooke^2)

John ALDEN^4 (Isaac^3) and 1st Hannah KINGMAN

John ALDEN^4 and 2nd Rebecca NIGHTINGALE

Cyrus ALDEN^6 (Jonathan^5, John^4) and Nabby Keith KINSLEY, 18 Sept. 1808

Hannah ALDEN and Izra BEAL, 30 Sept. 1821, Minot ME (VR)

Susannah ALDEN and Cyrus Bray HARRISON, 4 July 1822, Minot ME (VR)

Benjamin ALDEN and Sally TORRELL, 19 Sept. 1822, Minot ME (VR)

Elvina ALDEN and Martin CROFT, 27 Jan. 1827, Minot ME (VR)

Mary ALDEN and Artemus BROWN, 15 May 1828, Minot ME (VR)

Hannah K. ALDEN and Hiram C. BRIGGS, 29 Apr. 1830, Minot ME (VR)

Mehitable ALDEN and Edwin KINGSLEY, 1 July 1832, Minot ME (VR)

Mary K. ALDEN and Libbeus LEAVITT, 23 Apr. 1835, Minot ME (VR)

Abigail V. ALDEN and Jeremiah D. ALLEN, 2 July 1837, Minot ME (VR)

Charles ALDEN and Eliza P. CROFT, 17 Jan. 1838, Minot ME (VR)

Mehitable ALDEN^4 (Isaac^3) and Benjamin RICHARDS, 1 Jan. 1711, Bridgewater (VR 2:25,321)

Benjamin RICHARDS and 2nd Lydia FAXON, 20 Nov. 1722 (MD 14:180)

James RICHARDS and Susanna PRATT, 15 May 1740, Abington (VR 2:166,182)[6]

James RICHARDS and Susanna PRATT, Int. 4 Apr. 1798, Bridgewater (VR 2:310,321)

James RICHARDS and Dorothy PACKARD, 8 May 1777, Bridgewater (VR 2:275,321)

Mercy ALDEN^4 (Isaac^3) and Zaccheus PACKARD, 21 Oct. 1725, Bridgewater (MD 16:45)

Eleazer PACKARD^5 (Mercy Alden^4) and Mercy RICHARDS

Simeon PACKARD^5 (Mercy Alden^4) and Mary PERKINS, 6 July 1761

Sarah ALDEN^4 (Isaac^3) and 1st Seth BRETT^5 (Sarah Hayward^4, Sarah Mitchell^3, Experience),
    13 Oct. 1712, Bridgewater (MD 16:104) (see p.152, <4>)

Sarah ALDEN^4 and 2nd Recompense CARY, 17 Jan. 1726/27

John ALDEN^3 and Hannah WHITE

Priscilla ALDEN^4 (John^3) and Abraham BORDEN, 1722 (Middleboro Ch. Book)

Thankful ALDEN^4 (John^3) and Francis EATON^4 (Ben.$^{3-2}$), 14 Dec. 1727, Middleboro (MD 5:39)

Francis EATON^4 and 2nd Lydia FULLER, 12 June 1733, Middleboro (MD 13:250)

David ALDEN^5 (David^4) and Rhoda LEACH^7 (Jos.^{6}, Hephzibah Washburn^5, Jos.^{4}, Eliz.
    Mitchell^3, Jane Cooke^2), 18 Dec. 1755 (Bridgewater VR)

Darius ALDEN^7 (Rufus^6, David^5) and Lydia HOLMES

Rosinda ALDEN^6 (Silas^5, David^4) and John FOBES, 12 Mar. 1783, Bridgewater (VR)

Enoch FOBES^7 (Rosinda^6) and Sabra SCOTT

Hannah ALDEN^4 (John^3) and Thomas WOOD, 30 Apr. 1729, Middleboro (MD 5:40)

Micro #11 of 16

John ALDEN^4 (John^3) and 1st Lydia LAZELL^5 (Margaret Cook^4, Jacob$^{3-2}$), 14 May 1739,
    (MD 6:111)

John ALDEN^4 and 2nd Rebecca WESTON^5 (Zachariah^4, Rebecca Soule^3, John^2), 12 July 1750
    (MD 6:112)

Betsey ALDEN^5 (John^4) and Daniel THOMAS

Elihu ALDEN^5 (John^4) and Lydia MITCHELL

Elijah ALDEN^5 (John^4) and Mary ALDEN^6 (Solomon^5, Daniel^4, John^3)

Jael ALDEN^5 (John^4) and Isaiah JONES (MD 6:113)

John ALDEN^5 (John^4) and Lois SOUTHWORTH (MD 6:112)

John ALDEN^6 (John^5) and Ruth POPE, 5 Dec. 1793

Lydia ALDEN^6 (John^5) and Gamaliel CHURCH (MD 6:113)

Mary ALDEN^6 (John^5) and Rev. Isaac TOMPKINS

Lucy ALDEN^5 (John^4) and Eleazer CAREY, Nov. 1791, (MD 6:113)

Lydia ALDEN^5 (John^4) and John SPOONER (MD 6:112)

Mary ALDEN^5 (John^4) and Calvin DELANO (MD 6:112)

Nathan ALDEN^5 (John^4) and Priscilla MILLER, 16 Oct. 1766, Middleboro (MD 26:27)

Earl ALDEN^6 (Nathan^5) and Mercy NELSON (MD 6:113)

John ALDEN^6 (Nathan^5) and Susanna DUNHAM, c1790 (MD 6:113)

Otis ALDEN^6 (Nathan^5) and Abigail BARROW (MD 6:113)

Ruth ALDEN^5 (John^4) and Walter HOWARD (MD 6:113)

Susanna ALDEN^5 (John^4) and 1st Joseph TRIPP (MD 6:112)

Susanna ALDEN^5 and 2nd Samuel PROCTER, 1 Feb. 1781, Dartmouth (VR)

Susanna PROCTOR^6 (Susanna Alden^5) and Levi JENNEY^7 (Levi^6, Cornelius^5, Desire Black-
    well^4, Sarah Warren^3, Nathaniel^2), 2 Oct. 1800, New Bedford (VR)

Joseph ALDEN^4 (John^3) and 1st Hannah HALL, 1 Apr. 1742, Middleboro (MD 15:219)

Joseph ALDEN^4 and 2nd Deborah WILLIAMSON, 3 Sept. 1757, Middleboro (MD 26:27)

Ebenezer ALDEN^5 (Jos.^{4}) and Ruth FOBES, 22 Dec. 1763, Middleboro (VR 1:51)

Ruth FOBES and 2nd Daniel FAUNCE, 24 Aug. 1777

Hannah ALDEN^6 (Ebenezer^5) and Simeon BACKUS

Orpah ALDEN^6 (Ebenezer^5) and Zadock PERSHO

Ruth ALDEN^6 (Ebenezer^5) and 1st Joseph HATHAWAY

Ruth ALDEN^6 (Eben.^{5}) and 2nd Simon BACKUS (above), 6 Mar. 1821

Polly ALDEN^6 (Eben.^{5}) and Nehemiah JONES

Ebenezer ALDEN^6 (Eben.^{5}) and Elizabeth AMES

Martha Eloise ALDEN^9 (Elihah A.^{8}, Elijah^7, Ebenezer^6) and Charles Haddon McINTYRE c1898

Lydia ALDEN^4 (John^3) and 1st Samuel EDDY, 5 Feb. 1732/33, Middleboro (MD 13:250)

Lydia ALDEN^4 and John FULLER^4 (John^3, Samuel^2, Samuel^1), 27 Apr. 1762, Halifax (VR:31)

Nathan EDDY^5 (Lydia Alden^4) and Eunice SAMSON^5 (Ephraim^4, Lydia Standish^3, Alexander^2)

Mary ALDEN^4 (John^3) and Noah THOMAS, 22 Feb. 1732/33, Middleboro (MD 13:250)

Noah ALDEN^4 (John^3) and Joanna VAUGHN, 4 Mar. 1744/45, Middleboro (MD 18:79)

Caleb THOMSON and Lydia ALDEN (Mrs.), 21 Dec. 1768, Bellingham (VR)

Joel THOMSON (Caleb) and Ruth THAYER, Int. 7 Nov. 1794

Joseph ALDEN^3 and Hannah DUNHAM, c1690 (MD 3:142)

Daniel ALDEN^4 (Jos.^{3}) and Abigail SHAW, 25 Dec. 1717, Bridgewater (MD 16:185)

Barnabas ALDEN^5 (Daniel^4) and Elizabeth PATTERSON, 21 Nov. 1758, Stafford CT (VR)

Susanna ALDEN^6 (Barnabas^5) and Mark HOWES

Barnabas Alden HOWES^7 (Susanna Alden^6) and Polly Clark LAWTON

Joseph ALDEN^5 (Daniel^4) and Susanna PACKARD

Eleazer ALDEN^4 (Jos.^{3}) and Martha SHAW, 11 May 172-, Bridgewater (MD 16:186)[7]

Jonathan ALDEN^5 (Eleazer^4) and Experience HAYWARD

Timothy ALDEN^5 (Eleazer^4) and Sarah WELD, c1770

Timothy ALDEN^6 (Timothy^5) and 1st Elizabeth Shepherd WORMSTED, Int. 3 Dec. 1796,
    Marblehead (VR 2:3, 468)

Timothy ALDEN^6 and 2nd Sophia Louisa LUKER

Hannah ALDEN^4 (Jos.^{3}) and Mark LATHROP, 29 Mar. 1722, Bridgewater (MD 16:188)

Mary ALDEN^4 (Jos.^{3}) and Timothy EDSON, 10 Feb. 1719, Bridgewater (MD 16:186)

Hannah EDSON^5 (Mary Alden^4) and Israel HOWE, 11 Feb. 1758, Stafford CT (ch. rcds.)

Samuel ALDEN^4 (Jos.^{3}) and Abiah EDSON, c1729 (Bridgewater VR 1:17)

Solomon ALDEN and Hannah STONE, 8 or 10 Sept. 1795, (Newton VR:231,383; Lynn VR 2:15,359)

Silas ALDEN^6 (Simeon^5) and 1st Polly FRENCH, c1785

Silas ALDEN^6 and 2nd Charlotte (   ) THAYER, aft. 1810

Seth ALDEN^4 (Jos.^{3}) and Mehitable CARVER, 1 Jan. 1739/40, Bridgewater (VR 2:21,73)

Joseph ALDEN^5 (Seth^4) and Bethiah CARVER, c1774

Oliver ALDEN^5 (Seth^4) and Experience LEONARD, 21 Nov. 1765, Bridgewater

Seth ALDEN^5 (Seth^4) and Mary CARVER, 3 Dec. 1767

Mary CARVER and 2nd Joshua ALDEN, aft. 1775

Mercy ALDEN^3 and John BURRILL, 26 June 1688, Taunton (Gen. Reg. 13:251)

John BURRILL^4 (Mercy Alden^3) and Mary HUMPHREY, 8 Jan. 1716, Weymouth (VR 2:41,98)

John BURRELL and Susanna RICHARDS, 22 June 1721, Weymouth (VR 2:39,165)

John BURRELL^5 (John^4) and Ann VINTON, 15 May 1740, Weymouth (VR 2:41,205)

Mary BURRILL and Josia RIPLEY, Int. 17 Aug. 1717, Weymouth (VR 2:43,166)[8]

Joseph HUMPHREY^3 and 1st Mary (   ), c1696

Joseph HUMPHREY^3 and 2nd Hannah (VICKERY) Langlee, 22 May 1743 (Hist. of Hingham 2:361)

Humphrey BURRELL^5 (John^4) and Hannah THAYER, Int. 27 Jan. 1744/45, Weymouth (VR 2:40,184)

Abraham BURRELL^5 (John^4) and Jane DYER, 23 Dec. 1746, Weymouth (VR)

Joseph DYER and Jane STEPHENS, 27 June 1726, Weymouth (VR 2:65,177)

Mary RIPLEY and James BURRELL, 15 or 28 May 1749

Rebecca ALDEN^2 (John^1)

Rebecca ALDEN^2 and Dr. Thomas DELANO, pre 30 Oct. 1667 [9]

Benoni DELANO^3 and Elizabeth DREW (MD 20:31-32)

Nathaniel TURNER^5 (Rebecca^4, Benoni Delano^3) and Anna GROSS, 12 Sept. 1758, Lancaster

Beriah DELANO^4 (Benoni^3) and Naomi MERRITT, c1734, Kingston (VR)

Lemuel DELANO^4 (Benoni^3) and Lydia BARTLETT^6 (Ebenezer$^{5-4}$, Ben.^{3}, Mary Warren^2),
     9 July 1741, Duxbury (MD 11:81)

Rebecca DELANO^4 (Benoni^3) and Amasa TURNER, 2 Mar. 1726/27, Duxbury (MD 11:80)

Amasa TURNER and 2nd Eunice SANDERSON, Int. 23 Jan. 1750/51, Lancaster (B.M.D.:33)

Amasa TURNER and 3rd Margaret GROSS, Int. 14 Sept. 1754, Lancaster (B.M.D.:23)

Amasa TURNER^5 (Rebecca Delano^4) and Lucy SMITH, 26 July 1777, Lancaster (B.M.D.:137)

Hannah DELANO^4 (Benoni^3) and Eleazer HARLOW^5 (Sam.^{4}, Rebecca Bartlett^3, Mary Warren^2),
     6 Oct. 1715, Duxbury (MD 11:24)

Eleazer HARLOW^5 and 2nd Hannah PRATT, 21 July 1720, Plympton (MD 3:91)

Jonathan DELANO^3 and Hannah DOTEN^3 (Thomas^2), 12 Jan. 1698, Duxbury (MD 12:33)

Amaziah DELANO^4 (Jonathan^3) and Ruth SAMSON^5 (Abraham^4, Lorah Standish^3, Alexander^2),
     8 Jan. 1729/30, Duxbury (MD 11:240)

Ezekiel DELANO^5 (Amaziah^4) and Martha CHANDLER

Cornelius DELANO^5 (Amaziah^4) and Sarah PETERSON, 24 June 1762, Duxbury (VR)

Jonathan DELANO^4 (Jonathan^3) and 1st Elizabeth WINSLOW

Jonathan DELANO^4 and 2nd Elizabeth SPRAGUE, 3 Dec. 1736, Rochester (VR 2:44)

Jonathan DELANO^4 and 3rd Rachel BUMP, Int. 10 Nov. 1741, Rochester (VR 2:47)

Jonathan DELANO/DELANOY and Abigail HAMMOND, Int. 7 Sept. 1734, Rochester (VR 2:44)

Mary DREW^4 (Sarah Delano^3) and Isaac BENNET^4 (Priscilla Howland^3, Isaac^2), 24 Aug.
     1732, Middleboro (MD 13:249)

Sarah DELANO^3 and John DREW (MD 6:23)

John DREW^4 (Sarah Delano^3) and Susanna BENNET^4 (Prisc. Howland^3, Isaac^2), 25 Jan.
     1727/28, Middleboro (MD 5:39)

Deborah DREW^5 (John^4) and Ebenezer BONNEY

Lydia DREW^5 (John^4) and Stephen POWERS, 20 Mar. 1760, Middleboro (MD 24:132)

Thomas DREW^4 (Sarah Delano^3) and Abigail HARRIS^6 (Samuel^5, Mercy Latham^4, Susanna
     Winslow^3, Mary Chilton^2), 16 Aug. 1739, Bridgewater (VR 2:112,158)

Abigail DREW^5 (Thomas^4) and Samuel LUCAS, 21 Nov. 1771, Halifax (VR:29)

Thomas DREW^5 (Thomas^4) and Lucy TOMSON^5 (Reuben^4, Tho.^{3}, Mary Cooke^2), 2 May 1776,
     Halifax (MD 7:50)

Jemima DREW^5 (Tho.^{4}) and Peleg BARROWS, 4 May 1775, Halifax (MD 7:50)

Thomas DELANO^3 and Hannah (   ) BARTLETT, 24 Oct. 1699, Duxbury (MD 9:109)

Elkanah DELANO^4 (Tho.^{3}) and Mary SANDERS, 31 Oct. 1728, Plymouth (MD 14:72)

John RICHARDS (Sarah Delano) and Abigail DYER, 7 Nov. 1790, poss. Cape Elizabeth

Ruth ALDEN^2 (John^1)

Ruth ALDEN^2 and John BASS, 12 May 1657, (Braintree VR:716)

John BASS and 2nd Hannah/Ann STURTEVANT, 21 Sept. 1675

Micro #13 of 16

Hannah BASS^3 and Joseph ADAMS, c1687/88 (Braintree VR:665; MD 4:206)

Joseph ADAMS^3 and 1st Mary CHAPIN, 20 Feb. 1682 (Braintree VR:719)

George K. HOOPER and Louisa R. ADAMS, 1 Oct. 1867, Dedham (VR:65)

Ebenezer ADAMS^4 (Hannah Bass^3) and Anne BOYLSTON, Int. 7 Mar. 1728/29, Braintree
    (VR:815)

Anne ADAMS^5 (Ebenezer^4) and 1st Elisha SAVIL, 18 Nov. 1751, Braintree (ch. rcds.)

Anne ADAMS^5 and 2nd Thomas THAYER, Int. 17 Aug. 1776, Braintree (VR:879)

Lucretia SAVIL^6 (Anne Adams^5) and Jeriah BASS, 25 Dec. 1783, (Braintree VR:885)

Jeriah BASS and Hannah PALMER, 23 Aug. 1804

Elisha BASS and Joanna HUNT, Int. 29 Aug. 1818, Wilton (VR)

Jeriah BASS and Polly HUNT, 22 Mar. 1920, Wilton (VR)$^{<10>}$

John A. BASS and Mary PUHAM/PERHAM, 2 Dec. 1830, Wilton (VR)

Seth BASS and Nancy RUSSELL, Int. 21 Sept. 1834, Wilton (VR)

Charles BASS^7 (Lucretia Savil^6) and Susanna LOVE, c1810

Boylston ADAMS^5 (Ebenezer^4) and Mary ALLEN, 28 Sept. 1754

Ebenezer ADAMS^5 (Eben.^{4}) and Mehitable SPEAR, c1758

Zabdiel ADAMS^5 (Eben.^{4}) and Elizabeth STEARNS

Hannah ADAMS^4 (Hannah Bass^3) and Benjamin OWEN, 4 Feb. 1724/25, Braintree (TR:747)

John BASS^3 and 1st Abigail ADAMS, c1687 (Braintree VR:665)

John BASS^3 and 2nd Rebecca SAVIL, 17 May 1698

Ebenezer BASS^4 (John^3) and Sarah MOSELEY, 3 July 1733, Dorchester

John BASS^4 (John^3) and 1st Lydia SAVIL, 18 Feb. 1713 (Braintree VR:743)

John BASS^4 and 2nd Hannah NEALE, 21 June 1716 (Braintree VR:743)

Benjamin BASS^5 (John^4) and 1st Mary BRACKET

Benjamin BASS^5 and 2nd Hannah JONES

Jedediah BASS^5 (John^4) and 1st Hannah TOLMAN

Jedediah BASS^5 and 2nd Sarah HALL

Joseph BASS^5 (John^4) and Hannah BANKS

Hannah BASS^5 (John^4) and Josiah RAWSON, 28 Aug. 1750

Elizabeth RAWSON^6 (Hannah Bass^5) and Seth ELLIS

Josiah RAWSON^6 (Hannah Bass^5) and Elizabeth BARROWS

John BASS^5 (John^4) and Mary DANIELSON

Rev. John BASS and Mary DENESON, 24 Nov. 1743, Ashford CT (VR 2:36)

Jonathan BASS^5 (John^4) and Hannah HAYWARD, 5 May 1762

Jonathan BASS^6 (Jonathan^5) and Elizabeth Marston CHANNEL, Int. 8 July 1792, Quincy
   (m. 2 Aug.) (VR)

Benjamin BASS^7 (Jonathan^6) and Grace Hall STEVENS

Mary Jane BASS^8 (Benjamin^7) and William ADAMS

Isaac BASS and Abigail POPE, 13 Apr. 1828, Quincy (VR 1:25)

Samuel BASS^4 (John^3) and 1st Sarah SAVIL, 15 Aug. 1723

Samuel BASS^4 and 2nd Hannah GOULD, c1726/27

Joseph BASS^3 and 1st Mary BELCHER, 5 June 1688, Braintree (VR:720)

Joseph BASS^3 and 2nd Lois ROGERS, 23 Feb. 1707/08

Mary BASS^4 (Jos.^{3}) and John MILLER, 27 Sept. 1716, Boston (Rcd. com. 28:65)

Ruth BASS^4 (Jos.^{3}) and Samuel TROTT, Int. 29 Jan. or Feb. 1722, Boston (Rcd. com.24:159)

Alden BASS^4 (Jos.^{3}) and Mercy DOWDING

Alden BASS^5 (Alden^4) and Hannah TYLER

Rev. Benjamin BASS^4 (Jos.^{3}) and Mary GARDNER, c1729

Benjamin BASS^5 (Ben.^{4}) and 1st Mercy TOLMAN

Benjamin BASS^5 and 2nd Mary EELLS, 3 Mar. 1793

Benjamin BASS^6 (Ben.^{5}) and Lucinda SYLVESTER

Robert BASS^7 (Ben.^{6}) and Lydia LOUD (Rockland VR 401:392)

Alden BASS^8 (Robert^7) and Phelinda R. GREY, 8 Dec. 1855, Abington (VR 88:225)

Elizabeth BASS^4 (Jos.^{3}) and Daniel HENSHAW, 30 Mar. 1724, Boston (Rcd. com. 24:113)

Joseph BASS^4 (Jos.^{3}) and 1st Elizabeth BRECK, 14 Sept. 1715, Dorchester (Rcd.com.21:107)

Capt. Joseph BASS^4 and 2nd Hannah GLOVER, 14 Nov. 1751, (Boston Rcd.com.21:225)

Mary BASS^5 (Jos.^{4}) and Joseph WILLIAMS, 1 Jan. 1750 (Boston Rcd.com.21:224)

Elizabeth BASS^5 (Jos.^{4}) and Rev. Philip CURTIS, 6 Sept. 1744 (Boston Rcd.com.21:120)

Benjamin BASS^5 (Jos.^{4}) and Mercy TOLMAN, 28 Oct. 1765, Scituate (MD 1:235)

Joseph BASS^5 (Jos.^{4}) and Lydia SEARL, 8 Mar. 1747, Dorchester (Rcd.com.21:223)

Elizabeth BASS^6 (Jos.^{5}) and Jonathan SCOTT, 8 Dec. 1783 (MD 8:82)

Moses BASS^4 (Jos.^{3}) and Hannah BUTLER, 28 Mar. 1729, Boston (Rcd.com.28:147)

Gillam BASS^5 (Moses^4) and Rebecca WIMBLE, c1768 (Northboro VR:18)

Moses Belcher BASS^5 (Moses^4) and 1st Elizabeth KIMBLE, Mar. 1769

Moses Belcher BASS^5 and 2nd Margaret SPRAGUE, 29 Apr. 1773

Mary BASS^3 and 1st Christopher WEBB, 24 (3rd m.) 1686, (Braintree VR:664)

Mary BASS^3 and 2nd William COPELAND, 13 Apr. 1694 (Braintree VR:721)

Christopher WEBB^4 (Mary Bass^3) and Anne WHITE, 30 Apr. 1713, Boston

Sarah WEBB^4 (Mary Bass^3) and Samuel ARNOLD, 13 Sept. 1711 (Braintree VR:742)

David ARNOLD^5 (Sarah Webb^4) and Phebe PRATT, Int. 9 Dec. 1756, Norton (VR:182,297)

Moses ARNOLD^6 (Jos.^{5}) and Sarah VINTON, c1773 (Braintree VR:845)

Samuel THORNDIKE and Elizabeth J. HAYDEN, 19 May 1859, Boston (VR128:119)

Benjamin COPELAND^4 (Mary Bass^3) and Sarah ALLEN, 21 Nov. 1734, Braintree (VR:752)

Jonathan COPELAND^4 (Mary Bass^3) and Bettie SNELL, 14 Jan. 1723/24, Bridgewater (MD16:187)

Abigail COPELAND^5 (Jonathan^4) and George HOWARD, c1745, prob. Bridgewater (VR 2:165)

Benjamin M. HOWARD and Sadie W. GREEN, 15 July 1882, Fall River (Mass.VR 334:118)

Henry A. HOWARD and Sally F. WOOD, Int. 16 Oct. 1847, Lancaster (VR:251)

Caleb HOWARD and Rebecca THURSTON, 31 Dec. 1845, Lancaster (VR:255)

George W. HOWARD amd Martha F. RUGG, 24 Apr. 1843, Lancaster (VR:253)

George W. HOWARD and Elizabeth HOUGHTON, Int. 14 Mar. 1835, Lancaster (VR:242)

Betsey HOWARD and David K. THURSTON, 4 Mar. 1824, Lancaster (VR:234)

Susan S. HOWARD and Edmund MOORE, 28 Nov. 1848, Lancaster (VR:257)

Sarah Ann HOWARD and William MOORE, 18 Dec. 1844, Lancaster (VR:254)

Patty HOWARD and Stedman NOURSE, 4 June 1826, Lancaster (VR:236)

Olive HOWARD and Andrew L. FULLER, 19 May 1845, Lancaster (VR:254)

Mary A. HOWARD and Nathaniel L. HOWE, 9 Apr. 1843, Lancaster (VR:253)

Charlotte HOWARD and Jonathan BUTTRICK, 18 Feb. 1839, Lancaster (VR:245)

Sarah M. HOWARD and William GREENE, 21 Apr. 1833, Lancaster (VR:241)

George HOWARD and Elizabeth BUSS, Int. 21 Mar. 1833, Lancaster (VR:240)

Hannah HOWARD^6 (Abigail Copeland^5) and Daniel LOTHROP^8 (Dan.^{7}, Tho. Willis^6, Sam.
    Kinsley^5, John Washburn^4, Experience Mitchell^3- ?), 23 Oct. 1764[11]

Daniel LOTHROP^8 and 2nd Lydia WILLIS, 1775

Daniel LOTHROP^8 and 3rd Mary TURNER, 1785

Elijah COPELAND^5 (Jonathan^4) and Rhoda SNELL, 31 Oct. 1765, Bridgewater (VR 3:188)

Joseph COPELAND^4 (Mary Bass^3) and Elizabeth TOLMAN, 23 July 1735, Scituate (MD 1:108)

Ruth COPELAND^5 (Jos.^{4}) and Robert Lenthal EELLS

Rhoda COPELAND^5 (Jos.^{4}) and Micah FORD^6 (Michael^5, James^4, Abigail Snow^3, Abigail Warren^2), 16 Feb. 1775, Scituate (VR 2:75,122)

Elizabeth COPELAND^5 (Jos.^{4}) and William BRIGGS, 6 June 1754, Scituate (VR 2:41,76)

Cornelius BRIGGS^6 (Elizabeth Copeland^5) and Nancy TUCKER

William COPELAND and Mary THAYER, 15 June 1718, Braintree (VR)

Ruth BASS^3 and Peter WEBB, c1683 (MD 4:204,206)

Peter WEBB and 2nd Amy HAYDEN, betw. 1700-1703 (Braintree VR:684,694)

Priscilla WEBB^4 (Ruth Bass^3) and Samuel HAYDEN

Samuel BASS^3 and 1st Mary ADAMS, pre 18 July 1694 (PN&Q 2:49,51)

Samuel BASS^3 and 2nd poss. Bethia NIGHTINGALE, betw. 1706-1710 (Braintree VR:695; Thayer Mem.1:59-60)

Jonathan BASS^4 (Samuel^3) and Susanna BYRAM

Mary BASS^4 (Sam.^{3}) and William BOWDITCH, 2 Apr. 1720 Braintree (VR:745)

Bathsheba BOWDITCH^5 (Mary Bass^4) and Ephraim GROVES, 1762, Braintree

William BOWDITCH^5 and poss. Susanna ALLEN

Susanna BOWDITCH^6 (Wm.^{5}) and Ebenezer HUNT, Int. 12 Oct. 1782, Braintree/Weymouth

Samuel BASS^4 (Sam.^{3}) and 1st Hannah WHITE, 4 Dec. 1723

Samuel BASS^4 and 2nd Jerusha WEBB, 16 Jan. 1744

Hannah BASS^5 (Sam.^{4}) and Jonathan WILD

John WILD^6 (Hannah Bass^5) and Jemima SPEAR, Int. 24 Dec. 1770, Braintree (VR:876)

Thomas CODMAN and 1st Hannah PARK, 7 June 1792

Thomas CODMAN and 2nd Mary DRAPER

Col. Jonathan BASS^5 (Sam.^{4}) and Susanna BELCHER, Int. 24 Jan. 1756, Braintree (VR:816)

Sarah BASS^3 and Ephraim THAYER, 7 Jan. 1691/92, Braintree (VR:720)

Ephraim THAYER and 2nd Mary (   ) (Burrill) KINGMAN, aft. Aug. 1751 (Thayer Mem.2:3)

Abigail THAYER^4 (Sarah Bass^3) and Dr. Benjamin RICHARDS

Christopher THAYER^4 (Sarah Bass^3) and Mary MORSE

Ephraim THAYER^4 (Sarah Bass^3) and Mary COPELAND

Esther THAYER^4 (Sarah Bass^3) and Moses FRENCH, 24 Dec. 1730, Braintree (VR:749)

Moses FRENCH^5 (Esther Thayer^4) and Elizabeth HOBART

Asa FRENCH^6 (Moses^5) and Mehitable HOLLIS

Jonathan FRENCH^7 (Asa^6) and Sarah Brackett HAYWARD

Hannah THAYER[4] (Sarah Bass[3]) and 1st Nathaniel BLANCHARD

Hannah THAYER[4] and 2nd William NOYES

James THAYER[4] (Sarah Bass[3]) and Deborah ARNOLD

Joseph THAYER[4] (Sarah Bass[3]) and 1st Sarah FAXON

Joseph THAYER[4] and 2nd Eunice LUDDEN

Naphtali THAYER[4] (Sarah Bass[3]) and Bathsheba BASS[4] (Samuel[3], Ruth Alden[2]), 3 Feb. 1732

Bathsheba THAYER[5] (Naphtali[4]) and Nathan BEALS, c1749/50

Daniel BEALL and Sally CHENEY, 26 Jan. 1797

Mary BEAL and Levi LEGG, Int. 4 Sept. 1767

Asa BEALS[6] (Bathsheba Thayer[5]) and Olive CHENEY, 2 Sept. 1790

Lucinda BEALS[7] (Asa[6]) and Nathan WHITE JR., 23 Nov. 1820

Peter THAYER[4] (Sarah Bass[3]) and Anna PORTER

Philip THAYER[4] (Sarah Bass[3]) and Mary WILSON, 1 Apr. 1718, Braintree (VR:744)

Priscilla THAYER[4] (Sarah Bass[3]) and 1st Elijah HAYDEN

Priscilla THAYER[4] and 2nd Joseph FORD, c1739, (Braintree VR:782)

Priscilla THAYER[4] and 3rd William SPEAR

Ruth THAYER[4] (Sarah Bass[3]) and John CAPEN, 20 Sept. 1722, Braintree (VR:746)

Sarah THAYER[4] (Sarah Bass[3]) and Seth DORMAN, 4 Aug. 1715, Braintree (VR:743)

Shadrach THAYER[4] (Sarah Bass[3]) and Rachel WHITE

NOTES

<1> p.2, Ruth died two weeks later (9 Apr. 1733) so it is unlikely they were married.

<2> p.2, Although this couple were not married they are included here because they had a child together (one month after Samuel's death in 1727) and therefore left descendants.

<3> p.5, Bowman questioned this date of 1715 but wrote "apparently OK". The problem? Benjamin and 1st wife Lorah had a child Content b. 16 Dec. 1715 (MD 12:162), so obviously (unless divorced) he could not have married a 2nd wife five months earlier in July. (A death date for Lorah would solve the question but it is not given.) Since Benjamin and Priscilla's first child was born in 1718, they were possibly married c1717.

<4> p.6, The last two numbers are worn in the records. However, since the entry falls between entries 1677-81 and their first child was born Oct. 1680, a date of c1679 is probable.

<5> p.6, Bowman suggests she may be the Mary Jarvis who married Luke Verdey, 13 July 1716, Boston (Rcd.com.28:67).

<6> p.12, Bowman suggests she married 2nd Silas Williams, 13 Oct. 1760, Bridgewater (VR 2:232,409) but questions this as fact since the records do not mention her being a widow.

<7> p.14, The last figure is worn in the records but is most likely 1720 since

their first child was born June 1721.

<8> p.14, Bowman later identifies her as Mary Burrill[4] (Mercy Alden[2]).

<9> p.15, It was not until after Bowman's death that it was established that Rebecca Alden married Thomas Delano. Bowman believed it was her sister Mary who married Delano, therefore the files pertaining to Rebecca are listed under Mary.

<10> p.16, The date of 1920 is clearly an error for 1820.

<11> p.18, Line of descent is shown as (Experience Mitchell[3], Jane Cooke[2]). See p.152 <4> which explains descent is not from Jane Cooke but from her husband Experience Mitchell and 2nd wife. To add to this confusion, despite what is shown here, Experience Mitchell did not have a namesake, it was his son John who had a son named Experience, therefore descent should be (Experience[4], John[3], Experience[2]).

Microfiche #1 of 9

Isaac ALLERTON and 1st Mary NORRIS, 4 Nov. 1611, Leyden, Holland (MD 7:129)

Isaac ALLERTON and 2nd Fear BREWSTER^2

Isaac ALLERTON and 3rd Joanna (   )$^{<1>}$

John ALLERTON Jr. and Rosanna (BURLINGAME) Cooper, 7 July 1754, Coventry RI (VR)

Sarah ALLERTON^3 (Isaac^2) and Hancock LEE

Mary ALLERTON^2 (Isaac^1)

Hushai THOMAS and Lucy VAUGHAN, 25 Nov. 1756, Middleboro (VR 2:2:111)

Edward THOMAS Jr. and Abigail PARLOUR, 11 July 1720, Middleboro (VR 1:54)

Mary ALLERTON^2 and Thomas CUSHMAN, c1636 (MD 4:38)

Eleazer CUSHMAN^3 and Elizabeth COOMBS, 12 Jan. 1687, Plymouth (MD 13:205)

Eleazer CUSHMAN^4 (Eleazer^3) and Eunice (   ), pre 7 Oct. 1748

John RICKARD and Eunice (   ) CUSHMAN, 2 Nov. 1758, Plympton (Plym.Co.45:97)

James CUSHMAN^4 (Eleazer^3) and Sarah HATCH, 24 Dec. 1722, Plymouth (MD 14:40)

Mary CUSHMAN^5 (James^4) and Philip CANON, 30 June 1751

Lydia CUSHMAN^5 (James^4) and Ephraim JENNE, 26 Nov. 1741, Dartmouth

James CUSHMAN^5 Jr. (James^4) and Hannah NEGUS, Int. 3 Apr. 1752, Dartmouth (VR 2:-)

Ebenezer CUSHMAN^5 (James^4) and Zerviah SHERMAN

Elisha CUSHMAN^5 (James^4) and Reliance EASTLIN, 26 Nov. 1760 (Cushman Gen.:141)

Thomas CUSHMAN^5 (James^4) and Ruth CARVER

John CUSHMAN^4 (Eleazer^3) and Joanna PRAT, 19 Jan. 1715, Plympton (MD 2:236)

John CUSHMAN^5 (John^4) and Deborah RAYMOND, 3 Feb. 1746, Middleboro (MD 16:109)

Lydia CUSHMAN^4 (Eleazer^3) and John WATERMAN, 29 Dec. 1709, Plympton (MD 3:165)

Anthony WATERMAN^5 (Lydia Cushman^4) and Hannah VAUGHAN, 26 Feb. 1735/36, Halifax (VR:32)

Anthony WATERMAN^6 (Anthony^5) and Sarah CURTIS, 15 Nov. 1764, Scituate (Int. 2 July, 1764, Halifax VR:62)

James WATERMAN^7 (Anthony^6) and 1st Hannah BATES, 20 Oct. 1790

James WATERMAN^7 and 2nd Polly PAYSON, 12 July 1795

John WATERMAN^5 (Lydia Cushman^4) and Fear STURTEVANT^5 (Fear Cushman^4, Isaac^3, Mary Allerton^2), 15 May 1740, Halifax (VR:34)

Isaac WATERMAN^6 (John^5) and Lucy SAMPSON^6 (Bethiah^5, Jonathan Samson^4, Lydia Standish^3, Alexander^2), c1780 (MD 7:111)

Lucy SAMPSON[6] and 2nd Daniel SOULE[6] (Ephraim[5], Zachariah[4], Ben.[3], John[2]), 10 Sept. 1818, Halifax (VR:86)

Lucy WATERMAN[7] (Isaac[6]) and Ephraim BARKER

Lucy Waterman BARKER[8] (Lucy Waterman[7]) and Benjamin Franklin STONE, 27 June 1837

Perez WATERMAN[6] (Perez[5]) and 2nd Ruth NYE, Int. 19 Nov. 1784, Bridgewater

Jonathan WATERMAN[6] (Perez[5], Lydia Cushman[4]) and 1st Abigail WASHBURN, 24 Oct. 1768, Bridgewater (VR)

Jonathan WATERMAN[6] and 2nd Hannah BARTLET, 18 Dec. 1796 (Brookfield VR:266,432)

Benjamin WATERMAN[7] (Perez[6]) and Lucy STONE, c1805

Moses CUSHMAN[4] (Eleazer[3]) and Mary JACKSON, 22 Aug. 1721, Plympton (MD 3:92)

Abner CUSHMAN[5] (Moses[4]) and Mary TILSON, 6 Feb. 1745/46, Halifax (VR:33)

Mary TILSON and 2nd James FAUNCE, 17 July 1777, Halifax (VR:20)

Micro #2 of 9

Deborah CUSHMAN[5] (Moses[4]) and 1st Thomas HOOPER, 4 Mar. 1762, Halifax (VR:31)

Deborah CUSHMAN[5] and 2nd William DUNHAM, 1 Feb. 1781 (Int. 13 Jan.; Plym.TR 2:146)

William BARNES and Jane FISH, Int. 6 Jan. 1781, Plymouth (TR 2:146)

Rebecca CUSHMAN[6] (Abner[5]) and Silvanus LEACH, 27 Feb. 1772, Halifax (VR:30)

Rebecca LEACH[7] (Rebecca Cushman[6]) and Asa PRATT, 3 Dec. 1818, Halifax (VR:86)

Asa PRATT and Lydia LYON, 8 Aug. 1802, Halifax (VR:79)

Asa PRATT and Sally LOVELL, 8 Nov. 1789, Weymouth (VR 2:146)

Asa PRATT 3d and Betsey R. LOVETT, Int. 1 Aug. 1807, Weymouth (VR 2:146)

Asa PRATT 4th and Sarah BATES, 10 Feb. 1811, Weymouth (VR 2:146)

Asa PRATT 4th and Rebecca BADLAM, 11 May 1814, Weymouth (VR 2:146)

Asa T. PRATT and Mercy CLAPP, Int. 13 Nov. 1842, Weymouth (VR 2:146)

Jonathan CUSHMAN and Rachel HOBART, 28 Sept. 1794 (Pembroke VR:264,290)

Elkanah CUSHMAN[3] and 1st Elizabeth COLE, 10 Feb. 1677, Plymouth (MD 13:203)

Elkanah CUSHMAN[3] and 2nd Martha COOKE[3] (Jacob[2]), 2 Mar. 1683, Plymouth (MD 13:203)

Hugh COLE and Elizabeth (   ) COOKE, 1 Jan. 1688/89, (Plym. TR:127)

Elizabeth CUSHMAN[4] (Elkanah[3]) and Robert WATERMAN, 5 Dec. 1723, Plympton (MD 2:139)

Allerton CUSHMAN[4] and 1st Mary BUCK, 11 Jan. 1710/11, Plympton (MD 2:235)

Allerton CUSHMAN[4] and 2nd Elizabeth SAMPSON, 15 Sept. 1726, Plympton (MD 1:247)

Allerton CUSHMAN[5] (Allerton[4]) and Alethea SOULE[4] (Jos.[3], John[2]), 30 Jan. 1734/35, Duxbury (MD 11:241)

Lydia CUSHMAN[6] (Allerton[5]) and Ephraim FOOT (MD 6:121-23)

Elkanah CUSHMAN[4] (Elkanah[3]) and Hester BARNES, 23 Feb. 1702/03, Plymouth (MD 14:35)

Hannah BARNES and 2nd Benjamin WARREN^3 (Joseph^2), 25 Oct. 1716, Plymouth (MD 14:38)

Elizabeth CUSHMAN^5 (Elkanah^4) and Ichabod DELANO, 20 May 1725, Plymouth (MD 14:71)

Elkanah CUSHMAN^5 (Elkanah^4) and Lydia BRADFORD^4 (David^3, Wm.^{2}), 31 Mar. 1740, Plymouth
  (MD 14:159)

Lydia BRADFORD^4 and 2nd Dr. Lazarus Le BARON, 2 May 1743, Plymouth (MD 14:160)

Hannah CUSHMAN^5 (Elkanah^4) and John WATERMAN, 17 Aug. 1731, Plymouth (MD 14:73)

James CUSHMAN^5 (Elkanah^4) and Hannah COBB, 11 Apr. 1737, Plymouth (MD 14:157)

Hannah COBB and 2nd Joseph RUGGLES, 13 Jan. 1742/43, Plymouth (MD 14:160)

Lieut. Josiah CUSHMAN^4 (Elkanah^3) and Susanna SHURTLEF, 29 Dec. 1709, Plympton
  (MD 2:235)

Anna CUSHMAN^5 (Josiah^4) and Robert AVERY (MD 21:103) <see p.288>

Elkanah CUSHMAN^5 (Josiah^4) and 1st Hannah STANDISH^5 (Zachariah^4, Ebenezer^3, Alexander^2)

Elkanah CUSHMAN^5 and 2nd Patience (   ) PERKINS

Isaiah CUSHMAN^5 (Josiah^4) and Sarah KING, 1 Nov. 1753

Sarah CUSHMAN^6 (Isaiah^5) and Joseph PERKINS^6 (Deborah Soule^5, Ebenezer^4, Ben.^{3}, John^2),
  5 Oct. 1780, Plympton

Josiah CUSHMAN^5 (Josiah^4) and 1st Sarah STANDISH^5 (Zachariah^4, Eben.^{3}, Alexander^2),
  10 July 1749

Josiah CUSHMAN^5 and 2nd Deborah RING, aft. Feb. 1752

Sarah CUSHMAN^6 (Josiah^5) and Daniel SOULE^6 (Ephraim^5, Zachariah^4, Ben.^{3}, John^2)

Susanna CUSHMAN^5 (Josiah^4) and Benjamin SHURTLEFF, 25 Mar. 1745 (Carver VR:99,128)

Martha CUSHMAN^4 (Elkanah^3) and Nathaniel HOLMES, 6 June 1717, Plympton (MD 2:237)

Rev. Isaac CUSHMAN^3 and Rebecca HARLOW^4 (Rebecca Bartlett^3, Mary Warren^2), c1675/76
  (MD 1:210)

Rebecca CUSHMAN^4 (Isaac^3) and Jacob MITCHELL^4 (Jacob^3,Experience), 18 Nov. 1701,
  Plymouth (MD 13:207) (see p.152, <4>)

Fear CUSHMAN^4 (Isaac^3) and William STURTEVANT, 12 Feb. 1707, Plymouth (MD 14:34)

Fear STURTEVANT^5 (Fear Cushman^4) and John WATERMAN^5 (Lydia Cushman^4, Eleazer^3, Mary
  Allerton^2), 15 May 1740, Halifax (VR:34)

Hannah STURTEVANT^5 (Fear Cushman^4) and Jonathan RIPLEY, 20 Jan. 1731, Plympton
  (MD 2:51)

Isaac STURTEVANT^5 (Fear Cushman^4) and Sarah FULLER^5 (Nathaniel^4, Samuel^{3-2-1}), 8 Apr.
  1731, Plympton (MD 2:50)

Sarah FULLER^5 and 2nd Austin BEARSE, Int. 19 Dec. 1756, Halifax (VR:59)

Simeon STURTEVANT^6 (Isaac^5) and Ruth TOMSON^5 (Amasa^4, Tho.^{3}, Mary Cooke^2), 29 Nov.
  1764, Halifax (VR:32)

Levi STURTEVANT^7 (Simeon^6) and Mary CHAMBERLAIN^6 (Freedom^5, Mary Soule^4, Aaron^3, John^2), c1793

Simeon STURTEVANT^7 (Simeon^6) and Margaret JOHNSON, 9 May 1790, Kingston (VR:23 - Int.)

Ichabod CUSHMAN^4 (Isaac^3) and 1st Esther BARNES

Ichabod CUSHMAN^4 and 2nd Patience HOLMES, 27 Nov. 1712, Plympton (MD 2:236)

Patience HOLMES and 2nd Elnathan WOOD, 23 Apr. 1735, Middleboro (MD 13:251)

Experience CUSHMAN^5 (Ichabod^4) and Jonathan SMITH, 6 Sept. 1737, Middleboro (MD 13:253)

Jonathan SMITH and 1st Susanna TURNER, 29 Jan. 1712/13, Middleboro (MD 2:158)

Jonathan SMITH and 2nd Sarah CHURCHILL, 8 June 1725, Middleboro (MD 4:73)

Holmes CUSHMAN^6 (Ichabod^5) and Molly PADDOCK, 18 Nov. 1787, Middleboro (VR 4:2:163)

Sarah CUSHMAN^5 (Ichabod^4) and Daniel VAUGHAN, 12 Aug. 1735, Middleboro (MD 13:251)

Jabez VAUGHAN^6 (Sarah Cushman^5) and Lois SOULE^5 (Zachariah^4, Ben.^{3}, John^2), 25 Aug. 1763, Middleboro (MD 19:174)

Lucy VAUGHAN^7 (Jabez^6) and John PADDOCK

Asenath VAUGHAN^7 (Jabez^6) and John DARLING

Deborah VAUGHAN^7 (Jabez^6) and Phineas RAYMOND

Jonah VAUGHAN^7 (Jabez^6) and Rebecca MORTON

Ira VAUGHAN^8 (Jonah^7) and 1st Abigail Luce JOHNSON, 28 May 1829[2]

Ira VAUGHAN^8 and 2nd Emily JOHNSON, 18 Jan. 1831[2]

Z. Morton VAUGHAN and Katherine JOHNSON, 30 July 1832[2]

Lois VAUGHAN^7 (Jabez^6) and Nehemiah COBB, c1806 (Cobb Gen.:169)

William CUSHMAN^5 (Ichabod^4) and 1st Susanna SAMPSON, 25 Dec. 1735, Middleboro (MD13:251)

William CUSHMAN^5 and 2nd Priscilla (TINKHAM^5) Cobb (Shubael^4, Ebenezer^3, Mary Brown^2), 11 Apr. 1751, Middleboro (MD 18:84)

Noah CUSHMAN^6 (William^5) and 1st Mercy SOULE^6 (Jabez^5, Zachariah^4, Ben.^{3}, John^2), c1768 (MD 29:185)

Noah CUSHMAN^6 and 2nd Zilpha THOMPSON^6 (Francis^5, Thomas^4, John^3, Mary Cooke^2), c1789 (MD 32:163)

Noah CUSHMAN^6 and 3rd Zerviah THOMAS, c1810 (Cushman Gen.:292)

Hercules CUSHMAN^7 (Noah^6) and 1st Mary WASHBURN^8 (Abiel^7, Edward$^{6-5}$, James^4, Eliz. Mitchell^3, Jane Cooke^2), c1811/12 (MD 15:3)

Hercules CUSHMAN^7 and 2nd Betsy P. WASHBURN^8 (Abiel^7), aft. 1813 (MD 15:3)

Jacob CUSHMAN^8 (Jacob^7, Noah^6) and Roxa SHAW, 22 Mar. 1824, Middleboro (VR 8:268)

Lieut. Isaac CUSHMAN^4 (Isaac^3) and 1st Sarah GIBBS^4 (Alice Warren^3, Nathaniel^2), 28 Jan. 1700/01, Plymouth (MD 13:207)

Lieut. Isaac CUSHMAN^4 and 2nd Mercy(BRADFORD^4) Freeman (John^3, Wm.^{2}), 10 Oct. 1717, Harwich (MD 7:197)

Phebe CUSHMAN[5] (Isaac[4]) and 1st Nathaniel SPOONER, 6 Nov. 1729, Plympton (MD 5:210)

Phebe CUSHMAN[5] and 2nd Barnabas HEDGE, aft. 1732 (Spooner Gen.:73)

Fear CUSHMAN[5] (Isaac[4]) and Nehemiah STURTEVANT, 11 Dec. 1734

Micro #3 of 9

Mary CUSHMAN[4] (Isaac[3]) and Robert WATERMAN. 19 Mar. 1702, Plymouth (MD 13:208)

Josiah WATERMAN[5] (Mary Cushman[4]) and Joanna BRIANT, 21 Feb. 1722/23, Plympton (MD2:139)

Ichabod WATERMAN[6] (Josiah[5]) and Hannah ROGERS[6] (Ben.[5], John[4-3], Jos.[2]), 15 Dec. 1757, Kingston (VR)

Robert WATERMAN[5] (Martha CUSHMAN[4]) and Martha CUSHMAN[5] (Josiah[4], Elkanah[3], Mary Allerton[2]), c1734 (Halifax VR:1,42)

Rebecca WATERMAN[6] (Robert[5]) and Rev. Ephraim BRIGGS, 5 Apr. 1768, Halifax (VR:30)

Samuel WATERMAN[5] (Mary Cushman[4]) and 1st Mary TOMSON[4] (Thomas[3], Mary Cooke[2]), 16 Mar. 1737, Halifax (VR:32)

Samuel WATERMAN[5] and 2nd Mary FULLER, 14 Sept. 1756, Halifax (VR:35)

Seth WATERMAN[6] (Sam.[5]) and Hannah PERKINS, Int. 26 July 1762, Halifax (VR:61)

Thomas WATERMAN[5] (Mary Cushman[4]) and Mercy FREEMAN[6] (Jonathan[5], Tho.[4], Mercy Prence[3], Patience Brewster[2]), c1729 (Freeman Gen.:99)

Thomas WATERMAN[6] (Thomas[5]) and Joanna TOMSON[5] (John[4], Jacob[3], Mary Cooke[2]), 18 Dec. 1766, Halifax (VR:30)

Priscilla WATERMAN[7] (Freeman[6]) and Josiah MARSHALL, Int. 26 Nov. 1798, Halifax (VR:67)

Sarah CUSHMAN[4] (Isaac[3]) and James BRYANT, 8 July 1708, Plympton (MD 3:165)

Lydia CUSHMAN[3] and William HARLOW[4] (Rebecca Bartlett[3], Mary Warren[2]) (MD 4:39)

Mary CUSHMAN[3] and ( ) HUTCHINSON (MD 4:39) [3]

Sarah CUSHMAN[3] and John HAWKS, 11 Apr. 1661 (MD 17:224)

Sarah CUSHMAN[3] and 2nd Daniel HUTCHINGS Sr., aft. Aug. 1694 (MD 17:224)

John HAWKS and 1st Rebecca MAVERICK[3] (Remember Allerton[2]), c1658

Anna HAWKS and James HINDS, 12 Dec. 1789, Marblehead (VR 2:212,204)

Elizabeth HAWKES and Andrew ALLEY, 23 Jan. 1820, Lynn

Esther HAWKES and Jonathan SHILEBER, Int. 7 Apr.1799, Lynn

Eunice HAWKES and Daniel HITCHINS, 18 July 1766, Lynn (VR)

Hannah HAWKES and Gidney WITT, Int. 26 Sept. 1756, Lynn

Love HAWK and Moses DOLE, 27 Sept. 1796, Lynn (VR)

Lydia HAWKES and Thaddeus RIDDAU, Int. 14 Aug. 1743, Lynn

Lydia HAWKS and Benjamin PERKINS, 4 Nov. 1768, Lynn (VR)

Lydia HAWKES and John HITCHINGS, 3 Dec. 1768, Lynn

Mary HAWKES and Thomas MANSFIELD, 27 July 1756, Lynn (VR)

Mercy HAWKS and Jonathan HART, Int. 2 Mar. 1734/35, Lynn (VR:95)

Sarah HAWKES and Ezra WAYT, 8 Mar. 1752, Lynn (VR)

Sarah HAWKS and Samuel MERRIT, 26 Apr. 1768, Lynn (VR)

Sarah HAWKES and Thomas HART, 10 or 20 Jan. 1767, Lynn (VR)

Sarah HAWKES and Richard SHUTE, 18 Sept. 1787, Lynn (VR)

Susanna HAWKS and Michal NEWHALL, 26 Apr. 1762, Lynn (VR)

Adam HAWKS^4 (Sarah Cushman^3) and Elizabeth (   ), c1689 (MD 17:225)

Elizabeth (   ) HAWKS and poss. 2nd George LILLY, 15 Oct. 1695, Salem (Lynn VR:30-Int)

John HAWKS^5 (Adam^4) and Mary WHITFORD, Int. 12 Aug. 1710, Lynn (VR:37)

Adam HAWKES^6 (John^5) and 1st Huldah BROWN, 29 Nov. 1739, Lynn (Reading VR:363)

Adam HAWKES^6 and 2nd Lydia WILEY, 11 June 1747, Reading (VR:353)

Huldah HAWKES^7 (Adam^6) and Jonathan BROWN, 1 Mar. 1764, Lynn (VR)

Elizabeth HAWKES^6 (John^5) and John MEAD, Int. 10 June 1750, Lynn

Eunice HAWKES^6 (John^5) and Jacob WALTON, 6 Mar. 1744, Reading (Lynn VR)

Eve HAWKES^6 (John^5) and John BAUCROFT$^{<4>}$

Lydia HAWKES^6 (John^5) and Thomas NORWOOD, Int. 8 Apr. 1744, Lynn

Mary HAWKES^6 (John^5) and Nathaniel FELCH, 2 Dec. 1732, Lynn (VR)

Ebenezer HAWKES^4 (Sarah Cushman^3) and 1st ELizabeth COGSWELL, 16 June 1701, Lynn
    (Ipswich VR 2:106,212)

Ebenezer HAWKES^4 and 2nd Sarah (BASSETT)(Griffin) Newhall, Int. 13 May 1719, Lynn

Ebenezer HAWKES^4 and 3rd Ruth (   ) GRAVES, 9 Nov. 1732, Boston (Lynn VR)

Elizabeth HAWKES^5 (Ebenezer^4) and Joseph GRIFFIN

Ebenezer HAWKES^5 (Ebenezer^4) and Anna BREED, Int. 11 Apr. 1725, Lynn (VR 2:55,177)

Benjamin HAWKES^6 (Ebenezer^5) and Deborah KIMBALL, 31 July 1760, Marblehead (VR)

Deborah KIMBALL and 2nd Edward BOWEN, 16 July 1774

Benjamin HAWKES^7 (Ben.^{6}) and Mehitable LASKEY, 19 Jan. 1790, Marblehead (VR)

Deborah HAWKES^7 (Ben.^{6}) and Samuel Fortin ROUNDEY

Ebenezer HAWKES^6 (Samuel^5) and Rebecca ALLEY, 17 Apr. 1765, Lynn (ch. rcd.)

Matthew HAWKES^6 (Sam.^{5}) and Ruth BREED, 1 June 1774, Lynn

Matthew HAWKES and Ruth COLLINS, 29 Apr. 1778, Lynn (ch. rcd.)

Matthew HAWKES and Betsey SWEETSER, 13 Nov. 1792, Lynn (ch. rcd.)

Micro #4 of 9

John HAWKS^4 (Sarah Cushman^3) and 1st Abigail FLOID, Int. 7 Jan. 1698/99, Lynn (VR:14)

John HAWKS^4 and 2nd Elizabeth (SCADLOCK) Curtis, 4 Sept. 1735, Lynn (VR)

William CURTICE and Elizabeth SCARLET, Int. 26 Mar. 1709, Lynn (Essex Inst. Hist. Coll. Vol. XVI, p.76)

Abigail HAWKES^5 (John^4) and Cornelius JONES, .22 Apr. 1729, Lynn (VR)

Sarah HAWKS^5 (John^4) and Thomas GOWING, 27 Dec. 1720, Lynn (VR 3:88)

Mercy HAWKS^4 (Sarah Cushman^3) and Nathaniel GOODHUE, Int. 28 Nov. 1696, Lynn (VR:26)

William GOODHUE^5 (Mercy Hawkes^4) and Ruth PRESTON, Int. 19 Aug. 1727, Ipswich (VR 2:191)

Thomas HAWKS^4 (Sarah Cushman^3) and Sarah HAVEN, 16 Feb.1702/03 Lynn (VR 2:44)

Sarah HAWKES^5 (Tho.^{4}) and Benjamin GRAY, 30 Oct. 1744, Lynn (VR)

Elkanah HAWKES^5 (Tho.^{4}) and Eunice NEWHALL, 4 May 1742, Lynn (VR 4:32)

Thomas HOAKS and Esther NEWHALL, 23 June 1768, Lynn (VR 4:518)

Joseph Haven HAWKS and Mary HITCHINS, 30 Apr. 1792, Lynn (VR 5:140)

Hannah HAWKS^6 (Jonathan^5, Tho.^{4}) and Samuel CHENEY

Hannah HAWKS^5 (Tho.^{4}) and Jonathan WAITE, 10 July 1734, Lynn (VR)

Jonathan HAWKES^5 (Tho.^{4}) and 1st Sarah NEWHALL, 16 Oct. 1735, Lynn (VR 3:42)

Jonathan HAWKES^5 and 2nd Abigail FARRINGTON, 11 Oct. 1743, Lynn (VR 3:218)

Elizabeth HAWKS^6 (Jonathan^5) and 1st Zachariah POOL

Elizabeth HAWKS^6 and 2nd Rev. Peter THACHER

Jonathan HAWKES^6 (Jonathan^5) and Rachel SPRAGUE, 20 May 1776, Chelsea (VR:386,422)

Abigail HAWKS^6 (Jonathan^5) and Thomas RUGGLES, 9 NOv. 1777, Boston (VR 30:388)

Thomas CUSHMAN^3 and 1st Ruth HOWLAND^2, 17 Nov. 1664, Plymouth (MD 17:185)

Thomas CUSHMAN^3 and 2nd Abigail FULLER^4 (Sam.^{3}, Mathew^2, Edw.^{1}), 16 Oct. 1679, Rehoboth (MD 22:115)

Desire CUSHMAN^4 (Tho.^{3}) and poss. Samuel KENT, aft. Dec. 1686

Benjamin CUSHMAN^4 (Tho.^{3}) and 1st Sarah EATON^4 (Ben.$^{3-2}$), 8 Jan. 1712, Plympton (MD 2:236)

Benjamin CUSHMAN^4 and 2nd Sarah (   ) BELL, aft. Sept. 1737 (MD 10:112)

Abigail CUSHMAN^5 (Ben.^{4}) and 1st Zabdiel SAMSON^5 (Hannah Soule^4, Ben.^{3}, John^2), 31 Dec. 1747

Abigail CUSHMAN^5 and 2nd Abiah WHITMARSH, aft. Sept. 1776 (MD 11:119)

Huldah CUSHMAN^5 (Ben.^{4}) and 1st David FEANING, 2nd John MILLARD

Joanna CUSHMAN^5 (Ben.^{4}) and George STURTEVANT

Benjamin CUSHMAN^5 (Ben.^{4}) and Zerviah SAMSON (Cushman Gen.:169)

Caleb CUSHMAN^5 (Ben.^{4}) and Sarah BARROWS, 11 Nov. 1742 (Cushman Gen.:161)

Jabez CUSHMAN^5 (Ben.^{4}) and Sarah PADELFORD, 2 Dec. 1736, Taunton (VR 2:132,353)

Jabez CUSHMAN^6 (John^5) and Ursula BEARCE, 14 July 1780 (Cushman Gen.:161,257)

Nancy RIDER^7 (Hannah Cushman^6) and Benjamin HUTCHINS, 5 Apr. 1790, New Gloucester ME

Zebedee CUSHMAN[6] (Jabez[5]) and Sarah PADELFORD, c1781 (Cush. Gen.:161,255)

Hannah CUSHMAN[6] (Jabez[5]) and James RIDER, 13 Aug. 1767, Middleboro (MD 29:183)

Samuel CUSHMAN[6] (Zebedee[5]) and Lydia GANO, c1770 (Cush. Gen.:161,254)

Lydia GANO and 2nd Edward THOMAS, 13 July 1794 (Cush. Gen.:161,254)

Phebe CUSHMAN[6] (Jabez[5]) and Joseph BASSETT, 2 Dec. 1756, Bridgewater (VR 2:43,103)

Joseph BASSETT and 2nd Sarah (PRIOR)(Fobes) Eaton, 1798 (Cush.Gen.:161)

Sarah CUSHMAN[6] (Jabez[5]) and John BASSETT (Cush.Gen.:161)

Thomas CUSHMAN[5] (Ben.[4]) and Anna CHIPMAN[5] (Jacob[4], Sam.[3], Hope Howland[2]), Int. 8 Sept.
    1751, Halifax (VR:58)

Job CUSHMAN[4] (Thomas[3]) and Lydia BREWSTER[4] (Wm.[3], Love[2]), c1705 (MD 7:176)[5]

Maria CUSHMAN[5] (Job[4]) and John BARKER, 10 Dec. 1732, Duxbury (Hist.Dux.:224)

Robert CUSHMAN[4] (Tho.[3]) and 1st Persis (   ), c1697, (MD 4:111)

Robert CUSHMAN[4] and 2nd Prudence SHERMAN, aft. Jan. 1743/44 (MD 7:28)

Joshua CUSHMAN[5] (Robert[4]) and 1st Mary SOULE[4] (Jos.[3], John[2]), 2 Jan. 1732/33, Duxbury
    (MD 11:81)

Joshua CUSHMAN[5] and 2nd Deborah FORD, 5 Mar. 1752, Marshfield (Duxbury VR)

Apollos CUSHMAN[6] (Joshua[5]) and 1st Eleanor KEEN[6] (Isaac[5], Josiah[4], Abigail Little[3],
    Anna Warren[2]), 1 Mar. 1768 (Cush. Gen.:149)

Apollos CUSHMAN[6] and 2nd Abigail PARTRIDGE

Cephas CUSHMAN[6] (Joshua[5]) and Judith CLARK, 7 Dec. 1766, Rochester (VR 2:81,99)

Joshua CUSHMAN[6] (Joshua[5]) and Mercy WADSWORTH

Soule CUSHMAN[6] (Joshua[5]) and 1st Lydia KEMPTON, c1773

Soule CUSHMAN[6] and 2nd Thankful DELANO, c1775

Robert CUSHMAN[5] (Robert[4]) and Mercy WASHBURN[5] (Lydia Billington[4], Isaac[3], Francis[2])

Mercy WASHBURN[5] and 2nd John FULLER[4] (Samuel[3-2-1]), aft. Sept. 1751 (MD 7:28)

Jerusha CUSHMAN[6] (Robert[5]) and Ebenezer COBB, 30 Oct. 1747, Kingston (Gen.Adv.3:22)

Ruth CUSHMAN[5] (Robert[4]) and Luke PERKINS, 28 Jan. 1716, Plympton (VR)

Thomas CUSHMAN[5] (Robert[4]) and 1st Alice HAYWARD[5] (Tho.[4], Sarah Mitchell[3], Experience)[6]

Thomas CUSHMAN[5] and 2nd Mehitable FAUNCE[5] (Lydia Cooke[4], Jacob[3-2]), Int. 18 Feb.
    1737/38, Kingston (Cush.Gen.:131,146)

Thomas CUSHMAN[6] (Tho.[5]) and Bethiah THOMPSON

Thomas CUSHMAN[7] (Tho.[6]) and Lucy PRATT

Samuel CUSHMAN[4] (Tho.[3]) and Fear CORSSER, 8 Dec. 1709, Plympton (MD 2:235)

Sarah PERKINS and Andrew BARRONS, 1 Aug. 1771, Plympton

Desire CUSHMAN[5] (Sam.[4]) and Ebenezer FOSTER, 17 Sept. 1730 (Foster Gen.<1899>:713-17)

Fear FOSTER[6] (Desire Cushman[5]) and Oliver PECK, 22 Apr. 1759, Cumberland RI
    (VR 3:5:32,51)

Ira PECK[7] (Fear Foster[6]) and Lydia PALMER, c1798 (Foster Gen.:714)

Jacob CUSHMAN[5] (Sam.[4]) and 1st Elizabeth READ, 2nd Hannah (   ) COBB

Mercy CUSHMAN[5] (Sam.[4]) and Noah FULLER, c1740 (Attleboro VR:67)

Chloe FULLER[6] (Mercy Cushman[5]) and John BATES, 26 Apr. 1770, Attleboro (VR)

Noah FULLER and Rachel PIDGE, 25 Feb. 1711/12, Attleboro (VR:12)

Thomas CUSHMAN[4] (Tho.[3]) and Sarah STRONG, pre 1703

Remember ALLERTON[2] (Isaac[1])

Remember ALLERTON[2] and Moses MAVERICK (MD 5:129)

Moses MAVERICK and 2nd Eunice (   ) ROBERTS, 22 Oct. 1656

Sarah MAVERICK and John NORMAN, 10 Nov. 1683, Marblehead (VR 2:286,306)

Mary MAVERICK and Archibald FERGUSON, pre 1686

Benjamin HAWKES and Abigail BECKET, c1781 (Essex Coll.8:142,143)

Sarah HAWKES and Richard SHUTE Jr., 18 Sept. 1787, Lynn (VR)[7]

Moses HAWKES and Susannah TOWNSEND, 22 Feb. 1729/30

Moses HAWKES and Susanna HICHINGS, 9 Apr. 1730

Micro #6 of 9

Abigail MAVERICK[3] and Samuel WARD (MD 5:132)

Samuel WARD and 2nd Sarah (BRADSTREET) Hubbard, aft. May 1681

Abigail WARD[4] (Abigail Maverick[3]) and William HINDS, c1680

Abigail HINDS[5] (Abigail Ward[4]) and Joseph HORMAN, 21 Dec. 1710, Marblehead (VR 2:212,219)

Abigail HINDS[6] (John[5], Abigail Ward[4]) and Thomas ROLLS, 19 Aug. 1729, Marblehead
    (VR 2:211,367)

John HINDS[5] (Abigail Ward[4]) and Constance BENNETT, 25 Nov. 1700, Marblehead
    (VR 2:324,211)

Susanna HINDS[6] (John[5]) and 1st John NORTHEY, 2 Mar. 1731/32, Marblehead (VR 2:211,307)

Susanna HINDS[6] and 2nd Roger VICKERY, 7 Apr. 1746, Marblehead (VR 2:307,444)

Susanna HINDS[6] and 3rd Samuel GARDNER, 31 Dec. 1767, Marblehead (VR 2:160,443)

John NORTHEY and Mary CROSS, 4 Jan. 1784, Marblehead (VR 2:104,307)

John NORTHEY and Mrs. Mary FOWLER, 26 Dec. 1802

Mercy Craw/Cross NORTHEY and Levi MORSE, 2 Feb. 1812, Marblehead (VR)

Joseph NORTHEY[7] (Susanna Hinds[6]) and Mercy LeCRAW 21 Jan. 1762, Marblehead
    (VR 2:258,307)

Mercy NORTHEY[8] (Jos.[7]) and Samuel BARTOL, 4 Dec. 1785, Marblehead (VR 2:27,307)

Samuel BARTOL and 2nd Hannah (CALLEY) Hanover, Int. 1 May 1795

Mercy Craw BARTOL and Levi WALLIS, 8 May 1817

Samuel BARTOLL and 1st Sally RUSSELL, 12 Mar. 1809, Marblehead (VR 2:27,375)

Samuel BARTOLL and 2nd Hannah RUSSELL, 5 Dec. 1833, Marblehead

Sarah NORTHEY[7] (Susanna Hinds[6]) and Richard WOOD, 11 Nov. 1756, Marblehead (VR)

Richard WOOD and 2nd Abigail MEEK(sp), 7 May 1769, Marblehead (VR)

Rebecca HINDS[5] (Abigail Ward[4]) and William GROSS, c1709 (Marblehead 1st ch. rcds.)

Martha WARD[4] (Abigail Maverick[3]) and John TUTTLE, 3 (Dec.?) 1689, Ipswich (VR 2:435,443)

Sarah TUTTLE[5] (Martha Ward[4]) and Nicholas NOYES (Noyes Gen. 1:310)

Martha TUTTLE[5] (Martha Ward[4]) and Mark HASKELL, Int. 14 Jan. 1709, Ipswich
    (VR 2:209,435)

Jonathan INGERSOLL and Sarah LORD, Int. 20 Nov. 1770, Ipswich (VR 2:238,285)

Mary TUTTLE[5] (Martha Ward[4]) and Nathaniel WARNER, Int. 28 (2nd m.) 1716, Ipswich
    (VR 2:435,445)

John WARNER[6] (Mary Tuttle[5]) and Susanna HODGKINS, Int. 24 Oct. 1747, Ipswich (VR)

Remember TUTTLE[5] (Martha Ward[4]) and Job HARRIS, c1722 (Ipswich VR)

Job HARRIS and 2nd Ruth (   ) GORDALE(sp), 30 Sept. 1735, Boston

Sally HARRIS[7] (Nathaniel[6], Remember Tuttle[5]) and Robert CALDER

Mary WOOD[4] (Abigail Maverick[3]) and 1st (Joseph?) DOLIVER (MD 5:132)

Mary WOOD[4] and 2nd William WATERS/WALTERS, 17 July 1699, Marblehead (VR:129,450)

Hannah WATERS and Philip TEWKSBERRY, 29 Nov. 1720, Marblehead

Micro #7 of 9

Joseph DOLIBER and Mary FURNACE, 19 Oct. 1704, Marblehead

Margaret DOLLIVER and John CURTIS, 25 Dec. 1707, Marblehead

Remember WARD[4] (Abigail Maverick[3]) and William WILSON, 1 May 1679, Charlestown

William WILSON and 2nd Mary PEARSE, 1-8-1685

Samuel WARD[4] (Abigail Maverick[3]) and Sarah TUTTLE, 13 Nov. 1699, Ipswich (VR:436,443)

Sarah TUTTLE and 2nd John DENNIS, Int. 1 June 1713, Ipswich (VR:324,443)

Elizabeth MAVERICK[3] and 1st Nathaniel GRAFTON, 6 Apr. 1665, Salem (Essex Inst. Hist.
    Coll.2:97)

Elizabeth MAVERICK[3] and 2nd Thomas SKINNER, c1676

ELizabeth GRAFTON[4] (Eliz. Maverick[3]) and William HEWES/HUGHES

Priscilla GRAFTON[4] (Eliz. Maverick[3]) and Thomas JACKSON

Abigail SKINNER[4] (Eliz. Maverick[3]) and 1st Ebenezer AGER

Rebecca MAVERICK^3 and John HAWKS, 3 June 1658, Lynn (MD 17:223,224)

John HAWKS and 2nd Sarah CUSHMAN^3 (Mary Allerton^2), 11 Apr. 1661 (MD17:224)

Moses HAWKS^4 (Rebecca Maverick^3) and Margaret COGSWELL, 10 May 1698,
    Lynn (MD 17:224)

Margaret HAWKS^5 (Moses^4) and Jeremiah EATON, 10 Apr. 1722, Lynn (VR)

Rebecca HAWKS^5 (Moses^4) and Samuel WHITFORD, 3 Dec. 1732, Lynn (VR)

Daniel HUCHINGS Sr. and Mrs. Sarah HAWKS, Int. 7 Nov. 1695, Lynn (VR)

John HAWKS^5 (Moses^4) and Hannah PREAST, 27 Apr. 1732, Lynn (VR 3:208)

Hannah PREAST and 2nd Thomas FULLER, 1 Nov. 1753, Lynn (VR 2:146,175)

John HAWKES^6 (John^5) and Hannah JAMES, Int. 5 Dec. 1770, Lynn (VR 2:176,204)

John HAWKS^7 (John^6) and Alice ALLEN, 26 Oct. 1795, Lancaster (VR;133)

Cynthia Austiss HAWKES^8 (John^7) and Benjamin F. FARNSWORTH, 22 Feb. 1841, Lancaster
    (VR:246)

Hannah HAWKES^7 (John^6) and Silas WILLARD, 24 Jan. 1793 (Lancaster VR:147- Int.)

Silas WILLARD and 2nd Hannah OSGOOD (Williard Gen.<1915>:202)$^{<8>}$

Mary HAWKES^7 (John^6) and Jonas WHITNEY, 2 June 1803, Lancaster (VR:165)

Sally HAWKES^7 (John^6) and Jonas LANE, 30 July 1809, Lancaster (VR:167)

Catherine HAWKES^7 (John^6) and Anthony PHELPS, 7 Apr. 1811, Lancaster$^{<9>}$

Samuel PHELPS and Lovenia MORSE, 21 Sept. 1785, Lancaster$^{<9>}$

Jonas PHELPS and Nancy PHELPS, 26 Mar. 1806, poss. Lancaster$^{<9>}$

Catherine May PHELPS^8 (Catherine Hawks^7) and Andrew Jackson FARNSWORTH, 11 Sept.
    1842, Lunenburg, VT (Bible)

Andrew J. FARNSWORTH and 2nd Mary C. POTTER, 8 Mar. 1848, Charlestown, Mass (Bible)

Benjamin HAWKES^7 (John^6) and Polly BALLARD, 11 June 1809, Lancaster (VR:167)

Adam HAWKES^6 (John^5) and Hannah NEWHALL, 10 July 1765, Lynn (VR 4:379)

Lydia HAWKES^7 (Adam^6) and 1st Simon FRANCIS, 10 May 1795

Lydia HAWKES^7 and 2nd Jonathan PEIRCE, 27 Apr. 1809

Moses HAWKES and Susanna TOWNSEND, 22 Feb. 1729/30, Lynn (VR)

Daniel HICHINS and Susanna TOWNSEND, 19 Oct. 1708, Lynn (VR)

Moses HAWKS^5 (Moses^4) and Susanna HICHINGS, 9 Apr. 1730, Lynn (VR 3:194)

Abijah HAWKS^7 (Abijah^6, Moses^5) and Lois FRIZZELL, 5 Jan. 1792, Petersham (VR:95,106)

Abijah HAWKS^8 (Abijah^7) and Susanna BOARDMAN

Lois HAWKS^8 (Abijah^7) and David TAFT, 1822

Amos HAWKS^7 (Abijah^6) and Harriet Arethusa HAWKS^8 (Abijah$^{7-6}$, Moses$^{5-4}$, Rebecca
    Maverick^3, Remember Allerton^2), c1818

Giles HAWKS^8 (Amos^7) and Harriet A. HOLLISTER

Laura HAWKS^9 (Giles^8) and F.P. SINCLAIR

Luretta HAWKS^9 (Giles^8) and Milan McCARTY

Hannah HAWKS^7 (Abijah^6) and John William THAYER

Mary Eliza THAYER^8 (Hannah Hawks^7) and John Livingston LOTT, 18 Sept. 1837

Abijah HAWKS^6 (Moses^5) and Hannah HICHINGS, Int. 27 Dec. 1761, Lynn (VR 2:177,184)

Nancy HAWKS^7 (Abijah^6) and Sanford BABBIT, 15 June 1759, Petersham (VR:66,106)

Daniel HAWKS^6 (Moses^5) and Rhoda PERHAM, 7 Nov. 1771, Pepperell

James HAWKS^6 (Moses^5) and Olive WILLIS, 7 Mar. 1776, Hardwick (VR)

Lois HAWKS^6 (Moses^5) and John HITCHINGS

Mary HAWKS^6 (Moses^5) and Thomas MANSFIELD, 22 July 1756, Lynn (VR)

Moses HAWKS^6 (Moses^5) and Mary RIDDAN, 9 Jan. 1755, Lynn (VR 2:176,330)

Benjamin HAWKES^7 (Moses^6) and Abigail BECKET

Nathan HAWKES^6 (Moses^5) and Sarah HITCHINGS, 3 Sept. 1769, Lynn (VR 4:527)

Daniel HAWKES^7 (Nathan^6) and Rachel ALLEN, 6 Dec. 1804, Lynn (VR)

Nathan HAWKES^7 (Nathan^6) and Elizabeth TARBELL, 22 Jan. 1805, Lynnfield

Susanna HAWKS^6 (Moses^5) and Michael NEWHALL, 26 Apr. 1762, Lynn (VR)

Michael NEWHALL and 2nd Joanna COLLINS, 11 July 1765, Lynn (VR)

Remember MAVERICK^3 and Edward WOODMAN (MD 5:137)

Remember WOODMAN^4 (Remember Maverick^3) and Thomas PERKINS, 26 July 1694, Boston
    (Rcd.Comm.9:218)

Elizabeth PERKINS^5 (Remember Woodman^4) and 1st James LOVEL, 10 June 1718, Weymouth (VR)

Elizabeth PERKINS^5 and 2nd John PHINNEY

Mary PERKINS^5 (Remember Woodman^4) and Joseph GURNEY, 10 June 1718, Weymouth (VR)

Lydia GURNEY^6 (Mary Perkins^5) and William HERASEY, 5 Nov. 1745, Abington (VR 2:91,102)

Perkins GURNEY^6 (Mary Perkins^4) and Jane DERBY, 8 Jan. 1746/47, Abington (VR 2:60,92)

Benoni GURNEY^6 (Mary Perkins^5) and Caroline WILKS

Lucins HARDING^9 (Zenas Harden^8, Lydia Hersey^7, Lydia Gurney^6) and Rebecca L. PRATT

Zenas HARDEN^8 (Lydia Hersey^7, Lydia Gurney^6) and Sally GANNETT^8 (Seth$^{7-6}$, Hannah
    Brett^5, Sarah Hayward^4, Sarah Mitchell^3, Experience) (see p.152, <4>)

Mary GURNEY^6 (Mary Perkins^5) and Isaac HERSEY, 5 Jan. 1743/44, Abington (VR)

David HERSEY^7 (Mary Gurney^6) and 1st Elizabeth JENKINS, 27 Dec. 1764, Abington (VR)

Desire HERSEY^8 (David Hersey^7) and Nathan STODDARD

Isaac HERSEY and Mary BICKNELL, 29 Dec. 1772, Abington (VR)

NOTES

<1> p.22, It has since been established that her surname is SWINNERTON. (NEHGR 124:133)

<2> p.25, Butler, Francis Gould. A History of Farmington, Franklin County, Maine..., 1776-1885. 1885. Farmington

<3> p.26, It has since been established that Mary's husband was Francis Hutchinson. (Mayflower Quarterly 52:28-32).

<4> p.27, Bowman questions whether she first married Ebenezer Giles, 7 Aug. 1739, Lynn (VR)

<5> p.29, Among Bowman's notes are references to Lydia as Lydia ARNOLD.

<6> p.29, Thomas and Alice were not married but had a son together, (Thomas, b. 25 Sept. 1736) therefore left descendants.

<7> p.30, Bowman questions whether he married second, Elizabeth Rhoades, 30 Oct. 1792.

<8> p.32, This second marriage appears highly unlikely. Silas died in 1819, 24 years before his first wife Hannah.

<9> p.32, Servin, Andrew T. and Judge Oliver Seymour. The Phelps Family of America. 2 Vols. 1899. Pittsfield, Mass.

JOHN BILLINGTON DESCENDANTS

Elinor (   ) BILLINGTON and 2nd Gregory ARMSTRONG, 1638 (PCR 12:33, 37)

Samuel BILLINGTON and Eliza NICKERSON (Bangor Hist.Mag. 4:216)

Olive BILLINGTON and 1st Richard SWETT (Bangor Hist.Mag 4:216)

Olive BILLINGTON and 2nd Nathaniel PEIRCE Jr., c1828 (Bangor Hist.Mag. 4:216)

Francis BILLINGTON[2] (John[1])

Francis BILLINGTON[2] and Christian (PENN) EATON, July 1634 (PCR 1:31)[<1>]

Martha BILLINGTON and Samuel EATON, 10 Jan. 1660, Plymouth (PCR 8:22)

Marcye BILLINGTON and John MARTIN, 27 June 1681, Plymouth (PCR 8:76)

Dorcas BILLINGTON[3] and Edward MAY

Elizabeth BILLINGTON[3] and 1st Richard BULLOCK, 21 Sept. 1660 (Rehoboth VR)[<2>]

John BULLOCK[4] (Elizabeth Billington[3]) and Elizabeth BARNES, 29 Jan. 1695, Swansea (VR)

Francis BILLINGTON[4] (Francis[3]) and Abigail CHURCHILL, 17 May 1702, Plymouth (MD 13:207)

Abigail CHURCHILL and 2nd Nathaniel HOWLAND[3] (Joseph[2]), 25 Jan. 1725/26, Plymouth
   (MD 14:71)

Sarah BILLINGTON[5] (Francis[4]) and James HOWARD, 3 May 1723, Plymouth (MD 14:40)

Content BILLINGTON[5] (Francis[4]) and Francis MERRIFIELD, 18 Oct. 1734, Plymouth (MD 14:75)

Jemima BILLINGTON[5] (Francis[4]) and Joseph BENT, 17 Oct. 1728, Plympton (MD 1:248)

Mercy BILLINGTON[5] (Francis[4]) and Matthew LEMOTE, 18 Feb. 1728/29, Plymouth (MD 14:72)

Mercy LEMOTE[6] (Mercy Billington[5]) and 1st William BARNES[6] (Seth[5], Mary Bartlett[4],
   Joseph[3], Mary Warren[2]), Int. 26 Apr. 1755, Plymouth (MD 25:52)

Mercy LEMOTE[6] and 2nd Richard HOLMES, Int. 31 Mar. 1764, Plymouth (MD 26:43)

Isaac BILLINGTON[3] and Hannah GLASS

Desire BILLINGTON[4] (Isaac[3]) and James BONNEY

Isaac BILLINGTON[4] (Isaac[3]) and Mary DUNHAM, 5 Mar. 1729/30, Middleboro (MD 8:250)

Mercy WASHBURN[5] (Lydia Billington[4], Isaac[3]) and 1st Robert CUSHMAN[5] (Robert[4], Tho.[3],
   Mary Allerton[2])

Mercy WASHBURN[5] and 2nd John FULLER[4] (Samuel[3-2-1])

Lydia BILLINGTON[4] (Isaac[3]) and John WASHBURN, c1698 (MD 2:165)

John WASHBURN and 2nd Wiborah BUMPAS, aft. 1716 (MD 16:85)

Barnabas WASHBURN[5] (Lydia Billington[4]) and Hannah SEARS

Ebenezer WASHBURN[5] (Lydia Billington[4]) and Lydia FAUNCE

Lydia FAUNCE and 2nd Thomas WATERMAN

Elisha WASHBURN[5] (Lydia Billington[4]) and Martha PERKINS

Ephraim WASHBURN[5] (Lydia Billington[4]) and Eglah STETSON

Ichabod WASHBURN[5] (Lydia Billington[4]) and Bethiah PHILLIPS, 2 June 1725 Marshfield (VR)

Jabez WASHBURN[5] (Lydia Billington[4]) and 1st Judith FAUNCE[5] (Lydia Cooke[4], Jacob[3-2])
   2 Dec. 1731, Kingston (Gen.Ad.2:125)

Jabez WASHBURN [5] and 2nd Deborah THOMAS, aft. Mar. 1752 (MD 7:223)

Jabez WASHBURN[6] (Jabez[5]) and Mary SHERMAN, 14 May 1756, Marshfield

John WASHBURN[5] (Lydia Billington[4]) and Abigail JOHNSON, Int. 28 May 1727, Kingston (VR)

John WASHBURN[6] (John[5]) and Lydia PRINCE[6] (Ben.[5], Ruth Turner[4], Mary Brewster[3],
   Jonathan[2]), Int. 14 Dec. 1754, Plymouth (MD 25:52)

Benjamin WASHBURN[7] (John[6]) and Bathsheba CHURCHILL, 17 Nov. 1785 (Int. - MD 29:126)

Benjamin WASHBURN[7] and 2nd Abigail BARTLETT, Int. 21 Apr. 1792, Plymouth (MD 30:76)

Seth WASHBURN[6] (John[5]) and Fear HOWARD, 31 Oct. 1765, Plymouth (ch.rcds.2:444)

Thankful WASHBURN[5] (Lydia Billington[4]) and John ADAMS, Int. 1 Mar. 1739/40, Kingston
   (VR:166,299)

Mary BILLINGTON[4] (Isaac[3]) and Elnathan WOOD, 13 Feb. 1711/12, Middleboro (MD 2:158)

Elnathan WOOD and 2nd Patience (HOLMES) Cushman, 23 Apr. 1735, Middleboro (MD 13:251)

Martha BILLINGTON[3] and Samuel EATON[2], 10 Jan. 1660, Plymouth (MD 17:183)

Mary BILLINGTON[3] and Samuel SABIN, 20 Jan. 1663, Rehoboth (VR)

Israel SABIN[4] (Mary Billington[3]) and Mary ORMSBEE, 20 May 1696, Rehoboth (VR:271,331)

Josiah SABIN[5] (Israel[4]) and Mary GAY, 18 Nov. 1724, Rehoboth (VR:150,331)

Mercy SABIN[4] (Mary Billington[3]) and James WELCH, 9 Nov. 1683, Rehoboth (VR:331,381)

Mercy BILLINGTON[3] and John MARTIN, 27 June 1681, Rehoboth (MD 21:152)

Desire CARPENTER[5] (Desire Martin[4], Mercy Billington[3]) and Hezekiah HIX, Int. 15 Apr.
   1738, Rehoboth (VR:437,460)

Renew CARPENTER[5] (Desire Martin[4], Mercy Billington[3]) and Jabez ROUND, 26 Apr. 1733,
   Rehoboth (VR:81,324)

NOTES

   <1> p.35, It has since been established that her maiden name was PENN.
(Mayflower Increasings:20,67)

   <2> p.35, Bowman lists a 2nd marriage to ( ) PATTE. It is now known she
married 2nd Robert BEERS, 25 June 1673, Rehoboth and 3rd Thomas PATTE, c1679
(Ibid.,:20)

WILLIAM BRADFORD DESCENDANTS

William BRADFORD[1] and 1st Dorothy MAY, 10 Dec. 1613, Amsterdam, Holland (MD 9:115)

William BRADFORD[1] and 2nd Alice (CARPENTER) Southworth, 14 Aug. 1623, Plymouth
    (MD 30:4)

Jane C. BRADFORD and John HARLOW, 20 Jan. 1831, Plymouth (BDM 2:247)

Josiah BRADFORD and Polly ROBBINS, 7 Dec. 1803, Plymouth (BDM 2:283)

William BRADFORD and Ruth DONHAM, 14 Nov. 1773, Plymouth (BDM 2:266)

John BRADFORD and Sarah CAPEN, Int. 21 Mar. 1716, Boston (Rcd.com.28:96)

Thomas BRADFORD and Abigail DYER, 11 Dec. 1721, Boston (Rcd.com.28:99)

Thomas BRADFORD and Mehitable ADAMS, Int. 27 July 1749, Boston (Rcd.com.28:291)

Robert BRADFORD and Lydia ROGERS, 6 Dec. 1722, Boston (Rcd.com.28:104)

Elizabeth BRADFORD and Richard HONIWELL, 12 Mar. 1723, Boston (Rcd.com.28:113)

Joseph BRADFORD and Ruth BAKER, 17 July 1729, Boston (Rcd.com.28:148)

James BRADFORD and Hephzibah WILLIAMS, 23 Oct. 1729, Boston (Rcd.com.28:148)

Elizabeth BRADFORD and Thomas NEWELL/NOWEL, 12 Aug. 1730, Boston (Rcd.com.28:156)

Sarah BRADFORD and Nathan PEABODY, 29 Nov. 1739, Boston (Rcd.com.28:212)

Sarah BRADFORD and Edward JENNINGS, Int. 22 Dec. 1739, Boston (Rcd.com.28:232)

Elizabeth BRADFORD and William DALL, 25 Apr. 1750, Boston (Rcd.com.28:244)

Anne BRADFORD and William ROSS, 13 July 1742, Boston (rcd.com.28:260)

Frances BRADFORD and David DOYLE, Int. 21 Jan. 1744, Boston (Rcd.com.28:280)

John BRADFORD and Margaret BARTON, Int. 30 Oct. 1746, Boston (Rcd.com.28:284)

Abigail BRADFORD and Peter SLATER, Int. 25 Dec. 1751, Boston (Rcd.com.28:299)

Peres BRADFORD and Mrs. Abigail BELCHER, 14 Apr. 1720, Dedham (Rcd.com.28:301)

Elijah BRADFORD and Mrs. Mary LINDSEY, 6 Feb. 1763, Bristol RI (VR 2:50)

Daniel BRADFORD and Susanna JARVIS, 25 Sept. 1773, Bristol RI (VR 2:57)

Priscilla BRADFORD and Sylvester CHILD, 15 Jan. 1775, Bristol RI (VR 2:58)

William BRADFORD and Betsy Bloom JAMES, 11 July 1777, Bristol RI (VR 2:62)

Elisabeth BRADFORD and Nathaniel FALES Jr., 26 Sept. 1773, Bristol RI (VR 2:60)

Daniel BRADFORD and Mrs. Mary CHURCH, 1 Oct. 1749, Bristol RI (VR 1:9)

Hopestill BRADFORD and Joseph NASH, 9 Jan. 1756, Bristol RI (VR 1:8)

Polly BRADFORD and Henry GOODWIN, 20 May 1782, Bristol RI (VR 1:46)

Anna BRADFORD and James DeWOLF, 7 Jan. 1790, Bristol RI (VR 1:30)

Lydia BRADFORD and Charles COLLINS, 8 Oct. 1797, Bristol RI (VR 1:21)

Mary BRADFORD and Elijah WILLARD, 28 Mar. 1799, Bristol RI (VR 1:129)

Daniel BRADFORD Jr. and Sarah REYNOLDS, 29 Nov. 1799, Bristol RI (VR 1:13)

William BRADFORD and Mary SMITH, 1 Feb. 1804, Bristol RI (VR 1:12)

Nancy BRADFORD and Nicholas PECK, 22 Oct. 1815, Bristol RI (VR 4:1)

Harriet DeWolf BRADFORD and William R. TAYLOR, 1 Sept. 1833, Bristol RI (VR 4:16)

Charles J. BRADFORD and Elizabeth SWAN, 28 Feb. 1838, Bristol RI (VR 4:28)

William BRADFORD and Ann W. NOONING, 28 Mar. 1839, Bristol RI (VR 4:36)

Peter J. BRADFORD and Lucretia COLT, 16 June 1839, Bristol RI (VR 4:32)

Walter BRADFORD and Sarah W. MACUMBER, 19 June 1845, Bristol RI (VR 4:57)

Hannah BRADFORD and George H. REYNOLDS, 9 June 1850, Bristol RI (VR 4:73)

Chloe BRADFORD and John STARBIRD, 2 APr. 1780, Arnold (VR 10:200)

Levi BRADFORD and Sally HEALEY, 9 May 1784, Arnold (VR 10:200)

Betsy BRADFORD and John BEZELY, 12 Mar. 1786, Arnold (VR 10:200)

Hannah BRADFORD and Solomon KIMBALL, 30 Apr. 1789, Arnold (VR 10:200)

Sally BRADFORD and Samuel HOW, 17 Sept. 1789, Arnold (VR 10:200)

Nabby BRADFORD and Joseph JOHNSON, 15 Aug. 1790, Arnold (VR 10:200)

John BRADFORD and Sarah DAGGETT, 28 Nov. 1771, Arnold (VR 9:538)

Theophilus BRADFORD and Ruth GOODSPEED, 24 Feb. 1731, Arnold (VR 4:10)

Stephen BRADFORD and Polly TUPPER, 20 May 1804 (Kingston VR)

Stephen BRADFORD Jr. and Rebecca M. HAYWARD, 16 Dec. 1834 (Kingston VR)

Peleg BRADFORD and Deborah SAMPSON, 7 Oct. 1813 (Kingston VR)

Joanna BRADFORD and Francis DREW, 1816 (Kingston VR)

David BRADFORD and Mrs. Betty THOMAS, 16 Feb. 1779 (Kingston VR)

Elizabeth BRADFORD and Melatiah HOLMES, 31 Jan. 1771, Kingston (VR)

Susanna HOLMES and Benjamin DELANO, 30 Jan. 1803, Kingston(VR)

Catherine DELANO and Oliver DITSON, 3 May 1842, Kingston (VR)

John BRADFORD^2 (William^1)

John BRADFORD^2 and Martha BOURNE (MD 16:24) <No issue.>
Martha BOURNE and 2nd Thomas TRACY

Joseph BRADFORD^2 (William^1)

Joseph BRADFORD^2 and Jael HOBART
Nathan BRADFORD and Elizabeth GROSS, 27 Oct. 1748, Hingham (VR 1:307)

Elisha BRADFORD^3 and 1st Hannah COLE, pre 28 Jan. 1702/03 (MD 8:256)

Elisha BRADFORD^3 and 2nd Bathshua BROCK, 7 Sept. 1719, Plymouth (MD 14:38)

Bathshua BROCK and 2nd Joshua OLDHAM, Int. 21 Mar. 1752, Kingston (Gen.Reg.4:47)

Alice BRADFORD^4 (Elisha^3) and Zebulon WATERS, 21 Sept. 1757, Stoughton (VR:172)

Chloe WATERS^5 (Alice Bradford^4) and Lemuel MONK, 4 Aug. 1794, Stoughton (VR:170)

Zebulon WATERS and Zilpha LOVEL(sp), 18 Mar. 1794 (Canton VR:268)

Asa WATERS^5 (Alice Bradford^4) and Lydia SMITH, 10 Nov. 1785, Stoughton (VR:149)

Asa WATERS and 2nd Mary LYON, aft. June 1809

Asa WATERS and 3rd Susan B. SHEPARD

Deborah BRADFORD^4 (Elisha^3) and Jonathan SAMPSON^5 (Jonathan^4, Lydia Standish^3, Alex.^{2})

Laurana BRADFORD^4 (Elisha^3) and Elijah MacFARLAND (Gen.Reg.4:48)

Mercy BRADFORD^2 (William^1)

Mercy BRADFORD^2 and Benjamin VERMAYES, 21 Dec. 1648, Plymouth (MD 15:28)

Edward HUTCHINSON Jr. and Catharine HAMBY, pre 1637 (Savage 2:509)

William BRADFORD^2 (William^1)

William BRADFORD^2 and 1st Alice RICHARDS, pre 28 Jan. 1650/51 (MD 9:65,90)

William BRADFORD and 3rd Mary (WOOD) Holmes

Micro #3 of 15

Alice BRADFORD^3 and 1st Rev. William ADAMS, 29 Mar. 1680 (Dedham BMD:17)

Alice BRADFORD^3 and 2nd James FITCH, 8 May 1687

Abiel ADAMS^4 (Alice Bradford^3) and Rev. John METCALF, Int. 3 Sept. 1707, Falmouth
    (Gen.Ad.4:113)

Elizabeth METCALF^5 (Abiel Adams^4) and Rev. Jonathan LEE

John COLLINS^5 (Alice Adams^4, Alice Bradford^3) and Mary MEACHAM

Mary MEACHAM and 2nd Joseph SEXTON

Ariel COLLINS and Mary STEBBINS, 12 Aug. 1762, Springfield (VR 2:143)

Hannah COLLINS and Jonathan PEASE, Aug. 1800, Springfield (VR 2:263)

Betsey C. PEASE and Charles BLAKE, 1 Dec. 1836, Springfield (VR 3:335)

Elizabeth ADAMS^4 (Alice Bradford^3) and 1st Rev. Samuel WHITING, 14 Sept. 1696

Sybil WHITING^5 (Eliz. Adams^4) and John BACKUS, 12 Jan. 1725[1]

Sylvanus BACKUS^6 (Sybil Whiting^5) and Elizabeth GAMBLE(sp), 12 Apr. 1758[1]

Abigail FITCH^4 (Alice Bradford^3) and John DYER, 22 Oct. 1713, Canterbury CT

James DYER^5 (Abigail Fitch^4) and Ann WHITING, 8 Dec. 1753

Sybil DYER[5] (Abigail Fitch[4]) and Benjamin THROOP

Anna DYER[6] (James[5]) and David BUTTS, 28 Jan. 1796

Samuel WHITING[5] (Elizabeth Adams[4]) and Elizabeth JUDSON, c1742 (Hist. Stratford CT:1345)

John WHITING[6] (Samuel[5]) and Mary DeFOREST, c1769 (Hist. Stratford:1345)[2]

Ephraim WHITING[7] (John[6]) and Sally YOUNGS, 10 Jan. 1796

Sarah Cornelia WHITING[8] (Ephraim[7]) and 2nd Charles BANKS

Eliza LEWORTHY[8] (Eliz. Whiting[7]) and Artemas TROWBRIDGE, 7 June 1827

Elizabeth WHITING[7] (John[6]) and James LeWORTHY, 1799

Ephraim BURTON and Betty WELLS, 2 Feb. 1748/49, Stratford CT (Hist. Stratford:1170)

Jabez FITCH[4] (Alice Bradford[3]) and Lydia GALE, 29 May 1722, Canterbury CT (ch.rcds.)

Jabez ADAMS[6] (Lydia Fitch[5], Jabez[4]) and Lucy SWIFT[7] (Barzillai[6], Rowland[5], Abigail[3]
    Gibbs[4], Alice Warren[3], Nathaniel[2]), 10 Apr. 1793, Mansfield CT (VR:201)

Jabez ADAMS[6] and 2nd Lucy ENSWORTH, 12 Apr. 1815[3]

Harriet ADAMS[7] (Jabez[6]) and James BREWER, 16 Oct. 1816, Mansfield CT (1st ch.rcds.:424)

Henry ADAMS[7] (Jabez[6]) and Francis BLISS, 10 Nov. 1825[3]

Lucy S. ADAMS[7] (Jabez[6]) and Reuben BISHOP, 3 Dec. 1828[3]

Eliza ADAMS[7] (Jabez[6]) and Ezra BINGHAM, 29 Sept. 1830[3]

David A. ADAMS[7] (Jabez[6]) and Harriet SWIFT, Dec. 1834[3]

Sarah F. ADAMS[7] (Jabez[6]) and Col. E.S. FITCH, 6 Sept. 1836[3]

Lydia FITCH[5] (Jabez[4]) and Phineas ADAMS, 31 Dec. 1751, Norwich CT (VR 1:315)

Maude Porter BREWER and Howard Witherell LANG, 14 Nov. 1908, Longmeadow/Springfield
    (Mass.VR 579:131,203)

David BRADFORD[3] and Elizabeth FINNEY, 23 Feb. 1713/14, Plymouth (MD 14:37)

Elizabeth FINNEY and 2nd Benjamin LUDDEN, aft. Mar. 1729/30 (Kingston VR:319)

Lydia BRADFORD[4] (David[3]) and 1st Elkanah CUSHMAN[5] (Elkanah[4-3], Mary Allerton[2]),
    31 Mar. 1740, Plymouth (MD 14:159)

Lydia BRADFORD[4] and 2nd Dr. Lazarus LeBARON, 2 May 1743, Plymouth (MD 14:160)

Isaac LeBARON[5] (Lydia Bradford[4]) and Martha HOWLAND[5] (Consider[4], Tho.[3], Jos.[2])

Priscilla LeBARON[5] (Lydia Bradford[4]) and Abraham HAMMETT[6] (Lucy Howland[5], Consider[4],
    Tho.[3], Jos.[2])

Nathan BRADFORD[4] (David[3]) and 2nd Sarah STURTEVANT, aft. Apr. 1773 (Kingston VR)

Nathaniel BRADFORD[4] (David[3]) and Sarah SPOONER, 24 Nov. 1746, Plymouth (MD 17:5)[4]

Lemuel BRADFORD[5] (Nathaniel[4]) and 1st Mary SAMSON, 23 Mar. 1775, Plymouth (VR 2:267)

Lemuel BRADFORD[5] and 2nd Lydia HOLMES, 28 Aug. 1791, Plymouth (VR 2:274)

Mary BRADFORD^6 (Lemuel^5) and 1st Capt. Ephraim HOLMES, 20 Mar. 1800

Mary BRADFORD^6 and 2nd John TRIBBLE, betw. 1811-1816

Maj. Ephraim HOLMES^7 (Mary Bradford^6) and Mary Ann ATWOOD, 26 Dec. 1830, poss. Plymouth

Ann Mana HOLMES^8 (Ephraim^7) and Frank LEWIS, 1856

Joan HOLMES^7 (Mary^6) and Jacob JACKSON, 7 NOv. 1824

Joan JACKSON^8 (Joan^7) and Lewis Gould LOW, 29 Apr. 1850

Mary Ann HOLMES^7 (Mary Bradford^6) and Corban BARNES, 7 May 1836

Cornelius BRADFORD^6 (Lemuel^5) and Elizabeth HINCKLEY

Cornelius BRADFORD^7 (Cornelius^6) and Mary BA(K)IN

Mary BA(K)IN and 2nd Francis NYE, aft. June 1829 (Nye Gen.:281)

Joseph Morey BRADFORD^8 (Cornelius^7) and Anna Roberson RAYMOND, 28 Mar. 1839, Plymouth
    (VR 2:221)

Capt. David BRADFORD^6 (Lemuel^5) and 1st Betsey BRIGGS, 30 Oct. 1819

Capt. David BRADFORD^6 and 2nd Louisa (PERKINS) Foster Bartlett

Betsey BRADFORD^7 (David^6) and 1st William BRIGGS, 20 Apr. 1848

Betsey BRADFORD^7 and 2nd William B. COREY, 20 Aug. 1857

Cornelius BRADFORD^7 (David^6) and 1st Hannah Jane RIPLEY, c1847

Cornelius BRADFORD^7 and 2nd Mary P. DELANO, aft. May 1857

Desire Harlow BRADFORD^7 (David^6) and Frederick LELAND, 27 May 1859

Lemuel BRADFORD^7 (David^6) and Elizabeth Bartlett WHITING, Aug. 1848

Nathaniel BRADFORD^7 (David^6) and Susanna LEIGHTON, poss. Machias ME

Eleanor BRADFORD^6 (Lemuel^5) and Solomon FAUNCE, Nov. 1806

Solomon FAUNCE^7 (Eleanor Bradford^6) and Mary Olive HARLOW, 4 July 1831

Lemuel Bradford FAUNCE^7 (Eleanor Bradford^6) and 1st Lydia Vaughn WOOD, 4 Nov. 1832

Lemuel B. FAUNCE^7 and 2nd Elizabeth A. MORTON, 24 Mar. 1846

Rev. William FAUNCE^7 (Eleanor Bradford^6) and Matilda Bradford BRADFORD$^{<5>}$

Matilda Bradford FAUNCE^8 (William^7) and Weston VAUGHAN

William Thomas FAUNCE^8 (William^7) and Hannah PIERCE

Capt. George BRADFORD^6 (Lemuel^5) and Harriet CHURCHILL

George BRADFORD^7 (Capt. George^6, Lemuel^5) and Sarah Prince BROWN, 30 Apr. 1832

Edmund BRADFORD^7 (George^6) and Mary E. HALL, 1834

Lemuel BRADFORD^7 (George^6) and Lucy Ann DAMON, c1835

Capt. Lemuel BRADFORD^6 (Lemuel^5) and Hetty HINCKLEY, 1799

Abigail Hinckley BRADFORD^7 (Lemuel^6) and Isaac Jackson BICKNELL, 5 Jan. 1824

Charles Augustus BRADFORD^7 (Lemuel^6) and Abagail Clapp BEAL, 12 Sept. 1843

Hetty Amelia BRADFORD^7 (Lemuel^6) and Dr. Andrew MACKIE, 4 Dec. 1821

Rev. Andrew MACKIE^8 (Hetty Bradford^7) and Sarah COWELL, 10 Oct. 1848

Thomas BRADFORD^6 (Lemuel^5) and 1st Mary HOLMES, c1799

Thomas BRADFORD^6 and 2nd Mrs. Sophia RUSSELL, c1822

James Russell BRADFORD^7 (Thomas^6) and Cervilla Frances OLDAKEN, 16 Jan. 1845

David BRADFORD^8 (Amos S.^{7}, Thomas^6) and Mary BURK, 23 Nov. 1848

Sarah Spooner BRADFORD^8 (Amos S.^{7}) and Thomas M. PIERCE, 2 Mar. 1853

Amos Sturtevant BRADFORD^7 (Thomas^6) and Elizabeth CLARK, 20 Aug. 1829

Sarah Spooner CAMPBELL^8 (Mary S.^{7}, Tho.^{6}) and John EXLINE, c1857

Elizabeth A. CAMPBELL^8 (Mary S.^{7}, Tho.^{6}) and Dr. A. TOLAN, 6 June 1854, Carrol Co.,OH

Thomas S.B. CAMPBELL^8 (Mary S.^{7}) and Delia HILL, Jan. 1852, poss. Kensia, Nebraska

Mary Jane CAMPBELL^8 (Mary S.^{7}) and David EXLINE, 2 Mar. 1858

Mary Sampson BRADFORD^7 (Thomas^6) and John CAMPBELL

William Holmes BRADFORD^6 (Lemuel^5) and Mary HOLMES, c1827

Mary Holmes BRADFORD^7 (William H.^{6}) and Samuel HARLOW, 28 Dec. 1851

Nathaniel BRADFORD^5 (Nathaniel^4) and Rebecca HOLMES, 28 May 1775, Plymouth

Joseph BRADFORD^6 (Nathaniel^5) and Nancy BARNES, 19 Feb. 1802

Edward Winslow BRADFORD^7 (Joseph^6) and Mary DILLARD, c1829

Catharine Edward BRADFORD^8 (Edward W.^{7}) and Charles Henry THOMAS, 16 Mar. 1858

Mary Winslow BRADFORD^8 (Edward W.^{7}) and William Alfred DIMON, 26 July 1861

James Madison BRADFORD^7 (Joseph^6) and Betsey Mason HOLMES

Joseph BRADFORD^7 (Joseph^6) and Joan BARNES, c1829

Nancy Barnes BRADFORD^8 (Joseph^7) and Josiah Carver FULLER, 6 June 1854

Benjamin Willis BRADFORD^6 (Nathaniel^5) and Hannah CLOW

Ephraim BRADFORD^6 (Nathaniel^5) and 1st Hannah MORTON, 6 Mar. 1806

Ephraim BRADFORD^6 and 2nd Lucy PETERSON, c1822

Ephraim BRADFORD^7 (Ephraim^6) and Lucy KEENE, 22 Feb. 1833

Sally BRADFORD and Briggs Bradford DELANO, 18 Dec. 1833

Morton BRADFORD^7 (Ephraim^6) and Elizabeth BURT, 1843

John BRADFORD^7 (Ephraim^6) and Jane West MAGLATHLIN, Dec. 1849

Rev. George BRADFORD^7 (Ephraim^6) and Ruth Ann FORD, 28 Feb. 1857

Lucy BRADFORD^7 (Ephraim^6) and Francis NICKERSON, 28 July 1850

Nathaniel BRADFORD^6 (Nathaniel^5) and Deborah (SAMPSON) Wright, 12 Dec. 1799

Benjamin Wright BRADFORD^7 (Nathaniel^6) and Catherine ALLEN, 29 Sept. 1831

Nathaniel Governeun BRADFORD^7 (Nathaniel^6) and Rachel MILLER, 2 Dec. 1830, N.Y. City

Nathaniel Barnes BRADFORD^8 (Nathaniel^7) and Abagail SACKET, 20 Oct. 1853, N.Y. City

Elizabeth Holmes BRADFORD[7] (Nathaniel[6]) and Martin WILLARD, 19 July 1838

Rebekah BRADFORD[6] (Nathaniel[5]) and Capt. Samuel DOTEN, 7 Jan. 1807

Ephraim BRADFORD[3] and Elizabeth BREWSTER[4] (Wrestling[3], Love[2]), 13 Feb. 1709/10,
     Plymouth (MD 14:36)

Abigail BRADFORD[4] (Ephraim[3]) and Peleg HOLMES, Int. 4 Oct. 1740, Kingston

Anna BRADFORD[4] (Ephraim[3]) and Ebenezer CHANDLER, 23 Feb. 1737, Kingston (VR)

Elizabeth BRADFORD[4] (Ephraim[3]) and Azariah WHITON, 12 July 1753, (Kingston VR:180,304)

Ezekiel BRADFORD[4] (Ephraim[3]) and Betty CHANDLER, 21 July 1750 (Duxbury VR:222,230)

Jesse BRADFORD[5] (Ezekiel[4]) and Judith WESTON, 1781

Philip BRADFORD[6] (Jesse[5]) and 1st Lucy GREENWOOD, pre 1819

Marcia BRADFORD[7] (Phillip[6]) and William Riley FRENCH, 13 APr. 1843, Turner Center ME

Lucy Greenwood FRENCH[8] (Marcia Bradford[7]) and Merritt Bradford COLIDGE, 8 Apr. 1876,
     Turner ME

Susanna BRADFORD[4] (Ephraim[3]) and Seth EVERSON, 28 Apr. 1752 (Kingston VR)

Ruth BRADFORD[4] (Ephraim[3]) and Nathan CHANDLER, 3 Aug. 1749 (Kingston VR)

Nathan CHANDLER and 2nd Esther GLASS, aft. Aug. 1767

Ephraim CHANDLER[5] (Ruth Bradford[4]) and Molly DOTEN, c1775

Simeon BRADFORD[4] (Ephraim[3]) and Phebe WHITON, 23 Jan. 1755, Plympton (VR:266,425)

Joel BRADFORD[5] (Simeon[4]) and Tryphena SMITH, 5 Oct. 1794, Springfield VT (VR)

Nabby BRADFORD[5] (Simeon[4]) and Walter HOLMES

Ruth BRADFORD[5] (Simeon[4]) and Isaac SMITH

Simeon BRADFORD[5] (Simeon[4]) and Mary SMITH, c1798

Wait BRADFORD[4] (Ephraim[3]) and Welthea BASSETT[6] (Lydia Cooke[5], Wm.[4], Jacob[3-2]), 1 Nov.
     1765 (Kingston VR:174,182)

Hannah BRADFORD[3] and Joshua RIPLEY, 28 Nov. 1682, Plymouth (MD 28:100-101)

Alice RIPLEY[4] (Hannah Bradford[3]) and Samuel EDGERTON, 18 Apr. 1703 (Norwich CT VR)

Ann RIPLEY[4] (Hannah Bradford[3]) and Solomon WHEAT, pre 1736

Dr. Solomon WHEAT and 2nd Margaret GREEN, 17 Feb. 1747, Windham (Bailey CT Mgs.4:71)

David RIPLEY[4] (Hannah Bradford[3]) and Lydia CARY, 21 Mar. 1720 (Windham CT VR:A:61)

Faith RIPLEY[4] (Hannah Bradford[3]) and Samuel BINGHAM, 5 Jan. 1708/09, (Windham CT VR:A:3)

Samuel BINGHAM and 2nd Elizabeth MANNING, 23 NOv. 1721 (Windham CT VR:A:3)

Abishai BINGHAM[6] (Abishai[5], Faith Ripley[4]) and Ann SAWYER, Feb. 1755, Windham CT

John Clark BINGHAM[7] (Abner[6], Abishai[5]) and 1st Caroline Charity BROCKWAY, 1786/87
     Marlow NH

John Clark BINGHAM^7 and 2nd Silence HARLOW^8 (Levi^7, Eliphaz^6, Eleazer^5, Sam.^{4},
 Rebecca Bartlett^3, Wm. Bradford^2), 9 Sept. 1806 or 28 Oct. 1810

Ripley BINGHAM^8 (Ripley^7, Abner^6, Abishai^5) and Betsey CARY, 1 Dec. 1811, Marlow NH

Clarissa BINGHAM^8 (Ripley^7) and Charles BALDWIN

Betsey Elizabeth BINGHAM^8 (Ripley^7) and Stephen Eldridge HARTSHORN, 5 Sept. 1808,
 Stanstead, Que.

Theresa Lucina Sobeiska HARTSHORN^9 (Betsey E. Bingham^8) and Faber Enos KINGSLEY,
 1 Dec. 1847, Mantua OH

Abner BINGHAM^8 (Ripley^7) and Gelpha BRIGGS

Sally BINGHAM^8 (Ripley^7) and Samuel HORTON

Jacob BINGHAM^8 (Ripley^7) and Laura HINNAN(sp)

Frank Clayton BALL^{10} (Maria Bingham^9, Ben.^{8}, Ripley^7) and Elizabeth Wolfe BRADY,
 1 Nov. 1893, Muncie, Ind.

Hannah WHEAT^5 (Ann Ripley^4) and Joseph TAYLOR, c1758 (Concord VR:202)

Hannah RIPLEY^4 (Hannah Bradford^3) and Samuel WEBB, 8 Oct. 1711, (Windham CT VR:A:7)

Joshua WEBB^5 (Hannah Ripley^4) and Hannah ABBE, 28 May 1744 (Windham CT VR:A:7)

Ebenezer WEBB^5 (Hannah Ripley^4) and Ruth CRANE

Darius WEBB^6 (Ebenezer^5) and Deborah PALMER, 8 Oct. 1767

Hezekiah RIPLEY^4 (Hannah Bradford^3) and 1st Miriam FITCH, 16 Oct. 1740 (Windham CT VR)

Hezekiah RIPLEY^4 and 2nd Mary SKINNER, 25 Nov. 1746 (Windham CT VR:A:256)

Irena RIPLEY^4 (Hannah Bradford^3) and Samuel MANNING, 27 Apr. 1719 (Windham CT VR:A:3)

David MANNING^5 (Irena Ripley^4) and 1st Anne HAMILTON, 1 Aug. 1751 (Sharon CT BM:84)

David MANNING^5 and 2nd Miriam SIMONSON, pre 1764

Maj. David MANNING and 1st Lucy PECK, 6 Oct. 1785, Southbury CT (Manning Gen.:251)$^{<6>}$

Maj. David MANNING and 2nd Anne JACKSON, 6 Oct. 1785 (Manning Gen.:251)$^{<6>}$

Jerusha RIPLEY^4 (Hannah Bradford^3) and Edward BROWN, 9 Sept. 1744 (Windham CT
 VR:A:253)

Joshua RIPLEY^4 (Hannah Bradford^3) and Mary BACKUS, 3 Dec. 1712 (Windham CT VR 1:39)

Joshua RIPLEY^5 (Joshua^4) and Elizabeth LOTHROP, 26 Mar. 1749 (Windham CT VR 1:290)

Ebenezer RIPLEY^5 (Joshua^4) and Mehitable BURBANK, 11 June 1752 (Windham CT VR:B:11)

Mary RIPLEY^5 (Joshua^4) and Joshua ABBE, 14 Apr. 1736 (Windham CT VR:A:164)

Nathaniel RIPLEY^5 (Joshua^4) and   Ann RIPLEY^5 (David^4, Hannah Bradford^3, Wm.^{2}),
 31 Oct. 1745 (Windham CT VR:A:273)

Ann RIPLEY^5 and poss. 2nd Capt. Samuel BINGHAM, 17 May 1769 (Windham CT VR:B:148)

Leah RIPLEY^4 (Hannah Bradford^3) and 1st Samuel COOK, 14 Mar. 1716 (Windham CT
 VR:A:38)

Rebecca COOK[5] (Leah Ripley[4]) and Caleb JEWETT, 19 Nov. 1735 (Norwich VR)

Caleb JEWETT and 2nd Faith (RIPLEY[5]) Brewster (David Ripley[4], Hannah Bradford[3]),
    26 May 1766

Welthean COOK[5] (Leah Ripley[4]) and Thomas PARDEE, 24 Nov. 1743, Scotland CT

Margaret RIPLEY[4] (Hannah Bradford[3]) and Benjamin SEABURY

Rachel RIPLEY[4] (Hannah Bradford[3]) and Winslow TRACY, 21 June 1714 (Norwich CT VR 1:24)

Hezekiah BRADFORD[3] and Mary CHANDLER

Israel BRADFORD[3] and Sarah BARTLETT[5] (Benjamin[4-3], Mary Warren[2]), 27 Nov. 1701,
    Plymouth (MD 13:207)

Abner BRADFORD[4] (Israel[3]) and Susanna PORTER, Int. 4 Nov. 1733, Kingston

Elisha BRADFORD[5] (Abner[4]) and Eunice BENNETT, 10 June 1781

Susanna BRADFORD[6] (Elisha[5]) and Isaac BROWNE, 21 Aug. 1800, Cheshire (TR 1:32)

Albert BROWNE[7] (Susanna Bradford[6]) and Adaline BABBITT, 29 Apr. 1837

Charles BROWN[8] (Albert[7]) and Susan McCALLUM, 9 June 1869

George Washington BRADFORD[6] (Elisha[5]) and 2nd Mary Louisa SMITH

Joseph BRADFORD[6] (Elisha[5]) and Lovina TAYLOR

Lucy BRADFORD[6] (Elisha[5]) and Simeon SAYLES

William BRADFORD[6] (Elisha[5]) and Mary Tillinghast RENINGTON

Levi BRADFORD[5] (Abner[4]) and Polly RIPLEY, 22 Aug. 1782, Kingston (VR 2:68)

Peggy BRADFORD[5] (Abner[4]) and Calvin RIPLEY, 8 Dec. 1774

Bathsheba BRADFORD[4] (Israel[3]) and Thomas ADAMS

Benjamin BRADFORD[4] (Israel[3]) and Zerash STETSON[5] (Abigail Brewster[4], Wrestling[3],
    Love[2]), c1731 (Kingston VR)

Elisha BRADFORD[4] (Israel[3]) and Mary STURTEVANT

Ichabod BRADFORD[4] (Israel[3]) and 1st Mary JOHNSON, 25 Nov. 1743 (Kingston VR:180,230)

Ichabod BRADFORD[4] and 2nd Mary COOK, 1763

Lemuel BRADFORD[6] (Israel[5], Ichabod[4]) and Bathsheba NELSON, 23 Aug. 1812, Plymouth
    (VR 2:339)

Joshua BRADFORD[4] (Israel[3]) and Hannah BRADFORD[4] (Elisha[3], Joseph[2]), 17 Feb. 1736,
    Kingston

Cornelius BRADFORD[5] (Joshua[4]) and Patience DAVIS

Joseph BRADFORD[5] (Joshua[4]) and Abigail STARLING (Sterling Gen.2:1036-37)

John BRADFORD[3] and Mercy WARREN[3] (Joseph[2]), 6 Jan. 1674, Plymouth (MD 13:205)

Priscilla BRADFORD^4 (John^3) and Seth CHIPMAN^4 (Sam.^{2}, Hope Howland^2)

Alice BRADFORD^4 (John^3) and 1st Edward MITCHELL^3 (Experience), 26 Aug. 1708, Plymouth
(MD 14:36) (see p.152 <4>)

Alice BRADFORD^4 and 2nd Joshua HENRY, Int. 20 Nov. 1718, Hingham (Hist.Hingham 2:300)

Rebecca BRADFORD^5 (John^4, John^3) and John BREWSTER^4 (Wrestling^3, Love^2)

John BRADFORD^4 (John^3) and Rebecca BARTLETT^5 (Ben.$^{4-3}$, Mary Warren^2), 27 Nov. 1701,
Plymouth (MD 13:207)

Robert BRADFORD^5 (John^4) and Sarah STETSON^5 (Abigail Brewster^4, Wrestling^3, Love^2),
4 Nov. 1726, (Kingston VR:182,284)

James BRADFORD and Mrs. Sarah ELLIS, Int. 30 Jan. 1773 (Kingston VR)

Spencer BRADFORD and Lydia FAUNCE, 16 Oct. 1814 (Kingston VR)

Peleg BRADFORD and Sally JOHNSON, May 1820 (Kingston VR)

Consider BRADFORD and Betsey WILDER, Int. 10 May 1807 (Kingston VR)

Elizabeth W. BRADFORD and Thomas S. CUSHMAN, 20 Sept. 1835 (Kingston VR)

John BRADFORD^6 (Robert^5) and Ruth COBB, Int. 17 Sept. 1754 (Kingston VR)

John BRADFORD^6 and 2nd Hannah EDDY, Int. Jan. 1765, Kingston

Lucy BRADFORD^7 (John^6) and Benjamin WATERMAN, 1791

Exuma BRADFORD^7 (John^6) and Benjamin WATERMAN, 1805

Stephen BRADFORD^7 (John^6) and 1st Polly TUPPER, 20 May 1804

Stephen BRADFORD^7 and 2nd Ruth CUSHING, Int. 25 Mar. 1809 (Kingston VR)

Stephen BRADFORD^7 and 3rd Martha MORTON, 13 Aug. 1821

Mary BRADFORD^8 (Stephen^7) and Charles BRADFORD, 30 Dec. 1832

Pelham BRADFORD^7 (John^6) and 1st Selah PACKARD

Pelham BRADFORD and 2nd Joanna DOWNS

John BRADFORD^7 (John^6) and Lucy BROOKS, 1799

Austin BRADFORD^8 (John^7) and Amelia C.E. BISSELL, 1827

Sophronia BRADFORD^8 (John^7) and Jonah BROOKS, 8 Apr. 1827

Elmira BRADFORD^8 (John^7) and Ehud DARLING, 7 Mar. 1833

Philander BRADFORD^8 (John^7) and 1st Susan EDSON, 1835

Philander BRADFORD^8 and 2nd Olive (CARPENTER) Moore, 1867

Sylvanus BRADFORD^7 (John^6) and Jane BRIGGS, 16 Dec. 1779, Halifax (VR:21)

Robert BRADFORD^6 (Robert^5) and Keziah LITTLE, 19 Feb. 1782, Kingston (ch.rcds.)

Peleg BRADFORD^6 (Robert^5) and Lydia STURTEVANT, 9 Mar. 1746, Halifax (VR:34)

James BRADFORD^7 (Peleg^6) and Sarah ELLIS, Int. 30 Jan. 1773, Kingston (VR:180)

Stetson BRADFORD^6 (Robert^5) and Lurana HOLMES, 31 Oct. 1771 (Kingston VR)

Charles BRADFORD^7 (Stetson^6) and Elizabeth P. (BROWN) Clark, 28 Oct. 1802

Mercy BRADFORD^4 (John^3) and 1st Jonathan FREEMAN^5 (Tho.^{4}, Mercy Prence^3, Patience
    Brewster^2), c1709 (MD 5:86)

Mercy BRADFORD^4 and 2nd Isaac CUSHMAN^4 (Isaac^3, Mary Allerton^2), 10 Oct. 1717, Harwich
    (MD 7:197)

Samuel BRADFORD^4 (John^3) and Sarah GRAY, 21 Oct. 1714, Plympton (MD 2:236)

Sarah GRAY and 2nd William HUNT, 7 Sept. 1749, Plympton (MD 28:105)

Mary BRADFORD^5 (Samuel^4) and Abial COOK, c1743 (Little Compton RI VR)

Abigail BRADFORD^5 (Samuel^4) and Caleb STETSON, Int. 7 Sept. 1754, Plymouth (MD 25:51)

Gideon BRADFORD^5 (Sam.^{4}) and Jane PADDOCK, 8 Oct. 1741, Plymouth (MD 14:159)

Calvin BRADFORD^6 (Gideon^5) and Lucy PRATT, c1778

Luther BRADFORD^7 (Calvin^6) and 2nd Mary STANDISH^7 (Jonathan^6, Moses$^{5-4}$, Ebenezer^3,
    Alexander^2), aft. Mar. 1815 (MD 8:154)

Gideon BRADFORD^6 (Gideon^5) and Abigail SAMPSON^6 (Zabdiel^5, Hannah Soule^4, Ben.^{3},
    John^2)

Zabdiel BRADFORD^7 (Gideon^6) and Mary STANDISH^7 (Shadrack^6, Ebenezer^5, Zachariah^4,
    Ebenezer^3, Alexander^2)

Zabdiel BRADFORD^8 (Zabdiel^7) and Ann Eliza HAYNES

John BRADFORD^5 (Samuel^4) and Elizabeth HOLMES^6 (Hannah Sylvester^5, Hannah Bartlett^4,
    Joseph^3, Mary Warren^2), 10 Nov. 1743, Plymouth (MD 14:160)

Mary BRADFORD^6 (John^5) and John CHURCHILL, Int. 9 Mar. 1771, Plymouth (MD 26:190)

Mary BRADFORD and Ellis STANDISH, 7 June 1796

Lydia BRADFORD^6 (John^5) and Levi BRYANT

Oliver BRADFORD^6 (John^5) and Sarah CHIPMAN^6 (Seth$^{5-4}$, Samuel^3, Hope Howland^2),
    21 Feb. 1782 (Plympton VR:265,279)

Samuel BRADFORD^5 (Samuel^4) and Lydia PEASE, 25 Nov. 1762 (Chilmark VR:43,67)

William BRADFORD^5 (Samuel^4) and Mary LeBARON, 22 Mar. 1750/51, Plymouth (MD 16:171)[7]

John BRADFORD^6 (William^5) and Jemima WARDWELL, 17 Nov. 1794 (Bristol RI VR 8:325)

Mary BRADFORD^6 (Wm.^{5}) and Henry GOODWIN

William BRADFORD^6 (Wm.^{5}) and Elizabeth Bloom JAMES, c1777 (Bristol RI VR 2:74)

William BRADFORD^4 (John^3) and Hannah FOSTER, 9 Dec. 1714, Plymouth (MD 14:37)

Hannah FOSTER and 2nd George PARTRIDGE, aft. 1731

Eliphalet BRADFORD^5 (Wm.^{4}) and 1st Hannah PRINCE^6 (Tho.^{5}, Ruth Turner^4, Mary Brewster^3,
    Jonathan^2), 8 Aug. 1751 (Duxbury VR:222,290)

Eliphalet BRADFORD[5] (Wm.[4]) and 2nd Hannah OLDHAM, 9 Feb. 1758 (Duxbury VR:222,281)

Zadock BRADFORD[6] (Eliphalet[5]) and Lucy GRAY, 24 Mar. 1795 (Kingston VR)

James BRADFORD[5] (Wm.[4]) and 2nd Zerviah THOMAS[5] (Lydia Waterman[4], Sarah Snow[3], Abigail Warren[2]), c1746

Keziah BRADFORD[6] (James[5]) and Waterman CLIFT

Joseph BRADFORD[3] and 1st Anne FITCH, 5 Oct. 1698, Lebanon CT (VR:20)

Alathea BRADFORD[4] (Jos.[3]) and David HYDE, c1740 (Hyde Gen.:16)

Anne BRADFORD[4] (Jos.[3]) and Timothy DIMMICK, 15 Aug. 1723 (Mansfield CT VR:231)

Ann DIMMICK[5] (Anne Bradford[4]) and Ebenezer CLARK, 2 Sept. 1740 (Mansfield CT VR:221)

Daniel CLARK[6] (Ann Dimmick[5]) and Rebecca DAVIS, 18 May 1780 (Mansfield CT 1st ch. rcds.:480)

Daniel CLARK and Mehitable SLATE, 19 Oct. 1780 (Mansfield CT 1st ch rcds.:480)

Timothy DIMMICK[5] (Anne Bradford[4]) and Desire DIMMICK[6] (Tho.[5], Desire Sturgis[4]), 11 Mar. 1749/50 (Coventry CT VR)

Daniel DIMMICK[6] (Timothy[5]) and Anne WRIGHT, 16 Nov. 1786 (Coventry CT VR:138)

Mason DIMMICK[6] (Timothy[5]) and Anna ROBERTSON, 18 Jan. 1787 (Coventry CT 1st ch.rcds:255)

Desiah DIMMICK[6] (Mason[6]) and Ralzamon BELKUAP, 14 Oct. 1824 (Coventry CT VR:129)

Irene BRADFORD[4] (Jos.[3]) and Jonathan JANES, 18 Mar. 1736 (Lebanon CT VR:160)

Joseph BRADFORD[4] (Jos.[3]) and Henrietta SWIFT, Mar. 1730 (New London CT VR:4)

Elisabeth BRADFORD and Richard MAYO, 3 May 1773 (Chatham CT VR 1:123)

Ann BRADFORD[5] (Jos.[4]) and Richard LYMAN, 15 June 1758 (Mansfield CT VR)

William BRADFORD[5] (Jos.[4]) and Sarah RICH, 13 Apr. 1762 (Chatham CT VR 1:60)

Henriette BRADFORD[6] (Wm.[5]) and Israel HIGGINS, 8 June 1788 (Chatham CT VR 1:189)

Priscilla BRADFORD[4] (Jos.[3]) and Samuel HIDE, 14 Jan. 1724/25 (Lebanon CT VR:146)

Sarah BRADFORD[4] (Jos.[3]) and 2nd Israel LOTHROP, 9 June 1747 (Norwich CT VR:285)

Mary BRADFORD[3] and William HUNT, c1686 (Gen.Reg.4:59)

✔ Melatiah BRADFORD[3] and 1st John STEELE, 2nd Samuel STEVENS (Steele Fam.:10)

Mercy BRADFORD[3] and Samuel STEELE, 16 Sept. 1680

Abiel STEELE[4] (Mercy Bradford[3]) and John WEBSTER

Daniel STEELE[4] (Mercy Bradford[3]) and Mary HOPKINS, 20 June 1725, Hartford

Josiah STEELE and Elizabeth COLTON

Rachel STEELE[6] (Josiah[5]) and Jonas BARNES, 19 Feb. 1789

Mercy WEBSTER and John Kellogg BELDING, 18 Sept. 1769, Hartford (W.Hfd.IV:120)[8]

John BELDING and Asenah FARROW(sp), Int. 20 Apr. 1795 (W.Hfd.V:138)[8]

Noah WEBSTER and Mercy STETSON, 12 Jan. 1749 (W.Hfd.IV:116)[8]

Sarah A. BELDEN and Lyman HOTCHKIN, 15 May 1844 (Hartford VR:208)

Samuel BRADFORD^3 and Hannah ROGERS^4 (John$^{3-2}$), 31 July 1689, prob. Duxbury
(MD 13:205)

Elizabeth BRADFORD^4 (Samuel^3) and 1st Charles WHITING

Elizabeth BRADFORD^4 and 2nd John NOYES, 13 Mar. 1739 (Hist. Montville CT:715)

Gamiel BRADFORD^4 (Sam.^{3}) and Abigail BARTLETT^5 (Ben.$^{4-3}$, Mary Warren^2), 30 Aug. 1728,
Duxbury (MD 11:80)

Abigail BRADFORD^5 (Gamiel^4) and Wait WADSWORTH, c1748

Gamiel BRADFORD^5 (Gamiel^4) and Sarah ALDEN^4 (Sam.^{3}, David^2), 10 Mar. 1757
(Duxbury VR:212,222)

Hannah BRADFORD^5 (Gamiel^4) and Joshua STANFORD, c1759 (Duxbury VR)

Paybodie BRADFORD^5 (Gamiel^4) and Lydia FREEMAN[9]

Paybodie BRADFORD^5 (Gamiel^4) and Welthea DELANO^6, Int. 14 Mar. 1760, Kingston[10]

Lucy Foster BRADFORD^6 (Paybodie^5) and Joseph BARTLETT^7 (Joseph^6), 22 Nov. 1798
(Kingston VR)[11]

Peabody BRADFORD^6 (Paybodie^5) and Hannah (BRADBURY) Freeman, 15 July 1788

Hannah BRADBURY and 1st Samuel FREEMAN, 10 Oct. 1784 (Bible rcd.)

Lewis BRADFORD^6 (Peabody^5) and Priscilla TUPPER

Charles BRADFORD^7 (Lewis^6) and Emeline INGRAHAM, c1842

Alden BRADFORD^8 (Charles^7) and Hattie H. SIMONDS, 1 Jan. 1866, Lynn (Mass.VR 189:224)

Pamelia BRADFORD^6 (Paybodie^5) and Nathaniel LITTLE, 16 Feb. 1792, Duxbury (MD 29:67)

Charles Jones PEMBROOK and Deborah SAMSON, 2 Feb. 1792 (Duxbury ch.rcds.)

Samuel BRADFORD^5 (Gamiel^4) and Grace RING^5 (Sam.^{4}, Eleazer^3, Deborah Hopkins^2),
1 Nov. 1749 (Kingston VR:182,268)

Isaiah BRADFORD^6 (Samuel^5) and Elizabeth DINGLEY

Seth BRADFORD^5 (Gamiel^4) and Lydia SOUTHWORTH^6 (Jedediah^5, Tho.^{4}, Mary Pabodie^3,
Eliz. Alden^2)

Gershom BRADFORD^4 (Sam.^{3}) and Priscilla WISWALL^4 (Priscilla Pabodie^3, Eliz. Alden^2),
23 Oct. 1716, Plymouth (MD 14:38)

Daniel BRADFORD^5 (Gershom^4) and 1st Mary CHURCH, 2nd Susanna JARVIS

Priscilla BRADFORD^6 (Daniel^5) and Col. Sylvester CHILD, 15 Jan. 1775, Bristol RI

Mary R. CHILD^7 (Prisc. Bradford^6) and Christopher CHILD

Priscilla Bradford CHILD^7 (Prisc. Bradford^6) and Shubael P. CHILD

Abigail Miller CHILD^7 (Prisc. Bradford^6) and John FESSENDEN

Noah BRADFORD^5 (Gershom^4) and Hannah CLARKE

Job BRADFORD^5 (Gershom^4) and Elizabeth PARKMAN

Dr. Jeremiah BRADFORD^5 (Gershom^4) and Rebecca DART, 3 June 1756, Middle Haddam CT

Priscilla BRADFORD^5 (Gershom^4) and Moses NORMAN, 1750

Hopestill BRADFORD^5 (Gershom^4) and Joseph NASH

Eliphalet BRADFORD^5 (Gershom^4) and Hannah PRINCE

Dr. Solomon BRADFORD^5 (Gershom^4) and 1st Elizabeth GREENWOOD

Dr. Solomon BRADFORD^5 and 2nd Mary (RICHTENBURG) Owen

Daniel BRADFORD^5 (Gershom^4) and Susanna JARVIS, 25 Sept. 1773, Bristol RI (VR 2:57)

Joel BRADFORD^6 (Jeremiah^5) and Sally STOCKING, 22 Sept. 1791, Middle Haddam CT
(Martin L. Roberts' Chatham Families:251)

Jeremiah BRADFORD^6 (Jeremiah^5) and Mary SMITH, 19 May 1782, Middle Haddam CT,
(Chatham Fam:251)

William BRADFORD^6 (Jeremiah^5) and Elizabeth SEARS, 1782 (Chatham Fam.)

William BRADFORD^5 and Sarah RICH, 13 Apr. 1762, M. Haddam CT (Chatham Fam.)[12]

Vienna BRADFORD^6 (Jeremiah^5) and George TALCOTT 16 Mar. 1777, M. Haddam CT
(Chatham Fam.:252)

Henrietta BRADFORD^6 (Wm.^{5}) and Israel HIGGINS Jr., 8 June 1788, M. Haddem CT
(Chatham Fam.:252)

William BRADFORD^6 (Wm.^{5}) and Concurrence BONFOY, 13 Nov. 1800, M. Haddem CT
(Chatham Fam.:252)

Rebecca BRADFORD^7 (Joel^6) and Diodate BRAINERD, 3 Dec. 1826, M. Haddam CT (Chat.
Fam.:252)

Susan BRADFORD^7 (Joel^6) and Hezekiah YOUNG, 6 Apr. 1828, M. Haddem CT (Chat.Fam.:252)

Harriet BRADFORD^7 (Jeremiah^6) and John VAN RIPER (Chat.Fam.)

Vienna BRADFORD^7 (Jeremiah^6) and Chester NYE (Chat.Fam.)

Ruth BRADFORD^7 (Jeremiah^6) and Chester NYE (Chat.Fam.)

Urtham Henry BRADFORD^7 (Jeremiah^6) and Emily SMITH (Chat.Fam.)

Halsey BRADFORD^7 (Joel^6) and Judith STOUTINBURGH (Chat.Fam.)[13]

Charles Mansfield BRADFORD^7 (Joel^6) and Lavina PEARSON, 26 Oct. 1841 (Chat.Fam.)[14]

Elizabeth BRADFORD^5 (Joseph^4) and Richard MAYO, 3 May 1773 (Chat.Fam.)

Robert BRADFORD^5 (Jos.^{4}) and Penelope (BONJOY) Rich, 15 Apr. 1768 (Chat.Fam.)

Peter RICH and Penelope BONJOY, 30 June 1763 (Haddem ch.rcd.)

Louisa Ellen BRADFORD^8 (Charles M.^{7}) and Lewis C. NELSON, 1 Oct. 1874, Missouri

Charles Hardeman BRADFORD^8 (Charles M.^{7}) and Suzan Lacy SMITH, 31 Dec. 1867, poss.
   Arrow Rock, Missouri

Grace BRADFORD^9 (Wm.$^{8-7-6}$, Jeremiah^5) and Lindsay FAIRFAX, 14 Feb. 1889, New York City

Job BRADFORD^5 (Gershom^4) and Elizabeth PARKMAN, 26 Jan. 1758, Boston (Rcd.com.30:370)

Joseph Nash BRADFORD^6 (Job^5) and Ann (TUFFTS) Merchant, 1 May 1800, Boston (Rcd.com.
   30:170)

Micro #11 of 15

Elizabeth BRADFORD^6 (Job^5) and Benjamin REYNOLDS

Dorcas BRADFORD^6 (Job^5) and Silas NOYES

William Barnes BRADFORD^6 (Job^5) and Mary TUFTS, 7 June 1785, Boston (Rcd.com.30:72)

Abigail BRADFORD^7 and Rev. John ALLYNE

Claudius BRADFORD^7 (Jos. N.^{6}) and Maria W. BRADFORD

Eleanor BRADFORD^7 (Jos.N.^{6}) and Benjamin KENT

Louise E. BRADFORD^7 (Jos.N.^{6}) and Charles H. THOMAS

Charles F. BRADFORD^7 (Jos.N.^{6}) and Eliza E. HICKLING

John TUFTS and Rebecca SENTER(sp), 4 Oct. 1759, Boston (Rcd.com.30:396)

John TUFTS and Mary READY, 7 Dec. 1768, Boston (Rcd.com.30:428)

Nathaniel TUFTS and Mary PIERCE, Int. 3 Oct. 1753, Boston (Rcd.com.30:8)

Ann TUFTS and John MERCHANT, 11 Feb. 1784 Boston (Rcd.com.30:93)

Peter TUFTS and Mary PIERCE

Peter TUFTS and 1st Elizabeth LYNDE, 26 Aug. 1670, 2nd Mercy COLTON, 3rd Prudence WYMAN

Simon TUFTS and Abigail SMITH, 24 Oct. 1725

Samuel TUFTS and Hannah TUFTS, Int. 1753

Mercy TUFTS and Thomas BROOKS, 29 Dec. 1762

Anna TUFTS and Peter JOMS(sp), 2 May 1765

John TUFTS and Mercy COLLINS, Int. 5 Nov. 1747, Boston (Rcd.com.38:287) [15]

John TUFTS and Abigail PECK, Int. 21 Jan. 1750, Boston (rcd.com.38:296)

Mary TUFTS and John MORSE, 14 Sept. 1743, Boston (Rcd.com.38:275)

Samuel TUFTS and Susanna PEMBERTON(sp), 23 Feb. 1748, Boston (Rcd.com.38:265)

Simon TUFTS and Ruth JACKSON, Int. 11 June 1747, Boston (Rcd.com.38:286)

Priscilla BRADFORD^5 (Gershom^4) and Moses NORMAN, 26 July 1750, Newport RI (VR 4:2:10,51)

Moses NORMAN^6 (Prisc. Bradford^5) and Sarah CORNELL

Ann NORMAN^6 (Prisc. Bradford^5) and Edward TALBEE

Priscilla NORMAN^6 (Prisc. Bradford^5) and William THURSTON

Hope NORMAN^6 (Prisc. Bradford^5) and Caleb HARGILL

Hope NORMAN^7 (Moses^6) and Jason BUTLER

Priscilla Bradford NORMAN^7 (Moses^6) and Philip STEVENS

Dr. Solomon BRADFORD^5 (Gershom^4) and 1st Bettey GREENWOOD, 5 Nov. 1749, Rehoboth
   (VR:55)

John BRADFORD and Sarah DAGGETT, 28 Nov. 1771, Rehoboth (VR:55)

Keziah BRADFORD and Nathaniel HIX, 15 Aug. 1784, Swansea (Rehoboth VR:55)

Dr. Solomon BRADFORD^5 (Gershom^4) and Mary (RUTTENBURG) Owen, 9 Nov. 1769, (Arnold
   (Arnold VR 2:9)

Hannah BRADFORD^4 (Samuel^3) and Nathaniel GILBERT, 16 June 1709, Duxbury (MD 11:23)

Hannah GILBERT^5 (Hannah Bradford^4) and Ebenezer SMITH, 26 Nov. 1730, Taunton (VR
   2:198,438)

Mary GILBERT^5 (Hannah Bradford^4) and James GODFREY, 17 Feb. 1737, Berkley (Taunton
   VR:198,202)

Col. Thomas GILBERT^5 (Hannah Bradford^4) and Mary GODFREY

Welthea GILBERT^5 (Hannah Bradford^4) and Ebenezer HATHAWAY, Int. 18 Feb. 1743, Freetown
(VR 1:182)

Ebenezer HATHAWAY^6 (Welthea Gilbert^5) and Mary HATHWAY, 30 Nov. 1769 (Freetown VR)

Micro #12 of 15

Thomas Gilbert HATHAWAY^7 (Ebenezer^6) and 1st Ann CANBY, 30 Apr. 1815, St. John N.B.

Thomas Gilbert HATHAWAY^7 and 2nd Harriet Eliza BATES, 28 Apr. 1831, Eastport ME

Thomas Ebenezer HATHAWAY^8 (Tho.^{7}) and Helen Scoullar BATES

Gilbert HATHAWAY^6 (Welthea Gilbert^5) and 1st Elizabeth WILLIAMS^6 (Nathaniel$^{5-4}$, Eliz.
   Rogers^3, John^2), c1767 (Freetown VR 3:151)

Gilbert HATHAWAY^6 and 2nd Mary (EVANS) Weaver, 24 Nov. 1779 (Freetown VR 2:243)

Mary EVANS and Jonathan WEAVER, 15 Jan. 1769, Freetown (VR 16:133)

Shadrack HATHAWAY^6 (Welthea Gilbert^5) and Hannah CHASE, 31 Oct. 1772, Freetown
   (VR 2:383)

Welthea HATHAWAY^6 (Welthea Gilbert^5) and Richard RUGGLES, c1771[16]

Bathsheba RUGGLES^7 (Welthea Hathaway^6) and John HUTCHINSON

Cynthia RUGGLES^7 (Welthea Hathaway^6) and John DURLAND

Sophia RUGGLES^7 (Welthea Hathaway^6) and John RYARSON

Wealthy RUGGLES^7 (Welthea Hathaway^6) and Charles TUCKER

Jerusha BRADFORD^4 (Samuel^3) and Ebenezer GAY, 13 Nov. 1719, Duxbury (MD 11:239)

Perez BRADFORD[4] (Samuel[3]) and Abigail BELCHER, 14 Apr. 1720, Dedham

Joseph BRADFORD[5] (Perez[4]) and Beulah MORCE, Int. 14 Jan. 1758, Attleboro (VR:497)

John BRADFORD[5] (Perez[4]) and Phebe STEARNS, Int. 14 Feb. 1761, Attleboro (VR:499)

George BRADFORD[5] (Perez[4]) and Sarah CARPENTER, Int. 28 Apr. 1756, Attleboro (VR:496)

Abby HOPPIN and Marcus MORTON Jr., 19 Oct. 1843, Providence (VR 3:358)

Henry HOPPIN and Almy H. BOWLES, 26 Nov. 1810, Providence (VR 5:210)

Abigail BRADFORD[5] (Perez[4]) and Samuel LEE

Hannah BRADFORD[5] (Perez[4]) and Jabez GAY, 30 Apr. 1747 (Attleboro VR 1:143)

Lucy GAY[6] (Hannah Bradford[5]) and Joel METCALF

John BRADFORD[5] (Perez[4]) and 2nd Sarah DAGGETT, 28 Nov. 1771 (Rehoboth VR:55,117)

Walter BRADFORD[6] (John[5]) and Sarah MANN, Int. 30 Aug. 1795, Medfield (VR:121,155)

Perez BRADFORD[5] (Perez[4]) and Mary JACKSON, 24 Jan. 1750, Cumberland RI (VR 3:5:15,40)

Betty BRADFORD[6] (Perez[5]) and James WALCOTT

Mary BRADFORD and Michael FOSTER, 24 Oct. 1764 (Cumberland RI VR 1:24)

Welthea BRADFORD[4] (Samuel[3]) and Peter LANE, c1723 (Hingham Hist.2:414)

Hannah LANE[5] (Welthea Bradford[4]) and Samuel JOHNSON, 18 Feb. 1744/45, Hingham (Hist. Hingham 2:386)

Hannah JOHNSON[6] (Hannah Lane[5]) and Peleg EWELL, c1768 (Hist. of Francestown NH:673-4)

Perez EWELL[7] (Hannah Johnson[6]) and Betsey LORD, 10 July 1794

Sarah BRADFORD[3] and Kenelm BAKER, c1687 (MD 5:234)

Alice BAKER[4] (Sarah Bradford[3]) and Nathan THOMAS, 4 Mar. 1713, Marshfield (MD 7:131)

Nathan THOMAS and 2nd Abiah SNOW[4] (Josiah[3], Abigail Warren[2])

Anna THOMAS[5] (Abigail Baker[4]) and 1st Nathaniel OLDS, 26 Dec. 1747, Duxbury (MD 11:78)

Anna THOMAS[5] and 2nd Elijah DAMON, 17 May 1753, Marshfield

Elijah DAMON[7] (Elijah[6], Anna Thomas[5]) and Emily JOSELYN, 26 June 1827 (Bible rcd.)

Elijah DAMON[6] (Anna Thomas[5]) and Deborah SOPER, 21 Mar. 1790, Pembroke (VR:333)

Kenelm BAKER[4] (Sarah Bradford[3]) and Patience DOTY[3] (John[2]), 22 Jan. 1718/19, Duxbury (MD 11:25)

Samuel BAKER[4] (Sarah Bradford[3]) and Hannah FORD[5] (James[4], Abigail Snow[3], Abigail Warren[2]), 9 Nov. 1726, Marshfield

Eleanor BAKER[5] (Samuel[4]) and Joseph THOMAS, 7 Nov. 1754, Marshfield (Duxbury VR:215,320)

Bethiah BAKER[5] (Samuel[4]) and Henry PERRY, 25 Dec. 1760, Duxbury

Charles BAKER[5] (Sam.[4]) and Deborah WILLIAMSON, 21 Jan. 1768, Marshfield

Sarah BAKER[4] (Sarah Bradford[3]) and John SHERMAN, 26 Mar. 1712, Marshfield (MD 7:132)

Micro #13 of 15

Thomas BRADFORD^3 and Ann RAYMOND, c1681

James BRADFORD^4 (Thomas^3) and 2nd Susanna ADAMS, 7 Dec. 1724 (Early Settlers of CT:313)

James BRADFORD^4 and 3rd Leah (RIPLEY) Cook, aft. Mar. 1752 (Canterbury CT VR)

Thomas BRADFORD^5 (James^4) and Eunice ADAMS, 2 May 1733,(Canterbury CT VR)

Jerusha BRADFORD^5 (James^4) and Jonathan PELLETT (Early Settlers of CT:313)

Sarah BRADFORD^5 (James^4) and Joseph ADAMS (Early Settlers:313)

Anna BRADFORD^5 (James^4) and Eleazer CLEAVELAND (Early Settlers:313)

Mary BRADFORD^5 (James^4) and Joseph WOODWARD (Early Settlers:313)

William BRADFORD^5 (James^4) and 1st Zerviah LOTHROP, 13 Dec. 1739, Canterbury CT (VR)

William BRADFORD^5 (James^4) and 2nd Mary CLEAVELAND^6 (Abigail Paine^5, Elisha^4, Mary
    Snow^3, Constance Hopkins^2), 6 Apr. 1743, Canterbury CT (MD 15:66)

William BRADFORD^5 and 3rd Martha WARREN

Olive BRADFORD^6 (William^5) and Hezekiah BARSTOW^6 (Eliz. Newcomb^5, Jerusha Bradford^4,
    Tho.^{3}, Wm.^{2}), 23 May 1776 (MD 15:65,66)

Jerusha BRADFORD^4 (Thomas^3) and Hezekiah NEWCOMB, 14 Nov. 1716, (Lebanon CT VR:223)

Jemima NEWCOMB^5 (Jerusha Bradford^4) and 2nd Joseph KINNEY

William BRADFORD^3 and Rebecca BARTLETT^4 (Ben.^{3}, Mary Warren^2), c1679 (MD 6:45)

Rebecca BARTLETT and 2nd Robert STANFORD, betw. 1691-97

Rebecca BARTLETT and 3rd Caleb SAMSON

Alice BRADFORD^4 (Wm.^{3}) and William BARNES, 20 Nov. 1704, Plymouth (MD 14:35)

Benjamin BARNES^5 (Alice Bradford^4) and Experience RIDER, 14 June 1742, Plymouth
    (MD 14:159)

Experience RIDER and 2nd Elisha CORBAN, aft. Apr. 1760 (MD 5:53)

Experience BARNES^6 (Ben.^{5}) and Elisha CORBAN, 19 July 1772, Plymouth (VR 2:258)

Alice BARNES^6 (Ben.^{5}) and Samuel BATTLES, Int. 20 Feb. 1762, Plymouth (MD 26:41)

Sarah BATTLES^7 (Alice Barnes^6) and John GRAY, Int. 9 Feb. 1804, Plymouth (MD 31:112)

Experience BATTLES^7 (Alice Barnes^6) and George PERKINS, 22 June 1800, Plymouth

Samuel BATTLES^7 (Alice Barnes^6) and Deborah ATWOOD, Int. 29 Mar. 1792, Plymouth
    (MD 30:76)

Benjamin BARNES^6 (Ben.^{5}) and Deborah HOLMES^7 (Ichabod^6, Hannah Sylvester^5, Hannah
    Bartlett^4, Jos.^{3}, Mary Warren^2), 13 Nov. 1774, Plymouth (ch.rcds.2:498)

Bradford BARNES^6 (Ben.^{5}) and Sarah HOWARD (Hist.Danby VT <1869>)

Hosea BARNES^7 (Bradford^6) and Hannah BREWSTER (Hist.Danby)

Bradford BARNES JR.^{7} (Bradford^6) and Rachael AUSTIN (Hist.Danby)

Benjamin BARNES[7] (Bradford[6]) and Zilphia GIFFORD (Hist.Danby VT <1869>)

Clarissa BARNES[8] (Ben.[7]) and Joel NICHOLS (Hist.Danby)

Isaac BARNES[6] (Ben.[5]) and Lucy HARLOW[7] (Jonathan[6], Tho.[5], Wm.[4], Rebecca Bartlett[3], Mary Warren[2])

Lemuel BARNES[5] (Alice Bradford[4]) and Lydia BARNES[5] (Mary Bartlett[4], Jos.[3], Mary Warren[2]), 21 May 1735, Plymouth (MD 14:156)

Mercy BARNES[5] (Alice Bradford[4]) and 1st Samuel COLE, 14 Nov. 1728, Plymouth (MD 14:72)

Mercy BARNES[5] and 2nd Barnabas HEDGE, Int. 21 Dec. 1733, Plymouth (MD 18:120)

Barnabas HEDGE[6] (Mercy Barnes[5]) and Hannah HEDGE, Int. 30 May 1761, Plymouth (MD 26:40)

Ellen H. HEDGE and Rev. William P. LUNT(sp), 14 May 1829 (Plymouth TR 2:414)

Barnabas HEDGE[7] (Barnabas[6]) and Eunice Dennie BURR, 9 Sept. 1789 (Burr Gen.:156)[17]

Barnabas HEDGE[8] (Barnabas[7]) and Tryphena COVINGTON (Burr Gen.:156)

James HEDGE[9] (Barnabas[8]) and Sarah HOLMES (Burr Gen.:156)

Sarah HEDGE[9] (Barnabas[8]) and Joseph CUSHMAN (Burr Gen.:156)

Nathaniel HEDGE[9] (Barnabas[8]) and Sarah SYLVESTER (Burr Gen.:156)

Thomas HEDGE[8] (Barnabas[7]) and Lydia Coffin GOODWIN, 2 Sept. 1824 (Plymouth ch.rcds.)

Mercy HEDGE[6] (Mercy Barnes[5]) and Thomas DAVIS, 24 May 1753, Plymouth (MD 18:141)

Sarah BRADFORD[4] (Wm.[3]) and Jonathan BARNES, c1708 (MD 7:176)

Jonathan BARNES and 2nd Mercy (   ) DOTY, Int. 25 Aug. 1722, Plymouth

Rebecca BARNES[5] (Sarah Bradford[4]) and Ebenezer PHINNEY[5] (Ebenezer[4], Mary Rogers[3], Jos[2]) 22 Sept. 1730, Plymouth

Hannah BARNES[5] (Sarah Bradford[4]) and 1st Stephen CHURCHILL, 4 July 1738, Plymouth (MD 14:158)

Hannah BARNES[5] and 2nd Jeremiah HOWES, aft. Sept. 1751

Hannah CHURCHILL[6] (Hannah Barnes[5]) and John OTIS, c1765 (MD 22:106)

Stephen CHURCHILL[6] (Hannah Barnes[5]) and Lucy BURBANK, 10 July 1766 (Churchill Gen.:61)

Zadock CHURCHILL[6] (Hannah Barnes[5]) and Bathsheba RIDER[7] (Jos.[6], Mary Southworth[5], Desire Gray[4], Mary Winslow[3], Mary Chilton[2]), 7 Oct. 1773, Plymouth (TR 2:258)

Lydia BARNES[5] (Sarah Bradford[4]) and Joseph SMITH, 2 May 1738, Plymouth (MD 14:158)

Elizabeth DOANE[6] (Sarah Barnes[5]) and Israel NICKERSON, c1767 (MD 7:67)

Sarah BARNES[5] (Sarah Bradford[4]) and Thomas DOANE, 20 May 1729, Plymouth (MD 14:72)

William BRADFORD[4] (Wm.[3]) and Elizabeth FINNEY[4] (Eliz. Warren[3], Jos.[2]), 18 Nov. 1712, Plymouth (MD 14:37)

Mercy BRADFORD[5] (Wm.[4]) and Samuel HARLOW[6] (Wm.[5], Sam.[4], Rebecca Bartlett[3], Mary Warren[2]), 15 Dec. 1746, Plymouth (MD 17:5)

Jerusha BRADFORD[5] (Wm.[4]) and 1st Edward SPARROW, 16 Apr. 1741, Plymouth (MD 16:254)

Jerusha BRADFORD[5] and 2nd Josiah CARVER, 22 Jan. 1746/47, Plymouth (MD 17:5)

Edward SPARROW[6] (Jerusha Bradford[5]) and Rhoda BUMPUS, 21 Feb. 1765

Edward SPARROW[7] (Edward[6]) and Bathsheba PORTER

Elizabeth SPARROW[7] (Edward[6]) and Gorham WOOD, 28 Nov. 1798, Marlboro

Jerusha SPARROW[7] (Edward[6]) and Joseph LOVELL

Rhoda SPARROW[7] (Edward[6]) and Alfred WOOD

Susanna SPARROW[7] (Edward[6]) and John MILLER

Josiah BRADFORD[5] (Wm.[4]) and Hannah RIDER[6] (Sam.[5], John[4], Sarah Bartlett[3], Mary Warren[2]), 6 Nov. 1746, Plymouth (MD 17:5)

William BRADFORD[6] (Josiah[5]) and Ruth DUNHAM, c1773

Micro #15 of 15

Sarah BRADFORD[5] (Wm.[4]) and Zephaniah HOLMES, 23 Jan. 1738/39, Plymouth (MD 14:158)

NOTES

<1> p.39, Weaver, William L. History of Ancient Windham CT. Willimantic. 1864. (p.61)

<2> p.40, The name DeForest is entered with a question mark; added in pencil is the name "Burton?".

<3> p.40, Weaver's History of Ancient Windham CT, p.29-30.

<4> p.40, Bowman questions whether she married 2nd Benjamin Willis, 17 Dec. 1761, Plymouth (Bridgewater VR 2:409)

<5> p.41, The files give no reason for the double Bradford name. If this is not an error, perhaps she was given the middle name of Bradford to ensure she would carry on the family name after she married.

<6> p.44, These two marriages are printed here as they appear, obviously one of the dates is wrong.

<7> p.47, A date of April 1751 is also given, the source being the bible of William[5] found in PN&Q 3:105.

<8> p.48-49, The "W.Hfd." source appears to be church records of West Hartford.

<9> p.49, Although this couple was not married they are included here because they had a child (Peabody[6], b. 1 Mar. 1758) and therefore left descendants.

<10> p.49, Welthea Delano[6] appears to be descended from a double Mayflower line: Paternal line - Joshua Delano[5], Martha Simmons[4], Mercy Pabodie[3], Eliz. Alden[2], John[1]. Maternal line - Hopestill Peterson[4], Jonathan[3], Mary Soule[2], George[1]. See p.4 for parent's marriage.

<11> p.49, Although his descent is not shown Joseph Bartlett[7] is a Mayflower descendant as follows: Joseph[6-5], Ichabod[4], Benjamin[3], Mary Warren[2]. See Warren Micro #19.

<12> p.50, Descent is later shown to be William Bradford[5], Joseph[4-3], Wm.[2].

<13> p.50, Unidentified manuscript records state Halsey Dart Bradford, son of Joel Bradford and <u>Sarah</u> Stocking married Judith Bogart (possibly the maiden name of Judith Stoutinburgh),

<14> p.50, Her full name is later given to be Lavinia Martha Pearson.

<15> p.51, Along with this and the following four Tufts marriages are four additional Tufts marriages. However the surnames of the grooms are illegible so are not included here.

<16> p.52, Source for this and the following four Ruggles marriages: Ruggles, Henry Stoddard. The Ruggles Family of England and America. Boston. 1893. (p.86-87)

<17> p.55, Todd, Charles Burr. Burr Genealogy. N.Y. 2nd Ed. 1891.

WILLIAM BREWSTER DESCENDANTS

William BREWSTER[1] and Mary (   ), c1592, England[1]

Stephen BREWSTER and Philippi SIMMONS, 20 July 1815, (Marshfield VR 3:65)

Joseph BREWSTER and Jedidah WHITE, 22 Nov. 1740 (Marshfield VR 2:159)

Seabury BREWSTER and Sally BRADFORD, 25 Dec. 1785 (Norwich CT BMD IV:139)

Seabury BREWSTER and Lucy LEFFINGWELL, 25 Oct. 1789 (Norwich CT BMD IV:139)

Jonah BREWSTER and Joanna WALDO, 25 Jan. 1743/44

Bethiah BREWSTER and William PARISH, 23 May 1738, Windham (Tho.S.Weaver's Windham Mgs.)

Mary BREWSTER and Reuben LILLY, 14 Feb. 1733/34, Windham (Weaver's Mgs.)

William PARISH and 3rd Jerusha AYER, 13 Apr. 1742, Windham (Weaver's Mgs.)

Jerusha BREWSTER and Zebulon RUDD, 4 June 1741, Windham (Weaver's Mgs.)

Grace BREWSTER and Nathaniel WALES, 9 Feb. 1755, Windham (Weaver's Mgs.)

Lydia BREWSTER and William RIPLEY, 11 Jan. 1757, Windham (Weaver's Mgs.)

Drusilla BREWSTER and William ELY, Oct. 1766, Windham (Weaver's Mgs.)

Asa BREWSTER and Ruth BADGER, 28 May 1766, Windham (Weaver's Mgs.)

John BREWSTER and Mary DURKEE, 6 Nov. 1760, Windham (Weaver's Mgs.)

Benjamin BREWSTER and Susannah GREEN, 8 Sept. 1786, Windham (Weaver's Mgs.)

Jonathan BREWSTER[5] (Jonathan[4], Wrestling[3], Love[2]) and Eunice KINGSLEY, 12 Feb. 1767, Windham (Weaver's Mgs.)

Dr. John FITCH and Sophia BROCKMAN, 15 Oct. 1851, Lebanon (Weaver)

Esther BREWSTER and Roger WALES, 24 Mar. 1778, Windham (ch.rcds.)

Hannah BREWSTER and Luther MARTIN, 14 Apr. 1778, Windham (ch.rcds.)

Elizabeth BREWSTER and Jeremiah STEBBIN, 29 Aug. 1779, Windham (ch.rcds.)

Abigail BREWSTER and William PIERCE, 25 July 1799, Windham (ch.rcds.)

David BREWSTER and Sally DORRAME(sp), 28 Feb. 1803, Windham (ch.rcds.)

William DURKEE and Rebecca GOULD, 13 Jan. 1704 (Weaver)

William DURKEE Jr. and Abigail HONEY, 8 Feb. 1732/33 (Weaver)

Abigail DURKEE and Josiah HAMMOND (Weaver)

Hannah DURKEE and William FOSTER (Weaver)

James BREWSTER and Faith RIPLEY, 15 Mar. 1738/39 (Weaver)

Darius WEBB and Deborah PALMER, 8 Oct. 1767, Windham (Weaver's Mgs.)

William BREWSTER and Esther SEABIN, 16 Jan. 1752, Scotland CT (Weaver)

James BRADFORD and Leah (   ) COOK, 9 Nov. 1752, Scotland CT (Weaver)

Capt. Caleb JEWETT and Faith (   ) BREWSTER, 26 May 1766, Scotland CT (Weaver)

William CUSHMAN and Ruth ROBINSON, 4 May 1775, Scotland CT (Weaver)

William CUSHMAN and Anna RINDGE(sp), 31 Jan. 1792, Scotland CT (Weaver)

David Bradford RIPLEY and Polly ROBINSON, 6 Feb. 1800, Scotland CT (Weaver)

Jonathan BREWSTER^4(Wrestling^3, Love^2) and Mary PARTRIDGE, 6 Mar. 1710 (Weaver)

Mary BREWSTER^5 (Jonathan^4) and Jeremiah BINGHAM (Weaver)

Benjamin BREWSTER and Betsey HUNTINGTON, 15 Oct. 1809 (Weaver)

Christopher YERGASON and Charlotte Ann SMITH, 28 May 1838, Windham CT (Weaver)

Jonathan BREWSTER^2 (Wm.^{1})

Jonathan BREWSTER^2 and Lucretia OLDHAM, 10 Apr. 1624, Plymouth (MD 32:2)

Benjamin BREWSTER^3 and Ann DARTE, last day of Feb. 1659/60 (MD 1:72)

Benjamin BREWSTER^4 (Ben.^{3}) and 1st Mary SMITH, 17 Dec. 1696 (MD 1:193)

Mary BREWSTER^5 (Ben.^{4}) and Benjamin PAINE, 19 Oct. 1726, Lebanon CT (Gen.Reg.53:44)

Stephen PAYNE and Rebecca BUSHNELL, 23 Sept. 1756 (Coventry CT VR:156)

Daniel PAYNE and Rebecca BACON, Int. 12 Oct. 1811

Ebenezer PAYNE and Delight CADY/CODY, Int. 16 Apr. 1809

Keziah PAYNE and Squire Haskell BARRETT, 16 Dec. 1828

Lyman K. PAYNE and Emily EMMONS(sp), 28 May 1837

Noah PAYNE and Dolly HATHAWAY, 18 Sept. 1822

Sally PAYNE and Eleazer LYMAN Jr., 27 Aug. 1819

Stephen PAYNE and Ruth SMITH, Oct. 1816

Daniel BREWSTER^4 (Ben.^{3}) and 1st Hannah GAGER, 23 Dec. 1686 (MD 1:168)

Daniel BREWSTER^4 and 2nd Dorothy WITTER, aft. Sept. 1727 (MD 1:173)

Hannah BREWSTER^5 (Daniel^4) and Joseph FREEMAN, 2 Dec. 1708 (MD 1:171)

Nathan FREEMAN^6 (Hannah Brewster^5) and 1st Lucy BLODGETT, 1748 (MD 1:195)

Nathan FREEMAN^6 and 2nd Lucy BARNS, 14 Feb. 1753 (MD 1:196)$^{<2>}$

Lucy FREEMAN^7 (Nathan^6) and Gideon SAFFORD, 10 Nov. 1774 (Preston VR 2:193)

Mary SAFFORD^8 (Lucy Freeman^7) and John McINTYRE

Elizabeth SAFFORD^8 (Lucy Freeman^7) and Daniel CARSWELL

Gideon SAFFORD^8 (Lucy Freeman^7) and Jane ORR(sp)

Chester SAFFORD^8 (Lucy Freeman^7) and Esther CARSWELL

Nathan SAFFORD^8 (Lucy Freeman^7) and Huldah ESLEN(sp)

Adin SAFFORD^8 (Lucy Freeman^7) and Mary MONCRIEF

Hannah SAFFORD^8 (Lucy Freeman^7) and John BRADFORD

Matilda SAFFORD^8 (Lucy Freeman^7) and James TURNER

Lucy SAFFORD[8] (Lucy Freeman[7]) and James GILLIS

Thomas SAFFORD[8] (Lucy Freeman[7]) and Isabel LIVINGSTON

Thomas SAFFORD[8] and 2nd Betsey MORE

Sarah SAFFORD[8] (Lucy Freeman[7]) and David STEWART

Phoebe SAFFORD[8] (Lucy Freeman[7]) and Elias RHODES

John BREWSTER[5] (Dan.[4]) and Dorothy TREAT, 20 Sept. 1725 (MD 1:194)

Jonathan BREWSTER and Mary PARRISH, 9 Nov. 1726 (Preston CT VR 1:58)

Jonathan BREWSTER Jr. and Zipporah SMITH, 28 Aug. 1755 (Preston CT VR 2:73)

Ruth BREWSTER[5] (Dan.[4]) and John FOBES, 14 Jan. 1718/19 (MD 1:197)

Jonathan BREWSTER[4] (Ben.[3]) and Judith STEVENS, 18 Dec. 1690 (MD 1:172)

Mary BREWSTER[4] (Ben.[3]) and Samuel FITCH, 28 Nov. 1678 (MD 1:75)

Jabez FITCH[5] (Mary Brewster[4]) and Anna KNOWLTON, Mar. 1719 (MD 2:21)

Jabez FITCH[6] (Jabez[5]) and Hannah PERKINS, 3 June 1760 (MD 2:21)

Ruth BREWSTER[4] (Ben.[3]) and Thomas ADGATE, 15 June 1692, Norwich CT

William BREWSTER[4] (Ben.[3]) and 1st Elizabeth READ

Elizabeth BREWSTER[3] and 1st Peter BRADLEY, 7 Sept. 1653 (MD 1:71)

Elizabeth BREWSTER[3] and 2nd Christopher CHRISTOPHERS, aft. July 1676 (Hist. New
    London CT:317)

Elizabeth BRADLEY[4] (Eliz. Brewster[3]) and Thomas DYMOND, 22 Sept. 1670, New London CT
    (MD 1:73)

Benjamin SHAPLEY and Mary PICKET, 10 Apr. 1672 (Calkins' Hist. New London CT:350)

Benjamin SHAPLEY Jr. and Ruth DYMOND (Calkins :350)

Hannah BRADLEY[4] (Eliz. Brewster[3]) and Andrew LESTER, aft. Aug. 1674

Lucretia BRADLEY[4] (Eliz. Brewster[3]) and Richard CHRISTOPHERS, 26 Jan. 1681 (New
    London CT VR)

Richard CHRISTOPHERS and 2nd Grace TURNER[4] (Mary Brewster[3], Jonathan[2]), 3 Sept. 1691

Peter BRADLEY[4] (Eliz. Brewster[3]) and Mary CHRISTOPHERS, 9 May 1678, New London CT
    (MD 1:77)

Christopher CHRISTOPHERS and Sarah PROUT(sp), 22 Jan. 1711/12, New Haven CT (New
    London CT)

Richard CHRISTOPHERS and Mrs. Elizabeth SALTONSTALL, 14 Aug. 1710 (New London CT VR)

John CHRISTOPHERS[4] (Eliz. Brewster[3]) and Elizabeth MULFORD, 28 July 1696 (New London VR)

Elizabeth MULFORD and 2nd John PICKET[5] (Adam[4], Ruth Brewster[3], Jonathan[2])

Hannah BREWSTER[3] and Samuel STARR, 23 Dec. 1664 (New London CT VR 4:326)

Charles HILL and Ruth (BREWSTER[3]) Pickett, 16 July 1668 (New London CT VR 4:324)

Charles HILL and Rachell MASON, 12 June 1678 (New London CT VR 4:314)

Ezeekiell TURNER and Susanna KEYNEY, 26 Dec. 1678 (New London CT VR 4:314)

Adam PICKETT and Hanna WETHERELL, 26 May 1680 (New London CT VR 4:311)

Mary/Marcy PICKETT and Samuell FOSDICK, 1 Nov. 1682 (New London CT VR 4:307)

Joseph MINOR and Susana ( ) TURNER, 20 Aug. 1706 (New London CT VR 4:256)

Mary CHRISTOPHERS and Amos CHEESEBROUGH, 23 Jan. 1755, New London CT (VR)

Lucrecia CHRISTOPHERS and John Henry BRADICK, 19 June 1726

Thomas FOSDICK and Esther UPDIKE, 29 June 1720

Ester CHRISTOPHERS and Thomas MANWARING, 14 Feb. 1721/22, New London CT

Grace BREWSTER[3] and Daniel WETHERELL, 4 Aug. 1659 (MD 1:71,74)

Hannah WETHERELL[4] (Grace Brewster[3]) and Adam PICKET[4] (Ruth Brewster[3], Jonathan[2]),
    26 May 1680, New London CT (MD 1:170)

Mary WETHERELL[4] (Grace Brewster[3]) and 1st Thomas HARRIS, c1689

Mary WETHERELL[4] and 2nd George DENISON, aft. June 1691

Jonathan STARR[4] (Hannah Brewster[3]) and Elizabeth MORGAN

Samuel STARR[5] (Jonathan[4], Hannah Brewster[3]) and Ann BUSHNELL, 29 Sept. 1726 (Norwich
    CT VR:36)

Anna STARR[6] (Sam.[5], Jonathan[4]) and Stephen PRENTICE

Anna PRENTICE[7] (Anna Starr[6]) and 1st Joseph CHAMPLIN

Anna PRENTICE[7] and 2nd Elnathan HATCH, 8 June 1794

Anna PRENTICE[7] and 3rd Gilbert DEVOL, 4 Apr. 1811

Nancy CHAMPLIN[8] (Anna Prentice[7]) and Alpha DEVOL, 8 June 1814

Hannah Prentice HATCH[8] (Anna Prentice[7]) and Philip DEVOL

Julia DEVOL[9] (Hannah Hatch[8]) and Jackson BEACH

Julia DEVOL and Andrew J. BEACH, 20 Aug. 1851, Marietta OH (Marr.Rcd.)

Silence HATCH[8] (Anna Prentice[7]) and Stephen DEVOL

Thomas STARR[4] (Hannah Brewster[3]) and Mary MORGAN

Mary BREWSTER[3] and John TURNER Sr., 10 or 12 Nov. 1645, Plymouth (MD 32:3)

Amos TURNER[4] (Mary Brewster[3]) and 1st Mary HILAND, 6 Apr. 1695, Scituate (MD 2:87)

Amos TURNER[4] and 2nd Hannah ( ) CLAP, 19 Nov. 1730 Scituate (MD 1:44)

Lydia TURNER[5] (Amos[4]) and Joseph WITHEREL, 3 Jan. 1739, Scituate (MD 1:46)

Mary TURNER[5] (Amos[4]) and James TURNER, 23 Nov. 1732 (Scituate VR 2:303,305)

Seth TURNER[5] (Amos[4]) and Mehitable GOULD

Amos TURNER^5 (Amos^4) and Elizabeth STOCKBRIDGE, 29 Jan. 1721, Scituate (MD 11:48)

Amos TURNER^6 (Amos^5) and Hannah BASS, c1759

Hannah BASS and 2nd Henry MELLEN, 31 Aug. 1783/85 (Medway VR:229,267)

Priscilla TURNER^6 (Amos^6) and William PEAKES, 15 Jan. 1740, Scituate (MD 1:46)

Ezekiel TURNER^5 (Amos^6) and 1st Bathsheba STOCKBRIDGE, 27 Dec. 1727, Pembroke

Ezekiel TURNER^5 and 2nd Ruth RANDALL, 17 June 1736, Hanover

Desire TURNER^6 (Mary^5) and Eli CURTIS, 14 Dec. 1758 (Scituate VR 2:84,301)

James TURNER^6 (Mary^5) and Deborah LINCOLN, 24 Oct. 1760 (Scituate VR 2:180,303)

Mercy Dwelly TURNER^7 (James^6) and Jonathan HATCH, 25 Feb. 1790 (Scituate VR 2:142,304)

Nathaniel TURNER^7 (James^6) and Sarah JAMES^8 (Ben.$^{7-6}$, John^5, Lydia Turner^4, Mary
    Brewster^3, Jonathan^2)

Mehitable TURNER^6 (Mary^5) and Gideon CHITTENDEN, 29 Apr. 1773 (Scituate VR 2:55)

Benjamin TURNER^4 (Mary Brewster^3) and Elizabeth HAWKINS, 14 Apr. 1692, Scituate
    (MD 2:87)

Elizabeth TURNER^5 (Ben.^{4}) and Joseph BREWSTER^4 (Wm.^{3}, Love^2)

Benjamin TURNER^5 (Ben.^{4}) and Mercy TURNER, c1723

Elisha TURNER^6 (Ben.^{5}) and 1st Abigail FOSTER, 29 Dec. 176(), Scituate (MD 1:234) $^{<3>}$

Elisha TURNER^6 and 2nd Prudence JAMES^7 (John$^{6-5}$, Lydia Turner^4, Mary Brewster^3,
    Jonathan^2), 18 Sept. 1766, Scituate (MD 1:235)

Elisha TURNER^7 (Elisha^6) and Elizabeth DILL, 1812 (Hull VR:45,57)

Mercy TURNER^6 (Ben.^{5}) and Benjamin STETSON, 14 June 1763, Scituate (MD 1:234)

Grace TURNER^5 (Ben.^{4}) and Richard DWELLY, 13 Oct. 1712 (Scituate VR)

Grace DWELLY^6 (Grace Turner^5) and Jesse TURNER^5 (Jonathan^4, Mary Brewster^3, Jonathan^2),
    18 Dec. 173(), (Scituate VR) $^{<4>}$

Grace DWELLY^6 and 2nd Joseph CHURCH^5 (Nath.$^{4-3}$, Eliz. Warren^2), Aug. 1742 (Scituate VR)

John TURNER^5 (Ben.^{4}) and Mercy BARTLETT^5 (Ben.$^{4-3}$, Mary Warren^2), 5 Aug. 1714, Duxbury
    (MD 11:24)

John TURNER^5 and 2nd Mary VINAL, 15 Mar. 1769 (Scituate VR)

Micro #4 of 18

Ezekiel TURNER^4 (Mary Brewster^3) and Susanna KEYNEY, 26 Dec. 1678 (New London CT VR)

Susanna KEYNEY and 2nd Joseph MINOR, 20 Aug. 1706 (New London CT VR)

Elisha TURNER^4 (Mary Brewster^3) and Elizabeth JACOB, 6 June 1687, Scituate (MD 2:36)

Josiah TURNER and Hannah HOLBROOK, 24 Jan. 1700 (Scituate VR 2:151,304)

Waitstill TURNER and Mary STAPLES, c1760 (Hanover VR:203)

Elisha TURNER^5 (Elisha^4, Mary Brewster^3) and Mary STUDLEY

Elizabeth TURNER^5 (Elisha^4) and Joshua TURNER, 20 Apr. 1711 (Scituate VR)

Jael TURNER^5 (Elisha^4) and John DILLINGHAM, 7 Aug.1715 (Scituate VR)

Lydia DILLINGHAM and Joseph RICHARDS, 10 June 1733/34 (Hanover VR:88)

Henry DILLINGHAM and Hannah PERRY, 1652

Lydia DILLINGHAM^6 (Jael Turner^5) and Joseph RECCORD

Elizabeth DILLINGHAM^6 (Jael Turner^5) and Joshua SIMMONS

Jael DILLINGHAM^6 (Jael Turner^5) and Jonathan PETERSON

Deborah DILLINGHAM^6 (Jael Turner^5) and Perez HOWLAND

Princess DILLINGHAM^6 (Jael Turner^5) and Nehemiah PETERSON

Mary TURNER^5 (Elisha^4) and Zebulon SILVESTER, 1 Jan. 1711/12, Scituate

Elisha SILVESTER^6 (Zebulon^5) and 1st Hannah HUNT, Int. 17 Jan. 1746, Scituate

Elisha SILVESTER^6 and 2nd Grace RUGGLES, 17 Dec. 1751, Norwell (ch.rcds.:39)

Elisha SILVESTER^6 and 3rd Lillis YOUNG, 12 Nov. 1776 (Scituate VR:110)

Elisha SILVESTER and Eunice PROUTY, 12 Dec. 1734, Scituate (MD 1:107)

Edward PROUTY and Elizabeth HOW, 2 Dec. 1701 (Scituate VR 2:154,241)

Zebulon SILVESTER^6 (Mary Turner^5) and Letitia SHIPPY, 30 Oct. 1752, Boston (28:344)

Nathaniel SILVESTER^6 (Mary Turner^5) and Sylvia SPRAGUE, 6 Dec. 1759, Duxbury

Martha SILVESTER^6 (Mary Turner^5) and Elisha PROUTY, 17 Mar. 1747 (Scituate VR 2:241)

James SYLVESTER and Joanna BROOKS, 20 Dec. 1764

Joanna BROOKS and 2nd Benjamin BOWKER

Eunice SYLVESTER and Michael CLAPP, 11 Mar. 1790 (Scituate VR 2:60,284)

Micro #5 of 18

John RUGGLES and Joanna BROOKS, 26 Oct. 1720 (Scituate VR)

Chloe SILVESTER^7 (Elisha^7) and 2nd Elisha BISBE

Elisha SILVESTER^7 (Elisha^6) and Abigail PALMER, 23 Nov. 1775, Hanover (Scituate VR)

Thomas SILVESTER^7 (Elisha^6) and Relief JORDAN, 18 Jan. 1773 (Scituate VR 2:169,258)

Warren SILVESTER and Hannah TURNER, 9 Mar. 1805 (Scituate VR 2:259,302)

Hannah SILVESTER^7 (Elisha^6) and Caleb TORREY, 13 Nov. 1781 (Scituate VR)

Lillis SILVESTER^7 (Elisha^6) and Elnathan CUSHING, 15 Apr. 1802 (Scituate VR 2:91,258)

Lurana SILVESTER^7 (Elisha^6) and Abiel TURNER, 13 Nov. 1766 (Scituate VR 2:258,299)

Jacob SILVESTER^6 (Mary Turner^5) and 1st Deborah LEWIS, 2 Apr. 1747, Hingham

Luke SILVESTER^6 (Mary Turner^5) and Mary DAMON, 31 Oct. 1751 (Scituate ch.rcds.)

Olive SILVESTER^6 (Mary Turner^5) and Edmund GROSS, 3 Mar. 1736/37, Scituate (MD 1:108)

Abigail TURNER^5 (Ezekiel Turner^4) and Clement MINER, Jr., 9 Jan. 1721/22, New
     London CT

Clement MINOR Jr. and 2nd Hannah MINER, 18 Apr. 1758

Abigail MINER^6 (Abigail Turner^5) and Richard SMITH, 1 Aug. 1745, Lyme CT

Richard SMITH and 2nd Grace (LEACH) Moore, 8 Jan. 1756, Lyme CT

Anna SMITH^7 (Abigail Miner^6) and Timothy FLOWER, 13 Sept. 1766, Feeding Hills MA

Timothy FLOWER and 2nd Hannah SPENCER, 24 May 1784

Timothy FLOWER and 3rd Martha JONES, 14 Dec. 1809

Timothy FLOWER^8 (Anna Smith^7) and Clarissa PHILLIPS, 17 Feb. 1800, Rupert VT

Ezekiel TURNER^5 (Ezekiel^4) and Theoda WILLIAMS, 29 Apr. 1723 (Groton CT VR 1:107)

Ezekiel TURNER^5 and 2nd Borodel DENISON^5 (Jos.^{4}, Mercy Gorham^3, Desire Howland^2),
    11 May 1729 (Goton CT VR 1:144)

Eunice TURNER^6 (Ezekiel^5) and Amos BROWN

Ezekiel TURNER^6 (Ezekiel^5) and Rebecca ALLEN

Prudence TURNER^6 (Ezekiel^5) and Samuel FOX, 6 Jan 1751, Groton CT

<u>Micro #6 of 18</u>

John FOX^7 (Prudence Turner^6) and Abigail BAYLEY, 3 Mar. 1794

Theody TURNER^6 (Ezekiel^5) and Daniel BROWN, 22 Mar. 1750 (Stonington CT VR 3:196)

Prudence TURNER and Moses PALMER, 8 May 1753 (Stonington CT VR 3:178)

Sarah TURNER^5 (Ezekiel^4) and Jonathan CALKINS

Susanna TURNER^5 (Ezekiel^4) and Samuel FOSDICK^5 (Mercy Pickett^4, Ruth Brewster^3,
    Jonathan^2)

Grace TURNER^4 (Mary Brewster^3) and Richard CHRISTOPHERS, 3 Sept. 1691 (New London VR)

Richard CHRISTOPHERS and 1st Lucretia BRADLEY^4 (Eliz. Brewster^3, Jonathan^2),
    26 Jan. 1681

Grace CHRISTOPHERS^5 (Grace Turner^4) and John COIT, 2 July 1719 (New London CT VR:76)

John COIT and 2nd Hannah (GARDINER) Potter, 20 June 1748 (New London CT VR:76)

Richard COIT^6 (Grace Christophers^5) and Abigail BRADICK

Joseph COIT^6 (Grace Christophers^5) and Sarah MOSIER

John COIT^6 (Grace Christophers^5) and Mary PEIRCE, 13 June 1742 (New London VR:79)

David COIT^7 (Sam.^{6}) and Sarah OGDEN, 4 Feb. 1789$^{<5>}$

David OGDEN and Mary WILKINSON$^{<5>}$

Samuel COIT^6 (Grace Christophers^5) and Elizabeth RICHARDS, 18 Feb. 1753 (New London
    CT VR 2:109)

Sarah COIT^8 (David^7) and Elisha Lothrop AVERY^8 (John W.^{7}, Ephraim$^{6-5}$, Ruth Little^4,
    Ephraim^3, Anna Warren^2), 12 Apr. 1839

John TURNER^4 (Mary Brewster^3) and Abigail PADISHAL, c1689

Lydia TURNER and Joseph SYLVESTER, 5 Nov. 1728 (Scituate VR 4:2:29)

Joseph SYLVESTER and Mehitable COLE, 10 Aug. 1771, Scituate

Lemuel SILVESTER and Lydia ROSE, Int. 10 Apr. 1756, Scituate

Abiel TURNER^5 (John^4) and Elizabeth ROBINSON, 16 May 1737, Falmouth (Scituate VR)

Abiel TURNER^6 (Abiel^5) and Lurana SILVESTER, 13 Nov. 1766 (Scituate VR)

Abigail TURNER^5 (John^4) and Samuel BRYANT, 14 Feb. 1711/12 (Scituate VR)

Richard TURNER^5 (John^4) and Ruth FOSTER, 23 Jan. 1735/36 (Scituate VR)

Jonathan TURNER^4 (Mary Brewster^3) and 1st Martha BISBEE, c1677 (Scituate VR 4:3:87)

Jonathan TURNER^4 and 2nd Mercy HATCH, c1689 (Scituate VR 4:3:87)

Jonathan TURNER^4 and 3rd Lydia VINTON, 12 Sept. 1721

Isaac TURNER^5 (Jonathan^4) and Ruth TURNER, 31 Oct. 1711 (Scituate VR 2:303,307)

Martha TURNER^5 (Jonathan^4) and Jonathan LOWELL, 17 Oct. 1723 (Scituate VR)

Deborah TURNER^5 (Jonathan^4) and Jonathan SMITH, 10 Aug. 1704, Scituate (MD 3:118)

Ignatius TURNER^5 (Jonathan^4) and Elizabeth WILSON, 28 Dec. 1724 (Scituate VR)

Jemima TURNER^5 (Jonathan^4) and Edward FOSTER, 21 June 1705, Scituate (MD 3:119)

Joshua CLAPP and 1st Lydia SHORT, 12 July 1756, Abington (Clapp Mem.)

Joshua CLAPP and 2nd Mrs. Hannah BRIGGS, 21 Oct. 1787

Lydia CLAPP and Polycarpus JACOBS, 22 Oct. 1792

Polycarpus JACOBS and 2nd Rebecca COFFIN (Starbuck's Hist. Nantucket:723)

Samuel COFFIN and Elizabeth GARDNER, 6 Sept. 1744 (Nantucket VR 3:310)

Elihu COFFIN and Jemima PEASE

Obed COFFIN and 1st Deborah COLEMAN, 2nd Phebe (COLEMAN) Joy

Rebecca COFFIN and Charles JACOBS

Simeon COFFIN and Eunice COFFIN

Thomas COFFIN and Sarah COFFIN

Tristram COFFIN and Abigail COFFIN

Mercy TURNER^5 (Jonathan^4) and Jonah STETSON, 31 May 1720 (Scituate VR)

Ruth TURNER^5 (Jonathan^4) and Amos PERRY, 8 June 1720 (Scituate VR 2:233,307)

Isaac PERRY^6 (Ruth Turner^5) and 1st Betty CHUBBUCK, Int. 16 Feb. 1760 (Scituate
    VR 2:56,234)

Isaac PERRY^6 and 2nd Jemima FARROW, 9 Mar. 1783

Joseph TURNER^4 (Mary Brewster^3) and Bathsheba (HOBART) Leavitt, 19 Nov. 1674
    (Hingham VR 1:33)

Bathsheba HOBART and 1st John LEAVITT, June 1664 (NEHGR 2:253)

Bathsheba TURNER[5] (Jos.[4]) and Hatherly FOSTER, 1 Dec. 1698, Scituate (MD 2:35)

Elizabeth FOSTER[6] (Bathsheba Turner[5]) and Joshua BARSTOW

Joseph FOSTER[6] (Bathsheba Turner[5]) and Abigail STEEL, 11 Jan. 1727 (Scituate VR
    2:124,266)

Margaret TURNER[5] (Jos.[4]) and Joseph STOCKBRIDGE, 20 Oct. 1697 (Scituate VR 2:273,304)

David STOCKBRIDGE[6] (Margaret Turner[5]) and Deborah CUSHING, 10 Jan. 1736/37 (Scituate
    ch.rcds.)

David STOCKBRIDGE[7] (David[6]) and Ruth CUSHING, 23 Dec. 1779 (Hanover TR:126)

Margaret STOCKBRIDGE[6] (Margaret Turner[5]) and Samuel BARSTOW

Lydia TURNER[4] (Mary Brewster[3]) and 1st John JAMES, c1675 (MD 5:42)

Lydia TURNER[4] and 2nd William BARRELL, 20 Apr. 1680, Scituate (MD 19:145)

James BARRELL and Betsey RUSSELL, 15 Sept. 1785, Bridgewater (VR 3:150)

Jonathan BARREL and Judith SNOW, 20 Apr. 1756, Bridgewater (VR 3:180)

Joshua BARREL Jr. and Olive BASS, 23 Nov. 1768, Bridgewater (VR 3:190)

Ruth BARREL and Robert PACKARD, 28 Nov. 1782, Bridgewater (VR 3:161)

Lydia BARREL and Eliphalet PACKARD, 24 Jan. 1782, Bridgewater (VR 3:161)

William BARREL and Sarah CARY, 19 Dec. 1749/50, Bridgewater (VR 3:176)

Susanna BARREL and Oakes WHITMAN, 16 June 1790, Bridgewater (VR 4:196)

Jannett BARREL and John LORING, 30 Sept. 1794, Bridgewater (VR 4:200)

Sarah BARRELL and Nathan ALDEN, 24 Jan. 1776, Bridgewater (VR 4:201)

William BARREL Jr. and Huldah BISBE, 4 June 1800, Bridgewater (VR 4:207)

Abigail BARRELL and Jared WHITMAN, 1 Apr. 1713, Bridgewater (VR 4:214)

Hannah BARRELL and Dr. Daniel SAWIN(sp), 18 Nov. 1810, Bridgewater (VR 4:214)

Ruth BARREL and Dr. Caleb SWAN, 3 Oct. 1816, Bridgewater (VR 4:216)

Elizabeth BARRELL and Joseph PORTER, 25 Jan. 1753 (Bridgewater VR 4:488)

William BARRELL and Rebecca WILDER, 23 Nov. 1775, Hingham

John JAMES[5] (Lydia Turner[4]) and 1st Eunice STETSON, 18 Mar. 1700, Scituate (MD 20:153)

John JAMES[5] and 2nd Lydia TURNER, 25 June 1718 (Scituate VR)

Benjamin JAMES[6] (John[5]) and Mercy STOCKBRIDGE[5] (Mercy Tilden[4], Hannah Little[3], Anna
    Warren[2]), c1735 (Scituate VR 4:134)

Benjamin JAMES[7] (Ben.[6], John[5]) and Sarah HOLMES, c1770 (Scituate TR 12:62)

Sarah JAMES[8] (Ben.[7]) and Nathaniel TURNER[7] (James[6], Mary Turner[5], Amos[4], Mary
    Brewster[3], Jonathan[2])

Sally James TURNER and Augustus COLE, 11 May 1815, Scituate

John JAMES^8 (Ben.^{7}) and Abigail TURNER, 12 June 1838

Eunice JAMES^6 (John^5) and Charles TURNER, 5 May 1729 (Scituate VR 2:161,300)

William TURNER^7 (Eunice James^6) and 1st Elizabeth OAKMAN

William TURNER^7 and 2nd Eunice CLAPP^6 (Nathaniel^5, Temperance Gorham^4, John^3, Desire
   Howland^2)

John JAMES^6 (John^5) and Rhoda KING, 16 July 1730 (Scituate VR)

John JAMES^6 and 2nd Prudence STANTON(sp), Int. 16 Aug. 1737, Scituate

Mary JAMES^6 (John^5) and Joshua JACOB, 7 Apr. 1726 (Scituate VR)

John JAMES^7 (John^6) and 1st Sarah TILDEN^5 (Desire Oldham^4, Mercy Sprout^3, Eliz.
   Samson^2), 3 Dec. 1755, Marshfield (VR 2:149)

John JAMES^7 and 2nd Hannah JACOB, 24 May 1723 (Scituate VR)

John JAMES^8 (John^7) and Patience CLAPP, c1788 (Scituate VR)

John JAMES and Sally Cole WADE, 6 Nov. 1814 (Scituate VR)

Zipporah JAMES^6 (John^5) and Elisha RANDALL, 20 Dec. 1739 (Scituate VR)

Lydia BARRELL^5 (Lydia Turner^4) and Samuel STOCKBRIDGE, 5 Aug. 1703, Scituate
   (MD 5:117)

Abigail STOCKBRIDGE^6 (Lydia Barrell^5) and Jonathan TURNER

Abiel STOCKBRIDGE^6 (Lydia Barrell^5) and 1st Joseph BENSON, 1 Dec. 1743, Scituate

Abiel STOCKBRIDGE^6 and 2nd John BRYANT, Int. 16 July 1748, Scituate

Abiel BRYANT^7 (Abiel Stockbridge^6) and Job TURNER

Elizabeth BRYANT^7 (Abiel Stockbridge^6) and Noah MERRITT, 11 Jan. 1787 (Scituate
   VR 2:47,208)

Mary BARRELL^5 (Lydia Turner^4) and James CUSHING, 10 Dec. 1713, Scituate (MD 9:87)

William BARRELL^5 (Lydia Turner^4) and 1st Elizabeth BAILEY, 2 July 1706

William BARRELL^5 and 2nd Abigail BOWKER, 1723/24 (Norwell ch.rcds.)

Colburn BARRELL^6 (William^5) and Desire BOWKER

Elisha BARRELL^6 (William^5) and Mary COLLAMORE, c1773

James BARRELL^6 (William^5) and Deborah BOWKER, 5 Apr. 1750 (Scituate VR)

James BARRELL^7 (James^6) and Martha FARROW, 10 Dec. 1772 (Scituate VR)

John BARRELL^6 (William^5) and Judith SNOW

Lydia BARRELL^6 (William^5) and Joseph YOUNG^4 (Sarah White^3, Peregrine^2), 5 Sept. 1729

William BARRELL^6 (William^5) and 1st Lydia SIMMONS, Int. 19 Oct. 1745, Scituate

William BARRELL^6 and 2nd Sarah CARY, 19 June 1751

James BARRELL^7 (William^6) and Betsy RUSSELL, 16 Sept. 1785

Ruth BARRELL^7 (William^6) and Robert PACKARD, 28 Nov. 1782

Sarah BARRELL^7 (William^6) and Nathan ALDEN^6 (Nathan^5, Ebenezer^4, Isaac^3, Jos.^{2})

Lydia BARRELL^7 (William^6) and Eliphalet PACKARD, 24 Jan. 1782

Joshua BARRELL^7 (William^6) and Olive BASS^6 (Jonathan$^{5-4}$, Sam.^{3}, Ruth Alden^2)

Susanna BARRELL^8 (Joshua^7) and Oakes WHITMAN, 17 June 1790

Jennet BARRELL^8 (Joshua^7) and John LORING

William BARRELL^8 (Joshua^7) and Huldah BISBEE, 4 June 1801

Samuel BARRELL^8 (Joshua^7) and Olive HOWARD, 5 Dec. 1822

Elijah BARRELL^8 (Joshua^7) and Adaline KIMBALL

Azor BARRELL^8 (Joshua^7) and Lurana CHAMBERLAIN

Charles BARRELL^8 (Joshua^7) and Abigail Stone CHASE

Paschal BARRELL^8 (Joshua^7) and 1st Salome BONNEY

Paschal BARRELL^8 (Joshua^7) and Betsey HAYFORD

Micro #8 of 18

Mary TURNER^4 (Mary Brewster^3) and Isaac PRINCE, 23 Dec. 1679 (Hull VR:55,72)

Joseph PRINCE^5 (Mary Turner^4) and Mary TOWNSEND

Mary PRINCE^5 (Mary Turner^4) and Joseph GOULD, 18 Oct. 1713 (Hull VR:47,55)

Elisha GOULD^6 (Mary Prince^5) and Experience LORING, 1744 (Gould Gen.:337-38)

Mary GOULD^6 (Mary Turner^5) and Nathaniel DILL, 29 Dec. 1743 (Gould Gen.<1895>)

Jane GOULD^6 (Mary Prince^5) and Samuel LORING, 16 Nov. 1749

Caleb GOULD^6 (Mary Prince^5) and Sarah BINNEY (Gould Gen.)

Joshua GOULD^6 (Mary Prince^5) and Lydia (VICKERY) Low, 17 Dec. 1757 (Gould Gen.)

Jane GOULD^7 (Elisha^6) and Stephen GREENLEAF Jr., 12 Sept. 1773 (Gould Gen.:339)

Mehitable GOULD^7 (Elisha^6) and John LORING, 27 Dec. 1800 (Gould Gen.)

Experience GOULD^7 (Elisha^6) and Abel BARKER, pre 1790 (Gould Gen.)

Elizabeth GOULD^7 (Elisha^6) and John FILLEBROWN, 10 May 1780 (Gould Gen.)

Olive GOULD^7 (Elisha^6) and Samuel LOVELL, 20 Feb. 1777 (Gould Gen.)

Lydia GOULD^7 (Elisha^6) and Jonathan LORING, 11 Dec. 1783 (Gould Gen.)

Sarah GOULD^7 (Elisha^6) and Ebenezer POOL, 28 Sept. 1794 (Gould Gen.)

Onner PRINCE^5 (Mary Turner^4) and Francis LOUD, Int. 20 Oct. 1722 (Weymouth VR
   2:117,156)

Mary LOUD^6 (Onner Prince^5) and poss. Elisha JONES, Int. 28 Jan. 1781

John LOUD and Mercy VINING, Int. 18 Mar. 1758 (Abington VR 2:133,220)

Caleb LOUD^6 (Onner Prince^5) and Susanna BATES, 26 Mar. 1772 (Weymouth VR 2:18,116)

Deborah LOUD^6 (Onner Prince^5) and Abel TIRRELL, Int. 12 Jan. 1750/51, Weymouth

Francis LOUD^6 (Onner Prince^5) and Joanna DYER, 13 Nov. 1755, Weymouth

 Debby LOUD and Benjamin SEAVER, 25 May 1794 (Seaver Fam.)

Charles SEAVER and Catherine VOSE(sp), 1 Jan. 1824 (Seaver Fam.)

Jacob LOUD^6 (Onner Prince^5) and Mary SMITH, 3 July 1746 (Weymouth VR 2:117,174)

Capt. Jacob LOUD and Ruth BLANCHARD, 20 Jan. 1800 (Weymouth VR 2:34,117)

John White LOUD and 1st Susan TORREY, 2nd Sarah H. BLANCHARD

Miriam TURNER and Nehemiah JOY, 15 Dec. 1747, poss. Weymouth (Thomas Joy and His
     Descendants<1900>:76)

Jacob LOUD Jr. and Lydia JOY, 17 May 1772 (Weymouth VR 2:106,117)

Esau LOUD^7 (Jacob^6) and Huldah PALMER, 3 Dec. 1781, Hanover (2nd ch.rcds.)[6]

Bezaleel LOUD^8 (Esau^7) and Abiah HARRIS, Int. May 1808, Abington (VR 2:132)

Sylvanus LOUD^7 (John^6) and Lydia LOVELL, c1781 (Weymouth VR)

Solomon LOUD^8 (Sylvanus^7) and Abigail KEITH, 19 Oct. 1809, Boston

Sarah LOUD^6 (Onner Prince^5) and Amasa WADE, 24 July 1755 (Weymouth VR)

William LOUD^6 (Onner Prince^5) and Lucy VINING, c1760 (Weymouth VR 1:171)

Ruth PRINCE^5 (Mary Turner^4) and John SOPHER, 29 Sept. 1718 (Hull VR:55)

Ruth TURNER^4 (Mary Brewster^3) and 1st Thomas PAINE, c1685

Ruth TURNER^4 and 2nd Israel SILVESTER, 3 Oct. 1701, Scituate (MD 5:117)

Benjamin PRINCE^6 (Ben.^{5}, Ruth Turner^4) and 1st Rebecca FISHER

Silvanus PRINCE^6 (Ben.^{5}, Ruth Turner^4) and Elizabeth JOHNSON (Gen.Reg.5:12)

Micro #9 of 18

Benjamin PRINCE^5 (Ruth Turner^4) and Abiel NELSON, 1 Apr. 1717, Duxbury (MD 11:24)

Paul PRINCE^6 (Ben.^{5}) and Hannah CUSHING, 8 Sept. 1743, N. Yarmouth ME (MD 1:35)

Paul PRINCE^7 (Paul^6) and Sarah SOUTHWORTH^6 (John^5, Jedediah^4, Sarah Alden^3, Jonathan^2)

Rachel PRINCE^7 (Paul^6) and 1st Salathiel SWEETSER, 2nd Nathaniel WEEKS

Job PRINCE^5 (Ruth Turner^4) and Abigail KIMBALL, 24 Dec. 1719, Plympton (MD 3:91)

Abigail KIMBALL and 2nd Ephraim EVERSON, 15 Mar. 1731/32, Kingston (MD 7:85)

Thomas PRINCE^7 (Job$^{6-5}$) and Rebecca CUTLER, 9 Jan. 1783, (Boston Rcd.com.30:410)

Job PRINCE^6 (Job^5) and Elizabeth ALLEN, 26 Dec. 1748, (Boston 28:259)

James PRINCE^7 (Job^6) and Agnes GORDON, 19 Feb. 1789, Charlestown (Rcd.com.30:290)

Thomas PRINCE and Anna McCARTHY, Int. 4 Mar. 1779 (Boston Rcd.com.30:443)

Thomas I. PRINCE and Caroline PRINCE, 8 Nov. 1809 (Boston Rcd.com.30:267)

Kimball PRINCE^6 (Job^5) and Deborah FULLER^5 (John^4, Sam.$^{3-2-1}$), 2 Nov. 1749, Kingston
    (Gen.Adv. 3:23)

Hezekiah PRINCE^7 (Kimball^6) and Isabella COOMBS

Job DREW^8 (Thankful D. Prince^7, Tho.^{6}, Job^5) and Sarah LAWRENCE, 18 Feb. 1799,
    Boston (Rcd.Com.30:178)

Thomas PRINCE^6 (Job^5) and Lydia DELANO^6 (Joshua^5, Martha Simmons^4, Mercy Pabodie^3,
   Eliz. Alden^2), 8 Dec. 1743, Duxbury

Abigail PRINCE^7 (Tho.^{6}) and Theophilus STETSON^6 (Elisha^5, Abigail Brewster^4,
   Wrestling^3, Love^2), 24 Nov. 1768

Thankful Delano PRINCE^7 (Tho.^{6}) and Job DREW, 21 May 1767

Thomas PRINCE^5 (Ruth Turner^4) and Judith FOX, 25 Nov. 1729, Duxbury (MD 11:240)

Grace SILVESTER^5 (Ruth Turner^4) and Isaac PARTRIDGE, 10 Mar. 1729/30, Dusbury
   (MD 11:240)

Israel SILVESTER^5 (Ruth Turner^4) and Abigail SNELL, 12 Dec. 1734

Ruth BREWSTER^3 and 1st John PICKETT, 14 Mar. 1651 (MD 1:8)

Ruth BREWSTER^3 and 2nd Charles HILL, 2 July 1668 (MD 1:73)

Charles HILL and 2nd Mrs. Rachel MASON, 12 June 1678 (Gen.Reg.9:49)

Adam PICKET^4 (Ruth Brewster^3) and Hannah WETHERELL^4 (Grace Brewster^3, Jonathan^2),
   26 May 1680, New London CT (MD 1:170)

Mary PICKETT^4 (Ruth Brewster^3) and Benjamin SHAPLEY, 10 Apr. 1672, New London CT

Ruth SHAPLEY^5 (Mary Pickett^4) and John MORGAN

Mercy PICKETT^4 (Ruth Brewster^3) and 1st Samuel FOSDICK, 1 Nov. 1682 (New London
   CT VR)

Mercy PICKETT^4 (Ruth Brewster^3) and 2nd John ARNOLD, 6 Dec. 1703 (New London CT VR)

Anna FOSDICK^5 (Mercy Pickett^4) and Thomas LATHAM

Samuel FOSDICK^5 (Mercy Pickett^4) and Susanna TURNER^5 (Ezekiel^4, Mary Brewster^3,
   Jonathan^2), 13 July 1706 (New London CT VR)

Ruth PICKETT^4 (Ruth Brewster^3) and Rev. Moses NOYES

Charles HILL^4 (Ruth Brewster^3) and Abigail FOX

Jonathan HILL^4 (Ruth Brewster^3) and Mary SHARSWOOD

William BREWSTER^3 and Mary PEAME, 15 Oct. 1651 (MD 1:8)

Love BREWSTER^2 (Wm.^{1})

Dr. John BREWSTER and 1st Mary DURKEE, 6 Nov. 1760 (Hinnan:330-31)

Dr. John BREWSTER and 2nd Ruth AVERY, 4 June 1789 (Hinnan:330-31)

Micro #10 of 18

Sarah BREWSTER^3 and Benjamin BARTLETT^3 (Mary Warren^2)

William BREWSTER^3 and Lydia PARTRIDGE, 2 Jan. 1672, Duxbury (MD 8:232)

Joseph BREWSTER^4 (Wm.^{3}) and Elizabeth TURNER^5 (Ben.^{4}, Mary Brewster^3, Jonathan^2),
   c1725 (MD 12:120)

Lemuel BREWSTER^5 (Jos.^{4}) and Abigail BREWSTER^5 (John^4, Wrestling^3, Love^2),
   29 Jan. 1756

Eunice BREWSTER^5 (Jos.^{4}) and Timothy WALKER

Joshua BREWSTER^4 (Wm.^{3}) and Deborah JACKSON, 13 Mar. 1721/22, Plympton (MD 2:138)

Nathan BREWSTER^5 (Joshua^4) and 1st Rachel PARTRIDGE, c1752 (MD 12:169)

Nathan BREWSTER^5 and 2nd Hannah KENT, c1760 (MD 12:169)

Nathaniel BREWSTER^4 (Wm.^{3}) and Mary DWELLY, 24 Dec. 1705, Scituate (MD 5:114)

Joseph BREWSTER^5 (Nathaniel^4) and Jedidah WHITE, 26 Nov. 1740, Marshfield

Ruth BREWSTER^5 (Nathaniel^4) and Joseph MORGAN, 8 May 1735, Duxbury (MD 11:81)

William BREWSTER^5 (Nathaniel^4) and Priscilla SAMPSON^4 (John^3, Stephen^2), 1 Jan.
   1746/47 (Brewster Gen.1:84)

William BREWSTER^4 (Wm.^{3}) and Hopestill WADSWORTH, 20 May 1708, Duxbury (MD 8:232)

Ichabod BREWSTER^5 (Wm.^{4}) and Lydia BARSTOW, 3 June 1735, Duxbury (MD 11:241)

John PARTRIDGE and Mary (   ) BREWSTER, 23 May 1700, Duxbury (MD 9:108)

Abigail BREWSTER^4 (Wrestling^3) and Elisha STETSON, 28 Oct. 1707, Duxbury (MD 9:108)

Eglah STETSON^5 (Abigail Brewster^4) and Ephraim WASHBURN^5 (Lydia Billington^4, Isaac^3,
   Francis^2), Int. 4 Nov. 1732

Zerash STETSON^5 (Abigail Brewster^4) and Benjamin BRADFORD^4 (Israel^3, Wm.^{2})

Sarah STETSON^5 (Abigail Brewster^4) and Robert BRADFORD^5 (John$^{4-3}$, Wm.^{2})

Elisha STETSON^5 (Abigail Brewster^4) and Sarah ADAMS, 26 Apr. 1742 (Kingston VR:167,283)

Hopestill STETSON^5 (Abigail Brewster^4) and John SIMMONS, 21 Oct. 1736 (Kingston VR)

Noah SIMMONS^6 (Hopestill Stetson^5) and 1st Lydia HOWLAND, c1763 (Kingston VR 2:52)

Elizabeth SIMMONS^7 (Noah^6) and Benjamin SNOW, Int. 8 Feb. 1782, Kingston (VR 2:79)

John BREWSTER^4 (Wrestling^3) and Rebecca BRADFORD^5 (John$^{4-3}$, Wm.^{2}), c1789

Jonathan BREWSTER^4 (Wrestling^3) and Mary PARTRIDGE, 6 Mar. 1709/10, Duxbury (MD 11:23)

Mary BREWSTER^4 (Wrestling^3) and Joseph HOLMES, c1696 (MD 13:170)

Ephraim HOLMES^5 (Mary Brewster^4) and Sarah TILDEN, 1 Jan. 1733/34

Jonathan HOLMES^5 (Mary Brewster^4) and 1st Mary WATERMAN^5 (Mary Cushman^4, Isaac^3,
   Mary Allerton^2)

Jonathan HOLMES^5 and 2nd Rebecca TILDEN

Joseph HOLMES^5 (Mary Brewster^4) and 1st Rebecca WATERMAN^5 (Mary Cushman^4, Isaac^3,
   Mary Allerton^2), 20 May 1731 (Plympton VR:333,420)

Rebecca WATERMAN^5 and 2nd Rev. William RAND, aft. Apr. 1756

Keziah HOLMES^5 (Mary Brewster^4) and Isaiah THOMAS, 3 Oct. 1745, Kingston (VR:289)

Holmes THOMAS and Susannah CHURCHILL, Int. 22 Mar. 1777 (Kingston VR:289)

Joseph BIMBALL(sp) and Mrs. Keziah THOMAS, Int. 30 Apr. 1768 (Kingston VR:289)

Nathaniel COOK and Mrs. Keziah THOMAS Jr., 27 Sept. 1770 (Kingston VR:289)

Mary HOLMES[5] (Mary Brewster[4]) and Jacob DINGLEY, c1726 (MD 30:156)

Jacob DINGLEY[6] (Mary Holmes[5]) and 1st Desire PHILLIPS, 2 Feb. 1748, Marshfield
 (Duxbury VR:247,289)

Jacob DINGLEY[6] and 2nd Susanna FULLER[5] (John[4], Sam.[3-2-1]), 5 Apr. 1752

Jacob DINGLEY[6] and 3rd Alethea (   )JOYCE, 24 Oct. 1782 (Mass.Mgs.2:48)

Micah HOLMES[5] (Mary Brewster[4]) and Rebecca BRADFORD[6] (Robert[5], John[4-3], Wm.[2])

Sarah HOLMES[5] (Mary Brewster[4]) and John BEARSE, 12 May 1720, Plymouth (MD 14:39)

Asa BEARS[6] (Sarah Holmes[5]) and Mary RANDALL, 28 Sept. 1760 (Halifax VR:60)

Gideon BEARSE[6] (Sarah Holmes[5]) and Abigail RIPLEY[6] (Hannah Sturtevant[5], Fear
 Cushman[4], Isaac[3], Mary Allerton[2]), 13 June 1751 (Halifax VR:34)

Asa BEARCE[7] (Asa[6]) and Rhoda WESTON, 1 Mar. 1790

Asa BEARCE[8] (Asa[7]) and Lucy Greenwood BRIDGHAM, 21 May 1843

Sarah BREWSTER[4] (Wrestling[3]) and Caleb STETSON, 4 Mar. 1705/06, Duxbury (MD 9:108)

Caleb STETSON and Deborah MORTON, 8 Nov. 1732, Plymouth (MD 18:123)

Barzillai STETSON[5] (Sarah Brewster[4]) and Ruth KEMPTON, 6 Sept. 1742, Plymouth
 (MD 14:160)

Barzillai STETSON[6] (Barzillai[5]) and Experience CROWELL, Int. 3 Nov. 1765, Rochester
 (VR 2:97,291)

Isaac BREWSTER[5] (Wrestling[4]) and Leonice SOULE[5] (Aaron[4-3], John[2]), 21 Nov. 1771

Wrestling BREWSTER[4] (Wrestling[3]) and Hannah THOMAS[5] (Mary Tilden[4], Hannah Little[3],
 Anna Warren[2]), 12 July 1722, Duxbury (MD 11:240)

Wrestling BREWSTER[5] (Wrestling[4]) and Deborah SEABURY[5] (Deborah Wiswall[4], Priscilla
 Pabodie[3], Eliz. Alden[2]), 12 July 1750, Kingston (VR:185,276)

Huldah BREWSTER[6] (Wrestling[5]) and Samuel STETSON

Patience BREWSTER[2] (Wm.[1])

Patience BREWSTER[2] and Thomas PRENCE, 5 Aug. 1624, Plymouth

Thomas PRENCE and 2nd Mary COLLIER, 1 Apr. 1635, Plymouth (MD 13:83)

Hannah PRENCE[3] and 1st Nathaniel MAYO, 13 Feb. 1649, Eastham (MD 17:200)

Hannah PRENCE[3] and 2nd Jonathan SPARROW, betw. 5 June 1667-11 Sept. 1671 (MD 14:197)

Jonathan SPARROW and 2nd Mrs. Sarah COB, 23 Nov. 1698 (Barnstable VR)

Priscilla SPARROW[5] (Richard[4], Hannah Prence[3]) and David SNOW, 5 Mar. 1746/47,
 Eastham (MD 28:83)

Nathaniel MAYO^4 (Hannah Prence^3) and 1st Elizabeth WIXAM, 28 Jan. 1678, Eastham
(MD 4:32)

Nathaniel MAYO^4 and 2nd Mercy (DAVIS) Young, 10 June 1708, Eastham (MD 4:33)

Alice MAYO^5 (Nathaniel^4) and John PAINE^4 (Mary Snow^3, Constance Hopkins^2)

Bathsheba MAYO^5 (Nathaniel^4) and Thomas FREEMAN^5 (Tho.^{4}, Mercy Prence^3, Patience
Brewster^2) (MD 4:33)

Hannah MAYO^5 (Nathaniel^4) and John HIGGINS, 5 Aug. 1713, Eastham (MD 15:54)

Ichabod HIGGINS^6 (Hannah Mayo^5) and Bethiah KNOWLES^7 (Enos^6, Sam.^{5}, Mercy Freeman^4,
Mercy Prence^3, Patience Brewster^2), 23 Jan. 1752, Eastham (MD 24:192)

John HIGGINS^7 (Ichabod^6, Hannah Mayo^5) and Sarah HIGGINS, 27 Apr. 1786, Eastham
(Orleans ch.rcds.)

Bethiah HIGGINS^8 (John^7) and Edmund FREEMAN, 27 Nov. 1806, Orleans

Elisha MAYO^5 (Nathaniel^4) and Hannah LINNELL, 20 Feb. 1716/17 (Eastham VR)

Nathaniel MAYO and Ruth DOANE, 13 July 1710 (Doane Gen.:30)

Elizabeth MAYO and Judah ROGERS, 24 Nov. 1739 (Eastham VR)

Nathaniel MAYO and 1st Hannah HORTON, 19 Sept. 1734 (Eastham VR)

Nathaniel MAYO and 2nd Mary RANDALL, 24 Jan. 1748 (Eastham VR)

Samuel MAYO^4 (Hannah Prence^3) and 2nd Mary SWEAT, 31 Aug. 1727/28, Eastham (MD 15:53)

Hannah MAYO^5 (Sam.^{4}) and Judah HOPKINS^4 (Stephen^3, Gyles^2)

Jonathan MAYO^5 (Sam.^{4}) and Thankful TWINING^5 (Ruth Cole^4, Ruth Snow^3, Constance
Hopkins^2), 9 Apr. 1719, Eastham (MD 15:140)

Ruth MAYO^6 (Jonathan^5) and Capt. Edward BANGS, 1739

Mary MAYO^5 (Sam.^{4}) and Ralph SMITH, 23 Oct. 1712, Eastham (MD 8:15)

Thomas SMITH^7 (Tho.^{6}, Mary Mayo^5) and Urania WRIGHT^6 (John$^{5-4}$, Adam^3, Hester Cooke^2),
20 Mar. 1766, CT

Thomas SMITH^6 (Mary Mayo^5) and Ruth MAYO^6 (Israel^5, Tho.^{4}, Hannah Prence^3, Patience
Brewster^2), 30 June 1743, Eastham (MD 20:156)

Ruth MAYO^6 and 2nd Israel HIGGINS, 9 Mar. 1769 (Higgins Gen.1:119)

Rev. Bela SMITH^8 (Tho.^{7}) and Rhoda MERWIN, 31 Dec. 1811

Zoeth SMITH^8 (Tho.^{7}) and Olive MERWIN

Thomas Barrett SMITH^9 (Bela^8) and Martha Morgan BUCK, 26 Nov. 1848

Bela SMITH^9 (Bela^8) and Amanda JEROME, 21 Sept. 1835

Fred Milton SMITH^{10} (Tho.B.^{9}, Bela^8) and Ella RUMBLE

Rebecca MAYO^5 (Sam.^{4}) and Stephen COLE, 20 May 1725, Eastham (MD 16:73)

Mercy MAYO^5 (Sam.^{4}) and John COLE, 8 Feb. 1726/27 (Eastham VR)

Samuel MAYO^5 (Sam.^{4}) and Abigail SPARROW, 6 Aug. 1713, Eastham (MD 3:229)

Sarah MAYO^5 (Sam.^{4}) and James HIGGINS

Thomas MAYO^4 (Hannah Prence^3) and Barbara KNOWLES, 13 June 1677, Eastham (MD 8:94)

Elizabeth AREY^7 (Oliver^6, Mary Mayo^5) and Nathaniel MYRICK, 2 Feb. 1769 (Eastham VR)

Lydia MAYO^5 (Tho.^{4}) and Joshua MERRICK^4 (Abigail Hopkins^3, Gyles^2), 4 June 1714,
    (Eastham VR)

Eli STARR and Sally HURLBURT, 5 Mar. 1816[7]

Harmon STARR and Marilla MILLS, 28 Sept. 1843[7]

Mercy MAYO^6 (Israel^5, Tho.^{4}) and Jonathan LINNELL, 8 Jan. 1747, Eastham (MD 28:83)

Jonathan LINNELL and 2nd Rachel ( ) SMITH, Int. 5 Aug. 1760, Eastham (MD 27:107)

Experience LINNELL^7 (Mercy Mayo^6) and James HICKMAN, 7 Oct. 1773, (Eastham VR)

James HICKMAN and Eusebia SAWYER

Israel MAYO^5 (Tho.^{4}) and Mercy RIDER, 2 Apr. 1724, Chatham (MD 5:141)

Micro #12 of 18

Alice MAYO^6 (Israel^5) and Thomas TWINING, 16 Jan. 1755, Eastham (MD 15:140)

Phebe MAYO^6 (Israel^5) and Nathaniel PAINE^6 (Theophilus^5, John^4, Mary Snow^3, Constance
    Hopkins^2), 17 Nov. 1757, Eastham (MD 27:105)

Esther MAYO^6 (Israel^5) and Samuel KENWRICK, 26 Feb. 1761 (Eastham VR)

Ruth MAYO^6 (Israel^5) and 1st Thomas SMITH^6 (Mary Mayo^5, Sam.^{4}, Hannah Prence^3, Patience
    Brewster^2), 30 June 1743, Eastham (MD 20:156)

Ruth MAYO^6 and 2nd Israel HIGGINS, 2 Mar. 1769 (Higgins Gen.:119)

Judah MAYO^5 (Tho.^{4}) and Mary HAMILTON^5 (Mary Smith^4, Mary Hopkins^3, Gyles^2), Int.
    27 Jan. 1721/22, Eastham

Mary MAYO^5 (Tho.^{4}) and Samuel AREY, 10 Mar. 1714/15, Eastham (MD 15:53)

Oliver AREY^6 (Mary Mayo^5) and Elizabeth GOULD, Int. 18 Feb. 1737/38, Harwich
    (MD 16:197)

Mary MYRICK^8 (Eliz. Arey^7, Oliver^6) and Jesse LIBBY, poss. Int. 21 Mar. 1795,
    Hampden, ME (VR)

Oliver AREY^7 (Oliver^6) and Mary COLE, 3 Nov. 1763, Eastham

Mercy MAYO^5 (Tho.^{4}) and Jonathan GODFREY, 30 Oct. 1707, Eastham (MD 5:195)

Jephthah GODFREY^6 (Mercy Mayo^5) and Bathsheba ELDRIDGE

Ruth GODFREY^6 (Mercy Mayo^5) and 1st John GOULD, Int. 18 Aug. 1739, Eastham (MD 28:182)

Ruth GODFREY^6 and 2nd Thomas MYRICK, Int. 2 Aug. 1750, Harwich (MD 33:147)

Abigail GOULD^7 (Ruth Godfrey^6) and Joseph DOANE, 25 Dec. 1766, Chatham (MD 17:95)

John GOULD^7 (Ruth Godfrey^6) and Apphia COLE, 23 Jan. 1766

Richard GOULD^7 (Ruth Godfrey^6) and Martha BEARSE

Thomas GOULD^7 (Ruth Godfrey^6) and Phebe COLE, 11 Nov. 1762, Eastham (MD 31:175)

Phebe COLE and 2nd James YOUNG, 1 May 1791 (Orleans ch.rcds.2:38)

Nathaniel GOULD^8 (Tho.^{7}) and 1st Mercy NICKERSON, c1792 (Gould Gen.<1895>:169)

Nathaniel GOULD^8 and 2nd Ruth (HIGGINS) (Godfrey) Smith, 2 Dec. 1830 (Gould Gen.:172)

Thomas GOULD^9 (Nathaniel^8) and Laura HOOKER, 3 Oct. 1832, (Sherborn/Norfolk VR:132)

David GOULD^9 (Nathaniel^8) and Hannah FRENCH

Phebe GOULD^8 (Tho.^{7}) and Benjamin HURD, 4 Oct. 1792, Eastham (MD 33:132)

Nathaniel GOULD and Hannah KNOWLES, c1805 (MD 34:61)

Nathaniel GOULD and Hannah K. CROSBY, 24 Dec. 1835 (Gould Gen.:166)

Joshua GOULD^6 (Nathaniel^5) and Mary HURD, c1770 (MD 33:183)

Thomas GOULD^7 (Joshua^6) and Thankful HURD, c1809 (MD 34:60)

Ruth HIGGINS and 1st David GODFREY, 15 Dec. 1794 (Higgins Gen.:173)

Ruth HIGGINS and 2nd Lewis SMITH, 18 Apr. 1797

Ruth HIGGINS and 3rd Nathaniel GOULD

Theophilus MAYO^5 (Tho.^{4}) and Rebecca SMITH, 16 Aug. 1705, Eastham (MD 7:12)

Asa MAYO^6 (Theo.^{5}) and Experience YATES^5 (Abigail Rogers^4, James^3, Jos.^{2}), Int.
    4 Sept. 1731, Harwich (MD 13:59)

Asa MAYO^7 (Asa^6) and Hannah COVEL, 16 Dec. 1762, Eastham (MD 31:125)

Asa MAYO^6(Theo^5) and Hannah (BASSETT) Covel, 25 July 1756, Eastham (MD 15:230)

Sarah MAYO^8 (Asa^7) and John HIGGINS

Thomas MAYO^5 (Tho.^{4}) and 1st Elizabeth HIGGINS, 3 Apr. 1701, Eastham (MD 9:9)

Thomas MAYO^5 and 2nd Elizabeth ROGERS, Int. 6 Oct. 1722, Eastham (MD 28:112)

Patience SPARROW^4 (Hannah Prence^3) and 1st Joseph PAINE^4 (Mary Snow^3, Constance
    Hopkins^2), 27 May 1691, Eastham (MD 7:235)

Patience SPARROW^4 and 2nd John JENKINS, 23 Nov. 1715, Barnstable (MD 14:227)

Richard SPARROW^4 (Hannah Prence^3) and Mercy COB, 4 Feb. 1701/02, Eastham (MD 7:19)

Mercy COB and 2nd Israel DOANE, 17 Apr. 1729, Eastham (MD 15:55)

Hannah SPARROW^5 (Richard Sparrow^4) and Josiah COOK^5 (Joshua^4, Deborah Hopkins^3,
    Gyles^2), 11 Feb. 1730/31, Eastham (MD 17:31)

Elizabeth SPARROW^5 (Richard^4) and Elisha DOANE, 14 Mar. 1733/34, Eastham (MD 17:140)

Sarah SPARROW^5 (Richard^4) and Edmund FREEMAN^5 (Edmund^4, Mercy Prence^3, Patience
    Brewster^2), 25 SEpt. 1729 (Eastham VR)

Edmund FREEMAN^5 and 1st Lois PAINE^5 (Nicholas^4, Mary Snow^3, Constance Hopkins^2),
    22 Apr. 1725 (Eastham VR)

Elisha DOANE^6 (Eliz.^{5}) and Mehitable NICKERSON, 18 Oct. 1764 (Doane Gen.:73,111)

Mary SPARROW^5 (Richard^4) and Isaac SMITH, 9 Mar. 1737/38 (Eastham VR:225)

Isaac SMITH and 2nd Mary FREEMAN^6 (Prince^5, Tho.^{4}, Mercy Prence^3, Patience Brewster^2)

Mercy SPARROW^5 (Richard^4) and Zebulon YOUNG, 22 Feb. 1725/26 (Eastham VR:69)

Zebulon YOUNG and 2nd Mrs. Abigail ROGERS, 23 Feb. 1748 (Eastham VR:153)

Isaac YOUNG^6 (Mercy Sparrow^5) and Priscilla HOPKINS, 20 Jan. 1763 (Eastham VR)

Rebecca SPARROW^5 (Richard^4) and Richard MAYO, 26 Dec. 1728, Eastham (MD 16:203)

Eunice MAYO and Simeon KNOWLES, Int. 12 Aug. 1758, Eastham (MD 28:9)

Eunice MAYO and Nathan WINSLOW, 12 Sept. 1760, Harwich (MD 34:69)

Eunice MAYO and Nathan BASSET, 22 Dec. 1763, Chatham (MD 17:93)

Micro #13 of 18

Richard SPARROW^5 (Richard^4) and Hannah SHAW, 16 Sept. 1723, Eastham (MD 16:33)

Isaac SPARROW^6 (Richard^5) and Rebecca KNOWLES^6 (Sarah Paine^5, John^4, Mary Snow^3, Constance Hopkins^2), 15 Jan. 1746/47, Eastham (MD 24:190)

Richard SPARROW^7 (Isaac^6) and Elizabeth PAINE^6 (John$^{5-4}$, Mary Snow^3, Constance Hopkins^2), c1770/71 (MD 33:81)

Jesse SPARROW^8 (Richard^7) and Sally GODFREY, 4 Apr. 1816, (Orleans ch.rcds.)

Sarah SPARROW^7 (Isaac^6) and Herman LINNELL, Int. 17 Dec. 1773, Eastham (VR:12:2)

Hannah SPARROW^6 (Richard^5) and Daniel HAMILTON, Int. 15 Nov. 1760, Eastham (MD 27:107)

Mercy PRENCE^3 and John FREEMAN, 13/14 Feb. 1649, Eastham/Sandwich (MD 17:199, 16:122)

Bennet FREEMAN^4 (Mercy Prence^3) and John PAINE^4 (Mary Snow^3, Constance Hopkins^2), 14 Mar. 1689/90 (MD 9:139)

Lieut. Edmund FREEMAN^4 (Mercy Prence^3) and Sarah MAYO

Thankful FREEMAN^5 (Edmund^4) and Jonathan SNOW^5 (Nicholas^4, Mark^3, Constance Hopkins^2), 16 Oct. 1718, Eastham (MD 15:74)

Ebenezer FREEMAN^5 (Edmund^4) and Abigail YOUNG, 12 Oct. 1710, Eastham (MD 6:13)

Isaac FREEMAN^6 (Ebenezer^5) and Thankful HIGGINS, 25 Nov. 1756, Eastham (MD 16:198)

Edmund FREEMAN^5 (Edmund^4) and Lois PAINE^5 (Nicholas^4, Mary Snow^3, Constance Hopkins^2), 22 Apr. 1725, Eastham (MD 16:74)

Edmund FREEMAN^5 and 2nd Sarah SPARROW^5 (Richard^4, Hannah Prence^3, Patience Brewster^2), 25 Sept. 1729, Eastham (MD 16:74)

Jonathan FREEMAN^6 (Edmund^5) and Thankful LINNELL, 12 Mar. 1752, Eastham (MD 24:192)

Abner FREEMAN^7 (Jonathan^6) and Sarah HIGGINS, 20 Nov. 1777 (Eastham VR 9:5)

John FREEMAN^7 (Jonathan^6) and Abigail HOPKINS^6 (Joshua^{5-4-3}, Gyles^2), 22 Jan. 1784, (Freeman Gen.:184)

Lois FREEMAN^6 (Edmund^5) and Jesse SNOW^5 (Micajah^4, Stephen^3, Constance Hopkins^2),

10 Nov. 1748, Eastham (MD 24:138)

Elizabeth FREEMAN[5] (Edmund[4]) and Isaac PEPPER, 21 Feb. 1716/17, Eastham (MD 15:68)

Experience FREEMAN[5] (Edmund[4]) and Thomas GROSS, 9 Jan. 1709, Boston

Hannah FREEMAN[5] (Edmund[4]) and Christian REMICK, 10 Oct. 1717, Eastham (VR:19)

Isaac FREEMAN[5] (Edmund[4]) and Bethia STURGIS[5] (James[4], Temperance Gorham[3], Desire Howland[2]), 16 Mar. 1715/16

Mary FREEMAN[5] (Edmund[4]) and Samuel HINCKLEY, c1706/07 (MD 4:208)

Aaron HINKLEY and Mary LARRABEE, 13 Feb. 1746 (Brunswick ME VR 1:374)

Aaron HINKLY and Bethiah LOMBARD, 26 June 1788 (Brunswick ME VR 1:473)

Edmund HINCKLEY[6] (Mary Freeman[5]) and Sarah SMITH, Int. 17 Sept. 1744 (Brunswick ME VR 1:518)

Isaac HINCKLEY[6] (Mary Freeman[5]) and Agnes SMITH, Int. 31 Dec. 1749, Brunswick ME (VR 1:525)

Agnes SMITH and 2nd Thomas COTTON, Int. 5 Nov. 1757, Brunswick ME

Mary HINCKLEY[6] (Mary Freeman[5]) and Joseph THOMPSON

Tobias LORD[8] (Mehitable Scammon[7], Mehitable Hinckley[6], Mary Freeman[5]) and Hannah PERKINS

Nathaniel LORD[8] (Mehitable Scammon[7]) and Phebe WALKER

Charles A. LORD[9] (Nathaniel[8]) and Ernestine LIBBY, 3 May 1831, Scarborough ME

Claire Austin LORD[10] (Charles A.[9]) and Rev. Charles Baker RICE, 7 June 1861, Portland

Rev. Charles Baker RICE and 2nd Henrietta Hyde STANWOOD, 24 Sept. 1895, Swampscott MA

Lily Sherman RICE[11] (Claire A.[10]) and Frank FOXCROFT, 9 Sept. 1891, Danvers Centre MA

Natalie Lord RICE[11] (Claire A.[10]) and Frank L. CLARK, 15 Aug. 1900

Austin RICE[11] (Claire A.[10]) and 1st Laura Agnes LYMAN, 19 July 1899, Cunnington MA

Austin RICE[11] and 2nd Mary Emma VINAL, 1 Aug. 1931, North Scituate

Ernestine LORD[10] (Charles A.[9]) and Rev. George Augustus BOWMAN, 31 May 1855, Portland [8]

Austin Lord BOWMAN[11] (Ernestine Lord[10]) and 1st Ida VanHORNE, 19 Jan. 1893, New York

Austin Lord BOWMAN[11] and 2nd Eleanor HEAGAN, 28 Dec. 1907, New York, N.Y.

Caroline North BOWMAN[11] (Ernestine Lord[10]) and William Dwight PARKINSON, 11 Nov. 1882, Fergus Falls, Minn.

Herman Owen PARKINSON[12] (Caroline N. Bowman[11]) and Constance DYER, 18 Sept. 1920, Waltham MA

Micro #14 of 18

Dana PARKINSON[12] (Caroline N. Bowman[11]) and Lucy Robinson BACON, 9 Jan. 1915, Waltham

Royal PARKINSON^{12} (Caroline N. Bowman^{11}) and 1st Loretta Catherine MUNRO, 8 June 1915, Berkeley CA

Royal PARKINSON^{12} and 2nd Ida (STUBBLEFIELD) Still, 11 Sept. 1927, Fitchburg MA

Lydia Arabelle LORD^{10} (Charles A.^{9}) and Stephen Albert EMERY, 24 Oct. 1867, Portland ME

Stephen EMERY^{11} (Lydia A. Lord^{10}) and Nellie Babbitt THALHEIMER, 21 July 1898, Pigeon Cove, Rockport MA

Sidney Sheppard EMERY^{11} (Lydia A. Lord^{10}) and Anna Payne BUTLER, 16 Dec. 1896, Newton MA

Moritz Hauptmann EMERY^{11} (Lydia A. Lord^{10}) and Margaret Agnes WEAVING, 25 May 1905, Woodbury N.J.

Ernestine EMERY^{11} (Lydia A. Lord^{10}) and Albert Funk MESCHTER, 2 Oct. 1908, West Newton MA

Samuel LORD^{8} (Mehitable Scammon^{7}, Mehitable Hinckley^{6}) and Hannah JEFFERDS

Reliance HINCKLEY^{6} (Mary Freeman^{5}) and James THOMPSON, 13 Apr. 1732 (Hist. Brunswick ME:857)

James THOMPSON and 2nd Lydia (BROWN) Harris, 13 Dec. 1751

James THOMPSON and 3rd Mary HIGGINS, 22 Mar. 1764

Samuel HINCKLEY^{6} (Mary Freeman^{5}) and Sarah MILLER, c1732

Samuel HINCKLEY and Sarah POPE, 13 Nov. 1676 (Annals of Warren ME:552)

James HINCKLEY^{7} (Shubael Hinckley^{6}, Mary Freeman^{5}) and Mary McKENNY

James HINCKLEY^{8} (James^{7}) and Joanna NORCROSS, c1793 (Hallowell ME "Register of Families:90)

Oliver Osgood HINCKLEY^{8} (James^{7}) and Sarah PILSBURY (Hallowell ME Register:91)

Shubael HINCKLEY^{6} (Mary Freeman^{5}) and 2nd Sarah YOUNG, 11 May 1761 (Truro VR:91)

Shubael HINCKLEY^{6} and 1st Mary SMITH, c1732

Shubael HINCKLEY and Elizabeth WORSTER, Int. 8 Apr. 1753, Georgetown

Shubael HINCKLEY and Mary SOLOU/SOLON, 28 Aug. 1761

Shubael HINCKLEY Jr. and Mary SLEW, 28 Aug. 1761

Shubael HINCKLEY Jr. and Mary SOLVE(sp), 15 Sept. 1761

Thomas HINKLEY and Mrs. Mary TAYLOR, 10 Mar. 1781 (Hallowell ME VR 1:52)

James HINKLEY and Mary MEGGS, 20 July 1792 (Hallowell ME VR 1:42)

James HINKLEY Jr. and Joanna NORCROSS, 7 Nov. 1793 (Hallowell ME VR 1:42)

Stephen HINKLEY and Lucy NYE, 5 Oct. 1794 (Hallowell ME VR 1:43)

Shubael HINCKLEY^{7} (Shubael^{6}) and 1st Mary CLEW, c1759

Shubael HINCKLEY^{7} and 2nd Abigail (NORCROSS) Robinson, Int. 11 Dec. 1785, Hallowell

Shubael HINCKLEY^{8} (Shubael^{7}) and Betsey SPADE, Int. 20 June 1813, Hallowell ME

(Hallowell Register of Fam.:142)

Thomas HINCKLEY[7] (Shubael[6]) and 1st Elizabeth MITCHELL, 8 Dec. 1761

Thomas HINCKLEY[7] and 2nd Mary TAYLOR, Int. 19 Feb. 1781

Mary HINKLEY and Daniel NORCROSS, 31 Mar. 1814 (Bible)

Mary HINKLEY and Elijah COUCH, 1 Oct. 1820 (Bible)

Mercy FREEMAN[5] (Edmund[4]) and Thomas COBB, 14 Oct. 1717, Eastham (MD 15:69)

Lucy COBB and Silas RYDER/RIDER, 4 Feb. 1852, Truro (Mass.VR 60:16)

Joseph COBB[6] (Mercy Freeman[5]) and Rachel (TREAT) Mulford, 19 Mar. 1750/51, Truro
    (VR:77)

Hope COBB and Nehemiah RICH, 24 Dec. 1818 (Truro VR:227)

Martha A. RICH and George S. FARRAR, 27 Nov. 1849 (Bible)

Tamson/Thomasine COBB[7] (Joseph[6]) and Daniel LOMBARD, 15 Apr. 1779 (Truro VR:129)

Tamsin COBB[6] (Mercy Freeman[5]) and Lot HARDING, 23 Oct. 1746 (Truro VR:51)

Rachel FREEMAN[5] (Edmund[4]) and Thomas GRAY, 2 Oct. 1729

Elizabeth GRAY[6] (Rachel Freeman[5]) and Ebenezer BANGS[7] (Ann Sears[6], Mercy Freeman[5],
    Tho.[4], Mercy Prence[3], Patience Brewster[2])

Ruth FREEMAN[5] (Edmund[4]) and Israel DOANE, pre Feb. 1701

Edmund DOANE[6] (Ruth Freeman[5]) and Elizabeth (OSBORN)(Merrick) Paine, 10 Nov. 1749,
    Eastham (MD 24:88)

Samuel Osborn DOANE[7] (Edmund Doane[6]) and Sarah HARDING, c1774 (MD 8:141)

Prence DOANE[6] (Ruth Freeman[5]) and Elizabeth GODFREY, 3 Feb. 1725/26, Eastham
    (MD 16:75)

Sarah FREEMAN[5] (Edmund[4]) and Benjamin HIGGINS, 22 May 1701, Eastham (MD 7:15)

Benjamin HIGGINS and 2nd Mercy HOPKINS, 28 June 1749, Truro (VR:57)

Micro #15 of 18

Experience HIGGINS and 1st Israel COOMBS, Int. 3 May 1734 (Higgins Gen.:88)

Benjamin HIGGINS[6] (Sarah Freeman[5]) and 1st Hannah HIGGINS, 7 Feb. 1739/40, poss.
    Eastham

Benjamin HIGGINS[6] and 2nd Margery (HORNER) Sears, 19 May 1774

Isaac HIGGINS and Rebecca MAYO, 15 Apr. 1749

Paul HIGGINS and Rebecca MAYO, 3 Oct. 1737

Priscilla HIGGINS[6] (Sarah Freeman[5]) and Jonathan SMITH, Int. 15 Sept. 1722, Eatham
    (MD 28:112)

Thomas HIGGINS[6] (Sarah Freeman[5]) and Abigail PAINE[5] (Nicholas[4], Mary Snow[3], Constance
    Hopkins[2]), 12 Oct. 1727, Eastham (MD 16:197)

Solomon HIGGINS^5 (Tho.^{4}) and Margaret HOLBROOK, 24 Jan. 1760, Eastham (MD 15:230)

Solomon HIGGINS^5 and 2nd Abigail PIERCE 28 Oct. 1773

Solomon HIGGINS^6 (Solomon^5) and Elizabeth DYER, 20 Mar. 1794, Truro (VR:158)

Zaccheus HIGGINS^6 (Sarah Freeman^5) and 1st Bethiah CHASE, 13 Jan. 1758

Zaccheus HIGGINS^6 and 2nd Esther DEAN, c1773

Zaccheus HIGGINS and Rebecca YOUNG, 2 Feb. 1737/38 (Eastham VR:125)

Zaccheus HIGGINS and Mary CROSBY, Int. 10 June 1749 (Eastham VR:199)

Israel HIGGINS and Mary SNOW (Higgins Gen.:126,128)

Mary HIGGINS^6 (Sarah Freeman^5) and Henry YOUNG, 8 Mar. 1731/32, Eastham (MD 17:35)

Freeman HIGGINS^6 (Sarah Freeman^5) and 1st Martha COLE, 13 Nov. 1747, Eastham
    (MD 24:91)

Freeman HIGGINS^6 and 2nd Thankful (HOPKINS^5) Paine (Caleb$^{4-3}$, Gyles^2), 14 July 1757,
    Eastham (MD 16:76)

Timothy HIGGINS^7 (Freeman^6) and Reliance YATES (Higgins Gen.:129-131)

Apphia HIGGINS^7 (Freeman^6) and Ithiel BLAKE, 13 July 1769 (Higgins Gen.:129-131)

Thankful HIGGINS^7 (Freeman^6) and Thomas Stoddard BOARDMAN, 12 Nov. 1781 (Higgins
    Gen.:129-131)

Priscilla HIGGINS^7 (Freeman^6) and Caleb HAYDEN, 21 Oct. 1784 (Higgens Gen.:129-131)

Timothy BLAKE^8 (Apphia Higgins^7) and Susanna HIGGINS, 29 Nov. 1810

Mercy HIGGINS^7 (Freeman^6) and David SPEAR, 3 May 1787, Eastham (Boston Rcd.Com.30:311)

Priscilla HIGGINS^7 (Freeman^6) and Caleb HAYDEN, poss. 21 Oct. 1784 (Boston Rcd.
    Com.30:86)

Ephraim HIGGINS and Rebecca HIGGINS, 15 Nov. 1798, Standish ME (VR 1:523)

Robert HIGGINS and Sarah WHITNEY, Int. 24 Sept. 1789, Standish ME (VR 1:409)

Martha HIGGINS and Nathaniel BOLTER, Int. 18 Mar. 1790, Standish ME (VR 1:410)

Elkanah HIGGINS and Mira COLE, Int. 26 June 1790, Standish ME (VR 1:410)

Lydia HIGGINS and Moses NASON, Int. 20 Sept. 1794, Standish ME (VR 1:414)

William HIGGINS and Phebe PAINE, Int. 20 Dec. 1794, Standish ME (VR 1:414)

Knowles HIGGINS and Mary RAND, Int. 20 Dec. 1794, Standish ME (VR 1:414)

Mary HIGGINS and Crosby WHITNEY, Int. 20 July 1795, Standish ME (VR 1:414)

Mary HIGGINS and George RACKLIFF, Int. 17 Nov. 1798, Standish ME (VR 1:418)

Marcy HIGGINS and Daniel LOWELL Jr., Int. 19 Jan. 1799, Standish ME (VR 1:418)

Experience HIGGINS and Richard BERRY, Int. 17 May 1800, Standish ME (VR 1:419)

Rebecca HIGGINS and Nathaniel FROST, Int. 8 Oct. 1801, Standish ME (VR 1:420)

Rebecca HIGGINS and Nathaniel BLAKE Jr., Int. 7 Nov. 1801, Standish ME (VR 1:420)

Happy HIGGINS and Levi WHITNEY, Int. 28 Aug. 1802, Standish ME (VR 1:421)

Seth HIGGINS and Experience HIGGINS, Int. 25 June 1803, Standish ME (VR 1:421)

Walter HIGGINS and Mary LIBBY, 29 Feb. 1788, Standish ME (VR 1:519)

Martha HIGGINS and Nathaniel BOLTER, 8 Apr. 1790, Standish ME (VR 1:520)

Robert HIGGINS and Sarah WHITNEY, 21 Jan. 1790, Standish ME (VR 1:520)

William HIGGINS and Phebe PAINE, 8 Jan. 1795, Standish ME (VR 1:521)

Lydia HIGGINS and Moses NASON, 12 Oct. 1794, Standish ME (VR 1:521)

Knowles HIGGINS and Mary RAN/RAND, 26 Mar. 1795, Standish ME (VR 1:521)

Ephraim HIGGINS and Rebecca HIGGINS, Standish ME (VR 1:523)

Mary HIGGINS and George RACKLIFF, 27 Dec. 1798, Standish ME (VR 1:523)

Experience HIGGINS and Richard BERRY, 14 July 1800, Standish ME (VR 1:523)

Isaac HIGGINS and Esther PARKER, 27 Nov. 1800, Standish ME (VR 1:523)

Rebecca HIGGINS and Nathaniel FROST, 27 Oct. 1801, Standish ME (VR 1:523)

Rebecca HIGGINS and Nathaniel BLAKE Jr., 26 Nov. 1801, Standish ME (VR 1:523)

Happy HIGGINS and Levi WHITNEY, 10 Nov. 1802, Standish ME (VR 1:524)

Seth HIGGINS and Experience HIGGINS, 10 July 1803, Standish ME (VR 1:524)

Prince HIGGINS^8 (Timothy^7, Freeman^6) and Selina HIGGINS, 25 Sept. 1799, Standish ME

Lewis HIGGINS^9 (Prince^8) and Susan WHITNEY, 25 Mar. 1828 (Standish ME VR 1:503)

Sarah HIGGINS^6 (Sarah Freeman^5) and Jesse SMITH, Sept. 1724, Eastham (MD 16:71)

Hannah FREEMAN^4 (Mercy Prence^3) and John MAYO, 14 Apr. 1681 (Hist.Hingham 3:66)

Abgail FREEMAN^5 (Nathaniel^4) and Samuel SMITH^5 (Sam.^{4}, Mary Hopkins^3, Gyles^2),
     9 Oct. 1712, Eastham (MD 6:206)

Elizabeth MAYO^5 (Hannah Freeman^4) and Ebenezer NICKERSON^5 (Mary Snow^4, Mark^3, Constance
     Hopkins^2), 18 Oct. 1726, Harwich (MD 8:218)

John MAYO^5 (Hannah Freeman^4) and Susanna FREEMAN^5 (John^4, Mercy Prence^3, Patience
     Brewster^2), 22 Oct. 1712, Eastham (MD 7:20)

Rebecca MAYO^6 (John^5) and Joshua SEARS, 10 Feb. 1731/32, Eastham

Joseph MAYO^5 (Hannah Freeman^4) and Abigail MYRICK^5 (Ben.^{4}, Abigail Hopkins^3, Gyles^2),
     20 Feb. 1717/18, Harwich (MD 6:83)

Moses MAYO^6 (Jos.^{5}) and Phebe FREEMAN^8 (Watson^7, Edmund^6, Tho.^{5}, John^4, Mercy Prence^3,
     Patience Brewster^2)

Thomas MAYO^6 (Jos.^{5}) and Elizabeth WING, 5 Oct. 1752

Isaac MAYO^7 (Tho.^{6}) and Hannah CAHOON, Aug. 1781, Harwich

Reuben MAYO^8 (Isaac^7) and Dorcas MORRILL, 1823

Sarah Thurston MAYO^9 (Reuben^8) and 1st Stephen HALL, 9 Feb. 1849

Sarah Thurston MAYO^9 and 2nd Henry THOMAS, 5 Nov. 1859

Emily Ann MAYO^9 (Reuben^8) and John McLELLAN, 28 Feb. 1848

Hannah Maria MAYO[9] (Reuben[8]) and Moses A. TIBBETTS, Sept. 1848

Reuben Morrill MAYO[9] (Reuben[8]) and Addie E. BURROWS, Jan. 1877

Charles Morrill MAYO[9] (Reuben[8]) and 1st Abby J. ROBERTS, Oct. 1856

Charles Hall MAYO[9] and 2nd Ella KILMARTIN, June 1872

George Fred MAYO[9] (Reuben[8]) and Sarah E. CORNING, 30 Oct. 1879

Ellen Mercy MAYO[9] (Reuben[8]) and Solon B. HEATH, 5 Dec. 1853

Frances Snow MAYO[9] (Reuben[8]) and Elnathan HEATH, Mar. 1865

Viola Adeli MAYO[9] (Reuben[8]) and John F. RIDGEWOOD, Mar. 1862

Thomas MAYO[6] (Jos.[5]) and Elizabeth RING, 5 Oct. 1752

Asa MAYO[7] (Tho.[6]) and Sally SEABURY[6] (Ichabod[5], Jos.[4], Martha Pabodie[3], Eliz. Alden[2]), c1778 (Brewster VR:24,54)

Asa MAYO[8] (Asa[7]) and Sally MYRICK, Int. 12 Oct. 1815, Brewster (VR:11)

Benjamin MAYO[8] (Asa[7]) and Hannah GRAY, 29 Jan. 1817 (Brewster VR:17)

Sally MAYO[8] (Asa[7]) and Samuel HIGGINS

John MAYO[8] (Asa[7]) and Lydia LAHA, Aug. 1802 (Brewster VR:14)

Desire MAYO[7] (Tho.[6]) and Jason WOOD, 3 Apr. 1797, Hallowell ME

John FREEMAN[4] (Mercy Prence[3]) and 1st Sarah MERRICK, 18 Dec. 1672, Eastham (MD 3:180)

John FREEMAN[4] and 2nd Mercy (HEDGE) Watson, c1696/97 (MD 31:151)

Sarah FREEMAN[5] (John[4]) and Edward SNOW[4] (Jabez[3], Constance Hopkins[2])

Benjamin FREEMAN[5] (John[4]) and Temperance DIMOCK[5] (Desire Sturgis[4], Temperance Gorham[3], Desire Howland[2]), 2 June 1709, Barnstable (MD 14:87)

Benjamin FREEMAN[6] (Ben.[5]) and Sarah DILLINGHAM, 15 Mar. 1738/39, Harwich (MD 23:57)

Mary FREEMAN[7] (Ben.[6]) and James CROSBY, 27 Oct. 1787

Elizabeth FREEMAN[5] (John[4]) and John BACON[5] (Mary Hawes[4], Desire Gorham[3], Desire Howland[2]), 2 May 1726, Harwich (MD 8:218)

John FREEMAN[5] (John[4]) and Mercy WATSON, c1702 (MD 4:175)

Sarah FREEMAN[6] (John[5]) and Constant MYRICK[5] (Nathaniel[4], Abigail Hopkins[3], Gyles[2]), Int. 17 Feb. 1726/27, Harwich (MD 8:218)

John FREEMAN[6] (John[5]) and Joanna RICKARD, Int. 29 Jan. 1730/31, Rochester (VR 2:132)

Thankful FREEMAN[6] (John[5]) and Barnabas SEARS

Phebe FREEMAN[6] (John[5]) and Thomas ASHLEY, prob. 16 Jan. 1728 (Rochester VR 2:18,133)

Mary FREEMAN[5] (John[4]) and Judah BERRY, c1713 (MD 5:204)

Lemuel BERRY[6] (Mary Freeman[5]) and Lydia CLARK, 20 May 1741

Scotto BERRY[7] (Lemuel[6]) and Hannah MAYO, 27 Feb. 1772[9]

Scotto BERRY^7 and poss. 2nd Bethia (   ) ALLEN, aft. 1806

Theophilus BERRY^6 (Mary Freeman^5) and Hannah LINCOLN, 8 Sept. 1737, Harwich
    (MD 23:57)

Mercy FREEMAN^5 (John^4) and Chillingsworth FOSTER, c1705 (MD 3:175)

Chillingsworth FOSTER and 2nd Susanna (GRAY) Sears, 10 Aug. 1721, Harwich (MD 7:198)

Chillingsworth FOSTER and 3rd Ruth (MERRICK) Sears, Int. 14 Oct. 1731, Harwich
    (MD 13:59)

Susanna FOSTER^7 (Nathan^6, Mercy Freeman^5) and Joseph GOULD, 23 Mar. 1769[10]

Susanna GOULD^7 (Susanna Foster^6) and Benjamin GRIFFITHS, 7 Nov. 1805[10]

Lucy GOULD^7 (Susanna Foster^6) and Thomas ALLEN, 10 Oct. 1811[10]

John ALLEN^8 (Lucy Gould^7) and Thankful ALLEN, 20 Sept. 1841[10]

Lucy G. ALLEN^8 (Lucy Gould^7) and Joseph O. BAKER, 9 May 1839[10]

Hannah Gould ALLEN^8 (Lucy Gould^7) and 1st William M. SPARROW, 29 May 1848[10]

Hannah Gould ALLEN^8 and 2nd Luther HAMMOND, 3rd Collins HOWES[10]

Chillingsworth FOSTER^6 (Mercy Freeman^5) and Mercy WINSLOW, Int. 30 May 1730, Harwich
    (MD 13:57)

Isaac FOSTER^6 (Mercy Freeman^5) and Hannah SEARS^5 (Ruth Merrick^4, Abigail Hopkins^3,
    Gyles^2), 2 Nov. 1738, Harwich (MD 23:58)

Seth FOSTER^7 (Isaac^6) and Sarah COBB^7 (Jonathan^6, Sarah Hopkins^5, Stephen$^{4-3}$, Gyles^2)
    c1773 (Brewster VR:61)

Hannah FOSTER^9 (Sears^8, Seth^7) and William Whittemore GOSS, c1826 (Brewster VR:102)

Isaac FOSTER^7 (Isaac^6) and Sarah THATCHER^5 (Ben.^{4}, Lydia Gorham^3, Desire Howland^2)

James FOSTER^6 (Mercy Freeman^5) and Lydia WINSLOW^4 (Edw.^{3}, Kenelm$^{2-1}$), 10 July 1729,
    (Rochester VR 2:130,329)

Lydia FOSTER^7 (James^6) and Nathaniel HASKELL, Int. 3 Apr. 1757

Mary FOSTER^6 (Mercy Freeman^5) and David PADDOCK, c1727 (MD 13:56)

Nathaniel FREEMAN^5 (John^4) and Mary WATSON, 24 Oct. 1706, Harwich (MD 13:66)

Mary WATSON and 2nd Joseph FREEMAN^5 (Tho.^{4}, Mercy Prence^3, Patience Brewster^2),
    9 Sept. 1736, Harwich (MD 20:26)

Mary FREEMAN^6 (Nathaniel^5) and Benjamin DOANE (MD 7:94)

Seth FREEMAN^7 (Lemuel^6, Nath.^{5}) and Temporance BANGS, 14 Oct. 1773

Prence FREEMAN^6 (Nath.^{5}) and Abigail DILLINGHAM, 17 Nov. 1731, Harwich (MD 13:69)

Patience FREEMAN^5 (John^4) and Eleazer CROSBY, 24 Oct. 1706, Harwich (MD 13:66)

Eleazer CROSBY^6 (Patience Freeman^5) and Lydia GODFREE, 20 Oct. 1735, Harwich
    (MD 19:118)

Keziah CROSBY^7 (Eleazer^6) and Eleazer COBB^6 (Sarah Hopkins^5, Stephen$^{4-3}$, Gyles^2)

Lydia CROSBY^7 (Eleazer^6) and James LAHA, c1775 (Brewster VR:23)

Lydia LAHA^8 (Lydia Crosby^7) and John MAYO, Aug. 1802 (Brewster VR:14)

Phebe CROSBY^6 (Patience Freeman^5) and Joseph CLARK, 5 Nov. 1740, Harwich (MD 23:117)

Phebe CLARK^7 (Phebe Crosby^6) and Solomon CROSBY, pre 21 May 1787

Mercy FREEMAN^4 (Mercy Prence^3) and Samuel KNOWLES, Dec. 1679, Eastham (MD 6:204)

Amos KNOWLES^5 (Mercy Freeman^4) and Rebecca DILLINGHAM, 29 Jan. 1729/30, Harwich
   (MD 13:55)

Amos KNOWLES^6 (Amos^5) and 1st Abigail PEPPER^6 (Phebe Paine^5, Jos.^{4}, Mary Snow^3,
   Constance Hopkins^2), 30 Dec. 1765, Eastham (MD 32:64)

Amos KNOWLES^6 and 2nd Mary BROWN, Int. 17 Feb. 1787, Eastham (VR 12:16)

Phebe KNOWLES^7 (Amos^6) and Elisha SMITH, 29 Nov. 1798, Orleans (ch.rcds.)

Paulina SMITH^8 (Phebe Knowles^7) and Gould LINNELL, 25 Apr. 1823, Orleans

Mercy KNOWLES^5 (Mercy Freeman^4) and Thomas RICH, 23 July 1702, Eastham (MD 7:236)

Sarah RICH^6 (Mercy Knowles^5) and Jonathan SHAW, 5 Oct. 1731, Eastham (VR:99)

Mercy RICH^6 (Mercy Knowles^5) and George SHAW, Int. 22 Aug. 1724, Eastham (VR:211)

Richard KNOWLES^5 (Mercy Freeman^4) and Martha COBB, pre 2 July 1712 (MD 18:194-6)

Mercy KNOWLES^6 (Richard^5) and George GODFREE^5 (Deborah Cook^4, Deborah Hopkins^3,
   Gyles^2), 1 Nov. 1733, Chatham (MD 4:185)

Samuel KNOWLES^5 (Mercy Freeman^4) and Bethiah BROWN, 7 Nov. 1709, Eastham (MD 7:239)

Enos KNOWLES^6 (Sam.^{5}) and Sarah SPARROW^5 (Rebecca Merrick^4, Abigail Hopkins^3,
   Gyles^2), 12 Apr. 1733, Eastham (MD 17:37)

Bethiah KNOWLES^7 (Enos^6) and Ichabod HIGGINS^6 (Hannah Mayo^5, Nath.^{4}, Hannah Prence^3,
   Patience Brewster^2), 23 Jan. 1752, Eastham (MD 24:192)

Samuel KNOWLES^6 (Sam.^{5}) and Hannah FREEMAN, 16 Oct. 1735, Eastham (MD 17:143)

Seth KNOWLES^6 (Sam.^{5}) and Ruth FREEMAN^6 (Nath.$^{5-4}$, Mercy Prence^3, Patience Brewster^2),
   21 Feb. 1744/45, Eastham (MD 20:158)

Freeman KNOWLES^7 (Seth^6) and Esther MYRICK, 23 Nov. 1769, (Eastham VR)

John FREEMAN^5 (Nath.^{4}) and Thomison SEARS, 19 Mar. 1718/19 (Freeman Gen.:68-9)

John FREEMAN^5 and 2nd Elizabeth MERRICK, 26 Oct. 1761 (Freeman Gen.)

Nathaniel FREEMAN^5 (Nath.^{4}) and Hannah MERRICK, 6 Apr. 1721, Eastham (MD 15:230)

Martha FREEMAN^6 (Nath.^{5}) and Prince FREEMAN^6 (Eleazer^5, Nath.^{4}, Mercy Prence^3,
   Patience Brewster^2), 1768

Joseph FREEMAN^6 (John^5) and Phebe PAINE^6 (Richard^5, Jos.^{4}, Mary Snow^3, Constance

Hopkins^2), c1748 (Freeman Gen.:114)

Eliezer FREEMAN^5 (Nath.^{4}) and Rebecca YOUNG, 31 Mar. 1726, Eastham (MD 16:144)

Eleazer FREEMAN^6 (Eliezer^5) and 1st Elizabeth SNOW^6 (Jabez^{5-4-3}, Constance Hopkins^2)

Eleazer FREEMAN^6 and 2nd Ruth KNOWLES^7 (Seth^6, Sam.^{5}, Mercy Freeman^4, Mercy Prence^3, Patience Brewster^2)

Elisha FREEMAN and Phebe NICKERSON, 15 June 1812 (Sampler)

Lydia FREEMAN^5 (Nath.^{4}) and Elisha FREEMAN^4 (Sam.$^{3-2-1}$), 7 May 1725, Eastham (MD 16:74)

Elisha FREEMAN and 2nd Maria ALLEN, Int. 23 Apr. 1758 (Rochester VR 2:15,132)

Barnabas FREEMAN^6 (Lydia^5) and Thankful DENNIS, 16 Dec. 1761 (Rochester Gen'l. rcds. 2:43)

Patience FREEMAN^4 (Mercy Prence^3) and Samuel PAINE^4 (Mary Snow^3, Constance Hopkins^2), 31 Jan. 1682, Eastham (MD 6:12)

Thomas FREEMAN^4 (Mercy Prence^3) and Rebecca SPARROW, 31 Dec. 1673, Eastham (MD 8:93)

Edmund FREEMAN^5 (Tho.^{4}) and Phebe WATSON, c1703 (MD 3:175)

Edmund FREEMAN^6 (Edmund^5) and Mary CLARK, 7 Oct. 1731, Harwich (MD 13:69)

Seth FREEMAN^7 (Edmund^6) and Abigail ROGERS, 30 Sept. 1773 (Freeman Gen.:177)

Joshua FREEMAN^6 (Edmund^5) and Patience ROGERS

Watson FREEMAN^6 (Edmund^5) and Sarah GRAY, 30 Jan. 1723/24, Harwich (MD 8:159)

Elkanah FREEMAN^7 (Watson^6) and Abigail MAYO, 11 Oct. 1750

Isaac FREEMAN^7 (Watson^6) and Elizabeth COB^6 (Sarah Hopkins^5, Stephen$^{4-3}$, Gyles^2)

Watson FREEMAN^7 (Edmund^6) and Thankful FREEMAN^7 (Ben.$^{6-5}$, John^4, Mercy Prence^3, Patience Brewster^2), c1762 (MD 12:252)

Watson FREEMAN^8 (Watson^7) and Experience FREEMAN, c1794

Henry Huggeford FREEMAN^{11} (Henry^{10}, Watson$^{9-8}$) and Caroline Stevens WESSON^{11} (James L.^{10}, Sarah C. Nye^9, Abram^8, Mary Freeman^7, Seth^6, Mary Perry^5, Hester Taber^4, Hester Cooke^3, John^2), c1898 (PN&Q 1:5)

Lucy FREEMAN^{12} (Henry H.^{11}) and Felix Agnus LESER

Hatsuld FREEMAN^5 (Tho.^{4}) and Abigail HALLETT, 18 Jan./June 1719

Jonathan FREEMAN^5 (Tho.^{4}) and Mercy BRADFORD^4 (John^3, Wm.^{2}), c1708/09 (MD 5:86)

Mercy BRADFORD^4 and 2nd Isaac CUSHMAN^4 (Isaac^3, Mary Allerton^2), 10 Oct. 1717, Harwich (MD 7:197)

Joseph FREEMAN^5 (Tho.^{4}) and 1st Lydia THACHER^4 (Lydia Gorham^3, Desire Howland^2) c1709 (MD 5:87)

Joseph FREEMAN^5 and 2nd Mary (WATSON) Freeman, 9 Sept. 1736, Harwich (MD 20:26)

Mercy FREEMAN^5 (Tho.^{4}) and Paul SEARS, c1693 (MD 7:249)

Hannah SEARS^6 (Mercy Freeman^5) and Thomas HOWES, 4 July 1734, Yarmouth

Thomas HOWES and 2nd Bethia SEARS, 15 Oct. 1741

Ann SEARS^6 (Mercy Freeman^5) and Ebenezer BANGS, Int. 9 Dec. 1727, Harwich (MD 11:174)

Ruth BANGS and Gideon HIGGINS, 18 Apr. 1760, Eastham (MD 27:106)$^{<11>}$

Ruth HIGGINS and David GODFREY, Int. 31 Oct. 1794 (Eastham VR 12:25)

Ruth BANGS^7 (Ann Sears^6) and Solomon SAWYER (Bangs Gen.:50)

Jonathan BANGS^7 (Ann Sears^6) and Deborah HURD, c1766

Willard BANGS^8 (Jonathan^7) and Dorcus THOMPSON, 8 Jan. 1795, Buxton ME

Samuel BANGS^9 (Willard^8) and Rebecca HARMON, 19/20 Nov. 1820, Buxton ME

Harriet Frances BANGS^{10} (Sam.^{9}) and William Henry GREENE, 26 Mar. 1847, Sweden ME

Henry Eugene GREENE^{11} (Harriet F. Bangs^{10}) and Florence Adelaide KNIGHT, 1 July
    1879, Sweden ME

Ebenezer BANGS^7 (Ann Sears^6) and Elizabeth GRAY^6 (Rachel Freeman^5, Edmund^4, Mercy
    Prence^3, Patience Brewster^2), 31 Oct. 1754

Thomas BANGS^8 (Ebenezer^7) and 1st Ruth MYRICK, 25 May 1779, Harwich (Bangs Gen.:74)

Thomas BANGS^8 and 2nd Hannah MAYO (Bangs Gen.:74)

David SEARS^6 (Mercy Freeman^5) and Mercy SNOW^5 (Micajah^4, Stephen^3, Constance
    Hopkins^2), 13 Jan. 1736/37, Eastham (MD 17:146)

Paul SEARS^6 (Mercy Freeman^5) and Charity WHITTRIDGE, 30 May 1721, Rochester
    (VR 2:268,319)

Nathaniel SEARS and Elizabeth WINSLOW, 26 Nov. 1761 (Rochester VR 2:269)

Edmund SEARS^6 (Mercy Freeman^5) and Hannah CROWELL, c1743 (MD 6:93)

Hannah SEARS^7 (Edmund^6) and Willard SEARS

Jane SEARS and Roland HALLETT

Edmund SEARS^7 (Edmund^6) and Hannah TAYLOR

Elizabeth SEARS^7 (Edmund^6) and Thomas HOWES

Elkanah SEARS^7 (Edmund^6) and Mercy BRAY

Micro #18 of 18

Temperance SEARS^7 (Edmund^6) and Isaac CLARK

Prence FREEMAN^5 (Tho.^{4}) and Mary DOANE, 20 Mar. 1711/12, Eastham (MD 8:92)

Priscilla FREEMAN^6 (Prence^5) and Seth WINSLOW, 11 Mar. 1736/37 (Doane Gen.:51)

Hannah FREEMAN^6 (Prence^5) and poss. Theophilus MAYO, 16 Dec. 1742 (Doane Gen.:51)

Susanna FREEMAN^6 (Prence^5) and William TAYLOR, 24 Sept. 1747 (Doane Gen.:51)

Keziah FREEMAN^6 (Prence^5) and Johnson PELTON, 3 Mar. 1748 (Doane Gen.:51)

Moses FREEMAN[6] (Prence[5]) and Susanna BROOKS, 28 Aug. 1755 (Doane Gen.:51)

Elizabeth FREEMAN[6] (Prence[5]) and Isaac MERRICK, 25 July 1751 (Doane Gen.:51)

Mary FREEMAN[6] (Prence[5]) and James FREEMAN[6] (Thomas[5-4], Mercy Prence[3], Patience
   Brewster[2])<12>

Mary FREEMAN[6] (Prence[5]) and Isaac SMITH, Int. 2 Feb. 1744/45, Eastham (VR:233)

Nathaniel FREEMAN[6] (Prence[5]) and Martha BROWN, Int. 19 Feb. 1736/37, Eastham
   (MD 28:180)<13>

Sylvanus FREEMAN[7] (Nath.[6]) and Leah BRAINERD, 30 Oct. 1758<14>

Lydia FREEMAN[8] (Sylvanus[7]) and Abner COLE, 15 Dec. 1785<14>

Sylvanus FREEMAN[8] (Sylvanus[7]) and Huldah GOFF, 1 Jan. 1787<14>

Thankful FREEMAN[8] (Sylvanus[7]) and Enos BIGELOW, 10 Feb. 1803<14>

Philena/Paulina FREEMAN[8] (Sylvanus[7]) and Godfrey HOPKINS, 8 Nov. 1795<14>

Russell HOPKINS[9] (Philena Freeman[8]) and Hannah PADDOCK, 9 Feb. 1819<14>

Nathaniel FREEMAN[7] and Olivia CORNWELL

Olivia CORNWELL and 2nd Dr. Benejah(sp) MYNARD, 21 Aug. 1800

Annie FREEMAN[8] (Nath.[7]) and Stephen BRAINERD, 27 Nov. 1810 (Brainerd Gen.2:1:78,
   see <14> above)

Martha FREEMAN[7] (Nath.[6]) and Jabez ARNOLD

Mary Bowers ARNOLD[9] (Gideon[8], Martha Freeman[7]) and Warren Sylvester WILLIAMS

John WING and 1st Bethiah WINSLOW, 5 Mar. 1712/23

John WING and 2nd Rebecca (FREEMAN[5]) Vicory/Vickery (Tho.[4]), 24 July 1723, Harwich
   (MD 8:159)

David FOSTER and Lydia WHITE (Foster Gen.:562)

David FOSTER[8] (David[7], Phebe Wing[6], Rebecca Freeman[5]) and Polly TREADWELL c1804

Thomas FREEMAN[5] (Tho.[4]) and 1st Bathsheba MAYO[5] (Nath.[4], Hannah Prence[3], Patience
   Brewster[2]), 22 Aug. 1706, Eastham (MD 7:12)

Thomas FREEMAN[5] and 2nd Mary SMITH, 17 Oct. 1707, Eastham (MD 7:12)

Mary SMITH and 2nd Hezekiah DEANE, aft. Mar. 1716/17 (MD 6:56)

Thomas FREEMAN[6] (Tho.[5]) and Dorothy COLE, 6 Aug. 1730, Eastham (MD 17:33)

William FREEMAN[4] (Mercy Prence[3]) and Lydia SPARROW

Lydia SPARROW and 2nd Jonathan HIGGINS[4] (Eliz. Rogers[3], Jos.[2]), c1690

William FREEMAN[5] (Wm.[4]) and Mercy PEPPER, 16 Oct. 1711

William FREEMAN[6] (Wm.[5]) and Hannah ATWOOD, 1736

William FREEMAN[7] (Wm.[6]) and Mary COBB

Robert FREEMAN[8] (Wm.[7]) and Catharine FRASER, 1801

William Twining FREEMAN^9 (Robert^8) and Letitia FREEMAN^9 (Simeon^{8-7-6}, Lydia^4, Mercy Prence^3, Patience Brewster^2), 26 Nov. 1840

Lydia FREEMAN^5 (Wm.^{4}) and Richard GODFREE, 4 Feb. 1701/02, Eastham (MD 7:20)

Hannah GODFREE^6 (Lydia Freeman^5) and Edward GRAY, Int. 13 Apr. 1727, Harwich
(MD 8:219)

William FREEMAN^5 (Wm.^{4}) and Mercy PEPPER, 16 Oct. 1711, Eastham (MD 7:20)

Mercy FREEMAN^6 (Wm.^{5}) and 1st Nathaniel KNOWLES, 10 Jan. 1739/40, Eastham (MD 19:103)

Mercy FREEMAN^6 and 2nd Job CROCKER, 14 Jan. 1747/48, Harwich (MD 28:83)

Rebecca PRENCE^3 and Edmund FREEMAN, 22 Apr. 1646, Plymouth (13:86)

Edmund FREEMAN and 2nd Margaret PERRY, 18 July 1651, Sandwich (MD 14:109)

Patience FREEMAN^4 (Rebecca Prence^3) and Joseph BURGE, c1666/67 (MD 14:171)

Rebecca FREEMAN^4 (Rebecca Prence^3) and Ezra PERRY, 1672/73 (MD 14:110)

NOTES

<1> p.58, Although long sought after, Mary's identity remains a mystery. Wentworth has long been a possibility and more recently, Wyrall. See Dr. Jeremy Bangs in the Mayflower Quarterly 51:165-66.

<2> p.59, 1st wife Lucy Blodgett died 2 Nov. 1753 so Nathan's 2nd marriage to Lucy Barns should probably read 14 Feb. 1753/54.

<3> p.62, The last number is worn in the records but is undoubtedly 1763 - intentions were published 12 Nov. 1763 and Abigail died Apr. 1764 (Scituate VR 2:455)

<4> p.62, The last number is difficult to ascertain but is later shown in the files as 1734. Micro #6 shows Jesse remarried Lydia NEAL, 29 Mar. 1741 (Scituate VR). Jesse Turner and Grace Dwelly were divorced, no children are shown.

<5> p.64, Source: First Presbyterian Church, Morristown N.J, Combined Registers, 1742-1885, p.40,174.

<6> p.69, Their marriage in the 2nd Church Records spell his name "Cloud". The intentions in the Weymouth VR 2:117,130 and Hanover VR:253 spell it "Loud".

<7> p.74, Source: Starr, Burgis P. History of the Starr Family. Hartford CT. (p.336)

<8> p.77, Ernestine Lord and Rev. George Augustus Bowman were the parents of George Ernest Bowman, compiler of these Bowman Files.

<9> p.82, Hannah Mayo is descended from a double Mayflower line as follows: Paternal line - Moses Mayo^6 (Jos.^{5}, Hannah Freeman^4, Mercy Prence^3, Patience Brewster^2) Maternal line - Phebe Freeman^8 (Watson^7, Edmund^6, Tho.^{5}, John^4, Mercy Prence^3, Patience Brewster^2)

<10> p.83, Source: Gould, Benjamin Apthorp. The Family of Zaccheus Gould of Topsfield. Lynn. 1895 (p.73,107,174).

<11> p.86, On the same page is found - "Gideon Higgins and Mehitable Bangs^4 (Jonathan$^{3-2}$), 18 Apr. 1760 (Bangs Gen.:35)".

<12> p.87, Although not married this couple had a child together (James Freeman^7, bpt. 8 June 1740) (MD 7:99) and therefore left descendants.

<13> p.87, Evidence is cited proving this was not the Nathaniel Freeman (son

of Edmund and Keziah) who married Martha Dunham, 4 Sept. 1738 (MD 14:158).
     <14> p.87, Source: Brainard, Lucy Abigail. The Genealogy of the Brainerd/ Brainard Family in America. Hartford CT. 1908. (1:2:59)

PETER BROWN DESCENDANTS

Mary BROWN[2] (Peter[1])

Mary BROWN[2] and Ephraim TINKHAM, c1648 (MD 16:120)

Edward TINKAM and Lydia RYDER, Int. 17 July 1742 (Plymouth VR 1:251)

Elizabeth TINKHAM and Nathaniel HOOPER, 28 Mar. 1728, Middleboro (MD 5:39)

John TINKUM and Esther BLAIR 23 Sept. 1740 (Boston Rcd.Com.28:217)

Ebenezer TINKHAM and Abigail CLARK, 3 Oct. 1749 (Boston Rcd.Com.28:265)

John TINKUM and Mary KIDDER, Int. 28 July 1740 (Boston Rcd.Com.28:234)[1]

John TINCOM and Sarah DINSDALE, 14 May 1719 (Boston Rcd.Com.28:85)

John TINCOM and Susanna BRINNO, Int. 7 Apr. 1724 (Boston Rcd.Com.28:161)

Elizabeth TINKHAM and James GORDON, 14 Sept. 1721 (Boston Rcd.Com.28:101)

Isaac TINKHAM[3] and Sarah KING, 17 Nov. 1692, Plymouth (MD 13:206)

Mary TINKHAM[3] and John TOMSON[3] (Mary Cooke[2]), c1680 (MD 1:221)

Ebenezer TINKHAM[3] and Elizabeth BURROUGHS, pre 7 July 1676 (MD 17:186)

Ebenezer TINKHAM[4] (Ebenezer[3]) and 1st Patience PRATT, 28 Oct. 1703, Middleboro
    (MD 2:43)

Ebenezer TINKHAM[4] and 2nd Hannah (HATCH[3]) Turner (Mary Doty[2]), 9 July 1719, Scituate
    (MD 10:75)

Asel THOMAS and Phebe ELLIS, 26 May 2796, Middleboro (VR 4:179)

Patience TINKHAM[5] (Ebenezer[4]) and Edmund WOOD, 20 June 1744, Middleboro (MD 16:20)

Priscilla TINKHAM[5] (Ebenezer[4]) and John WOOD

Peter TINKHAM[5] (Ebenezer[4]) and Eunice THOMAS, 1 Apr. 1730, Middleboro (MD 8:250)

Joanna TINKHAM and Robert MACKFUN, 23 Dec. 1720, Marlboro (MD 4:72)

Jeremiah TINKHAM[5] (Jeremiah[4]) and Naomi WARREN[5] (John[4], Richard[3], Nathaniel[2]),
    c1739 (MD 15:221)

Ebenezer TINKHAM[5] (Jeremiah[4], Ebenezer[3]) and Hannah SHAW, c1738 (MD 14:246)

Elisha TINKHAM[6] (Jeremiah[5]) and 1st poss. Sarah GREEN, c1774

Elisha TINKHAM[6] and 2nd Reliance RICHMOND[7] (John[6-5], Jos.[4], Abigail Rogers[3], John[2]),
    13 Dec. 1777

Elisha TINKHAM[6] and 3rd Sarah RICHMOND[7] (John[6-5], Jos.[4], Abigail Rogers[3], John[2]),
    30 Nov. 1792

James TINKHAM[6] (Jeremiah[5]) and 1st Sarah REDDING, 20 Dec. 1770 (Middleboro VR)

James TINKHAM[6] and 2nd Chloe RICKARD, 21 Nov. 1777 (Middleboro VR)

Nancy TINKHAM and Nathaniel HOWARD, 6 Nov. 1810 (Middleboro VR 8:139)

Anna TINKHAM[7] (James[6]) and Nathaniel HOWARD, 6 Nov. 1810 (Middleboro VR)

Jane Tinkham HOWARD[8] (Anna Tinkham[7]) and Rev. James PORTER, 17 June 1833, Easton
(Marr.Cert.)

Enoch TINKHAM[7] (James[6]) and Rebecca WILLIAMS

Joanna TINKHAM[4] (Ebenezer[3]) and Thomas MACOMBER, 14 June 1709, Middleboro (MD 2:158)

Thomas MACOMBER Jr. and Betsy CURTIS, 3 Apr. 1794 (Hanover VR:101)

Simeon CURTIS and Lucy ( ) MACOMBER, 9 Jan. 1759 (Hanover VR:120)

Sarah MACOMBER and Elisha CURTIS, 22 Jan. 1778 (Hanover VR:121)

Mary MACOMBER and Solomon BATES Jr., 22 Dec. 1787 (Hanover VR:254)

Thomas MACOMBER[6] (Tho.[5]) and Prudence STETSON[6] (Mary Eames[5], Mary Oakman[4],
Eliz. Doty[3], Edw.[2]), 28 July 1768 (Marshfield VR 2:150)

Thomas MACOMBER[6] (Onesimus[5]) and Leah TILDEN, 12 July 1767 (Marshfield VR 2:150)

Onesimus MACOMBER[5] (Joanna Tinkham[4]) and Lucy BARKER, 15 Jan. 1744 (Marshfield
VR 2:172)

Lucy BARKER and 2nd Simeon CURTIS, 9 Jan. 1759

Elizabeth MACOMBER[5] (Joanna Tinkham[4]) and Job WINSLOW[5] (Mercy Snow[4], Josiah[3], Abigail
Warren[2]), 20 Mar. 1740

Sarah MACOMBER[5] (Joanna Tinkham[4]) and Josiah BARKER, c1738

Thomas MACOMBER[5] (Joanna Tinkham[4]) and Mercy TILDEN[5] (Desire Oldham[4], Mercy Sprout[3],
Eliz. Samson[2]), 9 May 1745 (Marshfield VR)

Mercy TILDEN[5] and 2nd David THOMAS Jr., 8 Jan. 1761

Shubael TINKHAM[4] (Ebenezer[3]) and Priscilla CHILDS, 17 Dec. 1718, Marshfield
(MD 7:131)

Priscilla TINKHAM[5] (Shubael[4]) and 1st John COBB[5] (John[4], Rachel Soule[3], John[2]),
c1744 (MD 16:134)

Priscilla TINKHAM[5] and 2nd William CUSHMAN[5] (Ichabod[4], Isaac[3], Mary Allerton[2]),
11 Apr. 1751, Middleboro (MD 18:84)

Joseph TINKHAM[5] (Shubael[4]) and Agnes MACKFUN, 5 June 1740, Middleboro (MD 15:218)

Ephraim TINKHAM[3] and Esther WRIGHT[3] (Hester Cooke[2]), aft. 9 June 1676 (MD 24:85)

John TINKHAM and Hannah HOWLAND, 11 Dec. 1716 (Middleboro VR 1:53)

John TINKHAM Jr. and Jerusha VAUGHAN, 27 Jan. 1742/43 (Middleboro VR 1:225)

John TINKHAM Jr. and Mary WOOD, 25 Mar. 1778 (Middleboro VR 4:14)

Joanna TINKHAM and Nathaniel THOMPSON, 12 Sept. 1805 (Middleboro VR 8:200)

Mary THOMPSON and David THOMAS, 25 Oct. 1832 (Middleboro VR 10:68)

Jacob TINKHAM Sr. and Hannah COBB, 16 Nov. 1721

Jacob TINKHAM Jr. and Lydia DONHAM, 5 Feb. 1746/47

Sebra CROOKER Jr. and Pamelia DURLAND, 9 Apr. 1829

Ephraim TINKHAM^4 (Ephraim^3) and Martha COBB^4 (Rachel Soule^3, John^2), 24 June 1708, Middleboro (MD 2:157)

Martha COBB^4 and 2nd Aaron SIMMONS, aft. 1713 (MD 17:163)

Martha TINKHAM^4 (Ephraim^3) and John SOULE^3 (John^2), 8 Dec. 1701, Middleboro (MD 1:220)

Isaac TINKHAM^4 (Ephraim^3) and Abijah WOOD, 12 Dec. 1717, Middleboro (MD 4:70)

Nathan TINKHAM^5 (Isaac^4) and Sarah SOULE^5 (Zachariah^4, Ben.^{3}, John^2), 10 Dec. 1746, (Halifax VR:34)

Noah TINKHAM^5 (Isaac^4) and Sarah PORTER, Int. 8 Feb. 1750/51 (Halifax VR:58)

Joseph TINKHAM^6 (Noah^5) and Lucy LUCAS, Int. 25 Jan. 1790, Halifax (MD 5:107)

John TINKHAM^4 (Ephraim^3) and Hannah HOWLAND^3 (Isaac^2), 11 Dec. 1716, Middleboro (MD 4:70)

Amos TINKHAM^5 (John^4) and Sarah TINKHAM, Int. 21 Sept. 1751, Middleboro (VR 2:1:56)

Zilpah TINKHAM^5 (John^4) and John MILLER^6 (John^5, Lydia Coombs^4, Francis^3, Sarah Priest^2)

John TINKHAM^5 (John^4) and Jerusha VAUGHAN, 27 Jan. 1742/43, Middleboro (MD 15:220)

Levi TINKHAM^6 (John^5) and Mary FOSTER^6 (Tho.^{5}, Faith Oakman^4, Eliz. Doty^3, Edw.^{2})

Mary TINKHAM^4 (Ephraim^3) and Henry WOOD, 24 Dec. 1717, Middleboro (MD 4:70)

Moses WOOD^5 (Mary Tinkham^4) and Lydia WATERMAN^6 (Jos.^{5}, Lydia Cushman^4, Eleazer^3, Mary Allerton^2), 12 Jan. 1761

Samuel TINKHAM^4 (Ephraim^3) and 1st Patience COBB^4 (Rachel Soule^3, John^2), 20 Feb. 1717/18, Middleboro (MD 4:70)

Samuel TINKHAM^4 and 2nd Melatiah EDDY, 22 Mar. 1730/31, Middleboro (MD 9:46)

Patience TINKHAM^5 (Sam.^{4}) and Samuel EATON^5 (Barnabas^4, Sam.$^{3-2}$)

Ephraim TINKHAM^5 (Sam.^{4}) and Sarah STANDISH^5 (Moses^4, Ebenezer^3, Alexander^2), 5 Jan. 1759 (Halifax VR:36)$^{<2>}$

Sarah STANDISH^5 and 2nd Adam WRIGHT^5 (John^4, Adam^3, Hester Cooke^2), 1 June 1773 (Plympton VR)

Abigail TINKHAM^6 (Ephraim^5) and Caleb LEACH, 17 Jan. 1782 (Plympton VR:339,412)

Caleb TINKHAM^4 (Helkiah^3) and Mercy HOLMES, 20 Oct. 1724, Plymouth (MD 14:70)

Eleanor TINKHAM^5 (Caleb^4) and Samuel BRYANT, c1758 (MD 20:71)

Sarah TINKHAM^5 (Caleb^4) and Benjamin SMITH, 13 Nov. 1749, Plymouth (MD 16:169)

Ebenezer TINKHAM^4 (Helkiah^3) and 1st Mary BONNEY, c1732 (MD 15:113)

Ebenezer TINKHAM^4 and 2nd Jane PRATT, 9 Nov. 1736, Plymouth (MD 14:157)

Helkiah TINKHAM^4 (Helkiah^3) and Elizabeth HESTER(sp), 15 Dec. 1709, Marblehead

Mary TINKHAM^5 (Helkiah^4) and Benjamin EATON, 28 Oct. 1746, Plymouth (Gen.Adv. 3:50)

Sarah TINKHAM and Charles COOK^5 (Robert^4, Francis^3, Jacob^2), 5 Oct. 1749 (Gen.Adv.3:23)

Isaac TINKHAM^5 (Helkiah^4) and Keziah WORMAL, 26 July 1739, Duxbury (MD 11:82)

Elizabeth TINKHAM^5 (Helkiah^4) and Jonathan SANDERS, 3 July 1741, Plymouth (MD 16:255)

Martha TINKHAM^5 (Helkiah^4) and Thomas SILVESTER, 23 Apr. 1750, Plymouth (MD 16:169)

Thomas SILVESTER and 2nd Elizabeth DUNHAM, 1766

Jacob TINKHAM^4 (Helkiah^3) and 1st Hannah COBB, 16 Nov. 1721, Plymouth (MD 14:39)

Jacob TINKHAM^4 and 2nd Judith HUNT, 18 Nov. 1725, Plymouth (MD 14:71)

Jacob TINKHAM^5 (Jacob^4) and Lydia DUNHAM, 5 Feb. 1746/47, Plymouth (MD 16:172)

Hannah TINKHAM^6 (Jacob^5) and William CURTIS, 17 Nov. 1768, Plymouth (Col.Soc.2:495)

John TINKHAM^4 (Helkiah^3) and Ann GRAY^5 (John^4, Mary Winslow^3, Mary Chilton^2),
    30 Dec. 1714, Plymouth (MD 14:37)

Joseph TINKHAM^5 (John^4) and Deborah FULLER, Int. 15 Sept. 1750

John TINKHAM^5 (John^4) and Sarah EVERSON, 2 Feb. 1747/48, Kingston (Gen.Adv.3:23)

Anne TINKHAM AND Samuel FULLER, 22 Oct. 1747, Kingston (Gen.Adv.3:23)

Edward TINKHAM^5 (John^4) and Lydia RIDER, 29 Sept. 1743, Plymouth (MD 17:4)

Hannah TINKHAM^6 (Edw.^{5}) and Lemuel BARTLETT, 24 Oct. 1774, Yarmouth (MD 9:42)

Mary TINKHAM^4 (Helkiah^3) and Ebenezer CURTIS, 19 Jan. 1709/10, Plymouth (MD 14:36)

Ebenezer CURTIS and 2nd Martha DOTY^3 (John^2), 7 Oct. 1718, Plymouth (MD 14:38)

Jacob CURTIS^5 (Mary Tinkham^4) and Fear DUNHAM, 1731

Peter TINKHAM^4 (Helkiah^3) and Mary BENNET, 6 Jan. 1736, Kingston (Gen.Adv.2:51,126)

<u>Micro #3 of 5</u>

Peter TINKCOM^4 (John^3) and Eunice CLARK, Int. 17 Mar. 1745/46 (Dartmouth VR:378)

Martha TINKHAM^4 (John^3) and Joseph ELLIS, Int. 4 Dec. 1742, Harwich (MD 23:122)

Luke ELLIS^5 (Martha Tinkham^4) and 1st Naomi BRIGGS, 3 Dec. 1780 (Dartmouth VR)

Luke ELLIS^5 and 2nd Elizabeth MACOMBER^6 (John^5, Eliz. Williams^4, Eliz. Rogers^3,
    John^2), 11 Mar. 1784 (Dartmouth VR 1:391)

Peter TINKHAM^4 (John^3) and Eunice CLARK, 6 Apr. 1746 (Rochester 1st ch.rcds.)

Charles TINKHAM^5 (Peter^4) and Jane ELLIS, Int. 22 Aug. 1774, Rochester (VR 2:125)

Andrew TINKHAM^6 (Charles^5) and Jemima WILBOR, 1812, Sydney ME

Peter TINKHAM^3 and Mercy MENDALL (PN&Q 2:55)

Joanna TINKHAM[4] (Peter[3]) and Joseph BATES, 16 Apr. 1716, Middleboro (MD 2:158)

Joseph BATES[5] (Joanna Tinkham[4]) and Eunice TINKHAM[6] (Peter[5], Ebenezer[4-3], Mary Brown[2]), c1749

Mercy TINKHAM[4] (Peter[3]) and James RAYMENT, 27 Dec. 1716, Middleboro (MD 4:70)

James RAYMENT and 2nd Elizabeth FULLER, 30 Jan. 1723/24, Plympton (MD 2:139)

Samuel TINKHAM[4] (Peter[3]) and Mary STAPLES, 1 Dec. 1719, Middleboro (MD 4:71)

Mercy TINKHAM[5] (Sam.[4]) and Ephraim DUNHAM, 30 Nov. 1741, Middleboro (Gen.Adv. 2:19)

Samuel TINKHAM and Hope COBB[5] (Gershom[4], Hope Chipman[3], Hope Howland[2]), 5 Apr. 1745, Middleboro (MD 16:108)

Deborah TINKHAM[5] (Sam.[4]) and Samuel SNOW[<3>]

Martha TINKHAM[5] (Sam.[4]) and Nathaniel WOOD, 1 June 1742, Middleboro (MD 15:219)

Nathaniel WOOD and 2nd Mary WINSLOW, 19 June 1744, Middleboro (MD 16:20)

Seth TINKHAM[5] (Seth[4], Peter[3]) and Eunice SOULE[5] (Zachariah[4], Ben.[3], John[2]), 22 Oct. 1761, Middleboro (VR 2:29)

Hazael TINKHAM[6] (Seth[5]) and Susanna PRATT, c1784 (MD 32:89)

Priscilla BROWN[2] (Peter[1])

Priscilla BROWN[2] and William ALLEN, 21 Mar. 1649, Sandwich (MD 16:122) -No issue

Rebecca BROWN[2] (Peter[1])

Rebecca BROWN[2] and William SNOW

Benjamin SNOW[3] and Elizabeth ALDEN[3] (Joseph[2]), 12 Dec. 1693, Bridgewater (MD 26:38)

Benjamin SNOW[4] (Ben.[3]) and Jemima SNELL, c1722

Ebenezer SNOW[4] (Ben.[3]) and Sarah PRATT

Elizabeth SNOW[4] (Ben.[3]) and Joseph CARVER, 4 May 1725 (Bridgewater VR 2:73,348)

Joseph CARVER[5] (Eliz. Snow[4]) and Sarah HARTWELL, 25 Dec. 1746 (Bridgewater VR 2:73,161)

Rhoda CARVER[6] (Jos.[5]) and William BARTON, 26 Apr. 1771 (Providence VR 2:90)

Anna Maria BARTON[7] (Rhoda Carver[6]) and Apollos CUSHMAN, 21 June 1809 (Arnold VR 14:507)

Sarah M. BARTON[7] (Rhoda Carver[6]) and Capt. Herman B. ADAMS, 3 Oct. 1812, Providence (Arnold VR 17:87)[<4>]

Sarah SNOW[4] (Ben.[3]) and Nathaniel PRATT

Seth PRATT[5] (Sarah Snow[4]) and Hannah WASHBURN[7] (Jos.[6], Josiah[5], John[4], Eliz.

Mitchell[3], Jane Cooke[2]), 24 Apr. 1753 (ch.rcds.)

Solomon SNOW[4] (Ben.[3]) and Bathsheba MALMIN(sp)

Hannah SNOW[3] and 1st Giles RICKARD[3] (Giles[2-1]), 7 Nov. 1683, Plymouth (MD 13:204)

Hannah SNOW[3] and 2nd Joseph HOWES

Joseph SNOW[3] and Hopestill ALDEN[3] (Joseph[2]), c1689 (MD 14:208)

David SNOW[4] (Joseph[3]) and Joanna HAYWARD , c1731

Isaac SNOW[4] (Jos.[3]) and Hannah SHAW, 19 Nov. 1722, Bridgewater (MD 16:187)

Hannah SHAW and 2nd John WHITMAN, 16 Mar. 1743

Isaac SNOW[5] (Isaac[4]) and 1st Elizabeth BOWDITCH[5] (Mary Bass[4], Sam.[3], Ruth Alden[2]),
    8 Sept. 1748 (Bridgewater VR)

Isaac SNOW[5] and 2nd Hannah HUNKINS, 7 July 1785

James SNOW[4] (Jos.[3]) and 1st Ruth SHAW, c1719

James SHAW[4] and 2nd Hannah HOVEY, 6 Aug. 1741, Weymouth (VR 2:96,175)

Ruth SNOW[5] (James[4]) and Perez BONNEY, 20 Apr. 1739 (Pembroke VR)

Jonathan SNOW[4] (Jos.[3]) and 1st Sarah SOULE[4] (John[3-2]), 18 Dec. 1728, Middleboro
    (MD 5:40)

Jonathan SNOW[4] and 2nd Ruth BENNET, 22 Jan. 1746, Middleboro (MD 18:79)

Samuel SNOW[5] (Jonathan[4]) and Deborah TINKHAM[5] (Sam.[4], Peter[3], Mary Brown[2])
    (MD 18:154)[3]

Samuel SNOW[5] (Jonathan[4]) and Jedidah BUMPAS, pre 8 Mar. 1769

Samuel SNOW[6] (Sam.[5]) and Bettie PERKINS, 15 June 1775 (Bridgewater VR 2:288,350)

Joseph SNOW[4] (Jos.[3]) and 1st Elizabeth FIELD, c1714 (MD 15:84)

James SNOW[5] (Jos.[4]) and Hannah SEARLE, 26 Mar. 1755, Providence

William Downing SNOW[7] (Jos.[6], James[5]) and Lydia HORSWELL, 25 Dec. 1806, Providence

Amanda SNOW[8] (Wm.[7]) and William READ

William Downing SNOW[8] (Wm.[7]) and Ann WARHURST, 16 Aug. 1835 (Bible)

Rev. Joseph SNOW[5] (Jos.[4]) and 1st Sarah FIELD, 1 Nov. 1737

Reve. Joseph SNOW[5] and 2nd Rebecca GRANT, 14 Mar. 1754 (Arnold VR 2:1:174)

Rev. Joseph SNOW[5] and 3rd Margaret PROCTOR, 24 Oct. 1775 (Arnold VR 2:1:174)

Mary SNOW[4] (Jos.[3]) and Joseph LOTHROP(sp), c1718

Rebecca SNOW[4] (Jos.[3]) and Thomas WADE, c1722

Rebecca SNOW[3] and Samuel RICKARD, 31 Dec. 1689, Plymouth (MD 13:205)

Hannah RICKARD[4] (Rebecca[3]) and Josiah BYRAM, 12 Apr. 1720, Plympton (MD 3:91)

William SNOW[3] and Naomi WHITMAN, 30 Nov. 1686, Bridgewater (MD 2:242)

Bethiah SNOW[4] (Wm.[3]) and Elisha HAYWARD, 1 Feb. 1720/21, Bridgewater (MD 16:187)

Eleazer SNOW[4] (Wm.[3]) and Mercy KING, 11 July 1728, Bridgewater (MD 16:45)

Reuben SNOW[5] (Eleazer[4]) and Hannah WILLIS, c1768

Bettie SNOW[5] (Eleazer[4]) and 1st Nathan AMES, 2nd William TOLMAN, 3rd Micah WHITE

Daniel SNOW[5] (Eleazer[4]) and Hannah DUNBAR, c1764

Eleazer SNOW[5] (Eleazer[4]) and Mary WOOD, c1757

Mercy SNOW[5] (Eleazer[4]) and 1st Jacob JOHNSON, 28 Feb. 1760, Bridgewater

Mercy SNOW[5] and 2nd Elijah CAPEN, 22 May 1789 (Sharon VR)

John SNOW[4] (Wm.[3]) and Hannah HAYWARD, 15 July 1731, Bridgewater (MD 16:98)

Susanna SNOW[4] (Wm.[3]) and Israel ALGER, 25 Dec. 1717, Bridgewater (MD 16:185)

William SNOW[4] (Wm.[3]) and Mary WASHBURN[5] (James[4], Eliz. Mitchell[3], Jane Cooke[2]),
    8 Nov. 1722, (Bridgewater VR 2:259)

NOTES

<1> p.90, The word "forbid" is added to this entry.

<2> p.92, It is possible the year 1759 is an error for 1758. Intentions were pub. 19 Dec. 1757 (Halifax VR:59) and their first child was born 20 July 1758 (MD 26:24)

<3> p.94,95, "Apparently not married" is written; they are included here because they had a child together (Samuel Snow[6], b. 10 May 1753 <MD 18:54>) and therefore left descendants.

<4> p.94, The entry in Arnold VR 19:333 differs slightly, giving his name as Capt. Herman B. Allen with the marriage date 1 Oct.

JAMES CHILTON DESCENDANTS

Mary CHILTON[2] (James[1])

Mary CHILTON[2] and John WINSLOW, pre 22 May 1627 (MD 1:150)

Mary WINSLOW and Jonathan POLLARD, 26 Dec. 1693

Eliza WINSLOW and Joseph SCOTT, 18 Jan. 1693

Hannah WINSLOW and John AUSTIN, Int. 7 Nov. 1754 (Wyman's Charlestown)

John WINSLOW and Sarah MOULTON, 5th day 3rd mth.1652 (Malden VR:324)[1]

Jacob WINSLADE and Elizabeth WHITTEMORE, 16 May 1690 (Malden VR:324)

Mary WINSLED and Patrick FLYNN, 16 July 1713 (Malden VR:324)

Mary WINSLOW and Silas SARGEANT, 14 Feb. 1745/46 (Malden VR:324)

Elizabeth WINSLOW and Jabez BURDETT, 3 May 1753 (Malden VR:324)

Capt. George WINSLOW and Elizabeth REID , 13 Feb. 1821 (Malden VR:324)

Caleb S. WINSLOW and Caroline BARRETT, 18 Mar. 1833 (Malden VR:324)

Sally M. WINSLOW and Peter J. BALLARD, 5 Mar. 1837, Marblehead (Malden VR:324)

Joshua WINSLOW and Sarah A. CLARK, Int. 17 Feb. 1849 (Malden VR:195)

Elizabeth WINSLOW and John SIMS, Int. 11 May 1720 (Malden VR:195)

Kenelm WINSLOW and Ann TAYLOR, 7 Sept. 1730

Joshua VAUGHAN and Anne TAYLOR, 1 Feb. 1747

John TAYLOR and Rebecca DINSDELL, 9 Aug. 1739

John TAYLOR and Hannah ELICE, 8 Sept. 1725

John TAYLOR and Ruth THOMPSON, 24 Feb. 1745

Elizabeth WINSLOW and Edward THOMAS, 4 Oct. 1689, Charlestown (Boston Rcd.Com.30:291)

Edward WINSLOW[3] and 2nd Elizabeth HUTCHINSON, 8 Feb. 1668 (MD 12:129)

Edward WINSLOW[3] and 1st Sarah HILTON, c1660 (Boston Rcd.Com.9:80)

Isaac WINSLOW and Sarah WENSLEY, 11 July 1700, Boston (Rcd.Com.28:2)

Abigall WINSLOW and James OBORN, 11 May 1702, Boston (Rcd.Com.:28:5)

Ann WINSLOW and John TAYLOR, 1 Nov. 1702, Boston (Rcd.Com.:28:6)

Capt. Edward WINSLOW and ELiza PEMBERTON, 22 May 1712, Boston (Rcd.Com.:28:43)

Edward WINSLOW JR. and Hannah SAVAGE, 1 Dec. 1726, Boston (Rcd.Com.28:158)

Edward WINSLOW and Susanna LYMAN, 27 Mar. 1744, Boston (Rcd.Com.28:267)

Joseph WINSLOW and Mary BONNER, 29 Jan. 1746, Boston (Rcd.Com.28:267)

Elizabeth WINSLOW and John WINNET, 15 Sept. 1746, Boston (Rcd.Com.28:267)

Isaac WINSLOW and Lucy WALDO, 14 Dec. 1747, Boston (Rcd.Com.28:267)

Elizabeth WINSLOW and Richard CLARKE, 3 May 1733, Boston (Rcd.Com.28:181)

Elizabeth WINSLOW and John SIMS, Int. 11 May 1720, Boston (Rcd.Com.28:98)

Hannah WINSLOW and William DAVIS, 26 Jan. 1715, Boston (Rcd.Com.28:57)

Joshua WINSLOW and Elizabeth SAVAGE, 8 Feb. 1720, Boston (Rcd.Com.28:90)

Jacob WINSLOW and Mary WINSLOW "forbid ye Banns", 27 Apr. 1713 (Rcd.Com.28:92)

Mary WINSLOW and Patrick FLING, Int. 2 July 1713, Boston (Rcd.Com.28:93)

Susanna WINSLOW and Capt. John ALDEN, 22 Nov. 1722, Boston (Rcd.Com.28:104)

John WINSLOW and Mary VRYLAND, 2 Jan. 1728, Boston (Rcd.Com.28:147)

John WINSLOW and Elizabeth MASON, Int. 28 Nov. 1751, Boston (Rcd.Com.28:299)

Faith WINSLOW and William TAYLOR, 19 Feb. 1735, Boston (Rcd.Com.28:194)

Samuel WINSLOW and Rebecca CLARKE, 8 June 1729, Boston (Rcd.Com.28:152)

Kenelm WINSLOW and Ann TAYLOR, 7 Sept. 1730, Boston (Rcd.Com.28:157)

Sarah WINSLOW and Tobias PAIN, Int. 25 Sept. 1728, Boston (Rcd.Com.28:165)

Sarah WINSLOW and John CORSER, 22 June 1742, Boston (Rcd.Com.28:240)

William WINSLOW and Elizabeth CLARKE, 11 Dec. 1735, Boston (Rcd.Com.28:194)

Rebecca WINSLOW and William LEE, 24 Aug. 1749, Boston (Rcd.Com.28:252)

Margaret WINSLOW and Benjamin POLLARD, 14 Aug. 1746, Boston (Rcd.Com.28:258)

Martha WINSLOW and John POWELL, 3 July 1748, Boston (Rcd.Com.28:343)

Katharine WINSLOW and Jaques HERBERT, Int. 16 July 1695, Boston (Rcd.Com.28:348)

Susanna WINSLOW and John RIDER, Int. 3 July 1754, Boston (Rcd.Com.30:11)

Mrs. Susanna WINSLOW and Nicholas SEVER, Int. 21 Sept. 1757, Boston (Rcd.Com.30:26)

Nathaniel WINSLOW and Ruth BONNER, Int. 9 Apr. 1757, Boston (Rcd.Com.30:23)

Joseph WINSLOW and Margaret CAZNEAN, Int. 11 Aug. 1757, Boston (Rcd.Com.30:25)

Katharine WINSLOW and Simon PEAS, Int. 29 Aug. 1757, Boston (Rcd.Com.30:25)

Hannah WINSLOW and John AUSTIN, Int. 7 Nov. 1754, Boston (Rcd.Com.30:13)

Joshua WINSLOW and Anna GREEN, Int. 7 Dec. 1757, Boston (Rcd.Com.30:27)

Elizabeth WINSLOW and Samuel GARDNER, Int. 20 May 1758, Boston (Rcd.Com.30:29)

John WINSLOW and Elizabeth WINSLOW, 3 July 1796, Boston (Rcd.Com.30:170)

Elizabeth WINSLOW and William PICKERING, 19 Nov. 1807, Boston (Rcd.Com.30:266)

Elizabeth WINSLOW and John HOLLAND, 17 Apr. 1787, Boston (Rcd.Com.30:130)

Elizabeth WINSLOW and Edward THOMAS, 4th day 8th mth. 1689, Boston (Rcd.Com.30:291)

Isaac WINSLOW and Jemima DEBUKE, 25 Nov. 1770, Boston (Rcd.Com.30:330)

Sarah WINSLOW and Tobias PAINE, 14 Oct. 1728, Boston (Rcd.Com.30:305)

John WINSLOW and Anna GARDNER, 18 May 1782, Boston (Rcd.Com.30:134)

Venus (negro servant of John Winslow) and Cole (negro servant of Henry Laughton),
    Int. 6 Feb. 1754, Boston (Rcd.Com.30:10)

John WINSLOW and Sarah TYNG, Int. 6 Aug. 1760, Boston (Rcd.Com.39:37)

Aaron WINSLOW and Elizabeth LEWIS, 18 May 1806, Boston (Rcd.Com.30:228)

Abigail WINSLOW and Samuel PIERCE, 17 Dec. 1809, Boston (Rcd.Com.30:265)

Abigail WINSLOW and Benjamin VEASEY, Int. 29 Apr. 1773, Boston (Rcd.Com.30:433)

Benjamin WINSLOW and Abigail Amory CALLAHAN, 28 Apr. 1807, Boston (Rcd.Com.30:279)

Betsy WINSLOW and Joseph RYWARD, Int. 5 Aug. 1805, Boston (Rcd.Com.30:489)

Celia WINSLOW and William NETTLETON, 27 Mar. 1785, Boston (Rcd.Com.30:412)

Edward WINSLOW and Mercy BOWLEY, 8 Nov. 1804, Boston (Rcd.Com.30:213)

Edward WINSLOW and Margaret RAYMOND, Int. 8 Nov. 1764, Boston (Rcd.Com.30:423)

Elizabeth J. WINSLOW and James F. TROTT, 22 Sept. 1808, Boston (Rcd.Com.30:276)

Mrs. Hannah WINSLOW and David JEFFRIES, Int. 25 July 1768, Boston (Rcd.Com.30:428)

Mrs. Lucy WINSLOW and George ERVING, Int. 19 Sept. 1768, Boston (Rcd.Com.30:428)

Hannah WINSLOW and Lewis HAMLIN, Int. 14 Sept. 1808, Boston (Rcd.Com.30:500)

Isaac WINSLOW Jr. and Mary DAVIS, 20 Apr. 1772, Boston (Rcd.Com.30:64)

Isaac WINSLOW and Mary RUSSELL, 11 May 1788, Boston (Rcd.Com.30:132)

Isaac WINSLOW Jr. and Margaret BLANCHARD, 24 Feb. 1801, Boston (Rcd.Com.30:172)

John WINSLOW Jr. and Sally BRAY, 27 Nov. 1808, Boston (Rcd.Com.30:278)

John WINSLOW and Mrs. Sarah TYNG, 4 Sept. 1760, Boston (Rcd.Com.30:291)

John WINSLOW and Elizabeth CREST, Int. 5 July 1766, Boston (Rcd.Com.30:425)

John WINSLOW Jr. and Mrs. Mary SIMPSON, Int. 25 June 1767, Boston (Rcd.Com.30:426)

John WINSLOW and Elizabeth BASS, Int. 25 Mar. 1771, Boston (Rcd.Com.30:430)

John WINSLOW and Fanny ODEN, Int. 8 Oct. 1783, Boston (Rcd.Com.30:452)

Joshua WINSLOW and Mrs. Anna GREEN, 3 Jan. 1758, Boston (Rcd.Com.30:326)

Joshua WINSLOW and Anna PERKINS, 19 Sept. 1771, Boston (Rcd.Com.30:330)

Joshua WINSLOW Jr. and Hannah LORING, 26 Dec. 1763, Boston (Rcd.Com.30:398)

Joshua WINSLOW and Sarah SHERBURNE, Int. 5 Aug. 1779, Boston (Rcd.Com.30:444)

Lidia WINSLOW and John MONGOMRY, 6 Feb. 1770, Boston (Rcd.Com.30:349)

Lucy WINSLOW and Thomas ALLINE/ALLEN, 27 Nov. 1808, Boston (Rcd.Com.30:230)

Maria WINSLOW and Nicholas BENEDICT, 15 Jan. 1801, Boston (Rcd.Com.30:169)

Maria WINSLOW and Thomas DISMORE, 20 Mar. 1804, Boston (Rcd.Com.30:180)

Maria WINSLOW and Isaac CALL, Int. 5 Aug. 1800, Boston (Rcd.Com.30:474)

Maria WINSLOW and Elijah KNIGHT, Int. 18 Nov. 1800, Boston (Rcd.Com.30:475)

Mary WINSLOW and Joseph DELGADO, 22 Nov. 1802, Boston (Rcd.Com.30:179)

Mary WINSLOW and Nathaniel BARBER, Int. 19 Dec. 1776, Boston (Rcd.Com.30:438)

Naomi WINSLOW and John DYER, 17 Apr. 1791, Boston (Rcd.Com.30:115)

Peggy (negro servant of Nathaniel Winslow), 8 Oct. 1761, Boston (Rcd.Com.30:379)

Nicholas WINSLOW and Elizabeth THOMAS, 26 Dec. 1773, Boston (Rcd.Com.30:110)

Sally WINSLOW and Samuel COVERLY, 27 Nov. 1787, Boston (Rcd.Com.30:161)

Sally WINSLOW and Otis GAY, 25 May 1806, Boston (Rcd.Com.30:247)

Samuel WINSLOW and Abigail ORCUT, 28 Mar. 1789, Boston (Rcd.Com.30:112)

Samuel WINSLOW and Martha SCOTT, 3 Sept. 1781, Boston (Rcd.Com.30:409)

Sarah WINSLOW and John BRADSHAW, Int. 8 July 1779, Boston (Rcd.Com.30:444)

Sarah (TYNG) Winslow and Samuel WALDO, Feb. 1789, Boston (Rcd.Com.30:343) [2]

Edward WINSLOW^4 (Edw.^{3}) and 1st Hannah MOODY, c1692 (Boston Rcd.Com.9:208)

Edward WINSLOW^4 and 2nd Elizabeth (DIXIE) Pemberton, 22 May 1712 (Boston Rcd.
    Com.28:43)

Edward WINSLOW^4 and 3rd Susanna (FARNUM) Lyman, 27 Mar. 1744 (Boston Rcd.Com.28:267)

Susanna FARNUM and Caleb LIMAN, 27 Sept. 1709 (Boston Rcd.Com.28:24)

Brimus and Floro (negro servants of Caleb Lyman), 9 Feb. 1720 (Boston Rcd.Com.28:89)

Edward WINSLOW^5 (Edw.^{4}) and Hannah SAVAGE, 1 Dec. 1726 (Boston Rcd.Com.28:158)

Elizabeth WINSLOW^5 (Edw.^{4}) and Richard CLARKE, 3 May 1733 (Boston Rcd.Com.28:181)

Susanna Farnum CLARKE^6 (Eliz.^{5}) and John Singleton COPLEY, 16 Nov. 1769, Boston
    (NEHGR 18:226)

Hannah WINSLOW^5 (Edw.^{4}) and William DAVIS, 26 Jan. 1715 (Boston VR)

Isaac WINSLOW^5 (Edw.^{4}) and 1st Lucy WALDO, 14 Dec. 1747 (Boston Rcd.Com.28:267)

Isaac WINSLOW^5 and 2nd Jemima DEBUKE, 25 Nov. 1770 (Boston Rcd.Com.30:330)

Hannah WINSLOW^6 (Isaac^5) and John WALL

Lucy WINSLOW^6 (Isaac^5) and George ERVING, Int. 19 Sept. 1768, Boston (Rcd.Com.30:428)

Joshua WINSLOW^5 (Edw.^{4}) and Elizabeth SAVAGE, 8 Feb. 1720 (Boston Rec.Com.28:90)

Margaret SAVAGE and John ALFORD

Mary WINSLOW^6 (Joshua^5) and Nathaniel BARBER, 2 Jan. 1777, Boston (NEHGR 22:463)

Rev.Edward WINSLOW^6 (Joshua^5) and Jane Isabella ALLEYNE, 16 July 1745, Barbados
    (Bible)

Mary WINSLOW^7 (Edw.^{6}) and James WYATT, 1783

Elizabeth WINSLOW^6 (Joshua^5) and John WINNIET, 15 Sept. 1746 (Boston Rcd.Com.28:267)

Hannah WINSLOW^6 (Joshua^5) and David JEFFRIES, Int. 25 July 1768, Boston (Rcd.
    Com.30:428)

Isaac WINSLOW^6 (Joshua^5) and 1st Margaret SPARHAWK

Isaac WINSLOW^6 and 2nd Mary DAVIS, 20 Apr. 1772 (Boston Rcd.Com.30:64)

Micro #2 of 7

Isaac WINSLOW^7 (Isaac^6) and 1st Margaret BLANCHARD

Joshua WINSLOW^7 (Isaac^6) and Sarah STARK

Katharine WINSLOW^6 (Joshua^5) and Francis MALBONE

Margaret WINSLOW^6 (Joshua^5) and Benjamin POLLARD, 14 Aug. 1746 (Boston Rcd. Com.28:258)

Samuel WINSLOW^5 (Edw.^{4}) and Rebecca CLARKE, 8 June 1729 (Boston Rcd.Com.28:152)

Rebecca CLARKE and 2nd William LEE, 24 Aug. 1749 (Boston Rcd.Com.28:252)

Rebecca WINSLOW^6 (Sam.^{5}) and John WILLIAMS, 3 Jan. 1771

Rebecca WILLIAMS^7 (Rebecca Winslow^6) and Stephen CHILDS

William WINSLOW^5 (Edw.^{4}) and Elizabeth CLARKE, 11 Dec. 1735 (Boston Rcd.Com.28:194)

Samuel HINCKS^5 (Eliz. Winslow^4, Edw.^{3}) and Susanna DYER, 10 Nov. 1755 (Truro VR:56)

Elizabeth WINSLOW^4 (Edw.^{3}) and 1st Joseph SCOTT, 18 Jan. 1693 (Boston Rcd.Com.9:210)

Elizabeth WINSLOW^4 and 2nd Samuel HINCKES, pre 1715 (NEHGR 29:315)

Jesse Young HINCKS^6 (Sam.^{5}) and Ruth P. RICH, 4 Apr. 1795

Mary HINKS^7 (Jesse^6) and Joshua NYE, 22 Jan. 1817 (Bible)

Ruth HINKS^7 (Jesse^6) and Sturgis NYE, 1 Nov. 1820 (Bible)

Eliza P. HINKS^7 (Jesse^6) and Walter GOODALE, 6 Mar. 1827 (Bible)

Rebeckah R. HINKS^7 (Jesse^6) and Nehemiah NICKERSON Jr., 31 Oct. 1827 (Bible)

Jesse HINKS^7 (Jesse^6) and Eliza ELDRIDGE, 6 Nov. 1827 (Bible)

Betsey HINKS^7 (Jesse^6) and Eli N. CROCKETT, 20 Jan. 1836 (Bible)

Reuben G. HINKS^7 (Jesse^6) and Eliva WARE, 15 Feb. 1837 (Bible)

John W. HINKS^7 (Jesse^6) and Sarah Ann BLODGET, 23 Aug. 1839 (Bible)

Hannah Jane HINKS^7 (Jesse^6) and William W. FRENCH, June 1852 (Bible)

Winslow HINCKS^6 (Sam.^{5}) and Thomasin COLLINGS, 15 June 1790 (Truro VR:149)

Samuel WINSLOW^3 and Hannah BRIGGS, pre 14 Feb. 1673 (Suffolk Co.Deeds 8:408)

Hannah BRIGGS and 2nd Thomas JOLLS, pre 31 Mar. 1697 (MD 10:56)

William TAYLOR^5 (Ann Winslow^4, Edw.^{3}) and 1st Faith WINSLOW^5 (Abigail Waterman^4, Sarah Snow^3, Abigail Warren^2)

William TAYLOR^5 and 2nd Sarah SAVAGE

Rebecca TAYLOR and Edward EMERSON, 2 Oct. 1744 (Milton VR)

Dorothy TAYLOR and Peter GILMAN, 1751 (Milton VR)

William TAYLOR and Polly HENSHAW, 22 May 1799 (Milton VR)

Col. William TAYLOR and Sarah TAYLOR, 19 May 1766 (Milton VR)

William TAYLOR and Sarah THOMAS, 1 Sept. 1768 (Milton VR)

Ann WINSLOW^4 (Edw.^{3}) and 1st John TAYLOR, 5 Nov. 1702, Boston (MD 1:90)

Ann WINSLOW^4 and 2nd Kenelm WINSLOW, 7 Sept. 1730, Boston (Rcd.Com.28:157)

Rebecca TAYLOR^5 (Ann Winslow^4) and Edward/Moses EMERSON, 2 Oct. 1744

Elizabeth TAYLOR^5 (Ann Winslow^4) and 1st Nathaniel GREENE, 27 June 1729, Boston
    (Rcd.Com.28:149)

Elizabeth TAYLOR^5 and 2nd Rev. Peter COFFIN, 7 July 1759 (MD 32:)

Rev. Peter COFFIN and 1st Dorothy GOOKIN, 20 Jan. 1740

Nathaniel GREENE^6 (Eliz. Taylor^5) and Annapel HENDERSON, 20 Sept. 1759, Boston
    (Rcd.Com.30:378)

John HENDERSON and Rachel CRANMER, 8 Jan. 1718 (Boston Rcd.Com.28:76)

John GREENE^6 (Elizabeth Taylor^5) and Aznbah WARD, 26 Dec. 1758, Worcester (Ward
    Family <1851>p.42,76-77)

Rev. John TAYLOR^5 (Ann Winslow^4) and 1st Elizabeth ROGERS, 9 Apr. 1730

Rev. John TAYLOR^5 and 2nd Dorothy (SHERBURNE)(Pymes) Rogers (Hist.Milton:256)

Dorothy (SHERBURNE)(Pymes) Rogers and 4th Peter GILMAN

Isaac WINSLOW^3 and Mary NOWELL, 14 Aug. 1666 (Savage 4:600)

Mary NOWELL and 2nd John LONG,10 Sept. 1674

Parnel WINSLOW^4 (Isaac^3) and Richard FOSTER, 4 May 1686 (Gen.Reg.25:69)

Elizabeth FOSTER^5 (Parnel Winslow^4) and Timothy McDANIEL

Mary FOSTER^5 (Parnel Winslow^4) and Samuel CARY

Parnel FOSTER^5 (Parnel Winslow^4) and John CODMAN

Anne FOSTER^5 (Parnel Winslow^4) and Rev. Daniel PERKINS, 6 Nov. 1721

Rev. Daniel PERKINS and 2nd Mary (HAWKE) (Thaxter) Hancock

Isaac FOSTER^5 (Parnel Winslow^4) and Eleanor WYER, (32?) Aug. 1732

Isaac FOSTER^6 (Isaac^5) and 1st Martha MASON, c1765

Isaac FOSTER^6 and 2nd Mary RUSSELL, aft. Sept. 1770

Mary RUSSELL and 2nd John HURD, 8 June 1783

Richard FOSTER^5 (Parnel Winslow^4) and 1st Sarah EMERSON, c1717

Richard FOSTER^5 and 2nd Mary FOYE, 21 Oct. 1725

Sarah FOSTER^5 (Parnel Winslow^4) and Dr. Peter CALEF

John WINSLOW^4 (John^3) and Abigail ATKINSON, c1692 (Boston Rcd.Com.9:208)

Abigail ATKINSON and 2nd Dr. James OSBORN

Abigail ATKINSON and 3rd Samuel PENHALLOW, 8 Sept. 1714 (Gen.Reg.32:31)

Micro #3 of 7

Elizabeth WINSLOW^5 (John^4) and Alexander TODD, pre 12 Oct. 1719 (Suffolk Deeds 34:268)

Joseph WINSLOW^3 and Sarah LAWRENCE

Mary WINSLOW[3] and Edward GRAY, 16 Jan. 1650, Plymouth (MD 16:235)

Edward GRAY and 2nd Dorothy LETTICE, 12 Dec. 1665, Plymouth (MD 18:56)

Sarah GRAY[4] (Mary Winslow[3]) and Samuel LITTLE[3] (Anna Warren[2]), 18 May 1682, Marshfield (MD 4:126)

Edward GRAY and Susanna TURELL, 15 Apr. 1790[3]

Mary Ann GRAY and William A. FALES[3]

Jane Mimot FALES and George LAMB[3]

Mary Turell FALES and Dr. Thomas GRAY, 1832, Brunswick ME[3]

Mary Ann GRAY and Guy Byram SCHOTT[3]

Alice GRAY and Sidney K. RICHARDSON[3]

Caroline Fales GRAY and J.B.F. DAVIDGE[3]

T. Fales GRAY and Elleanor Thompson POWELL, 4 Feb. 1885[3]

Rev. Thomas GRAY and Deborah STILLMAN, 23 May 1793[3]

Anna GRAY[4] (Mary Winslow[3]) and James LEBLOND pre 1690

Desire GRAY[4] (Mary Winslow[3]) and Nathaniel SOUTHWORTH, 10 Jan. 1671, Plymouth (MD 18:68)

Elizabeth SOUTHWORTH[5] (Desire Gray[4]) and James SPROUT[3] (Eliz. Samson[2]), 5 June 1712, Scituate (MD 9:87)

Edward SOUTHWORTH[5] (Desire Gray[4]) and Bridget BOSWORTH, 25 June 1711 (Hull VR:43,56)

Bridget BOSWORTH and 2nd Capt. John PHILLIPS, 19 Apr. 1749 (Bridgewater VR)

Bridget SOUTHWORTH[6] (Edw.[5]) and Thomas COLLIER, 20 Apr. 1734 (Hull VR:44,56)

Jerome WHEELOCK and Lydia Ann ROBINSON, 8 June 1858, Sudbury (Mass.VR 118:174)

Constant SOUTHWORTH[6] (Edw.[5]) and Martha KEITH, 18 Apr. 1734, Bridgewater (MD 16:100)

Ichabod SOUTHWORTH[5] (Desire Gray[4]) and Esther HODGES, c1706 (MD 3:24,8:28)

William SOUTHWORTH[6] (Ichabod[5]) and Bathsheba SMITH, 21 Dec. 1749, Middleboro (MD 18:83)

Bathsheba SMITH and 2nd Samuel RUGGLES, 26 May 1762, Middleboro (MD 19:174)

Desire SOUTHWORTH[6] (Ichabod[5]) and Samuel SHAW, 21 Apr. 1731, Middleboro (MD 9:47)

Nathaniel THOMAS and Jane JACKSON, 1 July 1796, Plymouth (VR 2:291)

Nathaniel THOMAS and Priscilla SHAW, 9 Dec. 1781, Plymouth (VR 2:269)

Elijah SHAW[7] (Desire Southworth[6]) and Phebe SAMPSON

Ichabod SHAW[7] (Desire Southworth[6]) and Priscilla ATWOOD, c1757 (MD 18:215)

Priscilla SOUTHWORTH[6] (Ichabod[5]) and Nathaniel MACUMBER, 13 Nov. 1735, Middleboro (MD 13:251)

Mary SOUTHWORTH[5] (Desire Gray[4]) and Joseph RIDER, 10 Mar. 1706/07, Plymouth (MD 14:36)

Mary RIDER and Paul LEONARD, 11 Jan. 1759, Plymouth (Raynham VR)

Polly LEONARD and Isaac HALL, 3 May 1787 (Raynham VR)

Micro #4 of 7

Hannah RIDER^6 (Mary Southworth^5) and John COOPER, 8 Dec. 1737, Plymouth (MD 14:158)

Richard COOPER^7 (Hannah Rider^6) and Hannah SAMSON^5 (Ebenezer^4, David^3, Caleb^2), 22 Jan. 1761 (Plymouth VR 2:256)

Calvin COOPER^8 (Richard^7) and Sarah MORTON

Sarah MORTON and 2nd Joseph ATKINS, 28 Apr. 1822, Plymouth (Old Colony Memorial, 4 May 1822)

Priscilla COOPER^8 (Richard^7) and 1st John VIRGIN

Priscilla COOPER^8 and 2nd Ezra WESTON, 4 July 1817, Bristol RI (MD 24:82)

Richard COOPER^8 (Richard^7) and Hannah SAMSON^6 (Zabdiel^5, Hannah Soule^4, Ben.^{3}, John^2), 7 Jan. 1784 (Plympton VR:286,380)

Jemima RIDER^6 (Mary Southworth^5) and Noah SAMSON^5 (Nathaniel^4, Lorah Standish^3, Alexander^2), c1734

Joseph RIDER^6 (Mary Southworth^5) and Elizabeth CROSSMAN, 17 May 1739, Taunton (VR 2:125,409)

Philippa RIDER^6 (Mary Southworth^5) and 1st Philip VINCENT, 9 Mar. 1743/44, Plymouth (MD 14:160)

Philippa RIDER^6 and 2nd Jonathan DEXTER, 1758, Yarmouth (Tho. Dexter Gen.<1905>:44)

Philippa RIDER^6 and 3rd David LORING, Int. 17 Dec. 1763, Barnstable (MD 19:127)

Benjamin DEXTER and Hannah BARROW, c1721

Jonathan DEXTER and 1st Hannah VINCENT

Nathaniel SOUTHWORTH^5 (Desire Gray^4) and Jael HOWLAND^3 (Isaac^2), c1709 (MD 2:107)

Fear SOUTHWORTH^6 (Nathaniel^5) and Joseph LEONARD, c1731 (MD 12:232)

Gideon SOUTHWORTH^6 (Nathaniel^5) and Rebecca ELLIS, 24 Dec. 1741, Middleboro (MD 15:218)

Hannah SOUTHWORTH^6 (Nathaniel^5) and Robert SPROUT^4 (James^3, Eliz. Samson^2), 10 Dec. 1741, Middleboro (MD 13:253)

Nathaniel SOUTHWORTH^6 (Nathaniel^5) and Susanna SMITH, 16 Feb. 1748, Middleboro (MD 18:81)

Samuel SOUTHWORTH^6 (Nathaniel^5) and Elizabeth CASWELL, 2 Jan. 1745/46, Middleboro (MD 16:20)

Elizabeth GRAY^4 (Mary Winslow^3) and Seth ARNOLD, c1679 (MD 2:249)

Desire ARNOLD^5 (Eliz. Gray^4) and Ichabod BARTLETT^4 (Ben.^{3}, Mary Warren^2), 14 Nov.

1709, Duxbury (MD 11:23)

Elizabeth ARNOLD[5] (Eliz. Gray[4]) and 1st Anthony WATERMAN[4] (Sarah Snow[3], Abigail
    Warren[2]), c1709 (MD 7:119)

Elizabeth ARNOLD[5] and 2nd Jonathan ALDEN[3] (Jonathan[2]), 17 Jan. 1717/18, Marshfield
    (MD 7:132)

Benjamin ARNOLD[5] (Eliz. Gray[4]) and Hannah BARTLETT[5] (Sam.[4], Ben.[3], Mary Warren[2]),
    8 Mar. 1713/14, Duxbury (MD 11:24)

Edward ARNOLD[5] (Eliz. Gray[4]) and Mercy BREWSTER[4] (Wm.[3], Love[2]), 8 Oct. 1706,
    Duxbury (MD 9:108)

Ezra ARNOLD[6] (Edw.[5]) and Rebecca SPRAGUE, 27 July 1732 (Duxbury VR)

James ARNOLD[5] (Eliz. Gray[4]) and Joanna SPRAGUE, 19 Feb. 1734/35, Duxbury (MD 11:241)

John GRAY[4] (Mary Winslow[3]) and Joanna MORTON, 9 Dec. 1686, Plymouth (MD 13:204)

Mercy GRAY[5] (John[4]) and Jabez FULLER[4] (Sam.[3-2]), Int. 13 Oct. 1733 (Kingston VR)

Jabez FULLER[4] and 1st Deborah SOULE[4] (Ben.[3], John[2])

Samuel GRAY[5] (John[4]) and Patience WADSWORTH, 7 Dec. 1727 (Duxbury VR)

John GRAY[6] (Sam.[5]) and Desire CUSHMAN[6] (Tho.[5], Robert[4], Tho.[3], Mary Allerton[2]),
    26 Jan. 1775 (Kingston VR)

Wait GRAY[6] (Sam.[5]) and Saba RIPLEY, 17 Dec. 1761 (Kingston ch.rcd.)

Saba RIPLEY and 2nd Zenas DREW, 15 Nov. 1764 (Kingston VR)

Mary GRAY[6] (Sam.[5]) and Benjamin COOKE[5] (Caleb[4], Francis[3], Jacob[2]), 2 Oct. 1754

Samuel GRAY[6] (Sam.[5]) and Eunice DELANO, Int. 11 Apr. 1761, Kingston

Sarah WINSLOW[3] and 1st Myles STANDISH[2], 19 July 1660, Boston (Rcd.Com.9:76)

Sarah WINSLOW[3] and 2nd Tobias PAYNE, Nov. 1666/67 (Paine Fam.1:46)

Sarah WINSLOW[3] and 3rd Richard MIDDLECOTT, 1672 (Payne Fam.)

Mary MIDDLECOTT[4] (Sarah Winslow[3]) and 1st Henry GIBBS (Savage 3:205)

Mary MIDDLECOTT[4] and 2nd Othniel HAGGETT (Savage 3:205)

Sarah MIDDLECOTT[4] (Sarah Winslow[3]) and Louis BOUCHER, 26 Mar. 1702 (Savage 3:205)

Jane MIDDLECOTT[4] (Sarah Winslow[3]) and Elisha COOKE Jr., 7 Jan. 1703 (Savage 3:205)

William PAYNE[4] (Sarah Winslow[3]) and 1st Mary TAYLOR, 11 Oct. 1694 (Boston VR)

William PAYNE[4] and 2nd Margaret STEWART, 12 May 1703

Rebecca PAYNE[6] (Edw.[5]) and Christopher GORE, 11 Nov 1783

William PAYNE[6] (Edw.[5]) and 1st Lucy (GRAY) Dobell, 26 June 1803

William PAYNE[6] and 2nd Catherine HALLETT, aft. Mar. 1809

Edward PAYNE[5] (Wm.[4]) and Rebecca AMORY, c1756

Margaret PAYNE[5] (Wm.[4]) and John PHILLIPS, 7 Oct. 1741

John PHILLIPS and 1st Sarah COOKE^5 (Jane Middlecott^4, Sarah Winslow^3, Mary Chilton^2)

Mary PAYNE^5 (Wm.^{4}) and Jonathan SEWALL, Oct. 1724

Sarah PAYNE^5 (Wm.^{4}) and John COLMAN, 26 Dec. 1734

Tobias PAYNE^5 (Wm.^{4}) and Sarah WINSLOW^5 (Abigail Waterman^4, Sarah Snow^3, Abigail Warren^2)

Sarah WINSLOW^5 and 2nd Samuel SMITH^5 (Sam.^{4}, Mary Hopkins^3, Gyles^2), 29 Dec. 1737, Eastham (MD 19:100)

Jane MIDDLECOTT^4 (Sarah Winslow^3) and Elisha COOKE, 7 Jan. 1702 (Boston Rcd. Com.28:3)

Jane COOK and John NEWPORT, Int. 7 Nov. 1750 (Boston Rcd.Com.28:295)

Mary COOKE^5 (Jane Middlecott^4) and Richard SALTONSTALL, 3 July 1744 (Bond's Watertown:927)

Sarah COOKE^5 (Jane Middlecott^4) and John PHILLIPS, May 1733

John PHILLIPS and 2nd Margaret PAYNE^5 (Wm.^{4}, Sarah Winslow^3, Mary Chilton^2), aft. July 1740

Mary MIDDLECOTT^4 (Sarah Winslow^3) and 1st Henry GIBBS, c1695 (Boston Rcd.Com.9:227)

Mary MIDDLECOTT^4 and 2nd Othniel HAGGET, 1702

Sarah MIDDLECOTT^4 (Sarah Winslow^3) and Louis BOUCHER, c1702

Ann BOUCHER^5 (Sarah Middlecott^4) and Nathaniel CUNNINGHAM, 27 Aug. 1722 (Boston Rcd.Com.28:105)

Nathaniel CUNNINGHAM and 2nd Susanna GERRISH, 28 Dec. 1738, Boston (Rcd.Com.28:330)

Ruth CUNNINGHAM^6 (Ann Boucher^5) and James OTIS^5 (Mary Allyn^4, Mary Doty^3, Edw.^{2}), 18 Mar. 1755 (Boston Rcd.Com.30:14)

Sarah BOUCHER^5 (Sarah Middlecott^4) and John FOYE, Oct. 1729

Ann FOYE^6 (Sarah Boucher^5) and Francis DISER, 28 Mar. 1759, Charlestown

John Foye DISER^7 (Ann Foye^6) and Anna SWAN^7 (Joshua^6, Ebenezer$^{5-4}$, Mary Pratt^3, Mary Priest^2)

Elizabeth FOYE^6 (Sarah Boucher^5) and David MUNROE, 17 Oct. 1765, Charlestown

Susanna WINSLOW^3 and Robert LATHAM, c1649 (MD16:235)

Arthur LATHAM and Allice ALLEN, 1 Feb. 1732/33 (Bridgewater VR 2:225)

Thomas LATHAM and Deborah HARDIN, 19 Mar. 1711/12 (Bridgewater VR 2:254)

Susanna LATHAM and Nathaniel HARDEN, 17 Feb. 1714/15 (Bridgewater VR 2:279/255)

Anne LATHAM and Nicholas WADE, 17 Feb. 1714/15 (Bridgewater VR 2:279/255)

Joseph LATHAM and Sarah HAYWARD, 27 Nov. 1717 (Bridgewater VR 2:280/256)

Hannah LATHAM and Josiah HATHAWAY Jr., 4 Dec. 1766 (Bridgewater VR 3:152)

Robert LATHAM and Jerusha HOOPER, 18 Nov. 1778 (Bridgewater VR 3:158)

Levi LATHAM and Hannah ALDEN, 30 July 1782 (Bridgewater VR 3:162)

Alice LATHAM and Matthew GANNETT, 20 Mar. 1783 (Bridgewater VR 3:163)

Ann LATHAM and Seth MITCHELL, 21 Dec. 1738 (Bridgewater VR 3:167)

Alice ( ) LATHAM and Jonathan ALLEN, 27 Mar. 1739 (Bridgewater VR 3:167)

Deliverance LATHAM and Daniel HOWELL, 18 Jan. 1743 (Bridgewater VR 3:169)

Mary LATHAM and Jonathan ALLEN, 3 June 1742 (Bridgewater VR 3:169)

Betty LATHAM and Joseph GANNET, 7 June 1744 (Bridgewater VR 3:171)

Rhoda LATHAM and David CONNANT, 29 Jan. 1748 (Bridgewater VR 3:172)

Joseph LATHAM Jr. and Mary PRYER, 27 Jan. 1747/48 (Bridgewater VR 3:173)

Robert LATHAM and Mary JOHNSON, 12 June 1751 (Bridgewater VR 3:177)

Thomas LATHAM and Abigail HAMNER, 8 June 1752 (Bridgewater VR 3:177)

Beriah LATHAM and Israel HILL, 27 June 1748 (Bridgewater VR 3:179)

Nathaniel LATHAM and Mercy LEACH, 11 Mar. 1756 (Bridgewater VR 3:180)

Nehemiah LATHAM and Lucy HARRIS, 26 May 1757 (Bridgewater VR 3:180)

Mary LATHAM and Benjamin WHITMAN, 3 Feb. 1757 (Bridgewater VR 3:180)

Jane LATHAM and Jonathan CONANT, 12 June 1759 (Bridgewater VR 3:182)

Jane LATHAM and Edward MITCHELL Jr., 30 Sept. 1762 (Bridgewater VR 3:187)

Arthur LATHAM and Margaret BEARSE, 17 Oct. 1765 (Bridgewater VR 3:187)

Mary LATHAM and William BRITTON Jr., 5 June 1766 (Bridgewater VR 3:187)

Susanna LATHAM and Seth BRETT Jr., (15?) Nov. 1768 (Bridgewater VR 3:190)

Chilton LATHAM and Mary HOWARD, 16 Aug. 1770 (Bridgewater VR 3:191)

Robert LATHAM and Bithia ( ) HARRIS, Int. 31 Mar. 1753 (Bridgewater VR 3:320)

Seth LATHAM and Rachel HOUSE, Int. 30 Apr. 1763 (Bridgewater VR 3:324)

Woodward LATHAM and Rebecca DEAN, Int. 13 June 1763 (Bridgewater VR 3:324)

James LATHAM and Esther BAKER, Int. 27 May 1769 (Bridgewater VR 3:331)

Lucenda LATHAM and Joshua POOL, Int. 11 July 1783 (Bridgewater VR 3:454)

Elizabeth LATHAM^4 (Susanna Winslow^3) and Francis COOKE^3 (Jacob^2), 2 Aug. 1687,
    Plymouth (MD 13:204)

Hannah LATHAM^4 (Susanna Winslow^3) and Joseph WASHBURN^4 (Eliz. Mitchell^3, Jane Cooke^2)

Chilton LATHAM^4 (Susanna Winslow^3) and Susanna KINGMAN, 6 Dec. 1699, Bridgewater
    (MD 2:146)

Arthur LATHAM^5 (Chilton^4) and 1st Alice ALLEN, 1 Feb. 1732/33, Bridgewater (MD 16:99)

Alice ALLEN and 2nd Jonathan ALLEN, 27 Mar. 1739 (Bridgewater VR 3:169)

Jane LATHAM^6 (Arthur^5) and Jonathan CONANT (see above)

Nehemiah LATHAM^6 (Arthur^5) and 1st Lucy HARRIS^7 (Arthur^6, Isaac^5, Mercy Latham^4,

Susanna Winslow^3, Mary Chilton^2), 26 May 1757 (Bridgewater VR 3:180)

Nehemiah LATHAM^6 (Arthur^5) and 2nd Hannah (PRATT) Allen, 6 Oct. 1801

Alice LATHAM^7 (Nehemiah^6) and Matthew GANNETT (see p.107)

Charles LATHAM^5 (Chilton^4) and Susanna WOODWARD, c1724 (Bridgewater VR 3:348)

Betty LATHAM^6 (Charles^5) and Joseph GANNETT (see p.107)

Chilton LATHAM^6 (Charles^5) and Mary HOWARD (see p.107)

Jane LATHAM^6 (Charles^5) and Edward MITCHELL^5 (Edw.$^{4-3}$, Experience) (see p.107,152)

Mary LATHAM^6 (Charles^5) and Benjamin WHITMAN (see p.107)

Woodward LATHAM^6 (Charles^5) and Rebecca DEAN (see p.107)

Barzillai LATHAM^7 (Woodward^6) and Mary WASHBURN^7 (Ben.$^{6-5}$, Jonathan^4, Eliz. Mitchell^3, Jane Cooke^2), 30 Nov. 1801 (Int.- Bridgewater VR 2:277,390)

Elias LATHAM^7 (Woodward^6) and Lucy LATHAM^7 (Nehemiah^6, Arthur^5, Chilton^4, Susanna Winslow^3, Mary Chilton^2)

Galen LATHAM^7 (Woodward^6) and Susanna KEITH

James LATHAM^5 (Chilton^4) and Abigail HARVEY, c1739 (Bridgewater VR 3:266)

Arthur LATHAM^6 (James^5) and Margaret BEARSE (see p.107)

Mary LATHAM^6 (James^5) and William BRITTON (see p.107)

Susanna LATHAM^6 (James^5) and Seth BRETT (see p.107)

Mary LATHAM^5 (Chilton^4) and Jonathan ALLEN (see p.107)

Robert LATHAM^5 (Chilton^4) and Mary JOHNSON (see p.107)

Robert LATHAM and Bethiah ( ) HARRIS, 17 Apr. 1753 (Bridgewater VR 3:177)

James LATHAM^4 (Susanna Winslow^3) and Deliverance ALGER

Anne LATHAM^5 (James^4) and Nicholas WADE (see p.106)

Amasa WADE^6 (Anne Latham^5) and Sarah LOUD^6 (Onner Prince^5, Mary Turner^4, Mary Brewster^3, Jonathan^2), 24 July 1755 (Weymouth VR 2:?)

Amasa WADE^7 (Amasa^6) and Mary TIRRELL, 16 Sept. 1790 (Weymouth VR 2:192,205)

Nabby WADE^7 (Amasa^6) and Asa COPELAND, 4 Sept. 1783 (Weymouth VR 2:205,53)

Polly WADE^7 (Amasa^6) and Job THAYER, 28 Apr. 1785 (Weymouth VR 2:205,184)

Lot WADE^7 (Amasa^6) and Naomi THAYER, Int. 13 Nov. 1790 (Weymouth VR 2:205,185)

Hannah WADE^7 (Amasa^6) and Asa FRENCH, 26 July 1781 (Weymouth VR 2:205,73)

Thomas WADE^7 (Amasa^6) and Mary AYERS, 29 Sept. 1785 (Weymouth VR 2:205,14)

Bettie LATHAM^5 (James^4) and Daniel JOHNSON, c1726 (MD 15:89)

Joseph LATHAM^5 (James^4) and Sarah HAYWARD (see p.106)

Joseph LATHAM^6 (Joseph^5) and Mary PRYER (see p.107)

James LATHAM^7 (Joseph^6) and Esther BAKER (see p.107)

Hannah LATHAM[7] (Joseph[6]) and Josiah HATHAWAY (see p.106)

Nathaniel LATHAM[6] (Joseph[5]) and Mercy LEACH, 11 Mar. 1756 (Bridgewater VR 3:180)

Levi LATHAM[7] (Nathaniel[6]) and Hannah ALDEN (see p.107)

Seth LATHAM[6] (Joseph[5]) and 1st Rachel HOUSE (see p.107)

Seth LATHAM[6] and 2nd Elizabeth ( ) HAWKS, 1800

Susanna LATHAM[5] (James[4]) and Nathaniel HARDEN (see p.106)

Thomas LATHAM[5] (James[4]) and Deborah HARDIN (see p.106)

Deliverance LATHAM[6] (Thomas[5]) and Daniel HOWELL (see p.107)

Beriah LATHAM[6] (Thomas[5]) and Israel HILL (see p.107)

Ann LATHAM[6] (Thomas[5]) and Seth MITCHELL[5] (Thomas[4], Jacob[3], Experience[2]) (see p.107)

Rhoda LATHAM[6] (Thomas[5]) and David CONANT (see p.107)

Joseph LATHAM[4] (Susanna Winslow[3]) and Phebe TURNER, pre 28 Feb. 1688/89

Mercy LATHAM[4] (Susanna Winslow[3]) and Isaac HARRIS, pre 29 Oct. 1668 (C.O.5:14,23)

Isaac HARRIS and 2nd Mary DUNBAR, 28 June 1698 (Hingham VR 1:109)

Samuel HARRIS and Mary COOK, 1755 (Hist. Annapolis Co., N.S.:523)

Samuel HARRIS and Abigail HARDEN, 1710 (Hist. Annapolis Co., N.S.:523)

Desire HARRIS[5] (Mercy Latham[4]) and John KINGMAN, c1689 (MD 5:249)

John KINGMAN and 2nd Bethiah NEWCOMB, 1 Dec. 1698 (MD 2:146)

Micro #6 of 7

Deliverance KINGMAN[6] (Desire Harris[5]) and Ebenezer ORCUTT, 22 Apr. 1725 (Bridgewater VR 2:222,269)

Micah ORCUTT[7] (Deliverance Kingman[6]) and Ann PHILLIPS, c1754

Anna ORCUTT[8] (Micah[7]) and 1st John HEWES, Int. 13 Mar. 1773, Boston (MD 8:104)

Anna ORCUTT[8] and 2nd Charles WILLIS, 23 Nov. 1779, Boston (MD 8:104)

Nathaniel Phillips HEWES[9] (Anna Orcutt[8]) and Sally EATON, 7 Feb. 1794 (Boston
Rcd.Com.30:131)

Charles WILLIS Jr.[9] (Anna Orcutt[8]) and Eliza EATON, 22 Apr. 1809 (Morse's Gen.
Reg.2:210-213)

Nancy WILLIS[9] (Anna Orcutt[8]) and Larkin SNOW[7] (Elisha[6], Isaac[5], John[4-3], Constance
Hopkins[2]), 24 Oct. 1802 (Boston Rcd.Com.30:204)

Sally Belknap WILLIS[9] (Anna Orcutt[8]) and John Phillips ORCUTT, 20 Nov. 1806 Boston
Rcd.Com.30:199)

Desire KINGMAN[6] (Desire Harris[5]) and John ORCUTT, 27 June 1721

Isaac COPELAND[7] (Mary Kingman[6], Desire Harris[5]) and Lydia THAYER, 15 Jan. 1745/46,
Braintree

Samuel COPELAND^8 (Isaac^7) and Ruth WHITMARSH, 11 Dec. 1783 (Braintree VR:868)

Nancy COPELAND^9 (Sam.^{8}) and Hezekiah ADAMS, 18 Nov. 1811

Mary KINGMAN^6 (Desire Harris^5) and Samuel COPELAND, c1710 (Braintree VR:691)

Samuel COPELAND^7 (Mary Kingman^6) and Mary OWEN, 2 Apr. 1736 (Braintree VR:752)

Isaac HARRIS^5 (Mercy Latham^4) and 1st Jane COOKE^4 (Caleb^3, Jacob^2), 27 Mar. 1707,
    Scituate (MD 5:116)

Isaac HARRIS^5 and 2nd Elizabeth (SHAW) Washburn, 22 July 1717, Bridgewater (MD 16:190)

Jane HARRIS^5 (Mercy Latham^4) and 1st James DUNBAR, c1688 (MD 2:243)

Jane HARRIS^5 and 2nd Pelatiah SMITH, c1691 (MD 2:243)

Smith THAYER and Abigail DRAKE, 14 Sept. 1793$^{<4>}$

Stephen THAYER and Johannah POND, 2 Feb. 1826$^{<4>}$

Joab POND and 1st Joanna PERRY, 9 Dec. 1779$^{<5>}$

Joab POND and 2nd Mary BALCH, 5 Nov. 1807$^{<5>}$

Samuel SMITH^6 (Jane Harris^5) and 2nd Agnes HENDERSON, 14 May 1724

Samuel SMITH^6 and 3rd Sarah CLARK, 9 Dec. 1725

Levina (COOK) Smith and Ezekiel BATES, 25 Apr. 1799

Rhoda BATES and Silas KENNEY, 6 Dec. 1824, Bellingham

Cyrus KENNEY and Lydia T. THOMPSON, 24 June 1823

Pelatiah SMITH^9 (Robert^8, Pelatiah^7, Sam.^{6}) and Joanna THAYER, Int. 6 Nov. 1796,
    Bellingham

Joanna SMITH^{10} (Pelatiah^9) and Jefferson B. DARLING, 1823

Levina Bates SMITH^{10} (Pelatiah^9) and Lyman A. COOK, 1830

Margaret SMITH^{10} (Pelatiah^9) and Samuel DARLING Jr., 1815

Milatiah Wales SMITH^{10} (Pelatiah^9) and Ebenezer H. FISHER, 1839

Olive Abigail SMITH^{10} (Pelatiah^9) and David H. BENEDICT, 1839

Pelatiah SMITH^{10} (Pelatiah^9) and Julia BATES, 1827

Ruth Alden SMITH^{10} (Pelatiah^9) and Thomas S. BENEDICT, 1835

Zilpha Thayer SMITH^{10} (Pelatiah^9) and Christopher C. DANIELL, 1831

Sarah SMITH^6 (Jane Harris^5) and Thomas BURCH, c1717/18 (Billingham VR)

Mary HARRIS^5 (Mercy Latham^4) and Daniel PACKARD, 2 Dec. 1713, Bridgewater (MD 16:189)

Sarah PACKARD^6 (Mary Harris^5) and Zachariah SHAW, 30 Aug. 1733

Judith SHAW^7 (Sarah Packard^6) and John EDSON, 3 May 1770, Bridgewater

Mary EDSON^8 (Judith Shaw^7) and John BISBEE

Sarah EDSON^8 (Judith Shaw^7) and 1st Paul HAMMOND, 9 Apr. 1795 (Rochester VR 2:121,156)

Sarah EDSON^8 and 2nd Jonathan RIDER, 21 Aug. 1796 (Rochester VR 2:157,257)

Sarah EDSON^8 and 3rd Joseph Bates SMITH, 20 Nov. 1800 (Rochester VR 2:258,280)

Jonathan RYDER and Almira Wheaton RICHMOND, 25 Jan. 1826 (Rochester VR 2:256,257)

Joseph Edson SMITH^9 (Sarah Edson^8) and Sarah Crandall SKIFFE, Int. 7 May 1830
    (Rochester VR 2:278,280)

Mercy HARRIS^5 (Mercy Latham^4) and Josiah SEARS

Mary PACKARD^6 (Mary Harris^5) and James ALLEN, 23 Nov. 1732 (Bridgewater VR)

Samuel HARRIS^5 (Mercy Latham^4) and Abigail HARDING, 10 Jan. 1709/10, Bridgewater
    (MD 16:103)

Abigail HARRIS^6 (Sam.^{5}) and Thomas DREW, 1739 (E. Bridgewater VR:217)

Seth HARRIS^6 (Sam.^{5}) and Abiah ALDEN, 1751 (E. Bridgewater VR:217)

Susanna HARRIS^6 (Sam.^{5}) and Joseph WILBOR, 1741 (E. Bridgewater VR:217)

Susanna HARRIS^5 (Mercy Latham^4) and Jeremiah NEWLAND, 7 Apr. 1696, Bridgewater
    (MD 3:9)

Sarah LATHAM^4 (Susanna Winslow^3) and John HOWARD

Edward HOWARD^5 (Sarah Latham^4) and Mary BYRAM, 7 Feb. 1710/11, Bridgewater
    (MD 16:104)

Mary HOWARD^6 (Edw.^{5}) and Henry HOWARD, c1732/33 (MD 15:200)

(The Peter Brown microfiche #5 contains 16 pages of data relating to the James
 Chilton family. The following marriages are taken from this fiche.)

Alice CHILTON and Stephen MORRIS, 21 June 1579, St. Paul's Church, Canterbury, Eng.

Annis CHILTON and Richard MILLER, 12 July 1584, St. Paul's, Canterbury, Eng.

Isabel CHILTON and Nicholas GRAUNT, 18 Jan. 1584, St. Paul's, Canterbury, Eng.

John CHILTON and Elizabeth BARNSLEY, 29 June 1602, St. Paul's, Canterbury, Eng.

Isaac CHILTON and Susanna (de la CLUSE) Bailey, Int. 6 May 1615 (Dexter)

Angelina CHILTON and Robert NELSON, 27 Aug. 1622 (Dexter)

Isabella CHILTON^2 (James^1)

Isabella CHILTON^2 and Roger CHANDLER, 21 July 1615, Leyden (NEHGR 44:314)

Mary BUNDEY and Andrew SMITH, 5 Jan. 1673 (PCR 8:58)

John BUNDEY and Ruth SURNEY, 9 Jan. 1676 (PCR 8:65)

NOTES

<1> p.97, NEHGR 10:239 shows 5th day 3rd mth. to be 5 May.

<2> p.100, Apparently Tyng was her middle name, not maiden name as given here. She is later identified as Sarah Tyng Winslow (Isaac[5]).

<3> p.103, Source: Raymond, M.D. Gray Genealogy. Tarrytown, N.Y. 1887 (p.195,197).

<4> p.110, Source: Chandler & Lee. History of New Ipswich NH (p.664).

<5> p.110, Source: Harris, E.D. Daniel Pond and His Descendants. 1873 (p.68-69)

FRANCIS COOKE DESCENDANTS

Francis COOKE[1] and Hester MAHIEU, 30 June 1603, Leyden (MD 8:48)

Ruhama COOKE and Robert SHATTUCK, 9 Sept. 1742, Plymouth (MD 14:160)

Damaris ( ) COOK and John DELANO, 15 Nov. 1749 (Gen.Adv.3:23)

Zibiah COOK and Joseph BISBE, 17 Apr. 1755 (Gen.Avd.3:25)

Abraham de MELAN and Catherine CHASTELET, 18 Feb. 1592/93

Alexandre WAUTIER and Magdelaine DESCHAMPS, 23 Nov. 1595

Gilles WILLAM and Debora le CLERC, 25 Sept. 1597

Arnold du FOREST and Judith DESCHAMPS, 20 Aug. 1598

Pierre POURTRAY(sp) and Geanne CORNAT, 16 Aug. 1606

Marie MAHIEU and Jaques VENIN(sp), 14 Oct. 1593

Anthoine MAHIEU and Marthe CONANT, 11 Nov. 1604

Marie MAHIEU and Marc de le MARLIERE, 8 July 1627

Mercy COOK and Jonathan KNAP, 13 Mar. 1760 (Norton VR:215,265)

Silas COOK and Elizabeth NIXON, 1 Apr. 1763, Shrewsbury (Norton VR:215,288)

Jonas COOK and Percis NEWTON, Int. 9 Dec. 1774, Norton (Shrewsbury VR:139,196)

Hester COOKE[2] (Francis[1])

Hester COOKE[2] and Richard WRIGHT, 1644, Plymouth (MD 13:86)

Caleb COOK Jr. and Sarah ADAMS, 11 Dec. 1753 (Gen.Adv.3:24)

Lydia COOK and 1st Elisha STETSON, 17 Dec. 1753 (Gen.Adv.3:24)

Lydia COOK and Ebenezer ADAMS, 3 Nov. 1766 (Gen.Adv.3:77)

Sarah COOKE and Periz RANDALL, 4 Nov. 1746 (Gen.Adv.3:22)

Sarah COOKE and Samuel KENT Jr., 28 Dec. 1752 (Gen.Adv.3:24)

Sarah COOKE and Gershom COBB, 19 Nov. 1766 (Gen.Adv.3:77)

Josiah COOKE and Lydia FAUNCE, 31 Mar. 1768 (Gen.Adv.3:77)

Esther WRIGHT and Daniel PRATT, 23 Jan. 1700 (Plymouth TR 1:133)

Daniel PRATT and Mary WASHBURN, 1 Oct. 1706 (Plymouth TR 1:135)

Esther WRIGHT[3] and Ephraim TINKHAM

Adam WRIGHT[3] and 1st Sarah SOULE[3] (John[2]) (MD 4:160)

Adam WRIGHT[3] and 2nd Mehitable BARROW, c1699 (MD 4:239)

Mehitable BARROW and 2nd John WASHBURN, 1744

Isaac WRIGHT and Mary COLE, c1718 (MD 5:209)

James WRIGHT^4 (Adam^3) and Elizabeth WATERMAN, 17 Nov. 1731, Plympton (MD 2:50)

Rachel WRIGHT^4 (Adam^3) and Ebenezer BARLOW, 18 Nov. 1719, Plympton (MD 2:50)

Sarah WRIGHT^4 (Adam^3) and Seth FULLER, 12 May 1720, Plympton (MD 3:91)[1]

Esther WRIGHT^4 and Daniel PRATT, 23 Jan. 1700/01

Daniel PRATT and 2nd Mary WASHBURN, c1706 (MD 5:183)

Esther PRATT^5 (Esther Wright^4) and John PRICE, Int. 9 Aug. 1728 (Plymouth TR 1:261)[2]

Sarah PRATT^5 (Esther Wright^4) and Joshua DUNHAM, Int. 16 Feb. 1722/23, Plymouth
    (Plymouth TR 1:265)

Isaac WRIGHT^5 (Isaac^4) and Faith CHANDLER

Joseph WRIGHT^5 (Isaac^4) and Sarah BREWSTER^5 (Joshua^4, Wm.^{3}, Love^2)

Rufus SAMPSON and Esther JORDAN, 26 June 1859, Plymouth (VR 5:22)

John WRIGHT^4 (Adam^3) and Mary LUCAS, 20 May 1708, Plympton (MD 3:165)

Esther WRIGHT^5 (John^4) and John HUNT, Int. 6 Apr. 1733, Plympton (VR:336,431)

John HUNT and Deborah SOULE^4 (Moses^3, John^2), 1 May 1746

Urania WRIGHT^6 (John^5) and Thomas SMITH^7 (Ruth Mayo^6, Israel^5, Tho.^{4}, Hannah
    Prence^3, Patience Brewster^2), 20 Mar. 1766

John WRIGHT^5 (John^4) and Mary COOMER, Int. 31 July 1736, Plympton (VR:295,432)

Adam WRIGHT^5 (John^4) and 1st Ruth SAMSON, 28 Feb. 1754, Plympton

Adam WRIGHT^5 and 2nd Sarah (STANDISH^5) Tinkham (Moses^4, Ebenezer^3, Alexander^2),
    1 June 1773 (Plympton VR:231)

Lydia WRIGHT^6 (Adam^5) and Daniel THRASHER, Int. 26 Sept. 1778, Plymouth (MD 28:35)

Benjamin WRIGHT^6 (Adam^5) and Sarah CROCKER, c1798

Asa WRIGHT^7 (Ben.^{6}, Adam^5) and 1st Mary CROCKER, Int. 8 Feb. 1828, Barnstable
    (VR 6:107)

Capt. Asa WRIGHT^7 and 2nd Hodiah J. CROCKER, 24 Dec. 1836, Barnstable
    (VR 6:170)

Esther WRIGHT^6 (Adam^5) and Asa HOOPER, c1773   (Plympton VR:120)

Levi WRIGHT^6 (Adam^5) and Betty WEST^7 (Sam.^{6}, Bethiah Keen^5, Josiah^4, Abigail Little^3,
    Anna Warren^2), 15 June 1779 (Plympton VR:422,432)

Levi WRIGHT^6 and 2nd Mercy ( ) TINKHAM, Int. 4 Mar. 1821, Plympton (VR:433)

Mary WRIGHT^4 (Adam^3) and Jeremiah GIFFORD, c1703

Elizabeth GIFFORD^5 (Mary Wright^4) and Jonathan SOULE^4 (Nathaniel$^{3-2}$)

Adam GIFFORD^5 (Mary Wright^4) and Ann FISH

David GIFFORD^5 (Mary Wright^4) and Deborah HART

Isaac GIFFORD^5 (Mary Wright^4) and Mary CORNELL(?)

Joseph GIFFORD^5 (Mary Wright^4) and Mary BRAYTON

Margaret GIFFORD^5 (Mary Wright^4) and John POTTER

Peleg GIFFORD^5 (Mary Wright^4) and Alice CORNELL, 19 Feb. 1740 (Cornell Fam.:41)

William CORNELL and Mehitable FISH, c1710 (Dartmouth VR 1:63)

Micro #3 of 30

Benjamin GIFFORD^5 (Mary Wright^4) and 1st Elizabeth PETTIS, 3 May 1739, Portsmouth
    RI (VR 4:1:24,35)

Benjamin GIFFORD^5 and 2nd Alice (FISH) Springer, 28 Mar. 1779, Tiverton RI
    (VR 4:7:27,49)

Ichabod GIFFORD^6 (Ben.^{5}) and Sarah PETTEY, 25 Dec. 1766, Dartmouth (VR 2:?)

Jeremiah GIFFORD^7 (Ichabod^6) and Judith REED, 21 Aug. 1794 (Dartmouth VR 3:?)

Benjamin GIFFORD^6 (Ben.^{5}) and Rhoda POTTER, 3 July 1783, Dartmouth (Friends'
    Rcds.:550)

James GIFFORD and Anner READ, Int. 15 Aug. 1789 (Dartmouth TR)

John GIFFORD^6 (John^5, Mary Wright^4) and Isabel MILK, 18 Sept. 1777 (Dartmouth VR)

Recompense GIFFORD and Phebe GRINELL(sp), 11 Mar. 1808 (Dartmouth VR 3:?)

Dr. Thomas RICHMOND and Mary SHEARMAN, Int. 14 Dec. 1811, poss. Westport

Rebecca M. GIFFORD^7 (John^6) and 1st Christopher CORNELL, Int. 16 Jan. 1815
    (Westport VR:139,167)

Rebecca M. GIFFORD^7 and 2nd John F. UNDERWOOD, Int. 13 Apr. 1828, Westport
    (VR:141,243)

Moses WRIGHT^4 (Adam^3) and Thankful BOALS, Int. 12 Jan. 1733 (Plympton VR:258,434)

Ebenezer WRIGHT^5 (Moses^4) and 1st Anna TRIP

Ebenezer WRIGHT^5 and 2nd Deliverance CHURCHILL, 7 Feb. 1776

Nathan WRIGHT^4 (Adam^3) and Hannah COOKE^5 (Wm.^{4}, Jacob$^{3-2}$), 7 Dec. 1736 (Kingston
    (VR 1:3)

Samuel WRIGHT^4 (Adam^3) and Ann TILSON, 2 Aug. 1722, Plympton (MD 2:138)

Samuel WRIGHT^5 (Sam.^{4}) and Abigail STANDISH^5 (Zachariah^4, Ebenezer^3, Alexander^2),
    1 Sept. 1752 (Plympton VR)

Samuel WRIGHT^6 (Sam.^{5}) and Sarah RICHMOND, 8 Nov. 1783, Plymouth (Plympton VR:434)

Abigail WRIGHT^6 (Sam.^{5}) and Ichabod HATCH, Int. 18 Mar. 1782, Halifax (VR:11)

Peleg WRIGHT^6 (Sam.^{5}) and Hannah DEANE, 9 Oct. 1796 (Plympton VR:434)

Sarah WRIGHT^5 (Sam.^{4}) and James HALL

Jacob COOKE[2] (Francis[1])

Jacob COOKE[2] and 1st Damaris HOPKINS[2], 1647 (MD 5:52)

Jacob COOKE[2] and 2nd Elizabeth (LETTICE) Shurtleff, 18 Nov. 1669, Plymouth
    (MD 18:57)

Elizabeth (LETTICE) Shurtleff and 2nd Hugh COLE, 1 Jan. 1688/89 (Plymouth VR:127)

Sarah COOKE and Perez RANDALL, 4 Nov. 1746 (Gen.Adv.3:22)

Micro #4 of 30

Francis COOK and Elizabeth LAYTHAM, 2 Aug. 1687 (Plymouth VR:128)

Anne COOK and James JONSON, 6 Feb. 1716/17 (Plymouth VR:138)

Sarah COOKE and Robert BARTLETT, 1 Apr. 1691 (Plymouth VR:130)

Elizabeth COOKE[3] and John DOTY[2], c1667 (MD 1:144)

John DOTY[2] and 2nd Sarah JONES[4] (Patience Little[3], Anna Warren[2]), 22 Nov. 1694

Martha COOKE[3] and Elkanah CUSHMAN[3] (Mary Allerton[2]), 2 Mar. 1683

Elkanah CUSHMAN[3] and 1st Elizabeth COLE, c1677

Sarah COOKE[3] and Robert BARTLETT[4] (Joseph[3], Mary Warren[2]) (see above)

Jane COOKE[4] (Caleb[3]) and Isaac HARRIS[5] (Mercy Latham[4], Susanna Winslow[3], Mary
    Chilton[2]), 27 Mar. 1707, Scituate (MD 5:116)

Isaac HARRIS[5] and 2nd Elizabeth (SHAW) Washburn, c1719 (MD 14:204)

Ann COOKE[4] (Caleb[3]) and James JOHNSON (see above)

Caleb COOKE[4] (Caleb[3]) and Abigail HOWLAND[4] (James[3], Joseph[2])

Elizabeth COOKE[4] (Caleb[3]) and Robert JOHNSON, 27 Oct. 1715, Plymouth (MD 14:37)

Ann JOHNSON and William KNIGHT, Int. 28 July 1757 (Old Times, N. Yarmouth ME:396)

Barnabas JOHNSON and Martha SOULE[6] (James[5], Jedidiah[4], Moses[3], John[2]), 16 Apr. 1812,
    (Old Times, N. Yarmouth ME:1014)

Content JOHNSON and Joseph GRAY (Old Times, N. Yarmouth ME:930)

Sophronia GRAY and Rudduck PRINCE (Old Times, N. Yarmouth ME:850)

Andrew GRAY and 1st Elizabeth BUCKNAM, 2nd Margaret (ADAMS) Johnson (Old Times)

Joseph JOHNSON and Mary RING, 20 Apr. 1742 (Old Times, N. Yarmouth:1158)

Jane JOHNSON[5] (Elizabeth Cooke[4]) and Cornelius MORTON, pre 8 Apr. 1736 (MD 15:139)

Joseph JOHNSON[5] (Elizabeth Cooke[4]) and Mary RING[5] (Andrew[4], Eleazer[3], Deborah
    Hopkins[2]), c1741 (Old Times, N. Yarmouth ME:613,1157)

Joseph JOHNSON[6] (Jos.[5]) and Abigail BUCKNAM

Joshua JOHNSON[7] (Jos.[6]) and Sarah RANDALL, 4 Mar. 1811, Cape Elizabeth ME (VR 1:499)

Elbridge JOHNSON[8] (Joshua[7]) and Joanna EDWARDS

Sarah JOHNSON^5 (Eliz.^{4}) and Thomas DAVEE, c1740 (MD 15:212)

Thomas DAVEE and 2nd Hannah ROGERS^6 (Tho.^{5}, Eleazer^4, Tho.^{3}, Joseph^2), 31 Dec.
    1761 (Plymouth Ch.Rcds.2:492)

Solomon DAVEE^6 (Sarah Johnson^5) and Jedidah SYLVESTER

Thomas DAVIE^6 (Sarah Johnson^5) and Jane HOLMES, 14 Apr. 1768 (Plymouth Ch.
    Rcds.2:495)

Thomas DAVIE^7 (Tho.^{6}) and Betsey BARNES^7 (Corban^6, John^5, Mary Bartlett^4, Jos.^{3},
    Mary Warren^2), 3 July 1794 (Plymouth VR 2:279)

William DAVIE^6 (Sarah Johnson^5) and Lydia HARLOW^7 (John$^{6-5}$, Sam.^{4}, Rebecca Bartlett^3,
    Mary Warren^2), 20 Oct. 1768 (Plymouth Ch.Rcds.2:495)

Isaac DAVIE^7 (Wm.^{6}) and Rhoda PERRY, 1816

Joseph DAVIE^7 (Wm.^{6}) and Hannah FAUNCE, 1803

Ebenezer DAVIE^7 (Wm.^{6}) and Lydia CURTIS, 28 Jan. 1798 (Plymouth Ch.Rcds.2:509)

John DAVIE^8 (Ebenezer^7) and Priscilla H. SNOW, c1838

Patience C. DAVIE^8 (Ebenezer^7) and George A. HATHAWAY

Susan DAVIE^8 (Ebenezer^7) and Oliver EDES, 1836

Lydia DAVIE^8 (Ebenezer^7) and Thomas TORREY, 26 July 1821, Plymouth

Jane DAVIE^8 (Ebenezer^7) and Frederick ROBBINS

Ebenezer DAVIE^8 (Ebenezer^7) and Mercy Bartlett BRADFORD, c1826 (MD 23:10)

Capt. William DAVIE^8 (Ebenezer^7) and 1st Marcia WESTON, 29 Nov. 1830

Capt. William DAVIE^8 and 2nd Lydia Ann BAKER, 21 Apr. 1850

William DAVIE^7 (Wm.^{6}) and Experience STETSON^7 (Barzillai$^{6-5}$, Sarah Brewster^4,
    Wrestling^3, Love^2), 4 June 1793 (Plymouth Ch.Rcds.2:506)

Eliza Bowes DAVIE^8 (Wm.^{7}) and Henry WHITMORE

James COOKE^4 (Caleb^3) and Abigail HODGES, c1732 (Kingston VR)

John COOKE^4 (Caleb^3) and Elizabeth SEARS, 22 Nov. 1705, Yarmouth (Sears Gen.:49)

John COOKE^4 and 2nd Hannah ( ) MORTON, pre 3 Apr. 1727 (MD 17:56)

Mercy COOKE^5 (John^4) and Edmund HODGES, 31 Jan. 1736, Kingston (Gen.Adv.2:126)

Paul COOKE^5 (John^4) and Joanna HOLMES, 29 Apr. 1734, Plymouth (MD 14:75)

Abigail COOK^6 (Paul^5) and James PEARSON, 23 June 1757 (Norton VR)

Sarah COOK^6 (Paul^5) and 1st Archelans JAY, 19 May 1774 (Billerica VR)

Sarah COOK^6 (Paul^5) and 2nd William LAWS, 4 Aug. 1779 (Billerica VR)

Mercy COOK^6 (Paul^5) and Jonathan KNAPP, 13 Mar. 1760 (Norton VR)

Micro #5 of 30

Phebe TOY and John Sheldon CENTER, 28 May 1778, Billerica

Sally TAY and Jonas CENTER, 16 June 1794, Woburn

Sally TAY and William HOLDEN, 4 May 1817, Woburn

William LAWS and Judith SPRAKE, 17 Mar. 1774, Billerica

John COOKE^6 (Paul^5) and Mary GODFREY, 22 Mar. 1759 (Norton VR:215,241)

Matilda COOKE and 1st Ebenezer BREWER, 24 July 1785

Matilda COOKE and 2nd Josiah STEVENS, Sept. 1790

Sears COOK^6 (Paul^5) and Abigail CROSBY, 10 Dec. 1771 (Billerica VR)

Silas COOKE^5 (John^4) and Elizabeth STETSON, Int. 9 Jan. 1730/31, Kingston
   (VR:199,283)

Joshua COOKE^6 (Silas^5) and Mary MOREY, Int. 23 Sept. 1769, Norton

Sarah COOKE^6 (Silas^5) and Joseph HART, 20 Feb. 1753 (Norton VR:215,248)

Elizabeth COOK^6 (Silas^5) and Samuel LANE, 21 Nov. 1751 (Norton VR:215,268,351)

Deborah COOKE^6 (Silas^5) and Zebediah SHEPARDSON, Int. 7 Aug. 1762 (Norton
   VR:215,306)

Joseph COOKE^4 (Caleb^3) and Experience HODGES, Int. 17 June 1732, Kingston

Mary CARVER^5 (Mary Cooke^4, Caleb^3) and Richard ADAMS, 18 Oct. 1744 (Kingston
   VR:167,188)

Mary COOKE^4 (Caleb^3) and Robert CARVER, 28 Mar. 1717, Plymouth (MD 14:38)

Francis COOKE^3 and Elizabeth LATHAM^4 (Susanna Winslow^3, Mary Chilton^2),
   2 Aug. 1687, Plymouth (MD 13:204)

Caleb COOKE^4 (Francis^3) and Hannah SHURTLEFF, 4 Mar. 1724/25, Plympton (MD 2:139)

Lydia COOKE and Ebenezer ADAMS, 3 Nov. 1766, Kingston (Gen.Adv.3:77)

Benjamin COOKE^5 (Caleb^4) and Mary GRAY^6 (Sam.^{5}, John^4, Mary Winslow^3, Mary
   Chilton^2), 2 Oct. 1754 (Kingston VR:195)

Elkanah COOK^6 (Ben.^{5}) and 1st Christiana HOLMES, 20 Jan. 1788 (Kingston VR:198)

Elkanah COOK^6 and 2nd Polly WASHBURN, 18 Oct. 1800 (Kingston VR:196)

Peleg COOK^7 (Elkanah^6) and Adaline STRANGER

Caleb COOKE^5 (Caleb^4) and Sarah ADAMS, 11 Dec. 1753, Kingston (Gen.Adv.3:24)

Sarah ADAMS and 2nd Gershom COBB, 19 Nov. 1766, Kingston (Gen.Adv.3:77)

Amos COOKE^6 (Caleb^5) and Eunice EATON^5 (David^4, Ben.$^{3-2}$), 11 Jan. 1787,
   (Kingston VR)

Elizabeth COOKE^4 (Francis^3) and David LEACH, 22 Jan. 1734 (Kingston VR)

Francis COOKE^4 (Francis^3) and   Ruth SILVESTER^5 (Ruth Turner^4, Mary Brewster^3,
   Jonathan^2), 4 Feb. 1719, Plympton (MD 3:91)

Ruth SILVESTER^5 and 2nd Samuel RING^4 (Eleazer^3, Deborah Hopkins^2), 28 Jan.

1724/25, Plympton (MD 2:139)

Susanna COOKE[5] (Francis[4]) and Gershom COBB, Int. 22 Sept. 1739 (Kingston VR:194)

Ruth COOKE[5] (Francis[4]) and Josiah HOLMES, Int. 29 Mar. 1740 (Kingston VR:199)

Robert COOKE[4] (Francis[3]) and 1st Abigail HARLOW[5] (Abigail Church[4], Nathaniel[3],
    Eliz. Warren[2]), 26 Nov. 1716, Plympton (MD 2:236)

Robert COOKE[4] and 2nd Lydia TILDEN, aft. Oct. 1727 (MD 7:26,16:150)

Francis COOKE[5] (Robert[4]) and Sarah BRYANT, 24 Sept. 1750 (Bridgewater VR 2:66)

Sarah COOKE[5] (Robert[4]) and poss. Perez RANDALL, 4 Nov. 1746, Kingston

Charles COOKE[5] (Robert[4]) and 1st Hannah FAUNCE[5] (Lydia Cooke[4], Jacob[3-2]),
    30 May 1738 (Kingston VR)

Charles COOKE[5] and 2nd Sarah TINKHAM, 5 Oct. 1749 (Kingston VR 1:5)

Micro #6 of 30

Zenas COOKE and Joanna FAUNCE

Josiah COOK[6] (Charles[5]) and Lydia FAUNCE, 31 Mar. 1768 (Gen.Adv.3:77)

Nathaniel COOKE[5] (Robert[4]) and Mary SAMSON[5] (Peleg[4], Lydia Standish[3], Alexander[2]),
    Int. 26 Sept. 1741, Kingston

Isaac COOKE and Rebecca BRADFORD, 13 Aug. 1778 (Kingston VR:178,198)

Mary COOK and Ichabod BRADFORD, 31 May 1763

Peleg COOKE[6] (Nathaniel[5]) and Hannah FULLER, Int. 1 Aug. 1767 (Kingston VR)

Hannah FULLER and 2nd Samuel DREW, 13 July 1774, Kingston

Robert COOKE[5] (Robert[4]) and Hannah BISBE, 25 Nov. 1742 (Plympton VR)

Hannah BISBE and 2nd John FAUNCE, 26 Dec. 1744, Plympton (Kingston VR:195,218)

Robert COOKE[6] (Robert[5]) and Lydia ADAMS[6] (Thankful Washburn[5], Lydia Billington[4],
    Isaac[3], Francis[2]), 1 Dec, 1774 (Kingston VR:167,199)

Robert COOK[7] (Robert[6]) and Judith ADAMS[7] (John[6], Thankful Washburn[5], Lydia
    Billington[4], Isaac[3], Francis[2]) (Adams Gen.:38,41)

Simeon COOKE and Mary DINGLEY, 1 Jan. 1756 (Duxbury VR:237,248)

Sarah COOKE[4] (Francis[3]) and Ephraim COLE, 16 May 1717, Plympton (MD 2:236)

Rebecca COLE[5] (Sarah Cooke[4]) and Richard DURFEE, 19 July 1750, Plymouth
    (MD 16:170)

Susanna COOKE[4] (Francis[3]) and James STURTEVANT, 15 Feb. 1710/11, Plympton
    (MD 2:235)

Caleb STURTEVANT[5] (Susanna Cooke[4]) and 1st Patience CUSHMAN[5] (Isaac[4-3], Mary
    Allerton[2]), 23 July 1739, Halifax (VR:32)

Caleb STURTEVANT[5] and 2nd Abigail BEARCE, 31 May 1770 (Halifax VR:31)

Jabez STURTEVANT^6 (Caleb^5) and Aznbah WOOD, 8 Mar.∴ 1764 (Halifax VR:32)

Jacob COOKE^3 and Lydia MILLER, 29 Dec. 1681, Plymouth

Jacob COOKE^4 (Jacob^3) and 1st Phebe HALL, 3 Apr. 1716 (Yarmouth VR 3:315)

Jacob COOKE^4 and 2nd Mary HERCY, 21 Jan. 1728/29 (Abington VR)

Jacob COOKE^4 and 3rd Rebecca AXTELL(sp), Int. 16 Oct. 1736, Abington

John COOKE^4 (Jacob^3) and Phebe CROSMAN, Int. 19 Dec. 1730, Kingston

Phebe CROSMAN and 2nd Samuel KENT, 8 Dec. 1748 (Kingston VR)

Molly COOKE and Cephas WADSWORTH, 5 Nov. 1767 (Gen.Adv.3:77)

Sarah COOKE^5 (John^4) and Samuel KENT, 28 Dec. 1752 (Kingston VR)

Sarah KENT^6 (Sarah Cooke^5) and Abner HOLMES

Lydia COOKE^4 (Jacob^3) and John FAUNCE, 23 Feb. 1709/10, Plymouth (MD 14:36)

John FAUNCE and 2nd Lydia (TILDEN) Cooke, aft. July 1738 (MD 7:85)

Judith FAUNCE^5 (Lydia Cooke^4) and Jabez WASHBURN^5 (Lydia Billington^4, Isaac^3,
    Francis^2)

Margaret COOKE^4 (Jacob^3) and Simon LAZELL, 5 Apr. 1716, Plymouth (MD 14:37)

Rebecca COOKE^4 (Jacob^3) and Benjamin SAMSON^3 (Stephen^2)

William COOKE^4 (Jacob^3) and Tabitha HALL, 18 Mar. 1706/07 (Yarmouth VR)

Tabitha COOK^5 (Wm.^{4}) and Benjamin ORCUTT, Int. 14 July 1738, Kingston

Hannah COOK^5 (Wm.^{4}) and Nathan WRIGHT^4 (Adam^3, Hester Cooke^2), 7 Dec. 1736
    (Kingston VR)

Elisha COOK^5 (Wm.^{4}) and Rebecca EGERTON, 5 Nov. 1741 (Halifax VR:33)

Levi COOKE^6 (Elisha^4) and Mary CORWIN

Sarah COOKE^7 (Levi^6) and Jacob RICE

Hannah COOKE^6 (Elisha^5) and Bernard HAGERMAN

Mary COOKE^6 (Elisha^5) and Webley EDWARD

James COOKE and Abigail HODGES, Int. 17 July 1731 (Kingston VR)

Robert COOKE and Patience FINEY, Int. 28 June 1735 (Kingston VR)

Mercy COOKE and Edmon HODGES, Int. 10 Nov. 1736 (Kingston VR)

Hannah COOKE and Nathan RITE, Int. 10 Nov. 1736 (Kingston VR)

Lydia COOKE and Moses BASSET, Int. 8 July 1738 (Kingston VR)

Lydia COOKE and Elisha STETSON, 17 Dec. 1753 (Kingston VR)

Damaris COOK and John Delano PEMBROKE, 15 Nov. 1749 (Kingston Ch.rcds.:227)

Sarah COOKE and Samuel HARRIS, 14 Dec. 1752 (Kingston Ch.rcds.:228)

Zebiah COOKE and Joseph BISBEE, 17 Apr. 1755 (Kingston Ch.rcds.:228)

Josiah COOKE and Huldah BASSET, 1 May 1760 (Kingston Ch.Rcds.:229)

Lydia ( ) COOKE and John FAUNCE, Int. 11 Apr. 1741 (Kingston VR) (see p.120)

Lydia COOKE[5] (Wm.[4]) and Moses BASSETT (see p.120)

Mary COOKE[3] and John RICKARD[3] (John[2], Giles[1]), c1678 (MD 1:144)

Mercy RICKARD[4] (Mary Cooke[3]) and Ignatius CUSHING, 4 Apr. 1710 (Plymouth VR)

Jane COOKE[2] (Francis[1])[<4>]

Thomas MITCHELL and Elizabeth TOTMAN, 28 Mar. 1756, Plymouth (Mass. Mgs.2:16)

Joseph MITCHEL and Mary TINKHAM, 3 Feb. 1760, Plymouth (Mass. Mgs.2:18)

Mary MITCHEL and Thomas PHILLIPS, 14 Sept. 1743, Kingston (Mass.Mgs.2:34)

Bersheba MITCHEL and Timothy BRIGGS, 14 Aug. 1746, Kingston (Mass.Mgs.2:35)

Job MITCHELL and Sarah BREWSTER, 1 Feb. 1769, Marshfield (Mass.Mgs.2:45)

Elizabeth MITCHELL and Job EWELL, 1 June 1769, Marshfield (Mass.Mgs.2:45)

John MITCHELL and Zilpha RICHARDS, 2 June 1763, Pembroke (Mass.Mgs.2:64)

Elisha MITCHELL and Hannah TOMSON, 21 Feb. 1781, Halifax (Mass.Mgs.2:113)

Seth MITCHELL and Ann LATHAM, 21 Dec. 1738, Bridgewater (Mass.Mgs.2:115)

John MITCHEL and Sarah MAKURIAN, 28 Nov. 1751, Bridgewater (Mass.Mgs.2:121)

Nathan MITCHELL and Ann CARY, 25 Apr. 1754, Bridgewater (Mass.Mgs.2:123)

Seth MITCHELL and Mary WADE, 21 Feb. 1760, Bridgewater (Mass.Mgs.2:125)

Elizabeth MITCHELL and Eleazer KEITH, 11 Sept. 1760, Bridgewater (Mass.Mgs.2:126)

Alice MITCHELL and John KEITH, 16 June 1763, Bridgewater (Mass.Mgs.2:127)

Edward MITCHELL JR. and Jane LATHAM, 30 Sept. 1762, Bridgewater (Mass.Mgs.2:129)

Jacob MITCHELL and Rebecca LORING, 26 Jan. 1763, Bridgewater (Mass.Mgs.2:129)

Cushing MITCHEL and Jennit ORR, 26 Sept. 1765, Bridgewater (Mass.Mgs.2:129)

Molly MITCHELL and James KEITH Jr., 4 May 1780, Bridgewater (Mass.Mgs.2:136)

Eus. Cushing MITCHELL and Hannah NEWTON, 15 Mar. 1780, Bridgewater (Mgs.2:136)

Mary MITCHELL and Luther JOTHAM, 8 Apr. 1778, Bridgewater (Mass.Mgs.2:137)[<3>]

Celia MITCHELL and Arthur HARRIS, 14 June 1781, Bridgewater (Mass.Mgs.2:139)

John MITCHELL and Anna BYRAM, 24 Sept. 1781, Bridgewater (Mass.Mgs.2:139)

Jenna MITCHELL and Edward HAYWARD, 16 Oct. 1782, Bridgewater (Mass.Mgs.2:140)

Susanna MITCHELL and Marlborough WILLIAMS, 20 Mar. 1783, Bridgewater (Mgs.2:140)

Timothy MITCHELL and Hannah LEONARD, 20 Aug. 1783, Bridgewater (Mass.Mgs.2:140)

Rothene MITCHELL and Hepza HAYWARD, 3 Apr. 1783, Bridgewater (Mass.Mgs.2:141)

Jacob MITCHELL and Sally ( ) WHITMAN, 4 Sept. 1783, Bridgewater (Mgs.2:141)

Reuben MITCHELL and Anna WADE, 23 Oct. 1783, Bridgewater (Mass.Mgs.2:141)

Thomas MITCHELL and Abigail HOWARD, 27 Oct. 1783, Bridgewater (Mass.Mgs.2:142)

Sylvia MITCHELL and Hugh ORR Jr., 9 Mar. 1785, Bridgewater (Mass.Mgs.2:143)

Susa MITCHELL and Asa FORREST, 20 Feb. 1787, Bridgewater (Mass.Mgs.2:146)

Nabby MITCHEL and James LINCOLN, Bridgewater (Mass.Mgs.2:147)

Alice MITCHELL and William HARRIS, 14 May 1788, Bridgewater (Mass.Mgs.2:148)

Joseph MITCHELL and Hannah HERSEY, 11 Jan. 1753, Abington (Mass.Mgs.2:152)

Hannah MITCHELL and John WHITMAN, 30 Sept. 1765, Abington (Mass.Mgs.2:153)

Thomas MITCHELL and Dinah NORTON, 29 Jan. 1766, Rochester (Mass.Mgs.2:190)

Thomas MICHELL and Mary MOLTON, Nov. 1655, Malden (NEHGR 10:162)

Abial MITCHEL Jr. and Sally OLIVER, 16 Sept. 1790, Easton

Samuel WASHBURN and Hannah HAVEN, Int. 6 June 1779 (Natick VR)

Edward MITCHELL^3 and 1st Mary HAYWARD $^{\langle 4 \rangle}$

Edward MITCHELL^3 and 2nd Alice BRADFORD^4 (John^3, Wm.^{2}), 26 Aug. 1708, Plymouth
   (MD 14:36)

Elizabeth MITCHELL^3 and John WASHBURN, 6 Dec. 1645, Plymouth (MD 13:86)

John WASHBURN and 2nd Elizabeth ( ) PACKARD, c1685

Joseph MITCHELL and Mary TINKHAM, Int. 2 Dec. 1758, Plymouth (MD 25:188)

Hannah WASHBURN and Nathan BASSETT, 15 Mar. 1733 (Bridgewater VR 2:42,382)

Joseph BASSETT and Hannah LOTHROP

Mary WASHBURN and Thomas PERKINS, 1716/17

Abigail WASHBURN and Josiah LEONARD, 1717

Rebecca WASHBURN and David JOHNSON, 1719

Hannah WASHBURN and Zachariah WHITMARSH, 28 Jan. 1729/30

Hannah WASHBURN and Nathan BASSETT, 15 Mar. 1733

Hannah WASHBURN and Thomas DAVIS, 2 June 1737

Alice MITCHELL^4 (Edw.^{3}) and Noah HERSEY, 12 Feb. 1735/36 (Hingham VR 2:302)$^{\langle 4 \rangle}$

Edward MITCHELL^4 (Edw.^{3}) and Elizabeth CUSHING, 14 Dec. 1738 (Hingham VR 2:154)$^{\langle 4 \rangle}$

William MITCHELL^5 (Edw.^{4}) and Elizabeth WARD

Cushing MITCHELL^5 (Edw.^{4}) and Jennet ORR (see p.121)

Edward MITCHELL^5 (Edw.^{4}) and Jane LATHAM (see p.121)

Mary MITCHELL^4 (Edw.^{3}) and Joshua HERSEY $^{\langle 4 \rangle}$

Jane COOKE^2 and Experience MITCHELL, c1628, Plymouth$^{\langle 4 \rangle}$

Benjamin WASHBURN and Bathsheba CHURCHILL, 17 Nov. 1785, Plymouth

Benjamin WASHBURN and Ella SHAW, 6 Aug. 1777 (Middleboro VR 4:150)

Benjamin WASHBURN and Hannah HALL, 11 July 1822 (Middleboro VR 8:225)

Abial WASHBURN and Abigail BRIGGS, Int. 22 July 1797, Plymouth (MD 30:118)

Abiel WASHBURN and Olive FINNEY, Int. 30 Apr. 1785, Plymouth (MD 29:127)

Jonathan WASHBURN and Judah WOOD, 23 May 1751, Middleboro (MD 18:84)

Jonathan WASHBURN and Rebecca JOHNSON, 17 Dec. 1719, Boston (Rcd.Com.28:86)

Jonathan WASHBURN and Thankful NEWTON, 9 Apr. 1724, Bridgewater (MD 16:188)

Nehemiah WASHBURN and Mary ELMES, 27 Dec. 1716 (Middleboro VR 1:53)

Edward WASHBURN and Elizabeth RICHMOND, 12 June 1728 (Middleboro VR 1:58)

Nathaniel WASHBURN and Mary PRATT, 28 Feb. 1739 (Middleboro VR 1:178)

Benjamin WASHBURN and Zerviah PACKARD, 1 Sept. 1740 (Middleboro VR 1:178)

Abishai WASHBURN and Hannah MORTON, 11 Aug. 1748 (Middleboro VR 2:28)

Abraham WASHBURN and Mary WESTON, 18 Oct. 1753 (Middleboro VR 2:45)

Isaac WASHBURN and Mary BENSON, 23 Nov. 1758 (Middleboro VR 2:47)

Josiah WASHBURN and Huldah SEARS, 7 July 1756 (Middleboro VR 2:85)

Edward WASHBURN Jr. and Hannah JONES, 29 Oct. 1765 (Middleboro VR 2:89)

Ezra WASHBURN Jr. and Lucy FULLER, 1767 (Middleboro VR 2:116)

Eleazer WASHBURN and Sarah SOUTHWORTH, 9 May 1771 (Middleboro VR 2:133)

Benjamin WASHBURN and Ella SHAW, 6 Aug. 1777 (Middleboro VR 4:150)

Jonah WASHBURN Jr. and Sally EDY, 3 Apr. 1783 (Middleboro VR 4:155)

Josiah WASHBURN and Phebe CUSHMAN, 26 Aug. 1784 (Middleboro VR 4:156)

Isaiah WASHBURN and Priscilla WOOD, 20 July 1775 (Middleboro VR 4:156)

Linus WASHBURN and Silence AMES, 2 Apr. 1789 (Middleboro VR 4:160)

Abiel WASHBURN and Betsey PEIRCE, 6 Jan. 1788 (Middleboro VR 4:160)

Isaac WASHBURN and Eunice CAREY, 13 Apr. 1786 (Middleboro VR 4:161)

Salmon WASHBURN and Ruth WHITE, 22 Mar. 1787 (Middleboro VR 4:162)

Ebenezer WASHBURN and Abigail WESTON, 23 Dec. 1787 (Middleboro VR 4:163)

Daniel WASHBURN and Melatiah KEITH, 30 Apr. 1795 (Middleboro VR 4:174)

Abial WASHBURN and Abigail BRIGGS, 13 Aug. 1797 (Middleboro VR 4:182)

Nathan WASHBURN and Sally BUMP, 15 Nov. 1804 (Middleboro VR 8:3)

Samson WASHBURN and Rebecca SOULE, 28 Jan. 1806 (Middleboro VR 8:76)

Linus WASHBURN and Hannah LEONARD, 17 Jan. 1809 (Middleboro VR 8:77)

Thomas WASHBURN Jr. and Huldah SAVERY, 30 May 1815 (Middleboro VR 8:112)

Cyrus WASHBURN and Betsey BUMP, 17 Sept. 1810 (Middleboro VR 8:138)

Luther WASHBURN and Hannah F. TERRY, 25 Dec. 1803 (Middleboro VR 8:200)

Linus WASHBURN and Lucy LEONARD, 16 Mar. 1807 (Middleboro VR 8:200)

Benjamin WASHBURN and Hannah HALL, 11 July 1822 (Middleboro VR 8:225)

Hiram WASHBURN and Olive WASHBURN, 27 Mar. 1827 (Middleboro VR 10:52)

Jonathan WASHBURN and Sarah K. PRATT, 8 Feb. 1827 (Middleboro VR 10:52)

Leonard WASHBURN and Elizabeth RICHMOND, 30 Sept. 1834 (Middleboro VR 10:74)

Seth WASHBURN Jr. and Casindana PRATT, 29 Nov. 1839 (Middleboro 10:262)

George B. WASHBURN and Catherine LEONARD, 29 May 1839 (Middleboro VR 10:263)

Capt. Linus WASHBURN and Huldah A. PERKINS, 30 Oct. 1825 (Middleboro VR 10:266)

Charles F. WASHBURN and Eliza MACOMBER, 20 Sept. 1841 (Middleboro VR 15:2)

Renel WASHBURN and Elisabeth M. HOARD, 1 Jan.1843 (Middleboro VR 15:3)

Bezaleel WASHBURN and Nancy T. VAUGHAN, 6 May 1838 (Middleboro VR 15:5)

Micro #9 of 30

Joanna WASHBURN and Ebenezer LEACH, 26 Dec. 1734 (Bridgewater VR 2:226)

Susanna WASHBURN and Timothy PERKINS, 18 Mar. 1735/36 (Bridgewater VR 2:226)

Tabitha WASHBURN and Solomon LEACH, 11 Apr. 1736 (Bridgewater VR 2:227)

Joanna WASHBURN and Samuel HACKET, 23 Sept. 1736 (Bridgewater VR 2:227)

Phoebe WASHBURN and Samuel KINGMAN, 3 Feb. 1736/37 (Bridgewater VR 2:227)

Lydia WASHBURN and Samuel WEST, 10 Mar. 1736/37 (Bridgewater VR 2:227)

Hannah WASHBURN and Thomas DAVIS, 2 June 1737 (Bridgewater VR 2:227)

Jane WASHBURN and Josiah DEANE, 18 Aug. 1737 (Bridgewater VR 2:227)

John WASHBURN and Bethiah KEITH, 12 Jan. 1737/38 (Bridgewater VR 2:212)

Sarah WASHBURN and Samuel CRANE, 13 Feb. 1737/38 (Bridgewater VR 2:212)

Eleazer WASHBURN and Anna ALDEN, 22 Nov. 1738 (Bridgewater VR 3:167)

Abigail WASHBURN and John FREELOVE, 10 May 1739 (Bridgewater VR 3:167)

Israel WASHBURN and Leah FOBES, 3 Jan. 1739 (Bridgewater VR 3:167)

Jemimah WASHBURN and Josiah LEONARD Jr., 24 Jan. 1739 (Bridgewater VR 3:167)

Deliverance WASHBURN and Joseph BOLTON, 6 Feb. 1739 (Bridgewater VR 3:167)

Robert WASHBURN and Mary FOBES, 6 Mar. 1739 (Bridgewater VR 3:167)

Elizabeth WASHBURN and Elisha HAYWARD Jr., 7 Oct. 1740 (Bridgewater VR 3:167)

Hannah WASHBURN and James Carkis WOODURS(sp), 12 Feb. 1770 (Bridgewater VR 3: 153)

Stephen WASHBURN and Sarah FAXON, 20 Nov. 1770 (Bridgewater VR 3:152)

Susanna WASHBURN and James HOOPER Jr., 6 Feb. 1772 (Bridgewater VR 3:192)

Ebenezer WASHBURN and Mary LEACH, 27 Apr. 1772 (Bridgewater VR 3:192)

Solomon WASHBURN and Anna MITCHELL, 17 Mar. 1773 (Bridgewater VR 3:154)

Alice WASHBURN and William FRENCH, 12 Aug. 1773 (Bridgewater VR 3:155)

Rebecca WASHBURN and Isaac POOL, 18 Oct. 1774 (Bridgewater VR 3:155)

Levi WASHBURN and Molly ALLEN, 22 Nov. 1774 (Bridgewater VR 3:148)

Josiah WASHBURN and Elizabeth SNOW, 6 July 1775 (Bridgewater VR 3:153)

Seth WASHBURN and Elizabeth DUNBAR, 21 July 1776 (Bridgewater VR 3:154)

Eliab WASHBURN and Molly LAZELL, 20 Feb. 1777 (Bridgewater VR 3:148)

Jeremiah WASHBURN and Kezia SNELL, 19 Aug. 1777 (Bridgewater VR 3:157)

Lydia WASHBURN and Simeon WOOD, 6 May 1778 (Bridgewater VR 3:157)

Jonathan WASHBURN and Hannah CONANT, 14 May 1778 (Bridgewater VR 3:157)

Deliverance WASHBURN and William SHAW Jr., 1 Oct. 1778 (Bridgewater VR 3:158)

Elizabeth WASHBURN and Nathaniel PRATT Jr., 12 Nov. 1778 (Bridgewater VR 3:157)

Zilpha WASHBURN and Noah WHITMAN, 1 July 1779 (Bridgewater VR 3:158)

Isaac WASHBURN and Huldah ALLEN, 6 Feb. 1781 (Bridgewater VR 3:161)

Oliver WASHBURN and Hannah GANNETT, 17 Mar. 1781 (Bridgewater VR 3:161)

Ezekiel WASHBURN and Naomi THAYER, 1 Nov. 1781 (Bridgewater VR 3:161)

Zerviah WASHBURN and Solomon HAYWARD, 16 Apr. 1782 (Bridgewater VR 3:162)

Eunice WASHBURN and Asa RICHMOND, 28 Nov. 1782 (Bridgewater VR 3:162)

Barnebas WASHBURN and Katurah CONANT, 5 Dec. 1782 (Bridgewater VR 3:162)

Solomon WASHBURN and Hannah ORCUTT, 15 Sept. 1785 (Bridgewater VR 3:150)

Elizabeth WASHBURN[4] (Eliz. Mitchell[3]) and 1st James HOWARD, c1685 (MD 5:247)

Elizabeth WASHBURN[4] and 2nd Edward SEALY, c1692 (MD 5:247)

Elizabeth HOWARD/HAWARD[5] (Eliz. Washburn[4]) and Thomas BUCK, 18 Dec. 1712, Bridge-
    water (MD 16:104)

Benjamin SILLEY[5] (Eliz. Washburn[4]) and Sarah LANE, 11 Dec. 1718, Norton (Lane Family,
    Exeter NH.<1897> 2:15)

James WASHBURN[4] (Eliz. Mitchell[3]) and Mary BOWDEN, 20 Dec. 1693, Bridgewater
    (MD 26:38)

Elizabeth WASHBURN[5] (James[4]) and Elisha HAYWARD, 7 Oct. 1740 (Bridgewater VR 3:167)

Martha WASHBURN[5] (James[4]) and Robert RICHMOND[5] (Ebenezer[4], Abigail Rogers[3], John[2]),
    17 May 1733 (Bridgewater VR 2:225)

Mary WASHBURN[5] (James[4]) and William SNOW[4] (Wm.[3], Rebecca Brown[2]), 8 Nov. 1722
    (Bridgewater VR 2:259)

Edward WASHBURN[5] (James[4]) and Elizabeth RICHMOND[5] (Ebenezer[4], Abigail Rogers[3],
    John[2]), 12 June 1728, Middleboro (MD 5:39)

Edward WASHBURN[6] (Edw.[5]) and Hannah JONES, 29 Oct. 1765, Middleboro (MD 25:87)

Gen. Abiel WASHBURN[7] (Edw.[6]) and Elizabeth PIERCE, 6 Jan. 1788 (MD 15:105)

Gideon WASHBURN^5 (James^4) and Mary PERKINS

James WASHBURN^5 (James^4) and Elizabeth LEONARD,* 23 Nov. 1720, Bridgewater
    (MD 16:186)

Elizabeth LEONARD and 2nd Joseph CROSSMAN, 20 Aug. 1752 (Bridgewater VR 2:100,385)

Jonah WASHBURN^6 (James^5) and Huldah SEARS, 7 July, Middleboro (MD 24:57)

Moses WASHBURN^5 (James^4) and Hannah CUSHMAN^5 (Robert^4, Tho.^{3}, Mary Allerton^2),
    23 May 1727 (Kingston VR:203,298)

Peter WASHBURN^6 (Moses^5) and Abigail POPE, 17 Jan. 1754 (Dartmouth VR 2:363,526)

Moses WASHBURN^6 (Moses^5) and Sarah POPE, 27 Nov. 1753 (Dartmouth VR 2:365,526)

Lettis WASHBURN^7 (Moses^6) and 1st Mercy SPOONER, 6 June 1779 (Dartmouth VR)

Lettis WASHBURN^7 and 2nd Sarah SPOONER, 24 Jan. 1782 (Dartmouth VR)

Lettice WASHBURN^8 (Lettis^7) and Annie CHASE

William WASHBURN^9 (Lettice^8) and Hannah ALLEN

Sarah WASHBURN^5 (James^4) and Henry CASWELL

Jane WASHBURN^4 (Eliz. Mitchell^3) and William ORCUTT, c1690-94

William ORCUTT and 2nd Hannah SMITH, 21 Sept. 1698, Bridgewater (MD 2:146)

John WASHBURN^4 (Eliz. Mitchell^3) and Rebecca LAPHAM, 16 Apr. 1679, Bridgewater
    (MD 2:92)

Abigail WASHBURN^5 (John^4) and Josiah LEONARD, 21 Nov. 1717 (Bridgewater VR 2:256)

John WASHBURN^5 (John^4) and Margaret PACKARD, 16 Feb. 1709/10 (Bridgewater VR 2:253)

Content WASHBURN^6 (John^5) and Joseph LATHROP^5 (Hannah Alden^4, Jos.$^{3-2}$), 24 Oct.
    1746 (Boston VR 2:230,385)

Nathaniel WASHBURN^6 (John^5) and Mary PRATT^5 (Sam.$^{4-3}$, Mary Priest^2)

Mary PRATT^5 and 2nd Eleazer CARY, 1753

Josiah WASHBURN^5 (John^4) and 1st Mercy TILSON, 11 Feb. 1702, Plymouth (MD 13:208)

Josiah WASHBURN^5 and 2nd Sarah RICHMOND^5 (Edw.^{4}, Abigail Rogers^3, John^2)

Josiah WASHBURN^5 and 3rd Susannah(?) CRANE, 13 Feb. 1737/38

Rebecca WASHBURN^5 (John^4) and David JOHNSON, 7 Jan. 1719, Bridgewater (MD 16:186)

Isaac JOHNSON^6 (Rebecca Washburn^5) and Mary WILLIS, Int. 21 June 1744, Bridgewater

Isaac JOHNSON^7 (Isaac^6) and Mary WRIGHT, Int. 15 July 1786, Bridgewater

Joseph WASHBURN^6 (Josiah^5) and Deliverance ORCUTT, c1728

Deliverance ORCUTT and 2nd Abiel PACKARD, aft. 1766

Josiah WASHBURN^6 (Josiah^5) and 1st Abigail CURTIS

Josiah WASHBURN^6 and 2nd Huldah LEONARD

Huldah WASHBURN and Solomon BARTLETT, c1782

Solomon BARLETT and 2nd Mercy OLDS(sp)$^{<5>}$

Lydia WASHBURN^6 (Josiah^5) and Samuel WEST, 10 Mar. 1736/37 (Bridgewater VR 2:389)

William WASHBURN^5 (John^4) and Experience MAN, 13 Jan. 1715, Bridgewater (MD 16:190)

Ezekiel WASHBURN^6 (Wm.^{5}) and Experience CURTIS, 4 Oct. 1749 (Bridgewater VR 2:101)

Ezekiel WASHBURN^7 (Ezekiel^6) and Naomi THAYER, 1 Nov. 1781 (Bridgewater VR 2:364)

Betty WASHBURN^7 (Ezekiel^6) and Lt. Nathaniel PRATT, 1778

Deliverance WASHBURN^7 (Ezekiel^6) and William SHAW, 1 Oct. 1778 (Bridgewater
    2:337,385)

Thankful WASHBURN^6 (Wm.^{5}) and John KINSLEY, 19 Feb. 1746 (Bridgewater VR)

Jonathan WASHBURN^4 (Eliz. Mitchell^3) and Mary VAUGHAN, c1683 (MD 15:48)

Josiah WASHBURN^5 (Jonathan^4) and Elizabeth DAVENPORT, 20 June 1723 (Bridgewater
    VR 2:259,388)

Zenas WASHBURN^8 (Solomon^7) and Lydia WHITMAN, 3 Feb. 1799 (Bridgewater VR 2:392)

Josiah WASHBURN^6 (Josiah^5) and Phebe HAYWARD, 3 May 1753 (Bridgewater VR 2:388)

Jonathan WASHBURN^5 (Jonathan^4) and Thankful NEWTON, 9 Apr. 1724, Bridgewater
    (MD 16:188)

Benjamin WASHBURN^5 (Jonathan^4) and Martha KINGMAN, 6 Aug. 1729, Bridgewater
    (MD 16:45)

Benjamin WASHBURN^6 (Ben.^{5}) and Desire SEARS, 29 Apr. 1762 (Halifax VR:31)

Daniel WASHBURN^6 (Cornelius^5, Jonathan^4) and Experience HARLOW, c1752

Elizabeth WASHBURN^5 (Jonathan^4) and John BENSON, 4 Dec. 1710 (Bridgewater VR 2:253)

Joseph WASHBURN^4 (Eliz. Mitchell^3) and Hannah LATHAM^4 (Susanna Winslow^3, Mary
    Chilton^2), pre 1674 (MD 21:40-42)

Micro #11 of 30

Benjamin WASHBURN^5 (Jos.^{4}) and Zerviah PACKARD, 1 Sept. 1740, Middleboro (MD 13:253)

Elizabeth WASHBURN^6 (Ephraim^5, Jos.^{4}) and Consider BENSON, 3 Dec. 1751 (Plymouth
    VR:255:418)

Ephraim WASHBURN^5 (Jos.^{4}) and Mary POLEN, 13 Jan. 1725/26, Plymouth (MD 14:71)

Phebe WASHBURN^6 (Ephraim^5) and David VAUGHAN

Japhet WASHBURN^6 (Ephraim^5) and Priscilla COOMBS

Lydia WASHBURN^6 (Ephraim^5) and Samuel NORRIS, 21 Dec. 1749 (Plympton VR:353,418)

Jemima NORRIS and Giddings LANE, 6 Sept. 1788 (Bible)

Uriah FOSS and Sarah GOODRIDGE, 16 Dec. 1779 (Bible)

Hephzibah WASHBURN^5 (Jos.^{4}) and Benjamin LEACH, 8 Sept. 1702, Bridgewater (MD 2:147)

Anne LEACH^6 (Hephzibah Washburn^5) and Samuel PACKARD, 3 July 1722, Middleboro
    (MD 4:72)

Benjamin LEACH^6 (Hephzibah Washburn^5) and Hannah KEITH, 10 Jan. 1739 (Bridgewater
    VR 3:167)

Joseph LEACH^6 (Hephzibah Washburn^5) and Anna HARRIS, 14 Jan. 1735/36, Bridgewater
    (MD 16:100)

Orpha LEACH^7 (Jos.^{6}) and Edward FOBES, 2 Apr. 1761 (Bridgewater VR 2:133,238)

Edward FOBES and 2nd Rebecca HADEN , Int. 30 Apr. 1787 (Chesterfield VR 2:53)

John FOBES^8 (Orpha Leach^7) and Nabbe BAILEY, Int. 16 Dec. 1782 (Chesterfield
    VR 1:37)

Clarissa FOBES^9 (John^8) and Oliver POST

Benjamin LEACH^7 (Jos.^{6}) and 1st Mary KEITH, 2 Oct. 1764

Benjamin LEACH^7 and 2nd Anna SHORT, Int. 20 Oct. 1792, Bridgewater

Dinah LEACH^7 (Jos.^{6}) and John SHAW, 8 Jan. 1761 (Bridgewater VR 2:235,335)

Sarah LEACH^6 (Hephzibah Washburn^5) and Timothy LEACH^3 (John^2, Giles^1), 5 Dec. 1732,
    Bridgewater (MD 16:99)

Sarah LEACH and Jonathan HAYWARD, 11 Nov. 1762 (Bridgewater VR 3:323)

Ann LEACH and James STURTEVANT, 19 Jan. 1769 (Bridgewater VR 3:189)

Levi LEACH and Hannah FOBES, 18 Nov. 1771 (Bridgewater VR 3:191)

Jonathan LEACH^7 (Sarah^6) and Abigail LEACH, 30 Nov. 1763 (Bridgewater VR 3:185)

Susanna LEACH^6 (Hephzibah Washburn^5) and Ezra WASHBURN, 20 July 1742 (Bridgewater
    VR 2:239,386)

Susanna WASHBURN^7 (Susanna Leach^6) and Zadock LEACH, 6 Dec. 1763 (Bridgewater
    VR 2:240,392)

Ezra WASHBURN^7 (Susanna Leach^6) and Lucy FULLER, 3 Nov. 1767 (Mass.Mgs.2:89)

Lucy FULLER and 2nd James PEARL, 16 July 1795 (Stafford CT VR:134)

Kezia WASHBURN and William NASON, 4 Sept. 1788 (Stafford CT VR:133)

Wealthy WASHBURN and Benjamin DUNBAR, 9 June 1774 (Bridgewater VR 2:392)

Seth WASHBURN and Elizabeth DUNBAR, 21 July 1772

Susanna WASHBURN^7 (Ezra?) and Zadock SEARS, 6 Dec. 1763 (Bridgewater VR)

Abraham LEACH^8 (Susanna Washburn^7) and Mary KEITH, c1796

Zadock LEACH^8 (Susanna Washburn^7) and Polly FROST

Beza LEACH^8 (Susanna Washburn^7) and Betsy SHAW, c1793

Jonathan WASHBURN^5 (Jos.^{4}) and Rebecca PERRY^5 (Rebecca Freeman^4, Rebecca Prence^3, Patience Brewster^2), 27 Dec. 1711, Sandwich

Joseph WASHBURN^5 (Jos.^{4}) and Hannah JOHNSON, c1722

Ebenezer WASHBURN^6 (Jos.^{5}) and Dorothy NEWHALL, 25 July 1757, Spencer (VR:212)

Cyrus WASHBURN^7 (Ebenezer^6) and 1st Electa STRATTON, c1799

Cyrus WASHBURN^7 and 2nd Rhoda FIELD, 19 Aug. 1806, Northfield

Cyrus WASHBURN^7 and 3rd Lucy HATHAWAY, Int. 24 Sept. 1827 (Hist.Hardwick:527,528)

Abiel WASHBURN^6 (Jos.^{5}) and Jacob WICKER, 15 Jan. 1745/46 (Leicester VR:226,233)

Ira WICKER^7 (Abiel Washburn^6) and Mary HASKELL, 1 Oct. 1812 (Hardwick VR:187,266)

Lemuel WICKER^7 (Abiel Washburn^6) and 1st Mary Parmer HUNT, 15 Jan. 1811 (Hardwick VR:195,266)

Lemuel WICKER^7 and 2nd Sarah HASKELL, 5 Oct. 1813 (Hardwick VR:187,266)

Sarah HASKELL and 2nd George H. ROWLEY, aft. July 1825 (Hist.Addison Co.:743)

David WICKER and Ann DAVIS, 21 May 1761 (Leicester VR:141,233)

John WICKER^8 (Wm.^{7}, Abiel Washburn^6) and Priscilla COLLINS, 13 Nov. 1803 (Hardwick VR:159,266)

William WICKER^7 (Abiel Washburn^6) and Susanna PARKER, Int. 23 Feb. 1772, Hardwick (VR:221,266)

Joseph WICKER^7 (Abiel Washburn^6) and Dorothy KNAPP

Dorothy KNAPP and 2nd Samuel JORDAN, aft. 1795 (Hardwick VR:335)

Seth WASHBURN^6 (Jos.^{5}) and 1st Mary HARWOOD, 12 Apr. 1750, Leicester (MD 2:66-68)

Seth WASHBURN^6 and 2nd Sarah (DENNY) Sargeant, 30 Apr. 1788 (MD 2:67)

Asa WASHBURN^7 (Seth^6) and 1st Sally UPHAM, 16 Nov. 1780, Spencer (MD 2:68)

Asa WASHBURN^7 and 2nd Persis BOUTELL, 26 Sept. 1805 (MD2:68)

Mary WASHBURN^4 (Eliz. Mitchell^3) and Samuel KINSLEY, pre 10 Sept. 1694 (MD 15:251)

Abigail KINSLEY^5 (Mary Washburn^4) and William HAYWARD, 17 Dec. 1728, Easton

Bethiah KINSLEY^5 (Mary Washburn^4) and William BRETT, 15 May 1732, Bridgewater (MD 16:98)

Hannah KINSLEY^5 (Mary Washburn^4) and Edward HAYWARD

Edward HAYWARD and 2nd Keziah ( ) WHITE

Mary KINSLEY^5 (Mary Washburn^4) and Thomas WILLIS, 18 Dec. 1716, Bridgewater (MD 16:191)

Edwin HOWARD and Sally COLE, 25 Dec. 1803 (Scituate VR 2:69,154)

Sally COLE and Benjamin MERRITT, 31 July 1814 (Scituate VR 2:69,204)

Sarah KINSLEY[5] (Mary Washburn[4]) and Josiah HAYWARD, 19 July 1715, Bridgewater
    (MD 16:190)

Josiah HAYWARD and 2nd Sarah (PRIOR) Moore, 11 Oct. 1738

Josiah HAYWARD[6] (Sarah Kinsley[5]) and 1st Mary PERKINS, 11 Feb. 1741 (Bridgewater VR)

Josiah HAYWARD[6] and 2nd Mary DUNHAM, 16 Nov. 1756, Bridgewater

Josiah HAYWARD[6] and 3rd Dinah MUXHAM, 22 Sept. 1768, Middleboro (VR 4:8)

Otis HAYWARD[7] (Josiah[6]) and Betsey PARRIS, 16 July 1804 (Halifax VR:78)

Independence HAYWARD[7] (Josiah[6]) and Hannah THORN, 7 Nov. 1799 (Halifax VR:78)

Kinsley HAYWARD[7] (Josiah[6]) and Hannah POOL, 9 Mar. 1806 (Halifax VR:81)

Cyrus HAYWARD and Silvia HOWARD, Apr. 1809 (Bridgewater VR 2:190,196)

Cyrus HAYWARD and Deborah RIPLEY, 18 Aug. 1804 (Bridgewater VR 2:169)

Sarah HAYWARD[7] (Josiah[6]) and Plato TURNER, Apr. 1803 (Bridgewater VR 2:176,376)

Lois HAYWARD[7] (Josiah[6]) and Moses SIMMONS, 23 Nov. 1769 (Bridgewater VR 2:173,361)

Thomas HAYWARD and Cynthia GARDNER, 17 Nov. 1791 (Middleboro VR 4:166)

James HAYWARD and Mercy WARREN, Int. 14 Mar. 1752 (Middleboro VR 2:96)

John R. HAYWARD and Nabby ROBINSON, Int. 13 June 1801 (Middleboro VR 4:16)

Benjamin HAYWARD and Phebe LEONARD, Int. 11 Jan. 1807 (Middleboro VR 8:29)

James HOLMES and Rhoda MUXHAM, Int. 9 July 1766 (Middleboro VR 2:212)

Isaac SHAW and Mrs. Hannah MUXHAM, Int. 29 Jan. 1783 (Middleboro VR 4:34)

William CHURCHILL and Lydia MUXHAM, Int. 28 Dec. 1783 (Middleboro VR 4:53)

Church HOLMES and Charity MUXHAM, Int. 20 July 1788 (Middleboro VR 4:75)

James RAYMOND Jr. and Patience MUXHAM, Int. 5 Apr. 1789 (Middleboro VR 4:80)

Lot COVELL and Mrs. Abigail MUXHAM, Int. 23 Sept. 1792 (Middleboro VR 4:101)

Lemuel RAYMON and Mrs. Abigail MUXHAM, Int. 17 Aug. 1793 (Middleboro VR 4:106)

William LITTLEJOHN and Deliverance MAXHAM, Int. 25 Jan. 1794 (Middleboro VR 4:109)

Isaac MUXHAM and Ruth MUXHAM, Int. 31 May 1794 (Middleboro VR 4:111)

Lazarus LeBARRON and Nabby MUXHAM, Int. 6 Oct. 1797 (Middleboro VR 4:132)

Beriah Dilino HATHAWAY and Fear MAXHAM, Int. 28 Apr. 1805 (Middleboro VR 8:6)

Tillson BARROWS and Hannah MAXHAM, Int. 23 Nov. 1806 (Middleboro VR 8:28)

Molly HAYWARD[7] (Josiah[6]) and Robert EDSON, 6 June 1782 (Bridgewater VR 2:174,126)

Phineas HAYWARD[7] (Josiah[6]) and Mehetabel GREEN, 16 Apr. 1797 (Windsor VR:88,91)

Nathan HAYWARD[6] (Sarah Kinsley[5]) and Susanna LATHAM[6] (Charles[5], Chilton[4], Susanna
    Winslow[3], Mary Chilton[2]), c1748

Sarah HAYWARD[6] (Sarah Kinsley[5]) and Silas WILLIS, c1745 (Bridgewater VR)

Susanna KINSLEY[5] (Mary Washburn[4]) and Samuel PACKARD, 22 July 1729, Bridgewater
    (MD 16:45)

Samuel WASHBURN[4] (Eliz. Mitchell[3]) and Deborah PACKARD, c1677 (MD 2:145)

Benjamin WASHBURN[5] (Sam.[4]) and Bethiah KINGMAN, 11 Feb. 1713/14, Bridgewater
(MD 16:189)

Benjamin WASHBURN[6] (Ben.[5]) and Susanna BATTLES, 23 Mar. 1743/44, Hingham (Bridgewater VR)

Benjamin WASHBURN[6] and 2nd Mary CUSHMAN[5] (Moses[4], Eleazer[3], Mary Allerton[2]),
5 Apr. 1748 (Halifax VR:34)

Joshua WASHBURN[7] (Ben.[6]) and Lovice RECORDS(sp), Int. 2 Mar. 1786 (Bridgewater
VR 2:324,388)

Eunice WASHBURN[8] (Joshua[7]) and Warren HUNT, 28 Oct. 1835 (Bridgewater VR 2:199)

Marsena WASHBURN[8] (Joshua[7]) and Lucy GIFFORD, 3 Dec. 1823 (Bible)

Hannah WASHBURN[5] (Sam.[4]) and John KEITH, 18 Apr. 1711, Bridgewater (MD 16:104)

Susanna KEITH[6] (Hannah Washburn[5]) and Ebenezer HINDS

Israel WASHBURN[5] (Sam.[4]) and Waitstill SUMMER, 3 Nov. 1708 (Bridgewater VR 2:360)

Waitstill SUMMER and 2nd Ebenezer PRATT, 15 Dec. 1720 (Bridgewater VR 2:305,392)

Israel WASHBURN[6] (Israel[5]) and Leah FOBES

Sarah WASHBURN[6] (Israel[5]) and Ephraim KEITH, 12 Sept. 1732 (Bridgewater VR 2:224)

Nehemiah WASHBURN[5] (Sam.[4]) and Jane HAWARD, 26 Mar. 1713, Bridgewater (MD 16:105)

Silence WASHBURN[6] (Nehemiah[5]) and Dr. Abiel HAWARD

Jane WASHBURN[6] (Nehemiah[5]) and Josiah DEAN

Zenas WASHBURN and Silence AMES, 2 Apr. 1789 (Bridgewater VR 2:33,392)

Zenas WASHBURN (Eleazer) and Sarah SHURTLIFF, 1 June 1804 (Plympton VR:392,419)

Noah WASHBURN[5] (Sam.[4]) and Elizabeth SHAW, 25 Jan. 1709/10, Bridgewater (MD 16:103)

Elizabeth SHAW and 2nd Isaac HARRIS[5] (Mercy Latham[4], Susanna Winslow[3], Mary
Chilton[2]), 22 July 1717, Bridgewater (MD 16:190)

Hannah WASHBURN[6] (Noah[5]) and Zachariah WHITMARSH, 28 Jan. 1729/30 (Bridgewater
VR 2:386,404)

Eleazer WASHBURN[6] (Noah[5]) and Anna ALDEN[5] (Ebenezer[4], Isaac[3], Jos.[2]), 22 Nov.
1738 (Bridgewater VR 3:167)

Eleazer WASHBURN[7] (Eleazer[6]) and 1st Huldah WOOD (Southworth Gen.:92)

Eleazer WASHBURN[7] and 2nd Sarah SOUTHWORTH[7] (Ebenezer[6], Edw.[5], Desire Gray[4], Mary
Winslow[3], Mary Chilton[2]), 9 May 1771

Sampson WASHBURN[8] (Eleazer[7]) and Rebecca SOULE[6] (John[5], James[4], John[3-2]), 28 Jan.
1806 (Bridgewater VR 2:351,391)

Samuel WASHBURN^5 (Sam.^{4}) and Abigail LEONARD, c1703 (MD 14:204)

Samuel WASHBURN and Deliverance LEONARD, 9 Jan. 1701, Bridgewater (MD 2:146)

Solomon WASHBURN^6 (Sam.^{5}) and Martha ORCUT, 13 Jan. 1731/32, Bridgewater (MD 16:98)

Sarah WASHBURN^4 (Eliz. Mitchell^3) and John AMES, 12 Jan. 1686/97, Bridgewater
    (MD 3:10)

Sarah AMES^5 (Sarah Washburn^4) and Abiel PACKARD, 11 Jan. 1722/23, Bridgewater
    (MD 16:187)

Abiel PACKARD and 2nd Deliverance (ORCUTT) Washburn, Int. 16 Nov. 1771, Bridgewater

Thomas PACKARD and 1st Mary HOWARD, 1 Jan. 1757, Easton

Thomas PACKARD and 2nd Martha (PERKINS) Packard, 18 Jan. 1780

Thomas WASHBURN^4 (Eliz. Mitchell^3) and Deliverance PACKARD, pre 29 Oct. 1684
    (MD 15:247,255)

Thomas WASHBURN^4 and 2nd Abigail ( ) HEFFORD, 24 July 1711, Bridgewater (MD 16:104)

Thomas WASHBURN and Sarah LEONARD, 22 July 1708 (Bridgewater VR)

Deliverance WASHBURN^5 (Tho.^{4}) and Ephraim JENNINGS, 18 Feb. 1718/19 (Bridgewater
    VR 2:257)

Prudence CONANT^6 (Eliz. Washburn^5, Tho.^{4}) and Thomas WESTON

Thomas WESTON and 1st Mary HOWLAND^4 (Nathaniel^3, Jos.^{2})

Thomas WESTON and Isabella CAMPBELL, 20 Dec. 1751, Boston (Rcd.Com.28:339)

Hephzibah WASHBURN^5 (Tho.^{4}) and John HUTCHINSON 29 Oct. 1708 (Bridgewater VR 2:252)

Thomas WASHBURN^5 (Tho.^{4}) and Elizabeth HOWLAND^4 (?James^3, Jos.^{2}), c1721 (MD 15:88)

Hannah MITCHELL^3 and Joseph HAYWARD, c1682 (MD 5:248)$^{<4>}$

Joseph HAYWARD and 1st Alice BRETT, pre 1673 (MD 5:248)

Edward HAYWARD^4 (Hannah Mitchell^3) and Keziah (HALL) White

Abigail HAYWARD^4 (Hannah Mitchell^3) and Zachariah SNELL, 11 Mar. 1730/31, Bridge-
    water (MD 16:98)

Alice HAYWARD^4 (Hannah Mitchell^3) and Israel ALGER, c1712 (MD 15:47)

Hannah HAYWARD^4 (Hannah Mitchell^3) and Ebenezer BYRAM, 9 Dec. 1714, Bridgewater
    (MD 16:190)

Mary HAYWARD^4 (Hannah Mitchell^3) and 1st Thomas AMES, 27 Feb. 1706, Bridgewater
    (MD 16:102)

Mary HAYWARD^4 and 2nd John BUCK, 1739

Joseph AMES^5 (Mary Hayward^4) and Susanna LITTLEFIELD, 6 July 1736 (MD 16:100)

Joseph AMES^5 and 2nd Ruth (FIELD) Packard, 30 Jan. 1754 (Bridgewater VR 2:32,282)

Joseph AMES^5 and 3rd Abihail (LATHROP)(Alger) Bozworth, Int. 12 Oct. 1768 (Bridgewater VR 2:32,58)

David GLAZIER and Cylinda MARCY, 19 Apr. 1808

Charles H. AMES and Caroline F. GLAZIER, 1 Dec. 1839, Willington (VR)

Thomas AMES^5 (Mary Hayward^4) and Keziah HOWARD

Peter HAYWARD^4 (Hannah Mitchell^3) and Abigail WILLIAMS, 14 Dec. 1732, Bridgewater (MD 16:99)

Susanna HAYWARD^4 (Hannah Mitchell^3) and Jonathan PACKARD, 24 Dec. 1719, Bridgewater (MD 16:186)

Thomas HAYWARD^4 (Hannah Mitchell^3) and Bethiah WALDO, c1719, Bridgewater (MD 15:89)

Edmund HAYWARD^5 (Tho.^{4}) and Anna SNELL, 22 Aug. 1751 (Bridgewater VR 2:170,343)

Waldo HAYWARD^6 (Edmund^5) and Lucy BARTLETT, 5 Dec. 1781 (Bridgewater VR 2:42,177)

Ira HAYWARD and Sarah EDSON

Samuel BARTLETT and Susanna DUNBAR, 12 May 1757 (Bridgewater VR 2:41,116)

Jacob MITCHELL^3 and Susanna POPE, 7 Nov. 1666, Plymouth (MD 18:56)

Jacob MITCHELL^4 (Jacob^3) and 1st Deliverance KINGMAN, 1 Jan. 1695/96, Bridgewater (MD 3:9)

Jacob MITCHELL^4 and 2nd Rebecca CUSHMAN^4 (Isaac^3, Mary Allerton^2), 18 Nov. 1701, Plymouth (MD 13:207)

Jacob MITCHELL^5 (Jacob^4) and Mary HOWLAND, 18 Jan. 1721 (Pembroke VR:294,319)

Jacob MITCHELL^5 and 2nd Rachel (LEWIS) Cushing, aft. Jan. 1726 (MD 10:158)

Mary MITCHELL^4 (Jacob^3) and Samuel KINGMAN, 1 Jan. 1695/96, Bridgewater (MD 3:9)

Jane KINGMAN^5 (Mary Mitchell^4) and Isaac KINGMAN, 13 Jan. 1729/30, Bridgewater (MD 16:45)

Joanna KINGMAN^5 (Mary Mitchell^4) and Akerman PETTINGALE, 17 Sept. 1723, Bridgewater (MD 16:188)

Mary KINGMAN^5 (Mary Mitchell^4) and Benjamin VICKERY, 21 Dec. 1739 (Bridgewater VR 2:223,377)

Benjamin VICKERY and Mary ALLEN, 3 Feb. 1736/37 (Bridgewater VR 2:28,377)

Benjamin VICKERY Jr. and Rhoda HOLBROOK, 12 Dec. 1776 (Mendon VR:323,417)

Lydia VICKERY and Isaiah CORBETT, 12 Jan. 1758 (Mendon VR:276,417)

Mary VICKERY and Jonathan HAYWARD JR., 25 Jan. 1769 (Mendon VR:315,417)

Rebecca VICKERY and Japhet TOFT, Int. 21 Feb. 1807 (Mendon VR:397,417)

Susanna KINGMAN^5 (Mary Mitchell^4) and Solomon PACKARD, c1718 (MD 15:168)

Solomon PACKARD and 2nd Dorothy (WHIPPLE) Perkins, 5 Oct. 1760

Asaba CHURCHILL^8 (Cynthia Packard^7, Solomon^6. Susanna Kingman^5) and Lewis L. KEITH

Thomas MITCHELL^4 (Jacob^3) and Elizabeth KINGMAN, 1 Jan. 1695/96, Bridgewater
(MD 3:9)

Seth MITCHELL^5 (Tho.^{4}) and 1st Ann LATHAM^6 (Tho.^{5}, James^4, Susanna Winslow^3, Mary Chilton^2), 21 Dec. 1738 (Bridgewater VR 3:163)

Seth MITCHELL^5 and 2nd Mary WADE, c1760

Rotheus MITCHELL^6 (Seth^5) and Hephzibah HAYWARD^7 (Josiah^6, Sarah Kinsley^5, Mary Washburn^4, Eliz. Mitchell^3, Jane Cooke^2), 3 Apr. 1783 (Bridgewater VR 2:171)

Thomas MITCHELL^6 (Timothy^5, Tho.^{4}) and Keziah SWIFT^6 (Wm.^{5}, Abigail Gibbs^4, Alice Warren^3, Nathaniel^2), Int. 1 Oct. 1757 (Plymouth VR 2:116)

John MITCHELL^3 and 1st Mary BONNEY, 14 Dec. 1675, Duxbury (MD 8:232)

John MITCHELL^3 and 2nd Mary LATHRUP, 14 Jan. 1679, Duxbury (MD 8:232)

John MITCHELL^3 and 3rd Mary PRIOR, 24 May 1682, Duxbury (MD 8:232)

Joseph MITCHELL^4 (John^3) and 1st Bathshua LUMBERT, 12 Oct. 1710, Plymouth (MD 14:36)

Joseph MITCHELL^4 and 2nd Hannah HERSEY, 11 Jan. 1753 (Abington VR 2:103,137)

Bathsheba MITCHELL^5 (Jos.^{4}) and Timothy BRIGGS, 14 Aug. 1746, Kingston (Gen.Adv. 3:22,52)

Martha MITCHELL^5 (Jos.^{4}) and Japhet RICKARD, 16 Mar. 1752, Kingston (Gen.Adv. 3:22,24)

Sarah MITCHELL^5 (Jos.^{4}) and Jonathan RING^4 (Eleazer^3, Deborah Hopkins^2), 21 Jan. 1747/48, Kingston (Gen.Adv.3:23)

Benjamin MITCHELL^5 (Jos.^{4}) and Mary PHILIPS, 27 Nov. 1750, Kingston (Gen.Adv.3:22)

Joseph MITCHELL^6 (Ben.^{5}) and Lucy SAMPSON^7 (Gideon^6, Zabdiel^5, Hannah Soule^4, Ben.^{3}, John^2), 3 Aug. 1806, Plympton (VR:351,380)

Mary MITCHELL^3 and James SHAW, 24 Dec. 1652, Plymouth (MD 16:239)[4]

Sarah MITCHELL^3 and John HAYWARD, c1661 (MD 2:92)[4]

Benoni HAYWARD^4 (Sarah Mitchell^3) and Hannah GOOLD, 11 Sept. 1717 (Bridgewater VR 2:280,256)[6]

Elizabeth HAYWARD^4 (Sarah Mitchell^3) and Edmund RAWSON, 22 May 1717, Bridgewater (MD 16:191)

John HAYWARD^4 (Sarah Mitchell^3) and Susanna EDSON, c1698 (MD 5:250)

Susanna EDSON and 2nd Elihu BRETT, 17 Dec. 1706, Bridgewater (MD 16:102)

Susanna HAYWARD^5 (John^4) and Joshua HAWARD, 6 May 1724 (Bridgewater VR 2:165,176)

Sarah HAYWARD[5] (John[4]) and Josiah WINSLOW[4] (Josiah[3], Kenelm[2-1]), 10 Jan. 1721/22, Bridgewater (MD 16:186)

Sarah HAYWARD[5] and 2nd Edward WENTWORTH, 22 Jan. 1745/46 (Bridgewater VR 2:394)

Joseph HAYWARD[4] (Sarah Mitchell[3]) and Mehitable DUNHAM, 30 May 1700, Bridgewater (MD 2:146)

Melatiah HAYWARD[5] (Jos.[4]) and Samuel DUNBAR[5] (Sarah Thaxter[4], Abigail Church[3], Eliz. Warren[2])

Samuel DUNBAR[5] and 2nd Mary HAYWARD[5] (Tho.[4], Sarah Mitchell[3], Experience)

Benjamin HAYWARD[5] (Jos.[4]) and Sarah CAREY, 6 Jan. 1741 (Bridgewater VR 2:76,168)

Joseph HAYWARD[6] (Ben.[5]) and Olive MANLEY, 20 Oct. 1768 (Bridgewater VR 2:173,254)

Mary HAYWARD[4] (Sarah Mitchell[3]) and William AMES, 13 Dec. 1698, Bridgewater (MD 2:146)

William AMES[5] (Mary Hayward[4]) and Elizabeth JENNINGS, 29 June 1721, Bridgewater (MD 16:187)

Martha AMES[5] (Mary Hayward[4]) and Thomas CONANT

Sarah AMES[5] (Mary Hayward[4]) and Jonathan NELSON

Hannah AMES[5] (Mary Hayward[4]) and Samuel KEITH, 20 Feb. 1733/34, Bridgewater (MD 16:99)

Bethiah AMES[5] (Mary Hayward[4]) and Timothy KEITH, 2 June 1737, Bridgewater (MD 16:101)

Mary AMES[5] (Mary Hayward[4]) and Joseph ALGER, 3 Sept. 1719, Bridgewater (MD 16:186)

Mercy HAYWARD[4] (Sarah Mitchell[3]) and John RAWSON

Sarah HAYWARD[4] (Sarah Mitchell[3]) and Nathaniel BRETT, 21 Nov. 1683, Bridgewater (MD 3:8)

Hannah BRETT[5] (Sarah Hayward[4]) and Joseph GANNETT, 2 Oct. 1732 (Bridgewater VR 2:224)

Mehitable BRETT[5] (Sarah Hayward[4]) and Samuel EDSON, 10 Jan. 1721/22 (Bridgewater VR 2:255)

Samuel EDSON and 2nd Mehitable HAYWARD, 1738

Nathaniel BRETT[5] (Sarah Hayward[4]) and 2nd Mary ( ) DYER, 1774

Seth BRETT[5] (Sarah Hayward[4]) and   Sarah ALDEN[4] (Isaac[3], Jos.[2]), 13 Oct. 1712, Bridgewater (MD 16:104)

Sarah ALDEN[4] and 2nd Recompense CARY, 17 Jan. 1726/27

Silas BRETT[6] (Seth[5]) and Thankful HOWARD

Simeon BRETT[6] (Seth[5]) and Mehitable PACKARD

William BRETT[5] (Sarah Haywood[4]) and Bethiah KINSLEY, 15 May 1732 (Bridgewater
    VR 2:225,61)

Mary BRETT[6] (Wm.[5]) and Jacob HAZZEN Jr., 12 Feb. 1752 (Norwich VR 2:178)

Susanna HAYWARD[4] (Sarah Mitchell[3]) and Thomas HAYWARD, 11 Nov. 1702, Scituate
    (MD 14:182)

Susanna HAYWARD[5] (Susanna[4]) and David DUNBAR[5] (Sarah Thaxter[4], Abigail Church[3],
    Eliz. Warren[2])

Alice HAYWARD[5] (Tho,[4]) and Thomas CUSHMAN[5] (Robert[4], Tho.[3], Mary Allerton[2])[7]

Alice HAYWARD[5] (Tho.[4]) and Joseph PRATT, 5 Apr. 1749, Bridgewater (VR 2:168,307)

Joseph PRATT and 1st Lydia LEONARD, 9 Dec. 1712 (Bridgewater VR)

Thomas HAYWARD[4] (Sarah Mitchell[3]) and Bethiah BRETT, 5 June 1706, Bridgewater
    (MD 16:102)

Mary HAYWARD[5] (Tho.[4]) and Samuel DUNBAR[5] (Sarah Thaxter[4], Abigail Church[3], Eliz.
    Warren[2])

John COOKE[2] (Francis[1])

John COOKE[2] and Sarah WARREN[2], 28 Mar. 1634, Plymouth (MD 13:83)

Ruth SPRAGUE and Eliezer SMITH, 12 Aug. 1680, Dartmouth (NEHGR 20:340)

Joannah SPRAGUE and John HATHAWAY, 15 Mar. 1682, Dartmouth (NEHGR 20:340)

Mahitable SPRAGUE and John RUSSELL, 17 July 16(), Dartmouth (NEHGR 20:340)

Patience SPRAGUE and John HATHAWAY, 29 Sept. 1696, Dartmouth (NEHGR 20:340)

Jonathan DELANO Jr. and Anne HATCH, 20 June 170(), Dartmouth (NEHGR 21:265)

Jonathan DELANO and Anne HATHAWAY (NEHGR 21:265)

Joseph TABER and Elizabeth HATHAWAY, 28 Jan. 1701/02, Dartmouth (NEHGR 21:265)

Jabez DELANO and Mary HATHAWAY, 8 Feb. 1709/10, Dartmouth (NEHGR 21:265)

Jonathan HATHAWAY and Susanna POPE, 31 Dec. 1701, Dartmouth (NEHGR 21:265)

John TRIPP and Rebecca SPOONER, 13 Jan. 1712/13, Dartmouth (NEHGR 21:265)

John HATHAWAY and Joanna POPE, 15 Mar. 1682/83, Dartmouth (NEHGR 21:266)

Elizabeth COOKE[3] and Daniel WILCOX, 28 Nov. 1661, Plymouth (MD 17:183)

Daniel WILCOX[4] (Eliz. Cooke[3]) and Hannah COOK, c1679 (Austin VR:423)

Hannah COOK and 2nd Enoch BRIGGS, 2 Mar. 1699/1700, Portsmouth RI

Samuel SANFORD and Deborah MANCHESTER, c1703[8]

Restcome SANFORD and 1st Elizabeth LAKE, 9 Dec. 1724[9]

Deborah SANFORD and Constant HART, 4 Feb. 1760[9]

William SANFORD and Mary WAIGHT, c1745$^{<8>}$

Peleg SANFORD and Lillis WILCOX, Oct. 1774 $^{<9>}$

Sarah ( ) WILCOX and 2nd Philip Marion SHEPUNGHS, 10 July 1728 (Friends Rcds.,
    New Bedford Library)

Sarah WILCOX and Love HOWLAND (Friends Rcds.)

William WILCOX and Dorathy ALLEN (Friends Rcds.)

Mary WILCOX and Isaac SMITH, 25 Apr. 1730 (Friends Rcds.)

Katherine WILCOX and Oliver BRIGGS (Friends Rcds.)

Edward WILCOX^4 (Eliz. Cooke^3) and Sarah MANCHESTER, c1700 (Arnold VR 4:7:115)

Ephraim WILCOX^5 (Edw.^{4}) and Mary PRICE, 28 Oct. 1729, Tiverton RI

Lydia WILCOX^4 (Eliz. Cooke^3) and 1st Thomas SHERMAN

Lydia WILCOX^4 and 2nd Thomas POTTER

Mary WILCOX^4 (Eliz. Cooke^3) and John EARLE, c1686

Benjamin EARLE^5 (Mary Wilcox^4) and Rebecca WESTGATE, 28 May 1726, Warwick RI (VR:93)

William EARLE and Mary BROWN, 10 Dec. 1752 (Earle Fam.:50)

Mary EARLE and Capt. Joseph TILLINGHAM(sp), 1776 (Earle Fam.:75)

John EARLE and Mary SPAULDING (Earle Fam.:76)

Sarah EARLE^6 (Ben.^{5}) and Benjamin GORTON, 6 Sept. 1757, Warwick RI (VR:53)

Daniel EARLE^5 (Mary Wilcox^4) and Grace HIX, 12 May 1716 (Tiverton VR)

Elizabeth EARLE^5 (Mary Wilcox^4) and George WESTGATE, 5 Oct. 1727, Portsmouth RI

Elizabeth ( ) WESTGATE and Capt. John ADAMS, 14 Nov. 1757$^{<10>}$

Earl WESTGATE^6 (Eliz. Earle^5) and Elizabeth GIFFORD, 17 Oct. 1756 (Tiverton RI VR)

George WESTGATE^6 (Eliz. Earle^5) and Elizabeth DURFEE, 26 July 1761 (Tiverton RI VR)

John WESTGATE^6 (Eliz. Earle^5) and Grace CHURCH, 6 June 1756 (Tiverton RI VR)

John EARLE^5 (Mary Wilcox^4) and Sarah POTTER, 19 Mar. 1711/12 (N. Kingstown RI VR)

Susanna EARL^6 (John^5) and Daniel SHERMAN, 22 May 1735 (S. Kingstown RI VR)

Abigail EARLE^6 (John^5) and Isaac SHELDON, 20 Dec. 1746 (S. Kingstown RI VR)

Benjamin WILCOX^6 (Jeremiah^5, Sam.^{4}, Eliz. Cooke^3) and Patience TUCKER, 19 Apr.
    1770 (Dartmouth VR)

Micro #18 of 30

Jeremiah WILCOX^7 (Ben.^{6}) and Ruth ALLEN, 29 Jan. 1809 (Westport VR:115,251)

Patience WILCOX^7 (Ben.^{6}) and Richard ALMY, Apr. 1799 (Westport VR:116,252)

Phebe WILCOX^7 (Ben.^{6}) and Christopher SLOCUM

Benjamin WILCOX^7 (Ben.^{6}) and 1st Sarah TABER, Int. 8 Sept. 1807, Westport

Benjamin WILCOX^7 and 2nd Patty BROWNEL, Int. 28 Oct. 1820, Westport

Jeremiah WILCOX[5] (Sam.[4]) and 2nd Judith BRIGGS[5] (Eliz. Fobes[4], Martha Pabodie[3], Eliz. Alden[2]), Int. 11 Feb. 1738

Willard WILCOX[7] (Ben.[6], Jeremiah[5]) and Ruth LAWRENCE, 21 Mar. 1795, Dartmouth (VR)

Henry WILCOX[8] (Willard[7]) and Hannah BAILEY, Int. 5 May 1821, Westport

Mary WILCOX[6] (Jeremiah[5]) and Humphrey SMITH, 1731

Sarah WILCOX[4] (Eliz. Cooke[3]) and Edward BRIGGS

Stephen WILCOX[4] (Eliz. Cooke[3]) and 1st Susanna BRIGGS

Esther COOKE[3] and Thomas TABER, c1667

Thomas TABER and 2nd Mary TOMSON[3] (Mary Cooke[2]), c1672

Thomas TABER[4] (Esther Cooke[3]) and Rebeckah HARLOW, 4 July 1700 (Dartmouth VR)

Esther TABER[4] (Esther Cooke[3]) and Samuel PERRY, 23 Oct. 1689, Sandwich (MD 14:171)

Elizabeth PERRY[5] (Esther Taber[4]) and Peleg BARLOW, 25 July 1717, Sandwich (VR 2:71)

Thomas BARLOW[6] (Eliz. Perry[5]) and Mehitable WING, 14 Feb. 1744, Sandwich (VR 2:131)

Mary BARLOW[7] (Tho.[6]) and James WITHERLY, 11 Mar. 1773, Sandwich (VR 2:207)

Obed BARLOW and Elizabeth BARLOW, 10 Sept. 1772 (Sandwich VR 2:197)

Mehitable BARLOW[7] (Tho.[6]) and Nathan HAMMOND, Oct. 1789 (Rochester VR 2:23,155)

Jesse BARLOW[7] (Tho.[6]) and Sarah NYE, 7 Dec. 1769 (Falmouth VR 2:18)

Arnold BARLOW[8] (jesse[7]) and Ann BRITTIN, 11 Dec. 1811, Philadelphia

Micro #19 of 30

Levi BARLOW[7] (Tho.[6]) and Rachel NYE, 29 Dec. 1768, Falmouth (Sandwich VR)

Thomas TABER[4] (Esther Cooke[3]) and Rebecca HARLOW (above) (MD 13:207)

Mary COOKE[3] and 1st Philip TABER, c1667 (Gen.Reg.35:32)

Esther TABER[4] (Mary Cooke[3]) and Thomas BROWNELL

Mary TABER[4] (Mary Cooke[3]) and Thomas EARLE

Bethiah TABER[4] (Mary Cooke[3]) and John MACOMBER, 11 Sept. 1711

Zebedee MACOMBER and Elizabeth CORNELL, Int. 30 Aug. 1755 (Dartmouth VR 2:456)

John TABER[4] (Mary Cooke[3]) and Susanna MANCHESTER

Lydia TABER[4] (Mary Cooke[3]) and Joseph MOSHER, c1694 (Dartmouth VR 1:170)

Benjamin MOSHER[5] (Lydia Taber[4]) and Abigail MAXFIELD, 12 Sept. 1728 (Dartmouth VR 2:312,323)

Benjamin MOSHER and Abigail MOSHER, 23 Nov. 1764 (Dartmouth VR 2:323)

Benjamin MOSHER and Phebe BROWNELL, 25 May 1755 (Little Compton RI VR 4:6:12,42)

Thomas BROWNELL and Mary CRANDALL, c1714 (Little Compton RI VR 4:6:86)

Charles BROWNELL and Mary WILBOR, c1718 (Little Compton RI VR 4:6:87)

Giles BROWNELL and Elizabeth SHAW, c1725 (Little Compton RI VR 4:6:87)

James MOSHER[5] (Lydia Taber[4]) and Sarah DIVEL, 25 Dec. 1729 (Dartmouth VR 2:164)

Jonathan MOSHER[5] (Lydia Taber[4]) and Isabel POTTER, 7 Jan. 1719/20 (Dartmouth VR)

Joseph MOSHER[6] (Jonathan[5]) and 1st Meribah ALLEN, 13 Feb. 1755 (Dartmouth VR
    2:28,327)

Joseph MOSHER[6] and 2nd Elizabeth BRIGGS, 22 May 1782, Dartmouth

Jonathan MOSHER[6] (Jonathan[5]) and Ann MOTT, 22 Mar. 1749/50, Dartmouth

Philip MOSHER[5] (Lydia TAber[4]) and 1st Abigail TRIPP, c1719 (Dartmouth VR 1:167)

Philip MOSHER[5] and 2nd Elinor ( ) HUDDLESTONE, Int. 20 Jan. 1759, Dartmouth

Maxon MOSHIER and Lydia BURGESS, 1750 (Newport RI VR 4:2:50)

Maxon MOSHIER and Hannah CLARKE, 8 Aug. 1754 (Newport RI VR 4:2:50)

Philip MOSHER[6] (Philip[5]) and Sarah BURGESS, 27 Sept. 1750 (MIddletown RI VR 4:3:14)

Micro #20 of 30

Caleb MOSHER[6] (Philip[5]) and Elizabeth WILLBOUR, Int. 26 Nov. 1743 (Little Compton
    RI VR 1:51)

Samuel WILBOR and Elizabeth CARR, 24 Dec. 1713 (Little Compton RI VR 4:6:17,67)

Maxson MOSHER and Rebecca MOSHER, Int. 18 Sept. 1822 (Dartmouth VR 2:328)

Maxson MOSHER and Phebe BEDON, 24 Feb. 1773 (Dartmouth VR 2:328)

Rebecca MOSHER[5] (Lydia Taber[4]) and Daniel TRIPP, c1720 (Dartmouth VR 1:279)

Ruth MOSHER[5] (Lydia Taber[4]) and William TRIPP, c1738 (Dartmouth VR 1:280)

Abigail MOSHER and Jonathan TRIPP, 23 Aug. 1764 (Dartmouth VR 2:322,509)

William TABER[5] and Hannah WHITE[6] (Eliz. Codman[5], Hannah Hathaway[4], Sarah Cooke[3],
    John[2]), 27 Dec. 1730 (Dartmouth VR)

Comfort TABER[5] (Philip[4]) and Benjamin BOWERS

Jonathan BOWERS[6] (Comfort Taber[5]) and Ruth SLADE

Mercy COOKE[3] and Stephen WEST, c1683 (Dartmouth VR)

Bartholomew WEST[4] (Mercy Cooke[3]) and Ann ELDRIDGE, 16 July 1747 (Dartmouth
    VR 2:176,531)

Stephen WEST[4] (Mercy Cooke[3]) and Susanna JENNEY, 15 Jan. 1718 (Dartmouth VR 2:533)

Micro #21 of 30

Samuel WEST[5] (Stephen[4]) and Salome ELDRIDGE, 17 Aug. 1749 (Dartomouth VR)

Hannah WEST and Jethro HATHAWAY, 3 Sept. 1741 (Dartmouth VR)

Jethro HATHAWAY and Judah HOWLAND, 22 Feb. 1782 (Dartmouth VR)

Jethro HATHAWAY and Abigail ( ) AKIN, 13 Nov. 1773 (Dartmouth VR)

Sarah COOKE[3] and Arthur HATHAWAY, 20 Nov. 1652, Plymouth (MD 16:238)

Stephen PECKHAM and 1st Content SISSON, c1715 (Peckham Gen.:234)

Stephen PECKHAM and 2nd Keturah ARTHUR, 8 Jan. 1739 (Peckham Gen.:234)

Stephen PECKHAM Jr. and Sarah BASS, 1739 (Peckham Gen.:272)

Seth PECKHAM and Mercy SMITH, 26 Jan. 1775 (Peckham Gen.:327)

Dr. Hazael PECKHAM and Susanna THORNTON, c1797 (Peckham Gen.:415)

Dr. F. Harris PECKHAM and Catharine Davis TORREY, 1840 (Peckham Gen.:493)

Hannah HATHAWAY[4] (Sarah Cooke[3]) and George CADMAN

Elizabeth CADMAN[5] (Hannah Hathaway[4]) and William WHITE[4] (Silvanus[3], Peregrine[2]), c1709

William WHITE and Abigail THURSTON, 2 Oct. 1729 (Little Compton RI VR 4:6:64,66)[11]

George WHITE and Deborah SHAW, 18 Feb. 1730 (Little Compton RI VR 4:6:53,66)[11]

Roger WHITE and Rebecca GRINNELL, 4 May 1736 (Little Compton RI VR 4:6:30,66)[11]

Elizabeth WHITE and Benjamin SLOCUM, 24 Apr. 1737 (Little Compton VR 4:6:58,66)[11]

Christopher WHITE and Elizabeth THURSTON, 4 Mar. 1739 (Little Compton VR 4:6:64,66)[11]

Abner WHITE and Ruth BROWNELL, 14 Apr. 1746 (Little Compton RI VR 4:6:11,66)[11]

Sarah WHITE and Noah STODDARD, 1747 (Little Compton RI VR 4:6:60,66)

Israel WHITE and Sybil HIX, 2 July 1754 (Little Compton RI VR 4:6:34,66)[13]

Sarah WHITE and Isaac HILLIARD, 28 Feb. 1759 (Little Compton RI VR 4:6:34,66)[12]

Noah WHITE and Rhoda SHAW, 16 Mar. 1777 (Little Compton RI VR 4:6:54,66)[12]

Elizabeth WHITE and George BROWN, 9 Nov. 1780 (Little Compton RI VR 4:6:15,66)[12]

Peregrine WHITE and Abigail ( ) SOULE, 10 Feb. 1782 (Little Compton VR 4:6:59,66)[12]

Thomas WHITE, and Ruth DURFEE, 11 Oct. 1789 (Little Compton RI VR 4:6:26,66)[12]

Peregrine WHITE and Patience TABER, 23 Dec. 1804 (Little Compton RI VR 4:6:61,66)

David D. WHITE and Patience BROWN, 12 May 1825 (Little Compton RI VR 4:6:16,66)

Mary A. (ALMY) White and Rev. Nathan B. SPAULDING, 11 Aug. 1830 (Little Compton
        RI VR 4:6:60,66)

Andrew WHITE and Louisa TRIPP, 17 Sept. 1839 (Little Compton RI VR 4:6:65,66)

Ruth D. WHITE and George W. STAPLES, 9 Mar. 1847 (Little Compton VR 4:6:60,66)

Harriet A. WHITE and George W. PEARCE, 28 Oct. 1849 (Little Compton VR 4:6:47,66)

Christopher T. WHITE and Mary G. BROWNELL, 21 Jan. 1850 (Little Compton VR 4:6:15)

Hannah WHITE[6] (Eliz. Cadman[5]) and William TABER[5] (Philip[4], Mary Cooke[3], John[2]),
        27 Dec. 1730 (Dartmouth VR)

Peleg WHITE[7] (George[6], Eliz. Cadman[5]) and Rachel CORNELL, Int. 2 Oct. 1754 (Dart-
        mouth VR 2:131,538)

Roger WHITE[8] (Peleg[7]) and 1st Lydia PECKHAM, 30 Jan. 1783 (Dartmouth VR)

Roger WHITE^8 and 2nd Lydia LAWTON, 30 Dec. 1802

Ruth WHITE^7 (George^6, Eliz. Cadman^5) and Culbert WILCOX, Int. 8 Jan. 1754 (Dartmouth VR 2:538,546)

Oliver WHITE^6 (Eliz. Cadman^5) and Mary HARMAN, c1747

Sarah WHITE^6 (Eliz. Cadman^5) and John BROWN, 23 May 1726 (Portsmouth RI VR 4:1:11)

Ruth BROWN^7 (Sarah White^6) and 1st Wanton HOWLAND, 12 Dec. 1754 (Tiverton RI VR 4:7:12,32)

Ruth BROWN^7 and 2nd Gilbert DEVOL

Thomas WHITE^6 (Eliz. Cadman^5) and Elizabeth JENNE, 25 Aug. 1751 (Dartmouth VR)

William WHITE^6 (Eliz. Cadman^5) and 1st Abigail THURSTON (see p.140)

William WHITE^6 and 2nd Abigail WHITE, Int. 20 Mar. 1766

John HATHAWAY^4 (Sarah Cooke^3) and 1st Joanna POPE, 15 Mar. 1682/83 (Dartmouth VR 2:232,364)

John HATHAWAY^4 and 2nd Patience POPE, 19/29 Sept. 1696, Dartmouth (Gen.Reg.20:340)

Ebenezer HATHAWAY^5 (John^4) and Ruth HATCH, 10 Sept. 1741 (Dartmouth VR)

Hunewell HATHAWAY^5 (John^4) and Mary WORTH, 5 Oct. 1731 (Nantucket VR 4:29,527)

William HATHAWAY^6 (Hunewell^5) and Ruth BARKER, 7 Feb. 1765 (Dartmouth VR)

Anna HATHAWAY^6 (Hunewell^5) and James BATES, Int. 30 Nov. 1759, Dartmouth

Lydia HATHAWAY^6 (Hunewell^5) and William RUSSEL, Int. 24 Mar. 1764, Dartmouth

Paul HATHAWAY^6 (Hunewell^5) and Sarah WINSLOW, 22 Apr. 1779 (Dartmouth VR 2:234)

Richard HATHAWAY^6 (Hunewell^5) and Sarah HATHAWAY, 25 Oct. 1772 (Dartmouth VR 2:234)

Richard HATHAWAY and Mary HATHAWAY, 10 Feb. 1783 (Dartmouth VR 2:234,233)

Ezra HATHAWAY^7 (Richard^6) and Abigail (WANTON) Thurston, 26 Nov. 1807

George W. HATHAWAY^8 (Ezra^7) and Betsey R. WASHBURN, 3 July 1831 (Dartmouth VR)

Sarah A. HATHAWAY^8 (Ezra^7) and Joseph C. TEW, 20 May 1832 (New Bedford VR 2:259)

Ann A. HATHAWAY^8 (Ezra^7) and James BEETLE, 1 Jan. 1854, New Bedford

James BEETLE and 1st Adelaide HATHAWAY^8 (Ezra^7)

Lydia Ann HATHAWAY^8 (Ezra^7) and Benjamin KING

Abigail WANTON and Latham THURSTON Jr., 1802

Elizabeth Thurston HATHAWAY^8 (Ezra^7) and George Cornell TEW, 20 June 1830, New Bedford

Patience HATHAWAY^5 (John^4) and Reuben PECKHAM

Sarah HATHAWAY^5 (John^4) and John CANNON, 11 Oct. 1709, Dartmouth (Gen.Reg.21:265)

Jonathan HATHAWAY^4 (Sarah Cooke^3) and Susanna POPE, 31 Dec. 1701, Dartmouth (Gen. Reg. 21:265)

Gamaliel HATHAWAY^5 (Jonathan^4) and Hannah HILLMAN, 16 June 1736 (Dartmouth VR:380)

Anna HATHAWAY^6 (Gamaliel^5) and Benjamin DILLINGHAM, Int. 3 July 1761 (Dartmouth VR:496)

Micah HATHAWAY^6 (Gamaliel^5) and Mary MYRICKS, aft. 1764

Nathan HATHAWAY^7 (Micah^6) and Elizabeth KEMPTON, 14 Oct. 1810 (New Bedford VR 2:193)

Phebe Kempton HATHAWAY^8 (Nathan^7) and Benjamin Jenne CRAPO

Obed HATHAWAY^6 (Gamaliel^5) and Desire HAWES, c1760

Lydia HATHAWAY^4 (Sarah Cooke^3) and James SISSON, c1681

Sarah SISSON^5 (Lydia Hathaway^4) and William DAVOL

Mary HATHAWAY^4 (Sarah Cooke^3) and Samuel HAMMOND, c1681 (Rochester VR 1:145)

<u>Micro #24 of 30</u>

Seth HAMMOND^5 (Mary Hathaway^4) and Mercy RANDEL, 4 Mar. 1705/06 (Rochester VR 2:159)

Jedediah HAMMOND^6 (Seth^5) and 1st Elizabeth JENNEY, 29 Mar. 1738 (Dartmouth VR 2:219,270)

Jedediah HAMMOND^6 and 2nd Mary BOWLS, Int. 16 July 1748 (Dartmouth VR 2:66,219)

Jeduthan HAMMOND^7 (Jedediah^6) and Mary JENNE, Int. 3 Nov. 1764 (Dartmouth VR 2:219)

Thomas HATHAWAY^4 (Sarah Cooke^3) and Hephzibah STARBUCK, c1697 (Dartmouth VR:207)

Thomas HATHAWAY^5 (Tho.^{4}) and Lois TABER^5 (Jacob^4, Mary Tomson^3, Mary Cooke^2), 25 Jan. 1753, Dartmouth

Antipas HATHAWAY^5 (Tho.^{4}) and Patience (COOK) Church, 13 Sept. 1729, Freetown

Nathaniel HATHAWAY^6 (Antipas^5) and Elizabeth PEIRCE, c1770

Elizabeth HATHAWAY^7 (Nath.^{6}) and Howard POTTER, 9 Apr. 1809

Martha HATHAWAY^7 (Nath.^{6}) and Noah GIFFORD, 20 June 1797

Nathaniel GIFFORD^8 (Martha Hathaway^7) and Mercy Anthony MACOMBER

Nathaniel HATHAWAY^7 (Nath.^{6}) and Susanna MAYHEW, Int. 30 Sept. 1815 (Nantucket VR 4:29,191)

Patience HATHAWAY^7 (Nath.^{6}) and Resolved HOWLAND, 14 Jan. 1796 (Dartmouth VR 2:234)

Apphia HATHAWAY^5 (Tho.^{4}) and Adam MOTT, 18 Dec. 1718, Dartmouth (Gen.Reg.20:340)

Jacob MOTT^6 (Apphia Hathaway^5) and Anne WEST^5 (Stephen^4, Mercy Cooke^3, John^2)

Hephzibah HATHAWAY^5 (Tho.^{4}) and Samuel WING

Jethro HATHAWAY^5 (Tho.^{4}) and 1st Hannah WEST^5 (Stephen^4, Mercy Cooke^3, John^2), 3 Sept. 1741 (New Bedford VR:37)

Hephzibah HATHAWAY^6 (Jethro^5) and Timothy DAVIS, 18 Oct. 1759, Dartmouth

Nicholas DAVIS^7 (Hephzibah^6) and Ruth SPOONER

Stephen HATHAWAY^6 (Jethro^5) and Abigail SMITH, 9 Aug. 1764, Dartmouth

Stephen HATHAWAY and Lydia SWAIN, 31 May 1804 (New Bedford TR 1:47)

Abigail HATHAWAY^7 (Stephen^6) and Weston HOWLAND, 10 Oct. 1793 (Howland Gen.:153)

Elizabeth HATHAWAY^7 (Stephen^6) and Jireh SWIFT, 10 Nov. 1805 (Swift Gen.:27,54)

Hannah HATHAWAY^7 (Stephen^6) and Thomas NYE, 6 Nov. 1791 (Nye Gen.:202)

Hephzibah HATHAWAY^7 (Stephen^6) and Pardon HOWLAND, 1 Sept. 1802 (Howland Gen.:161)

Humphrey HATHAWAY^7 (Stephen^6) and Abigail SMITH, 27 Dec. 1787 (Dartmouth VR 2:231)

Mary HATHAWAY^7 (Stephen^6) and John TABER, 26 Nov. 1800, New Bedford

Stephen HATHAWAY^7 (Stephen^6) and Lydia SWAIN (see above)

Sylvia HATHAWAY^7 (Stephen^6) and Gideon NYE, c1811 (Nye Gen.:310)

Mary HATHAWAY^5 (Tho.^{4}) and Thomas KEMPTON, 7 Nov. 1734, Dartmouth

Thomas KEMPTON and 2nd Phebe PRICE, Int. 23 Sept. 1758 (Dartmouth VR)

Ephraim KEMPTON^6 (Mary Hathaway^5) and Elizabeth TUPPER, 8 May 1774 (Dartmouth VR:207)

Ephraim KEMPTON and Ann NYE^4, 11 Jan. 1753, Dartmouth (Nye Gen.:77)

Lydia KEMPTON and Soule CUSHMAN, Int. 1 Aug. 1769 (Dartmouth VR)

David KEMPTON and Elizabeth GIFFORD, 21 Oct. 1787 (Dartmouth VR)

David KEMPTON^7 (Ephraim^6) and 1st Joanna MAXFIELD, 22 Dec. 1805

David KEMPTON^7 and 2nd Phebe KIRBY, 3 Feb. 1828 (Dartmouth VR)

Thomas KEMPTON and Ruth BALY, Int. 21 May 1770 (Dartmouth VR)

Phebe KIRBY and 2nd Cyrus MACOMBER (Kirby Gen.:297)

Lydia KEMPTON^7 (Ephraim^6) and Peter FOSTER

David Batchelder KEMPTON^8 (David^7) and Sarah Bates LINDSEY

Mary COOKE^2 (Francis^1)

Mary COOKE^2 and John TOMSON, 26 Dec. 1645, Plymouth (MD 13:86)

Cornelius TOMSON and Sarah PITTEY, Int. 31 July 1716 (Weymouth VR 2:193,140)

Andrew THOMPSON and Elizabeth MURDOCK, 14 July 1755, Plymouth (Early Mass.Mgs.2:16)

Jabdiel TOMSON and Clara STURTEVANT, 23 Feb. 1780, Plympton (Early Mass.Mgs.2:33)

Caleb TOMSON and Molly PERKINS, 23 Nov. 1775, Plympton (Early Mass.Mgs.2:33)

Ebenezer THOMSON Jr. and Elizabeth BESSEE, 1 May 1760, Wareham (Mass.Mgs.2:51)

Lidia TOMSON and James SOUL, 14 Dec. 1693, Duxbury (Mass.Mgs.2:54)

John THOMSON and Elizabeth BISBE, 13 Apr. 1762, Pembroke (Mass.Mgs.2:63)

Jacob TOMSON and Abigail WADSWORTH, 28 Dec. 1693, Middleboro (Early Mass.Mgs.2:70)

Ephraim TOMPSON and Joanna THOMAS, 6 Nov. 1734, Middleboro (Early Mass.Mgs.2:71)

Joseph TOMSON and Mary COX, 25 Apr. 1746, Middleboro (Early Mass.Mgs.2:74)

Elisabeth TOMSON and Edward RICHMOND, 6 Nov. 1750, Middleboro (Mass.Mgs.2:78)

Jacob TOMSON and Waitstill MILLER, 15 Apr. 1756, Middleboro (Mass.Mgs.2:83)

Sarah TOMSON and David MILLER Jr., 27 Aug. 1761, Middleboro (Mass.Mgs.2:85)

Susanna TOMSON and Silvanus THOMAS, 3 Dec. 1761, Middleboro (Mass.Mgs.2:85)

Nathaniel TOMSON and Phebe JONES, 1 Sept. 1767, Middleboro (Mass.Mgs.2:87)

Shubael TOMSON and Ruth HALL, 9 Oct. 1766, Middleboro (Mass.Mgs.2:88)

Francis TOMSON and Mary BUMPAS, 17 Dec. 1769, Middleboro (Mass.Mgs.2:92)

Abigail TOMSON and Seth MILLER, 17 Oct. 1771, Middleboro (Mass.Mgs.2:92)

Daniel TOMSON and Fear LION, 3 Dec. 1772, Middleboro (Mass.Mgs.2:92)

John TOMSON and Abigail TOMSON, 16 Feb. 1775, Middleboro (Mass.Mgs.2:95)

Nathaniel TOMSON and Hannah THOMAS, 1 Nov. 1775, Middleboro (Mass.Mgs.2:95)

Fear TOMSON and Abraham PERKINS, 23 Oct. 1777, Middleboro (Mass.Mgs.2:96)

Silva TOMSON and Elias THOMAS, 5 Feb. 1778, Middleboro (Mass.Mgs.2:96)

Jane TOMSON and Nathaniel BOLTON, 18 Dec. 1777, Middleboro (Mass.Mgs.2:99)

Susanna TOMSON and Daniel TUCKER, 30 May 1782, Middleboro (Mass.Mgs.2:100)

James THOMPSON and Jane HUTCHINSON, 22 June 1784, Middleboro (Mass.Mgs.2:104)

Esther TOMSON and Ebenezer BENNETT, 25 Oct. 1737, Halifax (Mass.Mgs.2:107)

Mary TOMSON and Samuel WATERMAN, 16 Mar. 1737, Halifax (Mass.Mgs.2:107)

John TOMSON and Lydia WOOD, 4 June 1741, Halifax (Mass.Mgs.2:107)

Elizabeth TOMSON and Samuel FULLER, 30 Sept. 1743, Halifax (Mass.Mgs.2:107)

Amasa THOMSON and Lydia COBB, 23 Feb. 1743/44, Halifax (Mass.Mgs.2:108)

Jebeda TOMSON and Zerviah STANDISH, 5 Dec. 1745, Halifax (Mass.Mgs.2:108)

Ruben TOMSON and Mary TOMSON, 8 Nov. 1739, Halifax (Mass.Mgs.2:109)

Francis TOMSON and Rebecca SNOW, 19 May 1761, Halifax (Mass.Mgs.2:110)

Nathan TOMSON and Mary HARLOW, 27 Oct. 1761, Halifax (Mass.Mgs.2:110)

Peter TOMSON and Rebecca THOMAS, 14 June 1763, Halifax (Mass.Mgs.2:110)

Deborah TOMSON and Micah REED, 24 Oct. 1768, Halifax (Mass.Mgs.2:111)

Noah TOMSON and Priscilla HOLMES, 27 Dec. 1768, Halifax (Mass.Mgs.2:111)

William TOMSON and Deborah STURTEVANT, 16 Nov. 1770, Halifax (Mass.Mgs.2:111)

Reuben TOMSON and Sarah TOMSON, 22 Jan. 1771, Halifax (Mass.Mgs.2:111)

Susanna TOMSON and Stephen ELLIS, 14 Nov. 1771, Halifax (Mass.Mgs.2:111)

Isaac TOMSON and Huldah STURTEVANT, 5 Dec. 1771, Halifax (Mass.Mgs.2:111)

Zerviah TOMSON and Ephraim FULLER, 9 July 1772, Halifax (Mass.Mgs.2:111)

Isaac TOMPSON and Lucy STURTEVANT, 19 June 1774, Halifax (Earley Mass.Mgs.2:112)

Lydia TOMPSON and Oliver HOLMES, 7 Feb. 1776, Halifax (Mass.Mgs.2:112)

Lucy TOMSON and Thomas DREW, 2 May 1776, Halifax (Mass.Mgs.2:112)

Adam TOMSON and Molly TOMSON, 18 Dec. 1777, Halifax (Mass.Mgs.2:112)

Ichabod TOMSON and Lydia HALL, 17 Dec. 1779, Halifax (Mass.Mgs.2:113)

Mercy TOMSON and Matthew PARRIS, 24 Feb. 1780, Halifax (Mass.Mgs.2:113)

Hannah TOMSON and Elisha MITCHELL, 21 Feb. 1781, Halifax (Mass.Mgs.2:113)

Lois TOMSON and Eliab KNAPP, 12 Mar. 1781, Halifax (Mass.Mgs.2:113)

Ezra TOMPSON and Sarah WHITTON, 5 Oct. 1781, Halifax (Mass.Mgs.2:113)

Jebadiah TOMSON and Phebe CURTIS, 13 Feb. 1782, Halifax (Mass.Mgs.2:113)

Martha TOMSON and Jonah BENSON, 6 Mar. 1783, Halifax (Mass.Mgs.2:113)

Sarah TOMSON and John PHINNEY, 16 Apr. 1780, Halifax (Mass.Mgs.2:114)

Levi TOMSON and Betty SNELL, 3 Dec. 1785, Halifax (Mass.Mgs.2:114)

Mary TOMSON and Elijah HOWARD, 5 Jan. 1786, Halifax (Mass.Mgs.2:114)

Eunice TOMSON and James SOUL, 20 Apr. 1786, Halifax (Mass.Mgs.2:114)

Thaddeus TOMSON and Ruth TILSON, 14 Sept. 1786, Halifax (Mass.Mgs.2:114)

Huldah TOMSON Jr. and Ephraim TINKHAM, 5 Apr. 1788, Halifax (Mass.Mgs.2:114)

Thomas THOMSON and Jane WASHBURNE, 31 Oct. 1745, Bridgewater (Mass.Mgs.2:119)

Betty TOMSON and Andrew GAMEL, 27 Oct. 1756, Bridgewater (Mass.Mgs.2:123)

Archibald TOMSON and Martha ROBINSON, 15 Oct. 1761, Bridgewater (Mass.Mgs.2:127)

Betty THOMSON and Nicholas WADE Jr., 25 Nov. 1762, Bridgewater (Mass.Mgs.2:128)

James THOMSON and Abigail ALLEN, 14 Nov. 1765, Bridgewater (Mass.Mgs.2:129)

Agnis THOMSON and Robert FULTON, 23 July 1767, Bridgewater (Mass.Mgs.2:131)

Sarah THOMPSON and Luther KEITH, 23 July 1767, Bridgewater (Mass.Mgs.2:132)

John THOMSON and Jennet ALLEN, 12 Mar. 1778, Bridgewater (Mass.Mgs.2:135)

Mary THOMSON and Cary HAYWARD, 29 Apr. 1779, Bridgewater (Mass.Mgs.2:137)

Elisabeth THOMSON and John PETTINGILL, 15 July 1784, Bridgewater (Mass.Mgs.2:145)

Nathaniel TOMSON and Sarah THAYER, 28 Apr. 1785, Bridgewater (Mass.Mgs.2:146)

Barnabas TOMSON and Hannah PORTER, 13 Mar. 1740, Bridgewater (Mass.Mgs.2:149)

Josiah THOMSON and Mary HA( )Y, 8 Nov. 1759, Bridgewater (Mass.Mgs.2:150)

Andrew THOMPSON and Judith NOYES, 3 May 1764, Bridgewater (Mass.Mgs.2:153)

Abigail THOMSON and Nehemiah NOYES, 21 Jan. 1782, Bridgewater (Mass.Mgs.2:157)

Peter TOMSON and Lydia COWING, 6 Jan. 1756, Rochester (Early Mass.Mgs.2:186)

John THOMPSON and Sarah SMITH, 19 Sept. 1682 (PCR 8:79)

Lydia TOMSON[3] and James SOULE[3] (John[2]), c1694 (MD 2:41)

Elizabeth TOMSON[3] and William SWIFT, c1678 (MD 14:172)

Thankful SWIFT[4] (Eliz. Tomson[3]) and Benjamin MOREY[5] (Jonathan[4], Mary Bartlett[3], Mary Warren[2]), 3 Nov. 1715, Sandwich

Benjamin SWIFT[4] (Eliz. Tomson[3]) and Hannah WING, 24 Feb. 1703/04, Sandwich (MD 30:60)

Zebulon SWIFT[5] (Ben.[4]) and Rebecca WING, Int. 30 Sept. 1739, Falmouth (Gen.Adv.3:81)

Ebenezer SWIFT[4] (Eliz. Tomson[3]) and Abigail GIBBS, 13 Feb. 1723/24

Jabez SWIFT[5] (Eben.[4]) and Hanny PARRY, Int. 25 May 1754, Falmouth (Gen.Adv.3:83)

Elizabeth SWIFT[4] (Eliz. Tomson[3]) and John GIBBS, 9 Nov. 1716 (Sandwich VR 2:63)

Joanna SWIFT[4] (Eliz. Tomson[3]) and Thomas GIBBS

Joseph SWIFT[4] (Eliz. Tomson[3]) and 2nd Rebecca (CLARKE) (Ellis) Morton, 14 Mar. 1730/31 (Swift Gen.:59)

Rebecca CLARK and 1st Mordecai ELLIS, 15 Oct. 1715, Plymouth (MD 14:37)

Rebecca CLARK and 2nd Nathaniel MORTON, 28 Apr. 1720, Plymouth (MD 14:39)

Jean SWIFT[5] (Joseph[4]) and Joseph BARTLETT[5] (Ben.[4], Jos.[3], Mary Warren[2]), Int. 2 Aug. 1735, Plymouth (MD 17:136)

Joanna SWIFT[5] (Jos.[4]) and Thomas GLOVER, 10 Feb. 1713/14 (Glover Gen.:512,515)

Joseph SWIFT[5] (Jos.[4]) and Sarah (BARTLETT[5]) Lebaron (Joseph[4-3], Mary Warren[2]), 21 Jan. 1736/37, Plymouth (MD 14:157)

Thomas SWIFT[5] (Jos.[4]) and Abigail PHILLIPS, 15 Nov. 1752, Sandwich

Maria SWIFT[6] (Tho.[5]) and Jonathan BEALE, Int. 20 Oct. 1787 (Braintree VR:888)

William Swift BEALE[7] (Maria[6]) and Elizabeth HOLBROOK, c1812

Elizabeth Holbrook BEALE[8] (Wm.[7]) and 1st Otis SPEAR, c1836

Elizabeth Holbrook BEALE[8] and 2nd Benjamin THAYER

Nancy Emogene SPEAR[9] (Eliz. H. Beale[8]) and John Winsor PRATT

William SWIFT[5] (Jos.[4]) and Lydia GIBBS, 2 Mar. 1731/32

Joshua SWIFT[5] (Jos.[4]) and Jane FAUNCE, 21/22 Mar. 1738/39, Plymouth (MD 16:254)

Abigail SWIFT[6] (Joshua[5]) and Nathaniel CORNISH, 12 Apr. 1768 (Plymouth Ch.rcds.2:495)

Joshua SWIFT and Nance CORNISH, Int. 6 Nov. 1779, Plymouth (MD 28:35)

Jane SWIFT[6] (Joshua[5]) and Samuel RIDER, 12 Apr. 1768 (Plymouth Ch.rcds.2:495)

Jane RIDER and Caleb BATTLES, c1797

Ezekiel RIDER[7] (Jane Swift[6]) and Polly HOLMES[8] (Peter[7], Jeremiah[6], Patience

Phinney^5, John^4, Mary Rogers^3, Jos.^{2}), Int. 20 Aug. 1803, Plymouth (MD 31:110)

James SWIFT and Elizabeth LORING, Int. 29 Mar. 1746, Plymouth (MD 17:134)

Samuel SWIFT and Thankful ASHLEY, Int. 22 June 1751, Plymouth (MD 16:168)

Elizabeth SWIFT and Joseph ASHLEY, Int. 4 Mar. 1748/49, Plymouth (MD 17:7)

Thomas SWIFT^4 (Eliz. Tomson^3) and Thankful MOREY^5 (Jonathan^4, Mary Bartlett^3, Mary Warren^2), 23 Jan. 1717/18, Plymouth (MD 14:38)

Thomas SWIFT^5 (Tho.^{4}) and Rebecca CLARK, 21 Oct. 1746, Plymouth (MD 16:172)

Jedidah SWIFT^6 (Phineas^5, Tho.^{4}) and Samuel NORRIS, Int. 11 Jan. 1772, Plymouth (MD 27:44)

Abiah SWIFT and Samuel GIBBS, Int. 26 June 1773, Plymouth (MD 27:46)

Phineas SWIFT and Sarah ELLIS, Int. 22 Apr. 1780, Plymouth (MD 28:35)

Micro #27 of 30

Lydia SWIFT^5 (Tho.^{4}) and Job BROWN, 19 Jan. 1737/38, Plymouth (MD 14:158)

Deborah SWIFT^5 (Tho.^{4}) and Jonathan TOBEY, 19 Feb. 1740, Plymouth (MD 17:4)

Elizabeth SWIFT^5 (Tho.^{4}) and Thomas TOBEY, 27 Feb. 1740/41 (Int.Plymouth-MD 18:32)

Jerusha SWIFT^5 (Tho.^{4}) and John MOREY, 17 Oct. 1751, Plymouth (MD 16:254)

Lemuel SWIFT and Rebecca WHITFIELD, Int. 11 Nov. 1756, Plymouth (MD 25:139)

Rhoda SWIFT^5 (Tho.^{4}) and Benjamin CORNISH, 22 Oct. 1750 (Int.Plymouth-MD 16:167)

Sarah CORNISH^6 (Rhoda Swift^5) and Nehemiah SAVERY, 1 Feb. 1794 (Plymouth VR 2:292)

Nehemiah SAVERY and 2nd Deborah SMITH, Int. 5 Mar. 1806 (MD 31:113)

Elizabeth SAVERY^7 (Sarah Cornish^6) and Sylvanus PRATT

William SWIFT^4 (Eliz. Tomson^3) and Lydia WEEKS, 9 Oct. 1707, Falmouth (Gen.Adv.4:113)

William SWIFT and Dorcas HATCH, 29 Nov. 1744, Falmouth (Gen.Adv.3:59)

Esther TOMSON^3 and William READ, c1679 (Weymouth VR 1:249)

Mary READ^4 (Esther Tomson^3) and Josiah ALLEN, 25 Dec. 1707 (Bridgewater VR 2:28)

Micah ALLEN^5 (Mary Read^4) and Hannah EDSON, 23 Feb. 1736/37, Bridgewater (MD 16:101)

Hannah EDSON and 2nd Thomas PHILLIPS, c1747

Dr. Micah ALLEN and Hannah CUSHING, 3 Nov. 1763 (Halifax VR:31)

Dr. Micah ALLEN and Margaret FORD, Int. 18 Oct. 1790 (Halifax VR:13)

Micah ALLEN and Catherine EVERITT, 24 Oct. 1764 (Canton VR:179)

Otis ALLEN and Susan DEANE, 20 Feb. 1806

Mary READ^4 (Esther Tomson^3) and Josiah ALLEN, 25 Dec. 1707, Bridgewater

Sarah REED^4 (Esther Tomson^3) and Hezekiah KING

Bathshua REED^4 (Esther Tomson^3) and Nicholas PORTER, c1699 (Weymouth VR 1:218)

Jacob REED^4 (Esther Tomson^3) and 1st Sarah HERSEY, c1717

Jacob REED^4 and 2nd Hannah ( ) NOYES

Ebenezer DRAKE and 1st Welthea SAMPSON, Int. 20 June 1824[14]

Ebenezer DRAKE and 2nd Lucy REED, 15 Feb. 1830[14]

Albert Henry DRAKE and Mary Ellen MARSHALL, 6 June 1869[14]

Ebenezer Hayward DRAKE and Phebe S. LUNN, 27 June 1852[14]

Sarah Elizabeth DRAKE and Ellery C. WRIGHT, 30 Nov. 1876[14]

Nellie Vernon DRAKE and Charles Edward BEALS, 30 June 1892[14]

William REED^5 (Jacob^4) and Silence NASH

James REED^6 (Wm.^{5}) and Ruth PORTER, 1 Jan. 1784 (Bridgewater VR 2:303,317)

James REED^7 (James^6) and Mehitable DYER, 19 Apr. 1810 (Abington VR 2:68,174)

John REED^4 (Esther Tomson^3) and 1st Sarah HERSEY, c1712

John REED^4 and 2nd Mary WHEELER, 1 Dec. 1715 (Rehoboth VR 1:159)

James REED^5 (John^4) and Ruth (FORD) Pool, 30 Aug. 1741 (Abington VR 2:159,174)

Ruth FORD and 3rd Samuel PORTER, betw. 1754-65

Hezekiah REED^6 (James^5) and Deborah M. TIRRELL, 21 Aug. 1766 (Reed Gen.<1901>:107)

Isaac REED^7 (Hezekiah^6) and Sally STETSON, 14 Apr. 1803 (Bridgewater VR 2:317)

James Thaxter REED^8 (Isaac^7) and 1st Eliza Ann KEITH, 5 June 1844 (Abington VR)

James Thaxter REED^8 and 2nd Mary Ann SEVERANCE, aft. 1851

Sarah Scott REED^9 (James^8) and Henry Cushman HARDING, 1 July 1866, E. Bridgewater

William REED^4 (Esther Tomson^3) and Esther NASH, c1703 (Boston Rcd.24:23)

Ebenezer REED^5 (Wm.^{4}) and Hannah TOMSON^4 (Jacob^3, Mary Cooke^2), 21 Feb. 1732/33, Middleboro (MD 13:250)

David REED^6 (Eben.^{5}) and Mercy FORD, 22 Apr. 1762 (Abington VR 2:76,172)

James REED^5 (Wm.^{4}) and Abigail NASH, 10 May 1739 (Abington VR 2:138,174)

Jacob TOMSON^3 and Abigail WADSWORTH, 28 Dec. 1693, Middleboro (MD 9:248)

Hannah TOMSON^4 (Jacob^3) and Ebenezer REED^5 (Wm.^{4}, Esther Tomson^3, Mary Cooke^2), 21 Feb. 1732/33, Middleboro (MD 13:250)

Mary TOMSON^4 (Jacob^3) and Reuben TOMSON^4 (Tho.^{3}, Mary Cooke^2)

Abigail TOMSON^4 (Jacob^3) and Jonathan PACKARD, 27 Nov. 1723, Middleboro (MD 4:73)[15]

Moses INGLEE^5 (Abigail Tomson^4) and Annah RANSOM, 10 Nov. 1757 (Halifax VR:35)

Barnabas TOMSON^4 (Jacob^3) and Hannah PORTER, 13 Mar. 1740 (Abington VR 2:161)

Adam TOMSON^5 (Barnabas^4) and Molly TOMSON^5 (Amasa^4, Tho.^{3}, Mary Cooke^2), 18 Dec.

Ichabod TOMSON^5 (Barnabas^4) and Lydia HALL, 17 Dec. 1779, Halifax (MD 7:51)

Isaac TOMSON^5 (Barnabas^4) and Huldah STURTEVANT, 5 Dec. 1771 (Halifax VR:30)

Jabez TOMSON^6 (Isaac^5) and Betsy WOOD, 31 Dec. 1799 (Middleboro VR 4:2:0)

Isaac TOMSON^6 (Isaac^5) and Phebe SOULE, Int. 9 Mar. 1801 (Halifax VR:67)

Noah TOMSON^5 (Barnabas^4) and Priscilla HOLMES, 27 Dec. 1768 (Halifax VR:31)

Caleb TOMSON^4 (Jacob^3) and Abigail CROSMAN, c1736 (MD 8:249)

Nathaniel THOMPSON^5 (Caleb^4) and Hannah THOMAS^5 (Mary Alden^4, John^3, Jos.^{2}),
    1 Nov. 1775 (MD 2:153)

Otis THOMPSON^6 (Nath.^{5}) and 1st Rachel CHANDLER, 3 Dec. 1801 (MD 2:153)

Otis THOMPSON^6 and 2nd Charlotte FALES, 30 Sept. 1828 (MD 2:153)

Otis THOMPSON^6 and 3rd Polly SHAW, 8 May 1850 (MD 2:153)

William TOMSON^5 (Caleb^4) and Deborah STURTEVANT, 16 Nov. 1770 (Halifax VR:29)

Esther TOMSON^4 (Jacob^3) and Ebenezer BENNET, 25 Oct. 1737 (Halifax VR:32)

Jacob TOMSON^4 (Jacob^3) and Elizabeth (TILSON) Holmes, 7 Jan. 1730/31, Middleboro
    (MD 9:46)

Jacob TOMSON^5 (Jacob^4) and Freelove PHINNEY^6 (Pelatiah^5, Jos.^{4}, Mary Rogers^3,
    Jos.^{2}), 27 Oct. 1761 (Bridgewater VR 2:298,368)

John TOMSON^4 (Jacob^3) and Joanna ADAMS, c1735 (MD 10:103)

Joanna TOMSON^5 (John^4) and Freeman WATERMAN^6 (Tho.^{5}, Mary Cushman^4, Isaac^3, Mary
    Allerton^2), 18 Dec. 1766 (Halifax VR:30)

Lydia TOMSON^4 (Jacob^3) and John PACKARD

Mercy TOMSON^4 (Jacob^3) and Nehemiah BENNET, 4 May 1721, Middleboro (MD 4:72)

Martha BENNET^5 (Mercy^4) and Nathan DARLING^5 (Eliz. Bennet^4, Priscilla Howland^3,
    Isaac^2)

John TOMSON^3 and Mary TINKHAM^3 (Mary Brown^2), c1680 (MD 1:221)

Ephraim TOMSON^4 (John^3) and Joanna THOMAS, 6 Nov. 1734, Middleboro (MD 13:251)

Joanna THOMAS and 2nd Joseph WORKS, 23 Oct. 1745 (Halifax VR:33)

John TOMSON^4 (John^3) and Elizabeth THOMAS^4 (Lydia Howland^3, John^2), c1724 (MD 2:51)

John TOMSON^5 (John^4) and Betty FULLER, Int. 2 Mar. 1760 (Halifax VR:60)

Shubael TOMSON^4 (John^3) and Susanna PARLOUR, 10 Dec. 1713, Middleboro (MD 2:158)

John TOMSON^5 (Shubael^4) and 1st Lydia WOOD, 4 June 1741 (Halifax VR:33)

John TOMSON^5 and 2nd Sarah (BRYANT) Soule, aft. Jan. 1761 (MD 14:219)

Sarah (BRYANT) Soule and 3rd Reuben TOMSON^4 (Tho.^{3}, Mary Cooke^2)

Thomas TOMSON^5 (Shubael^4) and Jane WASHBURN^6 (John$^{5-4}$, Eliz. Mitchell^3, Jane
    Cooke^2)

Thomas TOMSON^4 (John^3) and Martha SOULE^4 (John$^{3-2}$), 25 Apr. 1732, Middleboro
(MD 13:249)

Francis THOMPSON^5 (Tho.^{4}) and 1st Rebecca SNOW^5 (Jonathan^4, Jos.^{3}, Rebecca Brown^2)

Peter TOMSON^5 (Tho.^{4}) and Rebecca THOMAS, 14 June 1763 (Halifax VR:31)

Peter TOMSON and Rebecca STURTEVANT, Int. 8 Nov. 1761 (Halifax VR:61)

Ezekiel TOMSON^6 (Peter^5) and Mary BOSWORTH, 25 Nov. 1790 (Halifax VR:23)

Mary TOMSON^3 and Thomas TABER, c1672

Abigail TABER^4 (Mary Tomson^3) and Ebenezer TABER, c1715 (Tiverton VR)

Bethiah TABER^4 (Mary Tomson^3) and Caleb BLACKWELL^4 (Sarah Warren^3, Nath.^{2})

Jacob TABER^4 (Mary Tomson^3) and Sarah WEST^4 (Mercy Cooke^3, John^2), c1710

Lois TABER^5 (Jacob^4, Mary Tomson^3) and Thomas HATHAWAY^5 (Tho.^{4}, Sarah Cooke^3,
John^2), 25 Jan. 1753 (Dartmouth Friends VR)

John TABER^6 (Bartholomew^5, Jacob^4) and Mary HATHAWAY

Eunice TABER^5 (Jacob^4) and Benjamin AKIN

Benjamin AKIN and 2nd Lydia ALMY

Bartholomew AKIN^6 (Eunice Taber^5) and Mercy DELANO

Elizabeth AKIN^6 (Eunice Taber^5) and Edward BENNETT

Caleb BENNETT^7 (Eliz. Akin^6) and Ruth DAVIS, 6 Nov. 1791, New Bedford

John TABER^4 (Mary Tomson^3) and Phebe SPOONER, c1711 (Dartmouth VR 1:94)

Amaziah TABER^5 (John^4) and Sarah WING, 16 Nov. 1749 (Dartmouth VR 1:365)

Joseph TABER^4 (Mary Tomson^3) and Elizabeth SPOONER, 28 Jan. 1701/02, Dartmouth
(MD 3:218)

Joseph TABER^4 and 2nd Lydia ( ) GIFFORD, 30 Nov. 1738 (Taber Gen.:8)

Benjamin TABER^5 (Jos.^{4}) and Susanna LEWIS, 5 Feb. 1729/30

Jeduthan TABER^6 (Ben.^{5}) and Patience JENNEY^6 (Caleb^5, Desire Blackwell^4, Sarah
Warren^2)

Benjamin TABER^6 (Ben.^{5}) and 2nd Eunice (WORTH) Gardner, 28 July 1767

Barnabas TABER^7 (Ben.^{6}) and Mary CONGDON, 26 May 1796

Thomas TABER^6 (Ben.^{5}) and 1st Mary BENNET, Aug. 1766

Thomas TABER^6 and 2nd Hannah DAVIS, 20 Nov. 1777 (Bible)

Dr. Benjamin TABER^7 (Tho.^{6}) and 1st Phebe CARPENTER, 8 Dec. 1808$^{<16>}$

Sarah TABER^8 (Ben.^{7}) and Daniel GOVE

Adelbert Eugene TABER^9 (Ben.^{8}) and Lottie Ellen VAN CAMP, 24 Nov. 1880, Marion
  Minn.

Sarah TABER^5 (Jos.^{4}) and Preserved MERITHEW

Lydia TABER^4 (Mary Tomson^3) and John KINNEY (MD 16:233)

Mary TABER^4 (Mary Tomson^3) and Manasseh MORTON

Philip TABER^4 (Mary Tomson^3) and Susannah TUCKER (or Wilcox), c1710

Sarah TABER^4 (Mary Tomson^3) and William HART, 1 Dec. 1702, Dartmouth (MD 3:217)

William HART and Mary SHEPARD, 19 June 1740, Dartmouth

William HART and Esther SLADE, 15 July 1766, Dartmouth

Peter TOMSON^3 and Sarah (poss. Wood or Morton), c1699 (MD 4:111)

Peter TOMSON^4 (Peter^3) and 1st Hannah BOLTON, 18 Mar. 1740 (Halifax VR:32)

Peter TOMSON^4 and 2nd Lydia COWING, Int. 4 Jan. 1756 (Halifax VR:59)

Sarah TOMSON^4 (Peter^3) and Nehemiah BOZWORTH^4 (David^3, Hannah Howland^2), 26 Mar.
  1729, Plympton (MD 1:246)

Joseph TOMSON^4 (Peter^3) and Elizabeth BOLTON, 7 Feb. 1732/33, Bridgewater (MD 16:99)

Joseph TOMSON^5 (Jos.^{4}) and Jerusha WOOD, Int. 16 Nov. 1760 (Halifax VR:61)

Thomas TOMSON^3 and Mary MORTON^4 (Mary Ring^3, Deborah Hopkins^2), 13 Dec. 1715,
  Middleboro (MD 2:158)

Amasa TOMSON^4 (Tho.^{3}) and Lydia COBB^5 (John^4, Rachel Soule^3, John^2), 23 Feb.
  1743/44 (Halifax VR:33)

Ebenezer TOMSON^4 (Tho.^{3}) and Mary WRIGHT^5 (Isaac^4, Adam^3, Hester Cooke^2),
  13 July 1748 (Plympton VR)

Susanna TOMSON^5 (Eben^4) and Stephen ELLIS, 14 Nov. 1771 (Halifax VR:29)

Reuben TOMSON^4 (Tho.^{3}) and 1st Mary TOMSON^4 (Jacob^3, Mary Cooke^2), 8 Nov. 1739,
  (Halifax VR:34)

Reuben TOMSON^4 and 2nd Sarah (BRYANT)(Soule) Tomson, 22 Jan. 1771 (Halifax VR:29)

Deborah TOMSON^5 (Reuben^4) and Micah REED^6 (Dan.^{5}, Wm.^{4}, Esther Tomson^3, Mary
  Cooke^2), 24 Oct. 1768 (Halifax VR:31)

Lucy TOMSON^5 (Reuben^4) and Thomas DREW, 2 May 1776 (Halifax VR:20)

Andrew TOMSON^5 (Reuben^4) and Judith NOYES, Int. 2 Apr. 1764 (Halifax VR:62)

Joanna TOMSON^5 (Reuben^4) and Dr. Nathaniel MORTON, 5 Dec. 1790 (Halifax VR:23)

Thomas TOMSON^4 (Tho.^{3}) and Mary LORING, 25 Oct. 1745 (Plympton VR:343,410)

Thomas TOMSON^5 (Tho.^{4}) and Ruhamah BARROWS, Int 5 Jan. 1784 (Halifax VR:11)

Asa TOMSON^5 (Tho.^{4}) and 1st Rebecca CAMBELL, Int. 9 Dec. 1771 (Halifax VR:65)

Asa TOMSON^5 and 2nd Priscilla ( ) PHILLIPS, aft. Oct. 1803 (MD 14:9)

Zebadiah TOMSON^4 (Tho.^{3}) and Zerviah STANDISH^5 (Moses^4, Ebenezer^3, Alexander^2),
5 Dec. 1745 (Halifax VR:33)

NOTES

<1> p.114, Seth Fuller is descended from a double Mayflower line as follows:
Paternal line - Samuel Fuller^3 (Sam.$_1^{2-1}$)
Maternal line - Mercy Eaton^2 (Samuel^1)

<2> p.114, Included with this entry is "Daniel Prat forbid ye bands."

<3> p.121, The word "blacks" is written with this entry.

<4> p.121,122,134, Here is a good example of the progress that has been made in Mayflower research since Bowman's time.

Upon careful examination of the records, genealogists now feel that Jane Cook had only two (poss. three) children before her early death pre 1650/51 (the time of Bradford's writings). Thomas and Elizabeth Mitchell are now believed to be the only children of Experience and Jane (Cooke) Mitchell (with the possibility of Mary being a third). The remainder of the Mitchell children, namely Edward, Sarah, Jacob, John and Hannah are now believed to be Experience Mitchell's children by his second wife Mary ( ) and therefore do not have Mayflower lineage through Jane Cooke.

In an effort not to disrupt Bowman's files, descent for these Mitchell children is shown here as found, with the reminder that unless evidence surfaces to the contrary, line of descent is from Experience Mitchell, not Jane Cooke.

See NEHGR 127:94, "Comments on The Two Wives of Experience Mitchell of Plymouth, Mass.", by John B. Threlfall, F.A.S.G. and MQ 49:130-134, "Some Descendants of Francis Cooke, Mayflower Passenger", by Barbara L. Merrick.

<5> p.127, Solomon Bartlett married third, 20 Feb. 1814 and fourth, 23 Jan. 1820 but the names of his wives are not given.

<6> p.134, A second marriage for Benoni Hayward is given but is very hard to determine. It could read Hannah Page, 13 Oct. 1743 (Bridgewater VR 3:170)

<7> p.136, Although not married they are included here because they had a child together (Thomas Cushman^6, b.25 Sept. 1736) and therefore left descendants.

<8> p.136, Sanford, Carlton E. Thomas Sanford, The Emigrant to New England, 1632-34; Sketches of four other pioneer Sanfords and some of their descendants. Rutland VT. 1911. 2 Vols (2:1389).

<9> p.136, The Rhode Island Historical Magazine. Newport RI. 1886-87. (Vol 7:297,300,302,304).

<10> p.137, Ralph Earle and His Descendants. Worcester. 1888 (p.27,36) states this is the Elizabeth Earle who married first George Westgate. However, Bowman shows that George died after 7 Sept. 1765, so a second marriage of 1757 attributed to his wife ELizabeth is incorrect. (MD 18:253)

<11> p.140, Later shown to be the child of Elizabeth Cadman^5.

<12> p.140, Later shown to be the child of Christopher White^6 (Eliz.$_5$Cadman^5).

<13> p.140, His descent is later shown as (George^6, Elizabeth Cadman^5). His wife is later shown more fully as Sibyl (Woodward) Hicks.

<14> p.148, Drake, Louis Stoughton. The Drake Family in England and America, 1360-1895 and The Descendants of Thomas Drake of Weymouth, Mass., 1635-91. Boston, 1896. (p.163,250)

<15> p.148, Abigail Tomson had a child (Moses Inglee, b.c.1721) before this marriage, father's name unknown.

<16> p.150, History of Addison Co. VT. 1806. (p.509).

EDWARD DOTY/DOTEN DESCENDANTS

Edward DOTY and Faith CLARK, 6 Jan. 1634, Plymouth (MD 13:83)

Faith CLARK and 2nd John PHILLIPS, 14 Mar. 1666 (MD 18:56)

Elizabeth DOTY^2 (Edward^1)

Elizabeth DOTY^2 and John ROUSE, 13 Jan. 1674, Marshfield (MD 2:180)

Desire DOTY^2 (Edward^1)

Desire DOTY^2 and 1st William SHERMAN Jr., 25 Dec. 1667, Marshfield (MD 2:182)

Desire DOTY^2 and 2nd Israel HOLMES, 24 Nov. 1681 (MD 4:171)

Desire DOTY^2 and 3rd Alexander STANDISH^2, c1686 (MD 12:106)

Hannah SHERMAN^3 and William RING^3 (Deborah Hopkins^2), 13 July 1693, Plymouth
  (MD 13:206)

Experience SHERMAN^3 and Miles STANDISH^3 (Alexander^2), pre 5 July 1702

Ebenezer SHERMAN^3 and 1st Margaret DECRO, 18 Sept. 1702, Marshfield (MD 8:177)

Ebenezer SHERMAN^3 and 2nd Bathsheba FORD, 4 May 1730, Duxbury (MD 11:240)

Abigail SHERMAN^4 (Ebenezer^3) and Caleb CARVER, c1733 (MD 30:149)

Israel CARVER^5 (Abigail Sherman^4) and Margaret SHERMAN^5 (Elisha^4, Ebenezer^3,
  Desire Doty^2), Int. 4 Apr. 1764 (Marshfield VR 2:136)

Bathsheba SHERMAN^4 (Eben.^{3}) and Isaiah WALKER, 5 Apr. 1750

Ebenezer SHERMAN^4 (Eben.^{3}) and Elizabeth WORMALL, 1 Jan. 1749, Marshfield
  (VR 2:159)

Elisha SHERMAN^4 (Eben.^{3}) and Lydia WALKER, 5 Feb. 1744, Marshfield (VR 2:172)

Ebenezer SHERMAN^5 (Elisha^4) and Mary SIMMONS, 15 July 1773, (Marshfield VR 2:161)

Aaron SHERMAN^6 (Eben.^{5}) and Lydia MITCHELL, c1797 (Marshfield VR 3:13)

Elizabeth SHERMAN^4 (Eben.^{3}) and Joseph WITHERELL

Rachel SHERMAN^4 (Eben.^{3}) and Seth JOYCE, c1726/27 (Marshfield VR 2:106)

Patience SHERMAN^3 and Josiah WORMALL, 15 Jan. 1695, Duxbury (MD 9:108)

Josiah WORMALL and 2nd Grace ( ) SPRAGUE, 25 Dec. 1723, Middleboro (MD 4:72)

William SHERMAN^3 and Mercy WHITE^3 (Peregrine^2), 3 Feb. 1697, Marshfield (MD 5:237)

Sarah SHERMAN^4 (Wm.^{3}) and Adam HALL, c1725

Adam HALL^5 (Sarah Sherman^4) and Keziah FORD, c1752

Luke HALL^6 (Adam^5) and Anna TUELS

Luke HALL^7 (Luke^6) and Alice CARVER, 21 Sept. 1823

Thankful SHERMAN^4 (Wm.^{3}) and John POLDEN

Israel HOLMES^3 and Elizabeth TURNER

John HOLMES^3 and 1st Joanna SPRAGUE, 11 May 1710, Marshfield (MD 7:132)

John HOLMES^3 and 2nd Sarah THOMAS, 8 Sept. 1720 (Marshfield VR)

Edward DOTY^2 (Edward^1)

Edward DOTY^2 and Sarah FAUNCE, 26 Feb. 1662, Plymouth (MD 17:183)

Sarah FAUNCE and 2nd John BUCK, 26 Apr. 1693, Plymouth (MD 13:206)

Mercy DOTY^3 and Daniel PRATT, 13 Nov. 1713, Saybrook CT

Sarah DOTY^3 and 1st James WARREN^3 (Nathaniel^2)

Sarah DOTY^3 and 2nd John BACON, 28 Sept. 1726, Plymouth (MD 14:71)

Benjamin DOTY^3 and Hester BEMEN

Elizabeth DOTY^3 and Tobias OAKMAN, c1696 (MD 8:179)

Melzar OAKMAN and Persis ROGERS, Int. 16 Oct. 1779 (Marshfield VR 2:131)

Melzar Turner OAKMAN and Louisa OAKMAN, Int. 3 Sept. 1787 (Marshfield VR 2:162)

Abiah OAKMAN and Asa ROGERS, 13 Dec. 1781 (Marshfield VR 2:162)

Amos OAKMAN and Silvina THOMAS, 1 Feb. 1787 (Marshfield VR 2:174)

Christopher OAKMAN and Bethiah CLIFT Jr., Int. 7 Jan. 1807 (Marshfield VR 3)

Samuel OAKMAN and Catharine WHITE, Int. 22 Jan. 1821 (Marshfield VR 3)

Hiram OAKMAN and Jane S. ROGERS, Int. 17 Apr. 1826 (Marshfield VR 3)

Constant OAKMAN and Welthea CARVER, Int. 3 Dec. 1826 (Marshfield VR 3)

Edward OAKMAN^4 (Eliz. Doty^3) and Sarah DOGGETT^5 (Bethiah Waterman^4, Sarah Snow^3,
    Abigail Warren^2), c1736 (PN&Q 4:111)

Tobias OAKMAN^5 (Edw.^{4}) and Olive LITTLE^6 (Lemuel^5, John^4, Ephraim^3, Anna Warren^2),
    22 July 1779 (Int.- Marshfield VR 2:131)

Elizabeth OAKMAN^4 (Eliz. Doty^3) and Elisha FORD, 14 Jan. 1719/20 (Marshfield
    VR 2:147)

Tabitha FORD^5 (Eliz. Oakman^4) and Seth FORD, 13 Feb. 1766 (Marshfield VR 2:150)

Jerusha FORD^5 (Eliz. Oakman^4) and Arthur HOWLAND, 27 Dec. 1750 (Marshfield VR 2:160)

Elisha FORD^5 (Eliz. Oakman^4) and Elizabeth TILDEN

Lemuel FORD^5 (Eliz. Oakman^4) and Priscilla TURNER

Molbrough FORD^6 (Lemuel^5) and Mary TILDEN, 1 Mar. 1787 (Marshfield VR 2:153)

Faith OAKMAN^4 (Eliz. Doty^3) and Benjamin WHITE^4 (Dan.^{3}, Peregrine^2), 2 Dec. 1714,

Marshfield (MD 7:131)

Faith OAKMAN^4 and 2nd Thomas FOSTER, c1734 (Marshfield VR 2:165)

Thomas FOSTER^5 (Faith Oakman^4) and Mary THACHER, c1757 (PN&Q 4:36)

Mary FOSTER^6 (Tho.^{5}) and Levi TINKHAM^6 (John$^{5-4}$, Ephraim^3, Mary Brown^2)

Mary OAKMAN^4 (Eliz. Doty^3) and 1st Jedediah EAMES, c1733 (MD 31:22)

Mary OAKMAN^4 and 2nd Robert SHERMAN^4 (Ebenezer^3, Desire Doty^2), 23 Sept. 1740
    (Marshfield VR 2:172)

Betty Doty SHERMAN^5 (Robert^4) and Erastus RICHARDS, 16 May 1765 (Marshfield
    VR 2:150)

Jane EAMES^5 (Mary Oakman) and Seth EWELL

Mary EAMES^5 (Mary Oakman^4) and Joseph STETSON, 15 Sept. 1743, Marshfield
    (Scituate VR 2:269)

Penelope EAMES^5 (Mary Oakman^4) and Lemuel LITTLE^5 (John^4, Ephraim^3, Anna Warren^2)

Jedediah EAMES^5 (Mary Oakman^4) and Bethiah TILDEN, 7 Feb. 1753 (Marshfield VR2:152)

John Tilden EAMES^6 (Jedediah^5) and Sarah ROGERS Jr., 26 July 1792 (Marshfield VR 2:58)

Mercy OAKMAN^4 (Eliz. Doty^3) and 1st Matthew SIMONTON, 12 Mar. 1741 (Marshfield VR)

Mercy OAKMAN^4 and 2nd John HAMBELTON, 7 Feb. 1744 (Marshfield VR 2:172)

Samuel OAKMAN^4 (Eliz. Doty^3) and Elizabeth HATCH, 6 Jan. 1725 (Scituate VR 4:2:28)

Elizabeth HATCH and 2nd David HAYWARD, 12 Oct. 1748 (Marshfield VR 2:159)

Elizabeth HATCH and 3rd Peter RIPLEY, 22 June 1761 (Marshfield VR 2:149)

Samuel OAKMAN^5 (Sam.^{4}) and Deborah TURNER^6 (John^5, Ben.^{4}, Mary Brewster^3, Jonathan^2),
    9 June 1749 (Scituate VR 4:2:31)

Melzar Turner OAKMAN^6 (Sam.^{5}) and 1st Persis ROGERS (see p.154)

Melzar Turner OAKMAN^6 and 2nd Louisa OAKMAN^6 (Tobias^5, Sam.^{4}, Eliz. Doty^2) (see p.154)

Tobias OAKMAN^5 (Sam.^{4}) and Ruth LITTLE^5 (Constant Fobes^4, Martha Pabodie^3, Eliz.
    Alden^2), c1748 (Marshfield VR 2:114)

Constant Fobes OAKMAN^6 (Tobias^5) and Rachel HATCH, 11 Dec. 1783 (Marshfield VR 2:173)

Christopher OAKMAN^7 (Constant^6) and Bethiah CLIFT (see p.154)

Sarah OAKMAN^4 (Eliz. Doty^3) and Benjamin RANDALL, 17 May 1722 (Marshfield VR 2:147)

Susanna OAKMAN^4 (Eliz. Doty^3) and Anthony COLLAMORE, 4 May 1732 (Marshfield VR 2:143)

Martha DOTY^3 and Thomas MORTON, 23 Dec. 1696, Plymouth (MD 13:206)

Lydia MORTON^4 (Martha Doty^3) and Benjamin BARTLETT^5 (Jos.$^{4-3}$, Mary Warren^2),
    24 Sept. 1724, Plymouth (MD 14:70)

Micro #3 of 6

Mary MORTON^4 (Martha Doty^3) and John NELSON^5 (Sam.^{4}, Lydia Bartlett^3, Mary Warren^2),

c1732 (MD 15:43)

Sarah MORTON[4] (Martha Doty[3]) and Joseph BARTLETT[5] (Robert[4], Jos.[3], Mary Warren[2]),
4 Apr. 1727 (Plymouth VR)

Nathaniel MORTON[4] (Martha Doty[3]) and 1st Mary SHAW, Int. 21 Apr. 1733, Plymouth
(MD 17:134)

Nathaniel MORTON[4] and 2nd Mary ELLIS, 13 Nov. 1740, Plymouth (Int.-MD 18:31)

Thomas MORTON[4] (Martha Doty[3]) and Hannah NELSON[5] (Sam.[4], Lydia Bartlett[3], Mary
Warren[2]), 29 Mar. 1726, Plymouth (MD 14:71)

Hannah NELSON[5] and 2nd John DYER, 27 June 1734, Plymouth (MD 14:75)

Martha MORTON[5] (Tho.[4]) and Silas MORTON, 3 Nov. 1748, Plymouth (MD 17:7)

Mary DOTY[3] and Joseph ALLEN, 21 Dec. 1699, Plymouth (MD 13:207)

Elizabeth ALLYN[4] (Mary Doty[3]) and Hezekiah KILBOURN

Mary ALLYN[4] (Mary Doty[3]) and James OTIS, c1723/24 (Gen.Reg.2:289)

James OTIS[5] (Mary Allyn[4]) and Ruth CUNNINGHAM[6] (Ann Boucher[5], Sarah Middlecott[4],
Sarah Winslow[3], Mary Chilton[2]), 18 Mar. 1755 (Boston Rcd.com.30:14)

Mary OTIS[6] (James[5]) and Benjamin LINCOLN, 1 Feb. 1785, Boston

Sarah ALLYN[4] (Mary Doty[3]) and Nathaniel STILLMAN

Samuel DOTY[3] and Anne BUCKINGHAM

Isaac DOTY[2] (Edward[1])

Isaac DOTY[2] and Elizabeth ENGLAND, c1673

Samuel DOTY[3] and Charity MUDGE

Sarah DOTY[4] (Jos.[3]) and John JACKSON

Hannah JACKSON[5] (Sarah Doty[4]) and Taylor WEBSTER, 22 Feb. 1769

William WEBSTER[6] (Hannah Jackson[5]) and Mary MARSH, 30 Aug. 1795, Fayette Co. PA

Elias DOTY[4] (Sam.[3]) and Amy DEAN

Amy DOTY[5] (Elias[4]) and Thomas HALL, 9 Mar. 1786, Bagnall N.Y.

Mercy HALL[6] (Amy Doty[5]) and Winthrop ALLEN, 14 Mar. 1814

William Henry ALLEN[7] (Mercy Hall[6]) and 1st Charlotte AUSTIN

William Henry ALLEN[7] and 2nd Mary BARNES, c1863, Rose, Wayne Co. N.Y.

John DOTY[2] (Edward[1])

John DOTY[2] and 1st Elizabeth COOKE[3] (Jacob[2]), c1667 (MD 1:144)

John DOTY[2] and 2nd Sarah JONES[4] (Patience Little[3], Anna Warren[2]), 22 Nov. 1694,
Plymouth (PN&Q 3:121)

Sarah JONES^4 and 2nd Joseph PETERSON^3 (Mary Soule^2), 23 Apr. 1704 (Plymouth VR)

Desire DOTY^3 and George BARROWS, 23 Aug. 1722, Plymouth (MD 14:39)

Patience DOTY^3 and Kenelm BAKER^4 (Sarah Bradford^3, Wm.^{2}), 22 Jan. 1718/19, Duxbury (MD 11:25)

Elisha DOTY^3 and Hannah HORTON, 1 Feb. 1708/09, Marblehead (MD 19:177)

James DOTY^4 (Elisha^3) and 1st Ruth FINNEY^5 (John^4, Eliz. Warren^3, Joseph^2), 24 Apr. 1750, Plymouth (MD 16:169)

James DOTY^4 and 2nd Bathsheba DELANO, 26 Apr. 1753, Plymouth (MD 16:170)

Edward DOTY^4 (Elisha^3) and Phebe FINNEY, 3 Aug. 1738, Plymouth (MD 16:254)

Elisha DOTEN^4 (Elisha^3) and Deborah TUBBS, 6 Mar. 1728/29, Duxbury (MD 11:80)

Paul DOTEN^4 (Elisha^3) and Ruth (FAUNCE) Rider, c1749 (MD 3:113)

Stephen DOTEN^4 (Elisha^3) and 1st Hannah BARTLETT^6 (John^5, Robert^4, Jos.^{3}, Mary Warren^2), 10 Feb. 1745/46, Plymouth (MD 17:5)

Stephen DOTEN^4 and 2nd Jane DUNHAM, 16 Aug. 1784 (Plymouth VR 2:288)

James DOTEN^5 (Stephen^4) and Sarah ANDREWS, c1792, Boston (MD 17:182)

Sarah ANDREWS and 2nd Joshua TORREY, aft. June 1794 (Kingman:71)

John DOTEN^5 (Stephen^4) and Mary WRIGHT, 27 Nov. 1796 (Doty/Doten Fam.:173)

Joseph DOTEN^5 (Stephen^4) and Elizabeth ALLEN, 1794

Elizabeth ALLEN and 2nd Sylvanus STEPHENS

Stephen DOTEN^5 (Stephen^4) and 1st Betsey HOLMES

Stephen DOTEN^5 and 2nd Abigail CLARK

Elizabeth DOTY^3 and Joshua MORS, 12 Dec. 1698, Plymouth (MD 13:207)

Melatiah MORSE^6 (Joshua^5, Edw.^{4}, Eliz. Doty^3) and Joanna SWIFT, 7 Nov. 1788

Joshua MORSS and Mary GOODNUF, 8 Sept. 1763 (Rochester VR 2:156)

Newberry MORS^4 (Eliz. Doty^3) and Lydia BRIGGS

Isaac DOTY^3 and Martha FAUNCE, 17 Mar. 1702/03, Plymouth (MD 13:207)

Mary DOTY^4 (Isaac^3) and Lemuel BARTLETT^5 (Robert^4, Jos.^{3}, Mary Warren^2), 25 Nov. 1742, Plymouth (MD 14:160)

Rebecca DOTY^4 (Isaac^3) and 1st Benjamin WARREN^4 (Ben.^{3}, Jos.^{2})

Rebecca DOTY^4 and 2nd David TURNER

Elizabeth DOTY^4 (Isaac^3) and John STUDLEY

Isaac DOTEN^4 (Isaac^3) and Mary LANMAN, 5 Nov. 1734, Plymouth (MD 14:75)

James DOTEN^5 (Isaac^4) and Elizabeth KEMPTON, 8 Nov. 1764 (Plymouth Ch.rcds.)

John DOTEN^6 (James^5) and Sarah MORTON, 2 Nov. 1792 (Plymouth Ch.rcds.)

Hope DOTEN^6 and Samuel SMITH, 31 May 1791, Plymouth (Smithfield RI VR 3:6:31,68)

Jane DOTY[4] (ISaac[3]) and John PALMER

John DOTY[3] and 1st Mehitable NELSON, 2 Feb. 1692/93, Plymouth (MD 13:206)

John DOTY[3] and 2nd Hannah SHERMAN, 25 Apr. 1745 (Int.-MD 17:133)

Micro #4 of 6

John DOTY[4] (John[3]) and Lydia DUNHAM, 8 July 1724, Plympton (MD 2:139)

Ebenezer DOTEN[5] (John[4]) and 1st Mercy WHITTEN, 12 June 1750, Plymouth (MD 16:170)

Ebenezer DOTEN[5] and 2nd Mary RICKARD[6] (Theophilus[5], Sam.[4], Rebecca Snow[3], Rebecca Brown[2]), c1764

Susanna DOTY[4] (John[3]) and 1st Elkanah PRATT, 28 Mar. 1734

Susanna DOTY[4] and 2nd John FINNEY[4] (Eliz. Warren[3], Jos.[2]), Int. 31 Mar. 1739, Plymouth (MD 18:30)

Martha DOTY[3] and Ebenezer CURTIS, 7 Oct. 1718, Plymouth (MD 14:38)

Ebenezer CURTIS and 1st Mary TINKHAM[4] (Helkiah[3], Mary Brown[2]), 19 Jan. 1709/10, Plymouth (MD 14:36)

Samuel DOTY[3] and Mercy COBB, 10 Apr. 1727, Plymouth (MD 14:72)

Sarah DOTY[4] (Sam.[3]) and Benjamin SMITH, 4 Nov. 1757, Plymouth (MD 17:3)

Samuel DOTY[4] (Sam.[3]) and Mary COOKE[5] (Jacob[4-3-2])

Mary COOKE[5] and 2nd Cornelius HOLMES, 7 June 1743

Joseph DOTY[2] (Edward[1])

Joseph DOTY[2] and 2nd Sarah ( ) EDWARDS, 5 Mar. 1711/12 (Rochester VR 1:2)[1]

Joseph EDWARDS Jr. and Sarah BURGE, 13 July 1738, Rochester (Gen.Adv.1:108)

Deborah EDWARDS and Simon BURGE, 20 Dec. 1741, Rochester (Gen.Adv.2:81)

Joseph DOTY and Hannah EDWARDS, 2 July 1708, Rochester (Gen.Adv.4:66)

Deborah DOTY and Joseph LANDERS, 7 Feb. 1710, Rochester (Gen.Adv.4:66)

Edward DOTY and Mary ANDREWS, 17 Nov. 1726 (Rochester VR 1:28)

Barnabas DOTY and Sary TURNER, 24 Oct. 1728 (Rochester VR 1:27)

Faith DOTY and James SHAW, 14 Apr. 1719 (Rochester VR 1:26)

Elizabeth DOTY and John LEWIS, 28 Feb. 1705/06 (Rochester VR 1:1)

Mary DOTEN[3] and Samuel WATERMAN, 23 Aug. 1722, Plympton (MD 2:138)

Deborah DOTY[3] and Joseph LANDERS (see above)

Edward DOTY[4] (Ellis[3]) and Mary ANDREWS (see above)

Faith DOTY[3] and James SHAW (see above)

Samuel DOTY[4] (John[3]) and Zerviah LOVELL, c1749 (Sharon CT VR:36)

Joseph DOTY[3] and Hannah EDWARDS (see above)

Theophilus DOTY^3 and Ruth MENDALL, c1696/97 (Rochester VR 1:47)

Mary DOTY^2 (Edward^1)

Mary DOTY^2 and Samuel HATCH, c1677 (MD 5:111, 3:91)

Desire HATCH^3 and Joseph LOVELL, 23 Sept. 1731 (MD 1:106)

Ebenezer HATCH^3 and Abigail JONES, 10 Mar. 1719, Scituate (MD 10:76)

Elisha HATCH^3 and Patience KEEN, c1718

Elizabeth HATCH^3 and John BONNEY, 17 Dec. 1713

Ezekiel HATCH^3 and Ruth CHURCH^5 (Richard^4, Nathaniel^3, Eliz. Warren^2), 25 Sept.
    1718, Scituate (MD 10:75)

Hannah HATCH^3 and 1st Japhet TURNER, c1702 (Pembroke VR:211)

Hannah HATCH^3 and 2nd Ebenezer TINKHAM^4 (Ebenezer^3, Mary Brown^2), 9 July 1719,
    Scituate (MD 10:75)

Hannah HATCH^3 and 3rd Capt. Ichabod TUPPER, 23 Dec. 1729, Middleboro (MD 8:250)

Elizabeth TURNER^4 (Hannah Hatch^3) and John PRATT^5 (Sam.$^{4-3}$, Mary Priest^2)

Hannah TURNER^4 (Hannah Hatch^3) and William THOMAS, 22 June 1721, Middleboro
    (MD 4:72)

Sarah THOMAS^5 (Hannah Turner^4) and Thomas WOOD, 1 Nov. 1753, Middleboro (MD 19:46)

Thankful THOMAS^5 (Hannah Turner^4) and Christopher THRASHER, 14 May 1747, Middleboro
    (MD 18:82)

Hannah THOMAS^5 (Hannah Turner^4) and Thomas PADDOCK, 3 Dec. 1747, Middleboro
    (MD 18:80)

Ruth THOMAS^5 (Hannah Turner^4) and Thomas ELLIS, Int. 4 May 1757, Middleboro

William ELLIS^6 (Ruth Thomas^5) and Sarah RANSOM

Israel TURNER^4 (Hannah Hatch^3) and Abigail HOLMES^5 (Mary Brewster^4, Wrestling^3,
    Love^2), Int. 2 Jan. 1730/31, Kingston

Micro #5 of 6

Betty TURNER^5 (Israel^4) and Robert BARKER, 20 May 1759 (Pembroke VR:366)

Priscilla TURNER^5 (Israel^4) and Isaac PHILLIPS Jr., 27 Nov. 1754 (Pembroke VR:368)

Christiana TURNER^5 (Israel^4) and Poole SPEAR, 10 May 1761 (Pembroke VR:349,366)

Abigail SPEAR^6 (Christiana Turner^5) and Samuel ABBOTT, c1806

James P. ABBOT and Sarah Smith SIBLEY, 22 Sept. 1838, Bridgeton NJ (Bible)

Charles Sibley ABBOT and Marietta McMULLEN, 16 Apr. 1874, Louisville KY (Bible)

Marietta ABBOT and Joseph Henry BURNETT, 25 Jan. 1899, Louisville KY (Bible)

Elisha TURNER^5 (Israel^4) and Sarah KEEN, 26 Dec. 1781 (Pembroke VR:305,367)

Japhet TURNER^4 (Hannah Hatch^3) and Elizabeth MORSE, 17 Jan. 1724/25, Middleboro
(MD 4:73)

Samuel TURNER^5 (Japhet^4) and Lucy PRATT, c1762

Mary TURNER^5 (Japhet^4) and Job BRYANT, 3 May 1764 (Bridgewater VR 2:65,376)

Abigail TURNER^5 (Japhet^4) and Noah BENSON, 13 Dec. 1750, Middleboro (MD 18:83)

Betty TURNER^5 (Japhet^4) and Thomas REYNOLDS, 3 Nov. 1748 (Bridgewater VR 2:320)

Joseph REYNOLDS^6 (Betty Turner^5) and Jemima PERKINS, 17 Sept. 1772, Bridgewater

Thomas REYNOLDS^6 (Betty Turner^5) and Tabitha THAYER, 10 Feb. 1785, Bridgewater

Martha REYNOLDS^6 (Betty Turner^5) and Capt. Parmenas PACKARD, 9 Apr. 1778, Bridgew.

Susanna REYNOLDS^6 (Betty Turner^5) and Oliver HOWARD, 2 Nov. 1780, Bridgewater

Amy REYNOLDS^6 (Betty Turner^5) and Silas DUNBAR, 2 July 1772, Bridgewater

Josiah REYNOLDS^6 (Betty Turner^5) and Mary PHILLIPS, Int. 10 Dec. 1785, Bridgew.

Elizabeth TURNER and Thomas LINDSAY, 3 Oct. 1745 (Bridgewater VR 2:247,375)

Joseph TURNER^5 (Japhet^4) and Mercy FRENCH, 5 Oct. 1757, Middleboro (MD 19:174)

Hannah TURNER^5 (Japhet^4) and James LeBARON, 4 Feb. 1747, Middleboro (MD 18:80)

Issac HATCH^3 and 1st Lydia CLIFT, 9 Aug. 1716, Scituate (MD 9:80)

Isaac HATCH^3 and 2nd Penelope EWELL, 7 Jan. 1724/25

Isaac HATCH^4 (Isaac^3) and 1st Ann FISHER, 16 Dec. 1736 (Hampton Falls NH Ch.rcds.)

Isaac HATCH^4 and 2nd Sarah (HUMPHREYS) Cushing, 28 Nov. 1763 (Pembroke VR:264)

Samuel CANY and Susanna LATOUR, 19 Oct. 1735 (Hampton Falls NH Ch.rcds.)

Isaac HATCH^5 (Isaac^4) and Sarah HATCH^5 (Seth^4, Isaac^3, Mary Doty^2), 20 Sept.
1791 (Pembroke VR:285, 287)

Samuel HATCH^4 (Isaac^3) and Mary BARKER

Josiah HATCH and Mercy REDDING, 12 Nov. 1730, Middleboro (MD 9:46)

Mary HATCH^4 (Isaac^3) and Israel HATCH

Penelope HATCH^4 (Isaac^3) and Job CLAPP, 20 July 1758, Pembroke (Scituate VR 2:63)

Seth HATCH^4 (Isaac^3) and Mary TURNER, 9 Oct. 1754, Pembroke

Joseph HATCH^3 and Desire HAWES^4 (Desire Gorham^3, Desire Howland^2), 24 Feb. 1701/2

Desire HAWES^4 and 2nd John COWING, 19 June 1719 (Rochester VR)

Samuel HATCH^3 and 1st Elizabeth OLDHAM, 7 Mar. 1704/05 (MD 3:119)

Samuel HATCH^3 and 2nd Mary ( ) SYLVESTER, 27 Oct. 1747

Ruth HATCH^4 (Sam.^{3}) and John JONES^5 (Jos.^{4}, Patience Little^3, Anna Warren^2),
22 Mar. 1738/39 (Scituate VR)

Lydia HATCH^4 (Sam.^{3}) and John MITCHELL, 22 Mar. 1738/39 (Scituate VR 2:209)

Micro #6 of 6

Samuel DOTY[2] (Edward[1])

Samuel DOTY[2] and Jane HARMON

Thomas DOTY[2] (Edward[1])

Thomas DOTY[2] and Mary CHURCHILL, c1671

Mary CHURCHILL and 2nd Henry CHURCHILL, 8 Feb. 1687/88, Plymouth (MD 13:203)

Thomas DOTY[3] and 1st Elizabeth HARLOW[5] (Wm.[4], Rebecca Bartlett[3], Mary Warren[2]),
   24 Feb. 1702/03, Plymouth (MD 14:35)

Thomas DOTY[3] and 2nd Mercy ELLIS, 18 Apr. 1705, Sandwich (MD 14:127)

Hannah DOTY[3] and Jonathan DELANO[3] (Mary Alden[2]), 12 Jan. 1698, Duxbury (MD 12:33)

Thomas DOTY[4] (Tho.[3]) and Elizabeth COOK[5] (Richard[4], Deborah Hopkins[3], Gyles[2]),
   1 Nov. 1722 (Truro VR:39)

Elizabeth DOTY[5] (Tho.[4]) and Perez TILSON

Note: There are 12 pages at the end of this file pertaining to Richard Warren
      and his descendants, marriages are as follows:

Hannah BARNES[5] (Mary Bartlett[4], Jos.[3], Mary Warren[2]) and Lemuel DREW, 22 Dec.
   1715, Plymouth (MD 14:37)

Sarah DREW[6] (Hannah Barnes[5]) and Jonathan SAMSON

NOTES

<1> p.158, His first wife is now known to have been Deborah Ellis, c1674.
(MD 14:108; TAG 36:10-11)

FRANCIS EATON DESCENDANTS

Francis EATON and 3rd Christian (   ), c1624/25[1]

Christian (   ) EATON and 2nd Francis BILLINGTON, July 1634 (PCR 1:31)

Rachell EATON and Joseph RAMSDEN, 2 Mar. 1645/46 (PCR 2:94)

Benjamin EATON and Sarah HOSKINS, 4 Dec. 1660 (PCR 8:22)

Samuel EATON and Martha BILLINGTON, 10 Jan. 1660 (PCR 8:22)

Joseph RAMSDEN and Mary SAVORY, 16 Oct. 1661 (PCR 8:22)

Samuel EATON and Elizabeth FULLER, 24 May 1694, Middleboro

John EATON and Elizabeth FULLER, 1729, Middleboro

Francis EATON and Lydia FULLER, 12 June 1733, Middleboro

Benjamin EATON[2] (Francis[1])

Benjamin EATON[2] and Sarah HOSKINS, 4 Dec. 1660, Plymouth (MD 17:183)

Benjamin EATON[3] and 1st Mary COOMBS, 18 Dec. 1689, Plymouth (MD 13:205)

Benjamin EATON[3] and 2nd Susanna (LEWIS) Beal, 11 Mar. 1728/29, Hingham (Kingston
   VR:175,214)

Benjamin EATON and Mary TINKHAM, 28 Oct. 1746, Plymouth (MD 17:5)

Benjamin EATON and Mercy VAUGHAN, Int. 4 Oct. 1740, Kingston (see below)

Mary EATON and Jesse SNOW, 19 May 1757, Middleboro (MD 24:131)

Mary EATON and Micah TURNER, 1 Oct. 1761, Middleboro (MD 19:142)

Mercy (   ) FULLER and Capt. Jos. VAUGHAN, 2 Dec. 1720, Middleboro (MD 4:72)

Benjamin EATON and Mercy (   ) VAUGHAN, Int. 4 Oct. 1740, Kingston[2]

Andrew BEARCE and Margaret DAWES, 15 July 1736 (Bridgewater VR 2:48,106)

Andrew BEARCE and Mary (   ) EATON, 28 Jan. 1760, Kingston (Int.-Halifax VR:60)

John TILSON and Lydia RICKARD, 27 Mar. 1706 (Tilson Gen.:388)

Nehemiah STURTEVANT and Ruth SAMSON[3] (George[2], Abraham[1]), 9 Dec. 1703, Plymouth
   (MD 14:34)

Joseph VAUGHAN and 1st Joanna THOMAS, 7 May 1680, Middleboro (MD 2:157)

Joseph VAUGHAN and 2nd Mercy (   ) FULLER (see above)

Mary EATON[4] (Ben.[3]) and Zachariah SOULE[4] (Ben.[3], John[2]), 9 June 1720, Plympton
   (MD 3:91)

Sarah EATON[4] (Ben.[3]) and Benjamin CUSHMAN[4] (Tho.[3], Mary Allerton[2]), 8 Jan. 1712,
   Plympton (MD 2:236)

Benjamin EATON^4 (Ben.^{3}) and 1st Mercy STURTEVANT, 7 July 1726, Plympton (MD 2:50)

Benjamin EATON^4 and 2nd Mary TILSON, 7 Jan. 1742/43 (Kingston VR)

Benjamin EATON^5 (Ben.^{4}) and Hannah HOLMES, 1771

David EATON^4 (Ben.^{3}) and Deborah (?), Int. 24 Dec. 1743, Kingston

Deborah ( ) EATON and 2nd Ebenezer FULLER, 7 Apr. 1768 (Kingston VR)

Eunice EATON^5 (David^4) and Amos COOKE^6 (Caleb$^{5-4}$, Francis^3, Jacob^2), 11 Jan.
    1787 (Kingston VR)

Micro #2 of 4

Lot EATON^5 (David^4) and Elizabeth EVERSON, 23 July 1772 (Kingston VR)

Elisha EATON^4 (Ben.^{3}) and Katherine (BELCHER) Clough, 5 Dec. 1734 (Braintree VR:750)

Katherine BELCHER and 1st William CLOUGH, 30 Nov. 1732 (Braintree VR:750)

Elizabeth EATON^4 (Ben.^{3}) and Cornelius STURTEVANT, Int. 25 Jan. 1728/29, Kingston

Francis EATON^4 (Ben.^{3}) and 1st Thankful ALDEN, 14 Dec. 1727, Middleboro (MD 5:39)

Francis EATON^4 and 2nd Lydia FULLER, 12 June 1733, Middleboro (MD 13:250)

Elijah EATON^5 (Francis^4) and Sarah SHAW, 1 Nov. 1763, Middleboro (MD 24:55)

Joseph EATON^5 (Francis^4) and Hannah CROSSMAN, 22 Nov. 1750, Middleboro (MD 18:83)

Abigail EATON^6 (Jos.^{5}) and Abner SHAW, 16 Apr. 1770 (Middleboro VR 4:10)

Joel EATON^6 (Jos.^{5}) and Lucy LEONARD, c1774

Apollos EATON^7 (Joel^6) and Parna LEACH

Mary/Polly EATON^6 (Jos.^{5}) and John SHAW, 15 Dec. 1779 (Middleboro VR 4:144)

Hannah EATON^4 (Ben.^{3}) and Benjamin BRYANT, 31 July 1712, Plympton (MD 2:236)

Hannah BRYANT^5 (Hannah Eaton^4) and David CURTIS, c1734/35 (MD 15:163)

Jerusha BRYANT^5 (Hannah Eaton^4) and Solomon LEACH, c1738

Solomon LEACH and Hannah LEACH, Int. 6 Aug. 1743

Mercy BRYANT^5 (Hannah Eaton^4) and Nehemiah LEACH, pre July 1736

Phebe BRYANT^5 (Hannah Eaton^4) and David SEARS, c1733 (MD 13:6)

David SEARS and 2nd Hannah WESTON, 20 Dec. 1781, Middleboro

John EATON^4 (Ben.^{3}) and Elizabeth FULLER^4 (Sam.$^{3-2-1}$), July 1729, Middleboro
    (MD 8:250)

Ebenezer EATON^3 and Hannah RICKARD^3 (Giles$^{2-1}$), 24 Nov. 1701, Plymouth (MD 14:35)

Gideon EATON^4 (Eben.^{3}) and Hannah BAILEY

Joanna EATON^4 (Eben.^{3}) and Elisha FRENCH

Mercy EATON^4 (Eben.^{3}) and 1st Benjamin LAKE, 2nd Ebenezer BISHOP

Rebecca EATON^3 and Josiah RICKARD^3 (Giles$^{2-1}$), 21 Nov. 1699, Plymouth (MD 13:207)

Giles RICKARD^4 (Rebecca Eaton^3) and Mary EDDY, 18 Nov. 1724, Plympton (MD 2:139)

Benjamin RICKARD^4 (Rebecca Eaton^3) and Thankful PINCHEON, 12 Feb. 1729/30, Plympton
   (MD 5:210)

Rebecca RICKARD^4 (Rebecca Eaton^3) and 1st Seth ALLEN, c1735

Rebecca RICKARD^4 and 2nd Thomas WHITMAN, c1767

Samuel EATON^2 (Francis^1)

Samuel EATON^2 and 2nd Martha BILLINGTON^3 (Francis^2), 10 Jan. 1660 (MD 17:183)

Martha BILLINGTON^3 and 2nd Robert CROSSMAN (MD 17:183)

Samuel EATON^3 and Elizabeth FULLER^3 (Sam.$^{2-1}$), 24 May 1694, Middleboro (PN&Q 3:122)

Barnabas EATON^4 (Sam.^{3}) and 1st Mehitable ALDEN^4 (Jos.$^{3-2}$), c1729 (MD 12:131)

Barnabas EATON^4 and 2nd Elizabeth CLEMANS, 21 Feb. 1743, Middleboro (MD 15:220)

Nathan EATON^5 (Barnabas^4) and Margaret CHERRY, Int. 25 June 1774, Middleboro
   (VR 4:2:5)

Martha EATON and Abner LEONARD, 29 Apr. 1804 (Middleboro VR 8:76)

Samuel EATON^5 (Barnabas^4) and Patience TINKHAM^5 (Sam.^{4}, Ephraim^3, Mary Brown^2),
   8 Nov. 1753, Middleboro (MD 19:46)

Darius EATON^6 (Sam.^{5}) and Phebe RICHMOND, 8 Nov. 1789 (Middleboro VR 4:161)

Rufus EATON^7 (Darius^6) and Clarissa HORR

Louisa EATON^8 (Rufus^7) and Benjamin BOND, Aug. 1847

Eunice EATON^6 (Sam.^{5}) and Seth EDDY, Int. 22 Jan. 1792, Brookfield

Patience EDDY^7 (Eunice Eaton^6) and David BARLOW, 2 Apr. 1816 (Brookfield VR)

Salome E. BARLOW^8 (Patience Eddy^7) and Gilbert F. LINCOLN, 25 Apr. 1843 (Brook.VR)

Saloma EDDY^7 (Eunice Eaton^6) and Faxon NICKOLS, 11 Nov. 1818 (Brookfield VR)

Titus EDDY^7 (Eunice Eaton^6) and Elizabeth KENT, 1 Apr. 1817 (Brookfield VR)

Israel EATON^6 (Sam.^{5}) and Eunice RICKARD, c1781

Ziba EATON^5 (Barnabas^4) and Ruth LEONARD, 31 Aug. 1773 (Middleboro VR 4:10)

Micro #3 of 4

Ruth EATON^6 (Ziba^5) and George SPEAR

Solomon EATON^6 (Ziba^5) and Peggy RANDALL

Elizabeth EATON^4 (Sam.^{3}) and William KANNADY, 21 June 1727, Middleboro (MD 5:39)

John CANEDY and Anna HATHAWAY, 7 Nov. 1734 (Middleboro VR 1:140)

Hugh CANEDY and Bathsheba BAKER, 11 Apr. 1764 (Middleboro VR 2:83)

Isaac CANEDY and Deborah BENSON 2d, 30 Apr. 1769 (Middleboro VR 2:125)

Noble CANEDY and Hope NELSON, 4 Nov. 1784 (Middleboro VR 4:166)

John W. CANEDY and Abigail A. WESTON, 1 Feb. 1832 (Middleboro VR 10:259)

James C. CANEDY and Lydia ELLIOT, 24 Aug. 1833 (MIddleboro VR 10:269)

Capt. John W. CANEDY and Lucy McCULLEY, 15 Sept. 1838 (Middleboro VR 15:7)

William CANEDY and Sophronia W. SHAW, 14 Mar. 1847 (Middleboro VR 15:14)

Michael KENNEDY and Mary HOOPER, 31 May 1770 (Middleboro VR 2:132)

Lucy H. CANADY and Stephen HOAR, 24 Mar. 1820 (Middleboro VR 10:264)

Betsey CANEDY and Noah CLARK Jr., 27 Apr. 1806 (Middleboro VR 8:199)

Barnabas CANEDY^5 (Eliz. Eaton^4) and Elizabeth BARNABY^6 (Ambrose^5, James^4, Lydia Bartlett^3, Mary Warren^2), 9 Feb. 1763

Elizabeth BARNABY and 2nd Elijah BURT

Thankful CANEDY^5 (Eliz. Eaton^4) and Joseph MACOMBER^5 (Eliz. Williams^4, Eliz. Rogers^3, John^2)

Fear CANEDY^5 (Eliz. Eaton^4) and David PERKINS^7, pre 1773 (see below)

Hannah PERKINS^6 (Fear Canedy^5) and Thomas CAIN, pre 1801

William PERKINS^6 (Fear Canedy^5) and Parthenia MILLER

David PERKINS^6 (Martha HOWARD^5, Sarah Latham^4, Susanna Winslow^3, Mary Chilton^2) and Alice LEACH, 17 May 1738 (Bridgewater VR)

Hannah CANEDY^5 (Eliz. Eaton^4) and Abial PEIRCE

William CANEDY^5 (Eliz. Eaton^4) and Charity LEONARD, 6 Dec. 1753, Middleboro (MD 18:157)

Charity CANEDY^6 (Wm.^{5}) and Ebenezer HINDS Jr., 2 July 1775 (Middleboro VR 4:2:11)

Noble CANEDY^6 (Wm.^{5}) and Hope NELSON (see p.164)

Bathsheba CANEDY^6 (Wm.^{5}) and Rufus HOWLAND, 10 Nov. 1775 (Middleboro VR 4:2:11)

Alexander CANEDY^7 (Wm.$^{6-5}$) and Sally V. HOAR, Int. 25 Mar. 1821 (Middleboro VR 8:198)

John W. CANEDY^7 (Wm.^{6}) and 1st Abigail A. WESTON (see above)

John W. CANEDY^7 and 2nd Lucy McCULLY (see above)

Hannah CANEDY^7 (Wm.^{6}) and Asa Tyler WINSLOW, 6 Sept. 1823 (Middleboro VR 10:265)

Asa T. WINSLOW and Anna PICKENS, 21 Feb. 1831 (Middleboro VR 10:268)

William CANEDY^6 (Wm.^{5}) and Mary G. BROWN, Int. 17 Apr. 1784 (Middleboro VR 4:2:55)

Jane CANEDY^7 (Wm.^{6}) and William ASHLEY

Zebulon Leonard CANEDY^7 (Wm.^{6}) and Olive BISBEE, Int. 17 Nov. 1816 (Middleboro VR 8:147)

Sarah EATON^3 and Philip BUMPUS (MD 7:128)

Rachel EATON^2 (Francis^1)

Rachel EATON^2 and Joseph RAMSDEN, 2 Mar. 1645 (MD 8:18)

Joseph RAMSDEN and 2nd Mary SAVERY, 16 Oct. 1661, Plymouth (MD 8:18)

Abner RANDEL and Jerusa COLLINS, 26 Sept. 1786, Truro (VR:135)

Daniel RAMSDEN/RAMSDELL[3] and Hannah CASWELL, c1680

Thomas RAMSDELL[4] (Dan.[3]) and Sarah ALVERSON, 22 Mar. 1702/03, Scituate

Gideon RAMSDELL[5] (Tho.[4]) and Sarah FARRINGTON, 24 June 1736 (Bridgewater VR 2:313)

John RAMSDELL[6] (Gideon[5]) and Eunice COBB, 31 Dec. 1761, Abington

David RAMSDELL[7] (John[6]) and Polly CUDWORTH

Eunice RAMSDELL[7] (John[6]) and Ebenezer EATON, 28 Mar. 1808, Wardsboro VT

Gideon RAMSDELL[7] (John[6]) and Sarah UNDERWOOD, 12 Mar. 1805, Wardsboro VT

Joanna RAMSDELL[7] (John[6]) and Peter CLEVELAND

Job RAMSDELL[7] (John[6]) and Abigail WHITE, 26 May 1803, Wardsboro VT

John RAMSDELL[7] (John[6]) and Chloe PRICE, 12 Sept. 1784, Warwick

Robert RAMSDELL[7] (John[6]) and Mary JEFFERSON, Int. 23 June 1785, Warwick

Micro #4 of 4

Rosina Aurelia RAMSDELL[8] (Robert[7]) and Daniel Marshall BURNHAM (m. Washington VT)

Sarah RAMSDELL[7] (John[6]) and Nathaniel FITTS, 1793, prob. Wardsboro VT

NOTES

<1> p.162, His 3rd wife has been identified as Christian Penn.
<2> p.162, Bowman suggests the possibility that this was the 3rd marriage of Benjamin Eaton[3].

EDWARD FULLER DESCENDANTS

Consider FULLER and Hannah EATON, 13 July 1806 (Halifax VR:81)

Consider FULLER and Mercy THOMAS, 25 Mar. 1818 (Halifax VR:85)

Isaac FULLER and Susanna (NICHOLS) Wadsworth, 18 Apr. 1754 (Pembroke VR)

Susanna NICHOLS and 1st Isaac WADSWORTH, 16 Dec. 1730 (Pembroke VR)

Samuel FULLER[2] (Edward[1])

Samuel FULLER[2] and Jane LOTHROP, 8 Apr. 1635, Scituate

Hannah FULLER[3] and Nicholas BONHAM, 1 Jan. 1658, Barnstable (MD 18:198)

Mary BONHAM[4] (Hannah Fuller[3]) and Edmund DUNHAM

John FULLER[3] and Mehitable ROWLEY

Elizabeth FULLER[4] (John[3]) and Samuel ROWLEY

Joseph FULLER[4] (John[3]) and 1st Lydia DAY, 2nd Zerviah NOBLE

Shubael FULLER[4] (John[3]) and Hannah CROCKER

Thankful FULLER[4] (John[3]) and Jabez CRIPPEN

Mary FULLER[3] and Joseph WILLIAMS, 18 Nov. 1674 (Haverhill VR 2:126,336)

John WILLIAMS[4] (Mary Fuller[3]) and 1st Hannah KNOWLTON

Samuel FULLER[3] and Anne FULLER[3] (Matthew[2])

Desire FULLER[4] (Sam.[3]) and John TAYLOR

Joseph FULLER[4] (Sam.[3]) and Thankful BLOSSOM

Barnabas FULLER[4] (Sam.[3]) and Elizabeth YOUNG, 25 Feb. 1680, Barnstable (MD 4:226)

Ebenezer FULLER[5] (Barnabas[4]) and Martha JONES

Samuel FULLER[5] (Barnabas[4]) and 1st Ruth CROCKER[4] (Ruth Chipman[3], Hope Howland[2]), c1718 (MD 33:24)

Samuel FULLER[5] and 2nd Lydia LOVEL, 20 Dec. 1726, Barnstable (MD 33:27)

Hannah FULLER and Joseph BOURN, 25 July 1743, Barnstable (MD 33:124)

John FULLER[5] (Ben.[4], Sam.[3]) and Mary NYE, 7 Mar. 1728

James FULLER[5] (Ben.[4], Sam.[3]) and Temperance PHINNEY[5] (Ben.[4], Mary Rogers[3], Jos.[2]), c1733 (MD 32:53)

Matthew FULLER[4] (Sam.[3]) and Patience YOUNG, 25 Feb. 1692, Barnstable (MD 4:226)

Matthew FULLER[2] (Edward[1])[1]

Thomas FULLER[4] (Sam.[3]) and Elizabeth LOTHROP, 29 Dec. 1680, Barnstable (MD 4:226)

Elizabeth FULLER[3] and Moses ROWLEY, 22 Apr. 1652, Barnstable (MD 18:203)

Jabez FULLER^4 (Sam.^{3}) and Mary HALLETT^4 (Eliz. Gorham^3, Desire Howland^2), c1686 (MD 4:226)

Jonathan FULLER and Hannah HARLOW, 17 Dec. 1729, Middleboro (MD 8:250)

Jabez FULLER^6 (Jonathan^5, Jabez^4) and Hannah PRATT^6 (John^5, Sam.$^{4-3}$, Mary Priest^2), 27 Dec. 1744 (Middleboro VR)

Dr. John FULLER^3 and 2nd Hannah MORTON, 24 Mar. 1687, Plymouth (MD 13:203)

NOTES

<1> p.167, The files for Matthew Fuller^2 are not set out on their own but are mixed in with those of Samuel^2 so in this case it was necessary to take the marriages out of the order found in the files. It also appears that some of the files pertaining to Matthew clearly show him as Edward's son, while others show him as number one in the line of descent. In the latter cases, generation numbers have been changed to accurately reflect line of descent.

SAMUEL FULLER DESCENDANTS

Samuel FULLER[1] and 1st Alice GLASCOCK (MD 8:129)

Samuel FULLER and 2nd Agnes CARPENTER, 24 Apr. 1613, Leyden Holland (MD 8:129)

Samuel FULLER and 3rd Bridget LEE, 27 May 1617, Leyden Holland (MD 8:130)

Samuel FULLER[2] (Samuel[1])

Rev. Samuel FULLER[2] and 2nd Elizabeth ( ) BOWEN, c1665/66

Elizabeth FULLER[3] and Samuel EATON[3] (Sam.[2]), 24 May 1694, Middleboro (PN&Q 3:122)

Experience FULLER[3] and James WOOD, 12 Apr. 1693, Middleboro (PN&Q 3:122)

Abel WOOD[4] (Experience Fuller[3]) and Thankful LANDERS

Barnabas WOOD[4] (Experience Fuller[3]) and Hannah ROBBINS

Benjamin WOOD[4] (Experience[3]) and 1st Priscilla RICKARD, 12 Apr. 1733, Middleboro
(MD 13:250)

Benjamin WOOD[4] and 2nd Patience HASKELL

Ichabod WOOD[4] (Experience Fuller[3]) and 1st Christian WHEATON, 2nd Rebecca WOOD

James WOOD[4] (Experience Fuller[3]) and Deborah ( ) FISH, 21 Jan. 1735, Plymouth
(MD 16:254)

Jonathan WOOD[4] (Experience Fuller[3]) and Persis ROBBINS, 13 Jan. 1725/26, Middleboro (MD 8:250)

Jonathan WOOD and Betty THOMAS, 3 Mar. 1736/37, Middleboro (MD 8:30)

Lydia WOOD[4] (Experience Fuller[3]) and George HOLMES, 5 Feb. 1718/19, Plymouth
(MD 14:38)

Elizabeth HOLMES[6] (George[5], Lydia Wood[4]) and Caleb BARTLETT, c1778

George HOLMES[5] (Lydia Wood[4]) and Lydia WEST[6] (Bethiah Keen[5], Josiah[4], Abigail
Little[3], Anna Warren[2]), 21 Apr. 1741, Plymouth (MD 14:159)

Experience HOLMES[6] (George[5]) and Thomas COOPER, c1772

Joshua HOLMES[6] (George[5]) and Sarah BRYANT(?)

Rebecca HOLMES[6] (George[5]) and Richard AUSTIN, c1789

Barnabas HOLMES[6] (George[5]) and 1st Anna DAMON, c1787

Barnabas HOLMES[6] and 2nd Margaret (DREW) Rickard, c1812

Bethiah HOLMES[6] (George[5]) and Ansel CHURCHILL, 17 Oct. 1764 (Plymouth VR 2:262)

John CHURCHILL[7] (Bethiah Holmes[6]) and Nancy JACKSON, Int. 6 June 1801, Plymouth
(VR 2:176)

George HOLMES[6] (George[5]) and Anna RICH, 2 Dec. 1764 (Plymouth VR 2:262)

Lydia HOLMES[6] (George[5]) and 1st William SAVERY, c1766

Lydia HOLMES[6] and 2nd William ATWOOD, 3rd Benjamin CLARK, c1791

Mary HOLMES[6] (George[5]) and Peter LANMAN, c1783

Richard HOLMES[6] (George[5]) and Abigail DAMON, c1771

Abigail HOLMES[7] (Richard[6]) and 1st Ephraim BARTLETT, c1799

Abigail HOLMES[7] and 2nd William LEONARD, c1812

William LEONARD and 1st Rebecca BARTLETT, c1791

William LEONARD and 2nd Susanna BARTLETT, c1805

Sarah HOLMES[6] (George[5]) and 1st Nathaniel COBB, c1772

Sarah HOLMES[6] and 2nd Samuel LANMAN, c1780

Hannah FULLER[3] and Eleazer LEWIS

Hannah LEWIS[4] (Hannah Fuller[3]) and Thomas SNELL

Eleazer LEWIS and Mary EDDY, 27 Nov. 1755, Middleboro (MD 19:47)

Shubael LEWIS[4] (Hannah Fuller[3]) and Hasadiah EDDY, 14 Mar. 1733/34 (Int.- Plympton VR:312,340)

Samuel LEWIS and Mary NICHOLLS, 24 Dec. 1772 (Brimfield VR:212,226)

Isaac FULLER[3] and Mary PRATT, 1 Sept. 1709, Plympton (MD 2:235)

Isaac FULLER[4] (Isaac[3]) and Sarah PACKARD, 9 Nov. 1737, Bridgewater (VR 2:142)

Reliance FULLER[5] (Isaac[4]) and Josiah EDSON

Jabez FULLER[4] (Isaac[3]) and Elizabeth HILLIARD, 12 May 1747 (Boston Rcd.com.28:245)

Jonathan FULLER[5] (Jabez[4]) and Lucy EDDY

Jabez FULLER[5] (Jabez[4]) and Lucy LORING[5] (Anna Alden[4], John[3], Jonathan[2]), Aug. 1781, Duxbury (VR:256,274)

John FULLER[5] (Jabez[4]) and 1st Martha FULLER[6] (Barnabas[5], Nathaniel[4], Sam.[3-2-1]), 30 Dec. 1784 (Halifax VR:22)

John FULLER[5] and 2nd Hannah LOVELL, aft. Mar. 1804 (Fuller Gen.:172)

John FULLER[3] and Mercy NELSON, c1686

Mercy NELSON and 2nd William EATON

Jabez FULLER[4] (John[3]) and Priscilla SAMSON[4] (Lydia Standish[3], Alexander[2]), 12 Jan. 1726/27, Plympton (MD 1:247)

John FULLER[4] (John[3]) and 1st Hannah THOMAS, 1 Mar. 1719

John FULLER[4] and 2nd Lydia (ALDEN) Eddy, 27 Apr. 1762

Joanna FULLER[4] (John[3]) and Thomas DOGGETT

Mercy FULLER[3] and Daniel COLE, pre 1 Oct. 1695

Samuel FULLER^3 and Mercy EATON^3 (Sam.^{2}), 7 Jan. 1685, Plymouth (MD 13:204)

Jabez FULLER and Hannah PRATT, 27 Dec. 1744, Middleboro (MD 18:78)

James FULLER^4 (Sam.^{3}) and Judith RICKARD, 19 May 1725, Plympton (MD 1:246)

Samuel FULLER^5 (Ben.^{4}, Sam.^{3}) and Anna TINKHAM 27 Oct. 1747 (Plympton VR)

Ebenezer FULLER^4 (Sam.^{3}) and Joanna GRAY^5 (John^4, Mary Winslow^3, Mary Chilton^2),
    Int. 17 Mar. 1721, Plymouth (MD 18:143)

Eunice FULLER^5 (Eben.^{4}) and Ebenezer ROBBINS

Ansell ROBBINS and Hannah COBB, 27 Mar. 1791, Plymouth (VR 2:274)

Josiah FULLER^5 (Eben.^{4}) and Lydia CUSHMAN^6 (Robert$^{5-4}$, Tho.^{3}, Mary Allerton^2),
    21 Jan. 1746, Kingston (Gen.Adv.3:22)

John FULLER^5 (Jabez^4) and Rebecca ROBBINS

Jabez FULLER^4 (Sam.^{3}) and 1st Deborah SOULE^4 (Ben.^{3}, John^2), 12 Nov. 1724,
    Plympton (MD 2:139)

Jabez FULLER^4 and 2nd Mercy GRAY^5 (John^4, Mary Winslow^3, Mary Chilton^2), Int.
    13 Oct. 1733 (Kingston VR)

Ebenezer FULLER^4 (John^3) and Elizabeth SHORT, c1715 (MD 13:3)

Ebenezer FULLER^5 (Eben.^{4}) and 1st Lydia CHIPMAN^5 (Jacob^4, Sam.^{3}, Hope Howland^2),
    6 Jan. 1746 (Halifax VR:33,34)

Ebenezer FULLER^5 and 2nd Deborah (FULLER) Eaton, 7 Apr. 1768, Kingston (Gen.Adv.3:77)

Priscilla FULLER^6 (Eben.^{5}) and Ezekiel RIPLEY, c1788

Eunice FULLER^6 Eben.^{5}) and Joel PERKINS, Nov. 1789

Chipman FULLER^6 (Eben.^{5}) and Thankful WRIGHT^6 (Eben.^{5}, Moses^4, Adam^3, Hester
    Cooke^2), 9 Dec. 1779 (Plympton VR:435)

Nathan FULLER^7 (Chipman^6) and Faith SOULE^6 (Jacob$^{5-4}$, James^3, John^2), Int.
    7 Oct. 1808 (Halifax VR:71)

Micro #3 of 3

Priscilla FULLER and Noah BOSWORTH, 2 Oct. 1808 (Halifax VR:81)

Ebenezer FULLER and Rebecca FULLER, 30 Mar. 1809 (Halifax VR:82)

Capt. Ebenezer FULLER and Abigail SAMSON^7 (Gideon^6, Zabdiel^5, Hannah Soule^4,
    Ben.^{3}, John^2), 4 Dec. 1817 (Halifax VR:84)

Zerviah Nelson FULLER and Calvin GAMMONS, Int. 7 May 1832 (Rochester VR 2:134)

Ruth FULLER^6 (Eben.^{5}) and Elijah LEACH, 10 July 1771 (Halifax VR:29)

Nathan FULLER^5 (Eben.^{4}) and Mary PARLOW, 19 Sept. 1749, Middleboro (MD 18:82)

Ruth FULLER^5 (Eben.^{4}) and Joseph BOSWORTH, 6 Nov. 1741 (Halifax VR:33)

Joseph BOZWORTH and 2nd Sarah COBB, c1744 (Halifax VR:49)

Mercy FULLER^5 (Jabez^4) and Edmund WILLIS, 23 Feb. 1777

John FULLER^4 (Sam.^{3}) and 1st Deborah RING^4 (Eleazer^3, Deborah Hopkins^2), 7 Feb. 1722/23, Plympton (MD 2:139)

John FULLER^4 and 2nd Mercy (WASHBURN) Cushman, aft. Nov. 1763 (MD 7:87)

Susanna FULLER^5 (John^4) and Jacob DINGLEY^6 (Mary Holmes^5, Mary Brewster^4, Wrestling^3, Love^2), 5 Apr. 1752

Consider FULLER^5 (John^4) and Lydia BRYANT, 25 Feb. 1759

Issacher FULLER^5 (John^4) and 1st Elizabeth DOTEN^5 (John^{4-3-2}), 19 Jan. 1747 (Plympton VR 2:717)

Issacher FULLER^5 and 2nd Lucy TINKHAM^6 (Eben.^{5}, Jeremiah^4, Eben.^{3}, Mary Brown^2), 26 Dec. 1785 (Middleboro VR 4:2:162)

Issacher FULLER^6 (Issacher^5) and Matilda Crosby NICHOLS

Nathaniel FULLER^4 (Sam.^{3}) and Martha SAMPSON, 24 Jan. 1711/12, Plympton (MD 2:236)

Amos FULLER^5 (Nath.^{4}) and 1st Abigail HARLOW^6 (James^5, Abigail Church^4, Nath.^{3}, Eliz. Warren^2), c1744

Amos FULLER^5 and 2nd Rachel (STANDISH) Samson, 25 Oct. 1759 (MD 2:44)

Philemon FULLER^6 (Amos^5) and Mercy CHIPMAN

Sarah FULLER^5 (Nath.^{4}) and 1st Isaac STURTEVANT^5 (Fear Cushman^4, Isaac^3, Mary Allerton^2), 8 Apr. 1731, Plympton (MD 2:50)

Sarah FULLER^5 and 2nd Austin BEARCE, Int. 19 Dec. 1756 (Halifax VR:59)

STEPHEN HOPKINS DESCENDANTS

Damaris HOPKINS^2 and Jacob COOKE^2

Joseph HOPKINS and Mary HIGGINS, 12 Jan. 1770, Eastham (Higgins Gen.:128)

Mary HIGGINS and 2nd Levi HIGGINS

Constance HOPKINS^2 (Stephen^1)

Constance HOPKINS^2 and Nicholas SNOW, pre May 1627, Plymouth (MD 1:151)

Elizabeth SNOW^3 and Thomas ROGERS^3 (Jos.^{2}), 13 Dec. 1665, Eastham (MD 6:14)

Samuel SNOW and Sarah ATKINS, Int. 5 Dec. 1760 (Eastham VR:174)

Silvanus SNOW and 1st Hannah COLE, 1 Feb. 1733 (Eastham VR:107)

Silvanus SNOW and 2nd Mehitable WALKER, Apr. 1751 (Eastham VR:164)

Silvanus SNOW and 3rd Deborah COOK, 11 Nov. 1761 (Eastham VR)

Edward SNOW^4 (Jabez^3) and Sarah FREEMAN^5 (John^4, Mercy Prence^3, Patience
  Brewster^2), pre 1707 (MD 4:247,33:107,110)

Joseph SNOW^5 (Edw.^{4}) and Mary SEARS^5 (Ruth Merrick^4, Abigail Hopkins^3, Gyles^2),
  30 Nov. 1738, Harwich (MD 23:58)

Joseph SNOW^6 (Jos.^{5}) and Priscilla BERRY^7 (Theophilus^6, Mary Freeman^5, John^4,
  Mercy Prence^3, Patience Brewster^2), 4 Feb. 1762, Harwich (MD 34:69)

Nathaniel SNOW^5 (Edw.^{4}) and Thankful GAGE, 20 Aug. 1730, Harwich (MD 13:55)

Reuben SNOW^6 (Nath.^{5}) and Reliance WING^7 (Jos.^{6}, Rebecca Freeman^5, Tho.^{4}, Mercy
  Prence^3, Patience Brewster^2), 16 Nov. 1769

Grace SNOW^4 (Jabez^3) and 1st Samuel HEDGE, 8 Dec. 1698, Eastham (MD 9:11)

Grace SNOW^4 and 2nd George LEWIS, 21 July 1716, Eastham (MD 15:57)

Elisha HEDGE^5 (Grace Snow^4) and Martha JOHNSON, 30 Dec. 1728 (Ward Fam.<1851>:24)

Jabez SNOW^4 (Jabez^3) and Elizabeth TREAT, c1695 (Treat Gen.<1893>:168,178,187)

Elizabeth SNOW^5 (Jabez^4) and Thomas KNOWLES, 6 Aug. 1724, Eastham (MD 16:71)

Henry KNOWLES^6 (Eliz. Snow^5) and 1st Mary KNOWLES

Henry KNOWLES^6 and 2nd Phebe COOK, Int. 29 Aug. 1776, Eastham

Jabez SNOW^5 (Jabez^4) and Elizabeth PAINE^5, 27 Oct. 1720, Eastham (MD 15:230)[1]

Elizabeth SNOW^6 (Jabez^5) and Eleazer FREEMAN^6 (Eleazer^5, Nath.^{4}, Mercy Prence^3,
  Patience Brewster^2), 9 Mar. 1769

Eleazer FREEMAN^6 and 2nd Ruth KNOWLES^7 (Seth^6, Sam.^{5}, Mercy Freeman^4, Mercy
  Prence^3, Patience Brewster^2)

Eunice SNOW^6 (Jabez^5) and Nathaniel HORTON, Int. 10 Apr. 1742, Eastham (MD 29:13)

Hannah SNOW^6 (Jabez^5) and Edward HAWES

Joshua SNOW^6 (Jabez^5) and Mercy DOANE

Jabez SNOW^6 (Jabez^5) and Elizabeth DOANE, 22 May 1755, Eastham (MD 15:142)

Phebe SNOW^5 (Jabez^4) and John SMITH Jr., Int. 11 Sept. 1736 (VR:223)

Samuel SNOW^5 (Jabez^4) and Elizabeth FREEMAN^6 (Mary Paine^5, John^4, Mary Snow^3,
     Constance Hopkins^2), 12 Oct. 1732, Eastham (MD 17:79)

Betty SNOW^6 (Sam.^{5}) and John DOANE (Doane Gen.:98)

Silvanus SNOW^5 (Jabez^4) and 1st Hannah COLE, 1 Feb. 1733, Eastham (MD 17:80)

Silvanus SNOW^5 and 2nd Mehitable WALKER^6 (John^5, Wm.^{4}, Sarah Snow^3, Constance
     Hopkins^2), Apr. 1751 (Int.-10 Apr.), Eastham (MD 25:41)

Silvanus SNOW^5 (Jabez^4) and 3rd Deborah COOK, 11 Nov. 1761, Eastham (MD 32:41)

Mary SNOW^6 (Silvanus^5) and William DEAN, 14 Jan. 1762, Eastham (MD 32:41)

Tabitha SNOW^5 (Jabez^4) and John MAYO, 7 Oct. 1731 (Eastham VR:105)

Mercy SNOW^4 (Jabez^3) and John WITHEREL

William WETHEREL and Mary BROWN, 16 Nov. 1752, Eastham (VR:54)

Mercy WITHEREL and John CLARK, 20 Oct. 1732 (Eastham VR:107)

Rachel SNOW^4 (Jabez^3) and Thomas HUCKINS, 29 Aug. 1717, Harwich (MD 6:83)

Micro #2 of 18

John SNOW^3 and Mary SMALLEY, 19 Sept. 1667, Eastham (MD 7:17)

Mary SMALLEY and 2nd Ephraim DOANE

Amasa SNOW^5 (John^4) and Mary COLLINS, 19 Feb. 1740/41 (Truro VR:26)

Leonard SNOW^6 (Amasa^5) and Elizabeth ATKINS, 1 July 1776 (Truro VR:107)

Benjamin SNOW^6 (Amasa^5) and Mercy BAKER, 5 Feb. 1767 (Wellfleet VR 1:79)[2]

Cyprian SNOW and Sally BAKER, 12 Nov. 1801 (Orrington ME VR; Bangor Historical
     Magazine 1:111)

Ambrose SNOW^5 (John^4) and 1st Hannah COLLINGS, 29 Dec. 1742 (Truro VR:45)

Ambrose SNOW^5 and 2nd Elizabeth PAINE^6 (Barnabas^5, Tho.^{4}, Mary Snow^3, Constance
     Hopkins^2), 2 Apr. 1747 (Truro VR:52)

Ambrose SNOW^5 and 3rd Hannah RIDER, 13 June 1754 (Truro VR:52)

Ambrose SNOW^6 (Ambrose^5) and 1st Betty RICH, 2 Nov. 1772 (Truro VR:108)

Ambrose SNOW^6 and 2nd Huldah LOMBARD, 31 Oct. 1792 (Truro VR:153)

Lucinda SNOW^8 (Thankful^7, Ambrose^6) and Freeman LOMBARD Jr., 10 Dec. 1825
     (Truro VR:247)

Richard Rich SNOW^7 (Ambrose^6) and Dorcas COLLINGS, 23 Nov. 1807 (Truro VR:205)

Betsy SNOW and Richard RICH, 28 Apr. 1796 (Truro VR:163)

Hannah SNOW^6 (Ambrose^5) and John AVERY^6 (Job^5, Ruth Little^4, Ephraim^3, Anna
     Warren^2), 3 Dec. 1771 (Truro VR:108)

Josiah SNOW^6 (Ambrose^5) and Lydia DYER, 8 Sept. 1785 (Truro VR:136)

Lydia DYER and 2nd Silas ATKINS, Int. 11 Feb. 1804 (Truro VR:178)

Lydia SNOW^7 (Josiah^6) and John SWIFT, Int. 17 Oct. 1807 (Truro VR:185)

Elizabeth Atkins SNOW^7 (Josiah^6) and Thomas Rider WHORF, 28 Feb. 1811 (Truro:206)

Eunice SNOW^7 (Josiah^6) and Eldridge NICKERSON

John SNOW^7 (Josiah^6) and Sally LANCY, c1823 (Provincetown VR 4:75)

Josiah SNOW^7 (Josiah^6) and Ruth DYER, Int. 5 Nov. 1823, Provincetown (VR 2:66)

Obadiah SNOW^7 (Josiah^6) and Dorcas MYRICK

Anne SNOW^5 (John^4) and Leonard PIKE, 1 Apr. 1723 (Truro VR:39)

John SNOW^4 (John^3) and Elizabeth RIDLEY, 25 Feb. 1700/01, Eastham (MD 9:8)

Ambrose SNOW Jr. and Polly C. SWEET, Int. 14 Nov. 1833 (Truro VR:270)

Anthony SNOW^5 (John^4) and Sarah PAINE^6 (Jonathan^5, Tho.^{4}, Mary Snow^3, Constance
     Hopkins^2), 2 Mar. 1731/32 (Truro VR:24)

Anthony SNOW^6 (Anthony^5) and Tamsin HARDING, 17 Oct. 1771 (Truro VR:108)

Michael SNOW and Jenny LOMBARD, 12 Aug. 1819 (Truro VR:232)

Jesse SNOW^7 (Anthony^6) and Joanna COLE, 1 May 1804 (Truro VR:205)

Joanna Cole SNOW^8 (Jesse^7) and Isaiah KNOWLES, 15 Nov. 1828 (Truro VR:257)

Bethiah SNOW and Capt. William E. COLE, c1824

Sarah Elizabeth COLE and William Henry Harrison NEWMAN, 10 Dec. 1868, Boston

Emily A. COLE and Joshua Dorsey BALL

Betsey SNOW^8 (Jesse^7) and Barnabas SMITH

David SNOW^6 (Anthony^5) and 1st Sarah HATCH, 3 Feb. 1757 (Truro VR:88)

David SNOW^6 and 2nd Hannah COLLINGS, 7 June 1759 (Truro VR:89)

Ephraim SNOW and Hannah SNOW, 18 Nov. 1819 (Truro VR:232)

Ephraim SNOW^7 (David^6) and Mary RICH, 4 Sept. 1800 (Truro VR:204)

Hannah SNOW^7 (David^6) and James LOMBARD, 11 Sept. 1792 (Truro VR:157)

Stephen SNOW^7 (David^6) and Huldah LOMBARD, 21 Aug. 1794 (Truro VR:157)

Stephen SNOW^8 (Stephen^7) and Mary LEWIS, 9 July 1821 (Truro VR:232)

Freeman Atkins SNOW^8 (Stephen^7) and Drusilla ATKINS, 7 Dec. 1831 (Truro VR:268)

Richard SNOW and Mehitable KNOWLES, 4 Dec. 1823 (Truro VR:237)

Leonard SNOW^8 (Stephen^7) and Mary Wilson COLLINS, 19 Nov. 1818 (Truro VR:227)

Elisha SNOW^6 (Anthony^5) and 1st Hannah RICH, 2 Dec. 1762 (Truro VR:89)

Elisha SNOW^6 and 2nd Keziah LOMBARD, 15 Jan. 1795 (Truro VR:157)

Jonathan SNOW^6 (Anthony^5) and Deliverance ATKINS, 27 Nov. 1766 (Truro VR:110)

Jonathan SNOW^7 (Jonathan^6) and Jane LOMBARD, 22 Sept. 1796 (Truro VR:158,203)

Shubael SNOW^7 (Jonathan^6) and 1st Betsey (SNOW) Lombard, 6 Jan. 1801 (Truro VR:204)

Shubael SNOW^7 and 2nd Thankful SNOW, 10 Oct. 1816 (Truro VR:218)

Betsey SNOW and 1st Ephraim LOMBARD, 26 Jan. 1797 (Truro VR:159,203)

Capt. Reuben SNOW^7 (Jonathan^6) and Rebecca SNOW, 2 Sept. 1806 (Truro VR:205)

Deliverance SNOW^7 (Jonathan^6) and Phineas PAINE, 13 May 1804 (Truro VR:205)

Isaiah SNOW^7 (Jonathan^6) and Christian COAN^7 (Christian Hinckley^6, Mary Snow^5, Tho.^{4}, Mark^3, Constance Hopkins^2), Int. 19 July 1788 (Truro VR:138)

Jaazamiah GROSS^7 (Sarah Snow^6, Anthony^5) and Anne LOMBARD, 20 Dec. 1792 (Truro VR:157)

Silvanus SNOW^6 (Anthony^5) and Jerusha HINCKLEY, 2 Feb. 1774 (Truro VR:107)

Elizabeth SNOW^5 (John^4) and John ANNABLE, 9 Feb. 1726/27 (Truro VR:10)

Isaac SNOW^5 (John^4) and Apphia ATWOOD, 5 July 1733 (Truro VR:8)

Micro #3 of 18

Rev. Elisha SNOW^6 (Isaac^5) and Betsey JORDAN, 6 Dec. 1759, Cape Elizabeth

Larkin SNOW^7 (Elisha^6) and Nancy WILLIS^9 (Anna Orcutt^8, Micah^7, Deliverance Kingman^6, Desire Harris^5, Mercy Latham^4, Susanna Winslow^3, Mary Chilton^2), 24 Oct. 1802 (Boston Rcd.com.30:204)

Mary Brown SNOW^8 (Larkin^7) and William Rufus HORTON

Sarah SNOW^6 (Anthony^5) and Jaazamiah GROSS, 16 July 1764 (Truro VR:92)

Rebecca SNOW^4 (John^3) and Benjamin SMALLEY

Mary SNOW^4 (Jos.^{3}) and poss. Nathaniel MAYO

Benjamin SNOW^4 (Jos.^{3}) and Thankful BOORMAN, 6 June 1700, Eastham (MD 8:247)

Jane SNOW^5 (Ben.^{4}) and Ichabod HIGGINS, 3 Dec. 1731, Eastham (MD 17:79)$^{<3>}$

Susanna SNOW^5 (Ben.^{4}) and Solomon SMITH^5 (Hannah Rogers^4, John^3, Jos.^{2}), 21Feb. 1739/40, Eastham (VR:134)

Benjamin SNOW^5 (Ben.^{4}) and Martha ELDRIDGE, 7 Aug. 1723 (Eastham VR:51)

Martha SNOW^6 (Ben.^{5}) and Simeon HIGGINS, Int. 3 May 1746 (Eastham VR:234)

Mary SNOW^5 (Ben.^{4}) and Robert PEPPER, 26 July 1732, Eastham (MD 17:79)

Thomas SNOW^5 (Ben.^{4}) and Sarah YOUNG^5 (Sarah Snow^4, Jos.^{3}, Constance Hopkins^2), 23 Sept. 1730 (Eastham VR:109)

Joseph SNOW^4 (Jos.^{3}) and Sarah SMITH, 15 Dec. 1690, Eastham (MD 6:201)

Sarah SMITH and 2nd Daniel HAMILTON, 5 Aug. 1708, Eastham (MD 4:30)

Josiah SNOW^4 (Jos.^{3}) and Elizabeth SNOW, 20 Oct. 1719, Eastham (MD 16:26)

Lydia SNOW^4 (Jos.^{3}) and James LINKHORNEW, 10 Feb. 1714/15 (Eastham VR:4)

James LINCOLN Jr. and Rebecca BROWN^5 (Ruth Snow^4, Jos.^{3}), Int. 2 Sept. 1738, Eastham (VR:225)

Lydia LINCOLN and Jeremiah SMITH 3d, Int. 11 Feb. 1737/38, Eastham (VR:225)

Ruth SNOW^4 (Jos.^{3}) and James BROWN Jr., 13 Apr. 1704, Eastham (MD 3:181)

Joseph BROWN and Susanna COLE, 20 Feb. 1735/36, Eastham (MD 17:142)

Mary BROWN^6 (George^5, Ruth Snow^4) and Benjamin KNOWLES, 17 Feb. 1763, Eastham (MD 31:177)

George BROWN^5 (Ruth Snow^4) and Alice FREEMAN^6 (Mary Paine^5, John^4, Mary Snow^3, Constance Hopkins^2), Int. 27 Sept. 1740, Eastham (MD 29:11)

Samuel BROWN^6 (George^5) and Priscilla HARDING^6 (Cornelius^5, Hannah Rogers^4, Tho.^{3}, Jos.^{2}), 10 Mar. 1768, Wellfleet (VR 1:80)

Dorcas BROWN^7 (Sam.^{6}) and Samuel Sprague FILLEBROWN, 1801, Orrington ME

Sarah SNOW^4 (Jos.^{3}) and Benjamin YOUNG, 15 Feb. 1699/1700, Eastham (MD 8:246)

Daniel YOUNG^5 (Sarah Snow^4) and Lydia PAINE^5 (Nicholas^4, Mary Snow^3, Constance Hopkins^2), 5 Mar. 1729/30, Eastham (MD 16:204)

Sarah YOUNG^5 (Sarah Snow^4) and Thomas SNOW, 23 Sept. 1730 (Eastham VR:98,109)

Thankful YOUNG^5 (Sarah Snow^4) and Moses WILEY, Int. 15 July 1724 (Eastham VR:210)

Stephen SNOW^4 (Jos.^{3}) and Margaret ELKINS, 12 July 1705, Eastham (MD 7:16)

Stephen SNOW^5 (Stephen^4) and Rebecca SNOW^5 (Ben.^{4}, Jos.^{3}), 8 Oct. 1730, Eastham (MD 17:32)

Lydia SNOW^6 (Stephen^5) and John HOPKINS, Int. 26 Feb. 1757, Eastham (MD 28:12)

John SNOW^5 (Stephen^4) and Phebe HATCH, Int. 24 Oct. 1746, Eastham (MD 29:17)

Sarah SNOW^5 (Stephen^4) and Samuel SMITH, Int. 25 Sept. 1736, Eastham (MD 28:179)

Jane SNOW^5 (Stephen^4) and Levi SMITH, Int. 8 Oct. 1737, Eastham (MD 28:180)

Ruth SNOW^5 (Stephen^4) and Benjamin SMITH, 30 Nov. 1745, Eastham (MD 24:87)

Elkins SNOW^5 (Stephen^4) and Susanna WALKER^6 (Wm.$^{5-4}$, Sarah Snow^3, Constance Hopkins^2), Int. 24 Sept. 1737, Eastham (MD 28:180)

Lydia SNOW^5 (Stephen^4) and John MOTT, 24 Feb. 1732, Eastham (MD 17:79)

Margaret SNOW^5 (Stephen^4) and 1st Eldad ATWOOD^5 (Anna Snow^4, Mark^3, Constance Hopkins^2), 15 Feb. 1727/28, Eastham (MD 15:70)

Margaret SNOW^5 and 2nd Isaac THAYER, 3rd Joseph LOVERING

Mark SNOW^3 and 1st Anna COOKE^2 (Josiah^1), 18 Jan. 1654, Eastham (MD 5:23)

Mark SNOW^3 and 2nd Jane PRENCE^2 (Tho.^{1}), 9 Jan. 1660, Eastham (MD 7:14)

Anna SNOW^4 and Eldad ATWOOD, 14 Feb. 1683, Eastham (MD 4:141)

Eldad ATWOOD^5 (Anna Snow^4) and 1st Sarah GRAY, 23 Oct. 1718, Harwich (MD 7:196)

Eldad ATWOOD^5 and 2nd Margaret SNOW^5 (see p.177)

Micro #4 of 18

Margaret ATWOOD^6 (Eldad^5) and Stephen BALLARD

Nathan LAMB and Lucy PEPPER, 29 Jan. 1784, Weston MA

Anna LAMB and Joseph LINCOLN, 3 Nov. 1809, Boston

Sarah ATWOOD^6 (Eldad^5) and Samuel LAMB, 17 Dec. 1747, Hopkinton

John ATWOOD^5 (Anna Snow^4) and Thankful WILLIAMSON, 28 Sept. 1721, Eastham
    (MD 15:232)

Mary ATWOOD^6 (John^5) and Richard ATWOOD, c1748 (Wellfleet VR 1:99)

Deborah ATKINS and Andrew Washington PRATT, 22 June 1820

Mary SNOW^4 (Mark^3) and William NICKERSON, 22 Jan. 1690, Eastham (MD 4:33)

Mary NICKERSON^5 (Mary Snow^4) and James HARDING, 8 Oct. 1724, Harwich (MD 8:160)

Thankful NICKERSON^5 (Mary Snow^4) and Benjamin BURG, Int. 22 Apr. 1727 (MD 8:219)

Ebenezer NICKERSON^5 (Mary Snow^4) and Elizabeth MAYO^5 (Hannah Freeman^4, Mercy
    Prence^3, Patience Brewster^2), 18 Oct. 1726, Harwich (MD 8:218)

Seth NICKERSON^6 (Eben.^{5}) and 1st Mary SMITH, 19 Mar. 1761, Chatham (MD 17:91)

Seth NICKERSON^6 and 2nd Isabel (ELDRIDGE) Dyer, c1780/81

Ebenezer NICKERSON^7 (Seth^6) and 1st Salome COLLINS

Ebenezer NICKERSON^7 and 2nd Endoxa WHITE, aft. June 1804 (MD 10:31)

Jane NICKERSON^5 (Mary Snow^4) and Judah BAKER, 18 June 1724, Harwich (MD 8:160)

Judah BAKER^6 (Jane Nickerson^5) and Mary ELDRIDGE, 18 Dec. 1760 (Yarmouth VR 3:225)

Nicholas SNOW^4 (Mark^3) and Lydia SHAW, 4 Apr. 1689, Eastham/Harwich (MD 3:180,4:20)

Prence SNOW^5 (Nicholas^4) and Mary STURDEVANT, 31 Aug. 1727 (Rochester VR 2:284)

Thankful SNOW^5 (Nicholas^4) and Joseph BURGE, 11 Apr. 1723, Eastham (MD 15:54)

Jonathan SNOW^5 (Nicholas^4) and Thankful FREEMAN^5 (Edmund^4, Mercy Prence^3,
    Patience Brewster^2), 16 Oct. 1718, Eastham (MD 15:73)

Isaac SNOW^6 (Jonathan^5) and Thankful KING, c1742 (Rochester VR)

Prince SNOW^7 (Isaac^6) and Content DOTY, 6 Dec. 1770 (Rochester ch.rcd.)

Joshua SNOW^5 (Nicholas^4) and Bathsheba ( ), c1726

Bathsheba ( ) SNOW and 2nd Ebenezer MEIGS, Int. 26 May 1739 (Rochester VR 2:210)

Joshua SNOW and Ruth BOLLES, 2 Jan. 1752 (Rochester VR)

Prence SNOW^4 (Mark^3) and Hannah STORRS, c1698 (MD 4:176)

Elizabeth HUCKENS^4 (Hope Chipman^3, Hope Howland^2) and John LEWES, 4 June 1695,
Barnstable (MD 10:250)

Jabez SNOW^5 (Prence^4) and Elizabeth LEWIS^5 (Eliz. Huckins^4, above), 2 Apr. 1724,
Barnstable (MD 32:148)

Mehitable SNOW^6 (Jabez^5) and 1st Samuel HOPKINS^5 (Nath.^{4}, Stephen^3, Gyles^2),
23 Aug. 1753, Harwich (MD 34:26)

Mehitable SNOW^6 and 2nd Reuben RYDER, aft. Nov. 1761

Mehitable SNOW^6 and 3rd Paul CROWELL

Jonathan SNOW^5 (Prence^4) and Sarah BANGS, 24 Feb. 1736/37, Harwich (MD 20:26)

David SNOW^6 (Jonathan^5) and Mary COLE^6 (Jos.$^{5-4}$, Ruth Snow^3, Constance Hopkins^2),
5 Dec. 1765(?)

Herman SNOW^7 (David^6) and 1st Dorcas HIGGINS, 20 Apr 1786, Eastham (Orleans ch.rcds.)

Herman SNOW^7 and 2nd Lydia (KNOWLES) Knowles, c1814

Col. Jonathan SNOW^6 (Jonathan^5) and 1st Mehitable HOPKINS, 14 Jan. 1768
(Brewster VR:87)

Col. Jonathan SNOW^6 and 2nd Elizabeth CROSBY, 24 July 1787 (Brewster VR:87)

Col. Jonathan SNOW^6 and 3rd Huldah COBB, 29 Mar. 1813 (Brewster VR:87)

Mercy SNOW^7 (Jonathan^6) and Stephen ELLIS, c1794 (Brewster VR:28)

Prence SNOW^5 (Prence^4) and Jeney COLLINS, Int. 10 Sept. 1737, Harwich (MD 19:59)

Prence SNOW^6 (Prence^5) and Sarah ATWOOD, 12 Jan. 1758, Chatham (MD 9:34)

Samuel SNOW^5 (Prence^4) and Mary HOPKINS^5 (Stephen$^{4-3}$, Gyles^2), 6 Mar. 1729/30,
Harwich (MD 11:249)

Mary HOPKINS^5 and 2nd Shubael LEWIS, 5 June 1735 (MD 8:192)

Thomas SNOW^4 (Mark^3) and 1st Hannah SEARS, 8 Feb. 1692, Eastham (MD 8:13)

Thomas SNOW^4 and 2nd Lydia (SEARS) Hamblen, 30 Sept. 1706, Harwich (MD 4:177)

Thomas SNOW^5 (Tho.^{4}) and Rachel NICKERSON, 19 Feb. 1729/30, Harwich (MD 13:55)

Silas SNOW^6 (Tho.^{5}) and Rebecca SNOW, Int. 16 Oct. 1762, Eastham (MD 27:188)

Thomas SNOW^6 (Tho.^{5}) and Rebecca SNOW, 20 Jan. 1752, Harwich (MD 34:25)

Rebecca SNOW^7 (Silas^6) and Mathias TAYLOR, 11 July 1786 (Harwich VR 2:283)

Aaron SNOW^5 (Tho.^{4}) and Hannah GAGE, 11 May 1732, Harwich (MD 13:70)

Phebe SNOW^6 (Aaron^5) and Jonathan CROWELL, 24 Jan. 1754, Harwich (Crowell Gen:26)

Jonathan CROWEL^7 (Phebe Snow^6) and Miriam BAKER, 26 Nov. 1778 (Crowell Gen:32)

Mary SNOW^5 (Tho.^{4}) and Shubael HINCKLEY, 7 Oct. 1718, Harwich (MD 7:196)

Christian HINCKLEY[6] (Mary Snow[5]) and Abraham COAN, 11 Oct. 1759 (Truro VR:90)

Benjamin COAN[7] (Christian Hinckley[6]) and Lucy NEWCOMB, Int. 12 Aug. 1796
(Truro VR:159)

Christian COAN[7] (Christian Hinckley[6]) and Isaiah SNOW[7] (Jonathan[6], Anthony[5],
John[4-3], Constance Hopkins[2]), Int. 19 July 1788 (Truro VR:111)

Elisha Davis COAN[7] (Christian Hinckley[6]) and Mary ATKINS, 8 July 1794 (Truro VR:158)

Hannah COAN[7] (Christian Hinckley[6]) and Israel LOMBARD, 25 Mar. 1800 (Truro VR:203)

Joanna COAN[7] (Christian Hinckley[6]) and Francis SMALL, c1783

Francis SMALL[8] (Joanna Coan[7]) and Anna STEVENS, 13 Dec. 1807 (Truro VR:185)

Francis SMALLEY 3d and Elizabeth YOUNG, 2 June 1743

Francis SMALLEY Jr. and Elizabeth SMITH, 25 Oct. 1750

Micro #5 of 18

Samuel COAN[7] (Christian Hinckley[6]) and Elizabeth DYER, 30 Nov. 1788 (Truro VR:144)

Emma COAN[8] (Sam.[7]) and Jonathan COLLINS, 22 Oct. 1818 (Truro VR:227)

Paul Dyer COAN[8] (Sam.[7]) and Abigail KNOWLES, 24 Nov. 1825 (Truro VR:247)

Samuel COAN and Betsey DYER, 18 Sept. 1817 (Truro VR:226)

Samuel COAN and Hannah AVERY, 24 Dec. 1822 (Truro VR:234)

Betsey COAN and David D. SMITH, 15 Apr. 1847 (Truro VR:388,389)

Rebecca COAN and Jeremiah HOPKINS, 2 Dec. 1847 (Truro VR:392,393)

Shubael COAN[7] (Christian Hinckley[6]) and Deliverance ATKINS, 11 Dec. 1788
(Truro VR:145)

Abigail COAN and Thomas SMITH, 21 Oct. 1817 (Truro VR:226)

Mary COAN[8] (Shubael[7]) and John STEVENS, Int. 8 Jan. 1817 (Truro VR:218)

Polly COAN and John STEVENS, 23 Jan. 1817 (Truro VR:225)

Rebecca COAN[8] (Shubael[7]) and 1st Stephen MILLS

Rebecca COAN[8] and 2nd David BROWN, 12 Aug. 1845 (Truro VR:384,385)

Mary PAINE[3] and Thomas PAINE, pre Apr. 1651 (MD 1:14,163)

Thomas PAINE and Reliance ROGERS[6] (Elkanah[5], Jos.[4], John[3], Jos.[2]), 20 Feb.
1770 (Eastham VR 6:12)

Mary PAINE and Warren GREEN[5] (Wm.[4], Eliz. Warren[3], Nathaniel[2]), 14 Mar. 1733/34
(Eastham VR:110)

Daniel FITCH and Anne COOK, 5 Mar. 1718/19 (Canterbury CT VR)

Elisha PAINE and Mary JOHNSON, 24 Nov. 1720 (Canterbury CT VR)

Mary PAINE and William FITCH, 27 Jan. 1740/41 (Canterbury CT VR)

Dorcas PAINE^4 (Mary Snow^3) and Benjamin VICKERIE, c1689 (Hull VR)

Benjamin VICKERIE and 2nd Mary COOMB, 7 July 1709 (Hull VR)

John BULL and 1st Mary PITTS, c1672 (Hist.Hingham 2:97)

John BULL and 2nd Margaret DAMON, c1696 (Hist.Hingham 2:97)

Elisha PAINE^4 (Mary Snow^3) and Rebecca DOANE, 20 Jan. 1685, Eastham (MD 6:16)

Solomon PAINE^5 (Elisha^4) and Sarah CARVER, 2 Mar. 1720/21 (Canterbury CT VR)

Elisabeth PAINE^7 (Elihu^6, Solomon^5) and Ezra ENSWORTH, 13 Oct. 1757 (Canterbury CT VR)

Rebecca PAINE^5 (Elisha^4) and Edward CLEVELAND

James PAINE^4 (Mary Snow^3) and Bethiah THACHER, 9 Apr. 1691, Barnstable (MD 11:131)

Experience PAINE^5 (James^4) and Samuel HUNT, Int. 25 Sept. 1724 (Weymouth VR 2:102,135)

Mary PAINE^5 (James^4) and 1st Nathaniel FREEMAN, 11 Oct. 1723 (Freeman Gen:367)

Mary PAINE^5 and 2nd Edmund HOWES, 11 Oct. 1729 (Freeman Gen:367)

John PAINE^4 (Mary Snow^3) and 1st Bennet FREEMAN^4 (Mercy Prence^3, Patience Brewster^2), 14 Mar. 1689/90 (MD 9:138,139)

John PAINE^4 and 2nd Alice MAYO^5 (Nath.^{4}, Hannah Prence^3, Patience Brewster^2), 3 Mar. 1719/20, Eastham (MD 15:143)

Rebecca SPARROW and Joshua HOPKINS Jr., 14 May 1747 (Eastham VR:152)

John PAINE^5 (John^4) and 2nd Mrs. Thankful LINNEL, 8 Dec. 1743, Eastham (MD 20:156)

John PAINE^5 and 3rd Mrs. Mercy TREAT, 28 Nov. 1754, Eastham (MD 16:70)

Mary PAINE^5 (John^4) and Samuel FREEMAN, 9 Oct. 1712, Eastham (MD 6:203)

Alice FREEMAN^6 (Mary Paine^5) and George BROWN^5 (Ruth Snow^4, Jos.^{3}, Constance Hopkins^2), Int. 27 Sept. 1740, Eastham (MD 29:11)

Mary BROWN^7 (Alice Freeman^6) and Benjamin KNOWLES, 17 Feb. 1763, Eastham (MD31:177)

Rebecca FREEMAN^6 (Mary Paine^5) and Samuel WALKER^6 (John^5, Wm.^{4}, Sarah Snow^3, Constance Hopkins^2), Int. 23 Jan. 1741/42, Eastham (VR:229)

Sarah PAINE^5 (John^4) and Joshua KNOWLES, 13 Mar. 1717/18, Eastham (MD 15:71)

Joshua KNOWLES and 2nd Phebe ATWOOD, 27 Dec. 1774 (Truro VR:108)

Jesse KNOWLES^6 (Sarah Paine^5) and Sarah WALKER, 30 Jan. 1752, Eastham (MD 25:42)

Joshua KNOWLES^6 (Sarah Paine^5) and Mary HARDING, 23 May 1754 (Truro VR:79)

Martha KNOWLES^7 (Joshua^6) and David DYER, 21 Apr. 1785 (Truro VR:135)

Henry DYER^8 (Martha Knowles^7) and Sally MAYO, 4 Mar. 1819 (Truro VR:232)

Sarah DYER^8 (Martha Knowles^7) and Isaac SMITH, 31 Dec. 1816 (Truro VR:218)

Mehitable KNOWLES^7 (Joshua^6) and Ephraim LOMBARD, 17 Nov. 1774 (Truro VR:108)

Josiah KNOWLES[6] (Sarah Paine[5]) and Rebecca HIGGINS, 29 Oct. 1761, Eastham
(VR 6:17d)

Rebecca KNOWLES[6] (Sarah Paine[5]) and Isaac SPARROW[6] (Richard[5-4], Hannah Prence[3],
Patience Brewster[2]), 15 Jan. 1746/47, Eastham (MD 24:190)

Sarah KNOWLES[6] (Sarah Paine[5]) and Elkanah HIGGINS, Int. 17 Sept. 1757, Eastham
VR:182)

Simeon KNOWLES[6] (Sarah Paine[5]) and Eunice MAYO[6] (Jos.[5], Hannah Freeman[4], Mercy
Prence[3], Patience Brewster[2](?)), Int. 12 Aug. 1758, Eastham (VR:181)

Susanna KNOWLES[6] (Sarah Paine[5]) and Zoeth SMITH, Int. 11 Apr. 1760, Eastham
(VR:174)

Theophilus PAINE[5] (John[4]) and Hannah BACON, c1735 (Paine Fam.2:166)

Thomas PAINE[5] (John[4]) and Phebe FREEMAN[6] (Eleazer[5], Nath.[4], Mercy Prence[3],
Patience Brewster[2])

Thomas PAINE[5] and 2nd Sarah ( ) MASON, 1786, Eden ME (Paine Fam.2:167-169)

William PAINE[5] (John[4]) and 1st Sarah BACON, Int. 2 Sept. 1727, Eastham (MD 28:116)

William PAINE[5] and 2nd Elizabeth (OSBORN) Myrick, 15 Jan. 1744/45 (Eastham VR:144)

Sarah PAINE[6] (Wm.[5]) and Thomas STURGIS, 24 Jan. 1744/45, Eastham (MD 20:158)

Joseph PAINE[4] (Mary Snow[3]) and Patience SPARROW[4] (Hannah Prence[3], Patience
Brewster[2]), 27 May 1691, Eastham (MD 7:235)

Patience SPARROW[4] and 2nd John JENKINS, 23 Nov. 1715, Barnstable (MD 14:227)

Joseph PAINE[5] (Jos.[4]) and Hannah HUCKENS

James PAINE[6] (Jos.[5]) and Patience CROSBY, 30 Aug. 1759 (Paine Gen.2:184)

Dorcas PAINE[5] (Jos.[4]) and Joseph JENKINS, Int. 5 Jan. 1722/23, Harwich (MD 8:36)

Solomon PEPPER and Mercy MAYO, Int. 27 May 1774, Eastham (VR 12:2)

Phebe PAINE[5] (Jos.[4]) and Solomon PEPPER, 15 Oct. 1724, Eastham (MD 16:72)

Abigail PEPPER[6] (Phebe Paine[5]) and Amos KNOWLES[6] (Amos[5], Mercy Freeman[4], Mercy
Prence[3], Patience Brewster[2])

Solomon PEPPER[6] (Phebe Paine[5]) and 1st Abiel HOPKINS[5] (Caleb[4-3], Gyles[2]),
16 Dec. 1762 (Eastham VR 6:8)

Solomon PEPPER[6] and 2nd Phebe KNOWLES, 16 Apr. 1772, Eastham (VR 6:54)

Reliance PAINE[5] (Jos.[4]) and 1st Eleazer COBB, Int. 18 Oct. 1724, Barnstable
(MD 34:116)

Reliance PAINE[5] and 2nd John COLEMAN, 5 Aug. 1736

John COLEMAN and 2nd Mary HAMBLIN, 2 Aug. 1743

Patience COBB^6 (Reliance Paine^5) and Nathaniel ALLEN, 18 Sept. 1764, Barnstable
    (MD 19:126)

Benjamin COBB^6 (Reliance Paine^5) and Ann DAVIS, 29 May 1749, Barnstable
    (MD 31:13)

Benjamin COBB^7 (Ben.^{6}) and Persis TAYLOR, 1783

Eleazer COBB^7 (Ben.^{6}) and 2nd Elizabeth DAVIS, 3rd Sarah HINCKLEY

Joseph COBB^7 (Ben.^{6}) and Elizabeth ADAMS, 19 June 1785 (Bible)

Benjamin COBB^8 (Jos.^{7}) and Sally HAWES, 5 Sept. 1822 (Bible)

Eliza COBB^8 (Jos.^{7}) and Isaac G. HEDGE, 24 Apr. 1825 (Bible)

Lot COBB^8 (Jos.^{7}) and Sabria OLIVER, 19 Nov. 1818 (Bible)

Lucy COBB^8 (Jos.^{7}) and Nathaniel STURGIS, 19 Oct. 1809 (Bible)

Lucy COBB^7 (Ben.^{6}) and Benjamin ALLEN

Reliance COBB^7 (Ben.^{6}) and James DAVIS

Reliance COBB^6 (Reliance Paine^5) and Paul CROWELL, Int. 6 Aug. 1747, Barnstable
    (MD 31:85)$^{\langle 4 \rangle}$

Joseph CROWEL^7 (Reliance Cobb^6) and Aznbah SMITH, 9 Dec. 1773

Richard PAINE^5 (Jos.^{4}) and Phebe MERRICK, 20 Oct. 1726, Eastham (MD 16:195)

Joseph PAINE^6 (Richard^5) and Phebe RICH, 20 Jan. 1767

Mary PAINE^4 (Mary Snow^3) and 1st James ROGERS^3 (Jos.^{2}), 11 Jan. 1670, Eastham
    (MD 5:195)

Mary PAINE^4 and 2nd Israel COLE, 24 Apr. 1679, Eastham (MD 5:195)

Hannah COLE^5 (Mary Paine^4) and Samuel HIGGINS, 4 Nov. 1703, Eastham (MD 8:94)

Benjamin COLE^6 (Israel^5) and Desire SMITH, 8 Mar. 1743/44 (Eastham VR:142)

Benjamin COLE^7 (Ben.^{6}) and Elizabeth TUPPER, 29 Dec. 1774, Liverpool N.S.

Nicholas PAINE^4 (Mary Snow^3) and Hannah HIGGINS^4 (Eliz. Rogers^3, Jos.^{2}), c1699
    (MD 4:33)

Lydia PAINE^5 (Nicholas^4) and Daniel YOUNG^5 (Sarah Snow^4, Jos.^{3}, Constance
    Hopkins^2), 5 Mar. 1729/30, Eastham (MD 16:204)

Priscilla PAINE^5 (Nicholas^4) and William NORKUT, 4 Aug. 1726, Eastham (MD 16:145)

William NORKUT and 1st Ruth MAYO, 5 Mar. 1718/19 (MD 15:75)

Samuel PAINE^4 (Mary Snow^3) and Patience FREEMAN^4 (Mercy Prence^3, Patience
    Brewster^2), 31 Jan. 1682, Eastham (MD 6:12)

Ebenezer PAINE^5 (Sam.^{4}) and Hannah HOPKINS^4 (Joshua^3, Gyles^2), 13 Dec. 1722,
    Eastham (MD 16:28)

Hannah HOPKINS^4 and 2nd Zachariah SMALL

Ebenezer PAINE^6 (Eben.^{5}) and 1st Mary ALLEN, Int. 18 Jan. 1750, Harwich (MD 33:147)

Ebenezer PAINE^6 and 2nd Thankful WHITE^5 (Eben.^{4}, Jonathan^3, Peregrine^2),
2 Sept. 1756 (Yarmouth VR 3:281)

Nathaniel PAINE^7 (Eben.^{6}) and Sarah YOUNG

Hannah PAINE^6 (Eben.^{5}) and John ALLEN, 25 June 1750, Harwich (MD 33:62)

Mercy ALLEN^8 (Seth^7, Hannah Paine^6) and Halsey BAKER

Seth ALLEN^7 (Hannah Paine^6) and 1st Anna GAGE

Joshua PAINE^5 (Sam.^{4}) and Phebe SNOW^5 (Micajah^4, Stephen^3, Constance Hopkins^2),
19 Mar. 1729/30, Eastham (MD 17:29)

Isaac PAINE^6 (Joshua^5) and Abigail SNOW^6 (Tho.^{5}, Eben.^{4}, Stephen^3, Constance
Hopkins^2), 9 Dec. 1762 (Eastham VR 6:7)

Ebenezer PAINE^7 (Isaac^6) and Sarah SMITH, c1788 (Eastham VR 6:69)

Thomas PAINE^4 (Mary Snow^3) and 1st Hannah SHAW, 5 Aug. 1678, Eastham (MD 4:31)

Thomas PAINE^4 and 2nd Elizabeth EAIRS, 8 Mar. 1714/15 (Truro VR:8)

Abigail PAINE^5 (Tho.^{4}) and Rev. Ebenezer WHITE

Hannah WHITE^6 (Abigail Paine^5) and Joseph GUILD, 11 Nov. 1741 (Hist.Attleboro:229)

Barnabas PAINE^5 (Tho.^{4}) and Mary PURINTON, 25 June 1724 (Truro VR:55)

Mercy PAINE^6 (Barnabas^5) and Matthias RICH, 31 Oct. 1751 (Truro VR:77)

Joshua RICH^7 (Mercy Paine^6) and Molly DYER, 10 Apr. 1775 (Truro VR:106)

Elkanah PAINE^5 (Tho.^{4}) and Reliance YOUNG, 10 Mar. 1719/20, Eastham (MD 15:142)

Elisha PAINE^6 (Elkanah^5) and Thankful HOPKINS^5 (Caleb$^{4-3}$, Gyles^2), 12 June
1746 (Truro VR:51)

Thankful HOPKINS^5 and 2nd Freeman HIGGINS^6 (Sarah Freeman^5, Edmund^4, Mercy
Prence^3, Patience Brewster^2), 14 July 1757, Eastham (MD 16:76)

Mary PAINE^7 (Elisha^6) and Samuel KING, Int. 4 Dec. 1766 (Boston Rcd.com.30:426)

Reliance PAINE^7 (Elisha^6) and Prince SNOW^6 (Micajah^4, Stephen^3, Constance
Hopkins^2), 9 Mar. 1769, Eastham (MD 32:115)

Eleazer FREEMAN Jr. and Elizabeth SNOW, 9 Mar. 1769, Eastham (MD 32:115)

Elkanah PAINE^6 (Elkanah^5) and Mary RICH

Joshua PAINE^6 (Elkanah^5) and Elizabeth ATKINS, 29 July 1759 (Truro VR:90)

Molly Lewis PAINE^7 (Joshua^6) and Ebenezer LOMBARD, 12 Dec. 1792 (Truro VR:157)

Benjamin PAINE^7 (Joshua^6) and Thankful SMALL, 29 Jan. 1793

Atkins PAINE^8 (Ben.^{7}) and Joanna SNOW, 25 Dec. 1838 (Truro VR:328)

Hannah PAINE^5 (Tho.^{4}) and John BINNEY, 31 May 1704, Eastham (MD 3:229)

Jonathan PAINE^5 (Tho.^{4}) and 1st Sarah MAYO, 27 Oct. 1709, Eastham (MD 8:14)

Jonathan PAINE^5 and 2nd Mary PURRINGTON, 29 June 1719 (Truro VR:38)

Jonathan PAINE^6 (Jonathan^5) and Hannah LOMBARD

Daniel PAINE^6 (Jonathan^5) and Elizabeth THATCHER, 25 June 1741 (Truro VR:24)

Barnabas PAINE^7 (Dan.^{6}) and Martha ATKINS, c1782 (Paine Fam.:204)

Joshua PAINE^5 (Tho.^{4}) and 1st Rebecca SPARROW, 20 Oct. 1720 (Eastham VR:35)

Joshua PAINE^5 and 2nd Constance (PAINE^5) Baker

Moses PAINE^5 (Tho.^{4}) and Margery MAYO, 14 Apr. 1720, Yarmouth (Paine Fam.2:84,85)

Silas KNOWLES^6 (Phebe Paine^5) and Mary FREEMAN, 6 Apr. 1761 (Truro VR:91)

Phebe KNOWLES^7 (Silas^6) and Benjamin HARDING, 12 Apr. 1792 (Truro VR:153)

Mary Knowles HARDING^8 (Phebe Knowles^7) and Caleb FISH, 28 Nov. 1815 (Truro VR:217)

Betsey Goddard FISH^9 (Mary Harding^8) and Isaac GREEN, 2 Apr. 1835 (Truro VR:321)

Phebe PAINE^5 (Tho.^{4}) and Paul KNOWLES, 28 Feb. 1722/23 (Truro VR:39)

Paul KNOWLES and 2nd Mercy ( ) HARDING, c1752 (NEHGR 80:17)

Abigail KNOWLES^6 (Phebe Paine^5) and Sylvanus HIGGINS, 13 Dec. 1764

Sylvanus HIGGINS and 2nd Hannah HIGGINS, 10 Nov. 1799 (NEHGR 80:18)

Ann KNOWLES^6 (Phebe Paine^5) and Uriah RICH, 16 Feb. 1743/44, Truro (NEHGR 80:17)

Hannah KNOWLES^6 (Phebe Paine^5) and 1st John WARREN, 12 Mar. 1752, Truro

Hannah KNOWLES^6 and 2nd Jonathan SPARROW Jr., 12 Mar. 1766 (Truro VR:110)

Hannah KNOWLES^6 and 3rd Zaccheus HIGGINS, 3 Dec. 1772

Mary KNOWLES^6 (Phebe Paine^5) and Joshua ATWOOD, 27 Nov. 1746, Truro

Paul KNOWLES^6 (Phebe Paine^5) and Mary (ATKINS) Dyer, 11 Nov. 1760, Truro (NEHGR80:18)

Phebe KNOWLES^6 (Phebe Paine^5) and 1st Joseph COLLINS, 16 Feb. 1743/44, Truro

Phebe KNOWLES^6 and 2nd Simon GROSS, 14 Feb. 1749/50, Truro (NEHGR 80:17)

Ruth KNOWLES^6 (Phebe Paine^5) and Col. Elisha TICKNOR, 1756

Silas KNOWLES^6 (Phebe Paine^5) and 1st Mary FREEMAN, 6 Apr. 1761, Truro

Silas KNOWLES^6 and 2nd Susanna COBB, 17 Nov. 1791, Truro (NEHGR 80:18,19)

Thomas KNOWLES^6 (Phebe Paine^5) and Lucy LEWIS, 11 Dec. 1760, Truro

Thomas PAINE^5 (Tho.^{4}) and Thankful COBB, 17 Mary 1705, Eastham (MD 6:206)

Hugh PAINE^6 (Tho.^{5}) and Jerusha RICH, 4 Sept. 1740 (Truro VR:26)

Jerusha RICH and 2nd Solomon HINCKLEY, 14 May 1752 (Truro VR:79)

Mary PAINE^6 (Tho.^{5}) and Samuel DYER, 5 Feb. 1746/47 (Truro VR:52)

Samuel DYER and 1st Mary BROWN

Thankful PAINE^6 (Tho.^{5}) and Joseph ATKINS, c1726 (MD 24:140)

Uriah ATKINS[7] (Thankful Paine[6]) and Deborah ATWOOD[7] (Mary Atwood[6], John[5], Anna
Snow[4], Mark[3], Constance Hopkins[2])

Ruth SNOW[3] and John COLE, 12 Dec. 1666, Eastham (MD 5:196)

John COLE[4] (Ruth Snow[3]) and 2nd Sarah ( ) HIGGINS, 15 Nov. 1732, Eastham (MD 17:36)

Joseph COLE[5] (John[4]) and Mary YOUNG, 2 Dec. 1736, Eastham (MD 19:104)

Keziah COLE[6] (Jos.[5]) and Nathaniel HARDING

Joseph COLE[4] (Ruth Snow[3]) and 1st Elizabeth COB, 4 Feb. 1701/02, Eastham (MD 7:19)

Joseph COLE[4] and 2nd Mercy HINCKLEY, 6 Oct. 1715, Harwich (MD 6:83)

Sarah COLE[5] (Jos.[4]) and Joshua COLE, 31 Jan. 1733/34, Eastham (MD 17:81)

Patience COLE[5] (Jos.[4]) and Judah ROGERS[5] (Judah[4], John[3], Jos.[2]), 12 Dec. 1728,
Eastham (MD 16:147)

Sarah COLE[5] (Jos.[4]) and Joshua COLE, 31 Jan. 1733/34, Eastham (MD 17:81)

Gershom COLE[5] (Jos.[4]) and Mary ROGERS[5] (Judah[4], John[3], Jos.[2]), c1729 (MD 17:31)

Ruth COLE[5] (Jos.[4]) and Daniel DOANE, 8 Mar. 1732/33, Eastham (MD 17:36)

Joseph COLE[5] (Jos.[4]) and 1st Sarah NICKERSON, 17 Nov. 1737, Harwich (MD 23:56)

Reuben COLE and Hannah COLE, Int. 27 Apr. 1762, Eastham (MD 27:187)

Ruth COLE[4] (Ruth Snow[3]) and William TWINING Jr., 21 Mar. 1688/89, Eastham (MD 4:142)

Hannah TWINING[5] (Ruth Cole[4]) and David YOUNG, 1 June 1731, Eastham (MD 17:83)

Nehemiah YOUNG[6] (Hannah Twining[5]) and Abigail TAYLOR[7] (Phebe Higgins[6], Rebecca
Hopkins[5], Stephen[4-3], Gyles[2]), 26 Apr. 1770, Eastham (MD 32:172)

Barnabas TWINING[5] (Ruth Cole[4]) and Hannah SWEET, 11 June 1731, Eastham (MD 17:33)

Jonathan TWINING[6] (Barnabas[5]) and 1st Tabitha HIGGINS, 28 Feb. 1754, Eastham
(MD 25:40)

Jonathan TWINING[6] and 2nd Sarah ROGERS, 18 May 1/75 (Twining Gen.:49)

William TWINING[5] (Ruth Cole[4]) and Apphia LEWIS, 21 Feb. 1727/28, Eastham (MD 15:71)

Abigail TWINING[6] (Wm.[5]) and 1st Joseph ROGERS[6] (Crisp[5], Jos.[4], John[3], Jos.[2])

Sarah SNOW[3] and William WALKER, 25 Jan. 1654, Eastham (MD 6:206)

John WALKER and Hannah REMICK, Int. 12 June 1744 (Eastham VR:232)

Deborah WALKER and Williams SMITH, 3 Oct. 1728, Eastham (MD 15:227)

Jabez WALKER and Sarah ATWOOD, 17 July 1748, Provincetown (MD 12:78)

Rejoyce WALKER[5] (Jabez[4]) and Joseph LEWEN, 9 Nov. 1732, Eastham (MD 17:37)

Joseph LEWEN and 1st Hannah ROGERS[5] (Eleazer[4], Tho.[3], Jos.[2])

Richard WALKER[5] (Jabez[4]) and Joanna TOMLIN, Int. 13 Feb. 1719/20 (Eastham VR:207)

Susan WALKER and Jonathan COLLINS, 27 June 1716, Eastham (MD 15:57)

Samuel WALKER^6 (John^5, Wm.^{4}, Sarah Snow^3) and Rebecca FREEMAN^6 (Mary Paine^5,
   John^4, Mary Snow^3, Constance Hopkins^2), Int. 23 Jan. 1741/42, Eastham (VR:229)

Susanna WALKER^7 (Sam.^{6}) and John KNOWLES, 19 June 1769 (Eastham VR 6:40)

Robert KNOWLES^8 (Susanna Walker^7) and Lydia KNOWLES^7 (Amos$^{6-5}$, Mercy Freeman^4,
   Mercy Prence^3, Patience Brewster^2), Int. 30 Aug. 1794 (Eastham VR 12:24)

William WALKER^5 (Wm.^{4}) and Anne YOUNG, 24 Oct. 1717, Eastham (MD 15:68)

Susanna WALKER^6 (Wm.^{5}) and Elkins SNOW^5 (Stephen^4, Jos.^{3}, Constance Hopkins^2),
   Int. 24 Sept. 1737 (Eastham VR:224)

David WALKER^6 (Wm.^{5}) and Thankful BROWN, Int. 20 May 1758 (Eastham VR:181)$^{<5>}$

Andrew WALKER^6 (Wm.^{5}) and 1st Sarah DOANE, 14 Nov. 1754, Eastham (MD 15:56)

Andrew WALKER^6 and 2nd Dorcas PAINE, Int. 1 Jan. 1763, Eastham (VR:179)

William WALKER^6 (Wm.^{5}) and Hannah HINCKLEY, 17 Nov. 1757 (Truro VR:167)

Stephen SNOW^3 and 1st Susanna (DEANE) Rogers, 28 Oct. 1663, Eastham (MD 8:15)

Stephen SNOW^3 and 2nd Mary BIGFORD, 9 Apr. 1701, Eastham (MD 8:15)

Bethiah SNOW^4 (Stephen^3) and John SMITH^4 (Mary Hopkins^3, Gyles^2), 14 May 1694,
   Eastham (MD 8:243)

Hannah SNOW^4 (Stephen^3) and William COLE, 2 Dec. 1686, Eastham (MD 9:9)

Bathshua SNOW^4 (Stephen^3) and John KING$^{<6>}$

John KING and 2nd Mary (BENJAMIN) Clark, 7 Oct. 1707

John KING and 3rd Hannah HAMBLIN, 9 Sept. 1714 (Barnstable VR)

John KING and 4th Rachel (MAKER) Nickerson, 6 July 1737, Eastham (MD 17:148)

Bathsheba KING and Gershom RIDER, c1731 (MD 9:102)

Nathaniel KING and Reliance CLARK, 1 Feb. 1749 (Harwich VR 2:41)

Ebenezer KING^5 (Bathshua Snow^4) and Mercy MYRICK^5 (Nath.^{4}, Abigail Hopkins^3,
   Gyles^2), 13 Oct. 1726, Harwich (MD 8:218)

Heman KING^6 (Eben.^{5}) and Elizabeth CARTWRIGHT, c1750

Joanna KING^5 (Bathshua Snow^4) and Eleazer COLE, 30 May 1728, Harwich (MD 11:249)

Stephen KING^7 (Heman^6) and Elizabeth DAKIN, 4 Mar. 1779

Samuel KING^5 (Bathshua Snow^4) and Abigail LINNELL, 16 Oct. 1720, Eastham (MD 15:230)

Elizabeth KING^6 (Sam.^{5}) and Zaccheus ROGERS, Int. 1 Oct. 1743 (Eastham VR:231)

Stephen KING^5 (Bathshua Snow^4) and Abigail ATWOOD, 13 Oct. 1715, Eastham (MD 15:53)

Stephen KING^6 (Stephen^5) and Hannah PEIRCE, 22 Jan. 1740/41, Eastham (MD 19:185)

Ebenezer SNOW^4 (Stephen^3) and Hope HORTON, 22 Dec. 1698, Eastham (MD 9:12)

Hope HORTON and poss. 2nd Thomas ATKINS, 28 June 1739, Eastham (MD 19:102,103)

Henry SNOW^5 (Eben.^{4}) and Rebecca BERRY, 30 Sept. 1736 (Eastham VR:117)

Nathaniel SNOW[5] (Eben.[4]) and Mary DOANE, 21 May 1731 (Eastham VR:98)

Susanna SNOW[5] (Eben.[4]) and Roger THOMAS, 14 May 1724 (Eastham VR:60)

Aaron SNOW[5] (Eben.[4]) and Sarah GROSS, 12 Aug. 1736, Eastham (MD 17:146)

Polly Maria SNOW and Asher Porter KELLOGG, 22 Nov. 1834, N. Fairfield,"O."
    (Kelloggs 2:1111)

Elisha SNOW[5] (Eben.[4]) and Abigail DOANE, 8 Oct. 1735, Eastham (MD 17:82)

Knowles SNOW[6] (Elisha[5]) and Mercy WING, Int. 16 Dec. 1791

Elisha SNOW[6] (Elisha[5]) and 1st Elizabeth SNOW, 26 Dec. 1771, Yarmouth

Elisha SNOW[6] and 2nd Mercy SMITH, 21 Apr. 1811, Harwich

Levi SNOW[7] (Elisha[6]) and Asenath BROOKS, 12 Nov. 1807

Isaiah SNOW[7] (Elisha[6]) and Mary BURGESS, 12 Mar. 1812

Jane SNOW[7] (Elisha[6]) and James CHASE, 27 Sept. 1808

Laban SNOW[7] (Elisha[6]) and Polly ROGERS, Dennis MA

Elisha SNOW[7] (Elisha[6]) and Betsey WING, Jan. 1800 (Harwich VR 3:146)

Hannah SNOW[6] (Elisha[5]) and Lot BAKER

Nathaniel SNOW[6] (Elisha[5]) and Rebecca DOANE, 1757

Thomas SNOW[5] (Eben.[4]) and Abigail DOANE[6] (Ruth Freeman[5], Edmund[4], Mercy Prence[3],
    Patience Brewster[2]), 27 Jan. 1731/32, Eastham (MD 17:34)

Abigail SNOW[6] (Tho.[5]) and Isaac PAINE[6] (Joshua[5], Sam.[4], Mary Snow[3], Constance
    Hopkins[2]), Int. Oct. 1762 (Eastham VR:177)

Elnathan SNOW[6] (Tho.[5]) and Phebe SPARROW[6] (Jonathan[5], Rebecca Merrick[4], Abigail
    Hopkins[3], Gyles[2]), 4 Dec. 1755, Eastham (MD 15:232)

Abigail SNOW and Benoni BAKER, Int. 16 Aug. 1783 (Eastham VR:13)

Dorcas Vickery SNOW[7] (Elnathan[6]) and 1st Peter NEWCOMB (Newcomb Gen<1923>:325)

Dorcas Vickery SNOW[7] and 2nd Jedediah YOUNG, 1 Jan. 1818

Aaron SNOW[7] (Elnathan[6]) and Abigail HIGGINS, Int. 30 Dec. 1786 (Eastham VR 12:16)

Isaac SNOW[7] (Elnathan[6]) and Hannah FREEMAN[7] (Jonathan[6], Edmund[5-4], Mercy Prence[3],
    Patience Brewster[2]), 16 Mar. 1786

Russell SNOW[8] (Isaac[7]) and Hannah Shaw SPARROW

Hannah COLE[5] (Hannah Snow[4], Stephen[3]) and Elisha DOANE

Micajah SNOW[4] (Stephen[3]) and Mercy YOUNG, 25 Nov. 1697, Eastham (MD 9:10)

David SNOW[5] (Micajah[4]) and Priscilla SPARROW

Mercy SNOW[5] (Micajah[4]) and Daniel SEARS, 13 Jan. 1736/37 (Eastham VR:120)

Phebe SNOW[5] (Micajah[4]) and Joshua PAINE[5] (Sam.[4], Mary Snow[3], Constance Hopkins[2]),
     19 Mar. 1727/30 (Eastham VR:92)

Ruth SNOW[5] (Micajah[4]) and Samuel AREY, 20 Feb. 1745 (Eastham VR:145)

Jesse SNOW[5] (Micajah[4]) and Lois FREEMAN[6] (Edmund[5-4], Mercy Prence[3], Patience
     Brewster[2]), 10 Nov. 1748, Eastham (MD 24:138)

Ephraim SNOW[6] (Jesse[5]) and Martha ROGERS[6] (Elkanah[5], Jos.[4], John[3], Jos.[2]), Int.
     22 Feb. 1777 (Eastham VR 12:6)

John SNOW[5] (Micajah[4]) and 1st Hannah MYRICK[5] (Nath.[4], Abigail Hopkins[3], Gyles[2]),
     12 Oct. 1721, Harwich (MD 7:198)

Micajah SNOW[5] (Micajah[4]) and Elizabeth FREEMAN[6] (Nath.[5-4], Mercy Prence[3], Patience
     Brewster[2]), 27 May 1742, Eastham (MD 20:94,156)

Prince SNOW[6] (Micajah[5]) and Reliance PAINE[7] (Elisha[6], Elkanah[5], Tho.[4], Mary Snow[3],
     Constance Hopkins[2]), 9 Mar. 1769, Eastham (MD 32:115)

Stephen SNOW[5] (Micajah[4]) and Mary COLE, 30 Jan. 1734, Eastham (MD 17:144)

Heman SNOW[6] (Stephen[5]) and Jedidah SMITH, 18 Dec. 1766, Eastham (MD 32:66)

Heman SNOW 3d and Lucia FREEMAN, 1 Aug. 1799 (Orleans Ch.rcds.)

Deborah HOPKINS[2] (Stephen[1])

Deborah HOPKINS[2] and Andrew RING, 23 Apr. 1646, Plymouth (MD 13:86)

Andrew RING and 2nd Lettice ( ) MORTON, aft. 1673

Eleazer RING[3] and Mary SHAW, 11 Jan. 1687, Plymouth (MD 13:204)

Deborah RING[4] (Eleazer[3]) and John FULLER[4] (Sam.[3-2-1]), 7 Feb. 1722/23, Plympton
     (MD 2:139)

Lydia RING[4] (Eleazer[3]) and Ephraim STURTEVANT[5] (Anna Jones[4], Patience Little[3],
     Anna Warren[2]), c1731

Mary RING[4] (Eleazer[3]) and Peleg SAMPSON[4] (Lydia Standish[3], Alexander[2]), 7 Nov.
     1722, Plympton (MD 2:138)

Phebe RING[4] (Eleazer[3]) and Ichabod STANDISH[3] (Alexander[2]), 26 Nov. 1719, Plympton
     (MD 3:91)

Susanna RING[4] (Eleazer[3]) and Nehemiah BOSWORTH, 27 Jan. 1725, Plympton (MD 1:246)

Nehemiah BOSWORTH and 2nd Sarah TOMSON, 26 Mar. 1729, Plympton (MD 2:51)

Andrew RING[4] (Eleazer[3]) and Zeruiah STANDISH[4] (Eben.[3], Alexander[2]), 20 May 1724,
     Plympton (MD 2:139)

Zeruiah STANDISH[4] and 2nd Andrew GRAY, 19 Dec. 1745

Sarah RING^5 (Andrew^4) and Isaiah CUSHMAN^5 (Josiah^4, Elkanah^3, Mary Allerton^2)

Mary RING^5 (Andrew^4) and Joseph JOHNSON^5 (Eliz. Cooke^4, Caleb^3, Jacob^2), c1741

Susanna RING^5 (Andrew^4) and 1st Joseph YORK, 2nd John LOCKE

Elizabeth RING^4 (Eleazer^3) and James CLAGHORN, 26 June 1736 (Kingston VR)

Jonathan RING^4 (Eleazer^3) and Sarah MITCHELL, 21 Jan. 1747/48, Kingston (Gen.
     Adv.3:23)

Eleazer RING^5 (Jonathan^4) and 1st Elizabeth SPALDING, 22 Jan. 1774 (Worthington VR:96)

Eleazer RING^5 and 2nd Damaris JOHNSON, 7 Sept. 1789 (Worthington VR:108,111)

Samuel RING^4 (Eleazer^3) and Ruth (SILVESTER^5) Cooke (Ruth Turner^4, Mary Brewster^3,
     Jonathan^2), 28 Jan. 1724/25, Plympton (MD 2:139) <see below>

Ruth (SILVESTER^5) Cooke and 3rd John PHINNEY^5 (Jos.^{4}, Mary Rogers^3, Jos.^{2}),
     25 Dec. 1770 (Kingston VR) <see below>

Grace RING^5 (Sam.^{4}) and Samuel BRADFORD^5 (Gamaliel^4, Sam.^{3}, Wm.^{2}), 1 Nov. 1749,
     Kingston (Gen. Adv.3:23)

Lydia RING^5 (Sam.^{4}) and William RIPLEY^5 (Hannah Bosworth^4, David^3, Hannah Howland^2),
     5 Jan. 1748/49, Kingston (Gen.Adv.3:23)

Ruth SILVESTER^5 and 1st Francis COOKE^4 (Francis^3, Jacob^2), 4 Feb. 1719, Plympton
     (MD 3:91) <see above>

Francis RING^5 (Sam.^{4}) and Mary WESTON

Rufus RING^6 (Francis^5) and Fanny SHAW, 21 Aug. 1803 (Middleboro VR 4:2:0)

George RING^5 (Sam.^{4}) and Lucy CHIPMAN, 14 Apr. 1747

Lucy RING^6 (George^5) and Jonathan SCOTT, 14 Mar. 1768 (MD 8:81)

Jonathan SCOTT and 2nd Elizabeth BASS, 8 Dec. 1783 (MD 8:82)

Elizabeth RING^3 and William MAYO (MD 4:193)

Hannah MAYO^4 (Eliz. Ring^3) and Samuel TUCKER, c1706 (MD 4:184)

Thankful MAYO^4 (Eliz. Ring^3) and Samuel HIGGINS, 20 Mar. 1717/18, Eastham (MD 15:72)

Mary RING^3 and John MORTON, 4 Mar. 1687, Plymouth (MD 13:204)

John MORTON and 1st Phebe SHAW, c1681 (MD 1:209)

Mary MORTON^4 (Mary Ring^3) and Thomas TOMSON^3 (Mary Cooke^2), 13 Dec. 1715, Middle-
     boro (MD 2:158)

Hannah MORTON^4 (Mary Ring^3) and John HODGES, c1723 (Norton VR)

Deborah MORTON^4 (Mary Ring^3) and Jonathan INGLEE, 27 Feb. 1723/24, Middleboro
     (MD 4:73)

Jonathan INGLEE and 2nd Martha REED, 5 Sept. 1727, Middleboro (MD 5:38)

Ebenezer MORTON^4 (Mary Ring^3) and Mercy FOSTER, 2 Feb. 1720, Plymouth (MD 14:39)

Deborah MORTON^5 (Eben.^{4}) and Ichabod MORTON^5 (Nath.^{4}, Eleazer^3, Ephraim^2, George^1),
   26 Oct. 1749, Middleboro (VR 2:2:29)

Eleazer MORTON^6 (Deborah^5) and Lucy DOTY^5 (Sam.^{4}, John^3, Jos.^{2}), 18 Aug. 1777
   (MD 15:129)

Sarah MORTON^6 (Deborah^5) and John BARROWS^6 (Eben.^{5}, Mercy Coombs^4, Francis^3,
   Sarah Priest^2), 16 Nov. 1769 (Middleboro VR)

Ebenezer MORTON^5 (Eben.^{4}) and Sarah COBB^5 (James^4, Rachel Soule^3, John^2),
   23 July 1753, Middleboro (MD 18:157)

John MORTON^5 (Eben.^{4}) and Elizabeth BENNET^5 (Jos.^{4}, Priscilla Howland^3, Isaac^2),
   21 Jan. 1747, Middleboro (MD 18:78)

Mercy MORTON^5 (Eben.^{4}) and Zechariah EDDY, 18 Nov. 1737 (Eddy Gen.:214)

Capt. Joshua EDDY^6 (Mercy Morton^5) and Lydia PADDOCK, Int. 24 Jan. 1778 (Middleboro VR 4:31)

William RING^3 and Hannah SHERMAN^3 (Desire Doty^2), 13 July 1693, Plymouth (MD 13:206)

Deborah RING^4 (Wm.^{3}) and Caleb SHERMAN, 12 May 1737, Plymouth (MD 14:157)

Caleb SHERMAN and 2nd Rebecca RYDER^5 (John^4, Sarah Bartlett^3, Mary Warren^2),
   15 Aug. 1745, Plymouth (MD 17:5)

Elizabeth RING^4 (Wm.^{3}) and Joseph PEARCE, c1722 (MD 13:116)

Gyles HOPKINS^2 (Stephen^1)

Gyles HOPKINS^2 and Katherine WHELDON, 9 Oct. 1639, Plymouth (MD 13:85)

Ruth HOPKINS^3 and Samuel MAYO

Abigail HOPKINS^3 and William MERRICK, 23 May 1667, Eastham (MD 5:198)

William MERRICK and 2nd Elizabeth (   ) SNOW, aft. 22 Apr. 1691

Benjamin MYRICK^4 (Abigail Hopkins^3) and 1st Rebecca DOANE, pre 1703

Benjamin MYRICK^4 and 2nd Rachel (HOLMES) Lincoln, 31 July 1740

John MERRICK^4 (Abigail Hopkins^3) and 1st Ann SEARS, 28 Jan. 1703

John MERRICK^4 and 2nd Hannah HARDING, 17 Dec. 1746 (Truro VR:52)

Joshua MERRICK^4 (Abigail Hopkins^3) and Lydia MAYO^5 (Tho.^{4}, Hannah Prence^3,
   Patience Brewster^2), 4 June 1714, Eastham (MD 3:230)

Nathaniel MYRICK^4 (Abigail Hopkins^3) and Alice FREEMAN

Constant MYRICK^5 (Nath.^{4}) and Sarah FREEMAN^6 (John$^{5-4}$, Mercy Prence^3, Patience
   Brewster^2), Int. 17 Feb. 1726/27, Harwich (MD 8:218)

Hannah MYRICK^5 (Nath.^{4}) and John SNOW^5 (Micajah^4, Stephen^3, Constance Hopkins^2),

12 Oct. 1721

Mercy MYRICK[5] (Nath.[4]) and Ebenezer KING[5] (Bathshua Snow[4], Stephen[3], Constance Hopkins[2]), 13 Oct. 1726, Harwich (MD 8:218)

Alice MYRICK[5] (Nath.[4]) and Benjamin RUGGLES, 19 Oct. 1736, Harwich (MD 20:26)

Priscilla MYRICK[5] (Nath.[4]) and Elisha COBB, 25 Mar. 1735, Harwich (MD 19:118)

Ruth MYRICK[5] (Nath.[4]) and Thomas HINCKLEY, 31 Mar. 1730, Harwich (MD 13:55)

Sarah MYRICK[5] (Nath.[4]) and Abner LEE, Oct. 1744 (Hardwick VR:210)

William MYRICK[5] (Nath.[4]) and Elizabeth OSBORN, 23 Jan. 1733/34, Eastham (MD 17:141)

Rebecca MERRICK[4] (Abigail Hopkins[3]) and Jonathan SPARROW

Rebecca SPARROW[5] (Rebecca Merrick[4]) and Joshua PAINE, 20 Oct. 1720 (Eastham VR:35)

Abigail SPARROW[5] (Rebecca Merrick[4]) and Samuel MAYO, 6 Aug. 1713, Eastham (MD3:229)

Hannah SPARROW[5] (Rebecca Merrick[4]) and John HURD, c1710 (MD 5:88)

John HURD[6] (Hannah Sparrow[5]) and Tabitha CROSBY, 31 Oct. 1745, Harwich (MD 25:101)

Jonathan SPARROW[5] (Rebecca Merrick[4]) and Dorcas VICKERY, 12 Oct. 1721, Harwich (MD 7:198)

Lydia SPARROW[6] (Jos.[5], Rebecca Merrick[4]) and Isaac KING, Int. 26 Oct. 1751 (Eastham VR:195)

Samuel KING[9] (Tho.[8], Isaac[7], Lydia Sparrow[6]) and Sarah SMITH, 28 Dec. 1829 (Bible)

Joseph SPARROW[5] (Rebecca Merrick[4]) and Hannah DOANE, 10 Mar. 1725/26, Eastham (MD 16:75)

Hannah SPARROW[6] (Jos.[5], Rebecca Merrick[4]) and Joshua HIGGINS, Int. 8 Jan. 1762 (Eastham VR:176)

Mary SPARROW[6] (Jos.[5]) and Elkanah LINNELL[6] (Thankful Hopkins[5], Stephen[4-3], Gyles[2]), Int. 17 Jan. 1752 (Eastham VR:194)

Abigail SPARROW[6] (Jos.[5]) and Moses CROSBY, Int. 11 Apr. 1747 (Eastham VR:235)

Ruth MERRICK[4] (Abigail Hopkins[3]) and 1st Samuel SEARS, 2 Nov. 1710, Harwich (MD 4:210)

Ruth MERRICK[4] and 2nd Chillingsworth FOSTER, aft. Nov. 1726

Mary SEARS[5] (Ruth Merrick[4]) and Joseph SNOW[5] (Edw.[4], Jabez[3], Constance Hopkins[2]), 30 Nov. 1738, Harwich (MD 23:58)

Stephen MERRICK[4] (Abigail Hopkins[3]) and Deborah SNOW[4] (Jabez[3], Constance Hopkins[2]), 21 Nov. 1706, Harwich (MD 4:207)

Caleb HOPKINS[3] and Mary WILLIAMS, pre 10 May 1692 (MD 8:240)

Caleb HOPKINS[4] (Caleb[3]) and Mercy FREEMAN, 8 Oct. 1719 (Truro VR:38)

Mercy FREEMAN and 2nd Benjamin HIGGINS, 28 June 1749, Truro (MD 18:189)

Thankful HOPKINS[5] (Caleb[4]) and 1st Elisha PAINE[6] (Elkanah[5], Tho.[4], Mary Snow[3], Constance Hopkins[2]), 12 June 1746 (Truro VR:51)

Thankful HOPKINS[5] and 2nd Freeman HIGGINS[6] (Sarah Freeman[5], Edmund[4], Mercy Prence[3], Patience Brewster[2]), 14 July 1757, Eastham (MD 16:76)

Abiel HOPKINS[5] (Caleb[4]) and Solomon PEPPER[6] (Phebe Paine[5], Jos.[4], Mary Snow[3], Constance Hopkins[2]), 16 Dec. 1762, Eastham (MD 31:175)

Caleb HOPKINS[5] (Caleb[4]) and 1st Mary PAINE, 4 Nov. 1747 (Boston Rcd.com.28:248)

Caleb HOPKINS[5] and 2nd Jane VERNON, 15 June 1777 (Boston Rcd.com.30:373)

Caleb HOPKINS[5] and 2nd Mary WILLIAMS, 22 Mar. 1781 (Boston Rcd.com.30:84)

Jane Vernon HOPKINS[6] (Caleb[5]) and Dr. Isaac RAND Jr., 29 Nov. 1796 (30:148)

Constant HOPKINS[5] (Caleb[4]) and Phebe PAINE[6] (Jonathan[5], Tho.[4], Mary Snow[3], Constance Hopkins[2]), 1 Dec. 1743 (Truro VR:53)

Constant HOPKINS[6] (Constant[5]) and Elizabeth PAINE, c1775

Micro #12 of 18

Capt. Caleb HOPKINS[6] (Constant[5]) and Bethiah SMITH, 16 Mar. 1780 (Truro VR:129)

Bethiah SMITH and David GREEN, 10 June 1801

Jonathan HOPKINS[7] (Constant[6]) and Elizabeth WHORF

William GLOVER and Mary CAPEN, 15 Oct. 1772 (Glover Gen.:281)

William GLOVER and Mary BILLINGS, 14 Jan. 1804 (Glover Gen.:281,333)

Eunice Billings GLOVER and William B. DUGGAN, 4 Nov. 1827 (Glover Gen.:333)

Mary Emma DUGGAN and William Henry QUINCY, 7 Aug. 1867

Elizabeth HOPKINS and James WALCOM, 27 May 1695 (Boston VR 9:225)

John HOPKINS and Sarah WHEATLEY, 22 May 1741 (Boston Rcd.com.28:248)

Christopher HOPKINS and Mary NORRIS, 14 Dec. 1743 (Boston Rcd.com.28:248)

Mary HOPKINS and John DUGGAN, 4 Apr. 1796

Sarah HOPKINS and John GOLDTHWAIT, 13 Mar. 1701 (Boston VR 28:4)

Mary HOPKINS and John GOODWYN, 23 May 1700 (Boston VR 28:1)

Mehitable HOPKINS and John HARWOOD, 25 Apr. 1706 (Boston VR 28:11)

Samuel HOPKINS and Eliphal STRATTON, 21 May 1708 (Boston VR 28:19)

Hannah HOPKINS and Jonathan KEMBALL, 28 July 1709 (Boston VR 28:24)

Eliphal HOPKINS and Ebenezer GRAVES, 21 Apr. 1715 (Boston VR 28:58)

Martyn HOPKINS and Hannah LEWIS, 15 Mar. 1716/17 (Boston VR 28:64)

John HOPKINS and Susanna BILL, 22 Dec. 1719 (Boston VR 28:82)

Bethiah HOPKINS and James MORCH, Int. 12 Jan. 1718 (Boston VR 28:97)

Peter HOPKINS and Mary BILL, 23 Nov. 1722 (Boston VR 28:107)

George HOPKINS and Rebecca WAKEFIELD, 16 Mar. 1724 (Boston VR 28:120)

Bethiah HOPKINS and Mathew CURTIS, 1 Jan. 1728 (Boston VR 28:142)

Susanna HOPKINS and Benjamin SWAIN, 30 Jan. 1728 (Boston VR 28:146)

Matthew HOPKINS and Jane MORISON, 8 June 1738 (Boston VR 28:206)

Sarah HOPKINS and John ALLEN, 31 July 1746 (Boston VR 28:235)

Mary HOPKINS and John CROSS, 21 Oct. 1747 (Boston VR 28:241)

William HOPKINS and Susanna HOSKINS, 10 Aug. 1749 (Boston VR 28:249)

Abigail HOPKINS and Thomas WALKER, 5 May 1743 (Boston VR 28:267)

Mrs. Experience HOPKINS and Samuel OSBORNE, Int. 19 Oct. 1743 (Boston VR 28:276)

Rebecca HOPKINS and Thomas ANDERSON, 4 Dec. 1743 (Boston VR 28:334)

Enoch HOPKINS and Mary SPRAGUE, Int. 29 Mar. 1746 (Boston VR 28:282)

Susanna HOPKINS and James SCOLLOY, Int. 29 Aug. 1751 (Boston VR 28:298)

Edward HOPKINS and Elizabeth LOVERIDGE, Int. 27 Sept. 1753 (Boston VR 30:8)

Mercy HOPKINS and John GROSER, Int. 3 June 1756 (Boston VR 30:20)

Martha HOPKINS and John VEIZIE, 16 Apr. 1772 (Boston VR 30:60)

Mehitable HOPKINS and James PERKINS, 24 June 1793 (Boston VR 30:99)

Betsey HOPKINS and Philip HITCHBORN, 16 June 1792 (Boston VR 30:120)

Frances HOPKINS and Mungo WILLIAMS, 31 May 1795 (Boston VR 30:134)

Mary HOPKINS and Samuel TOWNSEND, 5 Apr. 1802 (Boston VR 30:156)

Patty HOPKINS and Thomas Smith WEBB, 24 Oct. 1797 (Boston VR 30:171)

Mary HOPKINS and John DUGGAN, 4 Apr. 1796 (Boston VR 30:176)

Nathaniel HOPKINS and Hannah CHIPMAN, 23 Sept. 1797 (Boston VR 30:183)

Elizabeth HOPKINS and Moses HOYT, 5 Feb. 1801 (Boston VR 30:182)

Constant HOPKINS and Margaret CLOUGH, 23 Jan. 1803 (Boston VR 30:214)

Elizabeth HOPKINS and Marks MONSON, 29 May 1806 (Boston VR 30:228)

Thomas S. WEBB and Hitty HOPKINS, 9 Aug. 1808 (Boston VR 30:277)

Alexander HOPKINS and Elizabeth CHUBB, 26 Aug. 1767 (Boston VR 30:306)

Nathaniel HOPKINS and Hannah SMITH, 28 Oct. 1799 (Boston VR 30:310)

Keturah HOPKINS and John KENCY(sp), 9 Jan. 1770, Truro (Boston VR 30:320)

Mary HOPKINS and John AUGELL, 8 Oct. 1773 (Boston VR 30:365)

Margaret HOPKINS and Laurence SMITH, 3 Jan. 1775 (Boston VR 30:365)

Nathen HOPKINS and Elizabeth COMPTON, 30 July 1776 (Boston VR 30:388)

Daniel BARKER and Mary TOMKINS, 13 June 1779 (Boston VR 30:389)

John HOPKINS and Susanna FRASIER, 7 Mar. 1779 (Boston VR 30:407)

Sarah HOPKINS and Stephen LOCK, 2 July 1780 (Boston VR 30:408)

Priscilla HOPKINS and Joseph HATCH, Int. 14 May 1763 (Boston VR 30:421)

John HOPKINS and Naomi GERGG, Int. 14 Dec. 1772 (Boston VR 30:432)

Rebecca HOPKINS and Samuel SPRAGUE, Int. 4 May 1780 (Boston VR 30:446)

John HOPKINS and Habby HINXTON, Int. 27 Aug. 1791 (Boston VR 30:462)

Polly HOPKINS and Capt. John IRWIN, Int. 8 Feb. 1796 (Boston VR 30:467)

Mary HOPKINS and Samuel TOWNSEND, Int. 27 Jan. 1802 (Boston VR 30:478)

Meriam HOPKINS and Samuel STIBBINS, Int. 1 Sept. 1802 (Boston VR 30:480)

Hannah HOPKINS and William ORLOWSKE, Int. 20 Nov. 1805 (Boston VR 30:490)

Sally HOPKINS and Jonathan HOWE, Int. 6 Jan. 1807 (Boston VR 30:494)

Hetty HOPKINS and William WHITTEMORE Jr., Int. 6 May 1807 (Boston VR 30:495)

Mary HOPKINS and William CONSLER, Int. 1 Dec. 1808 (Boston VR 30:501)

Sarah HOPKINS and John THOMPSON, Int. 11 May 1809 (Boston VR 30:502)

Micah HOPKINS^6 (Constant^5) and Elizabeth HARDING, 3 Nov. 1789 (Truro VR:145)

Ephraim HARDING and Sarah COLLINGS, 19 Dec. 1751 (Truro VR:78)

Phebe HOPKINS^6 (Constant^5) and 1st Elijah DAVIS, 2nd Asa WHITNEY

James HOPKINS^5 (Caleb^4) and Mehitable FREEMAN

Caleb HOPKINS^6 (James^5) and Keturah HILL

Mercy HOPKINS^5 (Caleb^4) and John GROZER

Joshua Freeman GROZER^6 (Mercy Hopkins^5) and Martha COOK, 24 Mar. 1793 (MD 9:64)

William GROZER^7 (Joshua^6) and Rebecca PERRY, poss. 4 Dec. 1817

William GROZER^6 (Mercy Hopkins^5) and Ruth DYER, 1 Aug. 1786 (Truro VR:135)

Ruth DYER and poss. 2nd Reuben YOUNG, 2 Apr. 1795 (Truro VR:158)

Silvanus DYER^6 (Ambrose^5, Thankful Hopkins^4, Caleb^3) and Jemima DYER, 6 Mar. 1794 (Truro VR:157)

Simeon HOPKINS^5 (Caleb^4) and Betty COBB^6 (Mercy Freeman^5, Edmund^4, Mercy Prence^3, Patience Brewster^2), 28 Aug. 1755 (Truro VR:88)

Nathaniel HOPKINS^4 (Caleb^3) and 2nd Sarah HIGGINS, 26 Oct. 1749 (Truro VR:57)

Elisha HOPKINS^5 (Nath.^{4}) and Elizabeth SNOW Jr., 29 Jan. 1761 (Truro VR:89)

Isaac HOPKINS^5 (Nath.^{4}) and 1st Elizabeth HIGGINS Jr., 22 Aug. 1751, Eastham (MD 25:40)

Isaac HOPKINS^5 and 2nd Lydia NEWCOMB^6 (Simon^5, Eliz. Cook^4, Deborah Hopkins^3, Gyles^2), poss. 18 Aug. 1772

Simon HOPKINS^6 (Isaac^5) and Susanna THAYER, 26 Nov. 1801 (Truro VR:204)

Isaac HOPKINS and Hannah HOPKINS, 16 July 1801 (Bible)

Isaac HOPKINS and Ruth DYER, 10 Jan. 1843 (Bible)

John HOPKINS^5 (Nath.^{4}) and Lydia SNOW^6 (Stephen$^{5-4}$, Jos.^{3}, Constance Hopkins^2),
   Int. 26 Feb. 1757 (Eastham VR:184)

John HOPKINS^6 (John^5) and Priscilla BROWN^7 (Alice Freeman^6, Mary Paine^5, John^4,
   Mary Snow^3, Constance Hopkins^2), 3 Mar. 1778 (Eastham VR 9:7)

Thankful HOPKINS^4 (Caleb^3) and Ambrose DYER, 22 Jan. 1729/30 (Truro VR:22)

Ambrose DYER^5 (Thankful^4) and Mercy PAINE, 12 Sept. 1751 (Truro VR:77)

Naphthali DYER^5 (Thankful Hopkins^4) and Elizabeth BIGGS, 16 Feb. 1764 (Truro VR:92)

Naphthali DYER^6 (Naphthali^5) and Deliverance SWEAT, Int. 2 Nov. 1792 (Truro VR:152)

Naphthali DYER^7 (Naphthali^6) and Reliance KNIGHT, 19 May 1819 (Truro VR:232)

Sarah DYER^6 (Naphthali^5) and James RICH, 21 Dec. 1797 (Truro VR:203)

Naphthali RICH^7 (Sarah Dyer^6) and Anna RICH (Gen.Reg.84:129)

Naphtali RICH^8 (Naphthali^7) and Sarah Priscilla RICH, 11 May 1847 (Truro VR:392)

Thankful DYER^5 (Thankful Hopkins^4) and James LUMBART JR., 28 Mar. 1754 (Truro VR:79)

Thomas HOPKINS^4 (Caleb^3) and Deborah BICKFORD, 10 Feb. 1724/25 (Truro VR:55)

Caleb HOPKINS^5 (Tho.^{4}) and Thankful PAINE^7 (Hugh^6, Tho.$^{5-4}$, Mary Snow^3, Constance
   Hopkins^2), 21 Apr. 1766 (Truro VR:105)

Caleb HOPKINS^6 (Caleb^5) and Priscilla ATKINS, 28 Dec. 1797 (Truro VR:203)

Betsey HOPKINS^7 (Caleb^6) and Zenas BOWEN, poss. 7 May 1823 (Dorchester VR 21:348)

Priscilla HOPKINS^7 (Caleb^6) and Shadrack JENKINS, poss. 24 Sept. 1829, Dorchester
   (Rcd.com.36:145,150)

Thankful HOPKINS^7 (Caleb^6) and Ebenezer GLOVER, poss. 9 Oct. 1826, Dorchester
   (Rcd.com.36:134,145)

Deborah HOPKINS^6 (Caleb^5) and Lot HARDING, 31 Mar. 1796 (Truro VR:163)

Nathaniel HARDING^7 (Deborah Hopkins^6) and Lucinda LOMBARD, 18 Nov. 1823 (TruroVR:237)

James A.H. MAGOWN(sp) and Cornelia K. BRICKLEY, 1 Dec. 1887, Medford (Mass.VR:389)

Lemuel HOPKINS^6 (Caleb^5) and Hannah KNOWLES 2d, Int. 14 June 1806 (Truro VR:184)

Rebecca Lombard HOPKINS^7 (Lemuel^6)   and Archelans SMITH, 29 Nov. 1838
   (Truro VR:328)

Hannah HOPKINS^7 (Lemuel^6) and 1st Edward ARMSTRONG, Int. 16 Nov. 1833 (Truro VR:270)

Hannah HOPKINS^7 and 2nd Asa SELLEW, 18 Feb. 1849 (Truro VR:394,395)

Solomon HOPKINS^6 (Caleb^5) and Hannah DYER, 17 Dec. 1795 (Truro VR:163)

Hugh HOPKINS^7 (Solomon^6) and Sarah Hopkins SMITH, 24 Nov. 1825 (Truro VR:247)

Thomas HOPKINS^6 (Caleb^5) and Susanna BAKER, poss. 28 Feb. 1811

Jerusha HOPKINS^7 (Tho.^{6}) and Leonard P. RICH

Susan B. HOPKINS^7 (Tho.^{6}) and Bartholomew O. GROSS

Mattie Hanson GROSS^9 (George^8, Susan B. Hopkins^7) and Theodore Winthrop SWIFT,
      c1901 (PN&Q 3:120)

William Covil HOPKINS^6 (Caleb^5) and Polly Freeman KNOWLES, 28 Dec. 1809 (TruroVR:206)

Ethel Blanchard HOPKINS^8 (Smith K.^{7}, Wm. C.^{6}) and Marcus Hall HOWES, c1910 (PN&Q 1:33)

Hannah HOPKINS^5 (Tho.^{4}) and John LEWIS, 15 Jan. 1756 (Truro VR:88)

Rebecca HOPKINS^5 (Th.^{4}) and Philip COVIL

Samuel HOPKINS^5 (Tho.^{4}) and Peggy RICH, 13 June 1754 (Truro VR:79)

Thomas HOPKINS^6 (Sam.^{5}) and Sarah LOMBARD, 27 Oct. 1785 (Truro VR:136)

Sally HOPKINS^7 (Tho.^{6}) and Joseph Valentine BACON, c1814

Octavia Augusta BACON^8 (Sally Hopkins^7) and James Brander FORSYTH, 24 Aug. 1836,
      Boston

Thomas HOPKINS^5 (Tho.^{4}) and Keturah DYER, 25 Apr. 1754 (Truro VR:79)

Keturah HOPKINS and John KENNAY, 9 Jan. 1770 (Truro VR:114)

Keturah HOPKINS and Joshua SMALLEY, 27 Jan. 1774 (Truro VR:107)

Sarah Doane HOPKINS^6 (Tho.^{5}) and Archelans SMITH, c1775 (Truro VR:129)

Archelans SMITH^7 (Sarah D. Hopkins^6) and Abigail SMITH, Int. 18 Aug. 1804
      (Truro VR:178)

Deborah HOPKINS^3 and Josiah COOK^2 (Josiah^1), 17 July 1668, Eastham (MD 8:88)

Josiah COOK and Mary RIDDER, 2 Mar. 1767 (Chatham CT VR 1:70)

Barnabas COOK and Mercy WALKER, 4 Mar. 1746/47 (Eastham VR:202)

Benjamin COOK^4 (Deborah Hopkins^3) and Mercy PAINE^5 (Sam.^{4}, Mary Snow^3, Constance
      Hopkins^2), 23 Nov. 1710, Eastham (MD 6:14)

Caleb COOK^4 (Deborah Hopkins^3) and Deliverance CROWEL, 18 Oct. 1710, Yarmouth

Deborah COOKE^4 (Deborah Hopkins^3) and Moses GODFREY (MD 5:186)

Deborah GODFREY^5 (Deborah Cook^4) and Thomas BASSET

Desire GODFREY^5 (Deborah Cook^4) and Nathaniel RIDER

Elizabeth GODFREY^5 (Deborah Cook^4) and Benjamin BEARSE, 31 May 1733, Chatham
      (MD 4:185)

Mary GODFREY^5 (Deborah Cook^4) and Caleb NICKERSON

Moses GODFREY^5 (Deborah Cook^4) and Martha COLLINS, c1726/27 (MD 10:194)

George GODFREY^5 (Deborah Cook^4) and 1st Mercy KNOWLES^6 (Richard^5, Mercy Freeman^4,
      Mercy Prence^3, Patience Brewster^2), 1 Nov. 1733 Chatham (MD 4:185)

George GODFREY[5] and 2nd Jane BERCE, 9 Nov. 1758, Chatham (MD 9:35)

Richard GODFREY Jr. and Lydia DOANE, Int. 4 Dec. 1756 (Chatham VR 2:113)

Knowles GODFREY[6] (George[5]) and Jerusha RIDER, 23 Oct. 1760, Chatham (MD 17:91)

Knowles GODFREY[7] (Knowles[6]) and Molly RIDER, 19 Oct. 1786 (Chatham VR 2:130)

Jonathan GODFREE and Mercy NICKERSON, 2 Sept. 1725, Chatham (MD 5:141)

Elizabeth COOK[4] (Deborah Hopkins[3]) and Thomas NEWCOMB, Oct. 1693, Eastham (MD 8:92)

Simon NEWCOMB[5] (Eliz. Cooke[4]) and Lydia BROWN, 5 Apr. 1722, Eastham (MD 16:27)

Simon NEWCOMB[6] (Simon[5]) and 1st Grace HARDING, 17 Apr. 1757, Chatham (MD 9:33)

Simon NEWCOMB[6] and 2nd Rebecca SMITH, Int. 20 Aug. 1784

Thomas NEWCOMB[7] (Simon[6]) and Jemima NEWCOMB[6] (Jos.[5], Elizabeth Cook[4], Deborah Hopkins[3], Gyles[2]), c1785

Jemima NEWCOMB[6] and 2nd Richard RICH, 13 June 1813 (Truro VR:206)

Joshua COOKE[4] (Deborah Hopkins[3]) and Patience DOANE, 7 Feb. 1705/06, Eastham (MD 6:15)

Josiah COOKE[5] (Joshua[4]) and Hannah SPARROW[5] (Richard[4], Hannah Prence[3], Patience Brewster[2]), 11 Feb. 1730/31, Eastham (MD 11:2,17:31)

Solomon COOK[5] (Josiah[4]) and Rebecca COWELL, 4 June 1733 (Truro VR:7)

Micro #14 of 18

Deborah COOK[5] (Josiah[4], Deborah Hopkins[3]) and Joseph HATCH, 29 May 1718 (Truro VR:38)

Mary COOK[5] (Josiah[4]) and David VICKERY, poss. 24 Apr. 1718 (Truro VR:38)

John COOK[5] (Josiah[4]) and Desire HATCH, poss. 15 Mar. 1721/22 (Truro VR:39)

Elizabeth COOK and Thomas DOTY, 1 Nov. 1722 (Truro VR:39)

Hannah COOK and Isaiah ATKINS, 12 Nov. 1724 (Truro VR:55)

Joshua COOKE and Hannah ROGERS, 25 Dec. 1755 (Truro VR:56)

Joshua COOKE and Zerviah HATCH, 5 Aug. 1724 (Truro VR:8)

Solomon COOKE and Rebecca COWEL, 4 June 1733 (Truro VR:7)

Rebecca COOKE and Thomas RIDER, 15 Nov. 1759 (Truro VR:90)

Jacob COOKE and Mercy YOUNG, 18 Feb. 1730/31, Eastham (MD 17:33)

Hannah COOK[5] (Josiah[4], Deborah Hopkins[3]) and Isaiah ATKINS (see above)

Henry ATKINS[6] (Hannah Cook[5]) and Mary LOMBARD, 24 Oct. 1768 (Truro VR:114)

Nathaniel ATKINS[6] (Hannah Cook[5]) and Mary PARKER, 7 June 1759 (Truro VR:90)

Nathaniel ATKINS[7] (Nath.[6]) and 1st Hannah PIKE, 6 May 1790 (Truro VR:149)

Nathaniel ATKINS[7] and 2nd Rebecca (COLLINS) Dyer, 27 July 1801 (Truro VR:204)

Rebecca COLLINS and 1st John DYER, 24 Jan. 1793 (Truro VR:157)

Rebecca COLLINS and 2nd Nathaniel ATKINS, 27 July 1801 (Truro VR:204)

Hannah ATKINS^8 (Nath.^{7}) and 2nd Richard HAWES, 3rd Amos PERKINS

Jonathan COOK and Sabra BROWN, 23 Apr. 1802, Provincetown

Bethiah COOK^7 (Jonathan^6) and Thomas Smith SPARKS, c1802

Freeman Grozer SPARKS^8 (Bethiah Cook^7) and Emily TRUSSELL

David N. COOK and Saloma LOMBARD, 23 Nov. 1800 (Bible)

Emerson D. COOK and Kathleen O. LYNCH, 4 May 1877, Barbadoes (Bible)

Phillip COOK^7 (Jonathan^6) and Anna SMITH, 27 Feb. 1806 (Bible)

Benjamin LANCY and Lillian Prince CLEMENT

Rebecca COOK^6 (Solomon^5) and Thomas RIDER, 15 Nov. 1759, Truro

Servia COOK^8 (Paran^7, Solomon^6) and Elisha HOLMES

Elisha HOLMES and 2nd Sybil BROWN

Hannah COOK^8 (Paron^7, Solomon^6) and Elisha YOUNG

Elisha YOUNG^9 (Hannah Cook^8) and Betsy SPARKS^8 (Bethiah Cook^7, Jonathan^6,
    Solomon^5, Josiah^4, Deborah Hopkins^3, Gyles^2)

Paron Cook YOUNG^{10} (Elisha^9) and Susan Elizabeth JOHNSON

Rebecca COOK^7 (Solomon^6) and David KILBURN

Capt. Paron C. KILBOURNE and Eliza G. TREAT, 16 Feb. 1839, Hampden (Treat Gen:286)

Samuel COOK^6 (Solomon^5) and Jennie NICKERSON, 25 July 1777 (MD 28:130)

Eleanor COOK^7 (Sam.^{6}) and Cyrenus BROWN^7 (David^6, Mercy Newcomb^5, Mercy Oldham^4,
    Mercy Sprout^3, Eliz. Samson^2)

Jonathan COOK^6 (Solomon^5) and Mercy TILTON, 16 Apr. 1773, Provincetown (MD 12:78)

Solomon COOK^7 (Solomon^6) and poss. Susanna BATES, 22 Mar. 1787 (Scituate VR)

Joshua COOK^8 (Solomon^7) and Rebecca ATKINS, 1 Jan. 1817, Provincetown

Thomas COOK and Dinah DOANE, 22 Oct. 1722 (Doane Gen.:45)

Oliver AREY and Elizabeth GOULD, Int. 18 Feb. 1737/38, Harwich/Eastham

Abigel COOK and Simmeon SMITH, Int. 5 July 1735, Eastham

Nehemiah SMITH and Jedidah AREY, 28 Oct. 1773

Caleb COOK^5 (Richard^4, Deborah Hopkins^3) and 1st Hannah BROWN, 7 Apr. 1726,
    Eastham (MD 16:147)

Caleb COOK^5 and 2nd Lydia WALKER, 20 Feb. 1728/29, Eastham (MD 16:202)

Samuel COOK^6 (Caleb^5) and Deborah ATWOOD, 17 Apr. 1753, Eastham (MD 25:42)

Samuel COOK and Thankful BROWN, 11 June 1772, Eastham (MD 32:175)

John COOK^7 (Sam.^{6}) and Rachel DOANE, Int. 2 Feb. 1788 (Eastham VR 12:17)

Abigail COOK^5 (Richard^4, Deborah Hopkins^3) and Simeon SMITH, Int. 5 July 1735

Joshua HOPKINS^3 and Mary COLE, 26 May 1681, Eastham (MD 7:15)

Hannah HOPKINS^4 (Joshua^3) and 1st Ebenezer PAINE^5 (Sam.^{4}, Mary Snow^3, Constance
    Hopkins^2), 13 Dec. 1722, Eastham (MD 16:28)

Hannah HOPKINS^4 and 2nd Zachariah SMALL

Mary HOPKINS^4 (Joshua^3) and Joseph SMITH^5 (Sam.^{4}, Mary Hopkins^3, Gyles^2),
    24 June 1715 (Eastham VR:5)

Abigail HOPKINS^4 (Joshua^3) and John TAYLOR, 3 Sept. 1713, Eastham (MD 15:74)

John TAYLOR^5 (Abigail Hopkins^4) and 1st Phebe HIGGINS^6 (Rebecca Hopkins^5,
    Stephen$^{4-3}$, Gyles^2), 1 Apr. 1742, Eastham (MD 20:94)

John TAYLOR^5 and 2nd Susanna HIGGINS, 22 Apr. 1756 (Eastham VR:46)

Elisha HOPKINS^4 (Joshua^3) and Experience SCUDDER, 9 Oct. 1712, Barnstable (MD 14:225)

Elizabeth HOPKINS^5 (Elisha^4) and Benjamin GODFREE^5 (Deborah Cooke^4, Deborah
    Hopkins^3, Gyles^2), 23 Aug. 1738, Chatham (MD 5:142)

Barzillai HOPKINS^5 (Elisha^4) and 2nd Martha HOWES, 19 Aug. 1773 (Chatham VR 2:225)

Experience HOPKINS^5 (Elisha^4) and Joseph WING Jr., 22 Feb. 1749, Chatham (MD 7:139)

Joshua HOPKINS^4 (Joshua^3) and Priscilla CURTIS, 1 Oct. 1724 (Eastham VR:63)

Joshua HOPKINS^5 (Joshua^4) and Rebecca SPARROW^6 (Richard$^{5-4}$, Hannah Prence^3,
    Patience Brewster^2), 14 May 1747, Eastham (MD 24:91)

Leida HOPKINS^6 (Joshua^5) and Philip HIGGINS, 12 July 1770 (Eastham VR 6:39)

Mary HOPKINS^6 (Joshua^5) and Jesse KINNEY, 2 Nov. 1769, Eastham (MD 32:115)

Phebe HOPKINS^4 (Joshua^3) and Moses BIXBEE, 18 Mar. 1724/25 (Eastham VR:64)

John BIXBEE^5 (Phebe Hopkins^4) and Elizabeth WARING, poss. 17 Feb. 1758, Norwalk CT

Mary HOPKINS^3 and Samuel SMITH, 3 Jan. 1665, Eastham (MD 8:17)

John SMITH^4 (Mary Hopkins^3) and Bethiah SNOW^4 (Stephen^3, Constance Hopkins^2),
    14 May 1694, Eastham (MD 8:243)

Dean SMITH^5 (John^4) and poss. Hester RIDER, c1720 (MD 4:184)

Hester RIDER and poss. 2nd Eleazer CROSBY

Dean SMITH^6 (Dean^5) and Rachel ( ), c1744 (MD 10:196)

Rachel ( ) SMITH and 2nd Jonathan LINNELL, Int. 5 Aug. 1760, Eastham (MD 27:107)

John SMITH^5 (John^4) and 1st Elizabeth BROWN, 21 Sept. 1727, Eastham (MD 15:69)

John SMITH^5 and 2nd Lydia SNOW, Int. 18 Mar. 1763, Eastham

Mehitable SMITH^6 (John^5) and Barnabas BAKER, 3 Mar. 1754, Chatham (MD 7:141)

Mary SMITH^5 (John^4) and Obadiah CHASE, 10 June 1732 (NEHGR 87:133)

Bethiah CHASE^6 (Mary Smith^5) and Solomon HIGGINS, 13 Jan. 1758, Eastham (MD 16:143)

Solomon HIGGINS^7 (Bethiah Chase^6) and 1st Abigail TWINING, 7 Aug. 1777, Eastham
(Orleans Ch.rcds.9:7)

Solomon HIGGINS^7 and 2nd Mary TWINING, c1789

Solomon HIGGINS^7 and 3rd Temperance SMITH, 25 Nov. 1790, Eastham (Higgins Gen.:201)

Solomon HIGGINS^9 (Solomon$^{8-7}$), and Olive Smith SPARROW^9 (Jesse^8, Richard^7,
Isaac^7, Richard$^{5-4}$, Hannah Prence^3, Patience Brewster^2), 8 Feb. 1838,
Orleans (Bible)

Lucinda Linnell HIGGINS^{10} (Solomon^9) and Andrew Campbell BERRY, 13 Aug. 1862,
Orleans

Solomon S. HIGGINS^{10} (Solomon^9) and Julia Louisa NICKERSON, 15 June 1866, Harwich

Solomon S. HIGGINS^{10} and 2nd Abbie E. LAKIN, Nov. 1878, Somerville MA

Obadiah HIGGINS^7 (Bethiah Chase^6) and Sarah MAYO, 25 Feb. 1779 (Eastham Ch.rcds.)

Solomon HIGGINS^8 (Solomon^7) and Hannah Mayo HIGGINS, c1811 (MD 34:58)

Samuel SMITH^5 (John^4, Mary Hopkins^3) and Mercy HIGGINS, Int. 19 July 1718
(Eastham VR:206)

Seth SMITH^5 (John^4) and 2nd Mary (   ) NICKERSON, poss. 18 Nov. 1756 (MD 7:143)

Hugh SMITH^6 (Seth^5) and Lydia PAINE, 19 Jan. 1775 (Chatham VR 2:226)

Seth SMITH^6 (Seth^5) and Elizabeth ELDREDGE, 26 Apr. 1764 (Chatham VR 2:144)

Stephen SMITH^5 (John^4) and 1st Hannah COLLINS

Stephen SMITH^5 and 2nd Bathshua BROWN, 9 Apr. 1729, Eastham (MD 16:203)

Archelans SMITH^6 (Stephen^5) and Elizabeth NICKERSON, 16 July 1752, Chatham
(MD 7:140)

Elijah SMITH^6 (Stephen^5) and 1st Elizabeth MYRICK, 24 Aug. 1760

Elijah SMITH^6 (Stephen^5) and 2nd Mary (TAYLOR) Collins, 8 July 1766, Chatham
(MD 17:95)

Elizabeth SMITH^7 (Elijah^6) and Enoch HOWES, c1789 (Howes Gen.:67)

James SMITH^7 (Elijah^6) and 1st poss. Bethiah RIDER, c1799

James SMITH^7 and 2nd Susanna DAVIS, 22 July 1812 (Barnstable East Parish Ch.rcds)

Stephen SMITH^8 (James^7) and Eliza Davis LOTHROP, 31 Jan. 1830

George SMITH^6 (Stephen^5) and Barbara MAYO, 16 Oct. 1755, Chatham (MD 7:142)

Stephen SMITH^6 (Stephen^5) and Mehitable ELDREDGE, c1746

Tabitha SMITH^7 (Stephen^6) and William COHOON, poss. 10 Nov. 1774

Dorcas COHOON^8 (Tabitha Smith^7) and Asa MORINE

Lorinda MORINE[9] (Dorcas Cohoon[8]) and Ira PRIDE, 24 Jan. 1839

Ira PRIDE and 2nd Olivia MORINE[9] (Dorcas Cohoon[8]), 17 Apr. 1850

Althea Estelle PRIDE[10] (Olivia Morine[9]) and Frederick Masters BARNABY, 27 Apr. 1881, Lynn

Florence Wier BARNABY[11] (Althea Pride[10]) and Percy Martin ROOPE, 25 Nov. 1926, Worcester (Mass VR 61:321)

Mary SMITH[4] (Mary Hopkins[3]) and Daniel HAMILTON, c1693 (MD 8:246)

Mary HAMILTON[5] (Mary Smith[4]) and Judah MAYO[5] (Tho.[4], Hannah Prence[3], Patience Brewster[2]), Int. 27 Jan. 1721/22 (Eastham VR:209)

Thomas HAMILTON[5] (Mary Smith[4]) and Rebecca MAYO, 3 May 1716, Eastham (MD 15:57)

Jane HAMILTON[6] (Tho.[5]) and Jonathan SMITH, 9 Nov. 1752, Chatham (MD 7:141)

Mary HAMILTON[6] (Tho.[5]) and Henry SAUNDERS, 13 Dec. 1742, Plymouth (MD 14:160)

Nathaniel HAMILTON[6] (Tho.[5]) and Mehitable GODFREY, 7 Sept. 1749, Chatham (MD 7:139)

Thomas HAMILTON[6] (Tho.[5]) and Ruhamah DOANE, 19 Mar. 1759, Chatham (MD 9:35)

Zeruiah HAMILTON[6] (Tho.[5]) and Samuel SMITH, 3 Jan. 1750, Chatham (MD 7:140)

Samuel SMITH[4] (Mary Hopkins[3]) and Bathshua LOTHROP, 26 May 1690, Eastham (MD 6:13)

Joseph SMITH[5] (Sam.[4]) and 1st Mary HOPKINS[4] (Joshua[3], Gyles[2]), 24 June 1715, Eastham (MD 15:55)

Joseph SMITH[5] and 2nd Rebecca (KEEN?) Thacher, Int. 22 July 1738 (Eastham VR:225)

Mary SMITH[6] (Jos.[5]) and James HICKMAN, Int. 24 Sept. 1737, Eastham (MD 28:180)

Samuel SMITH[5] (Sam.[4]) and 1st Abigail FREEMAN[5] (Nath.[4], Mercy Prence[3], Patience Brewster[2]), 9 Oct. 1712, Eastham (MD 6:206)

Samuel SMITH[5] and 2nd Sarah (WINSLOW[5]) Payne (Abigail Waterman[4], Sarah Snow[3], Abigail Warren[2]), 29 Dec. 1737 (Eastham VR:129)

Abigail SMITH[6] (Sam.[5]) and Jesse ELDREDGE, 7 Nov. 1734, Eastham (MD 17:143)

Zoheth SMITH[6] (Sam.[5]) and 1st Hannah SEARS, 23 Feb. 1737/38 (Eastham VR:129)

Zoheth SMITH[6] and 2nd Ruth MAYO, aft. May 1746

Stephen HOPKINS[3] and 1st Mary MERRICK, 23 May 1667, Eastham (MD 7:16)

Stephen HOPKINS[3] and 2nd Bethiah ATKINS, 7/9 Apr. 1701 (MD 7:16)

Benjamin HOPKINS[4] (Stephen[3]) and Rachel LINCOLN, 13 Feb. 1717/18, Harwich (MD6:83)

Samuel HOPKINS[5] (Ben.[4]) and Sarah WILEY, 11 Mar. 1752, Eastham (MD 24:140)

Seth HOPKINS[5] (Ben.[4]) and Elizabeth COHOON, 14 Apr. 1748 (Eastham VR:202)

Benjamin HOPKINS[6] (Seth[5]) and poss. Jemima HIGGINS, pre 1788

Deliverance HOPKINS[6] (Seth[5]) and Freeman ATWOOD

Elizabeth HOPKINS[6] (Seth[5]) and poss. Nehemiah MURRY, poss. 14 Sept. 1786

Gyles HOPKINS^6 (Seth^5) and 2nd Poss. Deborah (ATWOOD) Atkins, aft. Dec. 1779

Hannah HOPKINS^6 (Seth^5) and David HOLBROOK, poss. 10 Sept. 1776

Rachel HOPKINS^6 (Seth^5) and David BAKER

Sarah HOPKINS^6 (Seth^5) and Isaac RICH, poss. 30 Oct. 1793

Solomon HOPKINS^6 (Seth^5) and Hannah HIGGINS, 10 Aug. 1785 (Int. Wellfleet)

Joseph HOPKINS^4 (Stephen^3) and Mary MAYO^5 (Hannah Freeman^4, Mercy Prence^3,
Patience Brewster^2), 17 Apr. 1712, Harwich (MD 5:89)

Jonathan HOPKINS^5 (Jos.^{4}) and Rebecca FREEMAN, 4 Oct. 1744, Harwich (Freeman
Gen.:59)

Mary HOPKINS^5 (Jos.^{4}) and Thomas FOSTER

Isaac HOPKINS^5 (Jos.^{4}) and Thankful SMITH, 5 Mar. 1740/41, Eastham (MD 19:185)

Isaac HOPKINS^5 and poss. 2nd Elizabeth AREY, poss. 27 Nov. 1760, Eastham (MD 17:32)

Jonathan HOPKINS^6 (Isaac^5) and Mary FREEMAN^7 (Edmund$^{6-5}$, Tho.^{4}, Mercy Prence^3,
Patience Brewster^2), c1759

Nathan HOPKINS^6 (Isaac^5) and 1st Desire LINNELL, 5 Nov. 1783, Orleans

Joseph HOPKINS^5 (Jos.^{4}) and Mary BERRY, poss. 16 Sept. 1736, Harwich

Prence HOPKINS^5 (Jos.^{4}) and Patience SNOW^6 (Nath.^{5}, Edw.^{4}, Jabez^3, Constance
Hopkins^2), 15 Feb. 1753, Harwich (MD 34:26)

Nathaniel HOPKINS^6 (Prince^5) and Anna ARMSTRONG, poss. 7 July 1799, Franklin CT
(CT Marriages 4:86)

Samuel Badger HOPKINS^7 (Nath.^{6}) and Lydia Thacher FOSTER^9 (Sam.^{8}, Isaac$^{7-6}$,
Mercy Freeman^5, John^4, Mercy Prence^3, Patience Brewster^2)

Judah HOPKINS^4 (Stephen^3) and 1st Hannah MAYO^5 (Sam.^{4}, Hannah Prence^3, Patience
Brewster^2), 14 Apr. 1702, Eastham (MD 7:236)

Judah HOPKINS^4 and 2nd Hannah MAYO^5 (Hannah Freeman^4, Mercy Prence^3, Patience
Brewster^2), 12 May 1720, Harwich (MD 7:197)

Martha HOPKINS^5 (Judah^4) and John PADDOCK, 13 Feb. 1728/29, Harwich (MD 11:249)

John HOPKINS^5 (Judah^4) and Mehitable CROSBY, 22 Feb. 1732/33 (Yarmouth VR)

Judah HOPKINS^5 (Judah^4) and Mercy LINCOLN, 24 Feb. 1731/32, Harwich (MD 13:69)

Hannah HOPKINS^6 (Judah^5) and Elisha CLARK, 14 Feb. 1760 (Harwich VR)

Thomas CLARKE^7 (Hannah Hopkins^6) and Ruth MORSE, 10 Feb. 1802 (Bible)

Joshua V. Hopkins CLARKE^8 (Tho.^{7}) and Phebe Adeline SIMS, 10 Feb. 1830 (Bible)

William Thomas CLARKE^9 (Joshua^8) and Mary Matilda STIMSON, 9 June 1855, Manlius
N.Y. (Bible)

Mercy HOPKINS^5 (Judah^4) and John LEWIS, 6 Oct. 1726, Harwich (MD 8:218)

Thankful HOPKINS and Thomas LINNELL, 6 Oct. 1726, Harwich (MD 8:218)

Timothy LEWIS^7 (Tim.^{6}, Mercy Hopkins^5) and poss. Molly BRADLEY

Silvanus HOPKINS^5 (Judah^4) and poss. Ruth BERRY, c1739

Mary HOPKINS^4 (Stephen^3) and John MAKER, 5 Nov. 1714, Harwich (MD 6:83)

Nathaniel HOPKINS^4 (Stephen^3) and Mercy MAYO^5 (Hannah Freeman^4, Mercy Prence^3,
 Patience Brewster^2), 26 May 1707, Harwich (MD 4:178)

Mercy HOPKINS^5 (Nath.^{4}) and poss. Elijah WHITE

Theophilus HOPKINS^5 (Nath.^{4}) and Tabitha KINWRICKS, 24 July 1754, Harwich
 (MD 34:27)

Theophilus HOPKINS Jr. and Thankful FREEMAN, 4 Jan. 1781 (Orleans Ch.rcds.)

Theophilus HOPKINS and Thankful HIGGINS, Int. 5 Dec. 1778 (Eastham VR 12:9)

Elizabeth HOPKINS^5 (Nath.^{4}) and Thomas CROSBY, 9 Aug. 1733, Harwich (MD 13:148)

Reuben HOPKINS^5 (Nath.^{4}) and Elizabeth CLARK, 26 Dec. 1751, Harwich (MD 34:25)

Samuel HOPKINS^5 (Nath.^{4}) and Mehitable SNOW^6 (Jabez^5, Prence^4, Mark^3, Constance
 Hopkins^2), 23 Aug. 1753, Harwich (MD 34:26)

Mehitable SNOW^6 and 2nd Reuben RYDER, Int. 27 Sept. 1766, Chatham (MD 24:66)

Mehitable SNOW^6 and 3rd Paul CROWELL

Sarah HOPKINS^5 (Sam.^{4}, Stephen^3) and poss. Abner BANGS

Lydia HOPKINS^5 (Sam.^{4}, Stephen^3) and Joshua CROSBY, 2 Aug. 1733, Harwich (MD 13:148)

Moses HOPKINS^5 (Sam.^{4}) and Hannah BERRY, 18 Sept. 1740, Harwich (MD 23:117)

Reliance HOPKINS^5 (Sam.^{4}) and David CROSBY, 19 June 1735, Harwich (MD 19:113)

Abner CROSBY^6 (Reliance Hopkins^5) and Ruth FOSTER (Foster Gen.:536)

Richard HOPKINS^5 (Sam.^{4}, Stephen^3) and Ruth GAGE, Nov. 1732 (Yarmouth VR)

Theodore HOPKINS^5 (Sam.^{4}) and Hannah HURD, 17 Dec. 1751, Harwich (MD 34:25)

Josiah HOPKINS^6 (Theodore^5) and Sarah RACKLIFF, c1790

Stephen HOPKINS^4 (Stephen^3) and Sarah HOWES, 19 May 1692, Eastham (MD 8:16)

Mary HOPKINS^5 (Stephen^4) and Samuel SNOW^5 (Prence^4, Mark^3, Constance Hopkins^2),
 6 Mar. 1729/30, Harwich (MD 11:249)

Mary HOPKINS^5 and 2nd Shubael LEWIS, poss. 5 June 1735

Phebe HOPKINS^5 (Stephen^4) and 1st Samuel BANGS Jr., 19 June 1729, Harwich
 (MD 11:249)

Phebe HOPKINS^5 and 2nd Jonathan BANGS, 4 Jan. 1732/33 (MD 13:68,70)

Phebe HOPKINS^5 and 3rd Rev. Josiah DENNIS, 1746 (MD 33:61)

Rebecca HOPKINS^5 (Stephen^4) and Jonathan HIGGINS, 5 Apr. 1722, Harwich (MD 8:159)

Phebe HIGGINS[6] (Rebecca Hopkins[5]) and John TAYLOR[5] (Abigail Hopkins[4], Joshua[3], Gyles[2]), 1 Apr. 1742, Eastham (MD 20:94)

Abigail TAYLOR[7] (Phebe Higgins[6]) and Nehemiah YOUNG[6] (Hannah Twining[5], Ruth Cole[4], Ruth Snow[3], Constance Hopkins[2]), 26 Apr. 1770, Eastham (MD 32:172)

Sarah HOPKINS[5] (Stephen[4]) and Jonathan COB, 20 Oct. 1715, Harwich (MD 6:83)

Jonathan COB and 2nd Mehitable HOPKINS, Int. 6 Dec. 1753, Harwich (MD 33:150)

Jonathan COB[6] (Sarah Hopkins[5]) and Sarah CLARK, 16 Oct. 1740, Harwich (MD 23:117)

Elkanah LINNELL[6] (Thankful Hopkins[5], Stephen[4]) and Mary SPARROW[6] (Jos.[5], Rebecca Merrick[4], Abigail Hopkins[3], Gyles[2]), Int. 17 Jan. 1752 (Eastham VR:194)

Thankful HOPKINS[5] (Stephen[4]) and Thomas LINNELL, 6 Oct. 1726, Harwich (MD 8:218)

Thomas HOPKINS[5] (Stephen[4]) and Thankful CLARK, 15 June 1727, Harwich (MD 11:174)

Micro #18 of 18

Samuel HOPKINS and Doratha CONKLYN, 20 Dec. 1733

NOTES

<1> p.173, Elizabeth Paine[5] is descended from a double Mayflower line:
Paternal - John Paine[4] (Mary Snow[3], Constance Hopkins[2])
Maternal - Bennet Freeman[4] (Mercy Prence[3], Patience Brewster[2]).

<2> p.174, A later note from the Town Clerk's office in Wellfleet states her name was Nancy Baker, not Mercy.

<3> p.176, MFIP, Hopkins:45 states Jane Snow was mentioned in will of her father dated 1747/48, therefore could not have married in 1731.

<4> p.183, Barnstable VR 2:346 give the marriage of Paul Crowel and Experience Cob, 27 Aug. 1747 (MD 33:165)

<5> p. 187, "Evidently never married", they are included here because they had a child together and therefore left descendants: "Son of Thankful Brown and Grand son to William Walker", David Walker[7] was born 6 Feb. 1759 (MD 15:144).

<6> p.187, The file on John King and his four marriages is very confusing and difficult to determine. With the help of MFIP, Hopkins:50, his marriages are shown here in their proper order. (Note: John was 89 years old at the time of his fourth marriage.)

JOHN HOWLAND DESCENDANTS

John HOWLAND and Elizabeth TILLEY[2], c1626, Plymouth (MD 2:70)

Mary HOWLAND and Lot JENKINS, 22 Oct. 1761, Barnstable (MD 19:156)

Josiah GORHAM and Hannah HALLETT, 9 Oct. 1755, Barnstable (MD 27:6)

Benjamin HOWLAND and Lydia BAKER, 30 Apr. 1772 (Yarmouth VR 4:110)

Desire HOWLAND[2] (John[1])

Desire HOWLAND[2] and John GORHAM, c1643 (MD 5:72,174-177)

Desire GORHAM[3] and John HAWES, 7 Oct. 1661, Barnstable (MD 5:72)[1]

Mary HAWES and John BACON, 17 June 1686 (Barnstable VR 1:343)

Bayes HAWES and Jean LEWES, 1 July 1744 (Barnstable VR 2:412)

David HAWES and Elizabeth COB, 10 Mar. 1736 (Barnstable VR 2:407)

Thomas HAWES and Thankful GORHAM, July 1730 (Barnstable VR 2:407)

Joshua HAWES and Abigail HAPE, 5 Mar. 1789 (Barnstable VR 3:296)

Mary HAWES and Silvanus HINCKLEY Jr., 5 Mar. 1787 (Barnstable VR 3:533)

Nancy HAWES and Joseph BASSETT, 22 Apr. 1808 (Barnstable VR 3:292)

Desire HAWES[4] (Desire Gorham[3]) and 1st Josiah HATCH[3] (Mary Doty[2]), poss. 24 Feb.
   1701/02

Desire HAWES[4] and 2nd John COWING, poss. 19 June 1719 (Rochester VR 2:170)

Experience HAWES[4] (Desire Gorham[3]) and 1st Ebenezer SPROUT[3] (Eliz. Samson[2]),
   1 Mar. 1703/04 (Yarmouth VR)

Experience HAWES[4] and 2nd Francis MILLER[5] (Lydia Coombs[4], Francis[3], Sarah Priest[2]),
   22 Nov. 1731, Middleboro (MD 13:249)

Benjamin HAWES[4] (Desire Gorham[3]) and Dorcas SMITH, poss. 24 July 1705 (Edgartown VR:131,176)

Dorcas SMITH and poss. 2nd John WORTH, 22 Dec. 1724

Ebenezer HAWES and Sarah NORTON, 23 Feb. 1699/1700 (Edgartown VR:131)

James CLAGHORN and Salome COTTLE, 17 Feb. 1774 (Chilmark VR:45)

Mathew CLAGHORN and Jane BARTLETT, 4 Oct. 1759, Plymouth (Chilmark VR:45)

Shobal CLAGHORN and Martha HILMAN, 7 Jan. 1748 (Chilmark VR:45)

Experience HAWES[5] (Ben.[4]) and Shubael CLAGHORN, pre 1725

Mary CLAGHORN[6] (Experience Hawes[5]) and John SKIFFE, c1753

John SKIFFE and 2nd Wealthea MAKEPEACE, 4 Jan. 1781

James SKIFFE[7] (Mary Claghorn[6]) and Elizabeth Freeman AMES, 23 Aug. 1798

Sarah Crandall SKIFFE[8] (James[7]) and Joseph Edson SMITH, 23 Mar. 1830, Rochester

Nathan SMITH[9] (Sarah C. Skiffe[8]) and Martha Mendall DEXTER, 15 Oct. 1861,
   Mattapoisett

Ebenezer HAWES[4] (Desire Gorham[3]) and Sarah NORTON, 23 Feb. 1699/1700 <see p.206>

Elizabeth HAWES[4] (Desire Gorham[3]) and Thomas DAGGETT, poss. 22 Jan. 1683
   (Bristol RI VR)

Elizabeth DAGGETT[5] (Eliz. Hawes[4]) and John BUTLER, poss. 16 Dec. 1708, Edgartown

Micro #2 of 18

Phebe BUTLER and Abner COFFIN, 9 Sept. 1731 (Edgartown VR:101)

Keziah BUTLER and Samuel OSBORN, 9 Sept. 1731 (Edgartown VR:101)

John BUTLER Jr. and Jedidah BEETLE, 5 Dec. 1749 (Edgartown VR:101)

Abigail BUTLER and Joseph SMITH, 18 Apr. 1764 (Edgartown VR:99)

Abigail OSBORNE and James FISH, 12 Dec. 1765 (Edgartown VR:159)

Mary OSBORN and William JARNEGAN, 8 Feb. 1749 (Edgartown VR:160)

Jemima DAGGETT[5] (Eliz. Hawes[4]) and Malachi BUTLER

Samuel DAGGETT[5] (Eliz. Hawes[4]) and poss. Mary PEASE, 11 July 1705 (Daggett/
   Doggett Gen.:98)

Thankful DAGGETT[5] (Eliz. Hawes[4]) and 1st Zephaniah BUTLER, 2nd Brotherton DAGGETT

Timothy DAGGETT[5] (Eliz. Hawes[4]) and poss. Mary SMITH, 6 May 1717 (Edgartown VR)

Isaac HAWES[4] (Desire Gorham[3]) and Bethiah HOWES

Joseph HAWES[4] (Desire Gorham[3]) and Mary HOWES, c1695 (MD 5:162)

Thomas HAWES[5] (Jos.[4]) and Thankful GORHAM <see p.206>

Elizabeth HAWES[5] (Jos.[4]) and Jonathan SEARS, c1721 (MD 8:160)

Prince SEARS[6] (Eliz. Hawes[5]) and Betsey HALL[7] (Rebecca Sears[6], Mercy Freeman[5],
   Tho.[4], Mercy Prence[3], Patience Brewster[2]), poss. Int. 17 June 1758

Mary HAWES[4] (Desire Gorham[3]) and John BACON, 17 June 1686, Barnstable (MD 2:215)

John BACON and 2nd Sarah (DOTY[3]) Warren (Edw.[2]), 28 Sept. 1726, Plymouth (MD 14:71)

Isaac BACON[5] (Mary Hawes[4]) and Keziah DOANE, 19 May 1728 (Eastham VR:15)

Keziah DOANE and 2nd Dr. John DUNKARD

Nathaniel BACON[5] (Mary Hawes[4]) and 1st Patience PARKER, c1711, Barnstable (MD 3:72)

Nathaniel BACON[5] and 2nd Anna ANNABLE, 19 Aug. 1720, Barnstable (MD 32:152)[2]

Nathaniel BACON[5] and 3rd Thankful LUMBERT, c1730

Thankful LUMBERT and 2nd Augustin BEARSE, 7 Sept. 1744, Barnstable (MD 33:164)

Mercy BACON[6] (Nath.[5]) and Jonathan HALLET, 24 Nov. 1744, Barnstable (MD 33:165)

Hannah BACON[6] (Nath.[5]) and David DUNHAM

Solomon BACON[5] (Mary Hawes[4]) and Ann CAPRON, Int. 16 July 1726, Barnstable
(MD 34:117)

Desire BACON[5] (Mary Hawes[4]) and William GREEN[4] (Eliz. Warren[3], Nath.[2]), 25 Mar.
1709, Barnstable (MD 14:226)

William GREEN[4] and 2nd Mary FULLER

Hannah BACON[5] (Mary Hawes[4]) and Ebenezer MORTON, 25 Mar. 1709, Barnstable
(MD 14:226)

John BACON[5] (Mary Hawes[4]) and Elizabeth FREEMAN[5] (John[4], Mercy Prence[3], Patience
Brewster[2]), 2 May 1726, Harwich (MD 8:218)

Isaac BACON[6] (John[5]) and Alice TAYLOR, 29 Oct. 1762, Barnstable (MD 33:164)

Ann C. BACON and David THURSTON, 23 July 1821 (Barnstable VR 5:344)

Mary BACON[6] (John[5]) and Joseph DAVIS[6] (Thankful Hinckley[5], Mary Gorham[4], John[3],
Desire Howland[2]), 28 Mar. 1776 (Barnstable VR 3:175)

Elizabeth BACON[6] (John[5]) and Thomas DIMOCK[6] (Edw.[5], Desire Sturgis[4], Temperance
Gorham[3], Desire Howland[2]), 6 Oct. 1755, Barnstable (MD 27:6)

Elizabeth GORHAM[3] and Joseph HALLETT, c1666/67

Mary HALLETT[4] (Eliz. Gorham[3]) and Jabez FULLER[4] (Sam.[3], Matthew[2], Edw.[1]), pre
1688 (MD 4:226)

Jonathan FULLER[5] (Mary Hallett[4]) and 1st Elinor BENNET, 14 Feb. 1711/12, Middleboro (MD 2:158)

Jonathan FULLER[5] and 2nd Hannah HARLOW, 17 Dec. 1729, Middleboro (MD 8:250)

Lois FULLER[5] (Mary Hallett[4]) and Thomas FOSTER, Int. 16 Oct. 1725, Plymouth
(MD 18:124)

Thomas FOSTER and 2nd Mary MORTON, 13 Nov. 1744, Plymouth (MD 14:161)

Micro #3 of 18

Lois FOSTER and Josiah STURTEVANT, 21 Nov. 1757, Plymouth (MD 17:3)

Thomas FOSTER and Mercy WETHERELL, 5 Nov. 1747, Plymouth (MD 17:6)

Mercy FULLER[5] (Mary Hallett[4]) and Jabez WOOD, 5 Apr. 1716, Middleboro (MD 2:158)

Hannah GORHAM[3] and Joseph WHEELDING (MD 5:177)

Jabez GORHAM[3] and Hannah (STURGIS) Gray (MD 5:180)

Elizabeth GORHAM[4] (Jabez[3]) and William DOWNS, c1700

Elizabeth GORHAM[4] and 2nd Shubael BAXTER[4] (Temperance Gorham[3], Desire Howland[2]),
c1711 (MD 13:226)

Barnabas DOWNS^6 (Wm.^{5}, Eliz. Gorham^4) and Mary COBB, 3 Sept. 1759, Barnstable
    (MD 23:128)

James GORHAM^3 and Hannah HUCKINS, 24 Feb. 1673, Barnstable (MD 5:72)

Mehitable GORHAM^4 (James^3) and poss. John OLDHAM

Desire GORHAM^4 (James^3) and 1st Edward SPRINGER, pre Nov. 1707

Desire GORHAM^4 and 2nd Daniel HAMILTON, 15 Dec. 1715, Barnstable (MD 14:87)

Ebenezer GORHAM^4 (James^3) and Temperance HAWES^5 (Jos.^{4}, Desire Gorham^3, Desire
    Howland^2), c1728 (MD 32:54)

Thankful GORHAM^5 (Eben.^{4}) and Josiah DAVIS, 3 May 1759, Barnstable (MD 23:128)

Sylvanus DAVIS^6 (Thankful Gorham^5) and 1st Hannah GORHAM, 19 Nov. 1789 (Hist.
    of Gorham ME:523)

Sylvanus DAVIS^6 and 2nd Phebe McDONALD, 24 Apr. 1808 (Hist. Gorham ME:465)

Ebenezer Gorham DAVIS^7 (Sylvanus Davis^6) and Catherine PROCTOR, poss. Apr. 1818,
    Fryeburg

Mark Hill DAVIS^8 (Eben.^{7}) and Hannah WILLEY, 11 Sept. 1850, Lowell

Experience GORHAM^4 (James^3) and Thomas LOTHROP, 23 Apr. 1697, Barnstable (MD 6:237)

Ebenezer LOTHROP Jr. and Temperance LEWIS, 20 Jan. 1799 (Barnstable E.ch.rcds:204)

Lydia LOTHROP^5 (Experience Gorham^4) and Ebenezer BACON

James LOTHROP^5 (Experience Gorham^4) and Patience COLEMAN, poss. 20 Jan. 1732

Deborah LOTHROP^6 (James^5) and 1st David TURNER, Int. 5 May 1753, Plymouth
    (MD 16:165)

Deborah LOTHROP^6 and 2nd Stephen SAMPSON (poss. Abraham^4, Lorah Standish^3,
    Alexander^2), betw. 1775-81

Jabez GORHAM^5 (Jabez^4, James^3) and Mary BURBANK, 15 Nov. 1750, Plymouth (MD 16:170)

James GORHAM and Mary HALLETT, Int. 11 Nov. 1738, Barnstable (MD 33:171)

James GORHAM^4 (James^3) and Mary JOYCE^4 (Eliz. Chipman^3, Hope Howland^2), 29 Sept.
    1709, Barnstable (MD 5:73)

Isaac GORHAM^5 (James^4) and 1st Hannah HALLETT, poss. 24 Jan. 1736

Isaac GORHAM^5 and 2nd Mary COBB, 1742

John GORHAM^4 (James^3) and Ann BROWN

Thomas GORHAM^4 (James^3) and Rachel TROTT

John GORHAM^3 and Mary OTIS, 24 Feb. 1674, Barnstable (MD 5:73)

Mercy GORHAM^4 (John^3) and Sylvanus BOURNE^4 (Desire Chipman^3, Hope Howland^2),
    20 Mar. 1717, Barnstable (MD 14:227)

Thankful GORHAM^4 (John^3) and John FULLER, 16 June 1710, Barnstable (MD 4:225)

Thankful FULLER^5 (Thankful Gorham^4) and Nathan BASSETT, poss. 25 Oct. 1739
(Barnstable Families 1:49,384)

Elizabeth DENISON^4 (Mercy Gorham^3) and Christopher CHAMPLIN, c1706 (Gen.Reg.35:277)

Nancy Ora CLARK and Salmon HEATH, c1838

William CLARK and Mercy A. CHAMPLIN

H. Perry CLARK, and Adaline TRYON, 20 Nov. 1846 (Tyringham VR)

Maria B. CLARK and Albert C. HEATH, 11 May 1843 (Tyringham VR)

Mary A. CLARK and Henry C. BATTELL, 21 May 1848 (Tyringham VR)

Micro #4 of 18

Job GORHAM^4 (John^3) and 1st Desire DIMOCK^5 (Desire Sturgis^4, Temperance Gorham^3,
Desire Howland^2) (MD 5:180)

Job GORHAM^4 and 2nd Bethiah (STURGIS) Freeman (MD 5:180)

John GORHAM^4 (John^3) and Prudence CROCKER^4 (Anne Howland^3, John^2), 2 Oct. 1712,
Barnstable (MD 32:151)

Deborah GORHAM^5 (John^4) and Samuel BARKER, 16 Nov. 1738, Barnstable (Scituate
VR 2:133)

Samuel BARKER and 2nd Patience HOWLAND^4 (Jabez$^{3-2}$), poss. 6 Dec. 1739

Mary GORHAM^4 (John^3) and Joseph HINKLEY, 21 Sept. 1699, Barnstable (MD 6:99)

Thankful HINKLEY^5 (Mary Gorham^4) and James DAVIS, 4 Jan. 1727/28 (Otis 2:283)

Joseph DAVIS^6 (Thankful Hinkley^5) and 1st Lucretia THACHER, 17 Nov. 1763, Barnstable (MD 19:126)

Joseph DAVIS^6 and 2nd Mary BACON^6 (John^5, Mary Hawes^4, Desire Gorham^3, Desire
Howland^2), 28 Mar. 1776 (Barnstable VR 4:175)

Joseph DAVIS and Mercy COBB, Int. 5 Sept. 1778, Barnstable

Abner DAVIS^7 (Jos.^{6}) and Nancy COBB^7 (Eliz. Easterbrook^6, Abigail Gorham^5,
Tho.^{4}, James^3, Desire Howland^2), c1809 (Barnstable VR 4:339)

Shubael GORHAM^4 (John^3) and Mary THACHER^4 (Lydia Gorham^3, Desire Howland^2),
23 Dec. 1708 (Barnstable VR 2:321)

Stephen GORHAM^4 (John^3) and Elizabeth GARDNER, poss. 25 Dec. 1703, Nantucket
(Barnstable Families 1:423,433)

Lois GORHAM^5 (Stephen^4) and Jonathan MACY (Otis 1:435)

Mary GORHAM^5 (Stephen^4) and Andrew GARDNER (Otis 1:434)

Nathaniel GORHAM^5 (Stephen^4) and Mary SOLEY

Temperance GORHAM^4 (John^3) and Stephen CLAP, 24 Dec. 1696, Barnstable (MD 14:88)

Joseph GORHAM[3] and Sarah STURGIS, c1677/78 (MD 5:160)

Josiah GORHAM[4] (Jos.[3]) and 2nd poss. Priscilla SEARS, aft. 2 Feb. 1719/20

Josiah GORHAM[4] and 3rd poss. Mercy HALLETT, 25 Oct. 1761

Barnabas GORHAM[6] (Stephen[5], Josiah[4]) and Jane JOHNSON, 7 July 1803 (Hallowell
    ME VR 2:147)

Samuel GORHAM[4] (Joseph[3]) and Elizabeth HEDGE, c1702-09

Sarah GORHAM[4] (Joseph[3]) and Ebenezer HOWES, c1698 (MD 11:114)

Ebenezer HOWES and 2nd Lydia JOYCE

Lydia GORHAM[3] and John THACHER, 1 Jan. 1683, Yarmouth (MD 13:221)

John THACHER and 1st Rebecca WINSLOW,

Benjamin THACHER[4] (Lydia Gorham[3]) and Hannah LUMBERT, c1734

Hannah THACHER[4] (Lydia Gorham[3]) and Nathaniel OTIS, c1716 (Gen.Reg.2:293)

Dorothy OTIS[5] (Hannah Thacher[4]) and 1st Asahel BIGELOW, 2nd Isaac DAY,
    3rd Joseph LANGRILL

Judah THACHER[4] (Lydia Gorham[3]) and Sarah CROSBY

Thomas THACHER[4] (Lydia Gorham[3]) and Thankful BAXTER[5] (Shubael[4], Temperance
    Gorham[3], Desire Howland[2]), poss. 11 Feb. 1730/31 (Thacher:40)

Thankful BAXTER[5] and 2nd Samuel LUMBERT, 28 Jan. 1747/48 (Thacher:40)

Mercy GORHAM[3] and George DENNISON

Shubael GORHAM[3] and Puella HUSSEY, May 1695, Nantucket (MD 5:73,180)

Desire GORHAM[4] (Shubael[3]) and Zachariah BUNKER

Batchelor BENNETT and Mary SAMSON, 1 Nov. 1764 (Middleboro VR 2:84)

Micro #5 of 18

Abigail GORHAM[4] (Shubael[3]) and James LOVEL, 25 Oct. 1716, Barnstable (MD 14:226)

Christopher LOVELL[6] (Dan.[5], Abigail Gorham[4]) and 1st Abigail STURGIS, 24 Nov.
    1774 (Barnstable VR 2:174)

Christopher LOVELL[6] and 2nd Mary HOLBROOK, c1794

Christopher LOVELL[6] and 3rd Sarah FISH, 30 Oct. 1818

Temperance GORHAM[3] and 1st Edward STURGIS

Temperance GORHAM[3] and 2nd Thomas BAXTER, 27 Jan. 1679, Yarmouth (MD 5:177)

Hannah STURGIS[5] (James[4], Temperance Gorham[3]) and John MATTHEWS, c1709 (MD 13:224)

Desire STURGIS[4] (Temperance Gorham[3]) and 1st Thomas DIMOCK, c1685 (MD 4:221)

Desire STURGIS[4] and 2nd John THACHER, 10 Nov. 1698, Barnstable (MD 14:87)

Temperance DIMOCK[5] (Desire Sturgis[4]) and Benjamin FREEMAN[5] (John[4], Mercy Prence[3],

Patience Brewster[2]), 2 June 1709, Barnstable (MD 14:87)

Thomas DIMOCK[6] (Edw.[5], Desire Sturgis[4]) and Elizabeth BACON[6] (John[5], Mary Hawes[4], Desire Gorham[3], Desire Howland[2]), 6 Oct. 1755, Barnstable (MD 27:6)

Mehitable DIMOCK[5] (Desire Sturgis[4]) and John DAVIS, 13 Aug. 1705, Barnstable (MD 14:87)

John DAVIS[6] (Mehitable Dimock[5]) and 1st Abigail OTIS, poss. 5 Feb. 1729/30 (Otis 1:284)

John DAVIS[6] and 2nd Anna ALLEN, poss. 25 Mar. 1736 (Otis 1:284)

Mehitable DAVIS[6] (Mehitable Dimock[5]) and 1st Dr. James HERSEY, 9 Apr. 1741

Mehitable DAVIS[6] and 2nd Capt. John RUSSELL, 21 Aug. 1744

Mehitable DAVIS[6] and 3rd John STURGIS

Mehitable DAVIS[6] and 4th Daniel DAVIS

Daniel DAVIS[7] (Mehitable Davis[6]) and Lois FREEMAN, c1786

Charles Henry DAVIS[8] (Dan.[7]) and Harriet Blake MILLS[7] (Harriet Blake[6], Deborah Smith[5], Bethiah Chipman[4], John[3], Hope Howland[2])

Thomas DIMOCK[5] (Desire Sturgis[4]) and Anna MASON, poss. 9 Nov. 1720 (Mansfield CT VR)

Jesse DIMMICK[6] (Tho.[5]) and Rachel RIDDER, poss. 19 May 1751 (Dudley VR:190,166)

Lot DIMMICK[6] (Tho.[5]) and Hannah GURLEY, 8 May 1760 (Mansfield CT VR:232)

Jonathan DIMMICK[7] (Lot[6]) and Achsah STORRS, 3 June 1787 (Mansfield CT VR:232)

Edward STURGIS[4] (Temperance Gorham[3]) and Mehitable HALLETT, poss. 25 Nov. 1703

Mary STURGIS[5] (Edw.[4]) and Benjamin GORHAM

Jerusha STURGIS[5] (Edw.[4]) and Samuel HOWES

Mehitable STURGIS[5] (Edw.[4]) and Ebenezer HINCKLEY, c1743

Temperance STURGIS[5] (Edw.[4]) and Heman STONE, Int. 14 Apr. 1727, Harwich (MD 8:219)

Fear STURGIS[4] (Temperance Gorham[3]) and Joshua HOLMES, 21 Nov. 1698, (Yarmouth VR 3:10)

John HOLMES[5] (Fear Sturgis[4]) and 1st Abigail FRINK, poss. 20 Apr. 1727 (Stonington VR 2:68)

John HOLMES[5] and 2nd Mary SMITH, aft. Mar. 1729/30

John HOLMES[5] and 3rd Hannah HALSEY

Abigail HOLMES[6] (John[5]) and Roger STERRY, 4 May 1748 (Preston CT VR 2:29)

Micro #6 of 18

James STURGIS and Rebecca THACHER, c1689 (MD 10:24)

Rebecca THACHER and 2nd Ebenezer LEWIS, aft. Jan. 1717/18

Samuel STURGIS[4] (Temperance Gorham[3]) and Mercy HOWES, 17 Oct. 1700, Yarmouth (MD 10:243)

Samuel STURGIS[5] (Sam.[4]) and 1st Lucretia WENDALL, c1735

Samuel STURGIS[5] and 2nd Olive ALEN, 28 Nov. 1754, Barnstable (MD 27:5)

Samuel STURGIS[5] and 3rd Abigail OTIS, aft. May 1756

Thankful STURGIS[4] (Temperance Gorham[3]) and Peter THACHER, c1693 (MD 13:225)

Peter THACHER[5] (Thankful Sturgis[4]) and Anner LEWIS, 24 Oct. 1734 (Thacher Gen:41)[3]

Thomas THACHER and Mary CHURCHILL, 11 Jan. 1787, Barnstable (Thacher Gen.:304)[3]

Sarah THACHER[5] (Thankful Sturgis[4]) and George LEWIS, poss. 12 Sept. 1727 (Int.-
    Barnstable VR:363)

John LEWIS[6] (Sarah Thacher[5]) and Deborah PHINNEY[6] (David[5], Ebenezer[4], Mary
    Rogers[3], Jos.[2]), 19 Oct. 1752, Barnstable (MD 31:7)

Peter LEWIS[7] (John[6]) and Mehitable HINCKLEY

Temperance THACHER[5] (Thankful Sturgis[4]) and Seth CROCKER, poss. 1 June 1734

Thankful THACHER[5] (Thankful Sturgis[4]) and John HALLET, poss. 24 Aug. 1716

John BAXTER[4] (Temperance Gorham[3]) and Desire GORHAM[4] (Jos.[3], Desire Howland[2]),
    11 June 1706 (Yarmouth VR 2:317)

Isaac BAXTER[5] (John[4]) and Abigail TAYLOR, 21 Feb. 1744 (Baxter Gen:34)[4]

Sarah BAXTER[5] (John[4]) and Gershom COBB, 20 Apr. 1732 (Baxter Gen.:34)

Shubael BAXTER[4] (Temperance Gorham[3]) and Elizabeth (GORHAM[4]) Downs (Jabez Gorham[3],
    Desire Howland[2]), c1711 (Baxter Gen.:34)

Richard BAXTER[5] (Shubael[4]) and 1st Jane BAXTER, 11 Apr. 1734 (Yarmouth VR)

Richard BAXTER[5] and 2nd Mary/Molly COFFIN, 2 Nov. 1775 (Nantucket VR 3:93,292)

Thankful BAXTER[5] (Shubael[4]) and 1st Thomas THACHER, 11 July 1730 (Baxter Gen.:35)

Thankful BAXTER[5] and 2nd Samuel LAMBERT, 28 Jan. 1747 (Baxter Gen.:35)

Jeney BAXTER[5] (John[4]) and Richard BAXTER, 26 Jan. 1733/34 (Baxter Gen.:34)

Temperance BAXTER[5] (John[4]) and Samuel DOWNS, 25 Feb. 1730 (Baxter Gen.:34)

Joseph BAXTER[5] (John[4]) and Hannah NORTH, 15 Nov. 1747 (Baxter Gen.:34)

Isaac BAXTER[5] (John[4]) and Abigail TAYLOR, 21 Feb. 1744 (Baxter Gen.:34)

Hezekiah BAXTER[5] (John[4]) and 1st Deborah NICKERSON, 1743 (Baxter Gen.:34)

Hezekiah BAXTER[5] and 2nd Thankful MERCHANT, 4 Oct. 1758 (Baxter Gen.:34)

Shubal BAXTER[5] (John[4]) and Mehitable HALLET, 5 Mar. 1746 (Baxter Gen.:34)

Thankful BAXTER[6] (Richard[5]) and Joseph HALLETT, 15 June 1760 (Yarmouth VR 2:284)

Hannah HALLETT[7] (Thankful Baxter[6]) and Jonathan LEWIS, 15 Apr. 1788 (Barnstable
    East Parish ch.rcds.)

Shubal BAXTER[6] (Richard[5]) and Elizabeth TAYLOR, 23 Oct. 1757 (Baxter Gen.:38)

Richard BAXTER[6] (Richard[5]) and Patience DAVIS, 21 Nov. 1771 (Baxter Gen.:38)

Desire BAXTER[6] (Richard[5]) and Leverett TAYLOR, 21 Jan. 1762 (Baxter Gen.:38)

Prince BAXTER[6] (Richard[5]) and Sarah BLISH, 3 Dec. 1778 (Baxter Gen.:38)

Jane BAXTER[6] (Richard[5]) and Thomas BRAGG, 20 Nov. 1777 (Baxter Gen.:38)

Edward BAXTER and Catharine RATHBON, Int. 26 Dec. 1795, Dennis (MD 13:124)

Obed BAXTER and Mary HOWES, Int. 13 Feb. 1795, Dennis (MD 13:123)

Thomas BAXTER and Mary LATTIMER, 3 May 1705 (Stiles' Wethersfield 2:51)

Thomas BAXTER and Zilpha NICKERSON, 8 Nov. 1740 (Stiles' Wethersfield 2:51)

Elizabeth HOWLAND[2] (John[1])

Elizabeth HOWLAND[2] and 1st Ephraim HICKS, 13 Sept. 1649

Elizabeth HOWLAND[2] and 2nd John DICKINSON, 10 July 1651

Elizabeth DICKINSON[3] and Caleb WRIGHT

Elizabeth WRIGHT[4] (Eliz. Dickinson[3]) and Joseph COLES

Daniel COLES[5] (Eliz. Wright[4]) and Ann CARPENTER

Jacob COLES[6] (Dan.[5]) and Sarah COCKS

Annie COLES[7] (Jacob[6]) and Divine HEWLETT

Hannah DICKINSON[3] and Isaac GIBBS

Isaac GIBBS Jr.[4] (Hannah Dickinson[3]) and Mary SHREVE, 5 June 1722, Chesterfield

Joshua GIBBS[5] (Isaac[4]) and Hannah BURROUGHS, 11 June 1757, Haddonfield NJ

Joshua GIBBS[6] (Joshua[5]) and Mary GASKILL

Joshua GIBBS[7] (Joshua[6]) and Barbara SHAEFFER, 4 Oct. 1829, Canton OH

Lewis GIBBS[8] (Joshua[7]) and Caroline BOWERISE

Elmer W. GIBBS[9] (Lewis[8]) and Louise VOGES, 1 Jan. 1887, Canton OH

Hazel Louise GIBBS[10] (Elmer[9]) and Wendell HERBRUSK, 14 Oct. 1916

Joseph DICKINSON[3] and Rose TOWNSEND, c1680

Zebulon DICKINSON[4] (Jos.[3]) and Rose TOWNSEND, pre 1710

Zebulon DICKINSON[5] (Zebulon[4]) and 1st Joyce HANCE, 5 May 1733

Zebulon DICKINSON[5] and 2nd Mary DOUGHTY, 10 Sept. 1747

Zebulon DICKINSON[6] (Zebulon[5]) and Rose TOWNSEND, c1759

Zebulon DICKINSON[7] (Zebulon[6]) and Elizabeth BRUSH, 22 July 1782

Hannah HOWLAND[2] (John[1])

Hannah HOWLAND[2] and Jonathan BOSWORTH, poss. 6 July 1661

David BOSWORTH[3] and 1st Mercy STURTEVANT, 18 Aug. 1698, Plymouth (MD 13:207)

David BOSWORTH[4] (David[3]) and Priscilla SHAW, 22 Dec. 1720, Plympton (MD 3:91)

David BOZWORTH and 1st Mary STRONG, 27 June 1743 (Lebanon CT VR:25)

David BOZWORTH and 2nd Ruth BINGHAM, 12 Dec. 1787 (Strong Gen.:804)[5]

Lydia BOZWORTH and Joseph LOOMIS, 5 May 1763 (Lebanon CT VR)

Lois BOZWORTH and Zina HYDE, 24 Feb. 1785 (Lebanon CT VR)

Priscilla BOZWORTH[5] (David[4]) and Andrew MINOR, 4 Nov. 1750 (Norwich CT VR)

David BOZWORTH Jr. and Mindwell FITCH, 24 Mar. 1773 (Goshen Ch.rcds.)

Jabin BOZWORTH and Luna(sp) WEST, 24 Mar. 1773 (Goshen Ch.rcds.)

Stephen STRONG and Abigail BUELL, 16 Jan. 1718 (Strong Gen.:773)[5]

Jonathan SHAW and Mehitable PRATT, 29 Dec. 1687, Plymouth (MD 13:204)

Ichabod BOZWORTH and Abigail CHAPPEL, 4 Apr. 1770 (Goshen Ch.rcds., Lebanon CT)

Zadock BOZWORTH[5] (David[4]) and Joanna RAYMOND(?) (Bosworth Gen.4:382)

Joel MOORE and Martha SPRING, 30 Sept. 1765, (Montgomery MA VR)

Charlotte BOZWORTH[6] (Zadock[5]) and Joel MOORE, Int. 23 July 1791 (Montgomery
    VR:38,48)

Hannah BOZWORTH[6] (Zadock[5]) and John BRANT, c1782 (Montgomery VR)

Joshua BOZWORTH[6] (Zadock[5]) and Rebecca SQUIRE, Int. 23 July 1791 (Montgomery
    VR:38,53)

Priscilla BOZWORTH[6] (Zadock[5]) and Gamaliel KING, Int. 18 July 1794 (Montgomery
    VR:38,46)

Raymond BOZWORTH[6] (Zadock[5]) and Rachel HINKSON, Int. 23 Nov. 1794 (Montgomery VR:14)

Persis BOZWORTH[7] (Raymond[6]) and Thaddeus ADAMS Jr., Int. 14 July 1816 (Montgomery
    VR:35,37)

Betsey BOZWORTH[7] (Raymond[6]) and Massillon CROW, 29 Jan. 1837 (Montgomery VR:37,41)

Orpha BOZWORTH[7] (Raymond[6]) and Charles GORHAM, 29 Feb. 1816 (Montgomery VR:38,43)

Sally BOSWORTH[7] (Raymond[6]) and Rufus GORHAM, Int. 1 Mar. 1828 (Montgomery VR:38,43)

Roswell BOSWORTH[7] (Raymond[6]) and Pamelia HERRICK, 31 Jan. 1837 (Montgomery VR:37,44)

Pamela BOSWORTH[7] (Raymond[6]) and Elisha GORHAM, c1815 (Montgomery VR:20)

Elisha GORHAM and Almira PELTON, 12 Mar. 1827 (Montgomery VR)

Octavia Wheeler GORHAM[8] (Pamela Bosworth[7]) and Rev. John CADWELL

George Washington GORHAM[8] (Pamela Bosworth[7]) and Lucy RANNEY

Chloe GORHAM[9] (Geo. W.[8]) and Walter MINER

Levi GORHAM[8] (Pamela Bosworth[7]) and Harriet PRESTON

Greve GORHAM[9] (Levi[8]) and Mary LINDSAY

French GORHAM[9] (Levi[8]) and Adella McARTHUR

Nelson BOZWORTH[7] (Raymond[6]) and Polly GORHAM, May 1823 (Montgomery VR:37,43)

Rebecca BOZWORTH[6] (Zadock[5]) and Daniel BARRET, 21 Aug. 1782 (Montgomery VR:36,38)

Zadock BOZWORTH[6] (Zadock[5]) and 1st Deborah BUNDY, 28 Feb. 1782 (Montgomery VR)

Zadock BOZWORTH[6] and 2nd Lucretia (ROGERS) Moor, Int. 9 Jan. 1802 (Montgomery VR)

Hannah BOSWORTH[4] (David[3]) and William RIPLEY, 24 Feb. 1725, Middleboro (MD 4:73)

William RIPLEY[5] (Hannah Bosworth[4]) and Lydia RING[5] (Sam.[4], Eleazer[3], Deborah
     Hopkins[2]), poss. 5 Jan. 1749, Plympton (Ripley Fam.:39)

David RIPLEY[6] (Wm.[5]) and Jane CHURCHILL, 3 Dec. 1772

David RIPLEY[7] (David[6]) and Hannah Wadsworth CUFFS, 14 June 1804, Plymouth
     (VR 2:373)

Alexander RIPLEY and Hannah Shaw FLEMMONS, 27 Oct. 1816, Plymouth (VR 2:380)

Jonathan BOSWORTH[4] (David[3]) and 1st Alice CUSHMAN[5] (Isaac[4-3], Mary Allerton[2]),
     19 Dec. 1723, Plympton (MD 2:139)

Jonathan BOSWORTH[4] and 2nd Ruth TILSON, 30 Sept. 1725, Plympton (MD 1:246)

Ichabod BOSWORTH[5] (Jonathan[4]) and Lydia STANDISH[5] (Miles[4-3], Alexander[2]), 24 Oct.
     1765 (Halifax VR:32)

Nehemiah BOSWORTH[4] (David[3]) and 1st Susanna RING[4] (Eleazer[3], Deborah Hopkins[2]),
     27 Jan. 1725/26, Plympton (MD 1:246)

Nehemiah BOSWORTH[4] and 2nd Sarah TOMSON[4] (Peter[3], Mary Cooke[2]), 26 Mar. 1729,
     Plympton (MD 5:209)

Hannah BOSWORTH[3] and Nathaniel JENCKES, 4 Nov. 1686, Swansea

Hannah JENCKS[4] (Hannah Bosworth[3]) and Banfield CAPRON, c1710

Banfield CAPRON and 2nd Sarah ( ) BROWN, Int. 2 Feb. 1744/45, Bellingham

Elizabeth CAPRON[5] (Hannah Jencks[4]) and 1st Elkanah SPEAR, 17 May 1750 (Capron
     Gen.:111)

Elizabeth CAPRON[5] and 2nd Seth HALL, 17 Dec. 1761 (Cumberland RI VR) <see below>

Elkanah SPEAR[6] (Eliz. Capron[5]) and Elizabeth ARNOLD, 18 Sept. 1779 (Capron Fam:111)

Zuriel HALL and 2nd Jane ( ) SMITH, Int. 14 Dec. 1742, Bellingham

Seth HALL and 1st Mrs. Abigail ALBEE, 28 May 1737 (Bellingham VR) <see above>

Leah CAPRON[5] (Hannah Jencks[4]) and Joseph SCOTT, Int. 2 June 1750, Bellingham

Joseph SCOTT and 2nd Lucy BROWN, 17 Jan. 1753, Cumberland RI

Jonathan JENCKS[4] (Hannah Bosworth[3]) and poss. Mary SLACK

Micro #8 of 18

Hannah JENCKS[5] (Jonathan[4]) and Benjamin DROWN, poss. 13 Oct. 1751, Warren RI

Jonathan Jenckes DROWN^6 (Hannah Jencks^5) and Hannah BARNES

Rebecca JENCKS^5 (Jonathan^4) and Jeremiah SCOTT, poss. 20 Apr. 1746 (Cumberland
    RI VR 3:5:40,56)

Nathaniel JENCKES^4 (Hannah Bosworth^3) and 1st Lydia ARNOLD, poss. 28 Feb. 1722/23
    (Providence VR 1:52)

Nathaniel JENCKES^4 and 2nd Bridget BLAKE, poss. 29 Mar. 1730 (Providence VR 1:57)

Elizabeth JENCKES^4 (Hannah Bosworth^3) and John OWEN

Stephen JENKES^5 (Nath.^{4}) and Sarah HAWKINS, 11 Jan. 1747 (MD 20:177)

Mary JENCKES^7 (Eleazer^6, Stephen^5) and Walker ARMINGTON, 19 Oct. 1800 (Providence
    RI VR 7:477,494)

Charles JENCKES and Deborah CADMAN, 1 Dec. 1774 (Providence RI VR 8:468)

Ebenezer JENCKS and Mary THROOP, 22 Sept. 1795 (Providence RI VR 12:20)

Ebenezer JENCKS and Sally SHELDON, 20 Aug. 1799 (Providence RI VR 12:20)

Mary ARMINGTON and Solomon H. KENYON

John BOSWORTH^3 and Elizabeth TOOGOOD, 10/16 June 1702 (Swansea VR A:79,95)

Elizabeth TOOGOOD and 2nd James THURBER, poss. Int. 19 Dec. 1723 (Rehoboth VR:429)

Anna BOSWORTH^4 (John^3) and Samuel BULLOCK, poss. 8 Dec. 1734, Barrington
    (Rehoboth VR:52,67)

David BOSWORTH^4 (John^3) and Mary STRONG, 27 June 1743 (Lebanon CT VR 1:31)

Nathaniel BOSWORTH^4 (John^3) and Bethiah HINCKLEY

Nathaniel BOZWORTH and Elizabeth ELY, 14 June 1750 (Middletown CT VR 2:252)

Jonathan BOSWORTH^3 and Sarah ROUNDS, 26 Nov. 1703 (Swansea VR A:95)

Ichabod BOSWORTH^4 (John^3) and 1st Mary BOWEN, 12 Jan. 1726/27 (Rehoboth VR:42)

Ichabod BOSWORTH^4 and 2nd Bethiah WOOD, Int. 10 Sept. 1748 (Rehoboth VR:429,514)

Ichabod BOSWORTH^4 and 3rd Waitstill HIGGINS, 23 Apr. 1761 (Rehoboth VR:53,175)

Peleg BOZWORTH^5 (Ichabod^4) and 1st Mary SMITH, 1 Sept. 1774 (Rehoboth VR:53,345)

Peleg BOZWORTH^5 and 2nd Levina ROUNDS, poss. 10 Jan. 1821 (Rehoboth VR:54,327)

Peleg BOZWORTH^6 (Peleg^5) and Susanna ROUNDS, poss. 7 Feb. 1803 (Rehoboth VR:53)

Hope HOWLAND^2 (John^1)

Hope HOWLAND^2 and John CHIPMAN, c1647 (MD 3:181)

John CHIPMAN and 2nd Ruth (SARGENT) (Winslow) Bourne, aft. Jan. 1683

Micro #9 of 18

Jabez DIMMOCK and Mary NEWCOMB, Int. 5 Dec. 1722, Boston

Benjamin CHIPMAN and Hannah WADSWORTH, 9 May 1751 (Kingston VR)

Deborah CHIPMAN and Nicholas NICKERSON, Int. 17 Mar. 1721/22, Harwich (MD 8:36)

James CHIPMAN and Hannah CURRIER, 25 July 1805 (MD 10:136)

Content CHIPMAN and Ellis HOLMES, 12 July 1808 (Halifax VR:80)

Luce CHIPMAN and George RING, 14 Apr. 1747, poss. Plympton

Bethia CHIPMAN[3] and 2nd Timothy DIMMOCK

Timothy DIMMOCK and 2nd Abigail DOANE, 17 Mar. 1702/03

Jabez DIMMOCK[4] (Bethiah Chipman[3]) and 1st Mary/Mercy NEWCOMB, Int. 5 Dec. 1722, Boston

Mary DIMMOCK[5] (Jabez[4]) and Edward GEARING, 22 June 1750, Gloucester

Desire CHIPMAN[3] and Melatiah BOURNE, 23 Feb. 1692/93, Sandwich (MD 29:70)

Melatiah BOURNE and 2nd Abigail ( ) SMITH, aft. Mar. 1705

Bathsheba BOURN[4] (Desire Chipman[3]) and 1st William NEWCOMB, c1723 (Hist.Hardwich)

Bathsheba BOURN[4] and 2nd Timothy RUGGLES, Int. 18 Sept. 1736, Rochester

Sarah NEWCOMB[5] (Bathsheba Bourn[4]) and Benjamin FESSENDEN

John BOURN[4] (Desire Chipman[3]) and Mercy HINCKLEY[5] (Mary Gorham[4], John[3], Desire Howland[2]), poss. 16 Mar. 1722

Rev. Shearjashub BOURNE[4] (Desire Chipman[3]) and 1st Abigail COTTON, poss. 16 June 1725, Boston

Rev. Shearjashub BOURNE[4] and 2nd Sarah BROOKS, Int. 27 Dec. 1735

Rev. Shearjashub BOURNE[4] and 3rd Deborah BARKER, 6 June 1750 (Scituate VR)

Rev. Shearjashub BOURNE[4] and 4th Joanna STEVENS, 10 Nov. 1757, Roxbury

Shearjashub BOURN[5] (Shearjashub[4]) and Sarah WOODARD, 19 Oct. 1769, Scituate (MD 1:236)

Silvanus BOURNE[4] (Desire Chipman[3]) and Mercy GORHAM[4] (John[3], Desire Howland[2]), 20 Mar. 1717, Barnstable (MD 14:227)

Abigail BOURNE[5] (Silvanus[4]) and Kenelm WINSLOW[5] (Abigail Waterman[4], Sarah Snow[3], Abigail Warren[2]), poss. 14 Mar. 1754 (Otis 1:120)

Desire BOURN[5] (Silvanus[4]) and Nathaniel CLAP[5] (Temperance Gorham[4], John[3], Desire Howland[2]), poss. 22 Dec. 1737

Hannah BOURN[5] (Silvanus[4]) and Isaac HINCKLEY[5] (Mary Gorham[4], John[3], Desire Howland[2]), poss. 18 Dec. 1748

Melatiah BOURNE[5] (Silvanus[4]) and Mary BAYARD

Mercy BOURN[5] (Silvanus[4]) and Samuel JORDAN, poss. 10 Apr. 1751

Silvanus BOURN[5] (Silvanus[4]) and Hannah STURGIS

Eunice BOURNE[5] (Silvanus[4]) and John GALLISON, 19 June 1755, Barnstable (Bible)

John GALLISON and 1st Abigail LEE, 1 Nov. 1750 (Bible)

Charlotte GALLISON^6 (Eunice Bourne^5) and Sylvanus GRAY, 31 Aug. 1794 (Bible)

Henry GALLISON and Catharine SEWALL, 24 May 1787

Henry GALLISON and Betsey LEW, 24 Apr. 1806, Boston

Joseph LEMMON and Jane GOODWIN, 1750 (Bible)

Mary BOURNE^5 (Silvanus^4) and Nathaniel STONE, c1742

William BOURN^5 (Silvanus^4) and 1st Sarah (WANTON) Legallais, 30 May 1756
    (Marblehead VR)

William BOURN^5 and 2nd Deborah (TASKER) Freeman, Int. 7 May 1768, Marblehead

Elizabeth CHIPMAN^3 and Hosea JOYCE, c1675, Yarmouth (MD 3:37)

Lydia JOYCE^4 (Eliz. Chipman^3) and Ebenezer HOWES, poss. 20 Nov. 1706

Ebenezer HOWES and 1st poss. Sarah GORHAM^4 (Jos.^{3}, Desire Howland^2), c1698

Mehitable JOYCE^4 (Eliz. Chipman^3) and Thomas STORRS, 14 Mar. 1708 (Mansfield
    CT VR:285)

Samuel STORES and 1st Mary HUCKENS, 6 Dec. 1666, Barnstable (MD 12:154)

Samuel STORES and 2nd Hester EGARD, 14 Dec. 1685, Barnstable (MD 12:154)

Dorothy JOYCE^4 (Eliz. Chipman^3) and John OATS, poss. 12 Dec. 1717

Thomas JOYCE^4 (Eliz. Chipman^3) and Mercy BACON, poss. 19 Mar. 1719

Hannah CHIPMAN^3 and Thomas HUCKENS, 1 May 1680, Barnstable (MD 6:139)

Thomas HUCKENS and 2nd Sarah (POPE) Hinckley, 17 Aug. 1698 (MD 10:12)

Joseph HUCKENS^4 (Hannah Chipman^3) and Sarah LOTHROP

Hope HUCKENS^4 (Hannah Chipman^3) and 1st Benjamin HAMLIN, 29 May 1709, Barn
    stable (MD 6:138)

Hope HUCKENS^4 and 2nd Ebenezer CHILDS, c1719 (Otis' Barnstable Families 1:184)

Thomas HUCKENS^4 (Hannah Chipman^3) and Rachel SNOW^4 (Jabez^3, Constance Hopkins^2),
    29 Aug. 1717, Harwich (MD 6:83)

Hope CHIPMAN^3 and 1st John HUCKENS, 10 Aug. 1670, Barnstable (MD 6:139)

Hope CHIPMAN^3 and 2nd Jonathan COB , 1 Mar. 1682/83, Barnstable (MD 3:149)

Gershom LEWIS^5 (Eliz. Huckens^4, Hope Chipman^3) and poss. Mary MALTBY

Nathaniel LEWIS and Esther TUTTLE, 16 Jan. 1767 (Woodruff's Gen.Reg. of
    Litchfield <1900>:132)

John LEWIS^5 (Eliz. Huckens^4, Hope Chipman^3) and Mercy HOPKINS^5 (Judah^4,
    Stephen^3, Gyles^2), 6 Oct. 1726, Harwich (MD 8:218)

Experience HUCKENS^4 (Hope Chipman^3) and Thomas LEWES, 28 Sept. 1698, Barnstable
    (MD 10:250)

Hope HUCKENS[4] (Hope Chipman[3]) and Thomas NELSON, 24 Mar. 1697/98, Middleboro
(MD 2:43)

Elizabeth NELSON[5] (Hope Huckens[4]) and Benjamin COLE

Mary COLE and William LEVERETT, 29 Mar. 1825 (Providence VR 5:315)

Hannah NELSON[5] (Hope Huckens[4]) and Jabez WOOD, Jan. 1719/20, Middleboro (MD 4:71)

John NELSON[5] (Hope Huckens[4]) and Abiah LEONARD, 13 Oct. 1726, Middleboro (MD 5:38)

Abiah LEONARD and 2nd Mark HASKALL, 18 June 1740, Middleboro (VR 1:177)

Abiah NELSON[6] (John[5]) and Seth HASKELL, 31 Aug. 1749, Middleboro (MD 18:83)

Job HASKELL[7] (Abiah Nelson[6]) and Elizabeth HAMMOND[5] (Abigail Swift[4], Alice Warren[3],
Nathaniel[2]), poss. 8 Dec. 1773

Zebulon HASKELL[7] (Abiah Nelson[6]) and 1st Thankful DEXTER, 3 Feb. 1782 (Rochester
VR 3:199)

Zebulon HASKELL[7] and 2nd Susanna SHERMAN, 20 Dec. 1792 (Rochester VR 3:201)

Charity NELSON[6] (John[5]) and George LEONARD, 5/17 Jan. 1764, Middleboro (MD 24:56,30:6)

Hope NELSON[6] (John[5]) and Jacob BENNETT, 22 Mar. 1750/51, Middleboro (VR 2:2:32)

Lois NELSON[5] (Hope Huckens[4]) and Jedediah THOMAS[4] (Lydia Howland[3], John[2]), 12 Mar.
1723/24, Middleboro (MD 4:73)

Daniel ELDREDGE and Abigail FISH, 26 June 1711 (Groton CT VR)

Daniel ELDREDGE and Sarah CHIPMAN, 17 Nov. 1739 (Groton CT VR)

Abigail ELDREDGE and Ichabod PACKER, 30 Oct. 1729 (Groton CT VR)

Charles ELDREDGE and Mary STARR, 23 Apr. 1741 (Groton CT VR)

Ruth NELSON[5] (Hope Huckens[4]) and Henry THOMAS, 30 Nov. 1726, Middleboro (MD 5:39)

Thomas NELSON[5] (Hope Huckens[4]) and Juda PEIRCE, 2 Dec. 1736, Middleboro (MD 8:30)

William NELSON[5] (Hope Huckens[4]) and Elizabeth HOWLAND, 2 Oct. 1740, Middleboro
(MD 13:252)

Amos NELSON[6] (Wm.[5]) and Eunice PEIRCE, poss. 25 May 1769

Rev. Samuel NELSON[6] (Wm.[5]) and Charity HASKELL[7] (Abiah Nelson[6], John[5], Hope
Huckens[4], Hope Chipman[3], Hope Howland[2])

Mary HUCKENS[4] (Hope Chipman[3]) and Nathan BASSETT

Jonathan COBB[4] (Hope Chipman[3]) and Elizabeth VAUGHAN, Dec. 1711, Middleboro
(MD 2:158)

Hannah COBB[5] (Sam.[4], Hope Chipman[3]) and 1st John SWETT, 2nd Zerubbabel HUNNEWELL

Hope COBB[5] (Sam.[4], Hope Chipman[3]) and Benjamin WINSLOW[4] (James[3], Job[2], Kenelm[1]),
Int. 11 Aug. 1738, Falmouth ME (Winslow Mem.:217)

John CHIPMAN^3 and 1st Mary SKIFF, c1693 (MD 29:70)

John CHIPMAN^3 and 2nd Elizabeth (HANDLEY) (Pope) Russell, c1716 <see below>

John CHIPMAN^3 and 3rd Hannah (HOXIE) (Griffin) Case, c1725

Lydia CHIPMAN^4 (John^3) and Zephaniah SWIFT^5 (Abigail Gibbs^4, Alice Warren^3, Nathaniel^2)

Bethiah CHIPMAN^4 (John^3) and Samuel SMITH, 6 Oct. 1717

Deborah SMITH^5 (Bethiah Chipman^4) and Joseph BLAKE, c1757 (Blake Fam.<1881>:34)

Joseph BLAKE and 2nd Thankful ( ) (Freeman) BATY$^{<6>}$

Joseph BLAKE and 3rd Huldah DIX

John Welland BLAKE^6 (Deborah Smith^5) and Abigail JONES, 24 May 1790, poss. Hinsdale VT (Blake Fam.<1881>:35)

Henry Jones BLAKE^7 (John^6) and Gertrude TRUAX, 18 Feb. 1816 (Blake Fam.:36)

Anna Sophia BLAKE^7 (John^6) and Henry CABOT (Blake Fam.:36)

Charlotte Smith BLAKE^7 (John^6) and Dexter CHAPIN, 15 Jan. 1822 (Blake Fam.:36)

Frances Williams BLAKE^7 (John^6) and Edward CLARKE, 13 Jan. 1823 (Blake Fam.:36)

Harriet Barker BLAKE^7 (John^6) and James HOUGHTON, 10 Dec. 1827 (Blake Fam.:36)

Mary Welland BLAKE^7 (John^6) and 1st Frederick S. HILL, 7 June 182(8?) (Blake Fam.:36)

Harriet BLAKE^6 (Deborah Smith^5) and Elijah Hunt MILLS

Harriet Blake MILLS^7 (Harriet Blake^6) and Charles Henry DAVIS^8 (Dan.^{7}, Mehitable^6, Mehitable Dimock^5, Desire Sturgis^4, Temperance Gorham^3, Desire Howland^2)

Micro #11 of 18

Anna Sophia CABOT^8 (Anna Sophia Blake^7) and John Ellerton LODGE

Handley CHIPMAN^4 (John^3) and 1st Jane ALLEN, 24 Apr. 1740

Handley CHIPMAN^4 and 2nd Nancy POST, 14 Dec. 1775, Cornwallis N.S. (Eaton's Hist. Kings' Co., N.S.:601)

Stephen POST and Elizabeth CLARK (Eaton's Hist.:782)

Sarah POST and Benjamin BELCHER, 1764 (Eaton's Hist.:782)

Jerusha POST and Duncan REID, 22 Sept. 1769 (Eaton's Hist.:782)

Elizabeth POST and Joseph SIBLEY, 6 Oct. 1783 (Eaton's Hist.:782)

Elizabeth HANDLEY and Thomas POPE, 16 July 1702 (Genealogy of Thomas Pope and His Descendants <1917>:16) <see above>

William CHIPMAN^5 (Ebenezer^4, John^3) and poss. Betsey MAYO, Int. 25 Jan. 1772, Wellfleet

David CHIPMAN^6 (Wm.^{5}) and Bathsheba ATWOOD, Int. 30 Nov. 1803, Wellfleet

Ebenezer CHIPMAN^6 (Wm.^{5}) and Martha Atwood HIGGINS, c1807

Lydia CHIPMAN^3 and John SARGENT, c1674

Jonathan SARGENT^4 (Lydia Chipman^3) and 1st Mary LYNDE, 2nd Mary SPRAGUE

Mercy CHIPMAN^3 and Nathan SKIFF, 13 Dec. 1699, Sandwich (Chilmark VR:72)

Nathan SKIFF and 1st Hephzibah CODMAN

Joseph SKIFF^4 (Mercy Chipman^3) and Remember GIBBS, 7 July 1740 (Chilmark VR:51,72)

Ruth CHIPMAN^3 and Eleazer CROCKER, 7 Apr. 1682, Barnstable (MD 4:120)

Eleazer CROCKER and 2nd Mercy PHINNEY^4 (Mary Rogers^3, Joseph^2), 26 Jan. 1715,
    Barnstable (MD 14:227)

Ruth CROCKER^4 (Ruth Chipman^3) and Samuel FULLER^5 (Barnabas^4, Sam.$^{3-2}$, Edw.^{1})

Sarah CROCKER^4 (Ruth Chipman^3) and Joseph BURSLEY^4 (Eliz. Howland^3, John^2),
    7 Nov. 1712 (Otis 1:218)

Abel CROCKER^4 (Ruth Chipman^3) and Mary ISUM, 16 Apr. 1718, Barnstable (MD 14:227)

Sarah CROCKER^5 (Abel^4) and Elijah PERRY

Bethiah CROCKER^4 (Ruth Chipman^3) and John WITTON, 13 Mar. 1709/10, Barnstable
    (MD 14:88)

Bethiah WITON^5 (Bethiah Crocker^4) and Abraham JACKSON, Int. 1 Sept. 1744, Plymouth
    (MD 17:132)

Isaac JACKSON^6 (Bethiah Witon^5) and Lydia BARROWS, c1764

Nathan CROCKER^4 (Ruth Chipman^3) and Joanna BARSLEY^4 (Eliz. Howland^3, John^2),
    10 Mar. 1708/09, Barnstable (MD 14:226)

Rebecca CROCKER^4 (Ruth Chipman^3) and Jeduthan ROBINS, c1718 (MD 2:52)

Dr. Leavitt T. ROBBINS and Lydia FULLER, 23 Oct. 1831 (Plymouth VR 2:247)

Nathan BACON and Mary TAYLOR, Int. 6 Apr. 1765, Barnstable (MD 19:154)

Molly BACON and Charles ROBBINS

Theophilus CROCKER^4 (Ruth Chipman^3) and Lydia EDDY, 19 Nov. 1730, Plympton (MD 5:210)

Samuel CHIPMAN^3 and Sarah COBB, 27 Dec. 1686, Barnstable (MD 4:121)

Abigail CHIPMAN^4 (Sam.^{3}) and Nathaniel JACKSON, c1712 (MD 16:66)

Hannah CHIPMAN^4 (Sam.^{3}) and Barnabas LOTHROP

Ann CHIPMAN^5 (Jacob^4, Sam.^{3}) and Thomas CUSHMAN^5 (Ben.^{4}, Tho.^{3}, Mary Allerton^2),
    Int. 8 Sept. 1751, Halifax (VR:58)

Bethiah CHIPMAN^5 (Jacob^4, Sam.^{3}) and John SMITH Jr., Int. 1 Oct. 1764, Halifax
    (VR:62)

Lydia CHIPMAN^5 (Jacob^4, Sam.^{3}) and Ebenezer FULLER, 6 Jan. 1746, Halifax (VR:34)

Jacob CHIPMAN[5] (Jacob[4], Sam.[3]) and Anna WATERMAN, Int. 5 May 1760, Halifax (VR:60)

Hannah CHIPMAN[6] (Jacob[5]) and Richard BOZWORTH, 10 Feb. 1780, Halifax (MD 7:51)

Mary CHIPMAN[5] (Jacob[4], Sam.[3]) and Jonathan PORTER, 16 Feb. 1764, Halifax (VR:32)

Rev. John CHIPMAN[4] (Sam.[3]) and 1st Rebecca HALE, 12 Feb. 1718/19, Beverly (MD 29:145)

Rev. John CHIPMAN[4] and 2nd Hannah WARREN, 20 Nov. 1751

Benjamin CHIPMAN[5] (John[4]) and Anna PORTER, poss. Int. 7 Jan. 1776, Beverly

Henry CHIPMAN[5] (John[4]) and Mary (CARR) Nowell

Joseph CHIPMAN[5] (John[4]) and 1st Elizabeth OBEAR, poss. 2 Jan. 1803 (Beverly 2d ch.)

Joseph CHIPMAN[5] and 2nd Elizabeth FOWLER, 7 Feb. 1809 (Beverly VR)

Abigail CHIPMAN[5] (John[4]) and Capt. William GROVES, poss. 9 Jan. 1776 (Beverly
    1st ch.)

Hannah CHIPMAN[5] (John[4]) and Miles WARD, poss 28 June 1772, Beverly

Mary CHIPMAN[5] (John[4]) and Timothy LEACH, poss. 5 Dec. 1775 (Beverly 2d ch.)

Jacob CHIPMAN[4] (Sam.[3]) and 1st Abigail FULLER, 25 Oct. 1721 (Barnstable VR 2:307)[7]

Jacob CHIPMAN[4] (Sam.[3]) and Bethiah THOMAS[4] (Lydia Howland[3], John[2]), c1726 (MD 20:131)

John CHIPMAN[5] (John[4]) and Elizabeth BROWN, c1744

Thomas CHIPMAN[4] (Sam.[3]) and Abigail LOTHROP

Elizabeth CHIPMAN[5] (John[4]) and 1st Rev. John WARREN, 21 Apr. 1737 (Beverly VR)

Elizabeth CHIPMAN[5] 2nd Rev. Joseph SWAIN, 3 July 1751, Beverly

Rebecca CHIPMAN[5] (John[4]) and Rev. Nehemiah PORTER, 14 Feb. 1749 (Beverly VR)

Samuel CHIPMAN[5] (John[4]) and Anstice MANNING, c1745

Sarah CHIPMAN[5] (John[4]) and John LEACH, 15 Mar. 1743/44 (Beverly ch.rcds.)

Samuel CHIPMAN[4] (Sam.[3]) and Abiah HINKLEY, 8 Dec. 1715, Barnstable (MD 14:227)

Seth CHIPMAN[4] (Sam.[3]) and Priscilla BRADFORD[4] (John[3], Wm.[2]), 17 Sept. 1721
    (Kingston ch.rcds.:182,191)

Benjamin CHIPMAN[5] (Seth[4]) and Hannah WADSWORTH

Seth CHIPMAN[5] (Seth[4]) and Sarah RIPLEY[5] (Hannah Bosworth[4], David[3], Hannah Howland[2]),
    3 Dec. 1746 (Kingston VR:191,269)

Isaac HOWLAND[2] (John[1])

Isaac HOWLAND[2] and Elizabeth VAUGHAN, c1676 (MD 1:220,18:115,116)

Hannah HOWLAND[3] and John TINKHAM[4] (Ephraim[3], Mary Brown[2])

Jael HOWLAND[3] and Nathaniel SOUTHWORTH[5] (Desire Gray[4], Mary Winslow[3], Mary Chilton[2])

Seth HOWLAND[3] and Elizabeth DELANO, 24 May 1728, Middleboro (MD 5:40)

Isaac HOWLAND^3 and Sarah THOMAS^4 (Lydia Howland^3, John^2), c1713

Sarah THOMAS^4 and 2nd Samuel WOOD, 7 Aug. 1730, Middleboro (MD 9:46)

Nathan HOWLAND^3 and Frances COOMBS^4 (Francis^3, Sarah Priest^2), c1712

Seth HOWLAND^4 (Nathan^3) and Lydia COBB, 25 Jan. 1738/39, Middleboro (MD 13:253)[8]

Drusilla HOWLAND^5 (Seth^4) and Archippus COLE, 19 Nov. 1761, Middleboro (MD 24:55)

Deborah HOWLAND^5 (Seth^4) and David THOMAS, 1 Nov. 1764, Middleboro (MD 24:57)

Priscilla HOWLAND^3 and Peter BENNET, 30 Oct. 1700, Bridgewater (MD 2:146)

Deborah BENNET^4 (Priscilla Howland^3) and Samuel THACHER, 24 Sept. 1747, Middle-
    boro (MD 18:78)

Elizabeth BENNET^4 (Prisc. Howland^3) and John DARLING, 17 Oct. 1721, Middleboro
    (MD 4:72)

Nathan DARLING^5 (Eliz. Bennet^4) and Martha BENNET^5 (Mercy Tomson^4, Jacob^3, Mary
    Cooke^2)

Isaac BENNET^4 (Prisc. Howland^3) and Mary DREW^4 (Sarah Delano^3, Mary Alden^2),
    24 Aug. 1732, Middleboro (MD 13:249)

Jael BENNET^4 (Prisc. Howland^3) and Abiezer EDSON, c1740

Joseph BENNET^4 (Prisc. Howland^3) and Thankful SPROUT^4 (Ebenezer^3, Eliz. Samson^2),
    18 Nov. 1724, Middleboro (MD 4:73)

Thankful SPROUT^4 and 2nd Seth SAMSON^3 (Geo.^{2}, Abraham^1), poss. 9 Oct. 1758,
    Middleboro (MD 24:131)

Elizabeth BENNET^5 (Jos.^{4}) and John MORTON^5 (Ebenezer^4, Mary Ring^3, Deborah Hopkins^2),
    21 Jan. 1747, Middleboro (MD 18:78)

Samuel BENNET^5 (Jos.^{4}) and Anna BENNET^5 (Peter^4, Prisc. Howland^3, Isaac^2),
    24 July 1764, Middleboro (MD 24:56)

Nathan BENNET^4 (Prisc. Howland^3) and Jemima SAMSON, 5 Dec. 1745, Middleboro
    (MD 16:108)

Jemima SAMSON and poss. 2nd Lemuel JACKSON

Peter BENNET^4 (Prisc. Howland^3) and Sarah STEPHENS, 11 Sept. 1735, Middleboro
    (MD 13:251)

Jael BENNET^5 (Peter^4) and Paul PRATT, 9 Feb. 1764, Middleboro (MD 24:185)

Rev. Benajah PRATT^6 (Jael Bennet^5) and Lovica WARREN^7 (Silvanus^6, Ben.^{5}, Sam.^{4},
    Richard^3, Nathaniel^2), 13 May 1792 (Middleboro VR 4:2:170)

Priscilla BENNETT^4 (Prisc. Howland^3) and John MILLER^5 (Lydia Coombs^4, Francis^3,
    Sarah Priest^2), 30 Oct. 1735, Middleboro (MD 13:251)

Susanna BENNET^4 (Prisc. Howland^3) and John DREW^4 (Sarah Delano^3, Mary Alden^2),

25 Jan. 1727/28, Middleboro (MD 5:39)

Susanna HOWLAND[3] and Ephraim WOOD, c1709 (MD 2:201,6:148)

Ephraim WOOD and 2nd Patience (NICHOLS) Holmes, c1723/24

Patience NICHOLS and 1st Experience HOLMES, 6 Jan. 1707, Scituate (MD 5:116)

Thomas NICHOLS and Sarah WHISTON, 25 May 1663 (Scituate VR)

Micro #13 of 18

Rebecca WOOD[4] (Susanna Howland[3]) and Robert BARTLETT[5] (Robert[4], Jos.[3], Mary
   Warren[2]), Int. 21 Nov. 1733, Plymouth (MD 18:120)

Ephraim WOOD and Mary LAZEL, 11 Nov. 1742 (Middleboro VR 1:224)

Josiah WOOD[4] (Susanna Howland[3]) and Mary (SPROUT[4]) Holmes (Ebenezer[3], Eliz.
   Samson[2]), 29 Jan. 1735/36, Middleboro (MD 13:252)

Mary SPROUT[4] and 1st Thomas HOLMES

Josiah WOOD[5] (Josiah[4]) and Salome WOODS, 31 Mar. 1768 (Bridgewater VR)

Josiah WOOD[6] (Josiah[5]) and Judith WOODBURY, 3 Mar. 1796, Bridgewater VT

Mary WOOD[6] (Josiah[5]) and Gains PADDOCK

Jabez HOWLAND[2] (John[1])

Jabez HOWLAND[2] and Bethiah THACHER, c1668 (MD 18:70)

Phebe WARDWELL and James SMITH, 2 Dec. 1767

Elizabeth HOWLAND[3] and Nathan TOWNSEND

Jabez HOWLAND[3] and Patience STAFFORD, c1701

Bethiall HOWLAND and Nicholas BRAGG, 19 May 1725, Bristol RI (ch.rcds.)<see below>

Bethiah BRAGG and Simon DAVIS, 29 Aug. 1733, Bristol RI (ch.rcds.)

Patience HOWLAND and Samuel BARKER, 6 Dec. 1739, Bristol RI (ch.rcds.)<see below>

Simon DAVIS and Elizabeth McINTOSH, 2 June 1728 (Bristol RI VR 1:27)

Simon DAVIS and Mrs. Hannah CHURCH, Int. 15 Apr. 1732 (Bristol RI VR 1:27)

Bethia DAVIS and Daniel GREEN, Int. 21 Nov. 1741 (Bristol RI VR 1:43)

Elizabeth HOWLAND[4] (Jabez[3]) and Otis LITTLE[5] (Isaac[4-3], Anna Warren[2]), 3 Oct.
   1733, Bristol RI

Mercy HOWLAND[4] (Jabez[3]) and 1st George PEARCE, 22 Nov. 1722 (Bristol RI VR)

Mercy HOWLAND[4] and 2nd Isaac MARTINDALE, 9 July 1724 (Bristol RI VR)

Patience HOWLAND[4] (Jabez[3]) and Samuel BARKER, 6 Dec. 1739 (Scituate VR) <see above>

Samuel BARKER and 1st Deborah GORHAM[5] (John[4-3], Desire Howland[2])

Sarah HOWLAND[4] (Jabez[3]) and Isaac LAWTON, 27 Aug. 1732 (Bristol RI VR)

Bethiah HOWLAND[4] (Jabez[3]) and 1st Nicholas BRAGG <see above>

Bethiah HOWLAND[4] (Jabez[3]) and 2nd Simon DAVIS,·29 Aug. 1733, Bristol RI

Nicholas BRAGG[5] (Bethiah Howland[4]) and Sarah GREENE, 23 June 1757, poss. Coventry
  (Arnold 7:132)

Joseph HOWLAND[3] and Bathsheba CARY, c1714 (Howland Gen.:333,334,341)

Lydia HOWLAND[4] (Jos.[3]) and Capt. Edward BELCHER

Joseph HOWLAND[4] (Jos.[3]) and Sarah BAKER

Elizabeth HOWLAND[4] (Jos.[3]) and Constant TABER

Josiah HOWLAND[3] and Yetmercy SHOVE, 24 Nov. 1709

Yetmercy HOWLAND[4] (Josiah[3]) and 1st Isaac PALMER, 2nd Nathaniel HOWLAND

Samuel HOWLAND[3] and 1st Abigail CARY, 6 May 1708, Bristol RI

Samuel HOWLAND[3] and 2nd Rachel ( ) ALLEN, Int. 19 Feb. 1741/42 (Barrington RI VR)

Tabitha HOWLAND[4] (Sam.[3]) and 1st Nathaniel CAREY, 12 May 1734, Bristol RI

Tabitha HOWLAND[4] and 2nd John PECKHAM, 22 Apr. 1742, Bristol RI

John HOWLAND[2] (John[1])

John HOWLAND[2] and Mary LEE, 26 Oct. 1651, Plymouth (MD 16:237)

Anne HOWLAND[3] and Joseph CROCKER, 18 Sept. 1691, Barnstable (MD 3:150)

Benjamin CROCKER[4] (Anne Howland[3]) and Priscilla HALL, 17 Sept. 1719, Yarmouth

Elizabeth HOWLAND[3] and John BURSLEY, Dec. 1673, Barnstable (MD 3:53)

Elizabeth BURSLEY[4] (Eliz. Howland[3]) and Jonathan CROCKER, 28 Nov. 1723, Barnstable
  (MD 14:89)

Joanna BURSLEY[4] (Eliz. Howland[3]) and Nathan CROCKER[4] (Ruth Chipman[3], Hope Howland[2]),
  10 Mar. 1708/09, Barnstable (MD 14:226)

Mary BURSLEY[4] (Eliz. Howland[3]) and Joseph SMITH

Abigail BURSLEY[5] (Jabez[4], Eliz. Howland[3]) and Benoni CROCKER, c1736

Hannah BURSLEY[5] (Jabez[4], Eliz. Howland[3]) and Solomon BODFISH, c1741

Joanna BURSLEY[5] (Jabez[4], Eliz. Howland[3]) and Charles CONET[5] (Mary Howland[4],
  Sarah Howland[3], Jos.[2]), c1743

John BURSLEY[5] (Jabez[4], Eliz. Howland[3]) and Elizabeth SAUNDERS, c1743

Barnabas BURSLEY[5] (Jabez[4], Eliz. Howland[3]) and Thankful SMITH, 16 May 1754
  (Barnstable VR)

Thankful BURSLEY[6] (Barnabas[5]) and Joseph LEE, 24 Dec. 1786 (Barre VR:118,166)

Hannah BURSLEY[6] (Barnabas[5]) and Seth RUGGLES, 22 Nov. 1792 (Hardwick VR:151,237)

Seth RUGGLES and 1st Hannah AMIDON(sp), 3rd Sukey JENKS

Benjamin BURSLEY[5] (Jabez[4], Eliz. Howland[3]) and 1st Joanna CANNON, 7 July 1735
  Barnstable (MD 33:169)

Benjamin BURSLEY^5 and 2nd Mary GOODSPEED, 2 Feb. 1743, Barnstable (MD 33:165)

Martha BURSLEY^6 (Ben.^{5}) and Benjamin SMITH, 4 Nov. 1762, Barnstable (MD 20:43)

Jabez BURSLEY and Susanna CROCKER, Apr. 1763, Barnstable (MD 19:156)

Jabez BURSLEY and Anna CROCKER, 5 Dec. 1757, Barnstable (MD 25:132)

Benjamin BURSLEY^6 (Ben.^{5}) and Elizabeth GOODSPEED, Int. poss. 16 Oct. 1773, Barnstable

Lemuel BURSLEY and Lavinia SPENCER, Int. 4 Feb. 1797, Provincetown

John BURSLEY^4 (Eliz. Howland^3) and Mary CROCKER, 11 Feb. 1702/03, Barnstable (MD 3:53)

Experience BURSLEY^5 (John^4) and Benjamin LOTHROP, 30 Apr. 1730, Barnstable (MD 34:20)

Mary LOTHROP^6 (Experience Bursley^5) and Nathan FOSTER, 21 May 1753, Barnstable (MD 31:10)

Nathan FOSTER and 2nd Mercy SMITH, 13 Mar. 1766 (Barnstable VR 3:171)

Micro #14 of 18

Mary FOSTER^7 (Mary Lothrop^6) and Abraham CROCKER, 11 Apr. 1784 (Barnstable VR 3:177)

Mercy FOSTER and Ephraim CROCKER, 22 Oct. 1786 (Barnstable VR 3:330)

Joseph BURSLEY^4 (Eliz. Howland^3) and Sarah CROCKER^4 (Ruth Chipman^3, Hope Howland^2), poss. 7 Nov. 1712

Mercy BURSLEY^5 (John^4) and John GOODSPEED, 29 May 1757, Barnstable (MD 25:132)

Bethiah BURSLEY and Joseph JENKINS

Sarah BURSLEY and Peleg NYE (Nye Gen.:97,155,156)

Joseph BURSLEY^5 (Jos.^{4}) and Bethiah FULLER^5 (John$^{4-3}$, Matthew^2, Edw.^{1}), poss. 20 Dec. 1739

John BURSLEY^6 (Jos.^{5}) and Mary HOWLAND^5 (Jabez^4, Shubael^3, John^2), poss. 20 Nov. 1766, Barnstable

Lemuel BURSLEY^7 (John^6) and Jemima FISH, 28 Oct. 1790 (Barnstable VR 3:331)

Abigail BURSLEY^8 (Lemuel^7) and Cornelius JONES, 23 July 1809, Barnstable (MD 19:77)

Mercy BURSLEY^8 (Lemuel^7) and Marsena JONES, 14 Sept. 1810, Barnstable (MD 19:77)

Ausmon BURSLEY^8 (Lemuel^7) and Huldah FISH, 19 Oct. 1817, Barnstable (MD 19:79)

Joseph BURSLEY^8 (Lemuel^7) and 1st Deborah LOTHROP, 22 Mar. 1813

Joseph BURSLEY^8 and 2nd Mary C. LOTHROP, June 1842 (Lothrop Gen.:141,142)

Hannah HOWLAND^3 and Jonathan CROCKER, 20 May 1686, Barnstable (MD 3:150)

Hannah CROCKER^4 (Hannah Howland^3) and Shubael FULLER, 7 Dec. 1708 (MD 14:226)[9]

James CROCKER^4 (Hannah Howland^3) and Alice SWIFT^5 (Abigail Gibbs^4, Alice Warren^3, poss. 21 Nov. 1721

Jonathan CROCKER^5 (James^4) and Rachel SKINNER, poss. 27 Mar. 1755 (Colchester CT VR)

Isaac HOWLAND^3 and Anne TAYLOR, 27 Dec. 1686, Barnstable (MD 5:75)

Ebenezer HOWLAND^4 (Isaac^3) and Elizabeth JUSTICE, poss. 26 June 1712

Isaac HOWLAND^4 (Isaac^3) and Elizabeth JENNINGS, poss. 14 May 1719

Sarah HOWLAND^5 (Isaac^4) and Edmund HINCKLEY^5 (Abigail Jenkins^4, Lydia Howland^3, Joseph^2)

Joseph HOWLAND^5 (Isaac^4) and Elizabeth LOVELL, Mar. 1763, Barnstable (MD 19:156)

Benjamin HOWLAND^5 (Isaac^4) and Anna CROCKER, 15 Mar. 1763, Barnstable (MD 19:156)

John HOWLAND^4 (Isaac^3) and Alice HAMLIN, c1728 (Barnstable Fam.1:534)

Alice HAMLIN and 2nd Samuel HINCKLEY, 22 May 1748

David HOWLAND^5 (John^4) and Mary COLEMAN, 15 Dec. 1763, Barnstable (MD 19:126)

Deborah HOWLAND^5 (John^4) and Richard SPARROW, Nov. 1763, Barnstable (MD 19:156)

Joseph HOWLAND^4 (Isaac^3) and 1st Rachel CROCKER, poss. 18 Jan. 1739 (Otis 2:51)

Joseph HOWLAND^4 and 2nd Maria FULLER, 16 May 1746 (Otis 2:51)

Rachel HOWLAND^5 (Jos.^{4}) and Nathan JENKINS, Int. 3 July 1762, Barnstable (MD 23:126)

Hannah HOWLAND^5 (Jos.^{4}) and Christopher TAYLOR, 15 Jan. 1761, Barnstable (MD 19:156)

John HOWLAND^3 and 1st poss. Abigail CROCKER, c1704

John HOWLAND^3 and 2nd Mary CROCKER, June 1719, Barnstable (MD 33:121)$^{<10>}$

Josiah HOWLAND and Yetmercy SHOVE, 24 Nov. 1709 (Barnstable Marr.:68)

George HOWLAND^4 (John^3) and Abigail CROCKER, poss. 28 Oct. 1731 (Otis 1:240)

Job HOWLAND^4 (John^3) and 1st Hannah JENKINS^5 (Ben.^{4}, Lydia Howland^3, Jos.^{2}), 6 Dec. 1753, Barnstable (MD 31:10)

Hannah HOWLAND^5 (Job^4) and 1st William CHIPMAN, poss. 11 Dec. 1783 (Howland Gen:341)

Hannah HOWLAND^5 and 2nd Lemuel NYE, poss. 5 June 1792 (Howland Gen.:341)

Timothy HOWLAND^5 (Job^4) and Lydia PUTNAM, 3 Feb. 1802 (Warren VR:114,134)

Rufus HOWLAND^6 (Timothy^5) and Mary BORDWELL

Rev. John HOWLAND^4 (John^3) and Elizabeth LEWIS, 21 Jan. 1747/48 (Pembroke VR:309)

Lydia HOWLAND^3 and Jeremiah THOMAS, 25 Feb. 1684, Middleboro (MD 1:219)

Jeremiah THOMAS and 2nd Mary DURFE, 29 Apr. 1720, Middleboro (MD 4:71)

Mary THOMAS^4 (Lydia Howland^3) and 1st Reuben BLISH, 25 Oct. 1735

Mary THOMAS^4 and 2nd Lt. John ANNABLE, 5 Mar. 1745 (Blish Gen.:35,36)

Reuben BLISH and 1st Elizabeth BODFISH, 25 Jan. 1717 (Blish Gen.:35,36)

Sarah THOMAS^4 (Lydia Howland^3) and 1st Isaac HOWLAND^3 (Isaac^2), 2nd Samuel WOOD

Ebenezer THOMAS^5 (Eben.^{4}, Lydia Howland^3) and Joanna CUSHMAN^6 (Wm.^{5}, Ichabod^4,

-228-

Isaac^3, Mary Allerton^2), 5 Nov. 1761, Middleboro (MD 24:134)

Lois THOMAS and James SHAW, 12 Oct. 1749, Middleboro (MD 18:82)

Lois THOMAS and William HOOPER, 30 Jan. 1728 (MD 5:40)

Jedediah THOMAS^4 (Lydia Howland^3) and Lois NELSON^5 (Hope Huckens^4, Hope Chipman^3, Hope Howland^2), 12 Mar. 1723/24, Middleboro (MD 4:73)

Abiah THOMAS^5 (Jedediah^4) and Nehemiah ALLEN^7 (Mary Packard^6, Mary Harris^5, Mercy Latham^4, Susanna Winslow^3, Mary Chilton^2), 23 Mar. 1758, Middleboro (MD 24:131)

Foxel THOMAS^5 (Jedediah^4) and Martha HOLMES, 22 Mar. 1770, Middleboro (MD 30:7)

Jedediah THOMAS^5 (Jedediah^4) and Keziah CHURCHELL, 28 Dec. 1749, Middleboro (MD 18:82)

Martha THOMAS^6 (Jedediah^5) and James THOMAS, 27 Nov. 1777 (Middleboro VR 4:157)

Jeremiah THOMAS^4 (Lydia Howland^3) and Miriam THOMAS, 12 Dec. 1718, Middleboro (MD 4:71)

Lydia THOMAS^4 (Lydia Howland^3) and 1st George HACKET, 13 Jan. 1723/24, Middleboro (MD 4:73)

Lydia THOMAS^4 and 2nd Jonathan COB^4 (Hope Chipman^3, Hope Howland^2), 26 Aug. 1736, Middleboro (MD 8:30)

Gideon HACKET^5 (Lydia Thomas^4) and Betty SAMSON^4 (Seth^3, George^2, Abraham^1), 3 Aug. 1749, Middleboro (MD 18:82)

Lydia HACKET^5 (Lydia Thomas^4) and poss. John HALL, 13 Dec. 1745, Middleboro (MD 16:20)

Mary HOWLAND^3 and John ALLYN, c1673 (MD 2:213)

Lemuel BURSLEY and Jemima FISH, 28 Oct. 1790 (Barnstable VR 3:331)

Shobal HOWLAND^3 and Mercy BLOSSOM, 13 Dec. 1700, Barnstable (MD 5:75)

Jabez HOWLAND^4 (Shobal^3) and Elizabeth PERCIVAL, 22 Dec. 1727, Barnstable (MD 33:28)

Nathaniel HOWLAND^5 (Jabez^4) and Martha THACHER, Int. 2 Oct. 1762, Barnstable (MD 23:126)

Mary HOWLAND and John BURSLEY, 20 Nov. 1766 (Barnstable VR 3:171)

Micro #15 of 18

Ansel HOWLAND^5 (Jabez^4, Shobal^3) and Elizabeth BODFISH

Zaccheus HOWLAND^5 (Jabez^4, Shobal^3) and Mary PALMER, c1768

Job P. HOWLAND^6 (Zaccheus^5) and Amanda LOVELL, c1813

Joseph HOWLAND^2 (John^1)

Joseph HOWLAND^2 and Elizabeth SOUTHWORTH, 7 Dec. 1664, Plymouth (MD 17:185)

Elizabeth HOWLAND[3] and 1st Isaac HAMLIN, 14 Sept. 1698, Barnstable (MD 6:137)

Elizabeth HOWLAND[3] and 2nd Timothy CANNON, 9 Nov. 1711

Joseph HAMLIN[4] (Eliz. Howland[3]) and Elizabeth MATHEWS, poss. 3 Mar. 1726/27

Hannah HAMLIN[5] (Jos.[4]) and Lot CROWELL, 1 Dec. 1747 (Yarmouth VR 3:294)

Capt. Lott CROWELL and Hannah BERRY, 9 Nov. 1788 (Yarmouth VR 4:112)

Sarah CROWELL[6] (Hannah Hamlin[5]) and Silas BAKER, 22 Jan. 1789 (Yarmouth VR 4:112)

Braddock BAKER[7] (Sarah Crowell[6]) and Caroline CROWELL

James HOWLAND[3] and Mary LOTHROP, 8 Sept. 1697, Barnstable (MD 14:225)

Hannah HOWLAND[4] (James[3]) and James RICKARD, 29 June 1720 (Plymouth VR 14:39)

John HOWLAND[4] (James[3]) and Patience SPOONER, 27 May 1742, Plymouth (MD 14:159)

Lydia HOWLAND[3] and Joseph JENKINS, Oct. 1694, Barnstable (MD 6:236)

Prudence JENKINS[4] (Lydia Howland[3]) and Samuel BAKER

Abigail JENKINS[4] (Lydia Howland[3]) and Benjamin HINCKLEY, 2 Nov. 1716, Barnstable
    (MD 14:227)

Edmund HINCKLEY[5] (Abigail Jenkins[4]) and Sarah HOWLAND[5] (Isaac[4-3], John[2]),
    6 Dec. 1744 (Barnstable VR 2:346)

Mary HINCKLEY[6] (Edmund[5]) and Joseph CROCKER, 22 Apr. 1770 (Barnstable VR 3:172)

Samuel CROCKER[7] (Mary Hinckley[6]) and 1st Hodiah JENKINS, c1805 (Barnstable VR 4:280)

Samuel CROCKER[7] and 2nd Thankful PERCIVAL, 11 Feb. 1813, Barnstable (MD 19:78)

Hodiah Jenkins CROCKER[8] (Sam.[7]) and Capt. Asa WRIGHT, Int. 17 Dec. 1836 (Barn-
    stable VR 6:170)

Silvanus HINCKLEY[5] (Abigail Jenkins[4]) and Sarah PHINNEY[6] (Tho.[5], John[4], Mary
    Rogers[3], Joseph[2]), 31 May 1753, Barnstable (MD 31:8)

Prince HINCKLEY[6] (Silvanus[5]) and Eunice GOODSPEED, 20 Oct. 1784 (Barnstable VR 3:177)

Sophia S. HINCKLEY[7] (Prince[6]) and Bridgham CROCKER, 17 Apr. 1832 (Barnstable VR 6:186)

Arthur B. CROCKER and Almira PARKER, 17 Apr. 1832 (Barnstable VR 6:186)

Joel HAMLIN and Phebe GOODSPEED, 22 Dec. 1831 (Barnstable VR 6:186)

Prince HINCKLEY and Susan CHILDS, Int. 2 Apr. 1825, Barnstable

Ann JENKINS[4] (Lydia Howland[3]) and Joseph LOTHROP

Benjamin JENKINS[4] (Lydia Howland[3]) and Mehitable BLUSH, poss. 29 Oct. 1730
    (Barnstable VR 2:357)

Hannah JENKINS[4] (Lydia Howland[3]) and Stephen FREEMAN, poss. 3 Oct. 1736

Lydia JENKINS[4] (Lydia Howland[3]) and Cornelius CROCKER

Mercy HOWLAND[3] and Joseph HAMLIN, 27 Apr. 1704, Barnstable (MD 6:137)

Nathaniel HOWLAND[3] and 1st Martha COLE, 16 Mar. 1696/97, Plymouth (MD 13:206)

Nathaniel HOWLAND[3] and 2nd Abigail (CHURCHILL) Billington, 25 Jan. 1725/26,
     Plymouth (MD 14:71)

Mary HOWLAND[4] (Nath.[3]) and Thomas WESTON, 19 Apr. 1723, Plymouth (MD 14:40)

Thomas WESTON and 2nd Prudence CONANT[6] (Eliz. Washburn[5], Tho.[4], Eliz. Mitchell[3],
     Jane Cooke[2]), aft. Feb. 1730

Nathaniel HOWLAND[4] (Nath.[3]) and 1st Yetmercy PALMER, Int. 24 Nov. 1723, Plymouth
     (MD 18:120)

Nathaniel HOWLAND[4] and 2nd Abigail (BURT?) Lane

Micro #16 of 18

Mary HOWLAND[4] (Sarah Howland[3]) and 1st George CONETT, 3 Nov. 1718, Plymouth
     (MD 14:38)[11]

Mary HOWLAND[4] and 2nd William GREEN

Charles CONET[5] (Mary Howland[4]) and Joanna BURSLEY[5] (Jabez[4], Eliz. Howland[3], John[2]),
     c1743 (MD 31:87)

George CONANT and Lydia FREEMAN, 10 Sept. 1761, Harwich (MD 34:69)

George CONANT and Sarah GOODSPEED, 20 June 1753 (MD 31:8)

George CONNEAT and Susanna CROCKER, 30 Jan. 1755 (MD 31:10)

Mary CONANT and William GREEN, Oct. 1745, Barnstable (MD 33:165)

Caleb CONANT and Hannah LUMBARD, c1720 (Truro VR:62)

Sarah CONANT and William ELDRED, 30 Jan. 1706/07, Eastham (MD 6:205)

John CONANT and Keziah LUMBART, 28 Oct. 1725 (Truro VR:13)

Hannah CONANT and Benjamin GREEN, 29 Apr. 1753 (Eastham VR:162)

Thomas HOWLAND[3] and Joanna COLE, c1699 (MD 4:112)

Thomas Southworth HOWLAND[5] (Consider[4], Tho.[3]) and Abial HOVEY, Int. 16 Feb. 1771,
     Plymouth (MD 26:190)

Consider HOWLAND[4] (Tho.[3]) and Ruth BRYANT, 10 May 1725, Plymouth (MD 14:71)

Lucy HOWLAND[5] (Consider[4]) and Abraham HAMMATT, Int. 3 Sept. 1748, Plymouth (MD 17:124)

Abraham HAMMETT[6] (Lucy Howland[5]) and Priscilla LeBARON[5] (Lydia Bradford[4], David[3],
     Wm.[2]), Int. 26 Nov. 1774, Plymouth (MD 27:176)

Experience HOWLAND[4] (Tho.[3]) and Benjamin LOTHROP, 22 Dec. 1727, Plymouth (MD 14:72)

Capt. Benjamin LOTHROP and Mrs. Deborah THOMAS, Int. 16 Apr. 1748 (Kingston VR:250)

Capt. Benjamin LOTHROP and Mrs. Ruth PUTNAM, Int. 17 Apr. 1757 (Kingston VR:250)

Benjamin LOTHROP and Mary HALLET, 23 Sept. 1779, Yarmouth (Kinston VR:250)

Benjamin LOTHROP and Mercy BAKER, 26 May 1720, Barnstable (MD 32:148)

Benjamin LOTHROP and Deborah THOMAS, 5 May 1748, Plymouth (MD 17:6)

Mary GORHAM^5 (James Gorham$^{4-3}$, Desire Howland^2) and 1st Thomas HEDGE, 25 Jan. 1739

Mary GORHAM^5 and 2nd Lt. Thomas HALLETT, aft. June 1764

Mary GORHAM^5 and 3rd Benjamin LOTHROP, 23 Sept. 1779, Yarmouth (see p.231)

Hannah HOWLAND^4 (Tho.^{3}) and 1st William DYRE, 29 Oct. 1734, Plymouth (MD 14:75)

Hannah HOWLAND^4 and 2nd Edward WINSLOW^4 (Isaac^3, Josiah^2), 10 Apr. 1741, Plymouth
(MD 14:159)

Lydia HOWLAND^2 (John^1)

Lydia HOWLAND^2 and James BROWN, c1654 (MD 7:164)

William BROWN and Rebekah FOLITT, 27 Oct. 1725 (Rehoboth VR 2:140)

Dorothy BROWN^3 and Joseph KENT, 12 Nov. 1690, Swansea (MD 7:163)

James KENT^4 (Dorothy Brown^3) and Martha BARSTOW

John BROWN Jr. and Abigail COLE, 2 July 1696, Swansea

Joseph KENT and 2nd Mary CARPENTER, poss. 4 Jan. 1727/28, Rehoboth

James BROWN^3 and Margaret DENNISON, 5 June 1678, Swansea

Dorothea KENT^4 (Dorothy Brown^3) and Noah NEWMAN, poss. 1 Mar. 1721/22 (Rehoboth
VR 2:136)

Hezekiah KENT^4 (Dorothy Brown^3) and Ruth COOPER

John KENT^4 (Dorothy Brown^3) and Rachel CARPENTER, c1726 (Rehoboth VR:659)

Joseph KENT^4 (Dorothy Brown^3) and Bethiah THURSTON

Micro #17 of 18

Lydia KENT^4 (Dorothy Brown^3) and Joseph BOSWORTH, 23 Aug. 1715 (Rehoboth VR 1:159)

Susanna KENT^4 (Dorothy Brown^3) and Peter BOWEN, 23 Mar. 1726/27 (Rehoboth VR 2:141)

Jane BROWN^4 (Jabez^3) and Nathaniel BOSWORTH

Ann BROWN^4 (James^3) and Samuel HILL, c1710

Benjamin HILL^5 (Ann Brown^4) and Elizabeth IDE, 11 July 1745, Rehoboth

Elizabeth IDE and 2nd John SMITH, 27 May 1755

James HILL^5 (Ann Brown^4) and Eunice WALKER, 11 May 1749, Rehoboth

Samuel HILL^5 (Ann Brown^4) and 1st Deborah CUSHING, 13 Nov. 1739, Rehoboth

Samuel HILL^5 and 2nd Sarah HARNDEN, 14 June 1752, Swansea

Dorothy BROWN^4 (James^3) and Nathaniel MEDBERY, 27 Mar. 1718, Providence RI

Edward MEDBURY and Anna SMITH, 5 Apr. 1770, Smithfield RI (VR 1:93)

Deliverance MEDBURY and Daniel BROWN, 25 Oct. 1747 (N. Kingstown RI VR)

Ebenezer MEDBURY and Mary IDE, 12 May 1751 (Warren RI VR 1:64)

Bethiah MEDBURY and William CAMP, 21 Jan. 1755 (Warren RI VR 1:65)

Sarah MEDBURY and James DENNIS, 12 Apr. 1761 (Warren RI VR 1:67)

John MEDBURY and Anna CAMP, Int. 4 Oct. 1740 (Barrington RI VR 1:149)

Thomas MEDBURY and Elizabeth PHILLIPS, 11 Apr. 1796, Providence RI (VR 7:448)

Susanna MEDBURY and Jeremiah MATTHEWS, 25 Jan. 1737/38, Barrington RI (VR 10:233)

Harris MEDBURY and Lydia IRONS, 16 Nov. 1811, Glocester RI (VR 17:485)

Harris MEDBURY and Betsey HAWKINS, 13 Oct. 1816, Johnston RI (VR 17:485)

Phebe MEDBURY and Samuel STEERE, 8 June 1817, Glocester RI (VR 17:485)

Ann MEDBURY and James OLNEY, 2 June 1754, Smithfield RI (VR 1:93)

Edward MEDBURY and Annie SMITH, 5 Apr. 1770, Smithfield RI (VR 1:93)

James BROWN^4 (James^3) and Elizabeth (BOWEN) Hunt, 2 Dec. 1711 (Rehoboth VR 1:177)

Abijah BROWN^5 (James^4) and Josiah HUMPHREY, poss. 12 Jan. 1737/38

Elizabeth BROWN^5 (James^4) and John ADAMS, pre 15 Jan. 1735/36

John ADAMS and 2nd Elizabeth (   ) WESTGATE, 14 Nov. 1751, Warwick RI

Avis ADAMS^6 (Eliz. Brown^5) and Matthew WATSON, c1770

John WATSON^7 (Avis Adams^6) and Ann WATERMAN, 20 Nov. 1803, Barrington RI (VR 6:3:19)

James BROWN^5 (James^4) and 1st Rebecca PERRY, 27 July 1737 (Rehoboth VR 2:149)

Cyril BROWN^6 (James^5) and Mary ALLEN

Lydia BROWN^5 (James^4) and William PEIRCE, 22 Apr. 1742 (Bristol VR 6:1:11)

William BROWN^4 (James^3) and 2nd Rebecca FOLLETT, 27 Oct. 1725 (Rehoboth VR 2:140)

Isaac BROWN and Dorothy PAINE, 31 Mar. 1768, Rehoboth

Amos BROWN and Rachel READ, 4 Apr. 1768, Rehoboth

Isaac BROWN and Alice BRIGGS, Int. 30 May 1752, Rebohoth

Isaac BROWN and Sarah BULLOCK, Int. 24 Feb. 1782, Rehoboth

Amos BROWN^5 (Wm.^{4}) and 1st Mary WILLMARTH, 14 Oct. 1736 (Rehoboth VR 2:149)

Amos BROWN^5 and 2nd Rebecca WILLMARTH, 13 Mar. 1739/40 (Rehoboth VR 2:153)

Huldah BROWN^6 (Amos^5) and Ebenezer PECK, c1785 (Barrington RI VR)

Bethiah BROWN^5 (Wm.^{4}) and Ebenezer WALKER, poss. 26 June 1737

Elizabeth BROWN^5 (Wm.^{4}) and Daniel BISHOP

Ezra BROWN^5 (Wm.^{4}) and Lydia WILLMARTH, 3 Apr. 1743 (Rehoboth VR)

Isaac BROWN^5 (Wm.^{4}) and Susanna MAY, Int. 28 Feb. 1756, Rehoboth

Noah BROWN^5 (Wm.^{4}) and Deborah WILLMARTH, 9 Apr. 1752 (Attleboro VR:177)

Noah BROWN^6 (Noah^5) and Judith SHORT, Int. 28 Sept. 1778 (Attleboro VR:513)

Hannah BROWN[7] (Noah[6]) and Timothy CARPENTER, 25 Aug. 1795, Rehoboth

Cyril CARPENTER and Mary TYLER, 1790

Daniel CARPENTER and Lydia THORNTON

Elkanah CARPENTER and Experience SWEET, 1794

Rev. Samuel CARPENTER and Rhoda CARPENTER

Nathan CARPENTER and Lydia PADDLEFORD

Lucy CARPENTER and Ezra FOLLETT, 1800

Davis CARPENTER and Abiah FOLLETT, 1811

Huldah CARPENTER and Lewis DARY, 1805

Hannah CARPENTER and Elisha BROWN, 1809

Ruth HOWLAND[2] (John[1])

Ruth HOWLAND[2] and Thomas CUSHMAN[3] (Mary Allerton[2]), 17 Nov. 1664, Plymouth
(MD 17:185)

Thomas CUSHMAN[3] and 2nd Abigail FULLER, 16 Oct. 1679, Rehoboth

NOTES

[1] p.206, This date of 7 Oct. 1661 is interesting as the records state their first child was born 5 Oct. 1661 (MD 2:207).

[2] p.207, Although the year of marriage is given as 1720 Bowman attributes son David, b. 17 Mar. 1717 (MD 3:72) to this second wife.

[3] p.213, Source: Totten, John R. Thacher/Thatcher Genealogy. 1910. New York Genealogical and Biographical Society.

[4] p.213, Source: Baxter, Joseph Nickerson. Memorial of the Baxter Family. 1879. Boston.

[5] p.215, Source: Dwight, Benjamin W. History of the Descendants of Elder John Strong of Northampton, Mass. 1871. 2 Vols. Albany NY.

[6] p.221, Thankful ( ) married 1st Watson Freeman, 18 Mar. 1762; 2nd Gideon Baty Sr., 23 Sept. 1777. (Blake Family. 1887. Boston.:35)

[7] p.223, The possible Mayflower descent of Abigail Fuller is given – (Tho.[3], Sam.[3], Matthew[2], Edw.[1]).

[8] p.224, The possible Mayflower descent of Lydia Cobb is given – (James[4], Rachel Soule[3], John[2]).

[9] p.227, Although not shown here his line of Mayflower descent is as follows – Shubael Fuller[4] (John[3], Sam.[2], Edw.[1]).

[10] p.228, Barnstable Marriages:68 later gives the date as 19 June.

[11] p.231, Mary Howland was the illegitimate daughter of Sarah Howland, the name of the father is not given.

[12] p.233, The first nine Brown marriages on this microfiche are duplicated at the beginning of micro #1 of the More family.

RICHARD MORE DESCENDANTS

Richard MORE[1] and 1st Christian HUNT, 20 Oct. 1636 (MD 13:84)[2]

Richard MORE[1] and 2nd Jane HOLLINGSWORTH, aft. Mar. 1676

Samuel MORE and Katherine MORE, 4 Feb. 1610/11, Shipton, Shropshire, Eng.[3]

Christian MORE[2] and Joshua CONANT, 31 Aug. 1676 (Salem VR)

Susanna MORE[2] (Richard[1])

Susanna MORE[2] and 1st Samuel DUTCH

Susanna MORE[2] and 2nd Richard HUTTON, betw. Mar.- Dec. 1694 (MD 3:200)

Susanna MORE[2] and 3rd John KNOWLTON, Int. 11 Apr. 1714 (MD 3:200)

Susanna DUTCH[3] and Benjamin KNOWLTON, 26 Dec. 1705, Beverly (Ipswich VR 2:262)

Benjamin KNOWLTON[4] (Susanna Dutch[3]) and Susanna POTTER, 28 Feb. 1738 (Ipswich 2:263,358)

Benjamin KNOWLTON[4] and 2nd Abigail DANE, Int. 22 Apr. 1756, Ipswich

Moses KNOWLTON and Abigail LUFKIN, 13 July 1806 (Ipswich VR)

Nehemiah KNOWLTON and 1st Elizabeth POTTER, 14 Nov. 1769, Ipswich

Nehemiah KNOWLTON and 2nd Susanna FELLOWS, 11 Oct. 1771 (Hamlet ch.rcds.)

Nehemiah KNOWLTON and 3rd Martha TILTON, 22 Nov. 1774 (Hamlet ch.rcds.)

Annis KNOWLTON[5] (Ben.[4]) and William FOSTER, 22 June 1797 (Hamilton ch.rcds.)

William FOSTER[6] (Annis KNowlton[5]) and Martha WOODBERRY, Int. 6 Dec. 1828, Hamilton

Ezra KNOWLTON[5] (Ben.[4]) and Abigail DODGE, 11 Feb. 1762 (Ipswich VR)

Emma KNOWLTON[6] (Ezra[5]) and Abraham HOBBS, 20 Oct. 1796 (Hamilton VR)

Hepsibah KNOWLTON[5] (Ben.[4]) and Jonas CUMMINGS, 16 Aug. 1787 (Ipswich VR)

Malachi KNOWLTON[5] (Ben.[4]) and Abigail PATCH, Int. 19 May 1781, Ipswich

Susanna KNOWLTON[5] (Ben.[4]) and Nathaniel POLAND, c1768

Elizabeth KNOWLTON[4] (Susanna Dutch[3]) and Nathan BROWN, Int. 19 Aug. 1737 (Ipswich VR 2:67,263)

Susanna KNOWLTON[4] (Susanna Dutch[3]) and Josiah DODGE, 30 Mar. 1738/39 (Knowlton Gen.:37)

NOTES

[1] p.235, The first three lines of this microfiche contain data on the

Howland family. See <12>, p.234.

    <2> p.235, It has since been established that Hunter, not Hunt, was her maiden name (TAG 40:77).

    <3> p.235, Although Bowman does not give the relationship here, Katherine More was the mother of Richard More. See NEHGR 114:163; 124:85.

DEGORY PRIEST DESCENDANTS

Degory PRIEST[1] and Sarah (ALLERTON) Vincent, 4 Nov. 1611, Leyden, Holland (MD 7:129)

Sarah ALLERTON and 3rd Godbert GODBERTSON, 13 Nov. 1621 (MD 1:149)

Mary PRIEST[2] (Degory[1])

Mary PRIEST[2] and Phineas PRATT

Aaron PRATT[3] and 1st Sarah PRATT, c1684

Aaron PRATT[3] and 2nd Sarah (WRIGHT) Cummings, 4 Sept. 1707 (Charlestown VR)

Sarah WRIGHT and Abraham CUMMINGS, 28 Feb. 1687 (Woburn VR:66,311)

Edward LEARNED and Sarah (FULLER) Pratt, 25 Aug. 1748 (Newton VR:328)

Henry PRATT and Elizabeth MURDOCK, 2 Oct. 1769 (Newton VR:358)

Henry PRATT[4] (Aaron[3]) and Sarah FULLER, 30 Sept. 1741 (Newton VR:358)

Phineas PRATT[4] (Aaron[3]) and Sarah LINCOLN, 28 July 1731 (Hingham VR)

Gerard PRATT[5] (Phineas[4]) and Dorcas ASHLEY, 19 July 1764

Rhoda PRATT[6] (Gerard[5]) and Col. James BARLOW, c1794/95

Margaret BARLOW[7] (Rhoda Pratt[6]) and Lyman ROOT, Int. 6 Dec. 1814 (Granville VR:98)

Tabitha PRATT[6] (Gerard[5]) and Azariah BANCROFT, poss. 17 Nov. 1791 (Granville VR)

John PRATT[3] and Ann BARKER, c1664

Ebenezer PRATT[4] (John[3]) and Mehitable MUDGE (MD 3:8)

Joseph PRATT[3] and Dorcas FOLGER, 12 Feb. 1674/75

Mary PRATT[3] and John SWAN, 1 Mar. 1655 (Cambridge VR 2:314,380)

Ebenezer SWAN[4] (Mary Pratt[3]) and Elizabeth BRUCE, c1698 (Woburn VR:36,267)

Ebenezer SWAN[5] (Eben.[4]) and Bathsheba GRANT, c1728

Joshua SWAN[6] (Eben.[5]) and Sarah CUTTER, poss. 20 July 1762

Mercy SWAN[4] (Mary Pratt[3]) and John PERRY, 19 Dec. 1706, Watertown

James PERRY[5] (Mercy Swan[4]) and Lydia TUFTS, 14 Oct. 1742, Charlestown (Hist. Arlington, Mass.<1880>:282)

Lydia TUFTS and poss. 2nd Josiah MIXER, 1773 (Hist. Arlington:282)

Elizabeth PERRY[6] (James[5]) and John TUFTS, 19 May 1778, Medford

James PERRY[6] (James[5]) and Sarah ADAMS, 19 Oct. 1773 (Cambridge VR)

Lydia PERRY[7] (James[6]) and Samuel WHITTEMORE, 19 July 1796 (Cambridge VR)

Lydia PERRY^6 (James^5) and Ephraim FROST, 6 June 1765 (Cambridge VR)

Mercy PERRY^6 (James^5) and William HILL, 3 Oct. 1767 (Cambridge VR)

James HILL^7 (Mercy Perry^6) and Anna ADAMS, 11 Oct. 1796 (Cambridge VR)

Ruth PERRY^6 (James^5) and John ADAMS, 2 Dec. 1773 (Cambridge VR)

Mercy PRATT^3 and Jeremiah HOLMAN

Jeremiah HOLMAN and Anna PRIEST, 23 Mar. 1720/21 (Lancaster VR:18)

Peter PRATT^3 and Elizabeth GRISWOLD, 5 Aug. 1679

Peter PRATT^4 (Peter^3) and Mehitable WATRONS, 9 Sept. 1709

Samuel PRATT^3 and Mary BARKER

Mary BARKER and 2nd Francis COOMBS^3 (Sarah Priest^2), 1678 (MD 3:128)

Mary BARKER and 3rd David WOOD, 5 Mar. 1684/85, Middleboro (MD 1:219)

Samuel PRATT and Wiboree BUMPUS, 18 Mar. 1740/41, Middleboro (MD 15:219)

Samuel PRATT^4 (Sam.^{3}) and Hannah MILLER, c1696 (MD 2:42)

Sarah PRATT^5 (Sam.^{4}) and Ebenezer BARROWS^5 (Mercy Coombs^4, Francis^3, Sarah Priest^2),
    29 Feb. 1727/28, Middleboro (MD 5:39)

John PRATT^5 (Sam.^{4}) and Elizabeth TURNER^4 (Hannah Hatch^3, Mary Doty^2)

Phineas PRATT^5 (Sam.^{4}) and Sarah WHITE, 5 Nov. 1741, Middleboro (MD 15:219)

Samuel PRATT^5 (Sam.^{4}) and Jerusha CONANT^6 (Eliz. Washburn^5, Tho.^{4}, Eliz. Mitchell^3,
    Jane Cooke^2), c1724

Sarah PRIEST^2 (Degory^1)

Sarah PRIEST^2 and John COOMBS

Joshua COOMBS and ELizabeth PRATT, 10 Sept. 1729 (Middleboro VR 1:59)

Benjamin COOMBS and Priscilla BENSON, 22 Oct. 1772 (Middleboro VR 4:151)

Asa COOMBS and Abigail CUSHMAN, 23 June 1802 (Middleboro VR 8:2)

Elizabeth COMBES and Eleazer CUSHMAN^3 (Mary Allerton^2), 12 Jan. 1687/88

Francis COOMBS^3 and 1st Deborah MORTON, c1672 (MD 1:221)

Francis COOMBS^3 and 2nd Mary (BARKER) Pratt (see above)

John COMBES and Elizabeth ( ) BARLOW, 24 Feb. 1661, Boston (Rcd.comm.9:82)

John COMBES and Elizabeth PICKERING, 9 Oct. 1740 (Boston rcd.comm.28:331)

John COOMBS and Elizabeth BENNET, 12 Apr. 1716 (Boston rcd.comm.28:62)

John COMB and Dorothy DAVIS, Int. 4 Mar. 1711, Boston (Rcd.comm.28:91)

John COOMBS and Susanna STRONG, 28 July 1718 (Boston rcd.comm.28:74)

Micro #3 of 3

Francis COOMBS^4 (Francis^3) and Nathan HOWLAND^3 (Isaac^2), c1712

Deborah COOMBS^4 (Francis^3) and Ralph JONES^4 (Mary Fuller^3, Matthew^2, Edw.^{1}),
   c1695 (MD 6:140)

Lydia COOMBS^4 (Francis^3) and John MILLER, 12 Feb. 1701/02, Middleboro (MD 1:220)

Francis MILLER^5 (Lydia Coombs^4) and Experience (HAWES^4) Sprout (Desire Gorham^3,
   Desire Howland^2), 22 Nov. 1731, Middleboro (MD 13:249)

Experience HAWES^4 and 1st Ebenezer SPROUT^3 (Eliz. Samson^2), 1 Mar. 1703/04,
   (Yarmouth VR)

David MILLER^5 (Lydia Coombs^4) and Susanna HOLMES, 31 Oct. 1728, Middleboro (MD 5:40)

John MILLER^5 (Lydia Coombs^4) and Priscilla BENNETT^4 (Prisc. Howland^3, Isaac^2),
   30 Oct. 1735, Middleboro (MD 13:251)

John MILLER^6 (John^5) and Zilpah TINKHAM^5 (John^4, Ephraim^3, Mary Brown^2), 6 Sept.
   1764, Middleboro (MD 24:185)

Mercy COOMBS^4 (Francis^3) and Samuel BARROWS, c1701 (MD 2:105)

Coombs BARROWS^5 (Mercy Coombs^4) and 1st Joanna SMITH, 15 May 1729, Middleboro
   (MD 8:250)

Coombs BARROWS^5 and 2nd Mary DWELLEY, 29 May 1732, Middleboro (MD 9:47)

Ebenezer BARROWS^5 (Mercy Coombs^4) and Sarah PRATT^5 (Sam.$^{4-3}$, Mary Priest^2),
   29 Feb. 1727/28, Middleboro (MD 5:39)

Deborah BARROWS^6 (Eben.^{5}) and Eleazer RICHMOND^6 (Josiah^5, Edw.^{4}, Abigail Rogers^3,
   John^2) (Richmond Gen.:52)

Hannah BARROWS^6 (Eben.^{5}) and Israel DEAN, 1 Jan. 1750/51, Middleboro (MD 18:84)

Mercy BARROWS^6 (Eben.^{5}) and Benjamin DEAN, Int. 14 Oct. 1749 (Middleboro VR 2:1:52)

Gideon DEAN^7 (Hannah Barrows^6) and Mary VICKERY

John BARROWS^6 (Eben.^{5}) and Sarah MORTON^6 (Deborah^5, Eben. Morton^4, Mary Ring^3,
   Deborah Hopkins^2), 16 Nov. 1769 (Middleboro VR 4:8)

Elisha BARROWS^7 (John^6) and Elizabeth ALLEN

Mercy BARROWS^6 (Eben.^{5}) and Benjamin DEAN, 16 Nov. 1749, Middleboro (MD 18:83)

Ruth COOMBS^4 (Francis^3) and Ebenezer BENNET, 26 Aug. 1702, Middleboro (MD 2:43)

Ebenezer BENNET and 2nd Sarah STETSON, 23 Apr. 1719, Scituate (MD 10:75)

Cornelius BENNET^5 (Ruth Coombs^4) and Ruth GORHAM^4 (Shubael^3, Desire Howland^2),
   12 Jan. 1731/32 (Barnstable VR 2:335)

Batchelor BENNET^6 (Cornelius^5) and Mary SAMPSON

Sally BENNET^6 (Cornelius^5) and Ebenezer WOOD, Int. 1 Aug. 1767 (Middleboro VR 2:215)

Gorham WOOD^7 (Sally Bennet^6) and Elizabeth SPARROW^7 (Edw.^{6}, Jerusha Bradford^5,
   Wm.$^{4-3-2}$), 28 Nov. 1798 (Middleboro VR 8:1)

THOMAS ROGERS DESCENDANTS

John ROGERS[2] (Thomas[1])

John ROGERS[2] and Ann CHURCHMAN, 16 Apr. 1639 (MD 13:85)

Abigail ROGERS[3] and John RICHMOND, c1662

Abigail RICHMOND[4] (Abigail Rogers[3]) and Nathan WALKER

Ebenezer RICHMOND[4] (Abigail Rogers[3]) and Anna SPROAT[3] (Eliz. Samson[2]), c1700
(MD 2:43)

Anna RICHMOND[5] (Eben.[4]) and Caleb COWING, 3 May 1734, Middleboro (MD 13:250)

James COWING[6] (Anna Richmond[5]) and 1st Mary COTTLE, 29 Dec. 1763 (Rochester VR2:53)

James COWING[6] and 2nd Sarah RANDALL, 31 Dec. 1780 (Rochester VR 3:199)

Eunice COWING[7] (James[6]) and Caleb BROWN

John Philo COWING[7] (James[6]) and Elizabeth MALAY, 1 Jan. 1833, Seneca NY

Edward RICHMOND[4] (Abigail Rogers[3]) and 2nd poss. Rebecca THURSTON

Nathaniel RICHMOND[5] (Edw.[4]) and Alice HACKET, 2 Nov. 1732, Middleboro (MD 9:47)

John RICHMOND[4] (Abigail Rogers[3]) and Hannah OTIS, 28 Nov. 1709, Scituate (MD 8:205)

Stephen RICHMOND[5] (John[4]) and Silence ROBINSON

Abiel RICHMOND[6] (Stephen[5]) and Joanna ORCUTT (Richmond Gen.:62)

Silence RICHMOND[7] (Abiel[6]) and 1st Wellman FROST (Richmond Gen.:62,149)

Silence RICHMOND[7] and 2nd Capt. Nathaniel HAMBLIN (Richmond Gen.:62,149)

Joanna RICHMOND[7] (Abiel[6]) and Job STAPLES

Joseph RICHMOND[4] (Abigail Rogers[3]) and Mary ANDREWS, 26 June 1685 (Taunton VR 2:22)

John GOODING and Deborah BARNES, Int. 9 Mar. 1805 (Plymouth VR 2:182)

Benjamin B. GOODING and Harriet GOODWIN, Int. 15 May 1841 (Plymouth VR 3:3)

Christopher RICHMOND[5] (Jos.[4]) and 1st Phebe WILLIAMS, c1716 (MD 6:179)

Christopher RICHMOND[5] and 2nd Susanna BARDEN, 15 Nov. 1750, Middleboro (MD 18:84)

Eliakim RICHMOND[6] (Christopher[5]) and Sarah HACKETT[5] (Lydia Thomas[4], Lydia Howland[3],
John[2]), poss. 19 Nov. 1747

Judith RICHMOND[7] (Eliakim[6]) and Benjamin RHOADES, c1780

Samuel RICHMOND[4] (Abigail Rogers[3]) and 1st Mehitable ANDREWS, 20 Dec. 1694

Samuel RICHMOND[4] and 2nd Elizabeth (KING) Hall

Lydia RICHMOND[5] (Sam.[4]) and Samuel THOMAS, 9 June 1732, Middleboro (MD 9:47)

Peter WALKER[5] (Sarah Richmond[4], Abigail Rogers[3]) and Helen BAYLIES

Elnathan WALKER^5 (Sarah Richmond^4) and 1st Hannah CROSSMAN, 2nd Bethiah TISDALE,
    3rd Phebe (LEONARD) King

James WALKER^5 (Sarah Richmond^4, Abigail Rogers^3) and Mary PITTS

Sarah WALKER^5 (Sarah Richmond^4) and Thomas LEONARD, 23 June 1726 (Raynham VR 1:22)

Paul LEONARD^6 (Sarah Walker^5) and Mary RIDER^7 (Jos.^{6}, Mary Southworth^5, Desire
    Gray^4, Mary Winslow^3, Mary Chilton^2), 11 Jan. 1759, Plymouth (Raynham VR)

Anna ROGERS^3 and 1st John TISDALE, 23 Nov. 1664, Taunton (MD 19:108)

Anna ROGERS^3 and 2nd Thomas TERRY, aft. 5 Mar. 1677/78

Anna ROGERS^3 and 3rd Samuel WILLIAMS, aft. Oct. 1691

Abigail TISDALE^4 (Anna Rogers^3) and William MAKEPEACE

Abigail MAKEPEACE^5 (Abigail Tisdale^4) and Emanuel WILLIAMS, c1703 (Gen.Reg.57:75)

Anne WILLIAMS^6 (Abigail Makepeace^5) and William BARNEY (Gen.Reg.57:76)

Gershom WILLIAMS^6 (Abigail Makepeace^5) and Abigail WALDRON, 2 Aug. 1729 (Gen.
    Reg.57:76)

David WILLIAMS^7 (Gershom^6) and Lois WEBSTER, Int. 20 Nov. 1770 (Dighton VR)

John WILLIAMS^6 (Abigail Makepeace^5) and Elizabeth CASWELL, c1727

Lydia WILLIAMS^6 (Abigail Makepeace^5) and John TERRY, poss. 10 Feb. 1731/32
    (Gen.Reg.57:76,77)

Job TERRY^7 (Lydia Williams^6) and Rebecca WINSLOW

Abner WINSLOW and Rebecca HATHAWAY, 1759

Martha WINSLOW and Ephraim JONES

Philip WINSLOW and Lucy CHASE

John WINSLOW and Keziah HINDS

Hannah WINSLOW and Silas COLLINS

Welthea TERRY^8 (Job^7) and Hezekiah WILSON, poss. 4 Oct. 1801

Job Terry WILSON^9 (Welthea Terry^8) and Deborah DURFEE, 2 July 1829, Fall River[1]

Cory DURFEE and Betsey HATHAWAY, 24 Apr. 1808, Fall River[1]

James H. WILSON^{10} (Job^9) and 2nd Abbie M. BOWEN, 28 Sept. 1875, Fall River
    (Mass. VR 271:107)

Job TERRY^8 (Job^7) and Ruth STRANGE

Amy TERRY^8 (Job^7) and Alonzo DAVENPORT

Abigail TERRY^8 (Job^7) and Thomas EVANS

Benjamin TERRY^4 (Anna Rogers^3) and Margaret HOLLOWAY

Benjamin TERRY^5 (Ben.^{4}) and Joanna POPE, 15 Dec. 1741, poss. Dartmouth

Elnathan POPE and Margaret POPE, 14 Mar. 1/15/16 (Dartmouth VR 1:364)

Thomas TERRY^6 (Ben.^{5}) and Sarah WINSLOW, 17 Nov. 1771 (Dartmouth VR 2:495,560)

Sarah TERRY^5 (Ben.^{4}) and Barnabas WINSLOW^4 (Geo.^{3}, Job^2, Kenelm^1), poss. 6 July
    1761 (Winslow Mem.1:234,235)

Elizabeth ROGERS^3 and Nathaniel WILLIAMS, 17 Nov. 1668

Elizabeth WILLIAMS^4 (Eliz. Rogers^3) and John MACOMBER, 17 Mar. 1707 (Macomber
    Gen.:12,13)

John MACOMBER and 2nd Lydia (RING) Williams, 12 July 1733 (Macomber Gen.:12,13)

James MACOMBER^5 (Eliz. Williams^4) and Rachel DRAKE, 4 Feb. 1747 (Macomber Gen.:17)

John MACOMBER^5 (Eliz. Williams^4) and Elizabeth PHINNEY, poss. 27 Jan. 1746
    (Macomber Gen.:17)

Elizabeth MACOMBER^6 (John^5) and Luke ELLIS^5 (Martha Tinkham^4, John^3, Mary Brown^2),
    11 Mar. 1784 (Dartmouth VR)

Josiah MACOMBER^5 (Eliz. Williams^4) and poss. Ruth PAUL

Elizabeth MACOMBER^6 (Josiah^5) and Samuel HASKELL

Abiel MACOMBER^6 (Josiah^5) and Phebe DEAN

Rebecca MACOMBER^6 (Josiah^5) and Joseph GOODING

John WILLIAMS^4 (Eliz. Rogers^3) and Hannah ROBINSON, c1701/02

Experience WILLIAMS^5 (John^4) and Nathan HODGES, 12 Dec. 1728, Taunton

Nathaniel WILLIAMS^5 (John^4) and Sarah DEAN

Silas WILLIAMS^5 (John^4) and 1st Mary DUNHAM, 19 July 1737

Silas WILLIAMS^5 and 2nd Susanna (PRATT) Richards/Rickard, 23 Oct. 1760

Simeon WILLIAMS^5 (John^4) and 1st Zipporah CRANE, 26 Aug. 1742 (Hodges Fam.:115)

Simeon WILLIAMS^5 and 2nd Waitstill HODGES, c1750 (Hodges Fam.<1896>:115)

Timothy WILLIAMS^5 (John^4) and Elizabeth BRETTUN, 18 Jan. 1736/37, Raynham (Gen.
    Reg.54:16)

Lemuel WILLIAMS^6 (Timothy^5) and Anna HILTON, poss. 28 Apr. 1777 (Wiscassett ME VR)

Elizabeth WILLIAMS^7 (Lemuel^6) and Ephraim SAWYER

William WILLIAMS^7 (Lemuel^6) and Amy GRAY, 22 Dec. 1807 (Woolwich VR)

Nathaniel WILLIAMS^4 (Eliz. Rogers^3) and   Lydia KING, poss. 2 Jan. 1709/10

Lydia KING and 2nd John MACOMBER, 12 July 1733 (NEHGR 53:436)

Lydia WILLIAMS^5 (Nath.^{4}) and 1st Ichabod KEITH, 17 Oct. 1734 (Raynham VR 1:19)

Lydia WILLIAMS^5 and 2nd Dr. Nathaniel WHITE

Lydia WILLIAMS^5 and 3rd Dr. David JONES, 24 Apr. 1759

Judith WILLIAMS^5 (Nath.^{4}) and Elijah MACOMBER^5 (Eliz. Williams^4, Eliz. Rogers^3, John^2)

Bethiah WILLIAMS^5 (Nath.^{4}) and Noah WILLIAMS

Edmund WILLIAMS^5 (Nath.^{4}) and 1st Lydia CRANE, 6 Nov. 1737, Raynham (Gen.Reg.54:16)

Edmund WILLIAMS^5 and 2nd Mary ( ) HARVEY, 20 Aug. 1781, Bridgewater

Edmund WILLIAMS^5 and 3rd Abia ATWOOD, 25 May 1790

Edmund WILLIAMS^6 (Edmund^5) and Susanna WILLIAMS, 28 Apr. 1768, Raynham (NEHGR 55:46)

Sarah WILLIAMS^6 (Edmund^5) and Jonathan PADELFORD, c1775

Anna PADELFORD^7 (Sarah Williams^5) and Ebenezer WILLIAMS, poss. 23 Feb. 1797

Ebenezer WILLIAMS^8 (Anna Padelford^7) and Caroline BRIGGS

Sarah PADELFORD^7 (Sarah Williams^6) and Reuben PADELFORD

Betsey PADELFORD^7 (Sarah Williams^6) and John PADELFORD

Lydia PADELFORD^7 (Sarah Williams^6) and Nathan CARPENTER, c1801 (Carpenter Mem.217,371)

Elizabeth WILLIAMS^5 (Nath.^{4}) and Henry PITTS Jr., 18 May 1742

Nathaniel WILLIAMS^5 (Nath.^{4}) and Mary ARTHERTON, 12 May 1737, Raynham (VR 1:36)

Elizabeth WILLIAMS^6 (Nath.^{5}) and Gilbert HATHAWAY^6 (Welthea Gilbert^5, Hannah Bradford^4, Sam.^{3}, Wm.^{2})

Hannah WILLIAMS^6 (Nath.^{5}) and Samuel ALDEN^5 (Sam.^{4}, Jos.$^{3-2}$), poss. 1 Nov. 1763

John WILLIAMS^6 (Nath.^{5}) and Silence HALL, Int. 12 Mar. 1780, Raynham (VR 1:249)

Joshua WILLIAMS^6 (Nath.^{5}) and Ruth BASS

Judith WILLIAMS^6 (Nath.^{5}) and Job DEAN, poss. Dec. 1772

Mary WILLIAMS^6 (Nath.^{5}) and Nathaniel HALL, poss. 16 Dec. 1756

Nathaniel WILLIAMS^6 (Nath.^{5}) and Jemima HALL, poss. 24 Aug. 1769, Raynham

Phebe WILLIAMS^6 (Nath.^{5}) and Amos WADE, poss. 7 Feb. 2758

Seth WILLIAMS^6 (Nath.^{5}) and Mary SNOW

John ROGERS^3 and 1st Elizabeth PABODIE^3 (Eliz. Alden^2), Nov. 1666, Duxbury (MD 8:232)

John ROGERS^3 and 2nd Hannah (HOBART) Browne, poss. 21 Oct. 1679

John ROGERS^3 and 3rd Marah (COBHAM) Browning

Hannah ROGERS^4 (John^3) and Samuel BRADFORD^3 (Wm.^{2})

Ruth ROGERS^4 (John^3) and James BENNET, 12 July 1694 (Warren RI VR 1:4)

Elizabeth ROGERS^4 (John^3) and Silvester RICHMOND, c1693

Ruth RICHMOND^5 (Eliz. Rogers^4) and Ephraim ATWOOD

Silvester RICHMOND^5 (Eliz. Rogers^4) and Elizabeth TALBOT

William RICHMOND[5] (Eliz. Rogers[4]) and Anna GRAY[5] (Anna Little[4], Ephraim[3], Anna Warren[2])

Sarah ROGERS[4] (John[3]) and Nathaniel SEARLE

Joseph ROGERS[2] (Thomas[1])

Joseph ROGERS and Sarah HARDING, 13 Apr. 1739, Eastham (VR:129)

Henry ROGERS and Deborah NICKERSON, Int. 7 July 1761, Eastham (MD 27:186)

Elizabeth ROGERS[3] and Jonathan HIGGINS, 9 Jan. 1660, Eastham (MD 17:201)

Jonathan HIGGINS and 2nd Hannah ROGERS[3] (Joseph[2])

Joseph HIGGINS and Mercy REMICK, Int. 31 Jan. 1718/19, Eastham (MD 28:109)

Hannah HIGGINS[4] (Eliz. Rogers[3]) and Nicholas PAINE[4] (Mary Snow[3], Constance Hopkins[2]), c1699 (MD 4:33)

Jonathan HIGGINS[4] (Eliz. Rogers[3]) and Lydia (SPARROW) Freeman, c1693 (Higgins Gen.:67)

Samuel HIGGINS[5] (Jonathan[4]) and Mehitable PHINNEY[5] (Eben.[4], Mary Rogers[3], Jos.[2]), 9 Oct. 1718, Barnstable (MD 14:227)

Samuel HIGGINS[6] (Sam.[5]) and Elizabeth BASSETT, 1 Mar. 1759

Samuel HIGGINS[6] and 2nd Eunice YOUNG, 12 Sept. 1795

Ruth HIGGINS[5] (Jos.[4], Eliz. Rogers[3]) and 1st Ebenezer STEWARD, 11 Oct. 1716 (Higgins Gen.:71,598)

Ruth HIGGINS[5] and 2nd James ELDREDGE, c1732 (MD 17:88)

Rebecca ELDREDGE[6] (Ruth Higgins[5]) and Cyrenus COLLINS, 13 July 1756, Chatham (MD 7:142)

Solomon COLLINS[7] (Rebecca Eldredge[6]) and Jerusha RYDER, c1787 (MD 14:150)

Jerusha COLLINS[8] (Solomon[7]) and 2nd William Blake FOSS, Int. 1819, Roxbury

Eliza Abbie FOSS[9] (Jerusha Collins[8]) and Charles Smith CLARK

Cyrena Shed FOSS[9] (Jerusha Collins[8]) and Abner L. COLBEY, 4 July 1847, Boston

George Walter CLARK[10] (Eliza A. Foss[9]) and Kathrine Ellen McKINNON, poss. 1 Oct. 1881, Gloucester

Hannah ROGERS[3] and Jonathan HIGGINS, c1679 (MD 6:15)

Jemima HIGGINS[4] (Hannah Rogers[3]) and John MULFORD, 1 Nov. 1699, Eastham (MD 8:245)

Thankful HURLBUT and Jacob HURD Jr., 28 Feb. 1746, Chatham CT [2]

Jacob HURD 3d and Abigail CARY, Oct. 1782 [2]

Rebecca HIGGINS and Jacob HURD, 11 Aug. 1715, Eastham (MD 15:55)

Mary HIGGINS^4 (Hannah Rogers^3) and James YOUNG, 12 Feb. 1706/07, Eastham (MD 6:205)

Mary YOUNG^5 (Mary Higgins^4) and 1st Reuben OKILLEY, 28 May 1734 (Truro VR:8)

Mary YOUNG^5 and 2nd Robert NEWCOMB^5 (Mercy Oldham^4, Mercy Sprout^3, Eliz. Samson^2),
    30 Nov. 1744 (Truro VR:50)

Phebe YOUNG^5 (Mary Higgins^4) and 1st Judah DYER, 18 Feb. 1724/25 (Truro VR:55)

Phebe YOUNG^5 and 2nd Nathaniel ATWOOD, aft. June 1742

James ROGERS^3 and Mary PAINE^4 (Mary Snow^3, Constance Hopkins^2), 11 Jan. 1670,
    Eastham (MD 5:195)

Abigail ROGERS^4 (James^3) and John YATES, 11 Jan. 1698/99, Eastham (MD 9:12)

Experience YATES^5 (Abigail Rogers^4) and Asa MAYO^6 (Theophilus^5, Tho.^{4}, Hannah
    Prence^3, Patience Brewster^2), Int. 4 Sept. 1731, Harwich (MD 13:59)

James ROGERS^4 (James^3) and Susanna TRACY, 17 Feb. 1697/98, Eastham (MD 9:11)

Abigail ROGERS^5 (James^4) and Zebulon YOUNG, 23 Feb. 1748, Eastham (VR:153)

Zebulon YOUNG Jr. and Elizabeth HIGGINS, 26 Jan. 1758, Eastham (VR:169)

James ROGERS^5 (James^4) and Hannah GODFREY^6 (Mercy Mayo^5, Tho.^{4}, Hannah Prence^3,
    Patience Brewster^2), 21 May 1730, Chatham (MD 17:30)

James ROGERS^6 (James^5) and Elizabeth LINNELL, 25 Oct. 1759, Eastham (VR:171)

Jonathan ROGERS^6 (James^5) and Hannah MAYO, 19 Dec. 1776, Orleans

Hannah ROGERS^7 (Jonathan^6) and John ELLIS, 31 Dec. 1801 (Dennis VR 1:181)

Timothy ROGERS^7 (Jonathan^6) and Reliance COBB, poss. 24 June 1814

Albert C. ROGERS^8 (Timothy^7) and Julia A.F. SMALL

Timothy Otis ROGERS^9 (Albert^8) and Harriet Matilda NICKERSON, 19 Dec. 1883,
    Boston (Mass VR 345:216)

Prince ROGERS^6 (James^5) and Susanna SNOW, 8 Apr. 1766, Eastham (VR 6:28)

Samuel ROGERS^6 (James^5) and 1st Deborah BASSET, 12 Nov. 1761, Eastham (MD 31:173)

Mary ROGERS^5 (James^4) and Jacob DAVIS, Int. 24 May 1733, Eastham (VR:219)

Susanna ROGERS^5 (James^4) and Judah ROGERS^5 (Judah^4, John^3, Jos.^{2}), 4 June 1741,
    Eastham (VR:136)

Thomas ROGERS^5 (James^4) and Rebecca HIGGINS^5 (James^4, Eliz. Rogers^3, Jos.^{2}),
    2 Dec. 1736, Eastham (MD 17:145)

Mary ROGERS^4 (James^3) and poss. Samuel COLE Jr.

John ROGERS^3 and Elizabeth TWINING, 19 Aug. 1669, Eastham (MD 8:90)

Jonathan ROGERS^5 (John$^{4-3}$) and Elizabeth COOKE, 18 Jan. 1727/28 (Eastham VR:14)

Martha ROGERS^5 (Jos.^{4}, John^3) and Daniel COLE, Int. 14 Nov. 1730, Eastham (VR:216)

Henry ROGERS and Deborah NICKERSON, Int. 7 July 1761 (Eastham VR:173)

Josiah ROGERS and Abigail AREY, 12 Jan. 1769, Eastham

Eleazer ROGERS^4 (John^3) and Martha YOUNG, 22 Aug. 1712, Eastham (MD 7:14)

Ensign ROGERS^5 (Eleazer^4) and Temperance NICKERSON, 13 Jan. 1753, Chatham
    (MD 13:28)$^{\langle 3 \rangle}$

Eleazer ROGERS^5 (Eleazer^4) and Ruth HIGGINS, 13 Nov. 1747, Eastham (MD 24:138)$^{\langle 4 \rangle}$

Moses ROGERS^5 (Eleazer^4) and Elizabeth SMITH, 10 Nov. 1748, Chatham (MD 4:182)

Jonathan ROGERS and Phebe SHEPARD, 12 May 1785, Holden

Abner ROGERS^6 (Moses^5) and Priscilla PAINE, 27 Mar. 1778, Harwich

Abner ROGERS and Dorothy NICKOLS, 29 Sept. 1782 (Holden VR:172,163)

Micro #6 of 10

Nathan ROGERS^7 (Abner^6) and 1st Phebe BOYNTON, 16 Apr. 1801 (Holden VR:107,172)

Nathan ROGERS^7 and 2nd Mary Cheney MOORE, 22 May 1816 (Holden VR:160,173)

Nathan ROGERS^7 and poss. 3rd Sally BLAIR, Int. 20 Aug. 1829 (Holden VR:105,173)

Hannah ROGERS^4 (John^3) and James SMITH, 19 Feb. 1712/13, Eastham (MD 5:197)

John ROGERS^4 (John^3) and 1st Priscilla HAMLIN, 23 Apr. 1696, Eastham (MD 9:10)

John ROGERS^4 and 2nd Sarah (BASSETT) Nickerson

Jonathan ROGERS^5 (John^4) and Elizabeth COOK^5 (Richard^4, Deborah Hopkins^3, Gyles^2),
    18 Jan. 1727/28, Eastham (MD 15:69)

Benjamin ROGERS^5 (John^4) and Phebe HARDING^5 (Hannah Rogers^4, Tho.^{3}, Joseph^2),
    13 Oct. 1732, Plymouth (MD 14:74)

Benjamin ROGERS^6 (Ben.^{5}) and 1st Mehitable FAY, 10 Sept. 1760 (Hardwick VR:172,234)

Benjamin ROGERS^6 and 2nd Temperance PHINNEY, 5 Apr. 1763 (Hardwick VR:173,234)

Hannah ROGERS^6 (Ben.^{5}) and Ichabod WATERMAN^6 (Josiah^5, Mary Cushman^4, Isaac^3,
    Mary Allerton^2), 15 Dec. 1757 (Kingston Ch.rcds.)

Ebenezer ROGERS^5 (John^4) and Hannah COOK^5 (Richard^4, Deborah Hopkins^3, Gyles^2),
    24 Mar. 1719/20, Eastham (MD 15:144)

Joshua ROGERS^6 (Eben.^{5}) and Elizabeth COLE, Int. 17 Mar. 1743, Harwich (MD 25:60)

Joshua ROGERS^7 (Joshua^6) and Mercy HIGGINS, Int. 26 Oct. 1771, poss. Harwich

Joshua ROGERS^8 (Joshua^7) and Deborah YOUNG, 5 Mar. 1795, Eastham

Zenas ROGERS^8 (Joshua^7) and Polly HARDING

Zenas ROGERS^9 (Zenas^8) and Caroline NICKERSON

Zaccheus ROGERS^6 (Eben.^{5}) and Elizabeth KING, 5 Jan. 1743, Harwich (MD 25:64)

Richard ROGERS^6 (Eben.^{5}) and Sarah HIGGINS^6 (Ruth Twining^5, Ruth Cole^4, Ruth
    Snow^3, Constance Hopkins^2), 26 Feb. 1746/47, Eastham (MD 28:83)

Priscilla ROGERS^5 (John^4) and Reuben NICKERSON

Joseph ROGERS[4] (John[3]) and 1st Mercy CRISP, 13 Oct. 1703, Eastham (MD 8:91)

Joseph ROGERS[4] and 2nd Sarah HARDING, 13 Apr. 1739, Eastham (VR:129)

Martha ROGERS[5] (Jos.[4]) and Daniel COLE, 10 Dec. 1730, Eastham (MD 17:33)

Crisp ROGERS[5] (Jos.[4]) and Mary YATES, 22 Feb. 1727/28, Harwich (MD 8:218)

Joseph ROGERS[6] (Crisp[5]) and Abigail TWINING[6] (Wm.[5], Ruth Cole[4], Ruth Snow[3], Constance Hopkins[2]), 6 Feb. 1749, Eastham (VR:155)

Apphia ROGERS and Ebenezer HARDING, 24 Dec. 1772 (Orleans Ch.rcds.)

Elkanah ROGERS[5] (Jos.[4]) and 1st Reliance YATES, 18 Feb. 1730/31, Harwich (MD 11:175)

Elkanah ROGERS[5] and 2nd Mercy (GODFREY[6]) Burges (Mercy Mayo[5], Tho.[4], Hannah Prence[3], Patience Brewster[2]), Int. 25 June 1748, Eastham (MD 28:82)

Reliance ROGERS[6] (Elkanah[5]) and Thomas PAINE, 20 Feb. 1770, Eastham (VR 6:12)

Joshua ROGERS[7] (Elkanah[6]) and Sarah REED, Int. 6 Oct. 1817, Hardwick

Mercy GODFREY and 1st Ebenezer BURGESS, Int. 22 Feb. 1734/35, Yarmouth

Jonathan GODFREY and Mercy MAYO, 30 Oct. 1707, Eastham (MD 5:195)

Elkanah ROGERS[6] (Elkanah[5]) and Tamsin SNOW[6] (Jesse[5], Micajah[4], Stephen[3], Constance Hopkins[2]), Int. 9 Mar. 1782 (Eastham VR 12:12)

Josiah ROGERS[6] (Elkanah[5]) and Abigail AREY, 12 Jan. 1769 (Eastham VR 6:43)

Zenas ROGERS[7] (Josiah[6]) and Sarah MAYO, 18 Dec. 1794, Eastham (MD 33:133)

Judah ROGERS[4] (John[3]) and Patience LUMBART, 6 Apr. 1704, Barnstable (MD 14:87)

Mary ROGERS[5] (Judah[4]) and Gershom COLE[5] (Jos.[4], Ruth Snow[3], Constance Hopkins[2]), Int. 3 Jan. 1729/30 (Eastham VR:215)

Patience ROGERS[5] (Judah[4]) and Isaac MAYO, Int. 6 May 1732, Eastham (MD 28:175)

Judah ROGERS[5] (Judah[4]) and Patience COLE[5] (Jos.[4], Ruth Snow[3], Constance Hopkins[2]), 12 Dec. 1728, Eastham (MD 16:147)

Judah ROGERS and Susanna ROGERS, 4 June 1741, Eastham (MD 19:186)

Judah ROGERS and Lois YOUNG, 24 Nov. 1743, Eastham (MD 20:156)

Judah ROGERS and Elizabeth ( ) NICKERSON, 29 Aug. 1751, Eastham (MD 16:68)

Judah ROGERS[6] (Judah[5]) and Rebecca LOTHROP, c1778 (MD 33:80)

Nathaniel ROGERS[4] (John[3]) and 1st Elizabeth CROSBY, 1 Feb. 1715/16, Harwich (MD 6:83)

Nathaniel ROGERS[4] and 2nd Silence DIMOCK, 1 Feb. 1721/22, Harwich (MD 8:157)

Jabez ROGERS[5] (Nath.[4]) and Lucy KEEP, Nov. 1753

Selden CURTIS and Mary BISHOP, 3 Dec. 1841 (Bolton CT VR:130)

Samuel ROGERS^6 (Jabez^5) and Sarah SKINNER, 24 Nov. 1785 (Stiles' Ancient Windsor
   2:662)

Gustavus Adolphus ROGERS^7 (Sam.^{6}) and Susan Ann CAMPBELL, 19 Apr. 1827, Bath NY

Russell ROGERS^6 (Jabez^5) and Esther SKINNER, 21 Feb. 1796

Joseph ROGERS^3 and Susanna DEANE, 4 Apr. 1660, Eastham (MD 17:201)

Mary ROGERS^3 and John PHINNEY, 10 Aug. 1664 (MD 11:130)

Thomas PHINNEY and Maria LUMBART, Nov. 1731 (Barnstable VR 2:332)

Thomas PHINNEY 3d and Abigail LUMBART, 24 Nov. 1748 (Barnstable VR 2:247)

Temperance PHINNEY and Ebenezer ISHAM, 5 Apr. 1772 (Barnstable VR 3:173)

Freelove PHINEY and Prince FISH, 26 Oct. 1775 (Barnstable VR 3:174)

Mercy PHINNEY^4 (Mary Rogers^3) and Eleazer CROCKER, 26 Jan. 1715, Barnstable
   (MD 14:227)

Eleazer CROCKER and 2nd Ruth CHIPMAN^3 (Hope Howland^2), 7 Apr. 1682, Barnstable
   (MD 4:120)

Benjamin PHINNEY^4 (Mary Rogers^3) and 1st Martha CROCKER, June 1709, Barnstable
   (MD 11:132)

Benjamin PHINNEY^4 and 2nd Elizabeth (YOUNG) Ames, poss. 5 Nov. 1747 (Barnstable
   VR 2:346)

Barnabas PHINNEY^5 (Ben.^{4}) and Mehitable MORTON, 14 Aug. 1745 (Halifax VR:34)

Zaccheus PHINNEY^5 (Ben.^{4}) and Susanna DAVIS, 3 Mar. 1742/43 (Falmouth VR 1:239)

Susanna DAVIS and 2nd Theodore MORSE, 6 Mar. 1763 (Falmouth VR 2:11)

Benjamin PHINNEY^6 (Zaccheus^5) and Susanna MORSE

Ebenezer PHINNEY^4 (Mary Rogers^3) and Susanna LINNELL, 14 Nov. 1695, Barnstable
   (MD 11:132)

David PHINNEY^5 (Eben.^{4}) and Mary POPE, 27 Sept. 1733 (Otis 2:226)

Deborah PHINNEY^6 (David^5) and John LEWIS^6 (Sarah Thacher^5, Thankful Sturgis^4,
   Temperance Gorham^3, Desire Howland^2), 19 Oct. 1752, Barnstable (MD 31:7)

Ebenezer PHINNEY^5 (Eben.^{4}) and Rebecca BARNES^5 (Sarah Bradford^4, Wm.$^{3-2}$),
   22 Sept. 1730, Plymouth (MD 14:73)

Mehitable PHINNEY^5 (Eben.^{4}) and Samuel HIGGINS, 9 Oct. 1718, Barnstable (MD 14:227)

Ebenezer HIGGINS^6 (Mehitable Phinney^5) and 1st Martha BURGESS, 8 Oct. 1742,
   Eastham (MD 20:94)

Ebenezer HIGGINS^6 and 2nd Hannah YATES, 27 Oct. 1763, Harwich (MD 32:62)

Ebenezer HIGGINS^7 (Eben.^{6}) and Rebecca DYER, 14 Apr. 1772 (Truro VR:108)

Rebecca DYER and 2nd Col. Nathaniel FROST, 7 Nov. 1801 (Higgins Gen.:217)

Ebenezer HIGGINS[8] (Eben.[7]) and Joanna (COLLINS)Atkins, aft. Jan. 1797

Joanna COLLINS and 1st John ATKINS, 17 Sept. 1795 (Truro VR:163)

Daniel HIGGINS[7] (Sam.[6], Mehitable Phinney[5]) and Betty Foster KENRICK, Apr. 1747

Martha HIGGINS[6] (Mehitable Phinney[5]) and Elisha LINNEL, 14 Mar. 1744/45, Eastham
   (MD 20:158)

Elisha LINNELL and 1st Rebecca PAINE[5] (John[4], Mary Snow[3], Constance Hopkins[2]),
   17 July 1735, Eastham (MD 17:144)

Samuel LINNELL[7] (Martha Higgins[6]) and 2nd Susanna NEWCOMB, 15 May 1823, Portland ME

John PHINNY[4] (Mary Rogers[3]) and Sarah LUMBART, 30 May 1689, Barnstable (MD 11:131)

Elizabeth PHINNY[5] (John[4]) and Nathan DAVIS, 25 Nov. 1714, Barnstable (MD 4:222)

Micro #8 of 10

Jabez DAVIS and Experience LINNELL, 20 Aug. 1689, Barnstable (MD 4:224)

Experience LINNELL and 2nd Benjamin HATCH, 13 Feb. 1711/12

Sarah PHINNEY[5] (John[4]) and Thomas ADAMS, Int. 27 Aug. 1724, Barnstable (VR:361)

Hannah PHINNEY[5] (John[4]) and Roger GOODSPEED, 6 Oct. 1720 (Otis 1:404)

Elizabeth GOODSPEED[6] (Hannah Phinney[5]) and Jedediah WINSLOW, Int. 24 Nov. 1750
   (Rochester VR 2:139,329)

Jabez PHINNY[5] (John[4]) and Jane TAYLOR, 5 Oct. 1732, Barnstable (MD 34:20)

John PHINNEY[5] (John[4]) and Martha COLEMAN, 25 Sept. 1718 (Barnstable VR 2:304)

Patience PHINNY[5] (John[4]) and Ebenezer HOLMES, 20 Aug. 1719, Plymouth (MD 14:39)

Jeremiah HOLMES[6] (Patience Phinny[5]) and Phebe CRYMBLE, 12 Oct. 1749, Plymouth
   (MD 17:7)

Peter HOLMES[7] (Jeremiah[6]) and Mary BROOKS, 18 June 1778, Plymouth (Ch.rcds.2:499)

Nathaniel HOLMES[6] (Patience Phinny[5]) and Chloe SEARS[6] (Eliz. Bartlett[5], Robert[4],
   Jos.[3], Mary Warren[2]), 17 Apr. 1760, Plymouth (Ch.rcds.2:492)

Elizabeth HOLMES[7] (Nath.[6]) and 1st Eleazer NICHOLS, 7 Dec. 1787, Plymouth (Ch.
   rcds., Colonial Soc. Mass.23:503)

Elizabeth HOLMES[7] and 2nd Joseph DURFEE, 29 Jan. 1819

Eleazer NICHOLS and Mary TISDALE, 15 Feb. 1749/50 (Freetown VR 16:115)

Mercy Margaret MALONEY and Edmund Howland PEIRCE, 14 Oct. 1854 (Freetown VR 5:143)

Chloe NICHOLS[8] (Eliz. Holmes[7]) and David HILL

Thomas PHINNEY[5] (John[4]) and Reliance GOODSPEED, 31 Mar. 1726, Barnstable (MD 33:28)

Eli PHINNEY[6] (Tho.[5]) and Mary PHINNEY[6] (Jabez[5], John[4], Mary Rogers[3], Jos.[2]),
   14 Mar. 1754, Barnstable (MD 27:5)

Paul PHINNEY[7] (Eli[6]) and Mehitable HATCH, 8 Apr. 1784 (Barnstable VR 3:332)

Deborah PHINNEY[8] (Paul[7]) and Lewis HATHAWAY, c1802 (Barnstable TR 3:305)

Lydia PHINNEY[6] (Tho.[5]) and 1st Benjamin HINCKLEY, 22 Nov. 1750 (Barnstable TR 2:247)

Lydia PHINNEY[6] and 2nd Hercules HODGES, 26 Oct. 1766 (Barnstable TR 3:170)

Lydia HODGES[7] (Lydia Phinney[6]) and Lemuel SNOW, 10 Mar. 1785 (Barnstable TR 3:332)

Hercules HODGES and Ester PARKER, 23 Dec. 1817, Barnstable (MD 19:79)

Lydia SNOW[8] (Lydia Hodges[7]) and Asa JONES Jr., Int. 27 Sept. 1806 (Barnstable
    VR 3:352)

Patience PHINNEY[6] (Tho.[5]) and Lemuel BEARSE, 30 Apr. 1761

Sarah PHINNEY[6] (Tho.[5]) and Silvanus HINCKLEY[5] (Abigail Jenkins[4], Lydia Howland[3],
    Jos.[2]), 31 May 1753, Barnstable (MD 31:8)

Jonathan PHINNEY[4] (Mary Rogers[3]) and 2nd poss. Deborah WADE, c1712 (MD 11:132)

Thankful PHINNEY[5] (Jonathan[4]) and John HAYFORD, 23 Nov. 1738, Middleboro (MD 13:252)

Joseph PHINNEY[4] (Mary Rogers[3]) and 1st Mercy BRYANT, 15 June 1693, Plymouth
    (MD 13:206)

Joseph PHINNEY[4] and 2nd Esther WEST, 19 Sept. 1706, Plymouth (MD 14:34)

John PHINNEY[5] (?Jos.[4]) and 1st Rebecca BRYANT, 1 Mar. 1721/22 (Kingston VR:187,220)[5]

John PHINNEY[5] and 2nd Bettie LOVELL, 5 Apr. 1743 (Kingston/Abington TR)[4]

John PHINNEY[5] and 3rd poss. Ruth (SILVESTER[5]) (Cooke) Ring, 25 Dec. 1770 (King-
    ston VR:262,268)[4]

Mary PHINNEY[5] (Jos.[4]) and Eleazer HAMLIN, 25 Feb. 1721, Barnstable (MD 14:89)

Joseph PHINNEY[5] (Jos.[4]) and Mary RICKARD, 9 Jan. 1734/35 (Plympton VR)

Pelatiah PHINNEY[5] (Jos.[4]) and Mercy WASHBURN[6] (Josiah[5], John[4], Eliz. Mitchell[3],
    Jane Cooke[2]), poss. 28 Dec. 1738 (Bridgewater ch.rcds.)

Mary PHINNEY[4] (Mary Rogers[3]) and John EASTLAND, 29 Oct. 1702, Plymouth (MD 14:34,35)

Reliance PHINNEY[4] (Mary Rogers[3]) and John MORTON, 27 Dec. 1705, Barnstable (MD 14:88)

Josiah MORTON[5] (Reliance Phinney[4]) and Maletiah FINNEY[5] (Ben.[4], Mary Rogers[3],
    Jos.[2]), Int. 14 Aug. 1731, Plymouth (MD 18:122)

Samuel PHINNEY[4] (Mary Rogers[3]) and Bethiah SMITH, 30 Apr. 1713, Eastham (MD 15:57)

Thomas PHINNY[4] (Mary Rogers[3]) and Sarah ( ) BEETLE, 25 Aug. 1698, Barnstable
    (MD 11:132)

Gershom PHINNEY[5] (Tho.[4]) and Rebecca GRIFFITH, 29 July 1725, Harwich (MD 8:160)

Thomas ROGERS[3] and Elizabeth SNOW[3] (Constance Hopkins[2]), 13 Dec. 1665, Eastham
    (MD 6:14)

Eleazer ROGERS[4] (Tho,[3]) and Ruhamah WILLIS, c1697 (MD 3:123)

Experience ROGERS[5] (Eleazer[4]) and 1st Samuel TOTMAN, 17 Apr. 1727, Plymouth
    (MD 14:72)

Experience ROGERS[5] and poss. 2nd Walter RICH, 19 Nov. 1751, Plymouth (MD 16:171)

Experience TOTMAN and Abraham TISDALE, 7 Nov. 1765 (Plymouth Ch.rcds.2:494)

Deborah TOTMAN[6] (Experience Rogers[5]) and Moses BARROWS, 29 Dec. 1748, Plymouth
    (MD 17:7)[<6>]

John TOTMAN and Elizabeth HARLOW, 29 Apr. 1759, Plymouth (MD 16:255)

Experience TOTMAN and John WASHBURN Jr., 30 Apr. 1778 (Plympton VR:414,418)

Stoddard TOTMAN and Rebecca COBB, 16 Mar. 1780 (Plympton VR:290,414)

Samuel TOTMAN and 1st Deborah BUCK, 3 June 1714, Plymouth (MD 14:37) <2nd marr. above>

Hannah ROGERS[5] (Eleazer[4]) and Joseph LEWEN, 4 Nov. 1723, Plymouth (MD 14:40)

John LEWEN[6] (Hannah Rogers[5]) and Sarah HOLMES, 25 Oct. 1751, Plymouth (MD 16:171)

Maria LEWEN[6] (Hannah Rogers[5]) and Isaac MORTON, 19 Mar. 1746/47, Plymouth (MD 17:6)

Benjamin HOLMES and Meriah THOMAS, 24 Nov. 1797 (Plymouth VR 2:277)

Thomas ROGERS[5] (Eleazer[4]) and Priscilla CHURCHILL, 31 Oct. 1721, Plymouth (MD 14:39)

Hannah ROGERS[6] (Tho.[5]) and poss. Thomas DAVEE, 31 Dec. 1761[<7>]

Thomas DAVEE and 1st Sarah JOHNSON[5] (Eliz. Cooke[4], Caleb[3], Jacob[2])

Desire ROGERS[6] (Tho.[5]) and Samuel BARROWS, 7 Mar. 1744/45 (Plympton VR:250,379)

Isaac BARROWS[7] (Desire Rogers[6]) and Anna BLACKMER, c1773

Branch BARROWS[8] (Isaac[7]) and Rebecca CLARK

Lurany BARROWS[7] (Desire Rogers[6]) and Timothy CHUBBUCK, 19 July 1776 (Wareham Ch.rcds)

Willis CHUBBUCK[8] (Lurany Barrows[7]) and Hannah SWIFT, 1 Sept. 1805, Wareham (MD 31:127)

Hannah Ellis CHUBBUCK[9] (Willis[8]) and Nathan Bourne ELLIS, c1834

Thomas BARROWS[7] (Desire Rogers[6]) and Bethiah BESSE

Ebenezer BARROWS[8] (Tho.[7]) and Mary FREEMAN

Micro #10 of 10

Hannah ROGERS[4] (Tho.[3]) and Amaziah HARDING

James HARDING[5] (Hannah Rogers[4]) and Mary NICKERSON, 8 Oct. 1724, Harwich (MD 8:160)

Elizabeth HARDING[5] (Hannah Rogers[4]) and Rowland FISH, 16 Feb. 1730, Eastham (MD 17:33)

Hannah HARDING[5] (Hannah Rogers[4]) and Bartholomew FISH, 9 Oct. 1716, Eastham (MD 15:55)

Nathan HARDING[5] (Hannah Rogers[4]) and Anne BROWN, Int. 8 Jan. 1736/37 (Eastham VR:223)

Nathan HARDING and Abigal WEST, 15 Nov. 1750 (Middletown CT VR 2:264)

Ebenezer HARDING[6] (Nathan[5]) and Huldah TRYON, 6 Nov. 1760, Middletown CT

Anna HARDING^7 (Eben.^{6}) and Asahel MATTHEWS, poss. 11 July 1787

Huldah HARDING^7 (Eben.^{6}) and Lot HUDSON, poss. 5 Oct. 1794

Martha HARDING^7 (Eben.^{6}) and Daniel ACKLEY, poss. 7 May 1799

Lydia HARDING^7 (Eben.^{6}) and Jonathan GOFF, poss. 3 Apr. 1796

Ebenezer HARDING^7 (Eben.^{6}) and Jerusha FOX, 29 Nov. 1785, Glastonbury CT (CT

    Mges.7:108)

Prudence ( ) ROGERS and Machiel ATWOOD, 25 Oct. 1700, Eastham (MD 9:7)[8]

Thomas ROGERS^4 (Tho.^{3}) and 1st Sarah TREAT, 10 Dec. 1700, Eastham (MD 9:13)

Thomas ROGERS^4 and 2nd Rebecca COLLINS, 11 Feb. 1730/31 (Eastham VR:97)

Elizabeth ROGERS^5 (Tho.^{4}) and Benjamin LEWIS, 13 June 1728 (Truro VR:21)

Benjamin LEWIS^6 (Eliz. Rogers^5) and poss. Priscilla (RICH) Rich, 1 July 1765

    (Truro VR:109)

Lucy ROGERS^5 (Tho.^{4}) and Nehemiah SOMES, 15 Oct. 1734 (Truro VR:39)

NOTES

    [1] p.241, Source: Reed, Wm.F. The Descendants of Thomas Durfee of Portsmouth RI. Vol. 1, 1902. Vol. 2, 1905, Washington D.C.

    [2] p.244, Source: Hurlbut, Henry Higgins. The Hurlbut Genealogy. 1888. Albany NY.

    [3] p.246, Intentions of marriage were also recorded 5 Aug. 1755, Chatham (MD 13:29)

    [4] p.246, She is recorded as Ruth Higgins in the intentions of marriage (Eastham VR:235), and is called Rebecca Higgins in the marriage records.

    [5] p.250, Bowman questions whether this John Phinney was the son of Joseph and is uncertain regarding attributing all marriages to him. He also questions the identity of the third wife who is listed in the marriage record as "Mrs. Ruth Ring" and wonders if she was Ruth (Silvester)(Cooke) Ring. However, as shown here on p.190, the Hopkins file contain the three marriages of Ruth Silvester including her marriage to John Phinney, as well as giving her line of descent to William Brewster. (See also p.118 for her Cooke marriage.)

    [6] p.251, An accompanying note states Bailey's Mass. Marriages 2:11 gives the date as 29 Nov. 1747. (The note also mentions that the above contains many errors.)

    [7] p. 251, Although there seems to be some question here regarding this marriage, it can be found on p.117 (Cooke file).

    [8] p.252, She was possibly the widow of Joseph Rogers^4 (Tho.^{3}, Jos.^{2}).

HENRY SAMSON DESCENDANTS

Henry SAMSON[1] and Anne PLUMMER, 6 Feb. 1635 (MD 13:84)

Caleb SAMSON[2] (Henry[1])

Caleb SAMSON[2] and 1st Mercy STANDISH[3] (Alex.[2]), c1684

Caleb SAMSON[2] and 2nd Rebecca STANFORD, 30 Jan. 1728/29, Duxbury (MD 11:80)[1]

Caleb SAMSON[3] and Mehitable FORD, 12 Feb. 1729 (Marshfield VR 2:148)

Michael SAMSON and Deborah GARDNER, 7 Feb. 1739/40 (Marshfield VR: 2:172)[2]

Micah SAMSON and Hannah POOL, 3 Nov. 1755 (Abington VR 1:249)

Michael SAMSON[4] (Caleb[3]) and Hannah POOL (prob. above)

Gideon SAMSON and 1st Keziah CARVER, 19 Mar. 1772, Marshfield (Duxbury VR:229)

Gideon SAMSON and 2nd Rebecca SOULE (Duxbury VR:298,312)

Micah SAMSOM and Deborah RICHMOND, 31 Nov. 1780 (Abington VR:340)

Paul SAMSON[4] (Caleb[3]) and Esther CHANDLER, 26 Feb. 1751 (Kingston VR)

Chandler SAMPSON[5] (Paul[4]) and Nancy THOMAS, 5 Mar. 1795 (Marshfield VR 2:167)

David SAMSON[3] and Mary CHAFFIN, 5 June 1712, Marshfield (MD 7:132)

Mary SAMSON[4] (David[3]) and John LITTLE[5] (John[4], Ephraim[3], Anna Warren[2])

Chaffin SAMSON[4] (David[3]) and Betty CLIFT, c1761 (Giles Mem.:382,394)

Chapin SAMSON[5] (Chaffin[4]) and Sarah SMITH, 13 July 1788 (Boston Rcd.comm.30:103)

Job SAMSON[5] (Chaffin[4]) and Betsey WINSOR, poss. 15 June 1787, Duxbury

Sally SAMSON[6] (Chapin[5]) and William STEVENS, c1807

Thomas B. SAMPSON[6] (Chapin[5]) and Harriet B. CURRIER, 15 May 1826 (Gardiner
    ME VR 2:257,453)

Charles SAMSON[4] (David[3]) and Mary CHURCH[5] (Nath.[4-3], Eliz. Warren[2]), 19 June
    1740 (Scituate 2d ch.)

Charles SAMSON[5] (Charles[4]) and Elisabeth SPRAGUE, c1774

Sarah SAMPSON and Willard HALL, Int. 15 Nov. 1845 (Waldoboro ME VR 6:)

James A. SAMSON and Caroline TROWBRIDGE, Int. 6 Feb. 1847 (Waldoboro ME VR 6:)

Charles SAMSON Jr. and Olive THOMAS, Int. 1 May 1847 (Waldoboro ME VR 6:)

Eliza H. SAMPSON and Lowell P. HASKELL, Int. 31 Aug. 1861 (Waldoboro ME VR 10:8)

Charles SAMSON Jr.[6] (Charles[5]) and Sally THOMAS, Int. 5 May 1798 (Waldoboro
    ME VR 1:)

Eliza SAMSON and Alfred HOVEY, 28 Sept. 1818 (Waldoboro ME VR 2:361)

Sarah Ann SAMSON and John BALCH, 27 Sept. 1827 (Waldoboro ME VR 2:)

Emily Ann SAMSON and James HALL, 28 Feb. 1832 (Waldoboro ME VR 2:)

Charles SAMSON Jr. and Lucy B. KENT, Int. 25 Nov. 1837 (Waldoboro ME VR 6:)

John D. SAMSON and Adriannah BRADFORD, 22 Sept. 1840 (Waldoboro ME VR 6:)

George N. SAMSON and Susan M. MILLER, 29 Sept. 1840 (Waldoboro ME VR 6:)

Charles SAMSON^7 (Charles^6) and Lucy B. KENT <above>

Lucy SAMSON^6 (Charles^5) and Church C. TRONANT

Sarah Dingley SAMSON^6 (Charles^5) and John HASKELL, c1809

Martha Brookhouse HASKELL^7 (Sarah D. Samson^6) and Shubael WALDO, c1837

Ebenezer SAMSON^4 (David^3) and Hannah HARLOW^6 (Wm.^{5}, Sam.^{4}, Rebecca Bartlett^3,
    Mary Warren^2), 14 Sept. 1739, Plymouth (MD 14:158)

Ebenezer SAMSON^5 (Eben.^{4}) and Susanna FINNEY

Hannah SAMSON^5 (Eben.^{4}) and Richard COOPER^7 (Hannah Rider^6, Mary Southworth^5,
    Desire Gray^4, Mary Winslow^3, Mary Chilton^2), 22 Jan. 1761 (Int.- Plymouth
    (MD 26:40)

Eleanor SAMSON^4 (David^3) and Joseph FARNUM, 5 July 1753 (Marshfield VR 2:146)

Jonathan FARNAM and Dorcas BARNES, 28 Apr. 1782 (Plymouth ch.rcds.2:501)

Elizabeth SAMSON^4 (David^3) and Peter PINEO, poss. 20 Dec. 1743

Jonathan SAMSON^4 (David^3) and poss. Sarah DREW

Lydia SAMSON^4 (David^3) and Nathaniel BOSWORTH

Mercy SAMSON^4 (David^3) and Timothy HUTCHINSON

Joshua SAMSON^3 and Mary OAKMAN, 24 May 1724, Marshfield (Gen.Reg.6:351)

Anthony SAMSON^4 (Joshua^3) and Anna SAMSON^5 (Nath.^{4}, Lorah Standish^3, Alex.^{2})

Dorcas SAMSON^2 (Henry^1)

Dorcas SAMSON^2 and Thomas BONNEY, pre 1684 (MD 2:143)

Thomas BONNEY and 2nd Sarah STUDLEY, poss. 18 July 1695 (Duxbury VR)

Micro #3 of 7

Job BONNEY and Ruth BISBE, 9 May 1733, Pembroke (Gen.Adv.1:110)

Abiah BONNEY and John BISBE Jr., 6 Sept. 1733, Pembroke (Gen.Adv.1:110)

Ezekiel BONNEY and Hannah BRYANT, 26 Dec. 1734, Pembroke (Gen.Adv.1:110)

Elijah BONNEY and Susanna TUBBS, 27 Juen 1737, Pembroke (Gen.Adv.1:111)

Ichabod BONNEY and Elisabeth HOWLAND, 29 Oct. 1724, Pembroke (Gen.Adv.1:109)

Ruth BONNEY and Samuel PARRIS, 21 Jan. 1725, Pembroke (Gen.Adv.1:109)

Mary BONNEY and Josiah FOSTER Jr., 29 July 1725, Pembroke (Gen.Adv.1:109)

Ebenezer BONNEY and Elisabeth PARRIS, 16 Oct. 1729, Pembroke (Gen.Adv.1:109)

Deborah BONNEY and Joseph CHANDLER, 27 Nov. 1729, Pembroke (Gen.Adv.1:109)

Ann BONNEY and Rouse HOWLAND, 27 Nov. 1729 (Gen.Adv.1:109)

Elisha BONNEY and Elisabeth LINCOLN, 10 Dec. 1729, Pembroke (Gen.Adv.1:109)

Elizabeth BONNEY[3] and Ephraim NORCUT, 30 Jan. 1712/13, Marshfield (MD 7:132)

Mercy BONNEY[3] and 1st Nathaniel DELANO, 14 Oct. 1714, Duxbury (MD 11:24)

Mercy BONNEY[3] and 2nd John CURTIS, pre 29 July 1735

Zeruiah DELANO[4] (Mercy Bonney[3]) and Joshua BRIGGS, 3 June 1742 (Pembroke VR:247)

Lydia DELANO[4] (Mercy Bonney[3]) and 1st Ichabod WORMALL, 13 Dec. 1736, Duxbury
    (MD 11:241)

Lydia DELANO[4] and 2nd Ebenezer DELANO, 16 May 1745, Duxbury (MD 11:78)

Mercy DELANO[4] (Mercy Bonney[3]) and 1st John PRIOR, 14 Oct. 1735, Duxbury (MD 11:241)

Mercy DELANO[4] and 2nd Joseph RAMSDELL, 25 Nov. 1755 (Hanover 1st Ch.1:92)

Mercy RAMSDEL[5] (Mercy Delano[4]) and 1st Richard ESTES, poss. 4 Nov. 1778

Mercy RAMSDEL[5] and 2nd Josiah ELLIS, poss. 23 May 1806

Elizabeth SAMSON[2] (Henry[1])

Elizabeth SAMSON[2] and Robert SPROUT, c1661 (MD 6:9)

Anna SPROUT[3] and Ebenezer RICHMOND[4] (Abigail Rogers[3], John[2]), c1700 (MD 2:43)

Ebenezer SPROUT[3] and Experience HAWES[4] (Desire Gorham[3], Desire Howland[2]), 1 Mar.
    1703/04, Yarmouth (MD 25:101)

Experience HAWES[4] and 2nd Francis MILLER[5] (Lydia Coombs[4], Francis[3], Sarah Priest[2]),
    22 Nov. 1731, Middleboro (MD 13:249)

Mary SPROUT[4] (Eben.[3]) and 1st Thomas HOLMES, 1 Apr. 1731, Middleboro (MD 9:47)

Mary SPROUT[4] and 2nd Josiah WOOD[4] (Susanna Howland[3], Isaac[2]), 29 Jan. 1735,
    Middleboro (MD 13:252)

Thankful SPROUT[4] (Eben.[3]) and 1st Joseph BENNET[4] (Prisc. Howland[3], Isaac[2]),
    18 Nov. 1724, Middleboro (MD 4:73)

Thankful SPROUT[4] and 2nd Seth SAMSON[3] (George[2], Abraham[1]), 9 Oct. 1758, Middle-
    boro (MD 24:131)

Abigail SPROUT[4] (Eben.[3]) and John WADSWORTH, 11 Dec. 1729, Middleboro (MD 8:250)

Ebenezer SPROUT[4] (Eben.[3]) and Bathsheba WOOD, 8 June 1749, Middleboro (MD 18:82)

James SPROUT[5] (Eben.[4]) and Ann DENNIS, c1787 (MD 33:45)

Rev. James SPROUT[4] (Eben.[3]) and Sarah SMITH

Hannah SPROUT[3] and Ephraim KEEN, 1 Apr. 1703, Scituate (MD 3:119)

Welthea KEEN^4 (Hannah Sprout^3) and Israel CHASE

Hannah KEEN^4 (Hannah Sprout^3) and John BLETHEN

Abigail KEEN^4 (Hannah Sprout^3) and William SPRAGUE

Robert KEEN^4 (Hannah Sprout^3) and Elizabeth SIMMONS

James SPROUT^3 and Elizabeth SOUTHWORTH^5 (Desire Gray^4, Mary Winslow^3, Mary Chilton^2), 5 June 1712, Scituate (MD 9:87)

James SPROUT^3 and 2nd Rachel (BUCK) Dwelly, 8 Jan. 1728/29 (Scituate VR)

Micro #4 of 7

Lemuel DWELLY and Bethiah DOGGETT, Int. 7 June 1740, Scituate$^{<3>}$

Nathaniel SPROUT^4 (James^3) and Esther THRASHER, 16 Feb. 1743/44, Middleboro (MD 15:220)

Nathaniel SPROUT^5 (Nath.^{4}) and Aznbah CUMMINGS, poss. 28 Dec. 1775, Greenwich (Hardwick VR:162,246)

Robert SPROUT^5 (Nath.^{4}) and Betsy LINCOLN, poss. 17 Sept. 1781 (Hardwick VR:205)

Ebenezer SPROUT^5 (Nath.^{4}) and 1st Mary THAYER, 11 Dec. 1783 (Hardwick VR:245,251)

Ebenezer SPROUT^5 and 2nd Miriam BARNES, 3 June 1790

Ezra SPROUT^6 (Eben.^{5}) and Dency NEWLAND

Dexter Brigham SPROUT^7 (Ezra^6) and Sarah A. POPE, 1 Sept. 1855, Enfield

Robert SPROUT^4 (James^3) and 1st Hannah SOUTHWORTH^6 (Nath.^{5}, Desire Gray^4, Mary Winslow^3, Mary Chilton^2), 10 Dec. 1741, Middleboro (MD 13:253)$^{<4>}$

Robert SPROUT^4 and 2nd Mercy SMITH, 27 Oct. 1785 (Middleboro VR 4:158)

Robert SPROUT^5 (Robert^4) and Hannah LEONARD, 21 Nov. 1771 (Middleboro VR 2:134)

Zebedee SPROUTT^5 (Robert^4) and Elizabeth ROBINSON, poss. 10 May 1763, Taunton

Robert SPROUT^5 (Robert^4) and Hannah LEONARD, 21 Nov. 1771, Middleboro (MD 30:13)

James SPROUT^6 (Robert^5) and Lucy CLARKE, c1800

Mercy SPROUT^3 and Thomas OLDHAM, 27 June 1683, Scituate (MD 2:87)

Thomas OLDHAM^4 (Mercy Sprout^3) and Desire WORMALL^4 (Patience Sherman^3, Desire Doty^2), 8 May 1727 (Marshfield VR 2:148)

Elizabeth OLDHAM^4 (Mercy Sprout^3) and John DAMON, poss. 12 Sept. 1717 (Scituate VR 2:99,222)

Mary OLDHAM^4 (Mercy Sprout^3) and John BISBEE, 31 Jan. 1710/11 (Scituate VR 4:2:20)

Ruth OLDHAM and Elias MAGOONE, 30 Jan. 1711/12 (Scituate VR 4:2:20)

Anna OLDHAM^4 (Mercy Sprout^3) and Joseph YOUNG, 13 Oct. 1718 (Scituate VR 2:221)

Caleb OLDHAM^4 (Mercy Sprout^3) and Bethiah STEPHENS, 21 Oct. 1724 (Marshfield VR 2:147)

Thomas OLDHAM and Jane ROGERS, 10 Dec. 1752 (Marshfield VR 2:160)$^{<5>}$

Abigail OLDHAM^4 (Mercy Sprout^3) and Nathaniel EAMES, 2 Jan. 1720, Marshfield
    (Scituate VR 2:111,222)

Desire OLDHAM^4 (Mercy Sprout^3) and Samuel TILDEN, poss. 14 Nov. 1717 (Scituate VR)

Samuel TILDEN and Sarah CURTICE, 25 July 1694, Scituate (MD 2:86)

Samuel TILDEN Jr. and Mercy HATCH, 10 Nov. 1763 (Marshfield VR 2:150)

Samuel TILDEN Jr. and Peggy FOSTER, Int. 1 Sept. 1790 (Marshfield VR 2:62)

Samuel TILDEN and Grace HATCH, Int. 28 June 1782 (Marshfield VR 2:66)

Luther TILDEN and Philenda BROOKS, Int. 10 Mar. 1800 (Marshfield VR 2:50)

Mercy TILDEN^5 (Desire Oldham^4) and Thomas MACOMBER^5 (Joanna Tinkham^4, Ebenezer^3,
    Mary Brown^2)

Sarah TILDEN^5 (Desire Oldham^4) and John JAMES^7 (John$^{6-5}$, Lydia Turner^4, Mary
    Brewster^3, Jonathan^2), 3 Dec. 1755 (Marshfield VR)

Ruth TILDEN^5 (Desire Oldham^4) and North EELLS

Grace OLDHAM^4 (Mercy Sprout^3) and Anthony EAMES, 11 Dec. 1724, Marshfield

Lemuel EAMES^5 (Grace Oldham^4) and Ruth PORTER, 16 May 1750, Marshfield

Mercy OLDHAM^4 (Mercy Sprout^3) and Andrew NEWCOMB, 4 Nov. 1708, Scituate (MD 8:204)

Abigail NEWCOMB^5 (Mercy Oldham^4) and Ebenezer BOURNE

Mercy NEWCOMB^5 (Mercy Oldham^4) and John BROWN, 30 Nov. 1732 (Truro VR:24)

David BROWN^6 (Mercy Newcomb^5) and Eunice HINKLEY, 10 Dec. 1771 (Truro VR:417)

Cyrenus BROWN^7 (David^6) and Eleanor COOK^7 (Sam.^{6}, Solomon^5, Josiah^4, Deborah
    Hopkins^2), 25 Apr. 1793 (MD 28:130)

Elmira BROWN^8 (Cyrenus^7) and Ivory Hovey LORD

David BROWN^7 (David^6) and 1st Mary COOK, 20 Dec. 1797

David BROWN^7 and 2nd Rebecca (COAN) Mills, 12 Aug. 1845 (Truro VR:384,385)

Eunice BROWN^7 (David^6) and Philip GROSS

Micro #5 of 7

Hannah SAMSON^2 (Henry^1)

Hannah SAMSON^2 and Josiah HOLMES, 20 Mar. 1665, Duxbury (MD 8:232)

John HOLMES^3 and poss. Susanna RANDALL

William HOLMES^3 and Bathsheba STETSON, 22 Nov. 1715 (Pembroke VR:291)

Hannah HOLMES^4 (Wm.^{3}) and Joseph BEARSE, 17 Nov. 1743 (Halifax VR:33)

Hezekiah HOLMES^4 (Wm.^{3}) and poss. Mercy BISBEE, c1755

Jane HOLMES^4 (Wm.^{3}) and Ephraim HOLMES, 26 June 1744 (Halifax VR:33)

Betty HOLMES^5 (Jane Holmes^4) and Ebenezer SUMNER

Simeon HOLMES^4 (Wm.^{3}) and Abiah STURTEVANT, c1744 (Halifax VR:56)

William HOLMES^4 (Wm.^{3}) and poss. Elizabeth HAMLIN

James SAMSON^2 (Henry^1)

James SAMSON^2 and Hannah ( ) WAIT, pre Oct. 1694 (NEHGR 73:292,293)

Penelope SAMSON^3 and Abraham SAMSON^4 (Lorah Standish^3, Alexander^2), c1712
    (MD 6:189, 10:185)

Anna SAMSON^3 and Shubael SMITH, 12 Oct. 1725 (Chilmark VR:71,73)

James SAMSON^3 and poss. Ruth SAWYER

Ruth·SAMSON^4 (James^3) and Stephen HARDING

Joseph SAMSON^3 and Sarah SAMSON^4 (Lorah Standish^3, Alexander^2), 6 May 1719,
    Duxbury (MD 11:25)

Sarah SAMSON^4 and 2nd John ROUSE, 18 Nov. 1739, Dartmouth (Gen.Adv.4:83-87)

Ruhamah SAMSON^4 (Jos.^{3}) and poss. Zaccheus TOBEY, Int. 1 Dec. 1756

Sarah SAMSON^4 (Jos.^{3}) and poss. Peleg DELANO^5 (Nath.^{4}, Mercy Warren^3, Nath.^{2})
    c1755

Joseph SAMSON^4 (Jos.^{3}) and Mercy ELDRIDGE, Int. 30 May 1746, Dartmouth (VR:362)

Edward SAMSON^5 (Jos.^{4}) and 1st Catherine SHARROW, Int. 29 Oct. 1768, Dartmouth
    (VR:548)

Edward SAMSON^5 and 2nd Sarah (CANNON) Atsatt, 8 Jan. 1792

Mercy SAMPSON^6 (Edw.^{5}) and John ATSATT, 5 Feb. 1797 (New Bedford VR:209)

Lois SAMSON^4 (Jos.^{3}) and Samuel GRAY, Int. 21/31 Jan. 1745/46 (Tiverton RI VR 2:174)

Priscilla SAMSON^3 and Samuel HAMMOND, pre 27 Dec. 1712

Susanna SAMSON^3 and Benjamin HILMON (MD 6:188)

Mary SAMSON^2 (Henry^1)

Mary SAMSON^2 and John SUMMERS (MD 2:143)

Stephen SAMSON^2 (Henry^1)

Micro #6 of 7

Abigail SAMSON^3 and George BRUCE, poss. 11 July 1727, Mendon

John Fremont HILL^7 (Wm.^{6}, Eliz. Rawson^5, Eliz. Bruce^4, Abigail Samson^3) and
    1st Lizzie G. VICKERY, 19 Mar. 1880, Augusta ME

John Freemont HILL^7 and 2nd Laura (COLMAN) Liggett, 27 Apr. 1897, St. Louis MO

Deborah SAMSON^4 (Ben.^{3}) and Samuel VEAZIE, 6 Aug. 1742 (Duxbury VR:323)

Cornelius SAMSON^4 (Ben.^{3}) and Desire CROCKER^5 (Ben.^{4}, Anne Howland^3, John^2),

    poss. 3 Oct. 1747 (Barnstable Fam.1:222)

Micah SAMSON and Deborah GARDNER, Int. 22 Dec. 1739 (Kingston TR 1:) <see below>

Mrs. Deborah SAMSON and Jacob GOOL, Int. 11 Aug. 1744 (Kingston TR 1:)$^{<6>}$

Benjamin SAMSON^3 and Rebecca COOKE^4 (Jacob$^{3-2}$), 19 Mar. 1716, Plymouth (MD 14:37)

Benjamin SAMSON^4 (Ben.^{3}) and 1st Deborah CUSHING, poss. 4 Jan. 1759, Pembroke

    (Kingston VR)

Benjamin SAMSON^4 and 2nd Esther WESTON, poss. 16 Sept. 1770 (Kingston VR:272,301)

Micah SAMSON^4 (Ben.^{3}) and Deborah GARDNER, 7 Feb. 1739/40 (Marshfield VR) <see above)

Dorcas SAMSON^3 and John PLUMLY, poss. 15 Apr. 1723 (Mendon VR:364,375)

Elizabeth SAMSON^3 and 1st Jonathan THAYER, 21 Feb. 1722/23, Duxbury (MD 11:240)

Elizabeth SAMSON^3 and 2nd Josiah NELSON, Int. poss. 5 Apr. 1754, Bellingham

    (Thayer Gen.:496)$^{<7>}$

Cornelius THAYER^4 (Eliz. Samson^3) and Abigail JONES, poss. 24 Dec. 1747 (Bellingham VR)

Abigail JONES and 2nd John HARWOOD, 8 Jan. 1792 (Warren VR:110,145)

Ezra THAYER^4 (Eliz. Samson^3) and poss. Judith WILLIAMS, c1761/62

Hopestill THAYER^4 (Eliz. Samson^3) and Joseph DAMON, poss. 7 June 1750, Mendon

Micah THAYER^4 (Eliz. Samson^3) and Lois THAYER, poss. 17 Nov. 1763

Sarah THAYER^4 (Eliz. Samson^3) and Benoni WRIGHT, 19 Apr. 1750 (Wrentham VR 2:379)

Hannah SAMSON^3 and Robert TYLER, 13 Dec. 1721, Duxbury (MD 11:239)

John SAMSON^3 and Priscilla BARTLETT^5 (Ben.$^{4-3}$, Mary Warren^2), 31 Dec. 1718,

    Duxbury (MD 11:25)

Elijah SAMSON^4 (John^3) and Ruth BRADFORD^5 (Gamaliel^4, Sam.^{3}, Wm.^{2}), poss. 3 Sept.

    1761 (Duxbury VR)

John SAMSON^4 (John^3) and 1st Rebecca BREWSTER^5 (John^4, Wrestling^3, Love^2)

John SAMSON^4 and 2nd Abigail STETSON^6 (Elisha^5, Abigail Brewster^4, Wrestling^3, Love^2)

Micro #7 of 7

Mary SAMSON^3 and Samuel THAYER, poss. 13 Aug. 1716

NOTES

    <1> p.253, Although her identity is not shown here, she was Rebecca (Bartlett)(Bradford) Stanford. For her Mayflower line of descent and first two marriages see p.54.

    <2> p.253, According to the church records his name is listed as Micah Samson not Michael Samson.

    <3> p.256, "Probaby did not marry" accompanies this entry. The will of

Lemuel Dwelly was administered four months later in October.

<4> p.256, Further in the files is another chart bearing Robert Sprout's name. On this sheet his first wife is given as Hannah Samson[3] (Isaac[4], Lydia Standish[3], Alexander[2]), 2 Feb. 1737/38, Middleboro (MD 13:151); second wife "(?) Hannah Southworth" (no date); third wife "(?) Mercy Smith" (no date).

<5> p.257, The marriage intentions give her name as Jean Rogers with the date of intentions 22 Dec. 1752, (Marshfield VR 2:152),twelve days after the date of marriage.

<6> p.259, She is later shown to be Deborah Gardner, widow of Micah Samson[4].

<7> p.259, Bowman is uncertain as to whether this intention of marriage belongs to Elizabeth (Samson) Thayer[3] (whose husband died in 1747), or her daughter Elizabeth Thayer[4] (age 19 at the time).

GEORGE SOULE DESCENDANTS[1]

Anne SOUL and William WOOD Jr., 28 May 1778, Dartmouth (Bristol Co. Court Rec.)

Elenor SOUL and Oliver SOUL, 5 Sept. 1776, Dartmouth (Bristol Co. CR)

James SOUL and Mary WHITE, 11 Apr. 1765, Dartmouth (Bristol Co. CR)

Jonathan SOUL and Elizabeth GIFFORD, 3 Dec. 1731, Dartmouth (Bristol Co. CR)

Joseph SOUL and Mary DAVIS, 8 Apr. 1736, Dartmouth (Bristol Co. CR)

Meribah SOUL and William TABER, 25 Oct. 1729, Dartmouth (Bristol Co. CR)

Nathaniel SOUL and Hannah MACOMBER, 13 Feb. 1732/33, Dartmouth (Bristol Co. CR)

Timothy SOUL and Elizabeth ALLEN, 6 ( ) 1736/37, Dartmouth (Bristol Co. CR)

Barbara SOULE and Ichabod DAVIS, 7 Oct. 1781, Dartmouth (Bristol Co, CR)

Charles SOULE and Mary RUSSELL, 25 Sept. 1788, Dartmouth (Bristol Co. CR)

David SOULE and Phebe KIRBY, 22 July 1791, Dartmouth (Bristol Co. CR)

Jethro SOWLE and Silvia RICKETSON, 25 Dec. 1789, Dartmouth (Bristol Co. CR)

Mary SOWLE and John BAKER, 20 Mar. 1791, Dartmouth (Bristol Co. CR)

Mary SOWLE and David MAXFIELD, 3 Jan. 1793, Dartmouth (Bristol Co. CR)

Nathaniel SOWLE and Deborah SIMMS, 13 Jan. 1793, Dartmouth (Bristol Co. CR)

Lilli SOULE and Jonathan PHILLIPS, 20 Dec. 1763, Swansea (Bristol Co. CR)

Susanna SOWL and Zadok MAXFEALD, 27 July 1791, Westport (Bristol Co. CR)

Benjamin SOWLE and Sarah POTTER, 4 July 1793, Westport (Bristol Co. CR)

David SOWLE and Peace SHEARMAN, 26 Apr. 1789, Westport (Bristol Co. CR)

Elizabeth SOWLE and James EARL, 22 May 1788, Westport (Bristol Co. CR)

James SOWLE and Patience MACOMBER, 6 Dec. 1789, Westport (Bristol Co. CR)

Mary SOWLE and Benjamin EARL, 18 Mar. 1794, Westport (Bristol Co. CR)

Susanna SOLE and Peter OLIVER, 3 Feb. 1704, Rochester (PN&Q 1:20)

Joseph LISBE and Ruth HOSKINS, Int. 17 Apr. 1736 (Rochester VR 2:45)

John SOULE and Mabel PARTRIDGE, 5 Aug. 1730, poss. Duxbury (:138)[2]

Sarah SOULE and Jonathan SNOW, 18 Dec. 1728, poss. Middleboro (:124)[2]

Jacob SOULE and Mary THOMAS, 31 Mar. 1731, poss. Middleboro [2]

Rachel SOULE and Ebenezer VAUGHN, 6 Jan. 1744, poss. Middleboro (1:288)[2]

Jabez SOULE and Abigail BENNET, 17 Oct. 1745, poss. Middleboro (1:288)[2]

John SOULE and Mary LEACH, 12 Apr. 1750, poss. Middleboro (1:296)[2]

Elizabeth SOULE[2] (George[1])

Elizabeth SOULE[2] and Francis WALKER, pre 23 July 1668 (Col.Deeds 3:126)

George SOULE[2] (George[1])

John SOULE and Meribah HOLWAY, 20 Sept. 1733 (Dartmouth VR)<see below>

Benjamin SOLE and Mary HOLWAY, 25 Oct. 1721, Sandwich

Micro #2 of 11

Lydia SOULE[3] and William BROWNELL Jr.

Mary SOULE[3] and Joseph DEVOL, c1699

Benjamin DEVOL[4] (Mary Soule[3]) and Sarah MOSHER, 22/28 Aug. 1731 (Dartmouth VR
    2:160,331)

Benjamin DEVOL and Silvia GRINNELL, Int. 17 Mar. 1790 (Dartmouth VR 2:)

John DEVOL and Mary BROWNELL, Int. 29 June 1765 (Dartmouth VR 2:)

Daniel HOWLAND and 1st Mary SLOCUM, 1741

Daniel HOWLAND and 2nd Edith POTTER, 13 July 1746

Nathan SOULE[3] and Mercy GIFFORD, 12/13 June 1704 (Dartmouth VR)

Content SOULE[4] (Nathan[3]) and George SHELDEN

Cornelius SOULE[4] (Nathan[3]) and Sarah DENNIS, 1 Msy 1735, Tiverton RI (Bristol Co.
    Mgs.1:240)

George SOULE[4] (Nathan[3]) and 1st Avis TIBBETTS, c1731

George SOULE[4] and 2nd Alice DAVIS, c1758 (RI VR 7:292)

John SOULE[4] (Nathan[3]) and poss. Meribah HOLWAY <see above>

Lt. Nathaniel SOULE and Merebah GIFFORD, 20 July 1708 (Portsmouth RI VR 4:1:24,43)

Sarah SOULE and John TIBBETS, 19 Apr. 1726, Dartmouth (Friends' Rcds.:222)

Mary SOULE[4] (Nathan[3]) and poss. Joseph DAVIS

Timothy SOULE[4] (Nathan[3]) and poss. Elizabeth ALLEN   Int. 9 Dec. 1736

Alice SOULE[4] (Wm.[3]) and Richard SISSON

Micro #3 of 11

George SOULE[4] (Wm.[3]) and Lydia HOWLAND, c1719

Daniel SOULE[5] (George[4]) and (?)Hannah SHERMAN

George SOULE[5] (George[4]) and Mary HOAG

Benjamin SOULE[5] (George[4]) and Abigail HOWLAND

William SOULE[6] (Rowland[5]) and Deborah Ann (PADDOCK) (?)Elliott

Rowland SOULE[5] (George[4]) and Mary IRISH, c1761

Rowland SOULE[6] (Rowland[5]) and Cynthia PHELPS

Elisha SOULE[7] (Rowland[6]) and Polly COLEGROVE

Jonathan SOULE[4] (Wm.[3]) and Lydia SISSON, 12 Feb. 1736

James SOULE^5 (Jonathan^4) and 1st Mary WHITE^7 (Geo.^{6}, Eliz. Cadman^5, Hannah
Hathaway^4, Sarah Cooke^3, John^2), 11 Apr. 1765 (Dartmouth VR 2:469,538)

James SOULE^5 and 2nd Jemima (COFFIN) Russell, 27 Sept. 1781 (Soule Gen.2:926)

Levinah SOULE^6 (James^5) and William PHILLIPS

James PHILLIPS and Anna LOCKWOOD

William SOULE^4 (Wm.^{3}) and Rachel ALLEN, Int. 17 (12 mth) 1717/18 (Dartmouth
Mthly. Meeting of Friends)

Thankful SOULE^5 (Wm.^{4}) and John BENNETT, poss. 4 Jan. 1739/40 (Leonard Papers)

John SOULE^2 (George^1)

John SOULE^2 and 1st Rebecca SIMMONS, c1655 (MD 4:160,19:96)

John SOULE^2 and 2nd Esther (NASH) Samson, c1678 (MD 8:185)

Sarah SOULE^3 and Adam WRIGHT^3 (Hester Cooke^2)

Adam WRIGHT^3 and 2nd Mehitable BARROWS

Aaron SOULE^3 and Mary WADSWORTH, pre 1699 (MD 9:248,11:39)

Deborah SOUL and David CUDWORTH, 3 June 1773 (Pembroke VR 3:329)

Betty SOUL and David RAMSDELL, 22 Aug. 1770 (Pembroke VR 3:330)

Charles Williams SOUL and Dorothy CLARKE, 28 Apr. 1790 (Pembroke VR 3:333)

Isaac SOUL and Agatha PARRY, 11 Mar. 1725 (Pembroke VR 3:372)

Alice SOULE and Barnabas PARRY, 30 Mar. 1792 (Pembroke VR 3:374)

Aaron SOUL Jr. and Lydia PETERSON Jr., 26 Dec. 1733 (Pembroke VR 3:377)<see below>

Gideon SOUL and Mercy SYLVESTER, 5 Mar. 1738/39 (Pembroke VR 3:379)

Mary SOUL and Abraham JOSELYN, 16 Dec. 1741 (Pembroke VR 3:379)

Mrs. Huldah SOUL and Capt. Thomas CHURCH, 24 Feb. 1760 (Pembroke VR 3:387)

Leonice SOUL and Isaac BREWSTER, 21 Nov. 1771 (Pembroke VR 3:395)

Aaron SOUL and Mrs. Orphus(sp) FOORD, 18 Dec. 1775 (Pembroke VR 3:396)$^{<3>}$

Lydia SOUL Jr. and Jedidiah DWELLE, 24 Feb. 1763 (Pembroke VR)

Joseph SOULE Jr. and Mercy FULLINGTON, 18 Mar. 1742 (Marshfield VR 2:159)

Moses SOULE and Eleanor WILLIAMS, 7 May 1761 (Marshfield VR 2:146)

Jonathan SOULE and Hannah SOUTHWORTH, 9 Feb. 1776 (Marshfield VR 2:173)

Aaron SOULE^4 (Aaron^3) and 1st Alice PETERSON, 5 May 1727, Duxbury (MD 11:80)

Aaron SOULE^4 and 2nd Lydia PETERSON <see above>

Mary SOULE^4 (Aaron^3) and Freedom CHAMBERLAIN, 5 Apr. 1722 (Pembroke VR 251,349)

Freedom CHAMBERLAIN^5 (Mary Soule^4) and Deborah TURNER^6 (Ezekiel^5, Amos^4, Mary
Brewster^3, Jonathan^2), 8 Jan. 1761 (Pembroke VR:251,366)

Mary CHAMBERLAIN^6 (Freedom^5) and Levi STURTEVANT^7 (Simeon^6, Isaac^5, Fear Cushman^4,

Isaac^3, Mary Allerton^2), 31 Aug. 1793 (Pembroke VR)

Job CHAMBERLIN^5 (Mary Soule^4) and Rachel BONNEY^4 (Eliz. Hatch^3, Mary Doty^2),
    8 Dec. 1748 (Pembroke VR)

Celia CHAMBERLIN^6 (Job^5) and Mark PHILLIPS Jr., 23 Apr. 1789 (Bridgewater VR)

Elizabeth CHAMBERLIN^6 (Job^5) and Joseph SIMMONS^6 (Nath.^{5}, Jos.^{4}, Mercy Pabodie^3,
    Eliz. Alden^2)

Rachel CHAMBERLIN^6 (Job^5) and Ichabod PACKARD

Zerviah CHAMBERLIN^6 (Job^5) and Daniel CUSHING

Nathaniel CHAMBERLIN^5 (Mary Soule^4) and 1st Sarah FOSTER, 15 Dec. 1743 (Pembroke VR)

Nathaniel CHAMBERLIN^5 and 2nd Deliverance SNELL, 19 Mar. 1767 $^{<4>}$

Rachel SOULE^4 (Aaron^3) and David MAGOON, 26 Sept. 1728 (Duxbury VR)

Micro #4 of 11

Benjamin SOULE^3 and Sarah STANDISH^3 (Alexander^2), c1694 (MD 4:113)

Benjamin SOULE^4 (Ben.^{3}) and Hannah WHITMAN, 31 Mar. 1730, Plympton (MD 5:210)

Hannah WHITMAN and 2nd Isaac LITTLE^5 (Tho.^{4}, Isaac^3, Anna Warren^2), 10 Jan. 1754

Abigail SOULE^5 (Ben.^{4}) and 1st George LITTLE^6, c1757 (Plympton Rcds.Book 1:590)$^{<5>}$

Abigail SOULE^5 and 2nd Luke PERKINS, c1765 (Plympton Rcds.Book 1:588)

Luke PERKINS and 1st Elizabeth CHURCHILL, c1757 (Plympton Rcds.Book 1:588)

Elizabeth PERKINS^6 (Abigail Soule^5) and Andrew RING (Plympton Rcds.Book 1:588)

Abigail PERKINS^6 (Abigail Soule^5) and Benjamin EATON (Plympton Rcds.Book 1:588)

Luke PERKINS^6 (Abigail Soule^5) and Hannah HARLOW^6 (Ansel^7, Jonathan^6, Tho.^{5},
    Wm.^{4}, Rebecca Bartlett^3, Mary Warren^2), 10 Nov. 1796 (Plympton VR 1:644)

Deborah SOULE^4 (Ben.^{3}) and Jabez FULLER^4 (Sam.$^{3-2-1}$), 12 Nov. 1724, Plympton
    (MD 2:139)

Jabez FULLER^4 and 2nd Mercy GRAY^5 (John^4, Mary Winslow^3, Mary Chilton^2)

Benjamin SOULE^5 (Ben.^{4}) and Mehitable BONNEY, 5 May 1757 (Plympton VR:395)

Samuel SOULE^6 (Ben.^{5}) and Lydia BRADFORD, 22 Apr. 1802, Kingston

Henry SOULE^7 (Sam.^{6}) and Zilpha COOKE, 6 Jan. 1834, Kingston

Mary Turner SOULE^8 (Henry^7) and Edgar REED, June 1876, Kingston

Eliza SOULE^7 (Ben.^{6}) and Ephraim Cushman RIPLEY, 16 Nov. 1834, Plympton

Aaron SOULE^6 (Ben.^{5}) and Ruth SAMSON, Int. 25 Dec. 1797 (Halifax VR:15)

Ebenezer SOULE^4 (Ben.^{3}) and Susanna COOMER, 9 Aug. 1733 (Plympton VR)

Sarah SOULE^5 (Eben.^{4}) and Samuel NICHOLS, 21 May 1767 (Plympton VR)

Deborah SOULE^5 (Eben.^{4}) and Josiah PERKINS, 26 Apr. 1753 (Plympton VR:360,394)

Hannah SOULE^4 (Ben.^{3}) and George SAMSON^3 (Geo.^{2}, Abraham^1), 10 Dec. 1718,

(Plympton VR:380,398)

Gideon SAMSON^5 (Hannah Soule^4) and 1st Abigail CUSHMAN^5 (Isaac$^{4-3}$, Mary Allerton^2),
    31 Dec. 1741 (Plympton VR:303,382)

Gideon SAMSON^5 and 2nd Rebecca SOULE, aft. Feb. 1784

Hannah SAMPSON^5 (Hannah Soule^4) and Joshua PERKINS, 8 Feb. 1749/50 (Plympton VR:382)

Gideon PERKINS^6 (Hannah Sampson^5) and 1st Desire DUNHAM, 23 May 1771 (Plympton
    VR:310,354)

Hannah PERKINS^6 (Hannah Sampson^5) and Peleg SAVERY, c1786

John SAVERY^7 (Hannah Perkins^6) and Polly ATWOOD, Int. 6 May 1815 (Carver VR:123)

William SAVERY^8 (John^7) and Mary Page VAN SCHAACK, 10 Sept. 1840, Albany NY

William Egbert SAVERY^9 (Wm.^{8}) and Sarah Louise BELCHER, June 1870

Joshua PERKINS^6 (Hannah Sampson^5) and Rebecca COBB, 26 Dec. 1782 (Plympton VR:360)

Lothrop PERKINS^7 (Joshua^6) and Anna FROST, 10 Apr. 1809, West Cambridge

Zabdiel SAMPSON^5 (Hannah Soule^4) and 1st Abigail CUSHMAN^5 (Ben.^{4}, Tho.^{3}, Mary
    Allerton^2), poss. 31 Dec. 1747

Zabdiel SAMPSON^5 and 2nd Abiah WHITMARSH, poss. 22 Aug. 1752

Gideon SAMPSON^6 (Zabdiel^5) and Lydia RIPLEY^6 (Wm.^{5}, Hannah Bosworth^4, David^3,
    Hannah Howland^2), c1780

Issacher SAMPSON^6 (Zabdiel^5) and Rachel GRINNELL, poss. Int. 22 Aug. 1790 (New
    Bedford VR 2:233,462)

Moses SAMPSON^7 (Issacher^6) and Ann Thomas WOOD, 18 July 1826 (New Bedford VR:463)

Ann Thomas WOOD and 2nd Samuel SWEETSER, 19 Jan. 1863, New Bedford (Mass.VR:162:87)

Josiah WOOD and Philadelphia THOMAS, 31 Oct. 1794 (New Bedford VR 2:546,609)

Caroline Frances SAMPSON^8 (Moses^7) and William Tennant HART, c1848

Caroline Sampson HART^9 (Caroline Sampson^8) and Otis KIMBALL, 20 Mar. 1877, Boston

Zachariah SOULE^4 (Ben.^{3}) and Mary EATON^4 (Ben.$^{3-2}$), 9 June 1720, Plymouth (MD 3:91)

Eunice SOULE^5 (Zachariah^4) and Seth TINKHAM^5 (Seth^4, Peter^3, Mary Brown^2),
    22 Oct. 1761

Hannah SOULE^5 (Zachariah^4) and Nathaniel HAYWARD, 24 Mar. 1769 (Plympton VR:335)

Lois SOULE^5 (Zachariah^4) and Jabez VAUGHAN^6 (Sarah Cushman^5, Ichabod^4, Isaac^3,
    Mary Allerton^2), 25 Aug. 1763, Middleboro (MD 19:174)

Sarah SOULE^5 (Zachariah^4) and Nathan TINKHAM^5 (Isaac^4, Ephraim^3, Mary Brown^2),
    10 Dec. 1746 (Halifax VR:34)

Ephraim SOULE^5 (Zachariah^4) and 1st Rebecca WHITMARSH, 10 Feb. 1757 (Plympton VR)

Ephraim SOULE^5 and 2nd Sarah (BONNEY) Harlow, 2 Oct. 1806

Daniel SOULE^6 (Ephraim^5) and 1st Sarah CUSHMAN^6 (Josiah$^{5-4}$, Elkanah^3, Mary Allerton^2), 1 May 1783, Plympton

Daniel SOULE^6 and 2nd Lucy (SAMPSON^6) Waterman (Bethiah^5, Jonathan^4, Lydia Standish^3, Alexander^2), 10 Sept. 1818 (Halifax VR:86)

Daniel SOULE^7 (Dan.^{6}) and Content HOLMES, poss. Mar. 1817, Plympton

Lydia SOULE^6 (Ephraim^5) and John BISBEE

Zachariah SOULE^6 (Ephraim^5) and Nancy DUNBAR, Plymouth

Jabez SOULE^5 (Zachariah^4) and Abigail BENNET^5 (Mercy Tomson^4, Jacob^3, Mary Cooke^2), 17 Oct. 1745, Middleboro (MD 18:79)

Abigail BENNET^5 and 2nd David WESTON, 11 July 1760 (Plympton VR:305,422)

Jacob SOULE^6 (Jabez^5) and Hannah THOMAS, Int. 1 Oct. 1769 (Halifax VR:64)

Charity SOULE^7 (Jacob^6) and Oliver PARKER, 29 Aug. 1794 (Plympton VR:357,396)

Zachariah SOULE^5 (Zachariah^4) and Sarah BRYANT, c1751

Sarah BRYANT and 2nd John TOMSON^5 (Shubael^4, John^3, Mary Cooke^2)

Sarah BRYANT and 3rd Reuben TOMSON^4 (Tho.^{3}, Mary Cooke^2)

Jabez SOULE^6 (Zachariah^5) and Lucy MORTON, 6 June 1779

Abigail SOULE^6 (Zachariah^5) and Ignatius LORING, 27 Nov. 1776 (Halifax VR:20)

George SOULE^7 (Jabez^6) and Mary ATWOOD, Int. 7 Feb. 1831 (Halifax VR:95)

Sarah SOULE^7 (Jabez^6) and Dependance STURTEVANT, 9 Mar. 1817 (Halifax VR:85)

James SOULE^3 and Lydia TOMSON^3 (Mary Cooke^2), c1693/94 (MD 4:24,27)

Jacob SOULE^4 (James^3) and Mary THOMAS, 31 Mar. 1731, Middleboro (MD 9:46)

Isaac SOULE^5 (Jacob^4) and 1st Lydia TOMSON^5 (John$^{4-3}$, Mary Cooke^2), 20 Dec. 1764 (Halifax VR:32)

Jacob SOULE^5 (Jacob^4) and Sarah SHAW, 21 Jan. 1762, Middleboro (MD 24:185)

Faith SOULE^6 (Jacob^5) and Nathan FULLER, poss. 23 Apr. 1809

Lydia SOULE^5 (Jacob^4) and William SHAW^7 (Desire Southworth^6, Ichabod^5, Desire Gray^4, Mary Winslow^3, Mary Chilton^2)

William SOULE^5 (Jacob^4) and Sarah BRIGGS, 30 Oct. 1760

Martha SOULE^4 (James^3) and Joseph FAUNCE, 14 Feb. 1722/23, Middleboro (MD 4:72)

James FAUNCE^5 (Martha Soule^4) and Abigail RICKARD, 26 Nov. 1747, Middleboro (MD 18:80)

Abigail RICKARD and 2nd John JACOBS, c1766

John SOULE^3 and Martha TINKHAM^4 (Ephraim^3, Mary Brown^2), 8 Dec. 1701, Middleboro (MD 1:220)

John SOULE^4 (John^3) and Mary LEACH

Mary LEACH and 2nd Ephraim WOOD, aft. Feb. 1750

Martha SOULE^4 (John^3) and Thomas TOMSON^4 (John^3, Mary Cooke^2), 25 Apr. 1732, Middle-
    boro (MD 13:249)

Mary SOULE^4 (John^3) and Obadiah SAMSON

Rachel SOULE^4 (John^3) and Ebenezer VAUGHAN

James SOULE^4 (John^3) and Deborah HOLMES, 31 Mar. 1744, Plymouth (MD 16:15)

John SOULE^5 (James^4) and Joanna PERKINS, Int. 16 Mar. 1782, Middleboro

Joanna PERKINS and 2nd Nathan ALDEN, 24 Jan. 1819 (Bridgewater VR 2:20,351)

James SOULE^6 (John^5) and Leah BENNETT, 27 Nov. 1819

Micro #6 of 11

Joseph SOULE^3 and Mary PETERSON^3 (Mary Soule^2), c1711 (MD 11:235)

Alethea SOULE^4 (Jos.^{3}) and Allerton CUSHMAN^5 (Allerton^4, Elkanah^3, Mary Allerton^2),
    30 Jan. 1734/35, Duxbury (MD 11:241)

Mary SOULE^4 (Jos.^{3}) and Joshua CUSHMAN, 2 Jan. 1732/33, Duxbury (MD 11:81)

Zeruiah SOULE^4 (Joshua^3) and Ebenezer SAMSON^4 (Lorah Standish^3, Alexander^2),
    23 Apr. 1728, Duxbury (MD 11:80)

Joshua SOULE^3 and Joanna STUDLEY, 15 Feb. 1704/05, Duxbury (MD 9:108)

Abigail SOULE^4 (Joshua^3) and Perez DREW, 3 Sept. 1730, Duxbury (MD 11:241)

Silvanus DREW^5 (Abigail Soule^4) and Mercy CLARK, c1764

Charles DREW^6 (Silvanus^5) and 1st Betsey ROSE, 5 Jan. 1794, Marshfield

Charles DREW^6 and 2nd Susan ( ) BAILEY, Dec. 1810, Brewster

Zilpha DREW^6 (Silvanus^5) and Jonathan SMITH

Ezekiel SOULE^4 (Joshua^3) and Hannah DELANO^4 (Jonathan^3, Mary Alden^2), 4 Jan.
    1732/33, Duxbury (MD 11:81)

John SOULE^5 (Ezekiel^4) and Patience WORMALL

John SOULE^4 (Joshua^3) and Mabel PARTRIDGE^6 (Lydia Keen^5, Josiah^4, Abigail Little^3,
    Anna Warren^2), 5 Aug. 1730 (Duxbury VR)

Mabel PARTRIDGE^6 and 2nd Samuel KEMPTON Jr., 9 Feb. 1736/37, Plymouth (MD 14:157)

Mabel PARTRIDGE^6 and 3rd William COOMER

Samuel SOULE^5 (John^4) and Mehitable WHITE, 1 Oct. 1756 (Duxbury VR)

Mehitable WHITE and 2nd Ichabod WESTON, poss. 7 Dec. 1769

Lydia SOULE^6 (Sam.^{5}) and Joseph BARSTOW, 16 Nov. 1787, Duxbury (MD 28:48)

Joseph SOULE^4 (Joshua^3) and Mercy FULLERTON, 18 Mar. 1742, Marshfield (Duxbury VR)

Olive SOULE^5 (Jos.^{4}) and Nathaniel WINSOR

Ezekiel SOULE^5 (Jos.^{4}) and Clynthia WADSWORTH^6 (Abigail Bradford^5, Gamaliel^4, Sam.^{3}, Wm.^{2}), 7 Feb. 1777, Duxbury

Otis SOULE^6 (Ezekiel^5) and Salumith W. SAMPSON

James SOULE^5 (Jos.^{4}) and Abigail (SEAVER) Bosworth, 17 Jan. 1773 (Duxbury VR)

Richard SOULE^6 (James^5) and 1st Prudence LORING, 10/24 June 1810 (Duxbury VR)

Richard SOULE^6 and 2nd Lucy LORING, 4 Nov. 1824 (Duxbury VR)

Joshua SOULE^6 (James^5) and Rebecca CHANDLER, c1802

Joshua SOULE^5 (Jos.^{4}) and Mary CUSHMAN^6 (Allerton$^{5-4}$, Elkanah^3, Mary Allerton^2), 14 Feb. 1765, Duxbury

Anne PRIOR^6 (Sarah Soule^5, Jos.^{4}) and Nathaniel HOLMES

William SOULE^5 (Jos.^{4}) and Priscilla SAMSON^5 (Elijah^4, John^3, Stephen^2), 16 Apr. 1785

Laura Louise SOULE^8 (Laurence P.^{7}, Stephen^6, Wm.^{5}) and Albert Stokes APSEY, c1901

Nathan SOULE^4 (Joshua^3) and Sarah SOUTHWORTH^6 (Jedediah^5, Tho.^{4}, Mary Pabodie^3, Eliz. Alden^2), 17 Dec. 1746 (Duxbury VR)

Levi SOUL and Abigail COLE, 15 Dec. 1776 (Waldoboro ME VR 1:)

Abigail SOUL and Capt. Joshua HOWARD, 9 Sept. 1794 (Waldoboro ME VR 1:)

Anna SOUL and Alexander TURNER, Int. 25 Dec. 1784 (Waldoboro ME VR 1:)

Levi SOUL and Abigail COLE, 21 Feb. 1811 (Waldoboro ME VR 2:274)

Josiah SOULE^3 and Lydia DELANO, 25 May 1704, Duxbury (MD 9:109)

Abishai SOULE^4 (Josiah^3) and Abigail DELANO, 14 May 1741, Duxbury

Micah SOULE^4 (Josiah^3) and Mercy SOUTHWORTH^5 (Constant^4, Mary Pabodie^3, Eliz. Alden^2), 31 May 1740, Duxbury (MD 11:81)

Sarah SOULE^4 (Joshua^3) and Aaron BISBEE, 26 Nov. 1747, Duxbury (MD 12:34)

Esther SOULE^5 (Micah^4) and poss. Darius BREWSTER^7 (Zadock^6, Jos.^{5}, Nath.^{4}, Wm.^{3}, Love^2), 8 May 1791 (Brewster Gen.1:258)

Nephele SOULE^5 (Micah^4) and Consider SIMMONS^6 (Ichabod^5, Moses^4, Mercy Pabodie^3, Eliz. Alden^2), 25 Feb. 1763 (Duxbury Ch.rcds.)

Asa SOULE^5 (Micah^4) and Olive SOUTHWORTH^6 (Ben.^{5}, Constant^4, Mary Pabodie^3, Eliz. Alden^2), 15 Oct. 1773 (Duxbury VR)

Thomas SOULE^6 (Constant S.^{5}, Micah^4) and Lois HOWARD, poss. 26 Feb. 1805

Thomas Howard SOULE^7 (Tho.^{6}) and Margaret Albertson DUNHAM

Micro #7 of 11

Jonathan SOULE^5 (Micah^4) and Honor SOUTHWORTH, 9 Feb. 1776 (Marshfield VR 2:173)

Josiah SOULE^5 (Micah^4) and poss. Alice SOULE^6 (Sam.^{5}, John^4, Joshua^3, John^2),
    c1782

Alice SOULE^6 and 2nd John HATCH, poss. 29 Dec. 1807

Micah SOULE^6 (Josiah^5) and Lucy ALDEN, poss. Aug. 1806 (Duxbury VR)

Nathaniel SOULE^5 (Nath.^{4}, Josiah^3) and Polly PARTRIDGE, 29 Sept. 1808 (Duxbury
    VR:283,312)

Moses SOULE^3 and 1st Mercy SOUTHWORTH^4 (Mary Pabodie^3, Eliz. Alden^2)

Moses SOULE^3 and 2nd Sarah CHANDLER, 15 Jan. 1729/30, Duxbury (MD 11:240)

Alice SOULE^4 (Moses^3) and 1st Barnabas PERRY, 2nd Edward KING

Deborah SOULE^4 (Moses^3) and John HUNT, poss. 1 May 1746

John HUNT and 2nd Esther WRIGHT^5 (John^4, Adam^3, Hester Cooke^2), Int. 6 Apr. 1733
    (Plympton VR:336,431)

Gideon SOULE^4 (Moses^3) and Mercy SILVESTER, 5 Mar. 1738/39 (Pembroke VR)

Gideon SOULE^5 (Gideon^4) and Ruth HARDEN, 22 Dec. 1763 (Halifax VR:32)

Asa SOULE^6 (Gideon^5) and Ruth Howland STETSON, 27 Dec. 1784 (Halifax VR:22)

Ichabod SOULE^4 (Moses^3) and Grace TURNER, poss. 25 Mar. 1734, Scituate

Isaac SOULE^4 (Moses^3) and Agatha PERRY, 11 Mar. 1725 (Pembroke VR:325,349)

Mary SOULE^5 (Isaac^4) and Abraham JOSSELYN, poss. 16 Dec. 1741, Pembroke

William COX and Mrs. Elizabeth PHIPPS, 7 Feb. 1802 (Chatham NH TR 1:337)

Mary JOSSLYEN Jr. and William COX Jr., 21 Jan. 1762

Jedediah SOULE^4 (Moses^3) and Tabitha BISHOP, 4 Nov. 1741, Duxbury (MD 11:239)

Deborah SOULE^5 (Jedediah^4) and Ambrose HAMILTON Jr., 28 Apr. 1763, Chebeague ME
    ("Old Times - N. Yarmouth:1012)

James S. HAMILTON^6 (Deborah Soule^5) and Mary WEBBER, Chebeague ME

Ichabod SOULE^5 (Jedediah^4) and Martha BARTON, 24 Nov. 1768

James SOULE^5 (Jedediah^4) and Martha CURTIS, 7 Apr. 1778

Jedediah SOULE^5 (Jedediah^4) and Mary PINKHAM, 7 Nov. 1776

Jesse SOULE^6 (Jonathan^5) and Abigail HILL, 21 Nov. 1782

Jonathan SOULE^5 (Jedediah^4) and Mary MITCHELL, 20 Nov. 1783

Elizabeth SOULE^6 (Jonathan^5) and Shubal DIXON, 7 Nov. 1815, Freeport ME (TR)

Rachel SOULE^3 and John COBB, 5 Sept. 1688, Middleboro (MD 2:43)$^{<6>}$

Rachel COBB^4 (Rachel Soule^3) and Moses STANDISH^4 (Eben.^{3}, Alexander^2)

James COBB^4 (Rachel Soule^3) and Thankful THOMAS^4 (Lydia Howland^3, John^2), 6 Mar.
    1717/18, Middleboro (MD 4:71)

Jacob WOOD and Lydia MILLER, Int. 25 July 1784 (Middleboro VR 4:56)

James COBB^5 (James^4) and Susanna TINKHAM^5 (John^4, Ephraim^3, Mary Brown^2), Int.
   25 Nov. 1749 (Middleboro VR 2:153)

Priscilla COBB^5 (James^4) and Silas WOOD, 24 Nov. 1752, Middleboro (MD 18:157)

Thankful COBB^5 (James^4) and Ichabod WOOD, 16 Feb. 1743

John COB^4 (Rachel Soule^3) and 1st Joanna THOMAS, c1713 (MD 6:226)

John COB^4 and 2nd Mary CONANT^6 (Eliz. Washburn^5, Tho.^{4}, Eliz. Mitchell^3, Jane
   Cooke^2), 26 Aug. 1725, Middleboro (MD 4:73)

John COBB^5 (John^4) and Priscilla TINKHAM^5 (Shubael^4, Eben.^{3}, Mary Brown^2), c1744

Priscilla TINKHAM^5 and 2nd William CUSHMAN^5 (Ichabod^4, Isaac^3, Mary Allerton^2),
   11 Apr. 1751, Middleboro (MD 18:84)

Martha COBB^4 (Rachel Soule^3) and 1st Ephraim TINKHAM^4 (Ephraim^3, Mary Brown^2),
   24 June 1708, Middleboro (MD 2:157)

Martha COBB^4 and 2nd Aaron SIMMONS, c1716 (MD 3:233)

Martha SIMMONS^5 (Martha Cobb^4) and Nelson FINNEY, 7 Dec. 1749, Middleboro (MD 18:82)

Rebecca SOULE^3 and Edmund WESTON, 13 Dec. 1688, Plymouth (MD 13:204)

Benjamin WESTON^4 (Rebecca Soule^3) and 2nd Hannah COMER, 15 Oct. 1731, Plympton
   (MD 2:50)

Benjamin WESTON^4 and 4th Mercy (STANDISH) Lobdell, aft. Mar. 1765[7]

William WESTON^5 (Ben.^{4}) and Mary WESTON^7 (Prudence Conant^6, Eliz. Washburn^5,
   Tho.^{4}, Eliz. Mitchell^3, Jane Cooke^2), 22 Nov. 1753, Plymouth (MD 18:141)

Micro #8 of 11

Lewis WESTON^6 (Wm.^{5}) and Lucy CHURCHILL^7 (Eliz. Silvester^6, Solomon^5, Hannah
   Bartlett^4, Jos.^{3}, Mary Warren^2) (Churchill Gen.:27)

William WESTON^6 (Wm.^{5}) and Mary CHURCHILL^7 (Eliz. Silvester^6, Solomon^5, Hannah
   Bartlett^4, Jos.^{3}, Mary Warren^2), 26 Nov. 1778 (Plymouth Ch.rcds.2:499)

Harvey WESTON^7 (Wm.^{6}) and 1st Lucy HARLOW

Harvey WESTON^7 and 2nd Sally CHURCHILL^8 (Dan.^{7}, Stephen^6, Hannah Barnes^5, Sarah
   Bradford^4, Wm.$^{3-2}$), aft. July 1818

Edmund WESTON^4 (Rebecca Soule^3) and Susanna JACKSON, 21 Jan. 1724/25, Plympton
   (MD 2:139)

Edmund WESTON^4 and poss. 2nd Elizabeth SMITH, 2 Mar. 1734/35 (Middleboro VR 1:140)

Edmund WESTON^5 (Edmund^4) and Mary TINKHAM^5 (John^4, Ephraim^3, Mary Brown^2),
   11 Sept. 1755, Middleboro (MD 19:48)

Abner WESTON^6 (Edmund^5) and Huldah WASHBURN^7 (Jonah^6, James$^{5-4}$, Eliz. Mitchell^3,
   Jane Cooke^2)

John WESTON[4] (Rebecca Soule[3]) and Content JACKSON, 29 Nov. 1723, Plympton (MD 2:139)

John WESTON[4] and poss. 2nd Hannah VAUGHAN, 8 July 1749 (Middleboro VR 2:52)[8]

John WESTON and 1st Elizabeth LEONARD, 14 Apr. 1757 (Middleboro VR 2:85)

John WESTON and 2nd Priscilla STURTEVANT, 6 Dec. 1776 (Middleboro VR 4:157)

Nathan WESTON[4] (Rebecca Soule[3]) and Desire STANDISH[3] (Alexander[2]), 21 Feb. 1715, Plympton (MD 2:236)

Isaac WESTON[5] (Nathan[4]) and Molly RIPLEY, 30 June 1748 (Plympton VR)

Nathan WESTON[5] (Nathan[4]) and Hannah EVERSON, 29 Aug. 1751, Kingston (Plympton VR)

Rebecca WESTON[4] (Rebecca Soule[3]) and Thomas DARLING, 18 Nov. 1725, Plympton (MD 1:246)

Lurana DARLING[6] (Tho.[5], Rebecca Weston[4]) and William WASHBURN, 9 Oct. 1783, New Braintree (VR:77,121)

Benjamin DARLING[5] (Rebecca Weston[4]) and Hannah HARRIS, 29 July 1756 (Halifax VR:35)

John DARLING[6] (Ben.[5]) and Mary WOOD, 27 Jan. 1780 (Middleboro VR 4:150)

Zachariah WESTON[4] (Rebecca Soule[3]) and Mehitable SHAW, 20 June 1717, Plympton (MD 2:237)

Mehitable WESTON[5] (Zachariah[4]) and poss. Lemuel THOMAS, 19 Apr. 1750, Middleboro (MD 18:83)

James WESTON[5] (Zachariah[4]) and Abigail DUNHAM, 9 Feb. 1748/49, Plymouth (MD 17:3)

John Granger WESTON[7] (Joshua[6], James[5]) and Adeline Augusta TIDD

Adeline Augusta TIDD and 2nd John PUTNAM

Zachariah WESTON[5] (Zachariah[4]) and 2nd Sarah WOOD, 6 Dec. 1770 (Middleboro VR 4:2:9)

Mary SOULE[2] (George[1])

Mary SOULE[2] and John PETERSON, pre 1668

Rebecca PETERSON[3] and John WESTON, 1 Oct. 1717

Benjamin PETERSON[3] and Hannah WADSWORTH, 9 Feb. 1698, Duxbury (MD 9:108)

Jacob PETERSON[4] (Ben.[3]) and Mary HARLOW[6] (Wm.[5-4], Rebeca Bartlett[3], Mary Warren[2])

Isaac PETERSON[3] and Mary HOBART, 28 Mar. 1711 (Hist.Hingham 2:337)

Jonathan PETERSON[3] and Lydia WADSWORTH, c1700/01 (MD 9:247, 8:233)

John PETERSON and Ruth DELANO, 21 Aug. 1726, Kingston (Gen.Adv.2:124)

Reuben PETERSON[4] (Jonathan[3]) and Rebecca SIMMONS[5] (Jos.[4], Mercy Pabodie[3], Eliz. Alden[2]), 6 July 1732, Duxbury (MD 11:80)

Sarah PETERSON[5] (Reuben[4]) and Timothy WILLIAMSON, , poss. 3 Dec. 1767 (Duxbury VR)

Joseph PETERSON[3] and Sarah (JONES[4]) Doty (Patience Little[3], Anna Warren[2]), 23 Aug. 1704, Plymouth (MD 14:35)

Susanna PETERSON^5 (Jos.$^{4-3}$) and Gershom EWELL, 8 Oct. 1767, Duxbury

Nathaniel SOULE^2 (George^1)

Jacob SOULE^3 and Rebecca GIFFORD, 22 Jan. 1709 (Dartmouth VR)

Stephen SOULE^4 (Jacob^3) and Sarah POTTER

Nathaniel SOULE^3 and 1st Meribah GIFFORD, 20 July 1708 (Dartmouth VR 1:55)

Nathaniel SOULE^3 and 2nd Hannah MACOMBER, 13 Feb. 1732/33 (Dartmouth VR 2:303)

Henry SOULE^4 (Nath.^{3}) and Barbara COTTRELL

Jonathan SOULE^4 (Nath.^{3}) and Elizabeth GIFFORD^5 (Mary Wright^4, Adam^3, Hester
    Cooke^2), 3 Dec. 1731 (Dartmouth VR 1:384)

Wesson SOULE^4 (Nath.^{3}) and Ruhama HICKS

Silvanus SOULE^3 and Sarah SLADE

Patience SOULE^2 (George^1)

Patience SOULE^2 and John HASKELL, Jan. 1666, Middleboro (MD 1:219)

Bethiah HASKELL^3 and poss. William SHERMAN

Mary HASKELL^3 and Scotaway CLARK, 17 Apr. 1706 (Rochester VR 1:1)

Elizabeth HASKELL^3 and Thomas DRINKWATER

Joseph DRINKWATER^4 (Eliz. Haskell^3) and Jennet LATHAM^6 (Tho.^{5}, James^4, Susanna
    Winslow^3, Mary Chilton^2)

Joseph DRINKWATER^5 (Jos.^{4}) and Mary LEACH

John HASKELL^3 and Mary SQUIRE, 2 Mar. 1698/99, Middleboro (MD 1:220)

Squire HASCALL and Esther HUMPHREY, c1788, Wethersfield CT (Gen.Reg.18:225)

Josiah HASKELL^3 and 1st Sarah KANADY, 26 Mar. 1718, Middleboro (MD 4:71)

Josiah HASKELL^3 and 2nd Sarah BRAYLEY, 27 Mar. 1729, Middleboro (MD 5:39)

Susanna HASKELL^3 and Thomas PAIN, poss. 21 Feb. 1711/12

Thomas PAIN and 2nd Annabel CANADAY, 19 Aug. 1731, Middleboro (Gen.Reg.15:235)

Ralph PAIN^4 (Susanna Haskell^3) and Elizabeth HARLOW, Int. 20 Apr. 1742
    (Freetown VR 1:178)

Elizabeth PAIN^4 (Susanna Haskell^3) and Hezekiah WINSLOW, 20 May 1737 (Gen.
    Reg.13:236)

Job PAIN^4 (Susanna Haskell^3) and Hannah TERRY, 30 July 1761 (Freetown VR 2:227)[9]

Silas PAIN^5 (Job^4) and Chloe CHACE, 3 Dec. 1801 (Freetown VR 3:88)

George Anson PAINE^6 (Silas^5) and Ann SPENCER, Int. 4 Feb. 1827 (Freetown VR 3:225)

John Brown PAINE^6 (Silas^5) and Rebecca Morton REED

Lloyd Bowers PAINE^6 (Silas^5) and Julia Ann LILLIBAR, Int. 8 July 1827 (Freetown VR 3:227)

Thomas Jefferson PAINE^6 (Silas^5) and Sarah Ann SMITH

Mercy PAIN^4 (Susanna Haskell^3) and Seth FARROW, c1736 (Freetown VR 1:173)[10]

Patience PAIN^4 (Susanna Haskell^3) and Jonathan WINSLOW, 26 Dec. 1743 (Freetown
VR 1:176)

Susanna SOULE^2 (George^1)

Susanna SOULE^2 and Francis WEST, pre 1660 (MD 26:1,10)

Susanna WEST^4 (Francis^3) and John TANNER, 9 May 1723 (N. Kingstown RI VR 1:3)

Peter WEST^4 (Francis^3) and Sarah BAKER, 7 Nov. 1731 (N. Kingston RI VR 1:45)

John WEST and Alice SWEET, Mar. 1730/31 (N. Kingston RI VR 1:44)

Martha WEST^3 and 1st James CARD, 4 Mar. 1702/03 (Arnold VR 5:1:12)

Martha WEST^3 and 2nd Jeremiah FONES, Nov. 1710, Jamestown RI (VR RI 4:5:8)

Susanna WEST^3 and Moses BARBER, 20/24 Mar. 1691/92 (N. Kingston RI VR 5:1:8,51)

Moses BARBER and Elizabeth ELDRED, 23 May 1705

Dinah BARBER^4 (Susanna West^3) and Edward WILCOX, 14 June 1716 (Westerly VR 5:4:9,69)

Joseph WILCOX^5 (Dinah Barber^4) and Mary BURDICK, 28 July 1748

Prudence WILCOX^6 (Jos.^{5}) and Nathan TAYLOR, c1772 (VR RI 5:5:27)

Sarah TAYLOR^7 (Prudence Wilcox^6) and David ROSS, 6 Feb. 1806 (Charlestown RI VR)

William WEST^3 and Jane TANNER, c1725-30

William SPRAGUE and 1st Deborah LANE (Hist.Hingham 3:165)

William SPRAGUE and 2nd Mary TOWER (Hist.Hingham 3:165)

William WEST and Abiah SPRAGUE, Int. 24 Dec. 1709 (Hist.Hingham 3:165)

Francis WEST^4 (Wm.^{3}) and Eunice FONES, 1 Oct. 1758, Exeter RI (RI VR 5:3:14,34)

Francis WEST and Mary LAWTON, 17 Feb. 1757, Westerly RI (VR RI 5:7:19,27)

Benjamin WEST and Mary ELDRED, 7 Oct. 1759 (Arnold VR 5:3:13,35)

Sarah WEST and John ELDRED, 29 Mar. 1762 (Arnold VR 5:3:13,35)

Elizabeth WEST and David BISSELL, 10 Mar. 1785 (Arnold VR 5:3:8,35)

George W. HULING and Joanna E. LILLIBRIDGE, 16 Dec. 1824 (Arnold VR 5:3:18)

Elder Thomas WEST^4 (Wm.^{3}) and Annie COLGROVE, c1753 (MD 26:2,10)

Charles WEST and Mary WILLIAMS, 6 Mar. 1782, Foster RI (VR RI 3:4:30)

Thomas WEST and Annie COLGROVE, 3 June 1785, Foster RI (VR RI 3:4:30)

Huldah WEST and William HOPKINS 2d, 12 Aug. 1820, Foster RI (VR RI 3:4:30)

Welthian COLEGROVE and Edward FENNER, 30 Mar. 1786, Foster RI (VR RI 3:4:9)[11]

Elder Samuel WEST[5] (Tho.[4]) and 1st Jerusha STANTON, 10 Mar. 1785 (MD 26:3)[12]

Elder Samuel WEST[5] and 2nd Mary (SMITH) Lester, 1 Aug. 1816 (MD 26:3,107)

Elder Samuel WEST[5] and 3rd Anna ARNOLD, 12 Sept. 1830 (MD 26:3,173)

NOTES

[1] p.261, George Soule's wife is listed here as Mary ( ). It is now known he married Mary Bucket/Becket, c1676. (Mayflower Increasings:116)

[2] p.261, These seven marriages are listed under the source heading, "Court Gen'l. Sessions 1733", name of town is not given.

[3] p.263, Her name is given as Orphan Ford in the marriage intentions, 16 Dec. 1775 (Marshfield VR 2:168)

[4] p.264, Nathaniel Chamberlin's "Account Book" provides the dates of both marriages.

[5] p.264, George Little[6] appears to have Mayflower descent to Richard Warren but line is not shown here.

[6] p.269, The marriage is recorded in the Plymouth VR as 7 Sept. 1688. (MD 13:204)

[7] p.270, Benjamin Weston's 1st wife was Hannah ( ), c1723; 3rd, Philomena ( ), aft. Nov. 1742.

[8] p.271, She appears to be Hannah Tinkham who married 1st Joseph Vaughan, 2nd John Weston, 3rd David Sears (aft. Aug. 1768).

[9] p.273, There is undoubtedly an interesting story behind these dates. Marriage intentions were initially published 15 Aug. 1759 (Freetown VR 1:217) followed by the birth of their first child, 11 Dec. 1759. The marriage of Job Pain and Hannah Terry finally took place 30 July 1761, six days **after** the recorded birth of their second child.

[10] p.273, Before her marriage, Mercy Pain had an illegitimate son, Nathan Pain[5], b. 19 June 1733. The father is not named. (Freetown VR 1:173)

[11] p.274, Apparently the same marriage is given (within the same source) with the year of marriage 1876, probably an error. (VR RI 3:4:12)

[12] p.274, He is the author of "Samuel Wests Memmorandum Book". A literal transcript can be found beginning in MD 26:2. The manuscript contains much genealogical and historical data concerning his family, his ministry and the time period in which he lived.

MYLES STANDISH DESCENDANTS

Alexander STANDISH^2 (Myles^1)

Alexander STANDISH^2 and 1st Sarah ALDEN^2 (MD 12:99)

Alexander STANDISH^2 and 2nd Desire (DOTY^2) Sherman, pre 13 June 1688 (MD 3:11)

Desire STANDISH^3 and Nathan WESTON^4 (Rebecca Soule^3, John^2), 21 Feb. 1715,
  Plympton (MD 2:236)

Ebenezer STANDISH^3 and Hannah STURTEVANT, c1697 (MD 5:183)

Hannah STANDISH^4 (Eben.^{3}) and Seth STAPLE, 4 Jan. 1721, Plympton (MD 2:138,5:184)

Hannah STAPLE^5 (Hannah Standish^4) and Abraham GUSHEE, 23 July 1741 (Taunton VR 2:142)

Abraham GUSHEE^6 (Hannah Staples^5) and Silvia FOBES

Silvia FOBES and 2nd Eleazer CLAP, 8 July 1784, Raynham (Gen.Reg.51:291)

Abraham GUSHEE^7 (Abraham^6) and Bathsheba TOBEY, 10/11 Oct. 1804, Berkley (Tobey
  Gen.:84)

Maria GUSHEE^8 (Abraham^7) and Levi Loukton CRANE, poss. 15 July 1832

Almond GUSHEE^7 (Abraham^6) and Nancy ROBBINS

Elijah GUSHEE^6 (Hannah Staple^5) and 1st Sarah KING, 16 Dec. 1782, Raynham (Gen.
  Reg.51:290)

Elijah GUSHEE^6 and 2nd Jemima WILLIAMS, 17 Mar. 1791 (Taunton VR 2:211,529)

Elijah GUSHEE^6 and 3rd Phebe MACOMBER^7 (Abiel^6, Josiah^5, Eliz. Williams^4, Eliz.
  Rogers^2) (Macomber Gen.:30)

Hannah GUSHEE^6 (Hannah Staple^5) and Luther ROBINSON, c1770 (Gen.Reg.53:438)

Mercy GUSHEE^6 (Hannah Staples^5) and poss. Samuel JONES

Samuel GUSHEE^6 (Hannah Staple^5) and 1st Hannah GILMORE, 26 Feb. 1784, Raynham
  (Gen.Reg.51:290)

Samuel GUSHEE^7 (Sam.^{6}) and Keziah DEAN, 1 Dec. 1811

Edward GUSHEE^8 (Sam.^{7}) and poss. Fanny Dean LEONARD, c1837

Rev. John STAPLES and Susanna PERKINS, c1772 (Gen.Reg.14:118)

Ruth STAPLES^5 (Hannah Standish^4) and Oliver SOPER, 8 Nov. 1763 (PN&Q 2:77)

Fanny SOPER^6 (Ruth Staples^5) and John PRESBREY

Oliver SOPER^6 (Ruth STaples^5) and Rebecca PAULL, 24 Oct. 1802

Sarah STAPLES^5 (Hannah Standish^4) and Daniel WILD

Susanna STAPLE^5 (Hannah Standish^4) and Job WHITE, c1750

John WHITE 2d and Susanna JACKSON, 13 Jan. 1758 (poss. Norton VR)

Job WHITE and Susannah WILLIAMS, 4 June 1765 (poss. Norton VR)

Zeruiah STAPLES[5] (Hannah Standish[4]) and Abiel WILLIAMS, c1758, poss. Raynham
(Gen.Reg.55:43,44)

Anna WILLIAMS and Jonathan P. ROBINSON, 24 Apr. 1804 (poss. Raynham VR:125)

Rev. Abiel WILLIAMS[6] (Zeruiah Staples[5]) and Sarah CARGILL, 14 Apr. 1802, Palmer

Jonathan WILLIAMS[6] (Zeruiah Staples[5]) and Polly DEAN

Hannah WILLIAMS[7] (Jonathan[6]) and Joseph BASSETT, Int. 23 Mar. 1816, Bridgewater

Mercy STANDISH[4] (Eben.[3]) and 1st Ebenezer LOBDELL

Mercy STANDISH[4] and 2nd Benjamin WESTON, aft. Mar. 1765

Moses STANDISH[4] (Eben.[3]) and Rachel COBB[4] (Rachel Soule[3], John[2]), 23 Nov. 1723,
Middleboro (MD 4:73)

Micro #2 of 4

Sarah STANDISH[5] (Moses[4]) and 1st Ephraim TINKHAM[5] (Sam.[4], Ephraim[3], Mary Brown[2]),
5 Jan. 1759 (Halifax VR:36)[1]

Sarah STANDISH[5] and 2nd Adam WRIGHT[5] (John[4], Adam[3], Hester Cooke[2]), 1 June 1773
(Plympton VR:231)

John STANDISH[5] (Moses[4]) and Rebecca ELLIS, Int. 28 Nov. 1763 (Halifax VR:62)

John STANDISH[6] (John[5]) and Jane CHURCHILL, Int. 3 June 1805 (Halifax VR:69)

Rachel STANDISH[6] (John[5]) and Levi LORING, 13 Sept. 1789 (Halifax VR:23)

Moses STANDISH[5] (Moses[4]) and Mary EDDY, Int. 25 July 1758 (Halifax VR:60)

Rachel STANDISH[5] (Moses[4]) and 1st Philemon SAMPSON[4] (Ben.[3], Geo.[2], Abraham[1]),
12 May 1742 (MD 2:44)

Rachel STANDISH[5] and 2nd Amos FULLER[5] (Nath.[4], Sam.[3-2-1]), 25 Oct. 1759 (MD 2:44)

Sarah STANDISH[4] (Eben.[3]) and Jabez NEWLAND

Zachariah STANDISH[4] (Eben.[3]) and Abigail WHITMAN, 13 Oct. 1720, Plympton (MD 3:91)

Ebenezer STANDISH[5] (Zachariah[4]) and Averick CHURCHILL, 27 Dec. 1739 (HalifaxVR:34)

Averick STANDISH[6] (Eben.[5]) and Zadock THOMAS, 23 Apr. 1761, Kingston

Levi THOMAS[7] (Averick Standish[6]) and Lydia THOMAS

Levi THOMAS[8] (Levi[7]) and Phebe Crocker TILLSON, 5 Jan. 1826, Hanson

Levi Zelida THOMAS[9] (Levi[8]) and 1st Harriet STOCKBRIDGE, 5 Oct. 1855, Randolph

Levi Zelida THOMAS[9] and 2nd Julia Edward SOPER, 18 Mar. 1877

Irving Levi THOMAS[10] (Levi[9]) and Hannah Ann HILL, 27 Sept. 1882, Wells ME

Annie Lincoln THOMAS[10] (Levi[9]) and Frank C. BUELL, 25 Dec. 1882, Missoula, Mont.

Bradford Wilson THOMAS[10] (Levi[9]) and Frances BURNETT, 24 Jan. 1887, Oregon

Sherman Tillson THOMAS^{10} (Levi^9) and Lizzie B. IRESON, 2 Oct. 1887, Lynn

Addie May THOMAS^{10} (Levi^9) and Nelson GETCHELL, 23 May 1891, Waltham

Shadrach STANDISH^6 (Eben.^{5}) and poss. Mary CHURCHILL, c1771 (Churchill Fam.:73)

Ellis STANDISH^7 (Shadrach^6) and Mary BRADFORD$^{<2>}$

Jane STANDISH^8 (Ellis^7) and Israel HEALD

Zachariah STANDISH^5 (Zachariah^4) and 2nd Olive POOL

Zeruiah STANDISH^4 (Eben.^{3}) and 1st Andrew RING^4 (Eleazer^3, Deborah Hopkins^2),
      20 May 1724, Plympton (MD 2:139)

Zeruiah STANDISH^4 and 2nd Andrew GRAY, 19 Dec. 1745

Elizabeth STANDISH^3 and Samuel DELANO, pre 1685 (MD 12:101,183-84)

Hazadiah DELANO^4 (Eliz. Standish^3) and Mary TAYLOR, 1 Apr. 1731, Marshfield
      (Duxbury VR:243)

Priscilla DELANO^4 (Eliz. Standish^3) and Benjamin SIMMONS^4 (Mercy Pabodie^3, Eliz.
      Alden^2), 7 July 1715, Duxbury (MD 11:24)

Rebecca DELANO^4 (Eliz. Standish^3) and Benjamin SOUTHWORTH^4 (Mary Pabodie^3, Eliz.
      Alden^2)

Sarah DELANO^4 (Eliz. Standish^3) and Joshua SIMMONS, 4 Apr. 1728, Duxbury
      (MD 11:80)$^{<3>}$

Elizabeth DELANO^4 (Eliz. Standish^3) and Joseph CHANDLER, 8 Sept. 1720, Duxbury
      (MD 11:80)

Joseph CHANDLER and 2nd Deborah BONNEY, 27 Nov. 1729 (Pembroke VR)

John CHANDLER^5 (Eliz. Delano^4) and Sarah WESTON, 4 Nov. 1743, Duxbury (MD 11:239)

Rebecca CHANDLER^6 (John^5) and David OLDHAM

Samuel DELANO^4 (Eliz. Standish^3) and Elizabeth BONNEY, 21 May 1719, Duxbury
      (MD 11:79)

Ichabod STANDISH^3 and Phebe RING^4 (Eleazer^3, Deborah Hopkins^2), 26 Nov. 1719,
      Plympton (MD 3:91)

Desire STANDISH^4 (Ichabod^3) and David HATCH Jr., 16 Jan. 1755 (Halifax VR:35)

Ichabod HATCH^5 (Desire Standish^4) and Abigail WRIGHT^6 (Abigail Standish^5, Zachariah^4,
      Eben.^{3}, Alex.^{2}), 4 July 1782 (Plympton VR)

Micro #3 of 4

Lydia HATCH^5 (Desire Standish^4) and Isaac HOBART, 17 Mar. 1780 (Halifax VR:21)

Isaac HOBART^6 (Lydia Hatch^5) and Lettice BARKER, 20 Dec. 1807 (Pembroke VR)

David H. HOBART^6 (Lydia Hatch^5) and Sarah N. PRATT, Int. 7 June 1816, Pembroke

Abraham SAMSON^4 (Lorah Standish^3) and 1st Penelope SAMSON^3 (James^2), c1712 (MD 10:185)

Hannah SAMSON^5 (Abraham^4) and Experience HOLMES, 13 Dec. 1737, Duxbury (MD 11:241)

Abraham HOLMES^6 (Hannah Samson^5) and Bethiah NYE, poss. 26 Dec. 1776

Stephen SAMSON^5 (Abraham^4) and 1st Abigail MORTON, 19 Jan. 1748/49, Plymouth
(MD 17:7)

Stephen SAMSON^5 and 2nd Deborah (LOTHROP^6) Turner (James^5, Experience Gorham^4,
James^3, Desire Howland^2), pre 18 Apr. 1781

James SAMSON^6 (Stephen^5) and Sarah SMITH, Int. 30 Dec. 1775, Plymouth (MD 27:177)

Henry SAMPSON^7 (James^6) and Hannah Moody PHILBROOK, 5 Feb. 1819

Ebenezer SAMSON^4 (Lorah Standish^3) and Zeruiah SOULE^4 (Joshua^3, John^2), 23 Apr.
1728, Duxbury (MD 11:80)

Andrew SAMSON^5 (Miles^4, Lorah Standish^3) and 2nd Abigail BISBEE

Nathaniel SAMSON^4 (Lorah Standish^3) and Keturah CHANDLER, 19 Jan. 1703, Duxbury
(MD 9:108)

Nathaniel SAMSON^5 (Nath.^{4}) and poss. Mary HOLMES

Abner SAMSON^5 (Nath.^{4}) and 1st Sarah SAMSON, 12 Oct. 1749 (Duxbury VR:302,303)

Abner SAMSON^5 and 2nd Deborah BISBEE, 20 Apr. 1756

Noah SAMSON^5 (Nath.^{4}) and Jemima RIDER^6 (Mary Southworth^5, Desire Gray^4, Mary
Winslow^3, Mary Chilton^2), c1734 (MD 15:44)

Sarah SAMSON^4 (Lorah Standish^3) and 1st Joseph SAMSON^3 (James^2)

Sarah SAMSON^4 and 2nd John ROUSE

Lydia STANDISH^3 and Isaac SAMSON, aft. 26 Oct. 1686 (Plym.Rcds.Quart.Sessions
1687-1721,:13)

Barnabas SAMSON^4 (Lydia Standish^3) and Experience ADKINS, 6 Nov. 1728, Plympton
(MD 1:248)

Priscilla SAMSON^4 (Lydia Standish^3) and Jabez FULLER^4 (John^3, Sam.$^{2-1}$), 12 Jan.
1726/27, Plympton (MD 1:247)

Ephraim SAMSON^4 (Lydia Standish^3) and Abigail HORREL, 15 Nov. 1728, Plympton
(MD 1:248)

Ephraim SAMSON and Ruth SHEPHERD, 14 Nov. 1728, Plymouth (MD 14:72)

Sarah SAMSON^5 (Ephraim^4) and John MURDOCK, 29 Mar. 1764, Middleboro (MD 24:185)

Isaac SAMSON^4 (Lydia Standish^3) and 1st Sarah BARLOW, 26 Oct. 1715, Plympton
(MD 2:236)

Isaac SAMSON^4 and 2nd Elizabeth (   ) SHAW, 12 June 1734, Raynham (Gen.Reg.53:439)

Elizabeth (   ) SHAW and 3rd Edward RICHMOND^5 (Edw.^{4}, Abigail Rogers^3, John^2),
Int. 6 Oct. 1750 (Middleboro VR 2:1:54)

Uriah SAMSON^5 (Isaac^4) and Anna WHITE, 25 Dec. 1746, Middleboro (MD 18:79)

Ezra SAMSON^6 (Uriah^5) and Mary BOURNE

Jacob SAMSON^5 (Isaac^4) and Alice CLARK, 12 Feb. 1761, Middleboro (MD 19:142)

Liscomb SAMPSON^6 (Jacob^5) and Cyrene DAVIS, 22 Dec. 1824, Prescott

Lydia Lucina SAMPSON (Liscomb^6) and Charles MALLERY, 19 July 1856, Pownal VT

John SAMSON^5 (Isaac^4) and Mary WALKER, 25 Mar.1747 (Taunton VR 2:420,494)

Jonathan SAMSON^4 (Lydia Standish^3) and Joanna LUCAS, 28 Sept. 1721, Plympton
    (MD 2:138)

Bethiah SAMPSON^5 (Jonathan^4) and Joseph SAMPSON

Lucy SAMPSON^6 (Bethiah^5) and 1st Isaac WATERMAN^6 (John^5, Lydia Cushman^4, Eleazer^3,
    Mary Allerton^2), "2/12/1781", Plympton

Lucy SAMPSON^6 and 2nd Daniel SOULE^6 (Ephraim^5, Zachariah^4, Ben.^{3}, John^2),
    10 Sept. 1818 (Halifax VR:86)

Mary SAMPSON^5 (Jonathan^4) and Nathan PERKINS

Peleg SAMSON^4 (Lydia Standish^3) and Mary RING^4 (Eleazer^3, Deborah Hopkins^2),
    7 Nov. 1722, Plympton (MD 2:138)

John SAMPSON and Abigail PUDNEY, 9 Dec. 1718 (Salem VR 4:223,284)

Micro #4 of 4

Mary SAMSON^5 (Peleg^4) and Nathaniel COOKE^5 (Robert^4, Francis^3, Jacob^2)

Miles STANDISH^3 and Experience SHERMAN^3 (Desire Doty^2), pre 5 July 1702 (MD 12:102)

Miles STANDISH^4 (Miles^3) and Mehitable ROBBINS, 17 Dec. 1738, Duxbury (MD 11:82)

Penelope STANDISH^5 (Miles^4) and 1st Nathaniel COBB, 19 Mar. 1764 (Middleboro VR 2:2:83)

Penelope STANDISH^5 and 2nd Ichabod LEACH, 11 Oct. 1770 (Cobb Gen.:131)

Patience STANDISH^4 (Miles^3) and Caleb JENNEY^5 (Desire Blackwell^4, Sarah Warren^3,
    Nath.^{2}), 6 Apr. 1738 (Duxbury VR:316,269)

Caleb JENNE and Mary EURE, Int. 23 June 1770 (Dartmouth VR 2:180,270)

Caleb JENNE and Silence HOUSE, Int. 20 May 1746 (Dartmouth VR 2:246,270)

Priscilla STANDISH^4 (Miles^3) and Elisha BISBEE

Sarah STANDISH^4 (Miles^3) and Abner WESTON, 2 Mar. 1729/30, Duxbury (MD 11:240)

Micah WESTON^5 (Sarah Standish^4) and Bethiah OLDHAM, poss. 3 Dec. 1761

William Henry Harrison PRIOR and 1st Isabelle A. BARTON

William Henry Harrison PRIOR and 2nd Grace Darling MacBRIDE, 20 Dec. 1905,
    Providence RI[4]

Joseph PETERSON and Rebecca DELANO, 4 Apr. 1773[5]

Sarah STANDISH[3] and Benjamin SOULE[3] (John[2]), c1694 (MD 4:113)

Thomas STANDISH[3] and Mary CARVER, 20 Jan. 1717/18, Marshfield (MD 7:132)

David STANDISH[4] (Tho.[3]) and Hannah MAGOON[5] (Rachel Soule[4], Aaron[3], John[2]),
     poss. 24 Jan. 1745/46 (Pembroke VR)

Thomas STANDISH[4] (Tho.[3]) and 1st Martha BISBEE, 10 Feb. 1747/48 (Pembroke VR)

Hadley STANDISH[5] (Tho.[4]) and Abigail GARNET, poss. 30 Nov. 1780 (Pembroke VR)

William STANDISH[4] (Tho.[3]) and Abigail STETSON, poss. 8 Dec. 1763 (Pembroke VR)

William STANDISH[5] (Wm.[4]) and Ruth BARSTOW

Josiah STANDISH[2] (Myles[1])

Josiah STANDISH[2] and 1st Mary DINGLY, 19 Dec. 1654, Marshfield (MD 2:4)

Josiah STANDISH[2] and 2nd Sarah ALLEN, aft. July 1655

Miles STANDISH[3] and 1st Mehitable (CARY) Adams, 5 Dec. 1700, Bristol RI

Mercy STANDISH[3] and Ralph WHEELOCK, 30 Sept. 1726

Israel STANDISH and Elizabeth RICHARDS, 8 Feb. 1703/04 ("Blackman & Allied Fam."
     <1928>:167)

Prudence STANDISH and Jacob SAWYER, 3 Sept. 1730 (Windham CT VR 1:123)

Prudence STANDISH and 2nd John BOND, aft. Aug. 1758

Hannah STANDISH[4] (Josiah[3]) and Nathan FOSTER, poss. 3 Nov. 1724

Sarah FOSTER[5] (Hannah Standish[4]) and Jonathan LILLY

Nathan FOSTER[5] (Hannah Standish[4]) and Elizabeth LANSFORD

Elijah HOWES and Ruth BARROWS, 24 Nov. 1831 (Hist.Goshen MA:140)

Mehitable STANDISH[4] (Josiah[3]) and Jabez ROOD, c1716

Jabez ROOD and 2nd Mindwell ALLIS

Jeremiah ROOD[5] (Mehitable Standish[4]) and Hannah (BRIGGS) Grover, 10 May 1753
     (Lebanon CT VR)

Briggs ROOD[6] (?Jeremiah[5]) and Elizabeth BELCHER

Dudley Belcher ROOD[7] (Briggs[6]) and Elizabeth HIMMES, 28 Aug. 1825, Franklin VT

Myles STANDISH[2] (Myles[1])

Myles STANDISH[2] and Sarah WINSLOW[3] (Mary Chilton[2]), 19 July 1660 (Boston Rcd.com.9:76)

Sarah WINSLOW[3] and 2nd Tobias PAYNE, 3rd Richard MIDDLECOTT

NOTES

<1> p.276, The dates tell an interesting story. Marriage intentions were
published 19 Dec. 1757 (Halifax VR:59). Their first child was born 20 July 1758
(MD 26:24), with the marriage finally taking place 5 Jan. 1759.

<2> p.277, Mary Bradford appears to have Mayflower descent. On her daughter Jane Standish's chart is the note "Jane descended also from Alden, Bradford and 2 Warren".

<3> p.277, Although not shown here his Mayflower descent to John Alden can be found on p.4.

<4> p.279, William Prior is later shown to be 9th in descent from Myles Standish.

<5> p. 279, So stated in a letter from the Dep't of the Interior, Bureau of Pensions.

RICHARD WARREN DESCENDANTS

Abigail WARREN[2] (Richard[1])

Abigail WARREN[2] and Anthony SNOW, 8 Nov. 1639, Plymouth (PCR 1:134)

Alice SNOW[3] and Robert BARKER

Abigail SNOW[3] and Michael FORD, 12 Dec. 1667, Marshfield (MD 2:182)

Michael FORD and 2nd Bethiah HATCH, 29 Mar. 1683 (MD 3:43)

Hannah FORD[4] (Abigail Snow[3]) and (?)Joseph ROSE Jr.[1]

James FORD[4] (Abigail Snow[3]) and Hannah DINGLEY, 28 Feb. 1698, Marshfield (MD 5:237)

Abigail FORD[5] (James[4]) and John JOYCE, c1728/29 (MD 9:185)

Barnabas FORD[5] (James[4]) and Hannah SPRAGUE

Michael FORD[5] (James[4]) and Orphan WATERMAN[5] (Anthony[4], Sarah Snow[3], Abigail
    Warren [2]), c1738

Orphan WATERMAN[5] and 2nd Aaron SOULE[4] (Aaron[3], John[2]), 16 Dec. 1775 (Pembroke VR)

Michael FORD[6] (Michael[5]) and Rhoda COPELAND[5] (Jos.[4], Mary Bass[3], Ruth Alden[2]),
    16 Feb. 1775 (Scituate VR 2:75,122)

Lydia FORD[4] (Abigail Snow[3]) and Experience BRANCH, c1692 (MD 3:187)

Abigail BRANCH[5] (Lydia Ford[4]) and William CARVER, 28 Feb. 1711/12, Marshfield
    (MD 7:132)

Thomas BRANCH[5] (Lydia Ford[4]) and Lydia BARROW, 11 Oct. 1720, Plymouth (MD 14:39)

Experience BRANCH[6] (Tho.[5]) and Samuel SHERMAN, 8 Nov. 1750, Plymouth (MD 16:170)

Lydia BRANCH[6] (Tho.[5]) and Nathaniel SHURTLEFF, 1 Jan. 1738/39, Plymouth (MD 14:158)

Mercy BRANCH[6] (Tho.[5]) and Ebenezer CHURCHILL, 23 Nov. 1747, Plymouth (MD 17:6)

Ebenezer CHURCHILL and 2nd Patience FAUNCE, 13 Feb. 1775 (Churchill Gen.:37,179)

Thankful BRANCH[6] (Tho.[5]) and James HOWARD, 11 Dec. 1746, Plymouth (MD 17:5)

Josiah SNOW[3] and Rebecca BARKER, c1669 (MD 3:42)

Rebecca BARKER and 2nd John SAWYER, 23 (worn) 1694, Marshfield (MD 4:126)

Abiah SNOW[4] (Josiah[3]) and Nathan THOMAS, 2 Jan. 1716/17, Marshfield (MD 7:131)

Nathan THOMAS and 1st Alice BAKER[4] (Sarah Bradford[3], Wm.[2]), 4 Mar. 1713

Nathan THOMAS and 3rd Sarah (FOSTER) Bartlett, 17 June 1719

Susanna SNOW[4] (Josiah[3]) and Joseph WATERMAN[4] (Sarah Snow[3], Abigail Warren[2]),
    16 June 1709, Marshfield (MD 7:132)

Bethiah SNOW[4] (Josiah[3]) and John SPRAGUE

Lydia SNOW[4] (Josiah[3]) and Nathaniel WINSLOW[3] (Nath.[2], Kenelm[1])

Nathaniel WINSLOW[3] and 2nd Deborah BRYANT, 17 Feb. 1717, Scituate (MD 9:89)

Lydia WINSLOW[5] (Lydia Snow[4]) and Joseph THOMAS, 10 Dec. 1718, Marshfield (MD 7:131)

Mercy SNOW[4] (Josiah[3]) and Gilbert WINSLOW[3] (Nath.[2], Kenelm[1]), 7 Feb. 1698,
    Marshfield (MD 5:237)

Anthony WINSLOW[5] (Mercy Snow[4]) and Deborah BARKER

Sarah SNOW[4] (Josiah[3]) and Samuel BAKER, c1699/1700, Marshfield (MD 4:126)

Lydia SNOW[3] and Stephen SKEFFE, c1665 (MD 29:70)

Abigail SKIFFE[4] (Lydia Snow[3]) and Shubael SMITH

Deborah SKIFF[4] (Lydia Snow[3]) and Stephen PRESBURY

Mary PRESBURY[5] (Deborah Skiff[4]) and Thomas WEST

Mary WEST[7] (Tho.[6], Mary Presbury[5]) and Luen POPE, 3 Dec. 1761 (Int.- Dartmouth
    VR 2:364,532)

Stephen SKIFF[4] (Lydia Snow[3]) and Sarah LOTHROP

Sarah SNOW[3] and Joseph WATERMAN, c1673 (MD 2:180)[<2>]

Elizabeth WATERMAN[4] (Sarah Snow[3]) and Ichabod BARTLETT[4] (Ben.[3], Mary Warren[2])

Ichabod BARTLETT[4] and 2nd Desire ARNOLD[5] (Eliz. Gray[4], Mary Winslow[3], Mary Chilton[2])

Abigail WATERMAN[4] (Sarah Snow[3]) and Kenelm WINSLOW[3] (Nath.[2], Kenelm[1]), c1703

Kenelm WINSLOW[3] and 2nd Ann (WINSLOW[4]) Taylor (Edw.[3], Mary Chilton[2]), poss.
    7 Sept. 1730, Boston (Winslow Mem.1:98)

Nathaniel WINSLOW[5] (Abigial Waterman[4]) and Susanna BRYANT, poss. 3 Feb. 1731/32

Susanna BRYANT and 2nd Ezekiel KENT, poss. 22 Dec. 1740 (Winslow Mem.1:209)

Sarah WINSLOW[5] (Abigail Waterman[4]) and 1st Tobias PAYNE[5] (Wm.[4], Sarah Winslow[3],
    Mary Chilton[2])

Sarah WINSLOW[5] and 2nd Samuel SMITH[5] (Sam.[4], Mary Hopkins[3], Gyles[2]), 29 Dec.
    1737, Eastham (MD 19:100)

Anthony WATERMAN[4] (Sarah Snow[3]) and Elizabeth ARNOLD[5] (Eliz. Gray[4], Mary Winslow[3],
    Mary Chilton[2]), c1709 (MD 7:119,25:35-37)

Elizabeth ARNOLD[5] and 2nd Jonathan ALDEN[3] (Jonathan[2]), 17 Jan. 1717/18, Marsh-
    field (MD 7:132)

Thomas WATERMAN[5] (Anthony[4]) and Abigail THOMAS, c1733 (MD 9:187)

Anthony WATERMAN[6] (Tho.[5]) and Deborah FOSTER[5] (Faith Oakman[4], Eliz. Doty[3], Edw.[2]),
    c1760

Micro #3 of 32

Anthony WATERMAN[7] (Anthony[6]) and Deborah WATERMAN, 31 July 1787

Rev. Jotham WATERMAN[7] (Anthony[6]) and Olive PHINNEY, poss. 8 Jan. 1803, Dennis

Bethiah WATERMAN[4] (Sarah Snow[3]) and Samuel DOGGETT, 20 Feb. 1710, Marshfield
(MD 7:132)

Joseph WATERMAN[4] (Sarah Snow[3]) and Lusanna SNOW[4] (Josiah[3], Abigail Warren[2]),
16/26 June 1709, Marshfield (MD 7:132,8:42)

Abiah WATERMAN[5] (Jos.[4]) and John EELLS, 4 June 1730

Abiah WATERMAN[5] and poss. 2nd Mordecai LINCOLN, 30 Nov. 1758 (Scituate VR)

Waterman EELLS[6] (Abiah Waterman[5]) and Sarah TUBBS

Hannah EELLS[6] (Abiah Waterman[5]) and Anthony EAIMES, 4 Jan. 1757, Scituate (MD 1:165)

Lydia WATERMAN[4] (Sarah Snow[3]) and John THOMAS, 23 Dec. 1714, Marshfield (MD 7:131)

Anthony THOMAS[5] (Lydia Waterman[4]) and Abigail ALDEN[4] (John[3], Jonathan[2]), 23 Jan.
1745/46, Marshfield (Duxbury VR:211,319)

Sarah WATERMAN[4] (Sarah Snow[3]) and Solomon HEWET, c1699 (MD 8:178)

Anna WARREN[2] (Richard[1])

Anna WARREN[2] and Thomas LITTLE, 19 Apr. 1633, Plymouth (MD 13:83)

Thomas LITTLE and Abigail HOWLAND, 9 Mar. 1742 (2:159)[3]

Constant LITTLE and Sarah BARKER, Int. 25 Jan. 1773 (2:124)[3]

George LITTLE and Rachel ROGERS, 24 June 1779, poss. Marshfield (2:162)[3]

Peabody LITTLE and Ruth KEEN, Int. 26 Aug. 1780 (2:134)[3]

James LITTLE and Lydia YOUNG

William Henry LITTLE and Rhoda THOMAS, 2 Sept. 1787 (2:153,163)[3]

Dotey LITTLE and Mercy TILDEN, 21 May 1798 (2:321)

Jedediah LITTLE and Betsey Niles TILDEN, Int. 15 Aug. 1790 (2:62)[3]

Thomas LITTLE Jr. and Nancy TILDEN, Int. 6 Dec. 1791 (2:60)[3]

Thomas LITTLE and Lucy BOURNE, 21 Nov. 1793 (2:139)[3]

Ephraim LITTLE and Mrs. Sarah POITER, 1 Oct. 1795 (2:139)[3]

Jedediah LITTLE and Bethiah HATCH Jr., 18 Apr. 1796 (2:139)[3]

Luther LITTLE and Hannah LOVEWELL, Int. 1 Jan. 1798 (2:53)[3]

Constant LITTLE and Patience TORREY, Int. 1 June 1812, poss. Scituate[3]

Abigail LITTLE[3] and Josiah KEENE, Marshfield

Josiah KEENE and 2nd Hannah DINGLEY (PN&Q 5:92)

Josiah KEEN[4] (Abigail Little[3]) and Lydia BAKER, c1681 (MD 9:174, 28:5,6)

Abigail KEEN[5] (Josiah[4]) and Nicholas DREW, c1708 (MD 12:225)

Nicholas DREW and 2nd Rebecca MORTON, c1716

Nicholas DREW and 3rd Lydia DOGGETT, c1730

Benjamin KEEN^5 (Josiah^4) and Deborah (BARKER) Howland, 15 Mar. 1719/20, Pembroke
    (Gen.Adv.1:64)

Bethiah KEEN^5 (Josiah^4) and Judah WEST, 3 Sept. 1718, Plymouth (MD 14:38)

Josiah WEST^6 (Bethiah Keen^5) and Elizabeth GRIFFEN, 28 Nov. 1755 (Plymouth VR 2:254)

Lydia WEST^6 (Bethiah Keen^5) and George HOLMES^5 (Lydia Wood^4, Experience Fuller^3,
    Sam.$^{2-1}$), 21 Apr. 1741, Plymouth (MD 14:159)

Samuel WEST^6 (Bethiah Keen^5) and Elizabeth RICH, 30 Oct. 1753 (Plymouth VR 2:254)

Elizabeth RICH and Richard DURFEY, 23 Nov. 1770 (Plymouth VR 2:264)

Betty WEST^7 (Sam.^{6}) and Levi WRIGHT^6 (Adam^5, John^4, Adam^3, Hester Cooke^2), c1779

Rebecca WEST^7 (Sam.^{6}) and Isaac BILLINGTON

Bethiah WEST^7 (Sam.^{6}) and Richard BAGNAL, Int. 15 Mar. 1777, Plymouth (MD 27:178)

Richard BAGNAL and Lydia SAMPSON, 19 July 1819 (Plymouth VR 2:382)

Samuel West BAGNAL^8 (Bethiah West^7) and 1st Lois THOMAS, 19 Aug. 1811 (Plymouth
    VR 2:377)

Samuel West BAGNAL^8 and 2nd Minerva THOMAS, 13 Oct. 1822 (Plymouth VR 2:215)

Eleanor KEEN^5 (Josiah^4) and Joseph THOMAS, 24 Apr. 1718, Pembroke (Gen.Adv.1:62)

Hezekiah KEEN^5 (Josiah^4) and Alice HOWLAND, c1729 (MD 28:3,5)

Daniel KEEN^6 (Hezekiel^5) and Lucy FREEMAN, 21 July 1784

Howland KEEN^7 (Dan.^{6}) and Fanny SOULE^7 (Asa^6, Gideon$^{5-4}$, Moses^3, John^2), 20 Apr.
    1815

Galen KEEN^8 (Howland^7) and Statira R. SPRAGUE, c1844

Isaac KEEN^5 (Josiah^4) and 1st Deborah DWELLY, 17 Feb. 1724/25 (Scituate VR)

Isaac KEEN^5 and 2nd Lydia JONES, 16 Nov. 1733

Isaac KEEN^5 and 3rd Abigail KENT, 16 Feb. 1773 (Marshfield VR 2:161)

Eleanor KEEN^6 (Isaac^5) and Apollos CUSHMAN, Int. 15 Feb. 1768[4]

Josiah KEEN^5 (Josiah^4) and Rebecca ROSE, c1719

Lydia KEEN^5 (Josiah^4) and George PARTRIDGE, 18 Mar. 1712/13 (Pembroke VR:6)

George PARTRIDGE and 2nd Hannah (FOSTER) Bradford, c1736

Mabel PARTRIDGE^6 (Lydia Keen^5) and 1st John SOULE^4 (Joshua^3, John^2), 5 Aug. 1730
    (Duxbury VR)

Mabel PARTRIDGE^6 and 2nd Samuel KEMPTON, 9 Feb. 1736/37, Plymouth (MD 14:157)

Mabel PARTRIDGE^6 and 3rd William COOMER, pre 14 May 1764

Sarah PARTRIDGE^6 (Lydia Keen^5) and 1st Asa HUNT, 2 Dec. 1736, Duxbury (MD 11:241)

Sarah PARTRIDGE^6 and 2nd John PARTRIDGE, pre 14 May 1764

James PARTRIDGE[6] (Lydia Keen[5]) and Thankful STEVENS, 24 Dec. 1744, N. Stonington CT

Nathaniel KEEN[5] (Josiah[4]) and Thankful WINSLOW[5] (Lydia Snow[4], Josiah[3], Abigail Warren[2]), 27 Oct. 1725 (Marshfield VR)

Asa KEEN[6] (Nath.[5]) and Zilpah HATCH, 18 Feb. 1762 (Pembroke VR)

Snow KEEN[6] (Nath.[5]) and Rebecca BURBANK, c1756

Micro #4 of 32

Snow KEENE Jr. and Sarah BRADFORD, 26 Oct. 1794, Turner ME

Snow KEENE and Sophronia N. MAXIM, 28 Oct. 1822, Turner ME (VR)

Herbert KEENE and Florence M. PRATT, 1 Jan. 1874 (Palmyra ME VR)

Samuel KEEN[5] (Josiah[4]) and 1st Ruth SPRAGUE, 18 Apr. 1719, Duxbury (MD 11:25)

Samuel KEEN[5] and 2nd Margaret REDDING, 4 Jan. 1737 (Pembroke VR 3:378)

Levi KEEN[6] (Sam.[5]) and Eunice JENNINGS, 19 Feb. 1746/47 (Pembroke VR:296,304)

Grace KEEN[6] (Sam.[5]) and Jabez COLE, 23 Aug. 1744, Duxbury (MD 11:239)

Moses KEEN[6] (Sam.[5]) and Maria FREEMAN, 15 Dec. 1768, Sandwich

Ephraim LITTLE[3] and Mary STURTEVANT, 22 Nov. 1672 (MD 34:146)

Ephraim LITTLE[4] (Ephraim[3]) and Sarah CLARKE, 29 Nov. 1698, Plymouth (MD 13:207)

Anna LITTLE[4] (Ephraim[3]) and Thomas GRAY, 3 July 1694, Boston (Rcd.com.9:217)

Thomas GRAY and 2nd Phebe ( ) WARREN, aft. Nov. 1706

Anna GRAY[5] (Anna Little[4]) and William RICHMOND[5] (Eliz. Rogers[4], John[3-2])

Rebecca GRAY[5] (Anna Little[4]) and John PABODIE[4] (Wm.[3], Eliz. Alden[2])

Edward GRAY[5] (Anna Little[4]) and Elizabeth PABODIE[4] (Wm.[3], Eliz. Alden[2]), poss. 9 Mar. 1716, Little Compton RI

David LITTLE[4] (Ephraim[3]) and 1st Elizabeth SOUTHWORTH[4] (Rebecca Pabodie[3], Eliz. Alden[2]), 2 Dec. 1703, Little Compton RI (MD 34:146)

David LITTLE[4] and 2nd Abigail BAILEY, 20 Nov. 1746 (MD 34:147)

David LITTLE[5] (David[4]) and Deborah CLAP, 19 Feb. 1734, Scituate (MD 1:45)

Elizabeth LITTLE[5] (David[4]) and Joseph OTIS, 6 June 1738, Scituate (MD 1:45)

Mary LITTLE[5] (David[4]) and Benjamin CUDWORTH, 13 Nov. 1740, Scituate (MD 1:46)

Mercy CUDWORTH[6] (Mary Little[5]) and Israel CUDWORTH

Mercy LITTLE[5] (David[4]) and Joseph OTIS, 2 Feb. 1740, Scituate (MD 1:46)

Mercy OTIS[6] (Mercy Little[5]) and Nathaniel WATERMAN, Int. 14 June 1766, Scituate

Molly OTIS[6] (Mercy Little[5]) and George PILLSBURY, 6 Jan. 1782/83 (Scituate VR 2:226,237)

John LITTLE[4] (Ephraim[3]) and Constant FOBES[4] (Martha Pabodie[3], Eliz Alden[2]),

8 Apr. 1708 (Little Compton RI VR 4:6:27,39)

Anna LITTLE^5 (John^4) and Abijah WHITE^5 (John^4, Dan.^{3}, Peregrine^2), 1 Feb. 1738

John LITTLE^5 (John^4) and Mary SAMSON^4 (David^3, Caleb^2)

Ruth LITTLE^5 (John^4) and Tobias OAKMAN^5 (Sam.^{4}, Eliz. Doty^3, Edw.^{2})

Ephraim LITTLE^5 (John^4) and Alice BAKER^5 (Kenelm^4, Sarah Bradford^3, Wm.^{2}), c1740
    (MD 30:147)

Lucy LITTLE^6 (Ephraim^5) and Joshua VINAL, 25 Dec. 1782, Marshfield (Bailey 2:47)

Lucy Little VINAL^7 (Lucy Little^6) and Isaac ROGERS, poss. 25 July 1808 (Rogers
    Fam.<1898>:81,127)

Patience Little VINAL^7 (Lucy Little^6) and Calvin CORTHELL, Int. 25 July 1807
    (Hanover VR:259)

Lucy L. COTHEREL and Francis B. ELLIS, 9 Jan. 1826 (Hanover VR:140)

Seth VINAL^7 (Lucy Little^6) and Hannah B. HATCH

Micro #5 of 32

Fobes LITTLE^5 (John^4) and Sarah BAKER^5 (Sarah Snow^4, Josiah^3, Abigail Warren^2),
    c1733 (MD 9:184)

Fobes LITTLE^6 (Fobes^5) and Sarah WILCOX, poss. 28/29 July 1758, Little Compton

Nancy LITTLE^7 (Fobes^6) and John IRISH, 11 Jan. 1795 (Little Compton VR 2:39)

Lemuel LITTLE^5 (John^4) and Penelope EAMES^5 (Mary Oakman^4, Eliz. Doty^3, Edw.^{2}),
    1747 (Marshfield VR 2:159)

George LITTLE^6 (Lemuel^5) and Rachel ROGERS, c1780 (MD 31:77)

James LITTLE^6 (Lemuel^5) and Lydia YOUNG^6 (Ezekiel^5, Jos.^{4}, Sarah White^3, Pere-
    grine^2), poss. 4 Apr. 1782, Scituate

Lydia YOUNG^6 and 2nd Simeon GANNETT, poss. 18 Oct. 1809

Luther LITTLE^6 (Lemuel^5) and 2nd Hannah LOVELL, 4 Jan. 1798 (Weymouth VR 2:114,120)

Penelope LITTLE^6 (Lemuel^5) and Calvin LEWIS, poss. c1788

Thomas LITTLE^5 (John^4) and 1st Sarah BAKER^5 (Kenelm^4, Sarah Bradford^3, Wm.^{2}),c1750

Thomas LITTLE^5 and 2nd Lucy ( ) BOURN, aft. Nov. 1792

Doty LITTLE and Hannah B. THOMAS, 15 Oct. 1818 (Waldoboro ME VR 2:361)

Rhoda LITTLE and Capt. Daniel WESTON, 24 May 1819 (Waldoboro ME VR 2:367)

Thomas LITTLE^6 (Tho.^{5}) and Anna TILDEN

Mercy LITTLE^4 (Ephraim^3) and Job OTIS, 1 Oct. 1699 (MD   34:146,148)

David OTIS^5 (Mercy Little^4) and poss. Susan HADDEN, c1767

Mercy OTIS^5 (Mercy Little^4) and John CLAPP^5 (Temperance Gorham^4, John^3, Desire
    Howland^2), 5 Nov. 1724 (Scituate VR 2:60,226)

Ruth OTIS[5] (Mercy Little[4]) and Benjamin STOCKBRIDGE, 3 June 1731 (Scituate
VR 2:227,272)

Abigail OTIS[5] (Mercy Little[4]) and Andrew HALLIBURTON, poss. 22 Feb. 1730
(Scituate VR)

Ephraim OTIS[5] (Mercy Little[4]) and Rachel HENRY, 6 Sept. 1733 (Hist.Hingham 2:301)

Anna OTIS[6] (Ephraim[5]) and Barney SMITH, Int. 8 Oct. 1783, Boston (Rcd.com.30:452)

Lydia OTIS[6] (Ephraim[5]) and Abiel SMITH

Lydia SMITH[7] (Anna Otis[6]) and Jonathan RUSSELL

Dr. Ephraim OTIS[6] (Ephraim[5]) and Sarah HARRIS, c1769

George Alexander OTIS[7] (Ephraim[6]) and Lucinda SMITH[7] (Anne Otis[6], Ephraim[5],
Mercy Little[4], Ephraim[3], Anna Warren[2]), 15 Sept. 1802 (Boston Rcd.com.30:199)

Susanna OTIS[6] (Ephraim[5]) and William HALLIBURTON

Mary OTIS[6] (Ephraim[5]) and William LINCOLN, c1760 (Hist.Hing.2:466)

Priscilla OTIS[6] (Ephraim[5]) and William CLAPP, c1767 (Clapp Gen.:168)

Rachel OTIS[6] (Ephraim[5]) and Benjamin DeWOLF

Job OTIS[5] (Mercy Little[4]) and Thankful OTIS, 16 Feb. 1726, Scituate (MD 1:43)

Sarah OTIS[5] (Mercy Little[4]) and Mordecai ELLIS, 30 Sept. 1740 (Scituate VR)

Jacob FORD Jr. and 1st Rachel EAGER, 14 May 1761 (Abington VR 2:68,75)

Jacob FORD Jr. and 2nd Ann (JENKINS) Ellis, 18 Apr. 1793 (Abington VR 2:277)

David ELLIS[6] (Sarah Otis[5]) and 2nd Ann JENKINS, 26 Aug. 1773 (Scituate VR 2:113,163)

John ELLIS[7] (David[6]) and Nabby SYLVESTER, 23 Apr. 1801 (Hanover VR:134)

Ruth LITTLE[4] (Ephraim[3]) and Rev. John AVERY, 23 Nov. 1710 (Little Fam.Rcd.)

Rev. John AVERY and 2nd Ruth KNOWLES[5] (Mercy Freeman[4], Mercy Prence[3], Patience
Brewster[2]), 26 June 1734, Eastham (MD 17:140)

Rev. John AVERY and 3rd Mary (   ) ROTCH, 24 June 1748, Boston (Rcd.com.28:236)

Job AVERY[5] (Ruth Little[4]) and Jane THATCHER, 30 Dec. 1742, Eastham (Truro VR:419)

Jane AVERY[6] (Job[5]) and John ATKINS, 10 Sept. 1778 (Truro VR:129)

John AVERY[6] (Job[5]) and Hannah SNOW[6] (Ambrose[5], John[4-3], Constance Hopkins[2]),
3 Dec. 1771 (Truro VR:108)

John AVERY[7] (John[6]) and Rebecca KNOWLES

Robert AVERY[5] (Ruth Little[4]) and Anna CUSHMAN, 23 Feb. 1741 (Plympton VR:248)[5]

Ruth AVERY[5] (Ruth Little[4]) and Rev. Jonathan PARKER

Hannah LITTLE[3] and Stephen TILDEN, 15/25 Jan. 1661, Scituate (MD 2:34,35;17:202)

David TILDEN[4] (Hannah Little[3]) and Abigail PITCHER, 11 Jan. 1710/11, Scituate
(MD 2:170)

Elijah TILDEN^5 (David^4) and Ruth WADSWORTH, 11 Jan. 1743/44 (Stoughton VR:33)

William TILDEN^6 (Elijah^5) and Mary WITTINGTON, 26 Mar. 1779 (Stoughton VR:148)

Hannah TILDEN^5 (David^4) and Elhanan LYON, Int. 7 Dec. 1734, Stoughton

Stephen TILDEN^5 (David^4) and Abigail PIERCE, 25 Oct. 1753 (Stoughton VR:64)

Abigail PIERCE and 2nd Samuel HOLMES, 7 Sept. 1780 (Sharon VR:268)

Jerusha TILDEN^6 (Stephen^5) and Eleazer CLAP, 10 Aug. 1780 (Stoughton VR:146)

Rebecca TILDEN^6 (Stephen^5) and 1st William SMITH, 2nd Peter DICKERMAN

Micro #6 of 32

Stephen TILDEN^6 (Stephen^5) and Hannah PERRY, 4 Oct. 1792 (Medfield VR:163,177)

Hannah PERRY and 2nd Amos KINGSBURY, c1836

Ebenezer TILDEN^4 (Hannah Little^3) and Mary VINAL, 23 Mar. 1713/14, Scituate
   (MD 9:87)

Mary TILDEN^5 (Eben.^{4}) and Azariah BLISS, 29 Apr. 1736 (Lebanon CT VR 1:30)

Azariah BLISS and 2nd Lydia (SOUTHWORTH) Storr, c1770 (Bliss Gen.<1881>:57)

Mary BLISS^6 (Mary Tilden^5) and Hezekiah WATERS, 23 June 1763 (Lebanon CT 1st Ch.)

Luther WATERS^7 (Mary Bliss^6) and Sally STORRS, 28 May 1801, Lebanon CT (Bible Rcd.)

Rev. Isaiah WATERS^7 (Mary Bliss^6) and Nancy BALLENTINE

Joseph TILDEN^4 (Hannah Little^3) and Joanna BOULS, 25 Jan. 1701, Marshfield
   (MD 5:236)

Christopher TILDEN^5 (Jos.^{4}) and Sarah PARROTT, 24 Apr. 1740 (Boston Rcd.com.28:217)

Joanna TILDEN and Charles TURNER, 26 June 1716 (MD 9:88)

David TILDEN^6 (Christopher^5) and Joanna THWING, 16 June 1763 (Boston Rcd.com.30:59)

Benjamin TILDEN and Polly WENTWORTH, 8 Nov. 1797 (Boston Rcd.com.30:155)

Christopher TILDEN and Elizabeth BAKER, 28 June 1795 (Boston Rcd.com.30:154)

David TILDEN and Abigail PARROTT, 9 May 1738 (Boston Rcd.com.28:208)

Elizabeth TILDEN and John Inman LINZEE, 19 May 1807 (Boston Rcd.com.30:257)

Joanna TILDEN and Dr. Galen OTIS, Int. 17 Sept. 1785 (Boston Rcd.com.30:455)[6]

Jonathan TILDEN and Mary RUCK, Int. 15 May 1740 (Boston Rcd.com.28:233)

Joseph TILDEN and Sarah WHITE, 30 Nov. 1740, Scituate (MD 2:170)

Joseph TILDEN and Sarah PARKER, Int. 21 Nov. 1777 (Boston Rcd.com.30:440)

Bryant Parrott TILDEN and Zebiah Craval BROWN, 23 Oct. 1803 (Boston Rcd.com.30:211)

Joseph TILDEN and Susanna LINZEE, 18 May 1802 (Boston Rcd.com.30:156)

Joseph TILDEN and Matilda COWLEY, 7 Apr. 1808 (Boston Rcd.com.30:213)

Martha TILDEN and John STINSON, 19 July 1796 (Boston Rcd.com.30:140)

Mary TILDEN and Henry PRICE, 25 May 1752 (Boston Rcd.com.30:392)

Mary TILDEN and James PHILLIPS, 1 Feb. 1801 (Boston Rcd.com.30:200)

Samuel TILDEN and Grace HATCH, 18 Sept. 1782 (Boston Rcd.com.30:410)

Sarah TILDEN and Josiah KEEN, Int. 9 Dec. 1756 (Boston Rcd.com.30:22)

Sarah TILDEN and John Hunt WENDELL, Int. 4 June 1761 (Boston Rcd.com.30:140)

Sarah TILDEN and George BLANCHARD, 20 June 1793 (Boston Rcd.com.30:144)

Sarah TILDEN and Nathaniel Walker APPLETON, 26 June 1806 (Boston Rcd.com.30:175)

Thomas TILDEN and Frances Burns FULTON, 16 Apr. 1797 (Medford VR:224,305)

William TILDEN and Hannah R. INMAN, 22 Oct. 1807 (Boston Rcd.com.30:275)

Mary TILDEN[4] (Hannah Little[3]) and James THOMAS, 3 Jan. 1692/93, Duxbury (MD 26:37)

Ebenezer THOMAS[5] (Mary Tilden[4]) and 1st Hannah HASKIN, 7 Mar. 1735 (Norwich
 CT VR:162)[7]

Ebenezer THOMAS[5] and 2nd Deborah HIDE, 5 Sept. 1748 (Norwich VR:268)

Ebenezer THOMAS[6] (Eben.[5]) and 1st Chloe ALLEN, 27 Mar. 1771 (Norwich CT VR:509)

Ebenezer THOMAS[6] and 2nd Hannah ( ) DOWGLASS, 9 May 1790 (Norwich CT VR:510)

John THOMAS[5] (Mary Tilden[4]) and Hannah SPAFFORD, c1733 (Hine's Early Lebanon:171)

Malachi THOMAS[6] (John[5]) and Mary McCALL, 3 Oct. 1770, Mansfield CT

Mercy TILDEN[4] (Hannah Little[3]) and Benjamin STOCKBRIDGE, 23 July 1701, Scituate
 (MD 5:117)

Ruth TILDEN[4] (Hannah Little[3]) and Nathaniel TILDEN, 18 Dec. 1700, Scituate (MD 3:118)

Nathaniel TILDEN and Margaret DODSUN, 3 Jan. 1673/74 (Scituate VR)

Nathaniel TILDEN and Mary SHARPE, 5 Nov. 1673 (Scituate VR)

Nathaniel TILDEN and Elizabeth TURNER, Int. 20 June 1734 (Scituate VR)

Ruth TILDEN and James LITCHFIELD, 15 June 1732 (Scituate VR 2:291)

Ruth TILDEN and North EELLS, Int. 24 June 1742 (Scituate VR 2:291)

Ruth ( ) TILDEN and Ebenezer PEIRCE, 16 Apr. 1752 (Scituate VR 2:291)

Ruth TILDEN[5] (Ruth[4]) and 1st James LITCHFIELD <see above>

Ruth TILDEN[5] and 2nd Benjamin BAILEY, 12 June 1735 (Scituate VR 2:13,193)<see below>

James LITCHFIELD Jr. and Mrs. Anna GORDIN, 2 Mar. 1760 (Scituate VR 2:188)

James LITCHFIELD and Hannah PRATT, 15 May 1760, Hingham (Scituate VR 2:188)

James LITCHFIELD and Elizabeth LITCHFIELD, 9 Jan. 1770 (Scituate VR 2:188)

James LITCHFIELD Jr. and Rachel MANSFIELD, Int. 27 May 1781 (Scituate VR 2:188)

Benjamin BAILEY and 2nd Desire RUSSELL, 17 Nov. 1757 (Scituate VR 2:16)<see above>

Benjamin BAILEY and Mary BAILEY, 26 Jan. 1775 (Scituate VR 2:13)

Ruth BAILEY[6] (Ruth Tilden[5]) and 1st Lemuel DWELLEY, Int. 26 Nov. 1766 (Scituate

Ruth BAILEY^6 and 2nd Meshach PENNIMAN, 20 Aug. 1777

Lemuel DWELLY and Bethiah DOGGETT, Int. 7 June 1740 (Scituate VR 2:110)

Meschach PENNIMAN and 2nd Betsey RANDALL, 12 May 1812 (Scituate VR 2:233,244)

Elisha PENNIMAN^7 (Ruth Bailey^6) and Sybil ALLEN, 27 Nov. 1805

Joseph TILDEN and Elisabeth WHITE, 14 June 1750 (Goshen Ch., Lebanon CT)

Hannah TILDEN^5 (Stephen^4, Hannah Little^3) and Caleb PIERCE, aft. May 1725

Mary PIERCE^6 (Hannah Tilden^5) and William MURDOCK

Isaac LITTLE^3 and Bethiah THOMAS, c1674

Abigail LITTLE^4 (Isaac^3) and John ARBUTHNOT, 14 June 1720 (Pembroke VR:228,310)

Bethiah LITTLE^4 (Isaac^3) and Thomas BARKER, 22 May 1712, Plymouth (MD 14:37)

Charles LITTLE^4 (Isaac^3) and Sarah WARREN^4 (James^3, Nath.^{2}), 9 Oct. 1712, Ply-
    mouth (MD 14:37)

Sarah WARREN^4 and 2nd Nicholas SEVER, 21 Nov. 1728 (Kingston VR)

Bethiah LITTLE^5 (Charles^4) and Thomas TYLER, 1 Sept. 1733 (Kingston VR:249,293)

Isaac LITTLE^4 (Isaac^3) and 1st Mary OTIS, c1703 (MD 6:70)

Isaac LITTLE^4 and 2nd Abigail (CUSHING) Thomas, 29 Nov. 1732 (Pembroke VR:311,359)

Lemuel LITTLE^5 (Isaac^4) and Mary LAPHAM

Mary LITTLE^5 (Isaac^4) and John WINSLOW^4 (Isaac^3, Josiah^2)

Isaac LITTLE^5 (Isaac^4) and Lydia HATCH^5 (Isaac$^{4-3}$, Mary Doty^2), 27 Oct. 1760
    (Pembroke VR:286,311)

Nathaniel LITTLE^5 (Isaac^4) and 1st Lydia BARKER, 25 July 1745 (Pembroke VR:232,310)

Nathaniel LITTLE^5 and 2nd Keziah (WOOD) Adams, Int. 22 Feb. 1755, Plymouth
    (MD 25:52)

Charles JONES and Deborah SAMPSON, 2 Feb. 1792 (Duxbury Ch.rcds.1:34)

Nathaniel LITTLE^6 (Nath.^{5}) and Pamela BRADFORD, Int. 29 Oct. 1791, Bridgewater$^{<8>}$

Barker LITTLE^6 (Nath.^{5}) and Elizabeth HOWLAND^5 (Nicholas$^{4-3}$, Zoeth^2, Henry^1),
    31 Jan. 1773 (Dartmouth VR 2:251,296)

Lydia LITTLE^7 (Barker^6) and Stephen GIFFORD, 5 Mar. 1795

Stephen Barker GIFFORD^8 (Lydia Little^7) and Pamelia TRIPP

Nathaniel LITTLE^7 (Barker^6) and Rebecca CUNDALL

Esek LITTLE^8 (Nath.^{7}) and Ruth H. (MACOMBER) Slade

Sarah A. LITTLE^9 (Esek^8) and Isaiah Francis SEARS

Otis LITTLE^7 (Barker^6) and Alice GIDLEY, 14 July 1814, Dartmouth (Westport
    VR:158,186)

Christian LITTLE^6 (Nath.^{5}) and 1st Henry Paul STERLING, 18 Nov. 1791 (Bridge
water VR 2:248,355)

Christian LITTLE^6 and 2nd Joseph TISDALE, 27 May 1805 (Hodges Gen.:157)

Lucy LITTLE^6 (Nath.^{5}) and John COTTON, Int. 29 June 1780, Plymouth (MD 28:70)$^{\langle 9 \rangle}$

John COTTON^7 (Lucy Little^6) and Catherine PARKHURST

Theophilus COTTON and Martha SAUNDERS, c1743 (MD 15:211)

Nathaniel LITTLE^6 (Nath.^{5}) and Pamela BRADFORD^6 (Paybodie^5, Gamaliel^4, Sam.^{3},
Wm.^{2}), 16 Feb. 1792 (Duxbury VR:223,273)

Silvester LITTLE^6 (Nath.^{5}) and Luther BAILEY, 21 Oct. 1784 (Hanover VR:127)

Otis LITTLE^5 (Isaac^4) and Elizabeth HOWLAND^4 (Jabez$^{3-2}$), 3 Oct. 1733, Bristol RI

Lemuel LITTLE^4 (Isaac^3) and Jane SARSON, 1 Oct. 1717 (Edgartown VR:140,173)

Abigail LITTLE^5 (Lemuel^4) and Joseph JENKINS Jr., 31 Oct. 1737 (Edgartown VR)

Thomas LITTLE^4 (Isaac^3) and Mary MAYHEW, 5 Dec. 1698, Marshfield (MD 5:237)

Mary MAYHEW and 2nd Jonathan BRYANT, 2 July 1716, Plymouth (MD 14:38)

Isaac LITTLE^5 (Tho.^{4}) and 1st Sarah CHURCH^5 (Jos.^{4}, Nath.^{3}, Eliz. Warren^2),
1 Dec. 1726, Plymouth (MD 14:71)

Isaac LITTLE^5 and 2nd Hannah (WHITMAN) Soule, poss. 10 Jan. 1754

George LITTLE^6 (Isaac^5) and Abigail SOULE^5 (Ben.$^{4-3}$, John^2)

Dr. Thomas LITTLE^5 (Tho.^{4}) and 2nd Lucy MAYHEW, 13 Dec. 1733 (Chilmark VR)

William LITTLE^4 (Isaac^3) and 1st Hannah WILLARD, 19 June 1712, Boston (Rcd.com.28:41)

William LITTLE^4 and 2nd Penelope GALE, aft. Apr. 1715

Mercy LITTLE^3 and John SAWYER, "last of" Nov. 1666, Marshfield (MD 2:111)

John SAWYER and 2nd Rebecca (BARKER) Snow, 23 (worn) 1694 (MD 4:126)

Mercy SAWYER^4 (Mercy Little^3) and Anthony EAMES, 2 Dec. 1686, Marshfield (MD 4:126)

Anthony EAMES^5 (Mercy Sawyer^4) and Anna BARKER, 25 Mar. 1725 (Marshfield VR 2:148)

Jerusha EAMES^5 (Mercy Sawyer^4) and Thomas SAWYER, 11 Sept. 1711

Jerusha SAWYER^6 (Jerusha Eames^5) and Joseph BULLOCK, 17 Apr. 1744 (Rehoboth
VR:68,334)

Joseph BULLOCK and poss. 2nd Mercy BULLOCK

Mercy SAWYER^6 (Jerusha Eames^5) and Daniel BULLOCK, 17 Apr. 1744 (Rehoboth VR:68,334)

Submit SAWYER^6 (Jerusha Eames^5) and Abiezer PECK, 11 June 1738 (Rehoboth VR:284,334)

Mary EAMES^5 (Mercy Sawyer^4) and 1st William SHERMAN, 8 Oct. 1719 (Marshfield VR 2:147)

Mary EAMES^5 and 2nd Thomas PHILLIPS, 23 Feb. 1724 (Marshfield VR 2:148)

William SHERMAN and Desire DOTY, 25 Dec. 1667 (Marshfield VR 1:6)

William SHERMAN and Mercy WHITE, 3 Feb. 1697 (Marshfield VR 1:18)

William SHERMAN and Elizabeth LAPHAM, 21 Oct. 1731 (Marshfield VR 2:143)

Mercy EAMES[5] (Mercy Sawyer[4]) and Joseph PHILLIPS, 19 July 1711, Marshfield
    (MD 7:132)

Mercy PHILLIPS[6] (Mercy Eames[5]) and Benjamin HATCH Jr., 25 June 1740, Marshfield
    (Scituate VR 2:140,236)

Elisha PHILLIPS[6] (Mercy Eames[5]) and Mary WADSWORTH, Int. 17 May 1756, Marshfield
    (VR 2:142)

Agatha PHILLIPS[6] (Mercy Eames[5]) and Jonathan HATCH, Int. 23 Feb. 1733, Scituate

Thankful HATCH[7] (Agatha Phillips[6]) and Samuel JONES

Jerusha PHILLIPS[6] (Mercy Eames[5]) and Benjamin HATCH, 7 Apr. 1741, Marshfield
    (Scituate VR 2:236,140)

Patience LITTLE[3] and Joseph JONES, 11 Nov. 1657 (Weymouth VR 2:105,114)

Benjamin JONES[4] (Patience Little[3]) and 1st Susanna BEALE, 14 Dec. 1686 (Hingham
    VR 1:72)

Ephraim JONES[4] (Patience Little[3]) and Margaret FEARING, 18 Nov. 1708 (Hingham
    (VR 1:144)

Sarah JONES[4] (Patience Little[3]) and 1st John DOTY[2], 22 Nov. 1694, Plymouth (MD 26:37)

Sarah JONES[4] and 2nd Joseph PETERSON[3] (Mary Soule[2]), 23 Apr. 1704, Plymouth
    (MD 14:35)

Anna JONES[4] (Patience Little[3]) and Joseph STURTEVANT, 5 Dec. 1693, Plymouth
    (MD 13:207)

Ephraim STURTEVANT[5] (Anna Jones[4]) and Lydia RING[4] (Eleazer[3], Deborah Hopkins[2])

Anna JONES[5] (John[4], Patience Little[3]) and Bezaleel PALMER, 19 Mar. 1727/28,
    Marshfield (Scituate VR 2:167,228)

Ann PALMER[6] (Anna Jones[5]) and Henry JOSSELYN, c1768

Benjamin PALMER[6] (Anna Jones[5]) and Anne THOMPSON

Huldah PALMER[6] (Anna Jones[5]) and Joshua LINCOLN, Int. 29 Sept. 1750 (Scituate VR)

Joshua LINCOLN and 1st Mercy DWELLY, 18 Feb. 1731, Scituate (MD 1:106)

Huldah LINCOLN[7] (Huldah Palmer[6]) and Robert RANDALL, c1771 (Bible)

Anna RANDALL[8] (Huldah Lincoln[7]) and William STORY, 7 Dec. 1803 (Boston Rcd.com.30:204)

Joanna Matilda STORY[9] (Anna Randall[8]) and Moses RICKER (Bible)

Nathaniel PALMER[6] (Anna Jones[5]) and Rachel LINCOLN, 13 June 1754 (Scituate C.R.1)

John JONES[5] (John[4]) and poss. 1st Jemima PERRY, 20 July 1726 (Scituate VR 2:168,234)

John JONES[5] and poss. 2nd Grace CUSHING

William PERRY and Elizabeh LOBDELL, 31 May 1681 (Scituate VR)

Jemima JONES[6] (John[5]) and Asa THOMAS

Ruth JONES[6] (John[5]) and John BAKER

Abigail JONES[5] (Joseph[4], Patience Little[3]) and 1st Ebenezer HATCH[3] (Mary Doty[2])

Abigail JONES[5] and 2nd Joseph STETSON

Amos JONES[5] (Joseph[4], Patience Little[3]) and Naomi PHILLIPS[6] (Mercy Eames[5], Mercy
      Sawyer[4], Mercy Little[3], Anna Warren[2])

Ebenezer JONES[5] (Jos.[4], Patience Little[3]) and poss. Jane KING

Elisha JONES[5] (Jos.[4], Patience Little[3]) and Sarah HYLAND, 16 Aug. 1725 (Scituate/
      Pembroke VR)

John JONES[5] (Jos.[4], Patience Little[3]) and Ruth HATCH[4] (Sam.[3], Mary Doty[2]),
      22 Mar. 1738/39 (Scituate VR)

Amos JONES[6] (John[5]) and Abigail CARVER, c1770

Elizabeth JONES[6] (John[5]) and Jonathan HATCH Jr., c1770

Ezekiel JONES[6] (John[5]) and Huldah SHERMAN, c1777

Samuel JONES[6] (John[5]) and Thankful HATCH[7] (Agatha Phillips[6], Mercy Eames[5], Mercy
      Sawyer[4], Mercy Little[3], Anna Warren[2])

Thomas JONES[4] (Patience Little[3]) and Katherine CASWELL, 15 Feb. 1703/04 (Hing-
      ham VR 1:128)

Samuel LITTLE[3] and Sarah GRAY[4] (Mary Winslow[3], Mary Chilton[2]), 18 May 1682,
      Marshfield (MD 4:126)

Edward LITTLE and Rhoda RANNEY, 23 Feb. 1775, Middletown CT[10]

Edward LITTLE[4] (Sam.[3]) and 1st Mary WALKER, 7 Nov. 1717 (Bristol RI VR 1:66)

Edward LITTLE[4] and 2nd Mary BURNHAM, 18 June 1741 (Bristol RI VR 1:66)[11]

Otis LITTLE and Elizabeth HOWLAND, 3 Oct. 1733 (Bristol RI VR 1:64)

Mary LITTLE[5] (Edw.[4]) and Nathaniel REYNOLDS, Int. 13 June 1741 (Bristol RI VR 1:99)

Micro #10 of 32

Sarah LITTLE[5] (Edw.[4]) and Nathaniel FALES, Int. 16 Aug. 1740, Bristol RI

Nathaniel FALES Jr. and Elisabeth BRADFORD, 26 Sept. 1773 (Bristol RI VR 2:60)

Samuel LITTLE[4] (Sam.[3]) and 1st Mary BRIGGS, 10 May 1714 (Little Compton RI VR)

Samuel LITTLE[4] and 2nd Hannah WILSON, 29 Oct. 1730, Bristol RI

Thomas LITTLE[5] (Sam.[4]) and Margaret LAWTON, Int. 5 Feb. 1735/6, Bristol (Arnold VR 1:64)[12]

Samuel LITTLE[5] (Sam.[4]) and Hannah CARR, Int. 8 Dec. 1739, Bristol (VR 1:64)

Sarah LITTLE[4] (Sam.[3]) and Richard BILLINGS, c1703 (Little Compton VR)

Richard BILLINGS[5] (Sarah[4]) and Abigail WOODMAN, 22 Sept. 1734, Little Compton RI

Abigail WOODMAN and 2nd Nathaniel FESTON, poss. 28 July 1748, Little Compton

Elizabeth WARREN[2] (Richard[1])

Elizabeth WARREN[2] and Richard CHURCH, pre 14 Mar. 1635

Sarah THAXTER and Peter DUNBAR, 25 Mar. 1691 <see below>

David THAXTER and Alice CHUBBUCK, 24 June 1695 <see below>

Deborah THAXTER and Joseph BEAL, 27 Aug. 1717

Abigail THAXTER and Edward WARD, 25 Feb. 1730/31

Elizabeth CHURCH[3] and Caleb HOBART, 20 Jan. 1657/58, Hingham

Abigail CHURCH[3] and Samuel THAXTER, 19 Dec. 1666, Hingham (MD 23:145)

Samuel THAXTER and 2nd Deborah LINCOLN, 13 June 1678, Hingham (MD 23:145)

David THAXTER[4] (Abigail Church[3]) and Alice CHUBBUCK <see above>

David THAXTER[5] (David[4]) and Deborah LINCOLN, 29 Nov. 1739

Sarah THAXTER[4] (Abigail Church) and Peter DUNBAR, 25 Mar. 1691, Hingham (MD 23:145)

Abigail DUNBAR[5] (Sarah Thaxter[4]) and Joshua FOBES, 4 Dec. 1711, Bridgewater (MD 16:104)

Joshua FOBES[6] (Abigail Dunbar[5]) and Esther PORTER[5] (Bathshua Reed[4], Esther Tomson[3], Mary Cooke[2])

David DUNBAR[5] (Sarah Thaxter[4]) and 1st Susanna HAYWARD, 16 Mar. 1737/38, Bridge-water (MD 16:44)

David DUNBAR[5] and 2nd Mercy SOULE, 11 Apr. 1763 (Bridgewater VR 2:117)

David DUNBAR and Sarah BLAKE, 21 Sept. 1749 (Bridgewater VR 2:113)

David DUNBAR Jr. and Joanna DUNBAR, 1 Dec. 1768, Halifax (Bridgewater VR 2:113)

David DUNBAR Jr. and Hariot BRYANT, 6 July 1801 (Bridgewater VR 2:113)

David DUNBAR and Sarah BLAKE, 21 Sept. 1749 (W. Bridgewater VR:133)

John FARM(sp) and Mercy (SOULE) Dunbar, 31 July 1781 (Bridgewater VR 2:115,129)

Susanna DUNBAR[6] (David[5]) and Samuel BARTLETT, 12 May 1757 (Bridgewater VR 2:41,116)

Elisha DUNBAR[5] (Sarah Thaxter[4]) and Mercy HAYWARD, 6 Apr. 1727 (Bridgewater VR)

Peter DUNBAR[5] (Sarah Thaxter[4]) and Hannah DUNBAR, Int. 21 Dec. 1728

Hannah DUNBAR[6] (Peter[5]) and Solomon LORING[13]

Huldah DUNBAR[6] (Peter[5]) and 1st Jonathan STUBS, 4 Nov. 1754, Hingham

Huldah DUNBAR[6] and 2nd Joseph PUNNERY

Mary DUNBAR[6] (Peter[5]) and Peter BURRELL, 19 Feb. 1761

Patience DUNBAR[6] (Peter[5]) and Theophilus CUSHING Jr., 6 Apr. 1768, Hingham

Abigail DUNBAR[6] (Peter[5]) and 1st Caleb HUMPHREY, 29 Aug. 1758, Hingham

Abigail DUNBAR[6] and 2nd Hosea ORCUTT, 16 Aug. 1762 (Hingham 2:361)

Sarah DUNBAR[6] (Peter[5]) and poss. Jonathan LOCK[14]

Peter DUNBAR[6] (Peter[5]) and Elizabeth ( ), c1768

Elizabeth ( ) DUNBAR and 2nd Benjamin LUNT

Mary DUNBAR[7] (Peter[6]) and Job POOL, 13 May 1788, Falmouth ME

Ebenezer POOL[8] (Mary Dunbar[7]) and Elmira Knight BUCKMAN

Samuel DUNBAR[5] (Sarah Thaxter[4]) and 1st Melatiah HAYWARD, 14 Dec. 1732 (Bridge-
    water VR 2:117,173)

Samuel DUNBAR[5] and 2nd Mary HAYWARD, 11 Feb. 1745

Sarah DUNBAR[5] (Sarah Thaxter[4]) and Thomas ALGER, 15 Jan. 1723/24, Bridgewater
    (MD 16:187)

Sarah ALGER[6] (Sarah Dunbar[5]) and Jeremiah BASSETT, poss. 24 Nov. 1748 (Alger
    Mem.:7,10)

Jeremiah BASSETT[7] (Sarah Alger[6]) and Hannah WOODWARD, 3 Feb. 1780,

Abner BASSETT and Zilpah Hicks THRASHER, 11 Oct. 1835, poss. Rehoboth

Isaac THRASHER and Lucy L. PEIRCE, 27 Jan. 1810

Helen Louisa BASSETT and Francis Baylis MACKER, c1858

Eugene Parker BASSETT and 1st Marcia TUTTLE, 2nd Mary Anderson CASEY

Mary Louisa MACKER and John Thomas MIDDLETON

Helen Francis MACKER and G.W. YEATON, c1880

Jeremiah BASSETT and Mary FELCH, c1721

Benjamin CHURCH[3] and Alice SOUTHWORTH, 26 Dec. 1667 (Gen.Reg.1:159)

Mary CHURCH and Benjamin BOSWORTH, 19 July 1764 (Bristol RI VR 2:52)

Thomas CHURCH and Molly TRIP, 26 Oct. 1794 (Bristol RI VR 2:91)

Deborah CHURCH and Joseph LINDSEY, 9 Aug. 1772 (Bristol RI VR 2:60)

Edward CHURCH and Hannah LEDBELTER, 5 May 1754 (Newport VR:171)

Nathaniel CHURCH and Sarah ASTIN, 15 Oct. 1741 (Jamestown VR)

Elizabeth CHURCH and Benjamin LINDSEY, Int. 7 Feb. 1732/33 (Bristol RI 14:1-64)

Mrs. Elizabeth CHURCH and Thomas GREENE, 9 Apr. 1732 (Bristol RI 14:1-42,43)

Benjamin CHURCH and Phebe PRATT, 14 May 1797, Newport RI

Samuel CHURCH and Elizabeth BROWN/BROWNELL, 14 June 1803, Newport RI

Benjamin CHURCH and Elizabeth PHILLIPS, 6 June 1807, Newport RI

Charles CHURCH[4] (Ben.[3]) and Hannah PAINE, 20 May 1708 (Bristol RI VR 6:1:13,41,69)

Peter CHURCH and Mrs. Sarah FALES, 22 Mar. 1764 (Bristol RI VR 2:51)

Constant CHURCH[5] (Charles[4]) and Mary REYNOLDS

Edward CHURCH[4] (Ben.[3]) and Martha BURTON, c1702

Abigail WANTON[5] (Edw.[4]) and George WANTON

Benjamin CHURCH[5] (Edw.[4]) and 1st Elizabeth VIALL, Int. 26 Oct. 1727, Bristol
    (Arnold VR 6:1:13)

Benjamin CHURCH[5] and 2nd Hannah DYER, 6 Mar. 1731, Boston (Rcd.com.28:170)

Micro #12 of 32

Abigail CHURCH[6] (Ben.[5]) and Turner PHILLIPS

Hannah CHURCH[6] (Ben.[5]) and Edward WELD, Int. 7 Apr. 1757, Boston (Rcd.com.30:23)

Martha CHURCH[6] (Ben.[5]) and 1st John CHALONER, 12 Oct. 1746, Newport

Martha CHURCH[6] and 2nd Maj. James CUNNINGHAM, 19 Jan. 1773, Boston (Rcd.com.

John CHALLONER and Nancy BLIGHT, 21 Jan. 1777 (Boston Rcd.com.30:72)

Elizabeth CHALONER and Daniel GROVER, 19 June 1804 (Boston Rcd.com.30:217)

Abigail CHALONER and Abraham ELLISON, 6 Feb. 1774 (Boston Rcd.com.30:402)

Thomas CHURCH and Nancy CHALONER, 26 May 1785 (Boston Rcd.com.30:450)

Martha CHALONGER and George ELLIS, 14 Dec. 1786 (Medfield VR:124)

Samuel CHURCH and Mrs. Ann DAVIS, 5 Jan. 1755 (Arnold VR 6:1:14,17)

Elizabeth CHURCH[4] (Ben.[3]) and 1st Joseph ROSBOTHAM, c1700

Elizabeth CHURCH[4] and 2nd John SAMPSON, 11 Sept. 1717 (VR RI 6:1:47)

Elizabeth CHURCH[4] and 3rd Capt. Samuel WOODBURY, 18 June 1739 (VR RI 6:1:47,60)

Samuel CLARKE and Mrs. Mary SAMSON, 18 Jan. 1747 (Bristol RI VR 6:1:47)

Hannah ROSBOTHAM[5] (Eliz. Church[4]) and John MUNRO, 29 Apr. 1728 (Bristol RI VR
    6:1:37,47)

Thomas CHURCH[4] (Ben.[3]) and 1st Sarah HAYMAN, 21 Feb. 1698 (Bristol RI VR 6:1:13,26)

Thomas CHURCH[4] and 2nd Edith WOODMAN, 16 Apr. 1712 (Bristol RI VR 4:6:18,72)

Thomas CHURCH[4] and 3rd Sarah HORSWELL, 10 Aug. 1719 (Hingham VR 1:180)

Abigail CHURCH and Samuel THAXTER, 19 Dec. 1666 (Hingham VR 1:10)

Caleb CHURCH and Joannah SPRAGUE, 16 Dec. 1667 (Hingham VR 1:14)

Sarah CHURCH and James BURROWES, 8 Dec. 1674 (Hingham VR 1:33)

Francis HOASWELL and Abigaell TOWER, Int. 13 Oct. 1711 (poss. Hingham VR 1:5)

Alice CHURCH[5] (Tho.[4]) and Paul EUNICE, 29 Sept. 1728 (Little Compton RI VR 4:6:19,27)

Elizabeth VUNIS[6] (Alice Church[5]) and John NORRIS, 17 Apr. 1757 (Bristol RI VR)

Paul Vannis NORRIS[7] (Elizabeth Vunis[6]) and Martha MANCHESTER, 3 Nov. 1790 (Bristol VR RI 8:344)

Benjamin NORRIS[7] (Eliz. Vunis[6]) and Mary COX, 17 Aug. 1794 (Int.-Bristol VR RI 8:313)

William COX and Mary BRISTOW(sp), 16 Jan. 1739 (Bristol VR RI 8:203)

Hannah COX and Samuel LITTLE Jr., 27 Dec. 1739 (Bristol VR RI 8:203)

William COX and Sarah PEARSE, 18 Mar. 1741/42 (Bristol VR RI 8:203)

Eliza COX and Nathaniel MANCHESTER, 8 June 1769 (Bristol VR RI 8:203)

William COX Jr. and Mary HOAR, 5 Nov. 1769 (Bristol VR RI 8:203)

Sarah COX and Joseph REYNOLDS Jr., 11 Dec. 1771 (Bristol VR RI 8:203)

Mary COX and Thomas MUNRO, 15 Dec. 1771 (Bristol VR RI 8:203)

Mary COX and Benjamin NOKES, 17 Aug. 1794 (Bristol VR RI 8:203)

Susan COX and James USHER 2d, 17 Jan. 1808 (Bristol VR RI 8:203)

Hannah NORRIS[8] (Ben.[7]) and Isaac Dennis HALL, 12 Dec. 1831

Caleb CHURCH[3] and 1st Joanna SPRAGUE, 16 Dec. 1667 (Hingham VR 1:14)

Caleb CHURCH[3] and 2nd Rebecca SCOTTO, 6 Nov. 1691[15]

Lydia CHURCH[4] (Caleb[3]) and Samuel HASTINGS, 4 Jan. 1686/87 (Watertown VR 4:96)

Samuel HASTINGS and 2nd Sarah COOLIDGE, 10 July 1701 (Bond's Watertown:286)

Hannah CHURCH[4] (Caleb[3]) and Matthew BOOMER, c1688 (Freetown VR 1:165)

Hannah BOOMER[5] (Hannah Church[4]) and John JENKS

Caleb BOOMER[5] (Hannah Church[4]) and Sarah MARTIN, 19 Aug. 1725 (Freetown VR 1:9)

James BOOMER and Susanna BORDEN, 11 Nov. 1792 (Freetown VR)

Martin BOOMER[6] (Caleb[5]) and 1st Jemima ELSBREE, 30 Nov. 1758 (Freetown VR 2:229)

Martin BOOMER[6] and 2nd Sarah STILWELL, 31 Oct. 1776 (Freetown VR 2:246)

Rev. James BOOMER[7] (Martin[6]) and Susanna BORDEN, poss. 11 Nov. 1792 (Freetown VR)

Rev. James Cushman BOOMER[8] (Wm.[7], Martin[6]) and Eliza J. LUCE

Sarah BOOMER[6] (Caleb[5]) and Thomas WEST, 18 Jan. 1748 (Freetown Ch.rcds.)

Mathew BOOMER[5] (Hannah Church[4]) and Hannah HATHAWAY, 28 Sept. 1719, Freetown

Deborah BOOMER[6] (Mathew[5]) and Nathaniel MASON, 29 Mar. 1747, Swansea

Nathaniel MASON and 2nd Lydia MARTIN, 22 Sept. 1763 (Gen. of Sampson Mason Fam.100)

Sampson MASON[7] (Deborah Boomer[6]) and 1st Mercy SHERMAN

Sampson MASON[7] and 2nd Celia (LINCOLN) Richmond, 13 June 1803

Isaiah MASON[8] (Sampson[7]) and 1st Sarah CHILDS, 15 Jan. 1807

Isaiah MASON[8] and 2nd Lucy (SAWYER) Fenton, 28 Jan. 1823

Russell Sawyer MASON[9] (Isaiah[8]) and Mary Ann CLARK, 15 Nov. 1849

Caleb CHURCH[5] (Isaac[4]) and Rebecca BRAND, 16 Sept. 1731 (Westerly VR RI 5:4:20)

Joshua CHURCH[6] (Caleb[5]) and Katherine KENYON, 29 Mar. 1756 (Westerly VR RI 5:4:20)

Jonathan CHURCH[5] (Isaac[4]) and Thankful BULLARD, 21 Aug. 1734 (Watertown VR 1:103)

Joshua CHURCH[5] (Isaac[4]) and Annis JOHNSON, poss. 19 Nov. 1728 (Lancaster VR)

Jonathan SMITH and Jane PEABODY, 16 Mar. 1682/83

Nathaniel SMITH and Priscilla HARRIS, 17 Dec. 1751 (Watertown VR 3:133)

Lydia CHURCH[5] (Isaac[4]) and Nathaniel SMITH, 5 Feb. 1722/23 (Lexington VR:148)

Nathaniel SMITH[6] (Lydia Church[5]) and Keziah HOW, 2 Jan. 1750/51 (Marlborough VR)

Jonas SMITH[7] (Nath.[6]) and Susanna BRUCE, 26 June 1777

Samuel SMITH[8] (Jonas[7]) and 1st Candace WHITCOMB, 14 May 1807

Samuel SMITH[8] and 2nd Eunice HOAR, 3 Feb. 1814

Samuel SMITH[9] (Sam.[8]) and Eveline WALKER, 15 Apr. 1832

William D. SMITH[9] (Sam.[8]) and Lucy A. WHITE, 18 Nov. 1838

Candace SMITH[9] (Sam.[8]) and George T. BANCROFT, 17 May 1838

Eunice W. SMITH[9] (Sam.[8]) and George J. SMITH, 6 Oct. 1841

Mary E. SMITH[9] (Sam.[8]) and C.E. GIBSON

Jonathan WHITCOMB and Sarah BAKER, 8 July 1779

Rebecca CHURCH[4] (Caleb[3]) and Joshua WARREN, c1695

Abigail WARREN[5] (Rebecca Church[4]) and Jedediah HOW, 27 Nov. 1728 (Westboro VR:171,214)

Solomon HOW[6] (Abigail Warren[5]) and Mary HOLMES, poss. c1778

Daniel WARREN[5] (Rebecca Church[4]) and Martha COOLIDGE Jr., 20 Dec. 1733 (Water-
    town VR 2:95)

Rebecca WARREN[6] (Dan.[5]) and Simeon BELLOWS, 10 Apr. 1766 (Westboro VR:123,216)

Hannah WARREN[6] (Dan.[5]) and Ezra BAKER, Int. 4 June 1763 (Westboro VR:118,216)

Martha WARREN[6] (Dan.[5]) and Isaac BARTLET, Int. 25 Nov. 1752 (Westboro VR:120,216)

Sarah WARREN and Stephen MAYNARD Jr., 15 Dec. 1783 (Westboro VR:183,216)

Mrs. Sarah MAYNARD and James OUTHANK, 31 Dec. 1809 (Westboro VR:183,192)

Thaddeus WARREN[6] (Dan.[5]) and 1st Abigail WHIPPLE, Int. 18 Aug. 1759 (Westboro
    VR 3:324)

Thaddeus WARREN[6] and 2nd Hannah GOULD, 5 May 1768 (Westboro VR 3:349)

Submit WARREN[7] (Thaddeus[6]) and Samuel M. SMITH, 11 June 1797 (Westboro VR:207,216)

Asaph WARREN[7] (Thaddeus[6]) and Anna WHITNEY, 30 Mar. 1814 (Westboro VR 2:215,219)

Isaac Forbush WARREN[8] (Asaph[7]) and Martha Ann CHAMBERLAIN, 9 Apr. 1845, Westboro
   (Bible)

Anson WARREN[8] (Asaph[7]) and Mary Elizabeth STONE, 1 Sept. 1841, Westboro (Bible)

John WARREN[7] (Thaddeus[6]) and Hannah BALL, 30 Apr. 1795 (Westboro VR 3:358)

John WARREN and Anna FORBUSH(sp), 28 Oct. 1779, poss. Westboro

John WARREN and Charlotte JOHNSON, 22 Jan. 1811 (Southboro Ch.rcd.)

John BALL and Lydia PRATT, 12 May 1763 (Westboro VR:119,198)

Betsey WARREN[8] (John[7]) and David FISHER, 20 Apr. 1817 (Westboro VR:150,215)

David Harrison FISHER[9] (Betsey Warren[8]) and Sarah HOSMER, poss. 10 Nov. 1845

Joshua WARREN[5] (Rebecca Church[4]) and Elizabeth HARRIS, poss. 29 Apr. 1724

Phineas WARREN[5] (Rebecca Church[4]) and Grace HASTINGS, 3 May 1739 (Waltham VR:167,235)

Grace WARREN[6] (Phineas[5]) and Samuel BARNES, 10 July 1775 (Waltham VR:113,234)

Andrew BARNES[7] (Grace Warren[6]) and Sarah DEAN, 21 Apr. 1807, Newton

Harriet Dean BARNES[8] (Andrew[7]) and Jacob Sanborn MERRILL

Josiah Mixer BARNES[8] (Andrew[7]) and Elizabeth Ann JONES, c1842

Harriet Ann BARNES[9] (Josiah[8]) and George Edward CHICKERING, 6 Oct. 1866

Phineas BARNES[7] (Grace Warren[6]) and Sally SPOFFORD, 22 Dec. 1807 (Boxford VR:115,202)

Mary BARNES[8] (Phineas[7]) and Elijah GOULD

Thomas BARNES[7] (Grace Warren[6]) and Adaline LAWRENCE, 21 Nov. 1822 (Lexington VR:96)

Micro #15 of 32

Prudence WARREN[5] (Rebecca Church[3]) and Phineas HARDY, 8 Mar. 1731/32 (Westboro
   Ch.rcds.)

Constantine HARDY[6] (Prudence Warren[5]) and Jemima BRIGHAM, Int. 14 Dec. 1762,
   Westboro

Joanna MADDOCK[5] (Ruth Church[4], Caleb[3]) and 1st Edward OAKES, 1721

Joanna MADDOCK[5] and 2nd Richard SPRAGUE, aft. Apr. 1752 (Medford VR:268)

Ruth CHURCH[4] (Caleb[3]) and 1st John MADDOCKS, 23 June 1689 (Watertown VR 1:62)

Ruth CHURCH[4] and 2nd Joseph CHILD, 25 July 1705 (Watertown VR 2:20)

Ruth CHURCH[4] and 3rd Thomas INGERSOLL, c1719/20

Nathan OAKES[6] (Joanna Maddock[5]) and Amy (WYMAN) Buckman, 7 Oct. 1751 (N. Yarmouth
   ME VR)

Lydia CHILD[5] (Ruth Church[4]) and James FAY, 19 Dec. 1727 (Watertown VR 2:82)

Joseph CHURCH[3] and Mary TUCKER, 13 Dec. 1660, Hingham (NEHGR 2:253)

Deborah CHURCH^4 (Joseph^3) and 1st Samuel GRAY, 13 July 1699 (Little Compton RI
    VR 4:6:18,29)

Deborah CHURCH^4 and 2nd Dan THORPE, 21 Jan. 1713 (NEHGR 36:125)

Elizabeth CHURCH^4 (Jos.^{3}) and Joseph BLACKMAN

Mary CHURCH^5 (John^4, Jos.^{3}) and Samuel TISDALE, 12 Aug. 1725, Little Compton RI

Mary TISDALE^6 (Mary Church^5) and Eleazer NICHOLS, 15 Feb. 1749/50 (Freetown VR)

Rebecca TISDALE^6 (Mary Church^5) and Benjamin PORTER (Gen.Reg.20:225,266)

Joseph CHURCH^4 (Jos.^{3}) and Grace SHAW, c1688 (Arnold VR 4:6:18)

Mary CHURCH^4 (Jos.^{3}) and John WOOD, c1688

Nathaniel CHURCH^3 and Sarah BARSTOW, c1666

Abigail CHURCH^4 (Nath.^{3}) and Nathaniel HARLOW, c1692 (PN&Q 5:92)

Abigail HARLOW^5 (Abigail Church^4) and Robert COOKE^4 (Francis^3, Jacob^2), 29 Nov.
    1716, Plympton (MD 2:236)

James HARLOW^5 (Abigail Church^4) and Hannah SHAW, 9 Apr. 1719 (Plympton VR 1:135)

Nathaniel HARLOW^5 (Abigail Church^4) and Patience LUCAS^4 (Patience Warren^3, Jos.^{2}),
    19 Dec. 1717, Plymouth (MD 14:38)

Nathaniel HARLOW^6 (Nath.^{5}) and Sarah BONNEY (Gen.Reg.14:231)

Sarah BONNEY and 2nd Ephraim SOULE^5 (Zachariah^4, Ben.^{3}, John^2), aft. Aug. 1795

Susanna HARLOW^6 (Nath.^{5}) and Noah STURTEVANT

Charles CHURCH^4 (Nath.^{3}) and Mary POPE, c1705 (MD 5:55)

Charles CHURCH^5 (Charles^4) and Frances TURNER

Deborah CHURCH^5 (Charles^4) and Wing SPOONER, 9 Mar. 1729 (Spooner Gen.:55,56)

Joseph CHURCH^4 (Nath.^{3}) and Judith HARLOW, 1 Nov. 1705/06, Plymouth (MD 14:35)$^{<16>}$

Judith HARLOW and 2nd Stephen BARNABY^4 (Lydia Bartlett^3, Mary Warren^2), 11 July
    1710, Plymouth (MD 14:36)

Nathaniel CHURCH^4 (Nath.^{3}) and Judith BOSWORTH, 7 Jan. 1696/97, Hull (Scituate VR)

Joseph CHURCH^5 (Nath.^{4}) and Grace DWELLY^6 (Grace Turner^5, Ben^4, Mary Brewster^3,
    Jonathan^2), 2 Aug. 1742 (Scituate VR)

Grace DWELLY^6 and 1st Jesse TURNER^5 (Jonathan^4, Mary Brewster^3, Jonathan^2),
    18 Dec. 1734$^{<17>}$

Mary CHURCH^5 (Nath.^{4}) and Charles SAMSON^4 (David^3, Caleb^2)

Abigail CHURCH^5 (Nath.^{4}) and William TURNER

Caleb CHURCH and Sarah WILLIAMSON, 20 Jan. 1736/37 (MD 1:!08)

Deborah CHURCH^5 (Nath.^{4}) and Ebenezer FISH

Judith CHURCH^5 (Nath.^{4}) and William CLIFT, 28 Apr. 1720, Scituate (MD 11:46)

Rhoda CLIFT^6 (Judith Church^6) and Samuel TRONANT, 26 June 1766 (Marshfield VR 2:150)

Huldah TRONANT^7 (Rhoda Clift^6) and Joel HATCH, 21 Apr. 1796 (Marshfield VR 2:139)

Micro #16 of 32

William CLIFT^6 (Judith Church^5) and Bethiah HATCH, 17 Apr. 1746, Marshfield
   (Scituate VR)

Nathaniel CHURCH^5 (Nath.^{4}) and 1st Jerusha PERRY, 24 Mar. 1719 (Scituate VR)

Nathaniel CHURCH^5 and 2nd Mary (FAUNCE) Curtis, 2 Nov. 1758

Ichabod DAMON Jr. and Judeth PEAKS, 1 Jan. 1718, Scituate

Roger NICOLS and Bethiah WINSLOW, 18 Feb. 1718, Scituate

Gilbert BROOKS and Abigail STOCKBRIDGE, 12 Mar. 1718, Scituate

Barnabas BARKER and Hannah TURNER, 13 Apr. 1719, Scituate

Dr. Isaac OTIS and Mrs. Deborah JACOB, 25 May 1719, Scituate

Caesar BURGES and Meriah WELLS ("negrows"), 12 Nov. 1719, Scituate

John SUTTON and Anne COLE, 3 Dec. 1719, Scituate

Benjamin BRIGGS and Leah MERRIT, 7 Dec. 1719, Scituate

Titus MOSES and Rebecca OPECHUS ("Indians"), 3 Jan. 1719, Scituate

Rebecca CHURCH and George REED, Sept. 1793 (Waldoboro ME VR 1:)

Abigail CHURCH^6 (Nath.^{5}) and Seth BRIGGS

Lydia CHURCH^6 (Nath.^{5}) and 1st Simeon NASH, 19 Feb. 1740/41, Scituate

Lydia CHURCH^6 and 2nd Ezekiel PALMER

Church NASH^7 (Lydia Church^6) and Eve C.M. REED

Jane NASH^8 (Church^7) and Jacob OVERLOCK

Samuel NASH^8 (Church^7) and 1st Lydia SPRAGUE

Samuel NASH^8 and 2nd Sarah Margaret (HAVENER) Sprague, 25 Nov. 1833

Isaac Randall NASH^9 (Sam.^{8}) and Mary Ann PARKER

Samuel NASH^9 (Sam.^{8}) and Marietta HALL, 1836

Melita Susan NASH^{10} (Sam.^{9}) and Henry Clay FLAGG

Samuel NASH^7 (Lydia Church^6) and Jerusha BRIGGS

Thomas NASH^7 (Lydia Church^6) and Betsy MAN

Nathaniel CHURCH^6 (Nath.^{5}) and Mehitable NORTH, 11 Aug. 1750 (Scituate VR 2:58,219)

Sarah CHURCH^6 (Nath.^{5}) and Josiah LATHROP, 21 June 1749 (Scituate VR)

William BASSETT^8 (Hannah Lathrop^7, Sarah Church^6) and Abiah WILLIAMS^6 (Zerviah
   Staple^5, Hannah Standish^4, Eben.^{3}, Alex.^{2}), 23 Oct. 1800 (Raynham VR 1:101)

Richard CHURCH^4 (Nath.^{3}) and Hannah ( ), 2 Feb. 1696/97, Scituate (MD 2:35)

Hannah ( ) CHURCH and 2nd poss. David BRYANT, 31 July 1706 (Scituate VR)

Church STURTEVANT[6] (Hannah Church[5]) and Sarah LEACH, Int. 3 Nov. 1760 (Halifax VR:61)

Lucy STURTEVANT[6] (Hannah Church[5]) and George HAMMOND, 16 Nov. 1758 (Halifax VR:36)

Lemuel CHURCH[6] (Richard[5-4]) and poss. Bethiah CLAPP

Ruth CHURCH[5] (Richard[4]) and Ezekiel HATCH[3] (Mary Doty[2]), 25 Sept. 1718, Scituate
(MD 10:75)

Hannah CHURCH[5] (Richard[4]) and Josiah STURTEVANT, 24 Dec. 1719, Scituate (MD 10:75)

Richard CHURCH[5] (Richard[4]) and Anna STURTEVANT, Int. 18 June 1720, Plymouth
(MD 18:143)

Richard CHURCH[6] (Richard[5]) and 1st poss. Lois DEXTER, c1747

Richard CHURCH[6] and 2nd poss. Sarah STEVENS, 15 Apr. 1750

Sarah CHURCH[4] (Nath.[3]) and John HOLMES, 7 Oct. 1709, Plymouth (MD 14:36)

Sarah CHURCH[3] and James BURROWES, 8 Dec. 1674, Hingham (VR 1:33)

Sarah BURROUGHS and John BROWN, 21 Apr. 1698 (Boston Rcd.com.9:243)

Joseph WARREN[2] (Richard[1])

Joseph WARREN[2] and Priscilla FAUNCE, c1652, Plymouth (MD 18:69)

Mercy WARREN[3] and John BRADFORD[3] (Wm.[2])

Benjamin WARREN[3] and 1st Hannah MORTON, 22 Apr. 1697, Plymouth (MD 13:206)

Benjamin WARREN[3] and 2nd Esther (BARNES) Cushman, 25 Oct. 1716, Plymouth (MD 14:38)

Abigail WARREN[4] (Ben.[3]) and Joseph RIDER, 1 Nov. 1722, Plymouth (MD 14:39)

Abigail RIDER[5] (Abigail Warren[4]) and Lemuel HOLMES, 28 Apr. 1746, Plymouth (MD 17:5)

Benjamin RIDER[5] (Abigail Warren[4]) and Patience HOWLAND[5] (John[4], James[3], Jos.[2]),
poss. 27 Aug. 1775

James SISSON and Freelove FISH, 12 Nov. 1741 (Newport VR 2:45)

Joseph RIDER and Barbara WILLIAMS, 26 Nov. 1741 (Newport VR 2:45)

Lydia RIDER[6] (Jos.[5], Abigail Warren[4]) and Jacob ALBERTSON, 30 Nov. 1775 (Bible)

Martha ALBERTSON[7] (Lydia Rider[6]) and 1st Amaziah HARLOW

Martha ALBERTSON[7] and 2nd William CHURCHILL, poss. 24 May 1807

Jane Spooner ALBERTSON[7] (Lydia Rider[6]) and Daniel LAMB

Benjamin WARREN[4] (Ben.[3]) and Rebecca DOTY[4] (Isaac[3], John[2]), 14 Dec. 1738, Plymouth
(MD 14:158)

Rebecca DOTY[4] and 2nd David TURNER, 1756 (Doty Gen.:154,155)

Benjamin WARREN[5] (Ben.[4]) and Jane STURTEVANT

Hannah WARREN[4] (Ben.[3]) and Eleazer FAUNCE, 6 Aug. 1724, Plymouth (MD 14:70)

Mary FAUNCE^5 (Hannah Waren^4) and Peleg FAUNCE, Int. 13 Aug. 1756, Plymouth
(MD 25:139)

Hannah FAUNCE^5 (Hannah Warren^4) and Benjamin MORTON, 20 Sept. 1753, Plymouth
(MD 18:141)

Patience FAUNCE^5 (Hannah Warren^4) and Josiah JOHNSON, 16 Nov. 1747, Plymouth
(MD 17:6)

Mercy WARREN^4 (Ben.^{3}) and Sylvanus BRAMHALL, poss. 7 Jan. 1762

Nathaniel WARREN^4 (Ben.^{3}) and Sarah MORTON, 23 May 1734, Plymouth (MD 14:75)

Ruth WARREN^5 (Nath.^{4}) and Thomas MORTON

Elizabeth WARREN^3 and Josiah FINNEY, 19 Jan. 1687, Plymouth (MD 13:205)

Josiah FINNEY and 2nd Marcy THOMAS, Int. 6 Aug. 1726, Plymouth (MD 18:125)

Elizabeth FINNEY^4 (Eliz. Warren^3) and William BRADFORD^4 (Wm.$^{3-2}$), 18 Nov. 1712,
Plymouth (MD 14:37)

Phebe FINNEY^4 (Eliz. Warren^3) and Jonathan BARNES^5 (Mary Bartlett^4, Jos.^{3}, Mary
Warren^2), 8 Sept. 1726, Plymouth (MD 14:71)

John FINNEY^4 (Eliz. Warren^3) and 1st Sarah BARTLETT^5 (Rob.^{4}, Jos.^{3}, Mary Warren^2),
22 Feb. 1721/22, Plymouth (MD 14:39)

John FINNEY^4 and 2nd Susanna (DOTY^4) Pratt (John$^{3-2}$), Int. 31 Mar. 1739, Plymouth
(MD 18:30)

Phebe PHINNEY and Edward DOTEN, 3 Aug. 1738, Plymouth (MD 16:254)[18]

Ezra FINNEY^5 (John^4) and Hannah LUCE, 12 Jan. 1769

Josiah FINNEY^5 (John^4) and Alice BARNES^6 (Lemuel^5, Alice Bradford^4, Wm.$^{3-2}$), c1763

Daniel FINNEY^6 (Josiah^5) and poss. Sarah COOPER, c1795

Robert FINNEY^5 (John^4) and Lydia CLARK, 12 Dec. 1765 (Plymouth Ch.rcds.<1920>:494)

Lydia FINNEY and William CASSADY, 21 Nov. 1784 (Plymouth Ch.rcds<1920>:502)[19]

Sarah FINNEY^5 (John^4) and Ephraim HOLMES, 19 May 1742, Plymouth (MD 16:255)

Joshua FINNEY^4 (Eliz. Warren^3) and Hannah CURTIS, 28 Sept. 1727, Plymouth (MD 14:72)

Joshua FINNEY and Elizabeth POPE, Int. 29 Nov. 1746, Plymouth (MD 18:119)

Josiah FINNEY^4 (Eliz. Warren^3) and Abigail BRYANT, 13 Dec. 1722, Plympton (MD 2:138)

Priscilla FINNEY^4 (Eliz. Warren^3) and Samuel MARSHALL, 23 May 1717 (MD 14:38)

Robert FINNEY^4 (Eliz. Warren^3) and Ann MORTON, 15 Nov. 1716, Plymouth (MD 14:38)

Jerusha FINNEY^5 (Robert^4) and Isaac HARLOW^6 (Robert^5, Wm.^{4}, Rebecca Bartlett^3,
Mary Warren^2), 4 Jan. 1749/50, Plymouth (MD 16:69)[20]

Joseph WARREN^3 and Mehitable WILDER, 20 Dec. 1692, Plymouth (MD 13:206)

Joseph WARREN^4 (Jos.^{3}) and Alathea CHITTENDEN, 22 Aug. 1722, Plymouth (MD 14:39)

Priscilla WARREN[5] (Jos.[4]) and Lemuel DREW[6] (Hannah Barnes[5], Mary Bartlett[4], Jos.[3], Mary Warren[2]), 4 Nov. 1751, Plymouth (MD 16:171)

William WARREN[5] (Jos.[4]) and 1st poss. Rebecca EASDELL 2nd poss. Elizabeth LOTHROP

Patience WARREN[3] and Samuel LUCAS, 16 Dec. 1686, Plymouth (MD 13:204,205)

Patience LUCAS[4] (Patience Warren[3]) and Nathaniel HARLOW[5] (Abigail Church[4], Nath.[3], Eliz. Warren[2]), 19 Dec. 1717, Plymouth (MD 14:38)

Joseph LUCAS[4] (Patience Warren[3]) and 1st Persis SHAW, 10 Mar. 1714,15, Plympton (MD 2:236)

Joseph LUCAS[4] and 2nd Malatiah CAREY, 1727 (MD 3:94)

John LUCAS[5] (Jos.[4]) and Lydia DOTY[4] (John[3-2]), 10 June 1739 (Plympton VR:309,345)

Levi LUCAS[7] (Jos.[6]) and 1st Hannah JACKSON, 12 May 1794 (Plymouth VR 2:279)

Levi LUCAS[7] and 2nd Betsey (BARNES) Davie, 5 Sept. 1802 (Plymouth VR 2:283)[21]

Allen LUCAS[8] (Levi[7]) and 1st Dorothy BARTLETT, c1823

William A. LUCAS and Sarah RUSSELL, c1846

Isaac Jackson LUCAS[8] (Levi[7]) and Catherine HOWLAND, 17 Oct. 1819 (Plymouth Ch. rcds.2:653)

Thomas Davie LUCAS[8] (Levi[7]) and 1st Susan Malvina FRENCH, c1837

Thomas Davie LUCAS[8] and poss. 2nd Abby FRENCH, c1855/56

Samuel LUCAS[5] (Jos.[4]) and Abigail SHAW, 9 Nov. 1749, Plympton

Abijah LUCAS[6] (Sam.[5]) and 1st Mary ROBBINS, c1781

Abijah LUCAS[6] and 2nd Ruth ( ) INCAS, Int. 23 Dec. 1820 (Carver VR:111,112)

Samuel LUCAS[6] (Sam.[5]) and Jemima ROBBINS, 21 Mar. 1776 (Plympton VR)

William LUCAS[4] (Patience Warren[3]) and Mehitable DOTY[4] (John[3-2])

Mary WARREN[2] (Richard[1])

Mary WARREN[2] and Robert BARTLETT, aft. 22 May 1627

Caleb BARTLETT and Elizabeth HOLMES[6] (Geo.[5], Lydia Wood[4], Experience Fuller[3], Sam.[2]), Int. 29 Nov. 1777, Plymouth (MD 28:34)

Caleb BARTLETT and Rebecca HOLMES, Int. 27 Aug. 1791, Plymouth (MD 30:76)

Nathaniel BARTLETT and Zenobe WADSWORTH, 10 June 1742, Duxbury (MD 11:81)

Solomon BARTLETT Jr. and Abigail TORREY, Int. 3 July 1773, Plymouth (MD 27:46)

Benjamin BARTLETT[3] and 1st Susanna JENNEY (MD 8:171;6:170)

Benjamin BARTLETT[3] and 2nd Sarah BREWSTER[3] (Love[2]), aft. Apr. 1654 (MD 6:44)

Rebecca BARTLETT[4] (Ben.[3]) and 1st William BRADFORD[3] (Wm.[2]), c1679

Rebecca BARTLETT^4 and 2nd Robert STANFORD, pre 30 Aug. 1697

Rebecca BARTLETT^4 and 3rd Caleb SAMSON^2<22>

Sarah BARTLETT^4 (Ben.^{3}) and Robert BARTLETT^4 (Jos.^{3}, Mary Warren^2), 28 Dec. 1687

Robert BARTLETT^4 and 2nd Sarah COOKE^3 (Jacob^2) <see p.311>

Benjamin BARTLETT^4 (Ben.^{3}) and Ruth PABODIE^3 (Eliz. Alden^2), Dec. 1676 or 1678,
    Duxbury (MD 8:232,18:242)

Abigail BARTLETT^5 (Ben.^{4}) and Gamaliel BRADFORD^4 (Sam.^{3}, Wm.^{2}), 30 Aug. 1728,
    Duxbury (MD 11:80)

Mercy BARTLETT^5 (Ben.^{4}) and John TURNER^5 (Ben.^{4}, Mary Brewster^3, Jonathan^2),
    5 Aug. 1714, Duxbury (MD 11:24)

Priscilla BARTLETT^5 (Ben.^{4}) and John SAMSON^3 (Stephen^2), 31 Dec. 1718, Duxbury
    (MD 11:25)

Rebecca BARTLETT^5 (Ben.^{4}) and John BRADFORD^4 (John^3, Wm.^{2}), 27 Nov. 1701, Plymouth
    (MD 13:207)

Sarah BARTLETT^5 (Ben.^{4}) and Israel BRADFORD^3 (Wm.^{2}), 27 Nov. 1701, Plymouth
    (MD 13:207)

William BARTLETT^5 (Ben.^{4}) and Sarah FOSTER, 5 July 1716, Plymouth (MD 14:38)

Sarah FOSTER and 2nd Nathan THOMAS, 17 June 1719, Plymouth (MD 14:38)

Sarah FOSTER and 3rd Jedediah BOURNE

Deborah BARTLETT^5 (Ben.^{4}) and Josiah THOMAS, 19 Dec. 1723, Duxbury (MD 11:240)

Prince THOMAS and Mary WEBB, 2 July 1809 (Weymouth VR)

Ruth BARTLETT^5 (Ben.^{4}) and John MURDOCK, c1710 (MD 12:11)

Ebenezer BARTLETT^4 (Ben.^{3}) and poss. Hannah BRYANT<23>

Micro #19 of 32

Ebenezer BARTLETT^5 (Eben.^{4}) and 1st Mary RIDER, 3 July 1718, Plymouth (MD 14:38)

Ebenezer BARTLETT^5 and 2nd Jerusha SAMSON, 8 Oct. 1730, Duxbury (MD 11:80)

Lydia BARTLETT^6 (Eben.^{5}) and Lemuel DELANO^4 (Benoni^3, Rebecca Alden^2), 9 July
    1741, Duxbury (MD 11:81)

Rebecca BARTLETT^6 (Eben.^{5}) and Charles RIDER, 8 Oct. 1741, Duxbury (MD 11:81)

Ichabod BARTLETT^4 (Ben.^{3}) and 1st Elizabeth WATERMAN^4 (Sarah Snow^3, Abigail
    Warren^2), 28 Dec. 1699, Marshfield (MD 8:177)

Ichabod BARTLETT^4 and 2nd Desire ARNOLD^5 (Eliz. Gray^4, Mary Winslow^3, Mary
    Chilton^2), 14 Nov. 1709, Duxbury (MD 11:23)

Joseph BARTLETT^5 (Ichabod^4) and 1st Dorothy WADSWORTH^5 (Mercy Wiswall^4, Priscilla
    Pabodie^3, Eliz. Alden^2), 25 Dec. 1729, Duxbury (MD 11:240)

Joseph BARTLETT^5 and 2nd Sarah ( ) BARTLETT, 22 Sept. 1774 (Kingston VR)

Uriah BARTLETT^6 (Jos.^{5}) and poss. 1st Lois WASHBURN, 21 Jan. 1765 (Kingston VR:172,298)

Uriah BARTLETT^6 and 2nd Susanna COOKE, 25 Aug. 1768 (Kingston VR:173,177)

Joseph BARTLETT^6 (Jos.^{5}) and Lurana DREW, 27 Nov. 1766, Kingston (Gen.Adv.3:77)

David Bradford BARTLETT^7 (Jos.^{6}) and Abigail FREEMAN

Josiah BARTLETT^5 (Ichabod^4) and Mercy CHANDLER, 3 Jan. 1722/23 (Marshfield VR 2:147)

Betty BARTLET^6 (Josiah^5) and Brotherton MARTIN, 2 Oct. 1746 (Lebanon CT VR 1:203)

Molly BARTLETT and Peleg THOMAS, 18 Nov. 1760 (Lebanon CT VR 1:314)

Chandler BARTLET^6 (Josiah^5) and Delight MACKALL, 7 Aug. 1777 (Lebanon CT VR)

Ichabod BARTLET^6 (Josiah^5) and poss. Desire OTIS^5 (Hannah Thacher^4, Lydia Gorham^3,
     Desire Howland^2), c1747

John BARTLETT^7 (Ichabod^6) and Desire LOOMIS, c1774

John BARTLET^6 (Josiah^5) and 1st Susanna SOUTHWORTH^6 (Jedediah^5, Tho.^{4}, Mary
     Pabodie^3, Eliz. Alden^2), Dec. 1753, Duxbury (Lebanon CT VR:16)

John BARTLET^6 and 2nd Lucretia STEWART (Hist. Stonington CT:605)

Mercy BARTLETT^6 (Josiah^5) and Patrick BUTLER, 16 Dec. 1756 (Lebanon CT VR 1:361)

Harriet M. BUTLER and Henry W. LAMB, 7 Dec. 1842 (Lebanon CT VR <1912> 2:8)

Laura BUTLER and Seth BARTLETT, 9 Dec. 1824 (Lebanon CT VR <1912> 1:94)

Lot McCall BUTLER and Mary LOOMIS, 1 Jan. 1829 (Lebanon CT VR <1912> 1:89)

John BUTLER^7 (Mercy Bartlett^6) and Anna EASTON, c1778

Betsey BUTLER and Asa MANNING, 27 Nov. 1817 (E.Hartford CT VR 1:68)

John Bartlett BUTLER^8 (John^7) and Catherine Selina GAZZAM

Lemuel BUTLER^8 (John^7) and poss. Elizabeth OLMSTEAD, 17 Oct. 1805

Micro #20 of 32

Molly BARTLET^6 (Josiah^5) and Peleg THOMAS, 18 Nov. 1760, Lebanon CT (Kingsley's:311)

Peleg THOMAS^7 (Molly Bartlet^6) and Sally YOUNG, 25 Mar. 1802, Lebanon CT
     (Kingsley's Rcd.:314)

Clarissa THOMAS^7 (Molly Bartlet^6) and 1st Joseph METCALF, 25 Nov. 1784, Lebanon
     (Kingsley' Rcd.:311)

Clarissa THOMAS^7 and 2nd David BOIES(sp), 15 Oct. 1809, Lebanon CT (Kingsley's:311)

Peleg George THOMAS^8 (peleg^7) and Mary S. CADY, 10 Mar. 18( ), Lebanon CT
     (Kingsley's Rcd.:314)

Jabez METCALF^8 (Clarissa Thomas^7) and Deborah McCALL, 25 Nov. 1813, Lebanon CT
     (Kingsley's Rcd.:223)

Charlotte METCALF[8] (Clarissa Thomas[7]) and Robert SESSIONS, 14 Apr. 1812, Lebanon
    CT (Kingsley's Rcd.:223)

Nathaniel BARTLETT[6] (Josiah[5]) and Mercy OTIS[5] (Hannah Thacher[4], Lydia Gorham[3],
    Desire Howland[2]), 14 Dec. 1753 (Lebanon CT VR:38)

Sarah BARTLETT[5] (Ichabod[4]) and Cornelius DREW, 27 Feb. 1728/29, Duxbury (MD 11:80)

Samuel BARTLETT[4] (Ben.[3]) and Hannah PABODIE[3] (Eliz. Alden[2]), 2 Aug. 1683, Duxbury
    (MD 8:232)

Hannah PABODIE[3] and 2nd Sgt. John CHURCHILL, 4 Mar. 1715, Plymouth (MD 14:37)

Lydia BARTLETT[5] (Sam.[4]) and Samuel MORTON, 22 July 1724, Plymouth (MD 14:70)

Hannah BARTLETT[5] (Sam.[4]) and Benjamin ARNOLD, 8 Mar. 1713/14, Duxbury (MD 11:24)

Sarah BARTLETT[5] (Sam.[4]) and Elisha HOLMES[5] (Sarah Bartlett[4], Jos.[3], Mary Warren[2]),
    7 Mar. 1720/21, Plymouth (MD 14:39)

Elisha HOLMES[5] and 2nd Mary ELLIS, aft. July 1738

Ichabod BARTLETT[5] (Sam.[4]) and Susanna SPOONER, 6 Nov. 1721, Plymouth (MD 14:39)

Ichabod BARTLETT[6] (Ichabod[5]) and Hannah ROGERS, 15 Nov. 1753, Plymouth (MD 18:141)

Joseph BARTLETT[5] (Sam.[4]) and Lydia NELSON, 9 Dec. 1714, Plymouth (MD 14:37)

Patience BARTLETT[6] (Jos.[5]) and Jethro SPRAGUE, 12 Dec. 1738, Duxbury (MD 11:82)

Samuel BARTLETT[5] (Sam.[4]) and Hannah CHURCHILL, 19 Aug. 1725, Plymouth (MD 14:71)

John BARTLETT[6] (Sam.[5]) and Sarah BARTLETT[6] (Jos.[5], Robert[4], Jos.[3], Mary Warren[2]),
    Int. 29 Nov. 1755, Plymouth (MD 25:53)

Sarah BARTLETT[7] (John[6]) and Thomas MORTON

Samuel BARTLETT[6] (Sam.[5]) and 1st Betty MOORE, c1754 (MD 21:166)

Samuel BARTLETT[6] and 2nd Elizabeth JACKSON, 7 Aug. 1766 (Plymouth Ch.rcds.2:494)

Joseph BARTLETT[7] (Sam.[6]) and 1st Rebecca CHURCHILL, 23 Dec. 1784 (Plymouth Ch.
    rcds.2:502)

Joseph BARTLETT[7] and 2nd Lucy DYER, 2 Dec. 1821 (Plymouth Ch.rcds.2:654)

William BARTLETT[6] (Sam.[5]) and Mary BARTLETT[6] (Nath.[5], Ben.[4], Jos.[3], Mary Warren[2]),
    28 July 1752, Plymouth (MD 16:170)

Elizabeth BARTLETT[3] and Anthony SPRAGUE, 26 Dec. 1661, Plymouth (MD 17:183)

Anthony SPRAGUE[4] (Eliz. Bartlett[3]) and Mary TILDEN (Gen.Reg.63:150)

Mercy SPRAGUE[5] (Anthony[4]) and Daniel JENCKS

Phebe SPRAGUE[5] (Anthony[4]) and Peter WHIPPLE

Sarah SPRAGUE[5] (Anthony[4]) and John WHITMAN

Elizabeth SPRAGUE[5] (Anthony[4]) and William WHIPPLE

Hope WHIPPLE and Nicholas BROWN

Nicholas BROWN and Susanna ARNOLD, c1772

Eleazer BROWN and Betsey COLE, 18 Aug. 1793, Cumberland RI

Betty BROWN and Joseph MATHEWSON, 8 Apr. 1773, Smithfield RI

Lydia SPRAGUE^5 (Anthony^4) and Richard HARRIS, 15 Dec. 1723 (Providence RI VR 1:43)

James SPRAGUE^4 (Eliz. Bartlett^3) and Elizabeth FEARING, 8 May 1702

Elizabeth SPRAGUE^5 (James^4) and 1st Bartholomew DOYLE, 1 Jan. 1727/28 (Hingham
    Hist.3:165)

Elizabeth SPRAGUE^5 and poss. 2nd Benjamin WILSON

Jerusha SPRAGUE^5 (James^4) and Joshua TOWER, 30 Aug. 1731 (Hist.Hingham 3:165)

Joshua TOWER and 2nd Huldah BLISS (Tower Gen.:97,98)

Jeremiah SPRAGUE^4 (Eliz. Bartlett^3) and Priscilla KNIGHT, 5 Mar. 1706, Boston
    (MD 20:100)

Priscilla SPRAGUE^5 (Jeremiah^4) and Michael HATCH, 27 Mar. 1733

Susanna SPRAGUE^5 (Jeremiah^4) and Caleb MARSH, 17 Sept. 1735

Elizabeth SPRAGUE^5 (Jeremiah^4) and Nathaniel STODDER Jr., 21 Dec. 1747

Deborah SPRAGUE^5 (Jeremiah^4) and James HOBART, 25 Dec. 1750

Joanna SPRAGUE^5 (Jeremiah^4) and Joseph BARNES, 23 Jan. 1748/49

Deborah HOBART^6 (Deborah Sprague^5) and Nathaniel FEARING, 17 Nov. 1774

Celia HOBART^6 (Deborah Sprague^5) and 1st Samuel LINCOLN, 9 Mar. 1784

Celia HOBART^6 and 2nd Capt. George PRICE, 8 May 1808

Olla HOBART^6 (Deborah Sprague^5) and Obadiah STOWELL, 30 Apr. 1784

Elizabeth STODDER^6 (Eliz. Sprague^5) and Jonathan FRENCH, 12 Dec. 1776

Abigail STODDER^6 (Eliz. Sprague^5) and 1st Daniel HERSEY, 1 Jan. 1784

Abigail STODDER^6 and 2nd Jeremiah HOBART, 17 Dec. 1797

Jacob SPRAGUE^5 (Jeremiah^4) and Sarah STODDER, 18 Feb. 1734

Sarah SPRAGUE^6 (Jacob^5) and Abisha LEWIS, 26 Dec. 1754

Priscilla SPRAGUE^6 (Jacob^5) and Israel HERSEY, 29 Jan. 1767

Abigail SPRAGUE^6 (Jacob^5) and Asa BATIS(sp), 5 Dec. 1765

Jeremiah SPRAGUE^5 (Jeremiah^4) and Elizabeth WHITON, 19 Dec. 1739

Susanna SPRAGUE^6 (Jeremiah^5) and James BEAL, 20 May 1777

Miles SPRAGUE^6 (Jeremiah^5) and Peggy LINCOLN, 29 Sept. 1793

John SPRAGUE^5 (Jeremiah^4) and Margaret WEBB, 20 May 1742

Lucy SPRAGUE^6 (John^5) and Knight SPRAGUE Jr., 26 Feb. 1761

Mary SPRAGUE^6 (John^5) and Isaac TOWER, 9 Jan. 1770

Joseph SPRAGUE^6 (John^5) and Chloe LANE, 10 May 1779

Grace SPRAGUE[6] (John[5]) and Daniel SOUTHER(sp), 15 Apr. 1784

Knight SPRAGUE[5] (Jeremiah[4]) and 1st Mary LEWIS, 26 May 1735 (Hingham VR 2:442,3:168)

Knight SPRAGUE[5] and 2nd Mary BEAL, Int. 23 Oct. 1747

Mary SPRAGUE[6] (Knight[5]) and John GROCE/GROSS, 21 Aug. 1755

Sarah SPRAGUE and Richard SOUTHGATE Jr., 2 June 1762 (Leicester VR:210,211)

Sarah SPRAGUE and Daniel UPHAM, 29 July 1766 (Leicester VR:211,221)

Celia SPRAGUE[6] (Nehemiah[5], Jeremiah[4]) and Laban STODDER, 14 Apr. 1795

Rhoda MARSH[6] (Susanna Sprague[5]) and Knight SPRAGUE, 13 May 1767

Deborah MARSH[6] (Susanna Sprague[5]) and Jesse FRENCH, 27 Sept. 1764

Josiah SPRAGUE[4] (Eliz. Bartlett[3]) and Elizabeth WILDER, 17 May 1705 (Hist.Hing.3:165)

Benjamin SPRAGUE[5] (Josiah[4]) and Deborah CORTHELL, 18 Dec. 1735

Persis SPRAGUE[6] (Ben.[5]) and Seth STODDER, 3 Sept. 1765

Daniel SPRAGUE[5] (Josiah[4]) and Anna (WILDER) Whiton, 9 Nov. 1758

Ephraim SPRAGUE[5] (Josiah[4]) and 1st Hannah LANE, 12 Aug. 1747

Ephraim SPRAGUE[5] and 2nd Anna HUMPHREY, 4 June 1751

Ephraim SPRAGUE[5] and 3rd Mary (ORCUTT) Humphrey, 21 Apr. 1774

Isaac SPRAGUE[5] (Josiah[4]) and 1st Leah STODDER, 15 Dec. 1737

Isaac SPRAGUE[5] and 2nd Sarah (HERSEY) Blossom, aft. June 1754

Leah SPRAGUE[6] (Isaac[5]) and Benjamin JONES, 25 Nov. 1761

Tamar SPRAGUE[6] (Isaac[5]) and Joshua LINCOLN, 23 Dec. 1762

Rebecca SPRAGUE[6] (Isaac[5]) and Isaiah HERSEY, 30 Oct. 1766

Matthew SPRAGUE[4] (Eliz. Bartlett[3]) and Sarah FEARING, 13 Sept. 1716 (Hist.Hingham
        2:218,3:166)

Sarah SPRAGUE[5] (Matthew[4]) and Samuel GILBERT, 25 Dec. 1739, Hingham

Noah SPRAGUE[5] (Matthew[4]) and Anna HATCH, 9 Oct. 1777

Margaret SPRAGUE[5] (Matthew[4]) and Isaiah HERSEY, 14 Dec. 1743 (Hingham 3:166,2:301)

Lydia SPRAGUE[5] (Matthew[4]) and Stephen STOWELL, 1 Jan. 1746/47

Mary HERSEY[6] (Margaret Sprague[5]) and Jeremiah HERSEY, 31 Dec. 1772, Hingham

Sarah SPRAGUE[4] (Eliz. Bartlett[3]) and Caleb BATE, 10 June 1716

Caleb BATE and 2nd Mary LANE, 14 Apr. 1691[24]

Caleb BATE[5] (Sarah Sprague[4]) and Lydia HOBART, 11 Nov. 1742

Mary BATE and Israel LEAVITT, 18 Oct. 1716

Ruth BATE and Joseph MANSFIELD, 15 Dec. 1727

Jesse BATE[6] (Caleb[5]) and Abigail BARNES, 3 Dec. 1767

Joseph BARTLETT[3] and Hannah POPE, c1662 (MD 12:14)

Robert BARTLETT[4] (Jos.[3]) and Sarah COOKE, 1 Apr. 1691 (Plymouth VR 1:130)

John BARTLETT and Sarah COB, 4 Apr. 1723 (Plymouth VR 1:140)

Sarah BARTLETT and Thomas FAUNCE 4th, 20 Jan. 1742/43 (Plymouth VR 1:151)

Thomas FAUNCE Jr. and Mary CURTIS, 26 Nov. 1767 (Plymouth VR 2:263)

Benjamin BARTLETT[4] (Jos.[3]) and Sarah BARNES, 15 Oct. 1702, Plymouth (MD 14:35)

Sarah BARNES and 2nd John STURTEVANT, 26 Mar. 1723, Plymouth (MD 14:40)

Benjamin BARTLETT[5] (Ben.[4]) and Hannah STEPHENS, 8 Apr. 1737, Plymouth (MD 14:157)

Jonathan BARTLETT[5] (Ben.[4]) and Thankful BARNES[5] (Mary Bartlett[4], Jos.[3], Mary
    Warren[2]), 15 July 1731, Plymouth (MD 14:73)

Mary BARTLETT and Lothrop HOLMES, 16 Nov. 1769 (Plymouth VR 2:264)

Jonathan BARTLETT[6] (Jonathan[5]) and Mary DOTY, 22 Nov. 1764 (Plymouth VR 2:262)

Jonathan BARTLETT[6] (Jos.[5], Ben.[4]) and Lydia ELLIS, 29 Sept. 1777, Plymouth

Lydia ELLIS and 2nd Nathan REED, c1787-92

Joseph BARTLETT[5] (Ben.[4]) and Jane SWIFT[5] (Jos.[4], Eliz. Tomson[3], Mary Cooke[2]),
    c1735 (MD 15:110)

Benjamin BARTLETT[6] (Jos.[5]) and Jemima HOLMES, Int. 24 Nov. 1759, Plymouth (MD 25:189)

Nathaniel BARTLETT[5] (Ben.[4]) and 1st Abigail CLARKE, 8 Apr. 1725, Plymouth (MD 14:71)

Nathaniel BARTLETT[6] (Nath.[5]) and Lydia BARNES[6] (Lemuel[5], Alice Bradford[4], Wm.[3-2])
    Int. 15 May 1756, Plymouth (MD 25:54)

Andrew BARTLETT[6] (Nath.[5]) and Lydia CHURCHILL, 12 Dec. 1764 (Plymouth VR 2:262)

Henry BARTLETT[7] (Andrew[6]) and Clarissa HARLOW[7] (Jonathan[6], Tho.[5], Wm.[4], Rebecca
    Bartlett[3], Mary Warren[2])

Stephen BARTLETT[7] (Andrew[6]) and Mary NYE, 24 Apr. 1799, Sandwich (Plymouth VR 2:344)

Capt. John BARTLETT[6] (Nath.[5]) and Mercy ELLIS, c1762 (MD 23:8)

Sarah BARTLETT[5] (Ben.[4]) and 1st John COBB, Int. 13 May 1735, Plymouth (MD 17:136)

Sarah BARTLETT[5] and 2nd Nathan DELANO, 11 Dec. 1755 (Cobb Gen.:91)

Elnathan BARTLETT[4] (Jos.[3]) and Hannah MANSFIELD, 24 Apr. 1712, Plymouth (MD 14:37)

Hannah MANSFIELD and 2nd Price NICHOLS, 16 June 1719, Plymouth (MD 14:38)

Hannah BARTLETT[4] (Jos.[3]) and Joseph SILVESTER, cApr. 1690 (MD 3:12)

Mary SILVESTER[5] (Hannah Bartlett[4]) and Samuel RIDER[5] (John[4], Sarah Bartlett[3],
    Mary Warren[2]), 2 Nov. 1722, Plymouth (MD 14:40)

Content SILVESTER[5] (Hannah Bartlett[4]) and James HOLMES, 30 Jan. 1728/29, Plymouth
(MD 14:72)

Hannah SYLVESTER[5] (Hannah Bartlett[4]) and Eleazer HOLMES, 6 Dec. 1711, Plymouth
(MD 14:36)

Lydia HOLMES[6] (Hannah Sylvester[5]) and Barnabas CHURCHILL[6] (Lydia Harlow[5], Wm.[4],
Rebecca Bartlett[3], Mary Warren[2]), 13 Nov. 1744, Plymouth (MD 14:161)

Ichabod HOLMES[6] (Hannah Sylvester[5]) and Rebecca ELLIS, 25 Oct. 1748, Plymouth
(MD 17:6)

Job HOLMES[6] (Hannah Sylvester[5]) and Mehitable STEWART, Int. 7 Mar. 1752, Plymouth
(MD 16:69)

Joseph SILVESTER[5] (Hannah Bartlett[4]) and Mercy HOLMES[5] (Sarah Bartlett[4], Jos.[3],
Mary Warren[2]), 14 July 1721, Plymouth (MD 14:39)

Mercy HOLMES[5] and 2nd Edward STEVENS, 3 Apr. 1729, Plymouth (MD 14:72)

Sarah SILVESTER[6] (Mercy Holmes[5]) and Eleazer STEPHENS, 29 Oct. 1747, Plymouth
(MD 17:6)

Eleazer STEVENS and Susanna SILVESTER, Int. 25 Jan. 1766, Plymouth (MD 26:85)

Joseph SILVESTER and Susanna COB, Int. 26 Nov. 1754, Plymouth (MD 25:52)

Solomon SILVESTER[5] (Hannah Bartlett[4]) and Elizabeth RIDER, 23 Oct. 1718, Plymouth
(MD 14:38)

Solomon SILVESTER[6] (Solomon[5]) and Hannah CHURCHELL, Int. 6 Aug. 1757, Plymouth
(MD 25:140)

Abner SILVESTER[6] (Solomon[5]) and   1st Jedidah HARLOW[6] (Tho.[5], Wm.[4], Rebecca
Bartlett[3], Mary Warren[2]), 10 Nov. 1748, Plymouth (MD 17:4)

Abner SILVESTER[6] and 2nd Abigail WASHBURN[6] (John[5], Lydia Billington[4], Isaac[3],
Francis[2]), 29 Oct. 1753 (Plymouth VR 2:254)

Elizabeth SILVESTER[6] (Solomon[5]) and Amaziah CHURCHILL, 31 Oct. 1745, Plymouth
(MD 16:171)

Amaziah CHURCHELL and Betty BARTLETT, 16 June 1776 (Plymouth VR 2:267)

Amaziah CHURCHELL and Polly HARLOW, Int. 26 Mar. 1808 (Plymouth VR 2:191)

Ichabod MORTON Jr. and Patty WESTON, 15 Nov. 1818 (Plymouth VR 2:382)

Ichabod MORTON and Zilpah THARE, 5 May 1758 (Plymouth VR 2:255)

Ichabod MORTON Jr. and Sarah CHURCHELL, 4 Nov. 1787 (Plymouth VR 2:272)

Solomon CHURCHILL[7] (Eliz. Sylvester[6]) and Elizabeth BARTLETT[7] (Tho.[6], Jos.[5],
Robert[4], Jos.[3], Mary Warren[2]), 28 Nov. 1784 (Plymouth VR 2:270)

Joseph SYLVESTER[6] (Solomon[5]) and Susanna (BLACKMER) Tupper[6] (Sarah Holmes[5], Sarah

Bartlett^4, Jos.^{3}, Mary Warren^2), 20 Dec. 1769, Plymouth (Col.Soc.Coll.23:496)

Nathaniel SYLVESTER^7 (Jos.^{6}) and 1st Betsy PERKINS, 25 Dec. 1825 (Plympton VR:358,406)

Nathaniel SYLVESTER^7 and 2nd Nancy SYLVIA, 15 Dec. 1836 (Halifax VR:113)

Nathaniel SYLVESTER^7 and poss. 3rd Saba STURTEVANT, 7 Jan. 1839 (Halifax VR:114)

Reuben SYLVESTER^7 (Jos.^{6}) and Desire TILSON, 19 Dec. 1805 (Halifax VR:80)

Almira SYLVESTER^8 (Reuben^7) and Benjamin Hill DEWING, 28 Oct. 1841 (Halifax VR:152)

Thankful SILVESTER^5 (Hannah Bartlett^4) and Ebenezer RIDER^5 (John^4, Sarah Bartlett^3, Mary Warren^2), 16 Mar. 1725/26, Plymouth (MD 14:71)

Joseph BARTLETT^4 (Jos.^{3}) and Lydia GRISWOLD, 6 June 1692, Plymouth (MD 13:205)

Lydia GRISWOLD and 2nd Joseph HOLMES, 25 Jan. 1705 (MD 14:35)

Benjamin BARTLETT^5 (Jos.^{4}) and 1st Lydia MORTON^4 (Martha Doty^3, Edw.^{2}), 24 Sept. 1724, Plymouth (MD 14:70)

Benjamin BARTLETT^5 and 2nd Abigail MORTON, 4 May 1741, Plymouth (MD 14:159)

Benjamin BARTLETT^6 (Ben.^{5}) and poss. Jean ELLIS, c1751 (MD 4:113)

Joseph BARTLETT^6 (Ben.^{5}) and Lydia COBB, 4 Feb. 1762 (Plymouth Ch.rcds:493)

Joseph BARTLETT^5 (Jos.^{4}) and Elizabeth BARTLETT^5 (Sam.^{4}, Ben.^{3}, Mary Warren^2), 18 Mar. 1716/17, Plymouth (MD 14:38)

Sylvanus BARTLETT^6 (Jos.^{5}) and Martha WAIT, 7 July 1743

Elizabeth BARTLETT^7 (Sylvanus^6) and Thomas BARTLETT^6 (Jos.^{5}, Rob.^{4}, Jos.^{3}, Mary Warren^2), 5 Dec. 1765 (Plymouth VR)

Zaccheus BARTLETT^6 (Jos.^{5}) and poss. Margaret BARNES, 12 Apr. 1753 (Plym.VR 21:262)

Isaac BARTLETT^7 (Zaccheus^6) and Mercy BRYANT, 2 Nov. 1797 (Halifax VR:16)

Joseph BARTLETT^7 (Zaccheus^6) and poss. Anna CLARK, 4 Nov. 1784 (Plymouth VR 2:288)

Lydia BARTLETT^5 (Jos.^{4}) and Lazarus LEBARON, 16 May 1720, Plymouth (MD 14:39)

Lazarus LEBARON and 2nd Lydia (BRADFORD) Cushman, aft. May 1742

Lydia LEBARON^6 (Lydia Bartlett^5) and Nathaniel GOODWIN, poss. 25 Dec. 1746

Thomas GOODWIN^7 (Lydia Lebaron^6) and Desire RYDER, 1 June 1779 (Plymouth VR 2:268)

Nathaniel GOODWIN^7 (Lydia Lebaron^6) and Molley JACKSON, Int. 7 Jan. 1769, Plymouth (MD 26:140)

Nathaniel GOODWIN^8 (Nath.^{7}) and Lydia GARDNER, poss. 16 Nov. 1794 (Nantucket VR 3:514,552)

Thomas GOODWIN^7 (Lydia Lebaron^6) and Desire RYDER^7 (Jos.^{6}, Mary Southworth^5, Desire Gray^4, Mary Winslow^3, Mary Chilton^2)<see above>

Samuel BARTLETT^5 (Jos.^{4}) and 1st Elizabeth LOTHROP, 22 Dec. 1721, Plymouth
(MD 14:39)

Samuel BARTLETT^5 and 2nd poss. Elizabeth (LOTHROP) Wetherell, 24 Nov. 1748,
Plymouth (VR 1:232)

Elizabeth BARTLETT^6 (Sam.^{5}) and Peleg WADSWORTH Jr., 18 June 1772 (Plymouth
VR 2:265)

Sarah BARTLETT^5 (Jos.^{4}) and 1st Francis LEBARON, 23 Nov. 1721, Plymouth (MD 14:39)

Sarah BARTLETT^5 and 2nd Joseph SWIFT, 21 Jan. 1736/37, Plymouth (MD 14:157)

Mary BARTLETT^4 (Jos.^{3}) and John BARNES, 6 July 1693, Plymouth (MD 13:206)

Thankful BARNES^5 (Mary Bartlett^4) and Jonathan BARTLETT^5 (Ben.^{4}, Jos.^{3}, Mary
Warren^2), 15 July 1731, Plymouth (MD 14:73)

Elizabeth BARNES^5 (Mary Bartlett^4) and Francis CURTIS, 23 Nov. 1731, Plymouth
(MD 14:74)

James DREW^6 (Hannah Barnes^5, Mary Bartlett^4) and Mary CHURCHILL, 4 Apr. 1751,
Plymouth (MD 16:171)

Lemuel DREW^6 (Hannah Barnes^5, Mary Bartlett^4) and 1st Priscilla WARREN^5 (Jos.$^{4-3-2}$)
4 Nov. 1751, Plymouth (MD 16:171)

Lemuel DREW^6 and 2nd Mary (WEST)(Waterman) Freeman, 1 Jan. 1760, prob. Liverpool N.S.

Mary DREW^6 (Hannah Barnes^5, Mary Bartlett^4) and John RIDER^5 (John^4, Sarah Bart-
lett^3, Mary Warren^2), 5 Dec. 1734, Plymouth (MD 14:76)

John BARNES^5 (Mary Bartlett^4) and Dorcas CORBEN, Int. 28 Apr. 1725, Plymouth
(MD 18:145)

Corban BARNES^6 (John^5) and 1st Rebecca ATWOOD, Int. 1 Nov. 1754, Plymouth (MD 25:52)

Corban BARNES^6 and 2nd Mary PHINNEY, Int. 23 Nov. 1765, Plymouth (MD 26:85)

Mary BARNES^6 (John^5) and John DYER, Int. 16 July 1757, Plymouth (MD 25:140)

John DYER^7 (Mary Barnes^6) and poss. Elizabeth POPKINS

Jonathan BARNES^5 (Mary Bartlett^4) and Phebe FINNEY^4 (Eliz. Warren^3, Jos.^{2}),
8 Sept. 1726, Plymouth (MD 14:71)

Lydia BARNES^5 (Mary Bartlett^4) and Lemuel BARNES^5 (Alice Bradford^4, Wm.$^{3-2}$),
21 May 1735, Plymouth (MD 14:156)

Mary BARNES^5 (Mary Bartlett^4) and Richard WAITE, 4 Dec. 1722, Plymouth (MD 14:40)

Elizabeth BARTLETT^5 (Robert^4, Jos.^{3}) and Thomas SEARS, 16 May 1734, Plymouth
(MD 14:75)

Hannah BARTLETT^5 (Robert^4, Jos.^{3}) and Eleazer CHURCHILL, c1711 (MD 12:84)

Josiah CHURCHILL^6 (Hannah Bartlett^5) and Patience HARLOW^6 (Eleazer^5, Sam.^{4},

Rebecca Bartlett^3, Mary Warren^2), 1 Dec. 1741, Plymouth (MD 14:159)

Jonathan CHURCHILL^6 (Hannah Bartlett^5) and Hannah FOSTER, 10 Dec. 1743 (Int.-
    (MD 17:131)

Eleazer CHURCHILL^6 (Hannah Bartlett^5) and Sarah HARLOW^6 (Wm.^{5}, Sam.^{4}, Rebecca
    Bartlett^3, Mary Warren^2), 19 Oct. 1738, Plymouth (MD 14:158)

John BARTLETT^5 (Robert^4, Jos.^{3}) and 1st Sarah COBB, 4 Apr. 1723, Plymouth (MD 14:40)

John BARTLETT^5 and 2nd Sarah GRAY, Int. 24 Aug. 1734, Plymouth (MD 17:135)

Maria BARTLETT^6 (John^5) and Richard BABB, c1769

Abigail BARTLETT^6 (John^5) and poss. Eleazer CHURCHILL^7 (Eleazer^6, Hannah Bartlett^5,
    Robert^4, Jos.^{3}, Mary Warren^2), 12 Feb. 1776

Jerusha BARTLETT^6 (John^5) and George PECKHAM

Hannah BARTLETT^6 (John^5) and Stephen DOTEN^4 (Elisha^3, John^2)

George BARTLETT^6 (John^5) and Sarah CHURCHILL^7 (Eleazer^6, Hannah Bartlett^5, Rob.^{4},
    Jos.^{3}, Mary Warren^2), poss. 16 Jan. 1776 (Churchill Gen.:24)

Charles BARTLETT^6 (John^5) and Abigail CHURCHILL^7 (Susanna Bartlett^6, Nath.^{5},
    Ben.^{4}, Jos.^{3}, Mary Warren^2), poss. 4 Dec. 1785 (Churchill Gen.:28)

John BARTLETT^6 (John^5) and Dorothy CARVER, c1769 (MD 22:181)

Sarah BARTLETT^6 (John^5) and Thomas FAUNCE^6 (Lydia Barnabe^5, Stephen^4, Lydia
    Bartlett^3, Mary Warren^2), 20 Jan. 1742/43, Plymouth (MD 14:160)

Joseph BARTLETT^5 (Robert^4, Jos.^{3}) and Sarah MORTON^4 (Martha Doty^3, Tho.^{2}),
    4 Apr. 1727, Plymouth (MD 14:72)

Lemuel BARTLETT^5 (Robert^4, Jos.^{3}) and Mary DOTY^4 (Isaac^3, John^2), 25 Nov. 1742,
    Plymouth (MD 14:160)

Rebecca BARTLETT^6 (Lemuel^5) and Lemuel HOLMES, 15 Nov. 1781 (Plymouth VR 2:269)

Lemuel BARTLETT^6 (Lemuel^5) and Hannah TINKHAM, 24 Oct. 1774, Yarmouth (MD 9:42)

Thomas BARTLETT^6 (Jos.^{5}) and Betty BARTLETT^7 (Sylvanus^6, Jos.$^{5-4-3}$, Mary Warren^2),
    5 Dec. 1765 (Plymouth VR 2:262)

Robert BARTLETT^5 (Robert^4, Jos.^{3}) and Rebecca WOOD^4 (Susanna Howland^3, Isaac^2),
    Int. 21 Nov. 1733, Plymouth (MD 18:120)

Ephraim BARTLETT^6 (Robert^5) and 1st Mercy CHURCHELL, Int. 21 Oct. 1758, Plymouth
    (MD 25:187)

Ephraim BARTLETT^6 and 2nd Elizabeth KEMPTON, 10 Apr. 1774 (Plymouth Ch.rcds.2:498)

Ephraim BARTLETT Jr. and Abigail HOLMES 2d, Int. 10 Nov. 1798, Plymouth (MD 30:189)

Micro #24 of 32

Susanna BARTLETT^7 (Ephraim^6) and William LEONARD, 28 Nov. 1805 (Plymouth Ch.
    rcds.2:498)

William LEONARD and 1st Rebecca BARTLETT^7 (Ephraim^6), 18 June 1791 (Plymouth
   Ch.rcds.23:504)

William LEONARD and 3rd Abigail BARTLETT, 8 Mar. 1812, Plymouth (MD 32:130)

Isaac BARTLETT^7 (Ephraim^6) and 1st Fear COBB, Int. 18 Apr. 1801, Plymouth (MD 31:3)

Isaac BARTLETT^7 and 2nd Rebecca BARTLETT (Cobb Gen.:137)

Isaac BARTLETT^8 (Isaac^7) and Mary Ann WARD, c1827

Mary C. BARTLETT^9 (Isaac^8) and William James FRANCIS, c1864

Sarah BARTLETT^4 (Jos.^{3}) and Elisha HOLMES, 2 Sept. 1695, Plymouth (MD 13:206)

Elisha HOLMES and 2nd Susanna CLARK, 4 Nov. 1719, Plymouth (MD 14:38)

Bartlett HOLMES^6 (Elisha^5) and Lucy BARTLETT^6 (Jonathan^5, Ben.^{4}, Jos.^{3}, Mary
   Warren^2)

Elisha HOLMES^6 (Elisha^5) and Sarah EWER, 23 Oct. 1757, Barnstable (MD 23:128)

Thomas EWER and Reliance TOBEY, 10 June 1718 (Toby Gen.:25)

Elisha HOLMES^7 (Elisha^6) and Elizabeth HALLETT, 21 Sept. 1786 (Barnstable VR 3:332)

Sarah HOLMES^8 (Elisha^7) and Hatsel K. HANDY, c1810 (Mass.VR 519:10)

Rhoda HANDY^9 (Sarah Holmes^8) and Leander GAGE, 27 Nov. 1834 (Barnstable VR 6:199)

Sarah Abigail GAGE^{10} (Rhoda^9) and Seth LEWIS, 10 Nov. 1859 (Gage Gen.:8)[25]

Grace Ella LEWIS^{11} (Sarah A. Gage^{10}) and Arthur Alton PHINNEY, 23 Sept. 1890,
   E. Boston (Gage Gen.)[25]

Seth Ames LEWIS^{11} (Sarah A. Gage^{10}) and Ella May SWINT, 14 Nov. 1900, E. Boston
   (Gage Gen.)[25]

Elizabeth HOLMES^5 (Sarah Bartlett^4) and Elkanah MORTON, 1 Oct. 1724, Plymouth
   (MD 14:70)

Elnathan HOLMES^5 (Sarah Bartlett^4) and Rebecca CHURCHELL, 7 Oct. 1731, Plymouth
   (MD 14:74)

Elnathan HOLMES^6 (Elnathan^5) and Bathsheba HOLMES^6 (Bathsheba Nelson^5, Sam.^{4},
   Lydia Bartlett^3, Mary Warren^2), Int. 21 Mar. 1761, Plymouth (MD 26:40)

Mary HOLMES^5 (Sarah Bartlett^4) and 1st Joseph SILVESTER^5 (Hannah Bartlett^4, Jos.^{3},
   Mary Warren^2), 14 July 1721, Plymouth (MD 14:39)

Mercy HOLMES^5 and 2nd Edward STEVENS, 3 Apr. 1729, Plymouth (MD 14:72)

Sarah HOLMES^5 (Sarah Bartlett^4) and John BLACKMER, 15 Mar. 1731/32, Plymouth
   (MD 14:74)

Betty BLACKMER^6 (Sarah Holmes^5) and Jonathan HARLOW^7 (Jonathan^6, Tho.^{5}, Wm.^{4},
   Rebecca Bartlett^3, Mary Warren^2), 8 Mar. 1770, Plymouth

Branch BLACKMER^6 (Sarah Holmes^5) and Sarah WAITE^6 (Mary Barnes^5, Mary Bartlett^4,

Jos.^{3}, Mary Warren^2), Int. 27 Nov. 1756, Plymouth (MD 25:139)

Jerusha BLACKMER^6 (Sarah Holmes^5) and poss. Nathaniel BARNES, 12 June 1766
(Plymouth Ch.rcds.23:494 <Col.Soc.Coll.>)

Susanna BLACKMER^6 (Sarah Holmes^5) and 1st Nathaniel TUPPER, 23 Apr. 1761 (Plymouth Ch.rcds.23:492 <Col.Soc.Coll.>)

Susanna BLACKMER^6 and 2nd Joseph SYLVESTER^6 (Solomon^5, Hannah Bartlett^4, Jos.^{3},
Mary Warren^2), 20 Dec. 1769 (Plymouth Ch.rcds.23:496 <Col.Soc.Coll.>)

Mary TUPPER^7 (Susanna Blackmer^6) and Seth CLARK, Int. 24 Oct. 1789, Plymouth
(MD 30:74)

Joseph Sylvester CLARK^8 (Mary Tupper^7) and Harriet Bates BOURNE, Int. 10 Dec. 1831
(Sturbridge VR:166,178)

Rev. Joseph Bourne CLARK^9 (Jos.^{8}) and 2nd Caroline Mackey ALLEN, 9 Oct. 1867,
Newton (Mass.VR 200:241)

Nathaniel CLARK^8 (Mary Tupper^7) and 1st Harriet WASHBURN

Israel CLARK^8 (Mary Tupper^7) and 1st Catherine DUNBAR, 2nd Laura PERKINS

Susanna CLARK^8 (Mary Tupper^7) and Howard NICHOLS, Int. 4 June 1820, Plymouth
(MD 34:9)$^{<26>}$

Hannah BARTLETT^6 (Nath.^{5}) and 1st Elkanah BARNES

Hannah BARTLETT^6 and 2nd Ansell HARLOW^7 (Jonathan^6, Tho.^{5}, Wm.^{4}, Rebecca Bart-
lett^3, Mary Warren^2), Int. 8 Dec. 1769, Plymouth (MD 26:140)

Lydia WAITE^6 (Mary Barnes^5) and 1st Isaac ATWOOD, 26 Aug. 1740, Plymouth (MD 14:159)

Lydia WAITE^6 and 2nd Ezekiel RIDER, 7 Nov. 1762 (Plymouth Ch.rcds.2:493,1:458)

Isaac ATWOOD^7 (Lydia Waite^6) and 1st Hannah CHUBBUCK, 21 Apr. 1770, Plymouth

Isaac ATWOOD^7 and 2nd Lydia WHITMARSH, 1800

Lydia ATWOOD^8 (Isaac^7) and Alexander PATTEN, c1800 (Bedford NH Hist.<1903>:1039)

David PATTEN^9 (Lydia Atwood^8) and Abbie BROWN (Bedford NH Hist.<1903>:1040)

Elizabeth PATTEN^9 (Lydia Atwood^8) and James MOORE, c1899 (Bedford NH Hist.:1039)

Hannah PATTEN^9 (Lydia Atwood^8) and 1st A. COOLEDGE, 2nd John DEAVALL (Bedford
NH Hist.:1039)

John PATTEN^9 (Lydia Atwood^8) and Sally HUTCHINSON (Bedford NH Hist.<1903>:1040)

Margaret PATTEN^9 (Lydia Atwood^8) and Robert BAKER, c1821 (Bedford Hist.:1040)

Susannah PATTEN^9 (Lydia Atwood^8) and Phineas BLUNT (Bedford Hist.:1040)

Submit Walker ATWOOD^8 (Isaac^7) and James DARRAH, 16 Sept. 1802 (Bedford NH
Hist.:855,892)

Clarissa DARRAH^9 (Submit Atwood^8) and Samuel CORNING, 19 Feb. 1829 (Bedford
Hist.:744)

Esther DARRAH[9] (Submit Atwood[8]) and Nathan S. COLBY, 11 Apr. 1833 (Bedford NH
    Hist. <1903>:746)

Ismena DARRAH[9] (Submit Atwood[8]) and Matthew PARKER, 25 June 1829 (Bedford NH
    Hist.:744)

James DARRAH[9] (Submit Atwood[8]) and 1st Frances BLOOD (Bedford NH Hist.:892)

James DARRAH[9] and 2nd Cynthia N. WALLACE, 27 Feb. 1845 (Bedford NH Hist:748)

Lucinda F. DARRAH[9] (Submit Atwood[8]) and Josiah H. FOLSOM, 21 Oct. 1841 (Bedford
    NH Hist.:748)

Mary DARRAH[9] (Submit Atwood[8]) and Samuel N. SOUTHWORTH, 23 Jan. 1840 (Bedford
    NH Hist. :747)

Sarah Kidder DARRAH[9] (Submit Atwood[8]) and 1st David McAFEE, 23 Feb. 1824 (Bedford
    NH Hist.:743,970)

Sarah Kidder DARRAH[9] and 2nd A. Chase DARRAH

Sophia P. DARRAH[9] (Submit Atwood[8]) and John SMITH, 14 Sept. 1834 (Bedford NH
    Hist.:746)

Zaccheus ATWOOD[7] (Lydia Waite[6]) and Chloe HOVEY, Int. 3 Dec. 1772 (Weymouth VR 2:14)

Elisha HOLMES[5] (Sarah Bartlett[4]) and 1st Sarah BARTLETT[5] (Sam.[4], Ben.[3], Mary
    Warren[2]), 7 Mar. 1720/21, Plymouth (MD 14:39)

Elisha HOLMES[5] and 2nd Mary ELLIS, Int. 7 July 1739, Plymouth (MD 18:31)

Micro #25 of 32

Seth BARNES[5] (Mary Bartlett[4]) and Sarah WOODEN, 20 Apr. 1722, Plymouth (MD 14:39)

William BARNES[6] (Seth[5]) and Mercy LEMOTE[6] (Mercy Billington[5], Francis[4-3-2]),
    c1754 (MD 18:214)

Mercy LEMOTE[6] and 2nd Richard HOLMES, Int. 31 Mar. 1764, Plymouth (MD 26:43)

Benjamin BARNES[6] (Seth[5]) and poss. Elizabeth HOLMES, 18 Mar. 1762, Plymouth

Thomas HOLMES and Elizabeth COBB, c1738

Joseph BARNES[6] (Seth[5]) and Hannah RIDER[7] (Jos.[6], Mary Southworth[5], Desire Gray[4],
    Mary Winslow[3], Mary Chilton[2]), Int. 19 Jan. 1760, Plymouth (MD 25:189)

Sarah BARNES[6] (Seth[5]) and John JONES, 18 Aug. 1740, Plymouth (MD 16:254)

Robert BARTLETT[4] (Jos.[3]) and 1st Sarah BARTLETT[4] (Ben.[3], Mary Warren[2]), 28 Dec.
    1687, Plymouth (MD 13:204)

Robert BARTLETT[4] and 2nd Sarah COOKE, 1 Apr. 1691, Plymouth (MD 13:205)[27]

Thomas BARTLETT[5] (Robert[4]) and Abigail FINNEY, 10 Jan. 1716/17, Plymouth (MD 14:38)

Sarah BARTLETT[5] (Robert[4]) and John FINNEY[4] (Eliz. Warren[3], Jos.[2]), 22 Feb.
    1721/22, Plymouth (MD 14:39)

-318-

John FINNEY^4 and 2nd Susanna (DOTY^4) Pratt, Int. 31 Mar. 1739, Plymouth (MD 18:30)

Ebenezer BARTLETT^5 (Robert^4) and 1st Rebecca DIMOND, Int. 5 Feb. 1731/32, Plymouth (MD 18:122)

Ebenezer BARTLETT^5 and 2nd Abigail FINNEY, 11 Jan. 1749/50, Plymouth (MD 17:7)

Lydia BARTLETT^3 and 1st James BARNABY, c1669

Lydia BARTLETT^3 and 2nd John NELSON, c1682 (MD 1:210)

James BARNEBE^4 (Lydia Bartlett^3) and Joanna HARLOW, c1697 (MD 2:79)

Ambrose BARNEBE^5 (James^4) and Elizabeth GARDNER, 14 June 1728 (Gen.Reg.18:361)

Ambrose BARNABY^6 (Ambrose^5) and 1st Elizabeth WILBUR, 3 Sept. 1769

Ambrose BARNABY^6 and 2nd Philena BURT, c1779

Ambrose BARNABY^6 and 3rd Abigail WILLIAMS, c1792

Stephen BARNEBE^4 (Lydia Bartlett^3) and 1st Ruth MORTON, 10 Dec. 1696, Plymouth (MD 13:206)

Stephen BARNEBE^4 and 2nd Judith (HARLOW) Church, 11 July 1710, Plymouth (MD 14:36)

Elizabeth BARNABE^5 (Stephen^4) and poss. Isaac SMALL, 28 Nov. 1722 (Small Gen.3:1532)

Hannah BARNEBE^5 (Stephen^4) and John SMALE, Int. 24 Feb. 1727/28, Plymouth (MD 18:140)

Lydia BARNABE^5 (Stephen^4) and Thomas FAUNCE, 29 May 1718, Plymouth (MD 14:38)

James FAUNCE^6 (Lydia Barnabe^5) and 3rd Mary CUSHMAN, 17 July 1777 (Halifax VR:20)

James FAUNCE^7 (James^6) and Thankful TOBEY, 4 Nov. 1773 (Sandwich VR:207)[28]

James FAUNCE and Jane TUPPER, 12 June 1796 (Sandwich VR:119)[28]

William FAUNCE^8 (James^7) and Mary BOURNE, 2 Dec. 1804 (Freeman's Cape Cod 2:153)

Thomas FAUNCE^6 (Lydia Barnabe^5) and Sarah BARTLETT^6 (John^5, Robert^4, Jos.^{3}, Mary Warren^2), 20 Jan. 1742/43, Plymouth (MD 14:160)

Ansell FAUNCE^7 (Tho.^{6}) and Hope BESSE, c1779

Samuel NELSON^4 (Lydia Bartlett^3) and 1st Bathsheba NICHOLS, 1 Apr. 1706, Plymouth (MD 14:35)[29]

Samuel NELSON^4 and 2nd Sarah HOLMES, 12 Sept. 1718, Plymouth (MD 14:38)[29]

John NELSON^5 (Sam.^{4}) and Mary MORTON^4 (Martha Doty^3, Edw.^{2}), Int. 25 Nov. 1732, Plymouth (MD 18:123)

Samuel Nichols NELSON^5 (Sam.^{4}) and Elizabeth WARREN, Int. 18 Feb. 1743/44, Plymouth (MD 17:132)

Bathsheba NELSON^5 (Sam.^{4}) and Abner HOLMES, 20 Oct. 1737, Plymouth (MD 14:158)

Hannah NELSON^5 (Sam.^{4}) and 1st Thomas MORTON^4 (Martha Doty^3, Edw.^{2}), 29 Mar. 1726, Plymouth (MD 14:71)

Hannah NELSON[5] (Sam.[4]) and 2nd John DYER, 27 June 1734, Plymouth (MD 14:75)

Sarah NELSON[5] (Sam.[4]) and 1st Seth COBB, c1738 (MD 15:113)

Sarah NELSON[5] and 2nd Joseph SHURTLEFF, c1742 (MD 13:113)

Mary BARTLETT[3] and 1st Richard FOSTER, 10 Sept. 1651, Plymouth (MD 16:237)

Mary BARTLETT[3] and 2nd Jonathan MOREY, 8 July 1659, Plymouth (MD 17:182)

Jonathan MOREY and poss. 2nd Hannah ( ) WETHERELL, pre 1700

Edmund MOREY and Sarah EWELL, 29 Dec. 1710, Scituate (MD 2:170)[30]

Susanna MOREY and Josiah LITCHFIELD, 4 July 1732, Scituate (MD 1:44)

Patience MORY and William BONNEY, 16 June 1730 or 31, Plympton (MD 5:210)

Hannah MOREY[4] (Mary Bartlett[3]) and John BUMPUS, c1694

John BUMPUS and 2nd Jean (COVEL) Claghorn, Int. 12 July 1729, Rochester

Sarah BUMPUS[5] (Hannah Morey[4]) and George WHITE, 17 Oct. 1728 (Rochester VR 2:63,317)

Jonathan MOREY[4] (Mary Bartlett[3]) and Hannah BOURNE, 24 Jan. 1689/90, Plymouth
     (MD 13:205)

Thankful MOREY[5] (Jonathan[4]) and Thomas SWIFT[4] (Eliz. Tomson[3], Mary Cooke[2]),
     23 Jan. 1717/18, Plymouth (MD 14:38)

Benjamin MOREY[5] (Jonathan[4]) and Thankful SWIFT[4] (Eliz. Tomson[3], Mary Cooke[2]),
     3 Nov. 1715 (Sandwich VR 2:63)

Cornelius MOREY and poss. Sarah JOHNSON, c1753 (Davis; MD 20:73)

Mercy MOREY and Silas VALLAR, Int. 23 Sept. 1769, Plymouth (MD 26:140)

Sarah MOREY and Elisha NYE, Int. 17 Apr. 1779, Plymouth (MD 28:35)

Cornelius MOREY and poss. 1st Mercy BATES, Int. 2 Nov. 1782, Plymouth (MD 29:90)

Cornelius MOREY and 2nd Jerusha HARLOW, Int. 8 Nov. 1783, Plymouth (MD 29:)

Cornelius MOREY and Ruth HOLMES, Int. 27 July 1771, Plymouth (MD 26:190)

Elijah MOREY[6] (Ben.[5]) and Rebecca (WETHERHEAD) WEST, 24 Mar. 1763 (Plymouth
     VR 2:261)

Elijah MOREY and Grace CORNISH, Int. 1 Oct. 1803 (Plymouth VR 2:179)

Elijah MOREY and Lucy MANTER, 28 Apr. 1825 (Plymouth Ch.rcds.<Col.Soc.23:697)

Silas MOREY[7] (Elijah[6]) and Eunice DONHAM, 2 Mar. 1786 (Plymouth Ch.<Col.Soc.23:502)

Deborah MOREY and Amasa MORTON, 9 Dec. 1818 (Plymouth Ch.rcds.<Col.Soc.23:652)

Mary MOREY[6] (Ben.[5]) and Josiah SWIFT, 26 May 1738, Plymouth (MD 14:157)

Jesse SWIFT[7] (Mary Morey[6]) and Elizabeth ELLIS, c1764 (Wareham VR 1:61)

Hannah SWIFT and Willis CHUBBUCK, 1 Sept. 1805 (Wareham VR 1:228-9)

Nathan B. ELLIS and Hannah E. CHUBBUCK, 19 Dec. 1832 (Wareham VR 1:252)

Elisha SWIFT[7] (Mary Morey[6]) and poss. Martha BRIGGS, Int. 2 Dec. 1775, Sandwich
(Wareham VR:256)[31]

Elisha SWIFT[8] (Elisha[7]) and Betsey CLARK, Int. 11 Jan. 1818 (Wareham VR:213)

Alexander SWIFT[9] (Elisha[8]) and Betsey Sturtevant HAMBLEN

Jonathan MOREY[5] (Jonathan[4]) and Elizabeth SWIFT, Int. 14 Sept. 1728, Plymouth
(MD 18:140)

Joseph MOREY[5] (Jonathan[4]) and Mary SWIFT, Int. 25 Apr. 1733, Plymouth (MD 17:134)

Mercy BARTLETT[3] and John IVEY, 25 Dec. 1668, Plymouth

Rebecca BARTLETT[3] and William HARLOW, 20 Dec. 1649, Plymouth (MD 16:121)

Rebecca HARLOW[5] (Sam.[4], Rebecca Bartlett[3]) and Thomas TABER[4] (Esther Cooke[3],
John[2]), 4 July 1700, Plymouth (MD 13:207)

Eleazer HARLOW[5] (Sam.[4], Rebecca Bartlett[3]) and 1st Hannah DELANO[4] (Benoni[3],
Rebecca Alden[2]), 6 Oct. 1715, Duxbury (MD 11:24)

Eleazer HARLOW[5] and 2nd Hannah PRATT, 21 July 1720, Plympton (MD 3:91)

Eliphaz HARLOW[6] (Eleazer[5]) and 1st poss. Hopestill BABBITT, 18 June 1738, Berkeley
(Taunton VR)

Eliphaz HARLOW[6] and 2nd Hannah PHILLIPS, 26 Nov. 1756, Berkely (Taunton VR 2:62)

Eliphaz HARLOW[6] and 3rd Phebe (HART) Tisdale, 27 Apr. 1763, Taunton (VR 2:159)

Abigail HARLOWE and Samuel WHEELER, 1 Apr. 1798, Rochester (Taunton VR)

George HARLOW and Lois HALL, 16 Aug. 1817, Taunton (VR)

Hopestill HARLOW[7] (Eliphaz[6]) and John CUDWORTH, 25 May 1773, Taunton (VR)

Josiah HARLOW and Mary WARD, 30 Mar. 1780 (Taunton VR)

Lois HARLOW and Ephraim PEIRCE, 17 Jan. 1793 (Taunton VR)

Sarah C. HARLOW and William GILBERT, 25 Sept. 1849, Taunton (VR)

Susan E. HARLOW and Perry H. WALDRON, 17 Feb. 1840, Canton (Taunton VR)

Thomas HARLOWE and Abigail LESCOMBE, 5 Sept. 1793, Taunton (VR)

Zilpha HARLOW and Simeon TISDALE, 20 Feb. 1769, Taunton (VR 2:168)

Micro #27 of 32

Phebe HART and 1st Simeon TISDALE, 15 Feb. 1759 <see above>[32]

Eleazer HARLOW[6] (Eleazer[5]) and 1st Abigail THOMAS[5] (Abigail Baker[4], Sarah Bradford[3], Wm.[2]), Mar. 1739/40, Duxbury (MD 11:239)

Eleazer HARLOW[6] and 2nd Abigail CLARK, 11 Sept. 1745, Duxbury

Eleazer HARLOW[6] and 3rd Elizabeth ( ) DABNEY, 23 Feb. 1758 (Boston Rcd.com.30:28)

Eleazer HARLOW[7] (Eleazer[6]) and Rhoda ALEXANDER, c1765

Levi HARLOW[8] (Eleazer[7]) and Elizabeth RANNEY, 18 Dec. 1794 (Bible)

Abigail HARLOW[8] (Eleazer[7]) and Waitstill RANNEY (Vermont Hist.Gazeteer 5:613)

Hannah HARLOW[8] (Eleazer[7]) and Alfred SPOONER

Lorina HARLOW[8] (Eleazer[7]) and Alvin POTTER

Anna HARLOW[8] (Eleazer[7]) and Giles MARSH

Hopestill HARLOW[7] (Eliphaz[6]) and John CUDWORTH, 25 May 1773 (Taunton VR 2:173)

Sally CUDWORTH[8] (Hopestill Harlow[7]) and Job KING (Gen.of Kings of Raynham
     <1866>:15)

Charlotte KING[9] (Sally Cudworth[8]) and Frank WILBUR (Gen.of Kings)

Elizabeth KING[9] (Sally Cudworth[8]) and William Whitman KING (Gen.of Kings)

William KING[9] (Sally Cudworth[8]) and Lucy Ann THOMPSON (Gen.of Kings)

Isaac KING[9] (Sally Cudworth[8]) and Harriet SMITH (Gen.of Kings)

Job KING[9] (Sally Cudworth[8]) and Mary B. ANTHONY (Gen.of Kings)

Simeon KING[9] (Sally Cudworth[8]) and Mary COLYER (Gen.of Kings)

Levi HARLOW[7] (Eliphaz[6]) and Silence COBB, c1770

Elias HARLOW[8] (Levi[7]) and Abigail HERRICK, 27 June 1821

John Marshall HARLOW[9] (Elias[8]) and Winnie Dorinda FLOWER, 10 Apr. 1858

Frank Edwin HARLOW[10] (John[9]) and Lillian C. SEARS, 28 July 1897

Levi HARLOW and Mercy BARNES, c1774 (Landmarks Plymouth)

William BARNES and Mercy LEMOTE, 1755 (Landmarks Plymouth)

Lemuel HARLOW[6] (Eleazer[5]) and Joanna PADDOCK, 1 Sept. 1740, Plymouth (MD 14:159)

John HARLOW[5] (Sam.[4], Rebecca Bartlett[3]) and Martha DELANO[3] (Phillip[2-1]), c1706
     (MD 5:54)

Amaziah HARLOW[6] (John[5]) and Lois DOTEN[4] (Elisha[3], John[2]), 30 May 1746, Plymouth
     (MD 16:172)

Amaziah HARLOW[7] (Amaziah[6]) and 1st Lucy TORREY

Amaziah HARLOW[7] and 2nd Martha ALBERTSON[7] (Lydia Rider[6], Jos.[5], Abigail Warren[4],
     Ben.[3], Jos.[2]), c1796

John HARLOW[6] (John[5]) and Mary RYDER[5] (John[4], Sarah Bartlett[3], Mary Warren[2]),
     4 Oct. 1731, Plymouth (MD 14:74)

Ezra HARLOW[7] (John[6]) and Susanna WARREN[5] (Nath.[4], Ben.[3], Jos.[2]), Int. 21 Mar.
     1767, Plymouth (MD 26:86)

Lydia HARLOW[7] (John[6]) and William DAVIE[6] (Sarah Johnson[5], Eliz. Cooke[4], Caleb[3],
     Jacob[2]), 20 Oct. 1768 (Plymouth Ch.rcds.2:495)

Ebenezer HARLOW[7] (John[6]) and Rebecca BARTLETT, 20 Apr. 1758 (Plymouth VR 2:255)

Lazarus HARLOW[7] (John[6]) and 1st poss. Sarah DARLING, c1779

Lazarus HARLOW[7] and 2nd poss. Lucy ( ) BRADFORD

Samuel HARLOW[5] (Sam.[4], Rebecca Bartlett[3]) and Mary BARSTOW, 3 Jan. 1715/16, Scituate (MD 9:88)

Mary HARLOW[6] (Sam.[5]) and Caleb ROGERS[4] (John[3-2]), poss. 28 Mar. 1741, Scituate

William HARLOW[5] (Sam.[4]) and Mercy RIDER[5] (John[4], Sarah Bartlett[3], Mary Warren[2]), 24 Feb. 1714/15, Plymouth (MD 14:37)

Josiah HARLOW[7] (Sam.[6]) and Olive HUNT, Int. 4 Nov. 1775, poss. Wareham (War rcd.- letter from Bureau of Pensions)

Samuel HARLOW[6] (Wm.[5]) and Mercy BRADFORD[5] (Wm.[4-3-2]), 15 Dec. 1746, Plymouth (MD 17:5)[33]

William HARLOW[6] (Wm.[5]) and Hannah LITTLEJOHN, 5 Apr. 1742, Plymouth (MD 14:159)

Zephaniah HARLOW[7] (Wm.[6]) and Patience JOHNSON, 12 Apr. 1772 (Plymouth 1st Ch. rcds.2:497)

Betsey HARLOW[8] (Zephaniah[7]) and William MORSE, 18 Mar. 1804

Sarah HARLOW[7] (Wm.[6]) and Isaac MACKEY, 7 Apr. 1763, Plymouth (MD 26:42)

William HARLOW[7] (Wm.[6]) and Sarah HOLMES, 5 Aug. 1764, Plymouth

Isaac HARLOW[7] (Wm.[6]) and Martha SWINNERTON, 18 Mar. 1770, Plymouth

Hannah HARLOW[7] (Wm.[6]) and Elkanah CORBIN, Int. 25 Sept. 1773, Plymouth (MD 27:46)

Simeon HARLOW[7] (Wm.[6]) and Susanna CHURCHILL, 30 Mar. 1775, Plymouth

James HARLOW[7] (Wm.[6]) and Hannah BAGNELL, 25 Dec. 1780, Plymouth

Zephaniah HARLOW[8] (Zephaniah[7]) and Sally THOMAS, 15 Dec. 1796 (Kingston VR:233,289)

Patience HARLOW[8] (Zephaniah[7]) and Lemuel HOLMES, 6 Nov. 1794 (Plymouth Ch.rcds.2:507)

Olive B. HARLOW and John RYAN, 30 Dec. 1849, Bath ME (ME Hist.Gen.Rec.6:485)

William HARLOW[4] (Rebecca Bartlett[3]) and Lydia CUSHMAN[3] (Mary Allerton[2]), Jan. 1683 (Plymouth Ch.rcds.<Col.Soc.Mass.22:251)

Elizabeth HARLOW[5] (Wm.[4]) and Thomas DOTY[3] (Tho.[2]), c1703 (MD 4:112)

Lydia HARLOW[5] (Wm.[4]) and Barnabas CHURCHILL, 4 Feb. 1714, Plymouth (MD 14:37)

Barnabas CHURCHILL[6] (Lydia Harlow[5]) and Lydia HOLMES[6] (Hannah Sylvester[5], Hannah Bartlett[4], Jos.[3], Mary Warren[2]), 13 Nov. 1744, Plymouth (MD 14:161)

Seth CHURCHILL[7] (Barnabas[6]) and Elizabeth SYLVESTER[7] (Solomon[6-5], Hannah Bartlett[4], Jos.[3], Mary Warren[2]), Int. 24 May 1783, Plymouth (MD 29:90)

Rebecca HARLOW[5] (Wm.[4]) and poss. Jabez HOLMES, c1730

Robert HARLOW[5] (Wm.[4]) and 1st Susanna COLE, 10 Oct. 1717 (Plympton VR 1:135)

Robert HARLOW[5] and 2nd Remembrance WETHERHEAD, 15 Sept. 1749, Plymouth (MD 17:5)

Benjamin HARLOW[6] (Robert[5]) and 1st Abigail HOBBS, 2nd Ruth JOHNSON

Ebenezer HARLOW[6] (Robert[5]) and Meriah MOREY, 24 Aug. 1740, Plymoth (MD 17:4)

Isaac HARLOW[6] (Robert[5]) and Jerusha FINNEY[5] (Robert[4], Eliz. Warren[3], Jos.[2]),
    4 Jan. 1749/50, Plymouth (MD 16:169)

Robert HARLOW[6] (Robert[5]) and Jean WEST, 27 Mar. 1740/50, Plymouth (MD 16:169)

Susanna HARLOW[6] (Robert[5]) and William KING, 30 Oct. 1770 (Plymouth VR 2:287)

William KING and Huldah BATTLES, Int. 3/22 May 1802 (Plymouth VR 2:177)

Sarah KING[7] (Susanna Harlow[6]) and Uriah RIPLEY, 1 Jan. 1795 (Plymouth VR 2:292)

Thomas HARLOW[5] (Wm.[4]) and Jedidah CHURCHILL, 1 Dec. 1709, Plymouth (MD 14:36)

Jonathan HARLOW[6] (Tho,[5]) and Sarah HOLMES[6] (Elisha[5], Sarah Bartlett[4], Jos.[3],
    Mary Warren[2]), 22 Apr. 1742, Plymouth (MD 17:4)

Lucy HARLOW[7] (Jonathan[6]) and Isaac BARNES[6] (Ben.[5], Alice[4], Wm. Bradford[3-2])

Jonathan HARLOW[7] (Jonathan[6]) and Betty BLACKMER[6] (Sarah Holmes[5], Sarah Bartlett[4],
    Jos.[3], Mary Warren[2]), 8 Mar. 1770 (Plymouth VR 2:264)

Thomas HARLOW[6] (Tho.[5]) and Patience TILSON, Int. 4 Sept. 1736, Plymouth (MD 17:138)

Mary HARLOW[7] (Tho.[6]) and Issacher BISBEE, 28 Apr. 1766 (Bisbee Fam.:18)

Hopestill BISBEE and Hannah CHURCHILL, 25 Nov. 1731, Plympton (Bisbee Fam.:14)

William HARLOW[5] (Wm.[4]) and Joanna JACKSON, 18 June 1713, Plymouth (MD 14:37)

Lydia HARLOW[6] (Wm.[5]) and poss. Benjamin PRATT, 22 Dec. 1741

William HARLOW[6] (Wm.[5]) and Hannah BARTLETT, 5 Sept. 1738 (Plymouth VR 1:227)

Sarah BARTLETT[3] and Samuel RIDER, 23 Dec. 1656, Plymouth (MD 11:182)

Samuel RIDER and 2nd Lydia TILDEN, 1680 (MD 11:182)

John RIDER[4] (Sarah Bartlett[3]) and 1st Hannah BARNES, c1694 (MD 12:223)

Mercy RIDER[5] (John[4]) and William HARLOW[5] (Sam.[4], Rebecca Bartlett[3], Mary Warren[2])

Ebenezer RIDER[5] (John[4]) and Thankful SILVESTER[5] (Hannah Bartlett[4], Jos.[3], Mary
    Warren[2]), 16 Mar. 1725/26, Plymouth (MD 14:71)

Hannah RIDER[5] (John[4]) and William FOSTER, 17 Mar. 1725/26, Plymouth (MD 14:71)

John RIDER[5] (John[4]) and Mary DREW[6] (Hannah Barnes[5], Mary Bartlett[4], Jos.[3], Mary
    Warren[2]), 5 Dec. 1734, Plymouth (MD 14:76)

Samuel RIDER[5] (John[4]) and Mary SILVESTER[5] (Hannah Bartlett[4], Jos.[3], Mary Warren[2]),
    2 Nov. 1722, Plymouth (MD 14:40)

Sarah RIDER[6] (Sam.[5]) and Ebenezer RIDER[6] (Ebenezer[5], John[4], Sarah Bartlett[3],
    Mary Warren[2]), 18 Apr. 1757 (Plymouth VR 2:255)

Nathaniel WARREN^2 (Richard^1)

Nathaniel WARREN^2 and Sarah WALKER, 19 Nov. 1645, Plymouth (MD 13:86)

Nathaniel WARREN^3 and Phebe MURDOCK (Davis:273)

Phebe MURDOCK and 2nd Thomas GRAY, pre 24 June 1709

Alice WARREN^3 and Thomas GIBBS, 23 Dec. 1674, Sandwich (MD 14:111)

Sarah GIBBS^4 (Alice Warren^3) and Isaac CUSHMAN^4 (Isaac^3, Mary Allerton^2),
   28 Jan. 1700/01, Plymouth (MD 13:207)

Isaac CUSHMAN^4 and 2nd Mercy (BRADFORD) Freeman, aft. Oct. 1716

Abigail GIBBS^4 (Alice Warren^3) and Jirah SWIFT, 26 Nov. 1697, Sandwich (MD 23:39)

Jirah SWIFT and 2nd Mary BESSE, 19 Nov. 1741 (Swift Gen.:3,6)

Nathaniel SWIFT^5 (Abigail Gibbs^4) and poss. Abiah TUPPER

Abigail SWIFT^5 (Abigail Gibbs^4) and Antipas HAMMOND, Int. 21 Dec. 1736, Plymouth
   (MD 17:138)

Jabez SWIFT^5 (Abigail Gibbs^4) and poss. Abigail POPE, 9 Oct. 1729

Jirah SWIFT^5 (Abigail Gibbs^4) and Deborah HATHAWAY^5 (Jonathan^4, Sarah Cooke^3,
   John^2), c1729 (Dartmouth VR 1:266)

Jonathan SWIFT^6 (Jirah^5) and Elizabeth BOURNE, 16 Oct. 1753, poss. Falmouth

Rowland SWIFT^5 (Abigail Gibbs^4) and Mary DEXTER, 5 Dec. 1745, poss. Wareham
   (Gen.Adv.3:52)

Zephaniah SWIFT^6 (Rowland^5) and 2nd poss. Lucretia WEBB (Swift Gen.:15,30)

William SWIFT^5 (Abigail Gibbs^4) and 1st Keziah RIDER^4 (Sam.$^{3-2-1}$), Int. 30 Mar.
   1733, Plymouth (MD 17:134)

William SWIFT^5 and 2nd Abigail BURGESS, c1743

Keziah SWIFT^6 (Wm.^{5}) and Thomas MITCHELL, Int. 1 Oct. 1757, Plymouth (MD 25:140)

Zephaniah SWIFT^5 (Abigail Gibbs^4) and Lydia CHIPMAN^4 (John^3, Hope Howland^2),
   c1727 (MD 14:239)

Warren GIBBS^4 (Alice Warren^3) and Abigail HILLIARD, 11 Nov. 1714[34]

Elizabeth WARREN^3 and William GREEN, c1683 (MD 1:146)

William GREEN^4 (Eliz. Bartlett^3) and 1st Desire BACON^5 (Mary Hawes^4, Desire
   Gorham^3, Desire Howland^2), 23 Mar. 1709, Plymouth (MD 14:36)[35]

William GREEN^4 and 2nd Mary FULLER, 1 Sept. 1731 (Barnstable VR 2:357)

Barnabas BARKER and 1st Hannah (JENKINS) Turner, 3 Apr. 1719 (Barker Fam.:75)

Barnabas BARKER and 2nd Mary NEAL, 24 May 1736 (Barker Fam.:75)

Sarah GREEN^5 (Wm.^{4}) and Barnabas BARKER, c1751 (Barker Fam.:78)

William GREEN and Mrs. Mary FULLER, 1 Sept. 1731 (Barnstable VR 2:357)

William GREEN and Mary CONANT, Oct. 1745 (Barnstable VR 2:346)

Desire GREEN^5 (Wm.^{4}) and Nathaniel HINKLEY, 24 July 1746 (Barnstable VR 2:345)

Desire GREEN and Samuel PAIN Int. 8 Mar. 1739 (Barnstable VR 2:349)

Mrs. Abigail GREENE and James WHIPPO, 25 Feb. 1692 (Barnstable VR 1:388)

Sarah GREEN and Jonathan CHASE, 6 July 1709 (Barnstable VR 2:384)

James GREEN^5 (Wm.^{4}) and Ruth MARSHALL

Mary GREEN^5 (Wm.^{4}) and Barnabas BARKER

Warren GREEN^5 (Wm.^{4}) and Mary PAINE^6 (?John$^{5-4}$, Mary Snow^3, Constance Hopkins^2),
    14 Mar. 1733/34, Eastham (MD 17:141)

Bathsheba GREEN^6 (Warren^5) and Stephen HOSMER, poss. 3 Oct. 1763

Anna HOSMER^7 (Bathsheba^6) and Samuel BEMENT, 25 Apr. 1793 (Ashfield Ch.rcds.:111)

Polly HOSMER and Severance BEMENT, 3 Feb. 1793, Ashfield

Desire GREEN^6 (Warren^5) and Philip GOFF (NEHGR 57:19)

Mary GREEN^6 (Wm.^{5}) and Thomas SMITH

Sarah GREEN^6 (Wm.^{5}) and David DIMOCK

Warren GREEN^6 (Warren^5) and poss. Lucy BRAINERD

James WARREN^3 and Sarah DOTY^3 (Edw.^{2}), 21 June 1687, Plymouth (MD 13:204)

Sarah DOTY^3 and John BACON, 28 Sept. 1726, Plymouth (MD 14:71)

Alice WARREN^4 (James^3) and Peleg FORD, 10 May 1716, Plymouth (MD 14:38)

Peleg FORD and 2nd Phebe HIGGINS, 3 July 1740, Eastham (MD 19:185)

Hope WARREN^4 (James^3) and Nathaniel THOMAS, 23 July 1722, Plymouth (MD 14:39)

James WARREN^4 (James^3) and Penelope WINSLOW^4 (Isaac^3, Josiah^2), Int. 27 Dec.
    1723, Plymouth (MD 18:144)

Sarah WARREN^5 (James^4) and William SEVER^5 (Sarah Warren^4, James^4, Nath.^{3}), Int.
    16 Aug. 1755, Kingston

James WARREN^5 (James^4) and Mercy OTIS

Patience WARREN^4 (James^3) and Joseph STACE, 11 Apr. 1721, Plymouth (MD 14:39)

Sarah WARREN^4 (James^3) and 1st Charles LITTLE^4 (Isaac^3, Anna Warren^2), 9 Oct.
    1712, Plymouth (MD 14:37)

Sarah WARREN^4 and 2nd Nicholas SEVER, 21 Nov. 1728 (Kingston VR)

John SEVER^5 (Sarah Warren^4) and Judith COOPER, 13 Dec. 1753, Boston (Kingston VR)

Judith COOPER and 2nd William RAND, 10 Sept. 1761 (Kingston Ch.rcds.)

William SEVER^5 (Sarah Warren^4) and 1st Sarah WARREN^5 (James$^{4-3}$, Nath.^{2}), Int.
    16 Aug. 1755, Plymouth (MD 25:53)

William SEVER[5] and 2nd Mrs. Mercy RUSSELL, aft. Mar. 1797

Jane WARREN[3] and Benjamin LOMBARD, 19 Sept. 1672, Barnstable (MD 11:98)

Benjamin LOMBARD and 2nd Sarah WALKER, 19 Nov. 1685, Barnstable (MD 11:98)

Benjamin LOMBARD and 3rd Hannah ( ) WHETSTONE, 24 May 1694, Barnstable (MD 11:98)

Benjamin LOMBARD[4] (Jane Warren[3]) and Hannah TREDDAWAY, 23 May 1711, Barnstable
   (MD 11:98)

Mercy LOMBARD[4] (Jane Warren[3]) and Ebenezer BURGE, 20 Mar. 1701, Barnstable
   (MD 14:88)

Samuel BURGES[5] (Mercy Lombard[4]) and Jedidah GIBBS, Int. 16 Feb. 1731/32, Plymouth
   (MD 18:122)[36]

Samuel BURGES[5] and 2nd poss. Deborah BESSE, 7 Nov. 1754[37]

Jabez BURGES[6] (Sam.[5]) and Hannah LOTHROP, 3 May 1754, Wareham (Burgess Gen.<1865>:39)

Lothrop BURGES[7] (Jabez[6]) and Betsey BAKER, 28 Dec. 1791 (Burgess Gen.:39)

Calvin BURGE[8] (Lothrop[7]) and Polly HOTCHKISS

Lothrop BURGE[8] (Lothrop[7]) and Lois HOTCHKISS

Ebenezer BURGE[5] (Mercy Lombard[4]) and Zerviah NYE, Int. 14 May 1739, Plymouth
   (MD 18:39)

Mercy WARREN[3] and Jonathan DELANO, 28 Feb. 1677/78 (MD 3:218)

Jabez DELANO[4] (Mercy Warren[3]) and Mercy DELANO, 8 Feb. 1709/10, Duxbury (MD 11:23)

Jabez DELANO[4] and 2nd Hannah PECKHAM, c1716 (Delano Gen.:420)

Jabez DELANO[5] (Jabez[4]) and 2nd Ruth GOODSPEED, 24 Aug. 1760 (Rochester VR 2:53)

Jethro DELANO[4] (Mercy Warren[3]) and Elizabeh POPE, 9 Oct. 1727, Dartmouth

Thomas DELANO and Mary WARREN, Int. 28 Mar. 1777 (Dartmouth VR)

Jonathan DELANO[4] (Mercy Warren[3]) and Amy HATCH, 20 June 1704, Falmouth (Gen.
   Adv.4:19)

Mercy DELANO[4] (Mercy Warren[3]) and Joseph HATCH, pre Dec. 1720

Nathan DELANO[4] (Mercy Warren[3]) and Elizabeth MILLER, 7 July 1709, Middleboro
   (MD 2:158)

Richard WARREN[3] and Sarah ( ), c1678[38]

Sarah ( ) WARREN and 2nd Thomas EWER, 18 Sept. 1712, Barnstable (MD 14:226)

Anne WARREN[4] (Richard[3]) and John MAY, 8 Apr. 1712, Plymouth (MD 14:36)

John MAY[5] (Anne Warren[4]) and Bathshua BLACKWELL, Int. 10 Aug. 1745, Plymouth
   (MD 17:133)

Sarah MAY[6] (John[5]) and Thomas JACKSON 3rd, 27 Dec. 1787 (Plymouth VR 2:272)

Bathsheba MAY[6] (John[5]) and David LOTHROP, 12 July 1770 (Plymouth VR 2:264)

Anna MAY[6] (John[5]) and Thomas WETHRELL, 8 Dec. 1768, Plymouth (VR 2:264)

Thomas WETHERELL and 2nd Sarah JACKSON, aft. Sept. 1778

John MAY[6] (John[5]) and Mercy FOSTER, 21 June 1778 (Plymouth VR 2:268)

Thomas MAY[7] (John[6]) and Cordelia HOWARD, 16 May 1827 (Plymouth VR 2:246)

Charles MAY[7] (John[6]) and poss. Mary Ann WILLIAMS, c1819

Charles J. MAY[8] (Charles[7]) and Harriet E. DAVEE, Int. 19 Aug. 1849 (Plymouth VR 3:50)

Harriet W. MAY[8] (Charles[7]) and Rev. R. TOMLINSON, Int. 5 Oct. 1849 (Plymouth VR 3:51)

Edwin MAY[7] (John[6]) and Rhoda FRENCH, 31 Dec. 1821, Enfield NH

Marcia Ann MAY[8] (Edwin[7]) and Caleb Colby CHENEY, 16 Sept. 1871, Canaan NH

Jared BATES[7] (Naomi Warren[6], John[5-4]) and Eunice ALLEN, poss. Rochester

Mary MAY[5] (Anne Warren[4]) and John VALLER, Int. 22 Sept. 1733, Plymouth (MD 18:120)

Hope WARREN[4] (Richard[3]) and David TORREY, 12 June 1710, Scituate (MD 8:206)

Joanna WARREN[4] (Richard[3]) and Samuel BUMPAS, 1 Aug. 1717, Barnstable (MD 14:227,256)

Joanna BUMPAS[5] (Joanna Warren[4]) and Samuel HAMLIN Jr., c1749

John WARREN[4] (Richard[3]) and 1st Naomi BATES, 12 Jan. 1713/14, Scituate (MD 9:87)

John WARREN[4] and 2nd Ann REED, 27 July 1737, Middleboro (MD 13:252)

John WARREN[5] (John[4]) and Elizabeth LEWIS, Int. 10 Aug. 1745 (Rochester VR 2:57)

Naomi WARREN[6] (John[5]) and David BATES, 16 Aug. 1770 (Rochester VR)

Elizabeth BATES[7] (Naomi Warren[6]) and Esek CARR, poss. Rochester

Samuel WARREN[4] (Richard[3]) and Eleanor BILLINGTON[4] (Isaac[3], Francis[2]), 26 Jan. 1703/04, Middleboro (MD 2:43)

Benjamin WARREN[5] (Sam.[4]) and Jedidah TUPPER, 31 Dec. 1741, Middleboro (MD 15:219)

Jedidah WARREN[6] (Ben.[5]) and Nathaniel TUCKER, 18 Aug. 1767, Middleboro (MD 29:183)

Silvanus WARREN[6] (Ben.[5]) and 1st Huldah PEIRCE, 2 Oct. 1774 (Middleboro VR 4:11)

Silvanus WARREN[6] and 2nd Sarah WASHBURN, 1 Aug. 1782 (Middleboro VR 4:142)

Silvanus WARREN[7] (Silvanus[6]) and poss. Mary BUMP, 24 Dec. 1826 (Middleboro VR 10:267)

Zenas WARREN[6] (Ben.[5]) and Susanna WESTON, poss. 1 Mar. 1781

Cornelius WARREN[5] (Sam.[4]) and Mercy WARD, 18 Jan. 1732/33, Plymouth (MD 14:74)

James WARREN[5] (Sam.[4]) and poss. Mary TERRY, 4 May 1735, Freetown

Joanna WARREN[5] (Sam.[4]) and William BARLOW, 15 Oct. 1735 (Plympton VR:249,418)

Josiah WARREN^5 (Sam.^{4}) and Joanna SPOONER, 5 Apr. 1747, Middleboro (MD 16:109)

Josiah WARREN and Susanna MAKEPEACE, 29 Mar. 1770, Middleboro (MD 30:12)

Sarah WARREN^5 (Sam.^{4}) and William REED, 24 June 1740, Middleboro (MD 15:219)

Priscilla REED^6 (Sarah Warren^5) and Abraham PEIRCE, 6 Aug. 1761, Middleboro
    (MD 19:143)

Sarah WARREN^3 and John BLACKWELL, c1674 (MD 14:166)

Alice BLACKWELL^4 (Sarah Warren^3) and William SPOONER

Caleb BLACKWELL^4 (Sarah Warren^3) and Bethiah TABER^4 (Mary Tomson^3, Mary Cooke^2),
    c1710

Desire BLACKWELL^4 (Sarah Warren^3) and Lettice JENNEY, c1696

Ruth JENNEY^5 (Desire Blackwell^4) and Jeduthan SPOONER, Int. 18 Jan. 1728/29
    (Dartmouth VR:7)

Elizabeth JENNE and Samuel HOUSE, Int. 25 Jan. 1736/37 (Dartmouth VR:29)

Penelope JENNINGS and Joseph PECKHAM, Int. 28 July 1738 (Dartmouth VR:35)

Elizabeth JENNE and Jedediah HAMOND, Int. 11 Feb. 1737/38 (Dartmouth VR:32)

Parnell JENNE^5 (Desire Blackwell^4) and William MITCHELL Jr., Int. 10 Feb. 1745
    (Dartmouth VR:59)

Caleb JENNE^5 (Desire Blackwell^4) and 1st Patience STANDISH^4 (Myles^3, Alex.^{2}),
    6 Apr. 1738, poss. Dartmouth

Caleb JENNE^5 and 2nd Silence ( ) HOUSE, Int. 20 May 1746

David HOUSE and Silence FRENCH, 29 Feb. 1727 (Scituate VR 2:126,153)

Cornelius JENNE^5 (Desire Blackwell^4) and 2nd Eleanor (COLE) Young, Int. 28 Nov.
    1745 (Dartmouth VR:62)

Micro #32 of 32

Jethro JENNE^6 (Cornelius^5) and Desire MITCHELL, 14 Feb. 1750 (Dartmouth VR 2:271)

Levi JENNE^6 (Cornelius^5) and poss. Mary BLOSSOM

Susan JENNEY and Daniel C. BURT, Int. 21 May 1836 (New Bedford rcds.:841)

Levi JENNEY^7 (Levi^6) and Susanna PROCTOR^6 (Susanna Alden^5, John$^{4-3}$, Jos.^{2}),
    2 Oct. 1800 (New Bedford rcds.:219)

Mary JENNEY^5 (Desire Blackwell^4) and Thomas WEST, c1729

Parnel WEST^6 (Mary Jenney^5) and Hezekiah MASON, 28 Nov. 1756 (Gen. of Consider
    Smith:17)

Ruth MASON^8 (Parnel West^7) and Joseph WHELDEN

Jane BLACKWELL^4 (Sarah Warren^3) and Philip PECKHAM (NEHGR 57:36)

John BLACKWELL^4 (Sarah Warren^3) and Lydia SKIFFE^4 (Lydia Snow^3, Abigail Warren^2)

<1> p.282, The name of Joseph Rose is accompanied by a question mark. According to MFIP Warren:88, Hannah Ford married Samuel Nelson, 13 Dec. 1704, Plymouth (MD 13:206).

<2> p.283, See also: Waterman, Charles E. The Maine Watermans. 1906. Mechanic Falls ME. (p.21)

<3> p.284, Fourteen marriages are listed on a page which gives volume and page number but omits name of source.

<4> p.285, Although not shown here, Apollos Cushman's Mayflower descent can be found on p.29.

<5> p.288, Anna Cushman's Mayflower descent can be found on p.24.

<6> p.289, Intentions were also published at Brookfield , 3 Oct. 1785.

<7> p.290, This marriage date of 1735 is interesting; their first child was born in 1733, second in 1734 (Norwich VR:162).

<8> p.291, Pamela Bradford's Mayflower descent can be found on p.292.

<9> p.292, Intentions were also recorded in Kingston, 27 July 1780 (VR: 200,249)

<10> p.294, His descent is later shown to be Edward Little^5 (Edw.^{4}).

<11> p.294, Data is also given stating that his second wife was Mary (Kinsman) Burham (no source listed).

<12> p.295, Intentions are also given for 29 Jan. 1736/37 (no source listed).

<13> p.295, An accompanying note states "Hist. Hingham says she married 27 Aug. 1762, John Stodder, widower".

<14> p.296, An accompanying note reads "Hist. Hingham says she married 19 Dec. 1754, Caleb Campbell". The name of Jonathan Lock appears with a question mark and the words "not Caleb Campbell".

<15> p.298, MFIP Warren:19 states she was his third wife and calls her Rebecca ( ) Scottow, widow of John.

<16> p.301, The marriage date of Nov. 1705/06 is interesting as their first (and only) child, Sarah, was born 4 Aug. 1706 (MD 4:113). A split year is not usually used for the month of November.

<17> p.301, Grace Dwelly and Jesse Turner were divorced.

<18> p.304, Edward Doten/Doty's Mayflower descent can be found on p.157.

<19> p.304, Bowman questions whether this was the second marriage of Lydia (Clark) Finney or that of her daughter, Lydia Finney.

<20> p.304, Jerusha Finney had a child before her marriage, Lydia "Finney", born 8 Dec. 1747 (MD 1:144), but the father is not named.

<21> p.305, For the first marriage and Mayflower descent of Betsey Barnes, see p.117.

<22> p.306, Although a question mark accompanies this marriage, it can be found on p.253.

<23> p.306, Hannah Bartlett, widow, married 2nd Thomas Delano, 24 Oct. 1699 (MD 9:109). See p.16.

<24> p.310, Caleb Bate married 1st Ruth ( ), 26 Aug. 1689; 2nd Mary Lane; 3rd Sarah Sprague.

<25> p.316, Lewis, Ella May. Gage Genealogy. Manuscript. 1924. Springfield MA

<26> p.317, Intentions were also published 29 July 1820, New Bedford (VR 2:122,386)

<27> p.318, The charts for Robert Bartlett and his children are out of sequence. Those that are not found immediately following will be found on pages 314 and 315. Sarah Cooke's Mayflower descent can be found on p.116.

<28> p.319, Bowman suggests this may have been a second marriage, with the first being to Sarah ( ). According to an accompanying note from Freeman's Cape Cod 2:153,154, James Faunce married 1st Sarah ( ), 2nd Thankful Tobey, 3rd Jane Tupper.

<29> p.319, An accompanying note reads "Davis' Landmarks:194 says he marr. 1st Hannah Ford, no children". MFIP Warren:48 affirms this first marriage with a marriage date of 13 Dec. 1704, Plymouth (MD 14:35)

<30> p.320, The accompanying note reads "? did she marry 2d 14 Jan. 1730, Joseph Briggs?" The Scituate records give her name as Sarah Morey, widow (MD 1:44)

<31> p.321, Intentions were also published at Rochester 18 Dec. 1775.

<32> p.321, Phebe Hart was possibly the second wife of Simeon Tisdale. Five Tisdale children are listed (no dates), of whom not all would likely be Phebe's since she married in 1759 and became a widow and remarried by 1763.

<33> p.323, A question mark accompanies the possibility of a second marriage to Mary Morton, c1763 (Davis:128).

<34> p.325, On a note a few pages further, the marriage date is given as 25 Apr. 1714 (no source).

<35> p.325, The Barnstable records give the marriage date as 25 Mar. 1709 (MD 14:226).

<36> p.327, Cutter's New England Fam. (below) states the marriage took place 30 Mar. 1732.

<37> p.327, Cutter's New England Families. Second Series. 1914. NY (2:692).

<38> p.327, She is now believed to have been Sarah Torrey (Mayflower Increasings:132).

WILLIAM WHITE DESCENDANTS

Penelope WHITE and John TRASK, 28 Feb. 1726/27 (Rochester VR 1:28)

John TRASK and 2nd Tabitha ORCUTT, 7 July 1764

Margret WHITE and Edward MORSS, Int. 26 Aug. 1727, Dartmouth (New Bedford "Copy":2)

George WHITE and Deborah SHAW, Int. 30 Jan. 1729/30, Dartmouth (New Bedford:11)

Hannah WHITE and William TABER, Int. 11 Dec. 1730, Dartmouth (New Bedford:13)

Samuel WHITE and Mary CHASE, Int. 23 Apr. 1731, Dartmouth (New Bedford:15)

Abner WHITE and Ruth BROWNELL, Int. 10 Mar. 1745/46, Dartmouth (New Bedford:64)

Samuel WHITE and Elizabeth JACKSON, Int. 10 Mar. 1745/46, Dartmouth (New Bedford:64)

Hannah WHITE and Weston KERBY, Int. 23 Feb. 1750/51, Dartmouth (New Bedford:84)

Thomas WHITE and Elizabeth JENNE, Int. 8 July 1751, Dartmouth (New Bedford:86)

William WHITE and Mercy SEARS, Int. 3 Dec. 1751, Dartmouth (New Bedford:89)

Ruth WHITE and Culbert WILLCOX, Int. 8 Jan. 1754, Dartmouth (New Bedford:98)

Israel WHITE and Sibbel ( ) HICKS, Int. 14 June 1754, Dartmouth (New Bedford:101)

Peleg WHITE and Rachel CORNELL, Int. 2 Oct. 1754, Dartmouth (New Bedford:102)

Jonathan WHITE and Abigail WING, Int. 1 Jan. 1756, Dartmouth (New Bedford:109)

Hannah WHITE and Thomas WING, Int. 16 Jan. 1762, Dartmouth (New Bedford:144)

Rebecca WHITE and Robert BENTLEY, Int. 5 June 1764, Dartmouth (New Bedford:161)

Mary WHITE and James SOUL, Int. 6 Mar. 1765, Dartmouth (New Bedford:167)

William WHITE 2d and Abigail WHITE, Int. 20 Mar. 1766, Dartmouth (New Bedford:174)

Elizabeth WHITE and Stephen PECKCOM, Int. 26 Sept. 1771, Dartmouth (New Bedford:218)

Mary WHITE and Seth HILMAN, Int. 23 Mar. 1773, Dartmouth (New Bedford:232)

Silvenus WHITE and Mary GIFFORD, Int. 30 Mar. 1773, Dartmouth (New Bedford:232)

Benjamin WHITE and Amy BALL, Int. 28 Dec. 1774, Dartmouth (New Bedford:254)

Anan WHITE and Jacob TABER 3d, Int. 14 Oct. 1775, Dartmouth (New Bedford:262)

Love WHITE and Jonathan TOBEY Jr., Int. 12 July 1777, Dartmouth (New Bedford:280)

Hannah WHITE and David SOUL, Int. 28 Sept. 1777, Dartmouth (New Bedford:282)

Ruth WHITE and Gideon CORNELL 2d, Int. 25 July 1778, Dartmouth (New Bedford:290)

Theophilus WHITE and Mary WILCOX, Int. 13 Mar. 1779, Dartmouth (New Bedford:297)

Obed WHITE and Sarah PECKCOM, Int. 2 July 1779, Dartmouth (New Bedford:299)

Rhoda WHITE and Stephen CORNELL, Int. 27 Apr. 1781, Dartmouth (New Bedford:316)

Roger WHITE and Lydia PECKCOM, Int. 4 Jan. 1783, Dartmouth (New Bedford:329)

William WHITE Jr. and Hannah STETSON, Int. 6 Mar. 1784, Dartmouth (New Bedford:337)

Samuel WHITE and Abigail ANNES, Int. 31 Mar. 1784, Dartmouth (New Bedford:337)

George WHITE and Mary SMITH, Int. 24 Dec. 1784, Dartmouth (New Bedford:345)

Humphry WHITE and Sibbel KERBY, Int. 11 Feb. 1786, Dartmouth (New Bedford:355)

Molly WHITE and Abraham HOWLAND, Int. 1 Sept. 1786, Dartmouth (New Bedford:359)

Peregrine WHITE[2] (William[1])

Peregrine WHITE[2] and Sarah BASSETT, C1648/49 (Plymouth Col.Court Orders 2:183)

Mercy WHITE[3] and William SHERMAN[3] (Desire Doty[2]), 3 Feb. 1697, Marshfield (MD 5:237)

Daniel WHITE[3] and Hannah HUNT, 19 Aug. 1674, Marshfield (MD 2:180)

Benjamin WHITE[4] (Dan.[3]) and Faith OAKMAN[4] (Eliz. Doty[3], Edw.[2]), 2 Dec. 1714,
     Marshfield (MD 7:131)

Faith OAKMAN[4] and 2nd Thomas FOSTER, betw. May 1724-1735

Benjamin WHITE[5] (Ben.[4]) and Mercy THOMAS[5] (Abigail Baker[4], Sarah Bradford[3], Wm.[2])
     c1748

Cornelius WHITE[4] (Dan.[3]) and Hannah RANDALL, 22 May 1706, Scituate (MD 8:205)

Benjamin WHITE[5] (Cornelius[4]) and poss. Hannah DECROW, c1744 (White Gen.:126)

Hannah WHITE[6] (Ben.[5]) and Daniel CROOKER, 19 Dec. 1776

Daniel CROOKER and 1st Abigail STUDLEY, 16 Feb. 1764, Hanover (Ch. & Cem.rcds.1:94)

Hannah CROOKER[7] (Hannah White[6]) and Matthew ESTES, 9 Aug. 1805 (Pembroke VR:260,271)

Mary CROOKER[7] (Hannah White[6]) and Nathaniel BRYANT, 1 Dec. 1803 (Pembroke VR:249,260)

Matilda CROOKER[7] (Hannah White[6]) and Walter STUDLEY, 18 May 1806, Pembroke

Sarah CROOKER[7] (Hannah White[6]) and David GARDNER, 8 Sept. 1805, Pembroke

Sarah GARDNER[8] (Sarah Crooker[7]) and Jesse BURRELL, 8 Dec. 1831, Braintree

Charles GARDNER[8] (Sarah Crooker[7]) and 1st Eliza TOLMAN, c1827

Charles GARDNER[8] and 2nd Ruth A. BOWDITCH, 7 Nov. 1838

Emily GARDNER[8] (Sarah Crooker[7]) and Calvin NICHOLS, 25 May 1837 (Wakefied VR:191,212)

David GARDNER[8] (Sarah Crooker[7]) and Emeline ROGERS

George GARDNER[8] (Sarah Crooker[7]) and Elmira KELLEY, 3 May 1847, New Bedford

Fidelia C. GARDNER[8] (Sarah Crooker[7]) and Amos Hobart HUNT, 13 July 1842

Amos Hobart HUNT and 1st Betsy (LEAVITT) Pratt, 22 Oct. 1822 (Hunt Gen.<1862-3>:257)

Elizabeth GARDNER[8] (Sarah Crooker[7]) and Daniel EDSON

Daniel WHITE[5] (Cornelius[4]) and Abigail TURNER, pre 1750

Abigail WHITE[6] (Dan.[5]) and John SOULE, c1780 (MD 8:198)

Daniel WHITE[6] (Dan.[5]) and poss. Margaret BELL

Kate WHITE^6 (Dan.^{5}) and James LEWIS

Urania WHITE^6 (Dan.^{5}) and Luther HAYWARD, c1794

Luther HAYWARD and 1st Betty WILLIS, c1786

Gideon WHITE^5 (Cornelius^4) and Joanna HOWLAND^4 (Tho.^{3}, Jos.^{2}), 23 Feb. 1743/44,
    Plymouth (MD 14:160)

Joanna WHITE^5 (Cornelius^4) and Nathaniel PHILLIPS, 16 Jan. 1734/35, Duxbury
    (MD 11:241)

Joanna PHILLIPS^6 (Joanna^5) and Thomas TURNER, c1765

Lemuel WHITE^5 (Cornelius^4) and Anna SCOTT, 3 Feb. 1731 (Marshfield VR 2:143)

Paul WHITE^5 (Cornelius^4) and poss. Elizabeth CURTIS, 24 Feb. 1737 (White Gen.:124)

Ebenezer WHITE^4 (Dan.^{3}) and Hannah DOGGETT, 9 Mar. 1712/13, Marshfield (MD 7:132)

Obadiah WHITE^5 (Eben.^{4}) and Elizabeth ALLEN

Eleazer WHITE^4 (Dan.^{3}) and Mary DOGGETT, 29 Sept. 1712, Marshfield (MD 7:132)

John WHITE^4 (Dan.^{3}) and Susanna SHERMAN, 18 Feb. 1700, Marshfield (MD 5:236)

Abijah WHITE^5 (John^4) and Anna LITTLE^5 (John^4, Ephraim^3, Anna Warren^2), 1 Feb.
    1738 (Marshfield VR 2:159)$^{<2>}$

Anna WHITE^6 (Abijah White^5) and Ezra EDSON (MD 8:196)

Micro #3 of 7

Christiana WHITE^6 (Jesse^5, John^4) and William LEWIS, c1773

John WHITE^5 (John^4) and Joanna SPRAGUE, c1731 (MD 29:158)

Sarah WHITE^5 (John^4) and Isaac PHILLIPS, 25 Jan. 1727 (Marshfield VR 2:148)

Isaac PHILLIPS^6 (Sarah White^5) and Priscilla TURNER, Int. 4 May 1754 (Marshfield
    VR 2:151)

Anna PHILLIPS^6 (Sarah White^5) and Thomas DINGLEY, 20 Jan. 1757 (Marshfield VR 2:175)

John DINGLEY^7 (Anna Phillips^6) and Elizabeth BLAKE

Joseph WHITE^4 (Dan.^{3}) and Elizabeth DWELLY, 21 Dec. 1710, Scituate (MD 8:206)

Thomas WHITE^4 (Dan.^{3}) and Martha BISBEE, 16 Apr. 1719 (Pembroke VR:27)

Thomas WHITE and Rachel HARTON, 2 Mar. 1726/27, Milton

Jonathan WHITE^3 and 1st Hester NICKERSON, 2 Feb. 1682, Yarmouth (MD 2:209)

Ebenezer WHITE^4 (Jonathan^3) and Mercy SMITH, 13 July 1727, Harwich (MD 11:175)

Thankful WHITE^5 (Eben.^{4}) and Ebenezer PAINE^6 (Eben.^{5}, Sam.^{4}, Mary Snow^3, Constance
    Hopkins^2), 2 Sept. 1756 (Yarmouth VR 3:281)

Daniel WHITE^5 (Eben.^{4}) and poss. Jennie (?DAVIS) Smith, c1776

Thomas WHITE^5 (Eben.^{4}) and Mercy SEARS, 1 July 1765 (Yarmouth VR 3:232)

Esther WHITE^4 (Jonathan^3) and 1st John JOYCE, 7 Nov. 1707 (Yarmouth VR 3:14)

Esther WHITE^4 and 2nd John DRAKE, c1724

Elizabeth DRAKE^5 (Esther White^4) and William COREY, 3 Apr. 1743 (Arnold VR 1:2:)

Desire JOYCE^5 (Esther White^4) and John ARNOLD, 1 Mar. 1732/33

Jonathan WHITE^4 (Jonathan^3) and Dorcas HAMLIN, c1716

Dorcas WHITE^5 (Jonathan^4) and poss. (?)Joseph THORP, (?)29 May 1740, Yarmouth
    (VR 3:29)

Joseph WHITE^4 (Jonathan^3) and Lydia BAKER, 21 June 1737 (Yarmouth VR 3:26)

Anne WHITE^5 (Jos.^{4}) and John CROWELL

Joseph WHITE^5 (Jos.^{4}) and Rebecca BRAY, 29 Nov. 1764 (Yarmouth VR 3:234)

Joseph WHITE^6 (Jos.^{5}) and Lucy HOWES, 13 Jan. 1791 (Yarmouth VR 4:115)

Mary WHITE^4 (Jonathan^3) and James RUSSEL, 14 Aug. 1729 (Yarmouth VR 3:21)

Sarah WHITE^3 and Thomas YOUNG, Jan. 1688/89, Scituate (MD 2:87)

George YOUNG^4 (Sarah White^3) and Mary STOCKBRIDGE, 5/25 Apr. 1722 (Scituate
    VR 2:273,339)

Reuben YOUNG^5 (George^4) and poss. Abigail BATES, c1780

Micro #4 of 7

Elisha YOUNG^6 (James^5, Geo.^{4}) and Hannah RUGGLES, Int. 28 Dec. 1782 (Scituate
    VR 2:253,337)

Susanna YOUNG^7 (Elisha^6) and Samuel WHITE Jr., Int. 4 Jan. 1816 (Groton VR 2:180,195)

Almira YOUNG and George A. DADMAN, 12 May 1831 (Groton VR 2:49,195)

Deborah YOUNG and George HARTWELL, 14 Oct. 1830 (Groton VR 2:82,195)

Hannah YOUNG and Moses BURNHAM, Int. 8 Oct. 1806 (Groton VR 2:37,195)

Joanna YOUNG and Willard DADMIN, 10 Feb. 1823 (Groton VR 2:49,195)

Samuel Leander WHITE^8 (Susanna Young^7) and Nancy Porter BARKER

James YOUNG^5 (George^4) and Mehitable HATCH, Int. 13 Jan. 1753 (Scituate VR 2:143,338)

Mehitable YOUNG^6 (James^5) and Samuel CURTIS, 9 Apr. 1778 (Deane's Scituate:254)

Mary CURTIS^7 (Mehitable Young^6) and Peter CUDWORTH, 25 June 1820 (Scituate VR)

Hannah Ruggles WHITE^8 (Susanna Young^7) and William Whittle MERRILL, 7 Dec. 1853,
    Groton

Lucy MERRILL^9 (Hannah White^8) and Edward Livingston UNDERWOOD, 23 July 1885,
    Boston

Joseph YOUNG^4 (Sarah White^3) and Lydia BARRELL^6 (Wm.^{5}, Lydia Turner^4, Mary Brew-
    ster^3, Jonathan^2), 5 Sept. 1729 (Scituate VR 2:21,338)

Ezekiel YOUNG^5 (Jos.^{4}) and Lusanna WHITE^6 (Lemuel^5, Cornelius^4, Dan.^{3}, Peregrine^2), c1754 (Scituate VR)

Lydia YOUNG[6] (Ezekiel[5]) and 1st James LITTLE[6] (Lemuel[5], John[4], Ephraim[3], Anna Warren[2]), Int. 26 Mar. 1782, Marshfield

Lydia YOUNG[6] and 2nd Simeon GANNETT, poss. 18 Oct. 1809

Gideon YOUNG[6] (Ezekiel[5]) and 2nd Elizabeth MANN, 29 Mar. 1795 (Scituate VR 2:200,338)

Ebenezer Scott YOUNG[6] (Ezekiel[5]) and 1st Mary LERMOND, 24 Jan. 1799

Ebenezer Scott YOUNG[6] and 2nd Molly (GLEASON) Miles, Int. 6 Sept. 1810

Joseph YOUNG[6] (Ezekiel[5]) and Desire NASH, 27 Sept. 1778, Scituate

Ezekiel YOUNG[7] (Jos.[6]) and Elizabeth POWERS, c1801 (Scituate VR)

Joseph Chester YOUNG[8] (Ezekiel[7]) and Lydia BAILEY, 4 Sept. 1826

Mary YOUNG and Moses Parker RICH, 19 Dec. 1830

Clarissa Gardner YOUNG[8] (Ezekiel[7]) and Thomas G. BATES, poss. 6 Mar. 1831

Resolved WHITE[2] (William[1])

Resolved WHITE[2] and 1st Judith VASSALL, 5 Nov. 1640, Scituate (MD 2:32)

Resolved WHITE[2] and 2nd Abigail ( ) LORD, 5 Oct. 1674, Salem (MD 2:120)

Hannah WHITE and William TABER, 27 Dec. 1730, Dartmouth (Bristol Crt.rcds.:162)

Thomas WHITE and Elizabeth JENNE, 25 Aug. 1751, Dartmouth (Bristol Crt.rcds.:78)

Experience WHITE and Philip CHACE, 28 Feb. 1790, Dartmouth (Bristol Crt.rcds.:24)

Peleg WHITE and Almy PECKHAM, 15 May 1791, Dartmouth (Bristol Crt.rcds.:44)

Benjamin WHITE and Almy BALL, 16 Mar. 1775, Dartmouth (Bristol Crt.rcds.:52)

Holder WHITE and Cynthia MILK, 30 Aug. 1788, Dartmouth (Bristol Crt.rcds.:63)

Mary WHITE and James SOUL, 11 Apr. 1765, Dartmouth (Bristol Crt.rcds.:65)

William WHITE 3d and Abigail WHITE, 17 Apr. 1766, Dartmouth (Bristol Crt.rcds.:66)

Ruth WHITE and Gideon CORNELL, 13 Sept. 1778, Dartmouth (Bristol Crt.rcds.:80)

Theophis WHITE and Mary WILCOX, 8 Apr. 1779, Dartmouth (Bristol Crt.rcds.:81)

Obed WHITE and Sarah PECKHAM, 29 July 1779, Dartmouth (Bristol Crt.rcds.:81)

William WHITE Jr. and Hannah STETSON, 24 Mar. 1784, Dartmouth (Bristol Crt.rcds.:87)

Haturah WHITE and Lathan KIRBY, 22 Sept. 1791, Dartmouth (Bristol Crt.rcds.:98)

Sally WHITE and Zenas RIPLEY, 11 Aug. 1793, Dartmouth (Bristol Crt.rcds.:157)

Jerathunael WHITE and Abiel HOWLAND, 21 Nov. 1793, Dartmouth (Bristol Crt.rcds.:157)

Samuel WHITE and Mary CHASE, 11 May 1731, Dartmouth (New Bedford "copy":17)

Elisabeth WHITE and Stephen PECKCOM, 16 Nov. 1771, Dartmouth (New Bedford:100)

Hannah WHITE and David SOUL, 23 Oct. 1777, Dartmouth (New Bedford:130)

Roger WHITE and Lydia PECKCOM, 30 Jan. 1783, Dartmouth (New Bedford "copy":171)

Love WHITE and Jonathan TOBEY, 28 Dec. 1777, Dartmouth (New Bedford:204)

John WHITE and Mary HATHWAY, Int. 20 Sept. 1765 (Freetown VR 2:372)

Samuel WHITE and Abigail ANNES, Int. 31 Mar. 1784, Dartmouth

Peregrine WHITE and Mary HOWLAND, 3 May 1770, Middleboro (Bailey's Plym.Co.Mgs:90)

Anna WHITE[3] and John HAYWARD, 2 June 1671, Concord

Elizabeth WHITE[3] and Obadiah WHEELER, 17 July 1672, Concord

Josiah WHITE[3] and Remember READ, pre 30 Dec. 1680 (MD 8:166)

Samuel WHITE and Martha PRITCHET, 10 May 1751, Salem

Josiah WHITE[4] (Josiah[3]) and Mary TAYLOR, 28 Apr. 1737 (MD 8:167)

Caleb WHITE[5] (Josiah[4]) and Rebecca MARSH, 26 Feb. 1767, Sutton (MD 8:167)

Micro #5 of 7

Martha WHITE and Robert JONES, Int. 1 Aug. 1734 (Rochester VR 2:44)

Deborah WHITE and Samuel LEWES, Int. 31 Jan. 1738 (Rochester VR 2:46)

Samuel WHITE and Elizabeth ASHLEY, 14 Mar. 1733, Rochester (Gen.Adv.1:35)

Nathaniel WHITE and Mary RAYMOND, 20 May 1745 (Rochester Crt.rcds.1:245)

George WHITE and Sarah BUMPUS, 17 Oct. 1728 (Rochester VR 1:27)

John WHITE[4] (Sam.[3]) and Martha DOTY[3] (Tho.[2]), pre 1696

Mary WHITE and Nathan ELIS, 23 May 1723 (Rochester VR 1:27)

Sylvanus WHITE and Anna WILLIAMS, 16 Nov. 1752 (Rochester VR 2:52)

Justice WHITE and Jane SHAREMAN, 20 June 1745 (Rochester VR 2:51)

Samuel WHITE and Elizabeth JACKSON, Int. 1 Apr. 1746 (Rochester VR 2:57)

Timothy WHITE and Sarah HASKELL, 27 Oct. 1761 (Rochester VR 2:53)

Thomas WHITE and Ruth MARCHANT, Int. 18 Aug. 1754 (Rochester VR 2:161)

Melletiah WHITE and Mary SPRAGUE, 12 Feb. 1756 (Rochester VR 2:43)

Resolved WHITE and Charity CLAP, 19 Dec. 1771 (Rochester VR 3:198)

Melatiah WHITE and Mercy SPRAGUE, 10 Jan. 1779 (Rochester VR 3:199)

Justus WHITE and Content CLARK, 8 Mar. 1784 (Rochester VR 3:200)

Ezra S. WHITE and Rebecca SHERMAN, 29 Feb. 1816 (Rochester VR 4:211)

James WHITE and Rachel GURNEY, Int. 26 Mar. 1810 (Rochester VR 4:82)

Capt. Resolved WHITE and Anna BRIGGS, Int. 17 June 1811 (Rochester VR 4:83)

Alvan WHITE and Eugenia BENNETT, 29 Mar. 1829 (Rochester VR 10:188)

William S. WHITE and Eliza Ann WILLIS, 18 Mar. 1834 (Rochester VR 12:358)

Rufus WHITE and Nancy RANDALL, Int. 5 Oct. 1829 (Rochester VR 5:368)

Jedidiah WHITE and Aaron HAMMOND, 25 Dec. 1784 (Rochester VR 11:51)

Susanna WHITE and Abraham ASHLEY, 9 Sept. 1703 (Rochester VR 11:40)

Minerva WHITE and John PURRINGTON, 27 Feb. 1840 (Rochester VR 12:358)

Lizzie F. WHITE and Charles CHURCH, 20 June 1855 (Rochester VR 12:361)

Pennelabe WHITE and Peroo CRAPOO, 31 May 1704 (Rochester VR 1:1)

Mary WHITE and Timothy RUGGLES, 27 Dec. 1710 (Rochester VR 1:1)

Mercy WHITE and Samuel LUMBARD, 8 Feb. 1782 (Rochester VR 3:199)

Hope WHITE and Barnabas CLARK, 11 Oct. 1782 (Rochester VR 3:199)

Jane WHITE and Ebenezer SEARS, 21 Oct. 1779 (Rochester VR 3:199)

Deborah WHITE and William RANDAL, 7 Dec. 1780 (Rochester VR 3:199)

Katharine WHITE and Isaac BOWLES Jr., Int. 24 Oct. 1809 (Rochester VR 4:80)

Mrs. Eliza A. WHITE and William J. MONROE, 8 Oct. 1839 (Rochester VR 12:350)

Priscilla WHITE and Ebenezer ELLIS, Int. 5 Sept. 1789 (Rochester VR 3:217)

Tabitha WHITE and Joel ELLIS, 27 Mar. 1786, Rochester (Bailey's Marr.:196)

Mary WHITE and Shubael NYE, 10 Aug. 1783, Rochester (Bailey's Marr.:196)

Deborah WHITE^5 (John^4) and poss. Samuel LEWIS, 12 Apr. 1739 (Rochester Ch.
    rcds.2:202,317)

Micro #6 of 7

John WHITE^5 (John^4) and Mercy JENKINS, 23 Dec. 1718, Barnstable (MD 14:227)

Mercy WHITE^6 (John^5) and Joseph CLARK, 29 Nov. 1750 (Rochester VR 2:80,317)

Thankful CLARK^7 (Mercy White^6) and Weston ALLEN

Thomas WHITE^6 (John^5) and Ruth MARCHANT, Int. 2 Sept. 1754 (Rochester VR 2:210,318)

Merchant WHITE^7 (Tho.^{6}) and Hannah BROWN, 22 July 1792, Freetown (Bristol Crt.
    rcds.:162)

David WHITE and Bethiah DAGET, 25 Jan. 1788, Freetown (Bristol Crt.rcds.)

Mary WHITE^8 (Tho.$^{7-6}$) and Daniel EDSON

Love WHITE^7 (Tho.^{6}) and Jonathan TOBEY

William WHITE^6 (John^5) and Mercy SEARS^7 (Paul^6, Mercy Freeman^5, Tho.^{4}, Mercy
    Prence^3, Patience Brewster^2), Int. 17 Nov. 1751, Rochester[3]

William WHITE^7 (Wm.^{6}) and Hannah STETSON, 24 Mar. 1784 (Dartmouth VR 2:478,539)[4]

Phineas WHITE^8 (Wm.^{7}) and Betsy WALKER, 28 Nov. 1813

Justus WHITE^5 (John^4) and Jane SHERMAN, 20 June 1745 (Rochester VR)

Justus WHITE^6 (Justus^5) and Content CLARK, 8 Mar. 1784 (Rochester VR)

Silvanus WHITE^5 (John^4) and Anna WILLIAMS, 16 Nov. 1752 (Rochester VR)

Resolved WHITE^6 (Justus^5) and Charity CLAP, 19 Dec. 1771 (Rochester VR)

Charity CLAP and 2nd Daniel VAUGHAN, aft. Mar. 1780

Jane WHITE^7 (Resolved^6) and Elisha MACK

Thomas WHITE[5] (John[4]) and Hope JENKINS, c1726 (MD 12:99)

Thomas WHITE and Elizabeth JENNE, 25 Aug. 1751, Dartmouth (Bristol Crt.rcds.)

John WHITE[6] (Tho.[5]) and poss. Mercy HATHAWAY

Anna WHITE[7] (John[6]) and poss. Daniel ALLEN

Seth WHITE[7] (John[6]) and poss. Hannah GLEASON

Malatiah WHITE[4] (Sam.[3]) and Mercy WINSLOW, c1698 (MD 12:98)

Mercy WINSLOW and 2nd Thomas JENKINS, aft. Dec. 1712

Judith WHITE[5] (Malatiah[4]) and Ebenezer JENKINS, 9 Nov. 1721, Barnstable (MD 14:89)

Malatiah WHITE[5] (Malatiah[4]) and poss. (?)Jane COOMBS, 28 Apr. 1737 (Tiverton RI
    VR 4:7:55)[5]

Margaret WHITE[5] (Malatiah[4]) and Edward MORSS, Int. 26 Aug. 1727, Dartmouth

Penelope WHITE[4] (Sam.[3]) and Pierre CRAPO, 31 May 1704 (Rochester VR)

Peter CRAPO and Ann LUCE, 23 Nov. 1738 (Rochester VR 2:50)

Peter CREAPO and Hannah AXDIL, 13 Feb. 1755 (Rochester VR 2:52)

Francis CRAPO[6] (Penelope White[5]) and Patience SPOONER, Int. 18 Dec. 1734,
    (Rochester VR 2:44)

Susanna CRAPO[5] (Penelope White[4]) and Louis DEMORANVILLE, 8 Dec. 1730 (Rochester
    VR 2:95,107)

Samuel WHITE[4] (Sam.[3]) and 2nd poss. Mary CHASE, 11 May 1731 (Dartmouth VR)

Samuel WHITE[5] (Sam.[4]) and 1st Elizabeth ASHLEY, 14 Mar. 1733/34 (Rochester VR)

Samuel WHITE[5] and 2nd Elizabeth JACKSON, Int. 1 Apr. 1746, Rochester

Susanna WHITE[4] (Sam.[3]) and Abraham ASHLEY, 9 Sept. 1703, Sandwich (VR:23)

NOTES

<1> p.332, The first marriage given is that of William White and Susanna Fuller, 11 Feb. 1612, Leyden, Holland. Since it is yet to be proven, and highly unlikely, that it was William White of the Mayflower who married Susanna Fuller, this marriage has not been included. (See NEHGR 109:242). Susanna ( ) White married 2nd Edward Winslow, 12 May 1621, Plymouth.

<2> p.334, Anna Little also has Mayflower descent to John Alden through her mother Constant Fobes. See p.4 for line of descent.

<3> p.338, Intentions were also published 3 Dec. 1751, Dartmouth (New Bedford "copy":89).

<4> p.338, An accompanying note gives the marriage of a William White and Hannah Stetson, 30 July 1778 (Pembroke VR:352,373)

<5> p.339, There seems to be some question regarding this marriage. Bowman is uncertain as to which Malatiah White married Jane Coombs - Malatiah[5] (Sam.[4]) or Malatiah[5] (Malatiah[4]).

Edward WINSLOW[1] and 1st Elizabeth BARKER, Int. 28 Apr. 1618, Leyden, Holland
    (MD 8:100)

Edward WINSLOW[1] and 2nd Susanna ( ) WHITE, 12 May 1621, Plymouth (see p.339,<1>)

Elizabeth WINSLOW[2] (Edward[1])

Elizabeth WINSLOW[2] and 1st Robert BROOKS, pre 1656

Elizabeth WINSLOW[2] and 2nd George CORWIN, 22 Sept. 1669 (MD 1:239)

Penelope CORWIN[3] and Josiah WALCOT, 19 Feb. 1686

Josiah WALCOT and 2nd Mary FREAKE, 6 May 1694

Susanna CORWIN[3] and 1st Edward LYDE, 29 Nov. 1694 (Salem VR)

Susanna CORWIN[3] and 2nd Benjamin WADSWORTH

Josiah WINSLOW[2] (Edward[1])

Josiah WINSLOW[2] and Penelope PELHAM, c1657

Elizabeth WINSLOW[3] and Stephen BURTON, 4 Sept. 1684, Marshfield (MD 2:183)

Thomas BURTON[4] (Eliz. Winslow[3]) and Alice WADSWORTH, 10 May 1722, Duxbury

Isaac WINSLOW[3] and Sarah WENSLEY, 11 July 1700, Boston (MD 5:236)

Penelope WINSLOW[4] (Isaac[3]) and James WARREN[4] (James[3], Nath.[2]), Int. 27 Dec. 1723,
    Plymouth (MD 18:144)

Elizabeth WINSLOW[4] (Isaac[3]) and Benjamin MARSTON, 20 Nov, 1729

Edward WINSLOW[4] (Isaac[3]) and Hannah (HOWLAND[4]) Dyre, 10 Apr. 1741, Plymouth
    (MD 14:159)

Hannah HOWLAND[4] and 1st William DYRE, c1735

Patience MARSTON[5] (Eliz. Winslow[4]) and Elkanah WATSON, Int. 19 Oct. 1754, Plymouth
    (MD 25:52)

John WINSLOW[4] (Isaac[3]) and 1st Mary LITTLE[5] (Isaac[4-3], Anna Warren[2]), 16 Feb.
    1725/26 (NEHGR 4:302)

Isaac WINSLOW[5] (John[4]) and 1st Elizabeth STOCKBRIDGE[5] (Ruth Otis[5], Mercy Little[4],
    Ephraim[3], Anna Warren[2])

Isaac WINSLOW[5] and 2nd Frances GAY, 10 Jan. 1805

Pelham WINSLOW[5] (John[4]) and Joanna WHITE[6] (Gideon[5], Cornelius[4], Dan.[3],

MAYFLOWER INTER-MARRIAGES

The following marriage partners are listed alphabetically by male surname under each generation heading. With each set of names is the page number(s) where the marriage and line of descent can be found. There are undoubtedly many more inter-marriages in the files but they are either not shown as such, or the line of descent was not known. (The name of John Alden has been added here to provide a full representation of first-generation marriages.)

1st GENERATION

John ALDEN[1] and Priscilla MULLINS[2]

Isaac ALLERTON[1] and Fear BREWSTER[2] <22>

John HOWLAND[1] and Elizabeth TILLEY[2] <206>

2nd GENERATION

Jacob COOKE[2] and Damaris HOPKINS[2] <173>

John DOTY[2] and Elizabeth COOKE[3] <116,156>

John DOTY[2] and Sarah JONES[4] <6,15,116>

Samuel EATON[2] and Martha BILLINGTON[3] <36,164>

Caleb SAMSON[2] and Mercy STANDISH[3] <253>

Caleb SAMSON[2] and Rebecca BARTLETT[4] <253>

Alexander STANDISH[2] and Sarah ALDEN[2] <275>

Myles STANDISH[2] and Sarah WINSLOW[3] <105,280>

3rd GENERATION

Benjamin ALDEN[3] and Hannah BREWSTER[4] <1>

John ALDEN[3] and Susanna WINSLOW[4] <9>

Jonathan ALDEN[3] and Elizabeth ARNOLD[5] <10,105>

Benjamin BARTLETT[3] and Sarah BREWSTER[3] <70,305>

Ephraim BRADFORD[3] and Elizabeth BREWSTER[4] <43>

Israel BRADFORD[3] and Sarah BARTLETT[5] <45>

Samuel BRADFORD[3] and Hannah ROGERS[4] <49,243>

William BRADFORD^3 and Rebecca BARTLETT^4 <54>

Francis COOKE^3 and Elizabeth LATHAM^4 <107,118>

Elkanah CUSHMAN^3 and Martha COOKE^3 <23,116>

Isaac CUSHMAN and Rebecca HARLOW^4 <24>

Thomas CUSHMAN^3 and Abigail FULLER^4 <28,234>

Thomas CUSHMAN^3 and Ruth HOWLAND^2 <28,234>

Thomas DOTY^3 and Elizabeth HARLOW^5 <161>

Samuel EATON^3 and Elizabeth FULLER^3 <164,169)

Samuel FULLER^3 and Anne FULLER^3 <167>

Ezekiel HATCH^3 and Ruth CHURCH^5 <159>

Joseph HATCH^3 and Desire HAWES^4 <160,206>

Isaac HOWLAND^3 and Sarah THOMAS^4 <224,228>

Nathan HOWLAND^3 and Frances COOMBS^4 <224,238>

Samuel LITTLE^3 and Sarah GRAY^4 <103,294>

Joseph PETERSON^3 and Sarah JONES^4 <271>

William RING^3 and Hannah SHERMAN^3 <153,191>

James ROGERS^3 and Mary PAINE^4 <183,245>

John ROGERS^3 and Elizabeth PABODIE^3 <3,243>

Thomas ROGERS^3 and Elizabeth SNOW^3 <173,250>

Benjamin SAMSON^3 and Rebecca COOKE^4 <120,259>

John SAMSON^3 and Priscilla BARTLETT^5 <259>

Joseph SAMSON^3 and Sarah SAMSON^4 <258,278>

William SHERMAN^3 and Mercy WHITE^3 <153>

Benjamin SNOW^3 and Elizabeth ALDEN^3 <11,94>

Joseph SNOW^3 and Hopestill ALDEN^3 <11,95>

Benjamin SOULE^3 and Sarah STANDISH^3 <264,180>

James SOULE^3 and Lydia TOMSON^3 <266>

John SOULE^3 and Martha TINKHAM^4 <92,266>

Joseph SOULE^3 and Mary PETERSON^3 <267>

Moses SOULE^3 and Mercy SOUTHWORTH^4 <5,269>

Ebenezer SPROUT^3 and Experience HAWES^4 <206,225,239>

James SPROUT^3 and Elizabeth SOUTHWORTH^5 <103,256>

Ichabod STANDISH^3 and Phebe RING^4 <189,277>

Miles STANDISH^3 and Experience SHERMAN^3 <153,279>

Ephraim TINKHAM^3 and Esther WRIGHT^3 <91>

John TOMSON[3] and Mary TINKHAM[3] <149>

Thomas TOMSON[3] and Mary MORTON[4] <151,190>

James WARREN[3] and Sarah DOTY[3] <154>

4th GENERATION

Benjamin BARTLETT[4] and Ruth PABODIE[4] <7,306>

Ichabod BARTLETT[4] and Desire ARNOLD[5] <104,283,306>

Ichabod BARTLETT[4] and Elizabeth WATERMAN[4] <283,306>

Robert BARTLETT[4] and Sarah BARTLETT[4] <306,318>

Robert BARTLETT[4] and Sarah COOKE[3] <116,283,306>

Samuel BARTLETT[4] and Hannah PABODIE[3] <3,308>

John BAXTER[4] and Desire GORHAM[4] <213>

Shubael BAXTER[4] and Elizabeth GORHAM[4] <208,213>

Isaac BENNET[4] and Mary DREW[4] <15,224>

Joseph BENNET[4] and Thankful SPROUT[4] <224,255>

Caleb BLACKWELL[4] and Bethiah TABER[4] <329>

John BLACKWELL[4] and Lydia SKIFFE[4] <329>

Jonathan BOSWORTH[4] and Alice CUSHMAN[5] <216>

Nehemiah BOSWORTH[4] and Sarah TOMSON[4] <151,216>

Nehemiah BOSWORTH[4] and Susanna RING[4] <216>

John BOURN[4] and Mercy HINCKLEY[5] <218>

Silvanus BOURN[4] and Mercy GORHAM[4] <209,218>

Wrestling BREWSTER[4] and Deborah SEABURY[5] <72>

Wrestling BREWSTER[4] and Hannah THOMAS[5] <72>

Joseph BURSLEY[4] and Sarah CROCKER[4] <222,227>

Seth CHIPMAN[4] and Priscilla BRADFORD[4] <46,223>

John COB[4] and Mary CONANT[6] <270>

Jonathan COB[4] and Lydia THOMAS[4] <229>

James COBB[4] and Thankful THOMAS[4] <269>

Benjamin COOKE[4] and Mercy PAINE[5] <197>

Caleb COOKE[4] and Abigail HOWLAND[4] <116>

Francis COOKE[4] and Ruth SILVESTER[5] <118,190>

Robert COOKE[4] and Abigail HARLOW[5] <119,301>

James CROCKER[4] and Alice SWIFT[5] <227>

Nathan CROCKER[4] and Joanna BARSLEY[4] <222,226>

-343-

Benjamin CUSHMAN[4] and Sarah EATON[4] <28,162>

Isaac CUSHMAN[4] and Mercy BRADFORD[4] <25,47,85>

Isaac CUSHMAN[4] and Sarah GIBBS[4] <25,325>

Job CUSHMAN[4] and Lydia BREWSTER[4] <29>

Amaziah DELANO[4] and Ruth SAMSON[5] <15>

Lemuel DELANO[4] and Lydia BARTLETT[6] <15,306>

Stephen DOTEN[4] and Hannah BARTLETT[6] <157,315>

James DOTY[4] and Ruth FINNEY[5] <157>

Samuel DOTY[4] and Mary COOKE[5] <158>

Thomas DOTY[4] and Mary COOKE[5] <158>

John DREW[4] and Susanna BENNET[4] <15,224>

Thomas DREW[4] and Abigail HARRIS[6] <15>

Joseph DRINKWATER[4] and Jennet LATHAM[6] <272>

Barnabas EATON[4] and Mehitable ALDEN[4] <164>

Francis EATON[4] and Thankful ALDEN[4] <12>

John EATON[4] and Elizabeth FULLER[4] <163>

John FINNEY[4] and Sarah BARTLETT[5] <304,318>

John FINNEY[4] and Susanna DOTY[4] <158,304,319>

Ebenezer FULLER[4] and Joanna GRAY[5] <171>

Jabez FULLER[4] and Mercy GRAY[5] <105,171,264>

Jabez FULLER[4] and Mary HALLETT[4] <168,208>

Jabez FULLER[4] and Priscilla SAMSON[4] <170>

Jabez FULLER[4] and Deborah SOULE[4] <105,171,264>

John FULLER[4] and Lydia ALDEN[4] <13>

John FULLER[4] and Deborah RING[4] <172,189>

John FULLER[4] and Mercy WASHBURN[5] <35>

Shubael FULLER[4] and Hannah CROCKER[4] <227>

Ebenezer GORHAM[4] and Temperance HAWES[5] <209>

James GORHAM[4] and Mary JOYCE[4] <209>

Job GORHAM[4] and Desire DIMOCK[5] <210>

John GORHAM[4] and Prudence CROCKER[4] <210>

Shubael GORHAM[4] and Mary THACHER[4] <210>

William GREEN[4] and Desire BACON[5] <208,325>

William HARLOW[4] and Lydia CUSHMAN[3] <26,323>

Joseph HOPKINS[4] and Mary MAYO[5] <203>

Judah HOPKINS[4] and Hannah MAYO[5] <73,203>

Judah HOPKINS[4] and Hannah MAYO[5] <203>

Nathaniel HOPKINS[4] and Mercy MAYO[5] <204>

Job HOWLAND[4] and Hannah JENKINS[5] <228>

Thomas HUCKENS[4] and Rachel SNOW[4] <219>

Charles LITTLE[4] and Sarah WARREN[4] <291,326>

David LITTLE[4] and Elizabeth SOUTHWORTH[4] <7,286>

John LITTLE[4] and Constant FOBES[4] <4,286>

William LUCAS[4] and Mehitable DOTY[4] <305>

Joshua MERRICK[4] and Lydia MAYO[5] <74,191>

Stephen MERRICK[4] and Deborah SNOW[4] <192>

Thomas MORTON[4] and Hannah NELSON[5] <156,319>

Edward OAKMAN[4] and Sarah DOGGETT[5] <154>

Thomas OLDHAM[4] and Desire WORMALL[4] <256>

John PABODIE[4] and Rebecca GRAY[5] <286>

John PAINE[4] and Bennet FREEMAN[4] <76,181>

John PAINE[4] and Alice MAYO[5] <73,181>

Joseph PAINE[4] and Patience SPARROW[4] <75,182>

Nicholas PAINE[4] and Hannah HIGGINS[4] <183,244>

Samuel PAINE[4] and Patience FREEMAN[4] <85,183>

Jacob PETERSON[4] and Mary HARLOW[6] <271>

Reuben PETERSON[4] and Rebecca SIMMONS[5] <4,271>

Adam PICKET[4] and Hannah WETHERELL[4] <61,70>

Ebenezer RICHMOND[4] and Anna SPROAT[3] <240,255>

Andrew RING[4] and Zeruiah STANDISH[4] <189,277>

Samuel RING[4] and Ruth SILVESTER[5] <118,190>

Caleb ROGERS[4] and Mary HARLOW[6] <323>

Abraham SAMSON[4] and Penelope SAMSON[3] <258,277>

Anthony SAMSON[4] and Anna SAMSON[5] <254>

Charles SAMSON[4] and Mary CHURCH[5] <253,301>

Cornelius SAMSON[4] and Desire CROCKER[5] <259>

Ebenezer SAMSON[4] and Hannah HARLOW[6] <254>

Ebenezer SAMSON[4] and Zeruiah SOULE[4] <267,278>

Elijah SAMSON[4] and Ruth BRADFORD[5] <259>

John SAMSON[4] and Rebecca BREWSTER[5] <259>

John SAMSON[4] and Abigail STETSON[6] <259>

Peleg SAMSON[4] and Mary RING[4] <189,279>

Robert SHERMAN[4] and Mary OAKMAN[4] <155>

Benjamin SIMMONS[4] and Priscilla DELANO[4] <5,277>

Joshua SIMMONS[4] and Sarah DELANO[4] <4,277>

Moses SIMMONS[4] and Rachel SAMSON[3] <4>

William SIMMONS[4] and Abigail CHURCH[4] <6>

John SMITH[4] and Bethiah SNOW[4] <187,200>

Edward SNOW[4] and Sarah FREEMAN[5] <82,173>

Jonathan SNOW[4] and Sarah SOULE[4] <95>

William SNOW[4] and Mary WASHBURN[5] <96,125>

Aaron SOULE[4] and Orphan WATERMAN[5] <282>

Ezekiel SOULE[4] and Hannah DELANO[4] <267>

John SOULE[4] and Mabel PARTRIDGE[6] <267,285>

Jonathan SOULE[4] and Elizabeth GIFFORD[5] <114,272>

Micah SOULE[4] and Mercy SOUTHWORTH[5] <268>

Nathan SOULE[4] and Sarah SOUTHWORTH[6] <268>

Zachariah SOULE[4] and Mary EATON[4] <162,265>

Benjamin SOUTHWORTH[4] and Rebecca DELANO[4] <5,277>

Constant SOUTHWORTH[4] and Rebecca SIMMONS[4] <5>

Edward SOUTHWORTH[4] and Mary FOBES[4] <5>

Stephen SOUTHWORTH[4] and Lydia WARREN[5] <7>

Thomas SOUTHWORTH[4] and Sarah ALDEN[3] <5,11>

Robert SPROUT[4] and Hannah SAMSON[5] <260>

Robert SPROUT[4] and Hannah SOUTHWORTH[6] <104,256>

David STANDISH[4] and Hannah MAGOON[5] <280>

Moses STANDISH[4] and Rachel COBB[4] <269,276>

Thomas SWIFT[4] and Thankful MOREY[5] <147,320>

Thomas TABER[4] and Rebecca HARLOW[5] <321>

Thomas THACHER[4] and Thankful BAXTER[5] <211>

Naphtali THAYER[4] and Bathsheba BASS[4] <20>

Jedediah THOMAS[4] and Lois NELSON[5] <220,229>

Ebenezer TINKHAM[4] and Hannah HATCH[3] <90,159>

Ephraim TINKHAM[4] and Martha COBB[4] <92,270>

John TINKHAM[4] and Ann GRAY[5] <93>

John TINKHAM^4 and Hannah HOWLAND^3 <92,223>

Samuel TINKHAM^4 and Patience COBB^4 <92>

Amasa TOMSON^4 and Lydia COBB^5 <151>

Ebenezer TOMSON^4 and Mary WRIGHT^5 <151>

John TOMSON^4 and Elizabeth THOMAS^4 <149>

Reuben TOMSON^4 and Mary TOMSON^4 <148>

Thomas TOMSON^4 and Martha SOULE^4 <150,267>

Zebadiah TOMSON^4 and Zerviah STANDISH^5 <152>

Isaac TURNER^4 and Abigail HOLMES^5 <159>

Joseph WASHBURN^4 and Hannah LATHAM^4 <107,127>

Anthony WATERMAN^4 and Elizabeth ARNOLD^5 <10,105,283>

Joseph WATERMAN^4 and Lusanna SNOW^4 <282,284>

Benjamin WARREN^4 and Rebecca DOTY^4 <157,303>

James WARREN^4 and Penelope WINSLOW^4 <326,340>

Samuel WARREN^4 and Eleanor BILLINGTON^4 <328>

Nathan WESTON^4 and Desire STANDISH^3 <271>

Benjamin WHITE^4 and Faith OAKMAN^4 <154,333>

John WHITE^4 and Martha DOTY^3 <337>

William WHITE^4 and Elizabeth CADMAN^5 <140>

Edward WINSLOW^4 and Hannah HOWLAND^4 <232,340>

John WINSLOW^4 and Mary LITTLE^5 <291,340>

Josiah WOOD^4 and Mary SPROUT^4 <225,255>

Nathan WRIGHT^4 and Hannah COOKE^5 <115,120>

Joseph YOUNG^4 and Lydia BARRELL^6 <67,335>

5th GENERATION

David ALDEN^5 and Rhoda LEACH^7 <12>

Elijah ALDEN^5 and Mary ALDEN^6 <12>

Samuel ALDEN^5 and Hannah WILLIAMS^6 <243>

Benjamin ARNOLD^5 and Hannah BARTLETT^5 <105>

Edward ARNOLD^5 and Mercy BREWSTER^4 <105>

Eldad ATWOOD^5 and Margaret SNOW^5 <177>

Robert AVERY^5 and Anna CUSHMAN^5 <24,288>

John BACON^5 and Elizabeth FREEMAN^5 <82,208>

Jonathan BARNES^5 and Phebe FINNEY^4 <304,314>

Benjamin BARTLETT[5] and Lydia MORTON[4] <155,313>

Jonathan BARTLETT[5] and Thankful BARNES[5] <311,314>

Joseph BARTLETT[5] and Elizabeth BARTLETT[5] <313>

Joseph BARTLETT[5] and Sarah MORTON[4] <156,315>

Joseph BARTLETT[5] and Jane SWIFT[5] <146,311>

Joseph BARTLETT[5] and Dorothy WADSWORTH[5] <7,306>

Lemuel BARTLETT[5] and Mary DOTY[4] <157>

Robert BARTLETT[5] and Rebecca WOOD[4] <225,315>

Ebenezer BARROWS[5] and Sarah PRATT[5] <238,239>

Joseph BATES[5] and Eunice TINKHAM[6] <94>

Cornelius BENNET[5] and Ruth GORHAM[4] <239>

Samuel BENNET[5] and Anna BENNET[5] <224>

Ichabod BOSWORTH[5] and Lydia STANDISH[5] <216>

Eliphalet BRADFORD[5] and Hannah PRINCE[6] <47>

Gamiel BRADFORD[5] and Sarah ALDEN[4] <49>

James BRADFORD[5] and Zerviah THOMAS[5] <48>

John BRADFORD[5] and Elizabeth HOLMES[6] <47>

Josiah BRADFORD[5] and Hannah RIDER[6] <56>

Paybodie BRADFORD[5] and Welthea DELANO[6] <49>

Robert BRADFORD[5] and Sarah STETSON[5] <71>

Samuel BRADFORD[5] and Grace RING[5] <49,190>

Seth BRADFORD[5] and Lydia SOUTHWORTH[6] <49>

William BRADFORD[5] and Mary CLEAVELAND[6] <54>

Isaac BREWSTER[5] and Leonice SOULE[5] <72>

Lemuel BREWSTER[5] and Abigail BREWSTER[5] <71>

William BREWSTER[5] and Priscilla SAMPSON[4] <71>

George BROWN[5] and Alice FREEMAN[6] <177,181>

Joseph BURSLEY[5] and Bethiah FULLER[5] <227>

Barnabas CANEDY[5] and Elizabeth BARNABY[6] <165>

Israel CARVER[5] and Margaret SHERMAN[5] <153>

Freedom CHAMBERLAIN[5] and Deborah TURNER[6] <263>

Job CHAMBERLAIN[5] and Rachel BONNEY[4] <264>

Seth CHIPMAN[5] and Sarah RIPLEY[5] <223>

Joseph CHURCH[5] and Grace DWELLEY[6] <62,301>

John CLAPP[5] and Mercy OTIS[5] <287>

Nathaniel CLAP[5] and Desire BOURN[5] <218>

James COBB[5] and Susanna TINKHAM[5] <270>

John COBB[5] and Priscilla TINKHAM[5] <91,270>

Gershom COLE[5] and Mary ROGERS[5] <186,247>

Charles CONET[5] and Joanna BURSLEY[5] <226,231>

Benjamin COOKE[5] and Mary GRAY[6] <105,118>

Charles COOKE[5] and Hannah FAUNCE[5] <119>

Josiah COOKE[5] and Hannah SPARROW[5] <75,198>

Nathaniel COOKE[5] and Mary SAMSON[5] <119,279>

Allerton CUSHMAN[5] and Alethea SOULE[4] <23,267>

Elkanah CUSHMAN[5] and Lydia BRADFORD[4] <24,40>

Elkanah CUSHMAN[5] and Hannah STANDISH[5] <24>

Isaiah CUSHMAN[5] and Sarah RING[5] <190>

Joshua CUSHMAN[5] and Mary SOULE[4] <29>

Robert CUSHMAN[5] and Mercy WASHBURN[5] <29,35>

Thomas CUSHMAN[5] and Anna CHIPMAN[5] <29,222>

Thomas CUSHMAN[5] and Mehitable FAUNCE[5] <29>

Thomas CUSHMAN[5] and Alice HAYWARD[5] <29>

William CUSHMAN[5] and Priscilla TINKHAM[5] <25,91,270>

Nathan DARLING[5] and Martha BENNET[5] <149,224>

Joshua DELANO[5] and Hopestill PETERSON[4] <4>

Peleg DELANO[5] and Sarah SAMSON[4] <258>

Timothy DIMMICK[5] and Desire DIMMICK[4] <48>

Ebenezer DOTEN[5] and Mary RICKARD[6] <158>

Thomas DREW[5] and Lucy TOMSON[5] <15>

Samuel EATON[5] and Patience TINKHAM[5] <92,164>

Nathan EDDY[5] and Eunice SAMSON[5] <13>

Luke ELLIS[5] and Elizabeth MACOMBER[6] <93,242>

Josiah FINNEY[5] and Alice BARNES[6] <304>

Michael FORD[5] and Orphan WATERMAN[5] <282>

Samuel FOSDICK[5] and Susanna TURNER[5] <64,70>

Benjamin FREEMAN[5] and Temperance DIMOCK[5] <82>

Edmund FREEMAN[5] and Lois PAINE[5] <75>

Jonathan FREEMAN[5] and Mercy BRADFORD[4] <47,85>

Joseph FREEMAN[5] and Lydia THACHER[4] <85>

Thomas FREEMAN[5] and Bathsheba MAYO[5] <73,87>

Amos FULLER[5] and Abigail HARLOW[6] <172>

Amos FULLER[5] and Rachel STANDISH[5] <276>

Ebenezer FULLER[5] and Lydia CHIPMAN[5] <171>

Issacher FULLER[5] and Elizabeth DOTEN[5] <172>

Issacher FULLER[5] and Lucy TINKHAM[6] <172>

Jabez FULLER[5] and Lucy LORING[5] <170>

James FULLER[5] and Temperance PHINNEY[5] <167>

John FULLER[5] and Martha FULLER[6] <170>

Josiah FULLER[5] and Lydia CUSHMAN[6] <171>

Samuel FULLER[5] and Ruth CROCKER[4] <167,222>

Benjamin GODFREE[5] and Elizabeth HOPKINS[5] <200>

George GODFREY[5] and Mercy KNOWLES[6] <84,197>

Edward GRAY[5] and Elizabeth PABODIE[4] <286>

Eleazer HARLOW[5] and Hannah DELANO[4] <15,321>

Nathaniel HARLOW[5] and Patience LUCAS[4] <301,305>

William HARLOW[5] and Mercy RIDER[5] <323,324>

Isaac HARRIS[5] and Jane COOKE[4] <110,116>

Isaac HATCH[5] and Sarah HATCH[5] <160>

Isaac HATCH[5] and Abigail WRIGHT[6] <277>

Jethro HATHAWAY[5] and Hannah WEST[5] <142>

Thomas HATHAWAY[5] and Lois TABER[5] <142,150>

Samuel HIGGINS[5] and Mehitable PHINNEY[5] <244,286>

Edmund HINCKLEY[5] and Sarah HOWLAND[5] <228,230>

Isaac HINCKLEY[5] and Hannah BOURN[5] <218>

Silvanus HINCKLEY[5] and Sarah PHINNEY[6] <230,250>

Elisha HOLMES[5] and Sarah BARTLETT[5] <308,318>

George HOLMES[5] and Lydia WEST[6] <169>

Jonathan HOLMES[5] and Mary WATERMAN[5] <71>

Joseph HOLMES[5] and Rebecca WATERMAN[5] <71>

Micah HOLMES[5] and Rebecca BRADFORD[6] <72>

Caleb HOPKINS[5] and Thankful PAINE[7] <196>

Constant HOPKINS[5] and Phebe PAINE[6] <193>

Isaac HOPKINS[5] and Lydia NEWCOMB[6] <195>

John HOPKINS[5] and Lydia SNOW[6] <196>

Joshua HOPKINS[5] and Rebecca SPARROW[6] <200>

Prence HOPKINS[5] and Patience SNOW[6] <203>

Samuel HOPKINS[5] and Mehitable SNOW[6] <179,204>

Simeon HOPKINS[5] and Betty COBB[6] <195>

Caleb JENNE[5] and Patience STANDISH[4] <279,329>

Joseph JOHNSON[5] and Mary RING[5] <116,190>

Amos JONES[5] and Naomi PHILLIPS[6] <294>

John JONES[5] and Ruth HATCH[4] <160,294>

Nathaniel KEEN[5] and Thankful WINSLOW[5] <286>

Ebenezer KING[5] and Mercy MYRICK[5] <187,192>

Joseph LATHROP[5] and Content WASHBURN[6] <126>

Isaac LeBARON[5] and Martha HOWLAND[5] <40>

John LEWIS[5] and Mercy HOPKINS[5] <219>

Fobes LITTLE[5] and Sarah BAKER[5] <287>

Isaac LITTLE[5] and Sarah CHURCH[5] <292>

Isaac LITTLE[5] and Lydia HATCH[5] <291>

John LITTLE[5] and Mary SAMSON[4] <253,287>

Lemuel LITTLE[5] and Penelope EAMES[5] <155,287>

Otis LITTLE[5] and Elizabeth HOWLAND[4] <225,292>

Thomas LITTLE[5] and Sarah BAKER[5] <287>

John LUCAS[5] and Lydia DOTY[4] <305>

Joseph MACOMBER[5] and Thankful CANEDY[5] <165>

Thomas MACOMBER[5] and Mercy TILDEN[5] <91,257>

John MAYO[5] and Susanna FREEMAN[5] <81>

Jonathan MAYO[5] and Thankful TWINING[5] <73>

Joseph MAYO[5] and Abigail MYRICK[5] <81>

Judah MAYO[5] and Mary HAMILTON[5] <74,202>

Francis MILLER[5] and Experience HAWES[4] <206,239,255>

John MILLER[5] and Priscilla BENNETT[4] <224,239>

Benjamin MOREY[5] and Thankful SWIFT[4] <146,320>

Ebenezer MORTON[5] and Sarah COBB[5] <191>

John MORTON[5] and Elizabeth BENNET[5] <191,224>

Josiah MORTON[5] and Maletiah FINNEY[5] <250>

Constant MYRICK[5] and Sarah FREEMAN[6] <82,191>

John NELSON[5] and Mary MORTON[4] <155,319>

-351-

Robert NEWCOMB[5] and Mary YOUNG[5] <245>

Ebenezer NICKERSON[5] and Elizabeth MAYO[5] <81,178>

Samuel OAKMAN[5] and Deborah TURNER[6] <155>

Tobias OAKMAN[5] and Olive LITTLE[6] <154>

Tobias OAKMAN[5] and Ruth LITTLE[5] <155,156>

James OTIS[5] and Ruth CUNNINGHAM[6] <106,156>

Ebenezer PAINE[5] and Hannah HOPKINS[4] <183,200>

Joshua PAINE[5] and Constance PAINE[5] <185>

Joshua PAINE[5] and Phebe SNOW[5] <184,189>

Thomas PAINE[5] and Phebe FREEMAN[6] <182>

Tobias PAYNE[5] and Sarah WINSLOW[5] <106,280,283>

Ebenezer PHINNEY[5] and Rebecca BARNES[5] <55,248>

John PHINNEY[5] and Ruth SILVESTER[5] <190,250>

Pelatiah PHINNEY[5] and Mercy WASHBURN[6] <250>

John PRATT[5] and Elizabeth TURNER[4] <159,238>

Samuel PRATT[5] and Jerusha CONANT[6] <238>

Seth PRATT[5] and Hannah WASHBURN[7] <95>

Ebenezer REED[5] and Hannah TOMSON[4] <148>

Robert RICHMOND[5] and Martha WASHBURN[5] <125>

William RICHMOND[5] and Anna GRAY[5] <244>

Benjamin RIDER[5] and Patience HOWLAND[5] <303>

Ebenezer RIDER[5] and Thankful SILVESTER[5] <313,324>

John RIDER[5] and Mary DREW[6] <314,324>

Samuel RIDER[5] and Mary SILVESTER[5] <311,324>

Nathaniel RIPLEY[5] and Ann RIPLEY[5] <44>

William RIPLEY[5] and Lydia RING[5] <190,216>

Benjamin ROGERS[5] and Phebe HARDING[5] <246>

Ebenezer ROGERS[5] and Hannah COOK[5] <246>

Elkanah ROGERS[5] and Mercy GODFREY[6] <247>

James ROGERS[5] and Hannah GODFREY[6] <245>

Jonathan ROGERS[5] and Elizabeth COOK[5] <246>

Judah ROGERS[5] and Patience COLE[5] <186,247>

Thomas ROGERS[5] and Rebecca HIGGINS[5] <245>

Zabdiel SAMPSON[5] and Abigail CUSHMAN[5] <28,265>

Gideon SAMSON[5] and Abigail CUSHMAN[5] <265>

Noah SAMSON^5 and Jemima RIDER^6 <104,278>

Stephen SAMSON^5 and Deborah LOTHROP^6 <278>

David SEARS^5 and Phebe TAYLOR^6 <1>

William SEVER^5 and Sarah WARREN^5 <326>

Joseph SILVESTER^5 and Mary HOLMES^5 <316>

Joseph SILVESTER^5 and Mercy HOLMES^5 <312>

Benjamin SIMMONS^5 and Fear SAMSON^5 <5>

Ichabod SIMMONS^5 and Lydia SOULE^4 <6>

Jedidiah SIMMONS^5 and Lydia SOULE^5 <4>

Nathaniel SIMMONS^5 and Mercy SIMMONS^5 <4>

Joseph SMITH^5 and Mary HOPKINS^4 <200,202>

Samuel SMITH^5 and Abigail FREEMAN^5 <81,202>

Samuel SMITH^5 and Sarah WINSLOW^5 <106,202,283>

Solomon SMITH^5 and Susanna SNOW^5 <176>

Ambrose SNOW^5 and Elizabeth PAINE^6 <174>

Anthony SNOW^5 and Sarah PAINE^6 <175>

Elkins SNOW^5 and Susanna WALKER^6 <177,187>

Isaac SNOW^5 and Elizabeth BOWDITCH^5 <95>

Jabez SNOW^5 and Elizabeth LEWIS^5 <179>

Jabez SNOW^5 and Elizabeth PAINE^5 <173>

Jesse SNOW^5 and Lois FREEMAN^6 <76,189>

John SNOW^5 and Hannah MYRICK^5 <189,191>

Jonathan SNOW^5 and Thankful FREEMAN^5 <76,178>

Joseph SNOW^5 and Mary SEARS^5 <173,192>

Micajah SNOW^5 and Elizabeth FREEMAN^6 <189>

Samuel SNOW^5 and Elizabeth FREEMAN^6 <174>

Samuel SNOW^5 and Mary HOPKINS^5 <179,204>

Samuel SNOW^5 and Deborah TINKHAM^5 <95>

Silvanus SNOW^5 and Mehitable WALKER^6 <174>

Stephen SNOW^5 and Rebecca SNOW^5 <177>

Thomas SNOW^5 and Abigail DOANE^6 <188>

Thomas SNOW^5 and Sarah YOUNG^5 <176>

Asa SOULE^5 and Olive SOUTHWORTH^6 <268>

Ezekiel SOULE^5 and Clynthia WADSWORTH^6 <268>

Isaac SOULE^5 and Lydia TOMSON^5 <266>

Jabez SOULE[5] and Abigail BENNET[5] <266>

James SOULE[5] and Mary WHITE[7] <263>

Joshua SOULE[5] and Mary CUSHMAN[6] <268>

Josiah SOULE[5] and Alice SOULE[6] <269>

William SOULE[5] and Priscilla SAMSON[5] <268>

Nathaniel SOUTHWORTH[5] and Jael HOWLAND[3] <104>

Caleb STURTEVANT[5] and Patience CUSHMAN[5] <119>

Ephraim STURTEVANT[5] and Lydia RING[4] <189, 293>

Isaac STURTEVANT[5] and Sarah FULLER[5] <24,172>

Jirah SWIFT[5] and Deborah HATHAWAY[5] <325>

Joseph SWIFT[5] and Sarah BARTLETT[5] <146>

Zephaniah SWIFT[5] and Lydia CHIPMAN[4] <221, 325>

William TABER[5] and Hannah WHITE[6] <139>

John TAYLOR[5] and Phebe HIGGINS[6] <200,205>

William TAYLOR[5] and Faith WINSLOW[5] <101>

Anthony THOMAS[5] and Abigail ALDEN[4] <10,284>

Ebenezer THOMAS[5] and Joanna CUSHMAN[6] <228>

Francis THOMPSON[5] and Rebecca SNOW[5] <150>

Nathaniel THOMPSON[5] and Hannah THOMAS[5] <149>

Ephraim TINKHAM[5] and Sarah STANDISH[5] <92, 276>

Jeremiah TINKHAM[5] and Naomi WARREN[5] <90>

Nathan TINKHAM[5] and Sarah SOULE[5] <92,265>

Seth TINKHAM[5] and Eunice SOULE[5] <94,265>

Adam TOMSON[5] and Molly TOMSON[5] <148>

Jacob TOMSON[5] and Freelove PHINNEY[6] <149>

Thomas TOMSON[5] and Jane WASHBURN[6] <149>

Ezekiel TURNER[5] and Borodel DENISON[5] <64>

Jesse TURNER[5] and Grace DWELLY[6] <301>

John TURNER[5] and Mercy BARTLETT[5] <62,306>

Peleg WADSWORTH[5] and Lusanna SAMPSON[4] <7>

Edward WASHBURN[5] and Elizabeth RICHMOND[5] <125>

Ephraim WASHBURN[5] and Eglah STETSON[5] <71>

Jabez WASHBURN[5] and Judith FAUNCE[5] <36,120>

Jonathan WASHBURN[5] and Rebecca PERRY[5] <129>

Josiah WASHBURN[5] and Sarah RICHMOND[5] <126>

Moses WASHBURN[5] and Hannah CUSHMAN[5] <126>

Thomas WASHBURN[5] and Elizabeth HOWLAND[4] <132>

John WATERMAN[5] and Fear STURTEVANT[5] <22,24>

Robert WATERMAN[5] and Martha CUSHMAN[5] <26>

Samuel WATERMAN[5] and Mary TOMSON[4] <26>

Thomas WATERMAN[5] and Mercy FREEMAN[6] <26>

Edmund WESTON[5] and Mary TINKHAM[5] <270>

William WESTON[5] and Mary WESTON[7] <270>

Abijah WHITE[5] and Anna LITTLE[5] <287,334>

Benjamin WHITE[5] and Mercy THOMAS[5] <333>

Gideon WHITE[5] and Joanna HOWLAND[4] <334>

Amos WHITMAN[5] and Anna WASHBURN[7] <11>

Jeremiah WILCOX[5] and Judith BRIGGS[5] <138>

Isaac WINSLOW[5] and Elizabeth STOCKBRIDGE[5] <340>

Job WINSLOW[5] and Elizabeth MACOMBER[5] <91>

Pelham WINSLOW[5] and Joanna WHITE[6] <340>

Moses WOOD[5] and Lydia WATERMAN[6] <92>

Adam WRIGHT[5] and Sarah STANDISH[5] <92,114,276>

Joseph WRIGHT[5] and Sarah BREWSTER[5] <114>

Samuel WRIGHT[5] and Abigail STANDISH[5] <115>

Daniel YOUNG[5] and Lydia PAINE[5] <177,183>

Ezekiel YOUNG[5] and Lusanna WHITE[6] <335>

6th GENERATION

Jabez ADAMS[6] and Lucy SWIFT[7] <40>

Nathan ALDEN[6] and Sarah BARRELL[7] <11,67>

John AVERY[6] and Hannah SNOW[6] <175,288>

Benjamin BARNES[6] and Deborah HOLMES[7] <54>

Isaac BARNES[6] and Lucy HARLOW[7] <55,324>

Joseph BARNES[6] and Hannah RIDER[7] <318>

William BARNES[6] and Mercy LEMOTE[6] <35,318>

John BARROWS[6] and Sarah MORTON[6] <191,239>

Hezekiah BARSTOW[6] and Olive BRADFORD[6] <54>

Ichabod BARTLET[6] and Desire OTIS[5] <307>

John BARTLET[6] and Susanna SOUTHWORTH[6] <307>

George BARTLETT[6] and Sarah CHURCHILL[7] <315>

John BARTLETT[6] and Sarah BARTLETT[6] <308>

Nathaniel BARTLETT[6] and Lydia BARNES[6] <311>

Nathaniel BARTLETT[6] and Mercy OTIS[5] <308>

Thomas BARTLETT[6] and Betty BARTLETT[7] <315>

William BARTLETT[6] and Mary BARTLETT[6] <308>

Gideon BEARSE[6] and Abigail RIPLEY[6] <72>

Branch BLACKMER[6] and Sarah WAITE[6] <316>

Gideon BRADFORD[6] and Abigail SAMPSON[6] <47>

Oliver BRADFORD[6] and Sarah CHIPMAN[6] <47>

John BURSLEY[6] and Mary HOWLAND[5] <227,229>

Barnabas CHURCHILL[6] and Lydia HOLMES[6] <312,323>

Eleazer CHURCHILL[6] and Sarah HARLOW[6] <315>

Josiah CHURCHILL[6] and Patience HARLOW[6] <314>

Zadock CHURCHILL[6] and Bathsheba RIDER[7] <55>

Eleazer COBB[6] and Keziah CROSBY[7] <84>

Amos COOKE[6] and Eunice EATON[5] <118,163>

Robert COOKE[6] and Lydia ADAMS[6] <119>

Apollos CUSHMAN[6] and Eleanor KEEN[6] <29,285>

Noah CUSHMAN[6] and Mercy SOULE[6] <25>

Noah CUSHMAN[6] and Zilpha THOMPSON[6] <25>

William DAVIE[6] and Lydia HARLOW[7] <117,322>

Joseph DAVIS[6] and Mary BACON[6] <208,210>

Thomas DIMOCK[6] and Elizabeth BACON[6] <208,212>

Jacob DINGLEY[6] and Susanna FULLER[5] <72>

Lemuel DREW[6] and Priscilla WARREN[5] <305,314>

Thomas FAUNCE[6] and Sarah BARTLETT[6] <315,319>

Joshua FOBES[6] and Esther PORTER[5] <295>

Michael FORD[6] and Rhoda COPELAND[5] <19,282>

Isaac FOSTER[6] and Hannah SEARS[5] <83>

Eleazer FREEMAN[6] and Ruth KNOWLES[7] <173>

Eleazer FREEMAN[6] and Elizabeth SNOW[6] <85,173>

James FREEMAN[6] and Mary FREEMAN[6] <87>

Joseph FREEMAN[6] and Phebe PAINE[6] <84>

Prince FREEMAN[6] and Martha FREEMAN[6] <84>

Chipman FULLER[6] and Thankful WRIGHT[6] <171>

Jabez FULLER[6] and Hannah PRATT[6] <168>

John GRAY[6] and Desire CUSHMAN[6] <105>

Elijah GUSHEE[6] and Phebe MACOMBER[7] <275>

Abraham HAMMETT[6] and Priscilla LeBARON[5] <40,231>

Amaziah HARLOW[6] and Lois DOTEN[4] <322>

Eleazer HARLOW[6] and Abigail THOMAS[5] <321>

Isaac HARLOW[6] and Jerusha FINNEY[5] <304,324>

John HARLOW[6] and Mary RYDER[5] <55,322>

Jonathan HARLOW[6] and Sarah HOLMES[6] <334>

Samuel HARLOW[6] and Mercy BRADFORD[5] <323>

Gilbert HATHAWAY[6] and Elizabeth WILLIAMS[6] <52,243>

Nathan HAYWARD[6] and Susanna LATHAM[6] <130>

Freeman HIGGINS[6] and Thankful HOPKINS[5] <80,184,193>

Ichabod HIGGINS[6] and Bethiah KNOWLES[7] <73,84>

Thomas HIGGINS[6] and Abigail PAINE[5] <79>

Bartlett HOLMES[6] and Lucy BARTLETT[6] <316>

Elnathan HOLMES[6] and Bathsheba HOLMES[6] <316>

Nathaniel HOLMES[6] and Chloe SEARS[6] <249>

John HOPKINS[6] and Priscilla BROWN[7] <196>

Jonathan HOPKINS[6] and Mary FREEMAN[7] <203>

Benjamin JAMES[6] and Mercy STOCKBRIDGE[5] <64>

Samuel JONES[6] and Thankful HATCH[7] <294>

Amos KNOWLES[6] and Abigail PEPPER[6] <84,182>

Enos KNOWLES[6] and Sarah SPARROW[5] <84>

Simeon KNOWLES[6] and Eunice MAYO[6] <182>

Nehemiah LATHAM[6] and Lucy HARRIS[7] <108>

Paul LEONARD[6] and Mary RYDER[7] <241>

John LEWIS[6] and Deborah PHINNEY[6] <213,248>

Elkanah LINNELL[6] and Mary SPARROW[6] <192,205>

George LITTLE[6] and Abigail SOULE[5] <264,292>

James LITTLE[6] and Lydia YOUNG[6] <287,336>

Nathaniel LITTLE[6] and Pamela BRADFORD[6] <291,292>

Thomas MACOMBER[6] and Prudence STETSON[6] <91>

Asa MAYO[6] and Experience YATES[5] <75,245>

Moses MAYO[6] and Phebe FREEMAN[8] <81>

John MILLER[6] and Zilpah TINKHAM[5] <92,239>

Eleazer MORTON[6] and Lucy DOTY[5] <191>

Samuel NELSON[6] and Charity HASKELL[7] <220>

Melzar Turner OAKMAN[6] and Louisa OAKMAN[6] <155>

Ebenezer PAINE[6] and Thankful WHITE[5] <184,334>

Elisha PAINE[6] and Thankful HOPKINS[5] <184,193>

Isaac PAINE[6] and Abigail SNOW[6] <184,188>

Nathaniel PAINE[6] and Phebe MAYO[6] <74>

Solomon PEPPER[6] and Abiel HOPKINS[5] <182,193>

Joseph PERKINS[6] and Sarah CUSHMAN[6] <24>

Luke PERKINS[6] and Hannah HARLOW[6] <264>

Eli PHINNEY[6] and Mary PHINNEY[6] <249>

Benejah PRATT[6] and Lovica WARREN[7] <224>

Kimball PRINCE[6] and Deborah FULLER[5] <69>

Thomas PRINCE[6] and Lydia DELANO[6] <70>

Micah REED[6] and Deborah TOMSON[5] <151>

Erastus RICHARDS[6] and Betty Doty SHERMAN[5] <5>

Eleazer RICHMOND[6] and Deborah BARROW[6] <239>

Eliakim RICHMOND[6] and Sarah HACKETT[5] <240>

Ebenezer RIDER[6] and Sarah RIDER[6] <324>

Elkanah ROGERS[6] and Tamsin SNOW[6] <247>

Joseph ROGERS[6] and Abigail TWINING[6] <247>

Richard ROGERS[6] and Sarah HIGGINS[6] <246>

Gideon SAMPSON[6] and Lydia RIPLEY[6] <265>

David SEARS[6] and Mercy SNOW[5] <86>

Prince SEARS[6] and Betsey HALL[7] <207>

Consider SIMMONS[6] and Aphelia SOULE[5] <6,268>

Joseph SIMMONS[6] and Elizabeth CHAMBERLIN[6] <264>

Abner SILVESTER[6] and Jedidah HARLOW[6] <312>

Abner SILVESTER[6] and Abigail WASHBURN[6] <312>

Thomas SMITH[6] and Ruth MAYO[6] <73>

David SNOW[6] and Mary COLE[6] <179>

Elnathan SNOW[6] and Phebe SPARROW[6] <188>

Ephraim SNOW[6] and Martha ROGERS[6] <189>

Joseph SNOW[6] and Priscilla BERRY[7] <173>

Prince SNOW[6] and Reliance PAINE[7] <184,189>

Reuben SNOW[6] and Reliance WING[7] <173>

Daniel SOULE[6] and Sarah CUSHMAN[6] <24,266>

Daniel SOULE[6] and Lucy SAMPSON[6] <23,266,279>

Isaac SPARROW[6] and Rebecca KNOWLES[6] <76,182>

Theophilus STETSON[6] and Abigail PRINCE[7] <70>

Simeon STURTEVANT[6] and Ruth TOMSON[5] <24>

Joseph SYLVESTER[6] and Susanna BLACKMER[6] <312,317>

Jeduthan TABER[6] and Patience JENNEY[6] <150>

Elisha TINKHAM[6] and Reliance RICHMOND[7] <90>

Elisha TINKHAM[6] and Sarah RICHMOND[7] <90>

Levi TINKHAM[6] and Mary FOSTER[6] <92,155>

Elisha TURNER[6] and Prudence JAMES[7] <62>

Jabez VAUGHAN[6] and Lois SOULE[5] <25,265>

Amasa WADE[6] and Sarah LOUD[6] <108>

Samuel WALKER[6] and Rebecca FREEMAN[6] <181,187>

Benjamin WASHBURN[6] and Mary CUSHMAN[5] <131>

Eleazer WAHSBURN[6] and Anna ALDEN[5] <131>

John WASHBURN[6] and Lydia PRINCE[6] <36>

Nathaniel WASHBURN[6] and Mary PRATT[5] <126>

Anthony WATERMAN[6] and Deborah FOSTER[5] <283>

Freeman WATERMAN[6] and Joanna TOMSON[5] <149>

Ichabod WATERMAN[6] and Hannah ROGERS[6] <26,146>

Isaac WATERMAN[6] and Lucy SAMPSON[6] <22,279>

Thomas WATERMAN[6] and Joanna TOMSON[5] <26>

Abner WESTON[6] and Huldah WASHBURN[7] <270>

Lewis WESTON[6] and Lucy CHURCHILL[7] <270>

William WESTON[6] and Mary CHURCHILL[7] <270>

William WHITE[6] and Mercy SEARS[7] <338>

Levi WRIGHT[6] and Betty WEST[7] <114,285>

Nehemiah YOUNG[6] and Abigail TAYLOR[7] <186,205>

7th GENERATION

Nehemiah ALLEN[7] and Abiah THOMAS[5] <229>

Uriah ATKINS[7] and Deborah ATWOOD[7] <186>

Ebenezer BANGS[7] and Elizabeth GRAY[6] <79,86>

Joshua BARELL[7] and Olive BASS[6] <67>

Henry BARTLETT[7] and Clarissa HARLOW[7] <311>

Joseph BARTLETT[7] and Lucy Foster BRADFORD[6] <49>

Scotto BERRY[7] and Hannah MAYO[7] <82>

John Clark BINGHAM[7] and Silence HARLOW[8] <44>

Luther BRADFORD[7] and Mary STANDISH[7] <47>

Zabdiel BRADFORD[7] and Mary STANDISH[7] <47>

Darius BREWSTER[7] and Esther SOULE[5] <268>

Cyrenus BROWN[7] and Eleanor COOK[7] <257>

Eleazer CHURCHILL[7] and Abigail BARTLETT[6] <315>

Seth CHURCHILL[7] and Elizabeth SYLVESTER[7] <323>

Solomon CHURCHILL[7] and Elizabeth BARTLETT[7] <312>

Robert COOKE[7] and Judith ADAMS[7] <119>

Richard COOPER[7] and Hannah SAMSON[5] <104,254>

Hercules CUSHMAN[7] and Mary WASHBURN[8] <25>

Thomas DAVIE[7] and Betsey BARNES[7] <117>

William DAVIE[7] and Experience STETSON[7] <117>

Abner DAVIS[7] and Nancy COBB[7] <210>

John Foye DISER[7] and Anna SWAN[7] <106>

Isaac FOSTER[7] and Sarah THATCHER[5] <83>

Seth FOSTER[7] and Sarah COBB[7] <83>

Isaac FREEMAN[7] and Elizabeth COB[6] <85>

John FREEMAN[7] and Abigail HOPKINS[6] <76>

Watson FREEMAN[7] and Thankful FREEMAN[7] <85>

Nathan FULLER[7] and Faith SOULE[6] <171>

Thomas GOODWIN[7] and Desire RYDER[7] <313>

Amaziah HARLOW[7] and Martha ALBERTSON[7] <322>

Ansell HARLOW[7] and Hannah BARTLETT[6] <317>

Ezra HARLOW[7] and Susanna WARREN[5] <322>

Jonathan HARLOW[7] and Betty BLACKMER[6] <316,324>

Job HASKELL[7] and Elizabeth HAMMOND[5] <220>

Nathaniel HOLMES[7] and Asenath CHANDLER[7] <7>

Samuel Badger HOPKINS^7 and Lydia Thacher FOSTER^9 <203>

John JAMES^7 and Sarah TILDEN^5 <67,257>

Levi JENNEY^7 and Susanna PROCTOR^6 <13,239>

Howland KEEN^7 and Fanny SOULE^7 <285>

Lewis L. KEITH^7 and Asaba CHURCHILL^8 <11>

Barzillai LATHAM^7 and Mary WASHBURN^7 <108>

Elias LATHAM^7 and Lucy LATHAM^7 <108>

Levi LUCAS^7 and Betsey BARNES^7 <117,305>

Asa MAYO^7 and Sally SEABURY^6 <82>

Thomas NEWCOMB^7 and Jemima NEWCOMB^6 <198>

George Alexander OTIS^7 and Lucinda SMITH^7 <288>

Paul PRINCE^7 and Sarah SOUTHWORTH^6 <67>

Ezekiel RIDER^7 and Polly HOLMES^8 <146>

William SHAW^7 and Lydia SOULE^5 <266>

Thomas SMITH^7 and Urania WRIGHT^6 <73,114>

Isaac SNOW^7 and Hannah FREEMAN^7 <188>

Isaiah SNOW^7 and Christian COAN^7 <176,180>

Larkin SNOW^7 and Nancy WILLIS^9 <109,176>

Richard SPARROW^7 and Elizabeth PAINE^6 <76>

Ellis STANDISH^7 and Mary BRADFORD <277>

Levi STURTEVANT^7 and Mary CHAMBERLAIN^6 <25,263>

Nathaniel TURNER^7 and Sarah JAMES^8 <62,66>

William TURNER^7 and Eunice CLAPP^6 <67>

Eleazer WASHBURN^7 and Sarah SOUTHWORTH^7 <131>

Harvey WESTON^7 and Sally CHURCHILL^8 <270>

Gorham WOOD^7 and Elizabeth SPARROW^7 <239>

8th GENERATION

Elisha Lothrop AVERY^8 and Sarah COIT^8 <64>

William BASSETT^8 and Abiah WILLIAMS^6 <302>

Richard COOPER^8 and Hannah SAMSON^6 <104>

Charles Henry DAVIS^8 and Harriet Blake MILLS^7 <212,221>

Zenas HARDEN^8 and Sally GANNETT^8 <33>

Ambrose HAYWARD^8 and Hannah HOWLAND^7 <10>

Robert KNOWLES^8 and Lydia KNOWLES^7 <187>

Sampson WASHBURN[8] and Rebecca SOULE[6] <131>

9th GENERATION

William T. FREEMAN[9] and Letitia FREEMAN[9] <88>

Solomon HIGGINS[9] and Olive Smith SPARROW[9] <201>

Elisha YOUNG[9] and Betsy SPARKS[8] <199>

11th GENERATION

Henry H. FREEMAN[11] and Caroline S. WESSON[11] <85>

Barrell (cont-d)
Samuel, 68
Sarah, 11, 66, 67, 355
William, 66, 67, 68
Barret, Daniel, 216
Barrett, Caroline, 97
Squire Haskell, 59
Barrons, Andrew, 29
Barrow, Abigail, 13
Hannah, 104
Lydia, 282
Mehitable, 113
Barrows, Branch, 251
Coombs, 239
Deborah, 239, 358
Ebenezer, 238, 239, 251, 348
Elisha, 239
Elizabeth, 17
George, 157
Hannah, 239
Isaac, 251
John, 191, 239, 355
Lurany, 251
Lydia, 222
Mehitable, 263
Mercy, 239
Moses, 251
Peleg, 16
Ruhamah, 151
Ruth, 280
Samuel, 239, 251
Sarah, 28
Thomas, 251
Tillson, 130
Barsley, Joanna, 222, 343
Barstow, Hezekiah, 54, 355
Joseph, 267
Joshua, 66
Lydia, 71
Martha, 232
Mary, 323
Ruth, 280
Samuel, 66
Sarah, 301
Bartlet, Betty, 307
Chandler, 307
Hannah, 23
Ichabod, 307, 355
Isaac, 299
John, 307, 355
Mahala, 7
Molly, 307
Batlett, Abigail, 36, 49, 306, 315, 316
Andrew, 311
Benjamin, 7, 70, 155, 305, 306, 311, 313, 341, 343, 348
Betty, 312, 315, 356
Caleb, 169, 305
Charles, 315
David Bradford, 307
Deborah, 306
Dorothy, 305
Ebenezer, 306, 319
Elizabeth, 308, 312, 313, 314, 348, 360
Elnathan, 311
Ephraim, 170, 315
George, 315, 356
Hannah, 16, 105, 157, 308, 311, 314, 315, 317, 324, 330, 344, 347, 360
Henry, 311, 360
Ichabod, 104, 283, 306, 308, 343
Isaac, 313, 316

Bartlett (cont-d)
Jane, 206
Jerusha, 315
John 307, 308, 311, 315, 356
John (Capt.), 311
Jonathan, 311, 314, 348
Joseph, 7, 49, 56, 146, 156, 306, 307, 308, 311, 313, 315, 348, 360
Josiah, 307
Lemuel, 93, 157, 315, 348
Lucy, 10, 133, 316, 357
Lydia, 2, 15, 306, 308, 313, 319, 344
Maria, 315
Mary, 308, 311, 314, 320, 356
Mary C., 316
Mercy, 62, 306, 307, 321, 354
Molly, 307
Nathaniel, 305, 308, 311 356
Patience, 308
Priscilla, 259, 306, 342
Rebecca, 46, 54, 170, 259, 305, 306, 316, 321, 322, 341, 342
Robert, 116, 225, 305, 306, 311, 315, 318, 330, 343, 348
Ruth, 306
Samuel, 3, 133, 295, 308, 314, 343
Sarah, 45, 146, 304, 306, 308, 311, 314, 315, 316, 318, 319, 324, 341, 343, 344, 350, 354, 356
Sarah ( ), 307
Sarah (Foster), 307
Seth, 307
Solomon, 127, 152
Solomon (Jr.), 305
Stephen, 311
Susanna, 315
Sylvanus, 313
Thomas, 313, 315, 318, 356
Uriah, 307
William, 306, 308, 356
Zaccheus, 313
Bartol, Mercy Craw, 31
Samuel, 31
Bartoll, Samuel, 31
Barton, Anna Maria, 94
Isabelle A., 279
Margaret, 37
Martha, 269
Sarah, 94
William, 94
Bass, Alden, 17
Bathsheba, 20, 346
Benjamin, 16, 17
Benjamin (Rev.), 17
Charles, 16
Ebenezer, 16
Elisha, 16
Elizabeth, 17, 18, 99, 190
Gillam, 18
Hannah, 16, 17, 19, 62
Isaac, 17
Jedidiah, 16, 17
Jeriah, 16
John, 16, 17
John A., 16
John (Rev.), 17
Jonathan, 17, 19
Jonathan (Col.), 19

Bass (cont-d)
Joseph, 17
Joseph (Capt.), 17
Mary, 17, 18, 19
Mary Jane, 17
Moses, 18
Moses Belcher, 18
Olive, 66, 360
Oliver, 68
Robert, 17
Ruth, 17, 19, 243
Samuel, 17, 19
Sarah, 19, 140
Seth, 16
Basset, Deborah, 245
Huldah, 121
Moses, 120
Nathan, 76
Bassett, Abner, 296
Elizabeth, 244
Eugene, Parker, 296
Hannah, 75
Helen Louisa, 296
Jeremiah, 96
John, 28
Joseph, 28, 122, 206, 276
Mary, 2
Moses, 121
Nathan, 122, 210, 220
Sarah, 27, 246, 333
Welthea, 43
William, 302, 361
Bate, Caleb, 310, 330
Jesse, 311
Mary, 310
Ruth, 310
Bates, Abigail, 335
David, 328
Elizabeth, 328
Ezekiel, 110
Hannah, 22
Harriet Elizabeth, 52
Helen Scoullar, 52
James, 141
Jared, 328
John, 30
Joseph, 94, 348
Julia, 110
Mercy, 320
Naomi, 328
Rhoda, 110
Sarah, 23
Solomon (Jr.), 91
Susanna, 68, 199
Thomas G., 336
Batis, Asa, 309
Battell, Henry C., 210
Battles, Caleb, 146
Experience, 54
Huldah, 324
Samuel, 54
Sarah, 54
Susanna, 131
Baty, Gideon (Sr.), 234
Thankful ( ) (Freeman), 221
Baucroft, John, 27
Baxter, Desire, 214
Edward, 214
Hezekiah, 213
Isaac, 213
Jane, 213, 214
Jeney, 213
John, 213, 343
Joseph, 213
Obed, 214
Prince, 214
Richard, 213
Sarah, 213

Baxter (cont-d)
Shubael, 08, 213, 343
Shubal, 213
Temperance, 213
Thankful, 11, 213, 346
Thomas, 211, 214
Bayard, Mary, 218
Baylies, Helen, 240
Beach, Andrew J., 61
Jackson, 61
Beal, Abigail Clapp, 41
Izra, 11
James, 309
Joseph, 295
Mary, 20, 310
Susanna (Lewis), 162
Beale, Elizabeth Holbrook,
146
Jonathan, 146
Susanna, 293
William Swift, 146
Beall, Daniel, 20
Beals, Asa, 20
Charles Edward, 148
Lucinda, 20
Nathan, 20
Bearce, Abigail, 119
Andrew, 162
Asa, 72
Austin, 172
Ursula, 28
Bears, Asa, 72
Bearse, Augustin, 207
Austin, 24
Benjamin, 197
Gideon, 72, 356
John, 72
Joseph, 257
Lemuel, 250
Margaret, 107, 108
Martha, 75
Becket, Abigail, 30, 33
Mary, 274
Bedon, Phebe, 139
Beers, Robert, 36
Beetle, James, 141
Jedidah, 207
Sarah ( ), 250
Belcher, Abigail, 53
Abigail (Mrs.), 37
Benjamin, 221
Edward (Capt.), 226
Elizabeth, 280
Katherine, 163
Mary, 17
Sarah Louise, 265
Susanna, 19
Belden, Louisa Mirands, 10
Belding, John, 49
John Kellogg, 48
Sarah A., 49
Belkuap, Ralzamon, 48
Bell, Margaret, 333
Sarah, 28
Bellows, Simeon, 299
Bemen, Hester, 154
Bement, Samuel, 326
Severance, 326
Benedict, David H., 110
Nicholas, 99
Thomas S., 110
Benjamin, Mary, 187
Bennet, Abigail, 261, 266
Anna, 224, 348
Batchelor, 239
Cornelius, 239, 348
Deborah, 224
Ebenezer, 149, 239

Bennet (cont-d)
Elinor, 208
Elizabeth, 191, 224, 351
Isaac, 15, 224, 343
Jael, 224
James, 243
Joseph, 224, 255, 343
Martha, 149, 224, 349
Mary, 93
Nathan, 224
Nehemiah, 149
Peter, 224
Ruth, 95
Sally, 239
Samuel, 224, 348
Susanna, 15, 224, 344
Bennett, Batchelor, 211
Caleb, 150
Constance, 30
Ebenezer, 144
Edward, 150
Eugenia, 337
Eunice, 45
Jacob, 220
John, 263
Leah, 267
Mary, 150
Priscilla, 224, 239, 351
Bensen, Joseph, 67
Wealthy, 7
Benson, Consider, 127
Deborah, 164
John, 127, 145
Mary, 123
Noah, 160
Priscilla, 238
Bent, Joseph, 35
Bentley, Robert, 332
Berce, Jane, 198
Berry, Andrew Campbell, 201
Hannah, 204, 230
Judah, 82
Lemuel, 82
Mary, 203
Priscilla, 173, 359
Rebecca, 187
Richard, 80, 81
Ruth, 204
Scotto, 82, 83, 360
Theophilus, 83
Besse, Bethiah, 251
Deborah, 327
Hope, 319
Mary, 325
Bessee, Elizabeth, 143
Betterly, Thomas, 9
Beull, Abigail, 215
Bezely, John, 38
Bickford, Deborah, 196
Bicknell, Isaac Jackson, 41
Mary, 33
Bigelow, Asahel, 211
Enos, 87
Bigford, Mary, 187
Biggs, Elizabeth, 196
Bill, Mary, 194
Susanna, 193
Billings, Mary, 194
Richard, 295
Billington, Abigail (Churchill),
231
Content, 35
Desire, 35
Dorcas, 35
Eleanor, 328, 347
Elinor ( ), 35
Elizabeth, 35
Francis, 35, 162

Billington (cont-d)
Isaac, 35, 285
Jemima, 35
John, 35
Lydia, 35
Marcye, 35
Martha, 35, 36, 162, 164,
341
Mary, 36
Mercy, 35, 36
Olive, 35
Samuel, 35
Sarah, 35
Bimball, Joseph, 72
Bingham, Abishai, 43
Abner, 44
Betsey Elizabeth, 44
Clarissa, 44
Ezra, 40
Jacob, 44
Jeremiah, 59
John Clark, 43, 44, 360
Ripley, 44
Ruth, 215
Sally, 44
Samuel, 43
Samuel (Capt.), 44
Binney, John, 184
Sarah, 68
Bisbe, Elisha, 63
Elizabeth, 143
Hannah, 119
Huldah, 66
John (Jr.), 254
Joseph, 113
Ruth, 254
Bisbee, Aaron, 268
Deborah, 278
Elisha, 279
Hopestill, 324
Huldah, 68
Isaacher, 324
Jemima, 5
John, 11, 110, 256, 266
Joseph, 121
Martha, 65, 280, 324
Mercy, 257
Olive, 165
Bishop, Daniel, 233
Deborah, 6
Ebenezer, 163
Mary, 247
Reuben, 40
Tabitha, 269
Bissell, Amelia C.E., 46
David, 273
Jonah, 46
Bixbee, John, 200
Moses, 200
Blackman, Joseph, 301
Blackmer, Anna, 251
Betty, 316, 324, 360
Branch, 316, 356
Jerusha, 317
John, 316
Susanna, 312, 317, 359
Blackwell, Alice, 329
Bathshua, 327
Caleb, 150, 329, 343
Desire, 329
Jane, 329
John, 329, 343
Blair, Esther, 90
Sally, 246
Blake, Anna Sophia, 221
Bridget, 217
Charles, 39
Charlotte Smith, 221

Bradford (cont-d)
Cornelius, 41, 45
Daniel, 37, 38, 49, 50
David, 38, 40, 42
David (Capt.), 41
Deborah, 39
Desire Harlow, 41
Dorcas, 51
Edmund, 41
Edward Winslow, 42
Eleanor, 41, 51
Elijah, 37
Eliphalet, 47, 48, 50, 348
Elisabeth, 48, 294
Elisha, 39, 45
Elizabeth, 37, 38, 43, 49,
  50, 51
Elizabeth Holmes, 43
Elizabeth W., 46
Elmira, 46
Ephraim, 42, 43, 341
Exuma, 46
Ezekiel, 43
Francis, 37
Gamaliel, 306
Gamiel, 49, 348
George, 41, 53
George (Capt.), 41
George (Rev.), 42
George Washington, 45
Gershom, 6, 49
Gideon, 47, 356
Grace, 51
Halsey, 50
Halsey Dart, 56
Hannah, 38, 43, 45, 49, 52,
  53
Hannah (Foster), 285
Harriet, 50
Harriet DeWolf, 38
Henrietta, 50
Henriette, 48
Hetty Amelia, 42
Hezekiah, 45
Hopestill, 37, 50
Ichabod, 45, 119
Irene, 48
Isaiah, 49
Israel, 45, 306, 341
James, 37, 46, 48, 54,
  348
James Madison, 42
James Russell, 42
Jane C., 37
Jeremiah, 50
Jeremiah (Dr.), 50
Jerusha, 52, 54, 56
Jesse, 43
Joanna, 38
Job, 50, 51
Joel, 43, 50, 56
John, 37, 38, 4, 45, 46,
  47, 52, 53, 59, 303, 306,
  348
Joseph, 37, 38, 4, 45, 48,
  53
Joseph Morey, 41
Joseph Nash, 51
Joshua, 45
Josiah, 37, 56, 348
Keziah, 48, 52
Laurana, 39
Lemuel, 40, 41
Lemuel (Capt.), 41, 45
Levi, 38
Lewis, 49
Louise E., 51
Lucy, 42, 45, 46

Bradford (cont-d)
Lucy ( ), 323
Lucy Foster, 47, 360
Luther, 47, 360
Lydia, 24, 38, 40, 47, 264,
  313, 349
Marcia, 43
Maria W., 51
Mary, 38, 46, 47, 48, 52,
  53, 54, 281, 361
Mary Holmes, 42
Mary Sampson, 42
Mary Winslow, 42
Matilda Bradford, 41
Melatiah, 48
Mercy, 25, 39, 47, 48, 55,
  85, 323, 325, 344, 349,
  357
Mercy Bartlett, 117
Morton, 42
Nabby, 38, 43
Nancy, 38
Nancy Barnes, 42
Nathan, 38, 40
Nathaniel, 40, 41, 42
Nathaniel Barnes, 42
Nathaniel Governeum, 42
Noah, 50
Olive, 54, 355
Oliver, 47, 356
Pamela, 291, 292, 330, 357
Pamelia, 49
Paybodie, 49, 348
Peabody, 49
Peggy, 45
Peleg, 38, 46
Pelham, 46
Peres, 37
Perez, 53
Peter J., 38
Philander, 46
Philip, 43, 46
Polly, 37
Priscilla, 37, 46, 48, 49,
  50, 51, 223, 343
Rebecca, 46, 50, 71, 72,
  119, 350
Rebecca (Bartlett), 259
Rebekah, 43
Robert, 37, 46, 50, 71,
  348
Ruth, 43, 50, 259, 345
Sally, 38, 42, 58
Samuel, 47, 49, 190, 243,
  341, 348
Sarah, 37, 48, 53, 54, 55,
  56, 286
Sarah Spooner, 42
Seth, 49
Simeon, 43
Solomon (Dr.), 50, 52
Sophronia, 46
Spencer, 46
Stephen, 38, 46
Stetson, 46
Susan, 50
Susanna, 43, 45
Sylvanus, 46
Theophilus, 38
Thomas, 37, 42, 54
Urtham Henry, 50
Vienna, 50
Wait, 43
Walter, 38, 53
Welthea, 53
William, 37, 38, 39, 45,
  47, 48, 50, 54, 55, 56,
  304, 305, 342, 348

Bradford (cont-d)
William Holmes, 42
Zabdiel, 47, 360
Zadock, 48
Bradick, Abigail, 64
John Henry, 61
Bradley, Hannah, 60
Lucretia, 60, 64
Molly, 204
Peter, 60
Bradshaw, John, 100
Bradstreet, Sarah, 30
Brady, Elizabeth Wolfe, 44
Bragg, Bethiah, 225
Nicholas, 225, 226
Thomas, 214
Brainerd, Diodate, 50
Leah, 87
Lucy, 326
Stephen, 87
Brame, Anna, 9
Bramhall, Sylvanus, 304
Branch, Abigail, 282
Experience, 282
Lydia, 282
Mercy, 282
Thankful, 282
Thomas, 282
Brand, Rebecca, 299
Brant, John, 215
Bray, Mercy, 86
Rebecca, 335
Sally, 99
Brayley, Sarah, 272
Brayton, Mary, 115
Breck, Elizabeth, 17
Breed, Anna, 27
Ruth, 27
Brett, Alice, 132
Charity (Kingman), 11
Elihu, 134
Hannah, 135
Mary, 135
Mehitable, 135
Nathaniel, 135
Seth, 12, 108, 135
Seth (Jr.), 107
Silas, 135
Simeon, 135
William, 129, 136
Brettun, Elizabeth, 242
Brewer, Elizabeth, 118
James, 40
Maude Potter, 40
Brewster, Abigail, 58, 71,
  348
Asa, 58
Benjamin, 58, 59
Bethiah, 58
Daniel, 59
Darius, 268, 360
David, 58
Drusilla, 58
Elizabeth, 43, 58, 60, 341
Esther, 58
Eunice, 71
Faith ( ), 59
Faith Ripley, 45
Fear, 22, 341
Grace, 58, 61
Hannah, 1, 54, 58, 59, 341
Huldah, 72
Ichabod, 71
Isaac, 72, 263, 348
James, 58
Jerusha, 58
John, 46, 58, 60, 71
John (Dr.), 70

Casewell, Elizabeth, 104
  Hannah, 166
Casey, Mary Anderson, 296
Cassady, William, 304
Caswell, Elizabeth, 241
  Henry, 126
  Katherine, 294
Caznean, Margaret, 98
Center, John Sheldon, 117
  Jonas, 118
Chace, Chloe, 272
  Philip, 336
Chadwick, Mary, 7
Chaffin, Mary, 253
Challoner, John, 297
Chaloner, Abigail, 297
  Elizabeth, 297
  Nancy, 297
Chalonger, Martha, 297
Chamber, John, 8
Chamberlain, Freedom, 263,
  348
  Job. 348
  Lurana, 68
  Martha Ann, 300
  Mary, 25, 263, 361
Chamberlin, Celia, 264
  Elizabeth, 4, 264, 358
  Job. 264
  Nathaniel, 264, 274
  Rachel, 264
  Zerviah, 264
Champlin, Christopher, 210
  Joseph, 61
  Mercy A., 210
  Nancy, 61
Chandler, Asenath, 7, 360
  Benjamin, 7
  Betty, 7, 43
  Edmund, 10
  Elizabeth (Arnold), 10
  Esther, 253
  Faith, 114
  John, 277
  Joseph, 255, 277
  Keturah, 278
  Martha, 4, 15
  Mary, 4, 45
  Mercy, 7, 306
  Nathan, 43
  Perez, 7
  Rebecca, 268, 277
  Roger, 111
  Sarah, 269
  Sceva, 7
  Wadsworth, 7
Channel, Elizabeth Marston,
  17
Chapin, Dexter, 221
  Mary, 16
Chapman, Isaac, 2
  Prudence, 10
Chappel, Abigail, 215
Chase, Abigail Stone, 68
  Annie, 126
  Bethiah, 80, 201
  Hannah, 52
  Israel, 256
  James, 188
  Jonathan, 326
  Lucy, 241
  Mary, 332, 336, 339
  Obadiah, 200
Chastelet, Catherine, 113
Cheesbrough, Amos, 61
Cheeseborough, Amos, 2
  Jabez, 2
  Priscilla, 2

Cheeseborough (cont-d)
  Prudence, 2
  Samuel, 2
Cheney, Caleb Colby, 328
  Olive, 20
  Sally, 20
  Samuel, 28
Cherry, Margaret, 164
Chickering, George Edward,
  300
Child, Abigail Miller, 49
  Christopher, 49
  Joseph, 300
  Lydia, 300
  Mary R., 49
  Priscilla Bradford, 49
  Sarah, 37
  Shubael P., 49
  Sylapen, 37
  Sylvester (Col.), 49
Childs, Ebenezer, 219
  Priscilla, 3, 91
  Richard, 3
  Sarah, 299
  Stephen, 101
  Susan, 230
Chilton, Alice, 111
  Angelina, 111
  Annis, 111
  Isaac, 111
  Isabel, 111
  Isabella, 111
  James, 97, 111
  John, 111
  Mary, 97
Chipman, Abigail, 222, 223
  Ann, 222
  Anna, 29, 349
  Benjamin, 217, 223
  Bethia, 218
  Bethiah, 221, 222
  Content, 218
  David, 222
  Deborah, 218
  Desire, 218
  Ebenezer, 222
  Elizabeth, 219, 223
  Handley, 221
  Hannah, 194, 219, 222, 223
  Henry, 223
  Jacob, 223
  James, 218
  John, 217, 221, 223
  John (Rev.), 223
  Joseph, 223
  Luce, 218
  Lucy, 190
  Lydia, 171, 221, 222, 325,
    354
  Mary, 223
  Mercy, 172, 222
  Rebecca, 223
  Ruth, 222, 248, 342
  Samuel, 222, 223
  Sarah, 47, 219, 223, 356
  Seth, 46, 223, 343, 348
  Thomas, 223
  William, 221, 228
Chittenden, Alathea, 304
  Gideon, 62
Christophers, Christopher, 60
  Ester, 61
  Grace, 64
  John, 60
  Lucrecia, 61
  Mary, 60, 61
  Richard, 60, 64
Chubb, Elizabeth, 194

Chubbuck, Alice, 295
  Betty, 65
  Hannah, 317
  Hannah E., 320
  Hannah Ellis, 251
  Timothy, 251
  Willis, 251, 320
Church, Abigail, 6, 297, 301
  302, 346
  Alice, 298
  Benjamin, 296, 297
  Caleb, 297, 298, 299, 301
  Charles, 297, 301, 338
  Constant, 297
  Deborah, 296, 301
  Edward, 296, 297
  Elizabeth, 295, 296, 297,
    301
  Elizabeth (Mrs.), 296
  Gamaliel, 13
  Grace, 137
  Hannah, 297, 298, 303
  Hannah ( ), 302
  Hannah (Mrs.), 225
  Jonathan, 299
  Joseph, 62, 300, 301, 348
  Joshua, 299
  Judith, 301
  Judith (Harlow), 319
  Lemuel, 303
  Lucy, 270
  Lydia, 298, 299, 302
  Martha, 297
  Mary, 49, 253, 270, 296,
    301, 345
  Mary (Mrs.), 37
  Nathaniel, 296, 301, 302
  Patience (Cook), 142
  Peter, 297
  Rebecca, 299, 302
  Richard, 295, 302, 303
  Ruth, 159, 300, 303
  Samuel, 297
  Sarah, 292, 302, 303, 351
  Thomas, 296, 297
  Thomas (Capt.), 263
Churchell, Amaziah, 312
  Hannah, 312
  Keziah, 229
  Mercy, 315
  Rebecca, 316
  Sarah, 312
Churchill, Abigail, 35, 231,
  315
  Amaziah, 312
  Ansel, 169
  Asaba, 11, 134, 361
  Averick, 276
  Barnabas, 312, 323, 356
  Bathsheba, 36, 122
  Deliverance, 115
  Ebenezer, 282
  Eleazer, 314, 315, 356,
    360
  Elizabeth, 264
  Hannah, 55, 308, 324
  Harriet, 41
  Henry, 161
  Jane, 216, 276
  Jedidah, 324
  John, 3, 47, 169
  John (Sgt.), 308
  Jonathan, 315
  Josiah, 314, 356
  Lucy, 270, 359
  Lydia, 311
  Mary, 161, 213, 270, 277,
    314, 359

Coombs (cont-d)
  Frances, 224, 342
  Francis, 238
  Isabella, 69
  Israel, 79
  Jane, 339
  John, 238
  Joshua, 238
  Lydia, 239
  Mary, 162
  Mercy, 239
  Priscilla, 127
  Ruth, 239
Coomer, Joanna, 8
  Mary, 114
  Susanna, 264
  William, 267, 285
Cooper, Calvin, 104
  John, 104
  Judith, 326
  Priscilla, 104
  Richard, 254, 360, 361
  Rosanna (Burlingame), 22
  Ruth, 232
  Sarah, 304
  Thomas, 169
Copeland, Abigail, 18
  Asa, 108
  Benjamin, 18
  Elizabeth, 19
  Isaac, 109
  Jonathan, 18
  Joseph, 19
  Mary, 19
  Nancy, 110
  Rhoda, 19, 282, 356
  Ruth, 19
  Samuel, 110
  William, 18, 19
Copley, John Singleton, 100
Corban, Elisha, 54
Corben, Dorcas, 314
Corbett, Isaiah, 133
Corbin, Elkanah, 323
Corey, William, 335
  William B., 41
Cornat, Geanne, 113
Cornell, Alice, 115
  Christopher, 115
  Elizabeth, 138
  Gideon, 332, 336
  Mary, 115
  Rachel, 140, 332
  Sarah, 51
  Stephen, 332
  William, 115
Corning, Samuel, 317
  Sarah E., 82
Cornish, Benjamin, 147
  Grace, 320
  Nance, 146
  Nathaniel, 146
  Sarah, 147
Cornwell, Olivia, 87
Corser, John, 98
Corsser, Fear, 29
Corthell, Calvin, 287
  Deborah, 310
Corwin, George, 340
  Mary, 120
  Penelope, 340
Cotherel, Lucy L., 287
Cottle, Salome, 206
Cotton, Abigail, 218
  John, 292
  Mary, 240
  Theophilus, 292
  Thomas, 77

Cottrell, Barbara, 272
Couch, Elijah, 79
Covel, Hannah, 75
  Hannah (Bassett), 75
  Jean, 320
Covell, Lot, 130
Coverly, Samuel, 100
Covil, Philip, 197
Covington, Tryphena, 55
Cowell, Rebecca, 198
  Sarah, 42
Cowing, Caleb, 240
  Eunice, 240
  James, 240
  John, 160, 206
  John Philo, 240
  Lydia, 146, 151
Cowley, Matilda, 289
Cox, Eliza, 198
  Hannah, 298
  Mary, 144, 298
  Sarah, 298
  Susan, 298
  William, 298
  William (Jr.), 269, 298
Crandall, Mary, 138
Crane, Laurance, 3
  Levi Loukton, 275
  Lydia, 243
  Ruth, 44
  Samuel, 124
  Susannah, 126
  Zipporah, 242
Cranmer, Rachel, 102
Crapo, Benjamin Jenne, 142
  Francis, 339
  Peter, 339
  Pierre, 339
  Susanna, 339
Crapoo, Peroo, 338
Crest, Elizabeth, 99
Crippen, Jabez, 167
Crisp, Mercy, 247
Crocker, Abel, 222
  Abigail, 228
  Abraham, 227
  Anna, 227, 228
  Arthur B., 230
  Benjamin, 226
  Benoni, 226
  Bethiah, 222
  Bridgham, 230
  Cornelius, 230
  Desire, 259, 345
  Eleazer, 222, 248
  Elizabeth, 3
  Ephraim, 227
  Hannah, 167, 227
  Hodiah Jenkins, 230
  James, 227, 343
  Job, 88
  Jonathan, 226, 227, 228
  Joseph, 226, 230
  Martha, 248
  Mary, 114, 227, 228
  Nathan, 222, 226, 343
  Prudence, 210, 344
  Rachel, 228
  Rebecca, 222
  Ruth, 167, 222, 350
  Samuel, 230
  Sarah, 114, 222, 227, 343
  Seth, 213
  Susanna, 227, 231
  Theophilus, 222
Crockett, Eli N., 101
Croft, Eliza P., 12
Crooker, Daniel, 333

Crooker (cont-d)
  Hannah, 333
  Mary, 333
  Matilda, 333
  Sarah, 333
  Sebra (Jr.), 92
Crosby, Abigail, 118
  Abner, 204
  David, 204
  Eleazer, 83, 200
  Elizabeth, 247
  Hannah K., 75
  James, 82
  Joshua, 204
  Keziah, 84, 356
  Lydia, 84
  Mary, 80
  Mehitable, 203
  Moses, 192
  Patience, 182
  Phebe, 84
  Sarah, 211
  Solomon, 84
  Tabitha, 192
  Thomas, 204
Crosman, Abigail, 149
Cross, John, 194
  Mary, 30
Crossman, Elizabeth, 104
  Hannah, 163, 241
  Joseph, 126
  Robert, 164
Crow, Massillon, 215
Crowel, Deliverance, 197
  Joseph, 183
  Paul, 205
Crowell, Caroline, 230
  Experience, 72
  Hannah, 86
  John, 335
  Jonathan, 179
  Lott (Capt.), 230
  Paul, 179, 183, 204
  Sarah, 230
Crymble, Phebe, 249
Cudworth, Benjamin, 286
  David, 263
  Israel, 286
  John, 321, 322
  Mercy, 286
  Peter, 335
  Polly, 166
  Sally, 322
Cuffs, Hannah Wadsworth, 216
Cumber, John, 8
Cummings, Abraham, 237
  Aznbah, 256
  Jonas, 235
  Sarah (Wright), 237
Cundall, Rebecca, 291
Cunningham, James (Maj.),
    297
  Nathaniel, 106
  Ruth, 106, 156, 352
Currier, Hannah, 218
  Harriet B., 253
Curtice, Sarah, 257
  William, 28
Curtis, Abiel, 126
  Betsy, 91
  David, 163
  Ebenezer, 93, 158
  Eli, 62
  Elisha, 91
  Elizabeth, 334
  Elizabeth (Scadlock), 27
  Experience, 127
  Francis, 314

Decrow, Hannah, 333
DeForest, Mary, 40
de la Cluse, Susanna, 111
de la Marliere, Marc, 113
Delano, Abigail, 268
  Amaziah, 15, 344
  Bathsheba, 157
  Benjamin, 38
  Benoni, 15
  Beriah, 15
  Briggs Bradford, 42
  Calvin, 13
  Catherine, 38
  Cornelius, 15
  Ebenezer, 4, 255
  Elizabeth, 223, 277
  Elkanah, 16
  Eunice, 105
  Ezekiel, 15
  Hannah, 15, 267, 321, 346,
    350
  Hazadiah, 277
  Hopestill, 4
  Ichabod, 24
  Jabez, 136, 327
  Jethro, 327
  John, 113
  Jonathan, 15, 161, 327
  Jonathan (Jr.), 136
  Joshua, 4, 349
  Judah, 6
  Lemuel, 15, 306, 344
  Lydia, 70, 255, 268, 358
  Martha, 322
  Mary P., 41
  Mercy, 150, 255, 327
  Nathan, 311, 327
  Nathaniel, 255
  Peleg, 258, 349
  Priscilla, 5, 277, 346
  Rebecca, 5, 15, 277, 279,
    346
  Ruth, 271
  Samuel, 277
  Sarah, 4, 15, 277, 346
  Thankful, 29
  Thomas, 16, 21, 327, 330
  Thomas (Dr.), 15
  Welthea, 49, 56, 348
  Zeruiah, 255
Delanoy, Jonathan, 15
Delgrado, Joseph, 99
de Melan, Abraham, 113
Deneson, Mary, 17
Denison, Boradel, 64, 354
  Elizabeth, 210
  George, 61, 211
Dennis, Ann, 255
  James, 233
  John, 31
  Josiah (Rev.), 204
  Sarah, 262
  Thankful, 85
Dennison, Margaret, 232
Denny, Sarah, 129
Derby, Jane, 35
Deshamps, Judith, 113
  Magdelaine, 113
Devol, Alpha, 61
  Benjamin, 262
  Gilbert, 61, 141
  John, 262
  Joseph, 262
  Julia, 61
  Philip, 61
  Stephen, 61
Dewing, Benjamin Hill, 313
DeWolf, Benjamin, 288

DeWolfe (cont-d)
  James, 38
Dexter, Benjamin, 104
  Jonathan, 104
  Lois, 303
  Martha Mendall, 207
  Mary, 325
  Mercy, 2
  Thankful, 220
Dickenson, Elizabeth, 214
  Hannah, 214
  John, 224
  Joseph, 224
  Zebulon, 224
Dickerman, Peter, 289
Dill, Elizabeth, 62
  Nathaniel, 68
Dillard, Mary, 42
Dillingham, Abigail, 83
  Benjamin, 142
  Deborah, 63
  Elizabeth, 63
  Henry, 63
  Jael, 63
  John, 63
  Lydia, 63
  Princess, 63
  Rebecca, 84
  Sarah, 82
Dimmick, Ann, 48
  Daniel, 48
  Desiah, 48
  Desire, 48, 349
  Jesse, 212
  JOnathan, 212
  Lot, 212
  Mason, 48
  Timothy, 48, 349
Dimmock, Ann(a) (Mrs.), 1
  Jabez, 217, 218
  Mary, 218
  Timothy, 218
Dimock, David, 326
  Desire, 210, 344
  Mehitable, 212
  Silence, 247
  Temperance, 82, 211, 349
  Thomas, 208, 211, 212, 356
Dimon, William Alfred, 42
Dimond, Rebecca, 319
Dingley, Elizabeth, 49
  Hannah, 282, 284
  Jacob, 72, 172, 356
  John, 334
  Mary, 119
  Thomas, 334
Dingly, Mary, 280
Dinsdale, Sarah, 90
Dinsdell, Rebecca, 97
Dinsmore, Thomas, 99
Diser, Francis, 106
  John Foye, 106, 360
Ditson, Oliver, 38
Divel, Mary, 139
Dix, Huldah, 221
Dixie, ELizabeth, 100
Dixon, Shubal, 269
Doane, Abigail, 188, 218, 353
  Benjamin, 83
  Daniel, 186
  Dinah, 199
  Edmund, 79
  Elisha, 75, 188
  Elizabeth, 55, 174
  Ephraim, 174
  Hannah, 192
  Israel, 75, 79
  Joan, 174

Doane (cont-d)
  Joseph, 74
  Keziah, 207
  Lydia, 198
  Mary, 86, 188
  Mercy, 174
  Patience, 198
  Prence, 79
  Rachel, 199
  Rebecca, 181, 188, 191
  Ruhama, 202
  Ruth, 73
  Sarah, 187
  Thomas, 55
Dobell, Lucy (Gray), 105
Dodge, Abigail, 235
  Josiah, 235
Dodsun, Margaret, 290
Doggett, Bethiah, 256, 291
  Hannah, 334
  Lydia, 285
  Mary, 334
  Samuel, 284
  Sarah, 154, 345
  Thomas, 170
Dole, Moses, 26
Doliber, Joseph, 31
Doliver, Joseph, 31
Dolliver, Margaret, 31
Donham, Eunice, 320
  Lydia, 92
  Ruth, 37
Dorman, Seth, 20
Dorrame, Sally, 58
Doten, Ebenezer, 158, 349
  Edward, 304, 330
  Elisha, 157
  Elizabeth, 172, 350
  Hannah, 15
  Hope, 157
  Isaac, 157
  James, 157
  John, 157
  Joseph, 157
  Lois, 322, 357
  Mary, 158
  Molly, 43
  Paul, 157
  Samuel (Capt.), 43
  Stephen, 157, 315, 344
Doty, Amy, 156
  Barnabas, 158
  Benjamin, 154
  Content, 178
  Deborah, 158
  Desire, 153, 157, 275, 293
  Edward, 153, 154, 157, 158,
    330
  Elisha, 157
  Elizabeth, 153, 154, 157,
    158, 161
  Faith, 158
  Hannah, 161
  Isaac, 156, 157
  James, 157, 344
  Jane, 158
  John, 116, 156, 158, 293,
    341
  Joseph, 158
  Lucy, 191, 358
  Lydia, 305, 351
  Martha, 93, 155, 158, 337,
    347
  Mary, 156, 157, 158, 311,
    315, 348
  Mehitable, 305, 345
  Mercy, 55, 154
  Patience, 53, 157

Doty (cont-d)
Rebecca, 157, 303, 347
Samuel, 156, 158, 161, 344
Sarah, 154, 156, 158, 207,
  326, 343
Sarah (Jones), 271
Susanna, 158, 304, 319, 344
Theophilus, 158
Thomas, 161, 198, 323, 342,
  344
Doughty, Mary, 214
Dowding, Mercy, 17
Dowglass, Hannah ( ), 290
Downs, Barnabas, 209
Elizabeth (Gorham), 213
Joanna, 46
Samuel, 213
William, 208
Doyle, Bartholomew, 309
David, 37
Drake, Abigail, 110
Albert Henry, 148
Ebenezer, 148
Ebenezer Hayward, 148
Elizabeth, 335
John, 335
Nellie Vernon, 148
Rachel, 242
Sarah Elizabeth, 148
Draper, Mary, 19
Drew, Abigail, 15
Charles, 267
Cornelilus, 308
Deborah, 15
Elizabeth, 15
Francis, 38
James, 314
Jemima, 16
Job, 69, 70
John, 15, 224, 344
Lemuel, 161, 305, 314, 356
Lurana, 306
Lydia, 15
Margaret, 169
Mary, 15, 314, 324, 343,
  352
Nicholas, 284, 285
Perez, 267
Samuel, 119
Sarah, 5, 161, 254
Silvanus, 267
Thomas, 15, 111, 145, 344,
  349
Zenas, 105
Zilpha, 267
Drinkwater, Joseph, 272, 344
Thomas, 272
Drown, Benjamin, 216
Jonathan Jenckes, 217
Drury, Mary, 9
du Forest, Arnold, 113
Duggan, John, 193, 194
Mary Emma, 193
William B., 193
Dunbar, Abigail, 295, 296
Benjamin, 128
Catherine, 317
David, 136, 295
David (Jr.), 295
Elisha, 295
Elizabeth, 125, 128
Elizabeth ( ), 296
Hannah, 96, 295
Huldah, 295, 296
James, 110
Joanna, 295
Mary, 109, 296
Mercy (Soule), 295

Dunbar (cont-d)
Nancy, 266
Patience, 296
Peter, 295, 296
Samuel, 135, 136
Sarah, 296
Silas, 160
Susanna, 133, 295
Dunham, Abigail, 271
David, 208
Desire, 265
Edmund, 167
Elizabeth, 92
Ephraim, 94
Fear, 92
Hannah, 14
Jane, 157
Joshua, 114
Lydia, 158
Margaret Albertson, 268
Martha, 89
Mary, 35, 130, 242
Mehitable, 135
Ruth, 56
Susanna, 13
William, 23
Dunkard, John (Dr.), 207
Durfe, Mary, 228
Durfee, Cory, 241
Deborah, 241
Elizabeth, 137
Joseph, 249
Richard, 119
Ruth, 140
Durfey, Richard, 285
Durkee, Abigail, 58
Hannah, 58
Mary, 58, 70
William, 58
William (Jr.), 58
Durland, John, 52
Pamelia, 92
Dutch, Samuel, 235
Susanna, 235
Dwelle, Jedidiah, 263
Dwelley, Deborah, 285
Elizabeth, 334
Grace, 62, 88, 301, 348,
  354
Lemuel, 256, 260, 290, 291
Mary, 71, 239
Mercy, 293
Rachel (Buck), 256
Richard, 62
Dyer, Abigail, 16, 37
Ambrose, 196
Anna, 40
Betsey, 180
Constance, 77
David, 181
Elizabeth, 80, 180
Hannah, 196, 297
Henry, 181
Isabel (Eldridge), 178
James, 39
Jane, 14
Jemima, 195
Joanna, 68
John, 39, 99, 156, 198,
  314, 320
Joseph, 14
Judah, 245
Lucy, 308
Lydia, 175
Mary ( ), 135
Mary (Atkins), 185
Mehitable, 148
Molly, 184

Dyer (cont-d)
Rebecca, 248
Rebecca (Collins), 198
Ruth, 175, 195, 196
Samuel, 185
Sarah, 181
Silvanus, 195
Susanna, 101
Sybil, 40
Thankful, 196
Dymond, Ruth, 60
Thomas, 60
Dyre, Hannah (Howland), 340
William, 232, 340

Eager, Rachel, 288
Eaimes, Anthony, 284
Eairs, Elizabeth, 184
Eames, Anthony, 257, 292
Jane, 155
Jedediah, 155
Jerusha, 292
John Tilden, 155
Mary, 155, 292
Mercy, 293
Nathaniel, 257
Penelope, 155, 287, 351
Earl, Benjamin, 261
James, 261
Susanna, 137
Earle, Abigail, 137
Benjamin, 137
Daniel, 137
Elizabeth, 137, 152
John, 137
Mary, 137
Sarah, 137
Thomas, 138
William, 137
Easdell, Rebecca, 305
Eastland, John, 250
Eastlin, Reliance, 22
Easton, Anna, 307
Eaton, Abigail, 163
Apollos, 163
Barnabas, 164, 344
Benjamin, 93, 163, 162,
  166, 264
Christian ( ), 35
Darius, 164
David, 163
Deborah ( ), 163
Deborah (Fuller), 171
Ebenezer, 163, 166
Elijah, 163
Elisha, 163
Eliza, 109
Elizabeth, 163, 164
Eunice, 118, 163, 164, 356
Francis, 12, 162, 163, 344
Gideon, 163
Hannah, 163, 167
Israel, 164
Jeremiah, 32
Joanna, 163
Joel, 163
John, 162, 163, 344
Joseph, 163
Lot, 163
Louisa, 164
Martha, 164
Mary, 162, 163, 265, 346
Mercy, 163, 171
Mercy ( ), 162
Nathan, 164
Polly, 163
Rachell, 162
Rebecca, 163

378

Eaton (cont-d)
  Rufus, 164
  Ruth, 164
  Sally, 109
  Samuel, 35, 36, 92, 162,
    164, 169, 341, 342, 349
  Sarah, 28, 162, 344
  Sarah (Prior)(Fobes), 29
  William, 170
  Ziba, 164
Eddy, Hannah, 46
  Hasadiah, 170
  Joshua (Capt.), 191
  Lucy, 170
  Lydia, 222
  Lydia (Alden), 170
  Mary, 170, 276
  Melatiah, 92
  Nathan, 13, 349
  Patience, 164
  Saloma, 164
  Samuel, 13
  Seth, 164
  Titus, 164
  Zechariah, 191
Edes, Oliver, 117
Edgerton, Samuel, 43
Edson, Abiah, 14
  Abiezer, 224
  Daniel, 333, 338
  Ezra, 334
  Hannah, 14, 147
  John, 110
  Josiah, 170
  Mary, 110
  Robert, 130
  Samuel, 135
  Sarah, 10, 110, 111, 133
  Susan, 46
  Susanna, 134
  Timothy, 14
Edward, Webley, 120
Edwards, Deborah, 158
  Hannah, 158
  Joanna, 116
  Joseph (Jr.), 158
  Sarah ( ), 158
Edy, Sally, 123
Eells, Hannah, 284
  John, 284
  Lenthal, 19
  Mary, 17
  North, 257, 290
  Waterman, 284
Egard, Hester, 219
Egerton, Rebecca, 120
Eldred, Elizabeth, 273
  John, 273
  Mary, 273
  William, 231
Eldredge, Abigail, 220
  Charles, 220
  Daniel, 220
  Elizabeth, 201
  James, 244
  Jesse, 202
  Mehitable, 201
  Rebecca, 244
Eldridge, Ann, 139
  Bathsheba, 74
  Elizabeth, 101
  Isabel, 178
  Martha, 176
  Mary, 178
  Mercy, 258
  Salome, 139
Elice, Hannah, 97
Eliot, Jacob (Rev.), 6

Elkins, Margaret, 177
Elliot, Lydia, 165
Elliott, Deborah Ann (Paddock),
  262
Ellis, Ann (Jenkins), 288
  David, 288
  Deborah, 161
  Ebenezer, 338
  Elizabeth, 320
  Francis B., 287
  George, 297
  Jane, 93
  Jean, 313
  Joel, 338
  John, 245, 288
  Joseph, 93
  Josiah, 255
  Luke, 93, 242, 349
  Lydia, 311
  Mary, 156, 308, 318
  Mercy, 161, 311
  Mordecai, 146, 288
  Nathan, 337
  Nathan B., 320
  Nathan Bourne, 251
  Phebe, 90
  Rebecca, 104, 276, 312
  Rebecca (Clarke), 146
  Ruth, 288
  Samuel, 8
  Sarah, 46, 147
  Sarah (Mrs.), 46
  Seth, 17
  Stephen, 144, 151, 179
  Thomas, 159
  William, 159
Ellison, Abraham, 297
Elmes, Mary, 123
Elsbree, Jemima, 298
Ely, Elizabeth, 217
  Robert, 3
  William, 58
Emerson, Edward, 101, 102
  Moses, 102
  Sarah, 102
Emery, Ernestine, 78
  Moritz Hauptmann, 78
  Sidney Sheppard, 78
  Stephen, 78
  Stephen Albert, 78
Emmons, Emily, 59
England, Elizabeth, 156
Ensworth, Ezra, 181
  Lucy, 40
Erving, George, 99, 100
Eslen, Huldah, 59
Estes, Matthew, 333
  Richard, 255
Eunice, Paul, 298
Eure, Mary, 279
Evans, Mary, 52
  Thomas, 241
Everill, Abiel, 8
  Elizabeth (Philips), 8
Everitt, Catherine, 147
Everson, Abigail, 4
  Elizabeth, 163
  Ephraim, 69
  Hannah, 271
  Sarah, 93
  Seth, 43
Ewell, Gershom, 272
  Job, 121
  Peleg, 53
  Penelope, 160
  Perez, 53
  Sarah, 320
  Seth, 155

Ewer, Sarah, 316
  Thomas, 316, 327
Exline, David, 42
  John, 42

Fairfax, Lindsay, 51
Fales, Charlotte, 149
  Jane Mimot, 103
  Mary Turell, 103
  Nathaniel, 294
  Nathaniel (Jr.), 294
  Nathaniel (Sr.), 37
  Sarah, 297
  William A., 103
Farm, John, 295
Farnam, Jonathan, 254
Farnsworth, Andrew J., 32
  Andrew Jackson, 32
  Benjamin F., 32
Farnum, Joseph, 254
  Susanna, 100
Farrar, George S., 79
Farrington, Abigail, 28
  Sarah, 166
Farrow, Jemima, 65
  Josiah, 5
  Martha, 67
  Seth, 273
Faunce, Ansell, 319
  Daniel, 13
  Eleazer, 303
  Hannah, 117, 119, 304, 349
  James, 23, 266, 319, 331
  Jane, 146
  John, 119, 120, 121
  Joseph, 266
  Judith, 36, 120, 354
  Lemuel B., 41
  Lemuel Bradford, 41
  Lydia, 35, 46, 113, 119
  Martha, 157
  Mary, 302, 304
  Matilda Bradford, 41
  Mehitable, 29, 349
  Patience, 282, 304
  Peleg, 304
  Priscilla, 303
  Ruth, 157
  Sarah, 154
  Solomon, 41
  Thomas, 311, 315, 319, 356
  Thomas (Jr.), 311
  William, 319
  William Thomas, 41
  William (Rev.), 41
Faxon, Lydia, 12
  Sarah, 20, 124
Fay, James, 300
  Mehitable, 246
Feaning, David, 28
Fearing, Elizabeth, 309
  Margaret, 293
  Nathaniel, 309
  Sarah, 310
Febes, Elizabeth, 4
Felch, Mary, 296
  Nathaniel, 27
Fellows, Susanna, 235
Fenner, Edward, 274
Fenton, Lucy (Sawyer), 299
Ferguson, Archibald, 30
Fessenden, Benjamin, 218
  John, 49
Feston, Nathaniel, 295
Field, Elizabeth, 95
  Rhoda, 129
  Ruth, 133
  Sarah, 95

Gilbert (cont-d)
  William, 321
Giles, Ebenezer, 34
Gillis, James, 60
Gilman, Peter, 101, 102
Gilmore, Hannah, 275
Glascock, Alice, 169
Glass, Esther, 43
  Hannah, 35
Glazier, Caroline F., 133
  David, 1
Gleason, Hannah, 339
  Molly, 336
Glover, Ebenezer, 196
  Hannah, 17
  Thomas, 146
Godbertson, Godbert, 237
Godfree, Benjamin, 200, 350
  George, 84
  Jonathan, 198
  Lydia, 83
  Richard, 88
Godfrey, David, 75, 86
  Deborah, 197
  Desire, 197
  Elizabeth, 79, 197
  George, 197, 198, 350
  Hannah, 245, 352
  James, 52
  Jephthah, 74
  Jonathan, 74
  Knowles, 198
  Mary, 52, 118, 197
  Mehitable, 202
  Mercy, 247, 352
  Moses, 197
  Richard (Jr.), 198
  Ruth, 74
  Ruth (Higgins), 75
  Sally, 76
Goff, Huldah, 87
  Jonathan, 252
  Philip, 326
Goldthwait, John, 193
Goodale, Walter, 101
Goodhue, Nathaniel, 28
  William, 28
Gooding, Benjamin B., 240
  John, 240
  Joseph, 242
Goodnuf, Mary, 157
Goodridge, Sarah, 127
Goodspeed, Elizabeth, 227, 249
  Eunice, 230
  John, 227
  Mary, 227
  Phebe, 230
  Reliance, 249
  Roger, 249
  Ruth, 38, 327
  Sarah, 231
Goodwin, Harriet, 240
  Henry, 37, 47
  Jane, 219
  Lydia Coffin, 55
  Nathaniel, 313
  Thomas, 313, 360
Goodwyn, John, 193
Gookin, Dorothy, 102
Gool, Jacob, 259
Goold, Hannah, 134
Gordale, Ruth ( ), 31
Gordin, Anna (Mrs.), 290
Gordon, Agnes, 69
  James, 90
Gore, Christopher, 104
Gorham, Abigail, 211

Gorham (cont-d)
  Barnabas, 211
  Benjamin, 212
  Charles, 215
  Chloe, 215
  Deborah, 210, 225
  Desire, 206, 209, 211, 213, 343
  Ebenezer, 209, 344
  Elisha, 215
  Elizabeth, 213, 343
  Experience, 209
  French, 215
  George Washington, 215
  Greve, 215
  Hannah, 208, 209
  Isaac, 209
  Jabez, 208, 209
  James, 209, 344
  Job, 210
  John, 206, 209, 210, 344
  Joseph, 206, 211
  Josiah, 211
  Levi, 215
  Lois, 210
  Lydia, 211
  Mary, 210, 232
  Mehitable, 209
  Mercy, 209, 211, 218, 343
  Nathaniel, 210
  Octavia Wheeler, 215
  Polly, 216
  Rufus, 215
  Ruth, 239, 348
  Samuel, 211
  Sarah, 211, 219
  Shubael, 210, 211, 344
  Stephen, 210
  Temperance, 210, 211
  Thankful, 206, 209
  Thomas, 209
Gorton, Benjamin, 137
Goss, William Whitemore, 83
Gould, Abigail, 74
  Caleb, 68
  David, 75
  Elijah, 300
  Elisha, 68
  Elizabeth, 68, 74, 199
  Experience, 68
  Hannah, 17, 299
  Jane, 68
  John, 74
  Joseph, 68, 83
  Joshua, 68, 75
  Lucy, 83
  Lydia, 68
  Mary, 68
  Mehitable, 61, 68
  Nathaniel, 75
  Olive, 68
  Phebe, 75
  Rebecca, 58
  Richard, 75
  Sarah, 68
  Susanna, 83
  Thomas, 75
Gove, Daniel, 150
Gowing, Thomas, 28
Grafton, Elizabeth, 31
  Nathaniel, 31
  Priscilla, 31
Grant, Bathsheba, 237
  Rebecca, 95
Graunt, Nicholas, 111
Graves, Ebenezer, 193
  Samuel, 9
Gray, Alice, 103

Gray (cont-d)
  Amy, 242
  Andrew, 116, 189, 277
  Ann, 93, 346
  Anna, 103, 244, 286, 352
  Benjamin, 28
  Caroline Fales, 103
  Desire, 103
  Edward, 88, 103, 286, 350
  Elizabeth, 79, 104, 360
  Hannah, 82
  Hannah (Sturgis), 208
  Joanna, 171, 344
  John, 10, 54, 105, 357
  Joseph, 116
  Lucy, 48, 105
  Mary, 105, 118, 349
  Mary Ann, 103
  Mercy, 105, 171, 264, 344
  Rebecca, 286, 345
  Samuel, 105, 258, 301
  Sarah, 47, 85, 103, 178, 294, 315, 342
  Sophronia, 116
  Susanna, 83
  Sylvanus, 219
  T. Fales, 103
  Thomas, 79, 286, 325
  Thomas (Dr.), 103
  Thomas (Rev.), 103
  Wait, 105
Green, Anna, 98
  Anna (Mrs.), 99
  Bathsheba, 326
  Benjamin, 231
  Daniel, 225
  David, 193
  Desire, 326
  Isaac, 185
  James, 326
  Margaret, 43
  Mary, 326
  Mehitable, 130
  Sadie W., 18
  Sarah, 90, 325, 326
  Susanna, 58
  Timothy, 8
  Warren, 180, 326
  William, 208, 231, 325, 326, 344
Greene, Abigail (Mrs.), 326
  Henry Eugene, 86
  John, 102
  Nathaniel, 102
  Sarah, 226
  Thomas, 296
  William, 18
  William Henry, 86
Greenleaf, Stephen (Jr.), 68
Greenwood, Bettey, 52
  Elizabeth, 8, 50
  Lucy, 43
Grey, Phelinda R., 17
Griffen, Elizabeth, 285
Griffin, Hannah (Hoxie), 221
  Joseph, 27
  Sarah (Bassett), 27
Griffith, Rebecca, 250
Griffiths, Benjamin, 83
Grinell, Daniel, 3
  George, 3
  Sarah, 3
Grinnell, Lydia, 3, 6
  Mary, 3
  Priscilla, 3
  Rachel, 265
  Rebecca, 140
  Silvia, 262

384

388

Jenkins (cont-d)
  Hodiah, 230
  John, 75, 182
  Joseph, 182, 227, 230
  Lot, 206
  Lydia, 230
  Mercy, 338
  Nathan, 228
  Prudence, 230
  Shadrack, 196
  Thomas, 339
Jenks, John, 298
  Sukey, 226
Jenne, Caleb, 279, 329, 351
  Cornelius, 329
  Elizabeth, 141, 329, 332,
    336, 339
  Ephraim, 22
  Jethro, 329
  Levi, 329
  Mary, 142
  Parnell, 329
Jenney, Caleb, 279
  Elizabeth, 142
  Lettice, 329
  Levi, 13, 329, 361
  Mary, 329
  Patience, 150, 359
  Ruth, 329
  Susan, 329
  Susanna, 139, 305
Jennings, Edward, 37
  Elizabeth, 135, 228
  Ephraim, 132
  Eunice, 286
  Penelope, 329
Jerome, Amanda, 73
Jewett, Caleb, 45
Johnson, Abigail, 36
  Abigail Luce, 25
  Ann, 116
  Annis, 299
  Barnabas, 116
  Charlotte, 300
  Content, 116
  Damaris, 190
  Daniel, 108
  David, 116, 122
  Elbridge, 116
  Elizabeth, 69
  Emily, 25
  Hannah, 53, 129
  Isaac, 126
  Jacob, 96
  James, 116
  Jane, 116
  Joseph, 38, 116, 190, 351
  Joshua, 116
  Josiah, 304
  Katherine, 25
  Lydia, 211
  Margaret, 25
  Margaret (Adams), 116
  Martha, 173
  Mary, 3, 45, 107, 108, 180
  Patience, 323
  Rebecca, 123
  Robert, 116
  Ruth, 324
  Sally, 46
  Samuel, 53
  Sarah, 117, 251, 320
  Susan Elizabeth, 199
Jolls, Thomas, 101
Joms, Peter, 51
Jones, Abigail, 159, 221,
    259, 294
  Amos, 294, 351

Jones (cont-d)
  Anna, 293
  Anthony, 9
  Asa, 9
  Asa (Jr.), 250
  Benjamin, 293, 310
  Charles, 291
  Cornelius, 28, 227
  David (Dr.), 243
  Ebenezer, 294
  Elijah, 9
  Elisha, 68, 294
  Elizabeth, 294
  Elizabeth Ann, 300
  Ephraim, 241
  Ezekiel, 294
  Hannah, 16, 123, 125
  Hepzebath, 9
  Isaiah, 13
  Jemima, 294
  John, 9, 160, 294, 318,
    351
  John H., 9
  Joseph, 293
  Lydia, 285
  Marsena, 227
  Martha, 64, 167
  Nehemiah, 13
  Phebe, 144
  Ralph, 239
  Robert, 337
  Ruth, 294
  Samuel, 9, 275, 293, 294,
    357
  Sarah, 9, 116, 156, 271,
    293, 341, 342
  Thomas, 294
Jonson, James, 116
Jordon, Betsey, 176
  Esther, 114
  Relief, 63
  Samuel, 129, 218
Joselyn, Abraham, 263
  Emily, 53
Josselyn, Abraham, 269
  Henry, 293
Josslyen, Mary (Jr.), 269
Jotham, Luther, 121
Joy, Lydia, 69
  Nehemiah, 69
  Phebe (Coleman), 65
Joyce, Alethea ( ), 72
  Desire, 335
  Dorothy, 219
  Hosea, 219
  John, 282, 335
  Lydia, 211, 219
  Mary, 209, 344
  Mehitable, 219
  Seth, 153
  Thomas, 219
Judson, Elizabeth, 40
Justice, Elizabeth, 228

Kanady, Sarah, 272
Kannady, William, 164
Keen, Abigail, 256, 284
  Asa, 286
  Benjamin, 285
  Bethiah, 285
  Daniel, 285
  Eleanor, 29, 285, 356
  Ephraim, 255
  Galen, 285
  Grace, 286
  Hannah, 256
  Herbert, 286
  Hezekiah, 285

Keen (cont-d)
  Howland, 285, 361
  Isaac, 285
  Josiah, 284, 285, 290
  Levi, 286
  Lydia, 285
  Moses, 286
  Nathaniel, 286, 351
  Patience, 159
  Rebecca, 202
  Robert, 256
  Ruth, 284
  Samuel, 286
  Sarah, 159
  Snow, 286
  Snow (Jr.), 286
  Welthea, 256
Keene, Josiah, 284
  Lucy, 42
Keep, Lucy, 247
Keith, Abigail, 69
  Anna, 11
  Bethiah, 124
  David, 11
  Eleazer, 121
  Eliza Ann, 148
  Ephraim, 131
  Hannah, 128
  Harriet L., 11
  Ichabod, 242
  James (Jr.), 121
  John, 121, 131
  Lewis L., 11, 361
  Luther, 145
  Martha, 103
  Mary, 128
  Melatiah, 123
  Rebecca, 11
  Samuel, 135
  Susanna, 108, 131
  Timothy, 135
Kelley, Elmira, 333
Kellogg, Asher Porter, 188
Kemball, Jonathan, 193
Kemp, Patience, 3
Kempton, David, 143
  David Batchelder, 143
  Elizabeth, 142, 157, 315
  Lydia, 29, 143
  Ruth, 72
  Samuel, 285
  Samuel (Jr.), 267
  Thomas, 143
Kency, John, 194
Kennay, John, 197
Kennedy, Michael, 165
Kenney, Cyrus, 110
  Silas, 110
Kenrick, Betty Foster, 249
Kent, Abigail, 285
  Benjamin, 51
  Dorothea, 232
  Elizabeth, 164
  Ezekiel, 283
  Hannah, 71
  Hezekiah, 232
  James, 232
  John, 232
  Joseph, 232
  Lucy B., 254
  Lydia, 232
  Samuel, 28, 120
  Samuel (Jr.), 113
  Susanna, 232
Kenwrick, Samuel, 74
Kenyon, Katherine, 299
  Solomon H., 217
Kerby, Sibbel, 333

Mosher (cont-d)
Philip, 139
Rebecca, 139
Ruth, 139
Sarah, 262
Moshier, Maxon, 139
Mosier, Sarah, 64
Mott, Adam, 142
Ann, 139
Jacob, 142
John, 177
Moulton, Sarah, 97
Mountjoy, Hephzibah, 9
Mudge, Charity, 156
Mehitable, 237
Mulford, Elizabeth, 60
John, 244
Rachel (Treat), 79
Mullins, Priscilla, 341
Munro, David, 106
John, 297
Loretta Catherine, 78
Thomas, 298
William J., 338
Murch, Polly, 10
Murdock, Elizabeth, 143, 237
John, 278, 306
Phebe, 325
William, 291
Murray, Mary Gordon, 10
Murry, Nehemiah, 202
Muxham, Abigail (Mrs.), 130
Charity, 130
Deliverance, 130
Dinah, 130
Fear, 130
Hannah, 130
Hannah (Mrs.), 130
Isaac, 130
Lydia, 130
Nabby, 130
Patience, 130
Rhoda, 130
Ruth, 130
Mynard, Benejah (Dr.), 87
Myrick, Abigail, 81, 351
Alice, 192
Benjamin, 191
Constant, 82, 191, 351
Dorcas, 175
Elizabeth, 201
Elizabeth (Osborn), 182
Esther, 84
Hannah 189, 191, 353
Mary, 74
Mercy, 187, 192, 351
Nathaniel, 74, 191
Priscilla, 192
Ruth, 86, 192
Sally, 82
Sarah, 192
Thomas, 74
William, 192
Myricks, Mary, 142

Nash, Abigail, 148
Desire, 336
Esther, 148, 263
Isaac Randall, 302
Jane, 302
Joseph, 50
Melita Susan, 302
Samuel, 302
Silence, 148
Simeon, 302
Thomas, 302
Nason, Moses, 80, 81
William, 128

Neal, Lydia, 88
Mary, 325
Neale, Hannah, 16
Negus, Hannah, 22
Nelson, Abiah, 220
Abiel, 69
Amos, 220
Bathsheba, 45, 319
Charity, 220
Elizabeth, 220
Hannah, 156, 319, 320, 345
Hope, 164, 165, 220
John, 155, 220, 319, 351
Jonathan, 135
Josiah, 259
Lewis C., 51
Lois, 220, 229, 346
Lydia, 308
Mehitable, 158
Mercy, 13, 170
Robert, 111
Ruth, 220
Samuel, 319, 330, 358
Samuel Nichols, 319
Samuel (Rev.), 220
Sarah, 320
Thomas, 220
William, 220
Nettleton, William, 99
Newcomb, Abigail, 257
Andrew, 257
Bethiah, 109
Hezekiah, 54
Jemima, 54, 198, 361
Lucy, 180
Lydia, 195, 350
Mary, 217, 218
Mercy, 218, 257
Peter, 188
Robert, 245, 352
Simon, 198
Susanna, 249
Thomas, 198, 361
William, 218
Newell, Thomas, 37
Newhall, Dorothy, 129
Esther, 28
Eunice, 28
Hannah, 32
Michael, 27, 33
Sarah, 28
Sarah (Bassett)(Griffin),
27
Newland, Dency, 256
Jabez, 276
Jeremiah, 111
Newman, Noah, 232
William Henry Harrison, 175
Newport, John, 106
Newton, Hannah, 121
Percis, 113
Thankful, 123, 127
Nicholls, Mary, 170
Nichols, Bathsheba, 319
Calvin, 333
Chloe, 249
Eleazer, 249, 301
Howard, 317
Joel, 55
Matilda Crosby, 172
Patience, 225
Price, 311
Roger, 302
Samuel, 264
Susanna, 167
Thomas, 225
Nickerson, Caleb, 197
Caroline, 246

Nickerson (cont-d)
Deborah, 213, 244, 245
Ebenezer, 81, 178, 352
Eldridge, 175
Eliza, 35
Elizabeth, 201
Elizabeth ( ), 247
Francis, 42
Harriet Matilda, 245
Hester, 334
Israel, 55
Jane, 178
Jennie, 199
Julia Louisa, 201
Mary, 175, 251
Mary ( ), 201
Mehitable, 75
Mercy, 75, 198
Nehemiah (Jr.), 101
Nicholas, 218
Phebe, 85
Rachel, 179
Rachel (Maker), 187
Reuben, 246
Sarah, 186
Sarah (Bassett), 246
Seth, 178
Temperance, 246
Thankful, 178
William, 178
Zilpha, 214
Nickols, Dorothy, 246
Faxon, 164
Nightingale, Bethia, 19
Rebecca, 11
Nixon, Elizabeth, 113
Noble, Zerviah, 167
Nokes, Benjamin, 298
Nooning, Ann W., 38
Norcross, Abigail, 78
Daniel, 79
Joanna, 78
Norcut, Ephraim, 255
Norkut, William, 183
Norman, Ann, 51
Hope, 52
John, 30
Moses, 50, 51
Priscilla, 52
Priscilla Bradford, 52
Norris, Benjamin, 298
Hannah, 298
Jemima, 127
John, 298
Mary, 22, 193
Paul Vannis, 298
Samuel, 127
North, Hannah, 213
Mehitable, 302
Northey, John, 30
Joseph, 30
Mercy, 31
Mercy Craw, 30
Mercy Cross, 30
Sarah, 31
Norton, Dinah, 122
Sarah, 206, 207
Norwood, Thomas, 27
Nourse, Stedman, 18
Nowel, Thomas, 37
Nowell, Mary, 102
Mary (Carr), 223
Noyes, Jeremiah, 145
John, 49
Judith, 145, 151
Moses (Rev.), 70
Nicholas, 31
Silas, 51

Shareman, Jane, 337
Sharpe, Mary, 290
Sharrow, Catherine, 258
Sharswood, Mary, 70
Shattuck, Robert, 113
Shaw, Abigail, 14
  Abner, 163
  Betsy, 128
  Deborah, 140, 332
  Elijah, 103
  Elizabeth, 110, 116, 130,
    139
  Elizabeth ( ), 278
  Ella, 123
  Fanny, 190
  George, 84
  Grace, 301
  Hannah, 76, 90, 95, 184,
    301
  Ichabod, 103
  Isaac, 130
  James, 95, 134, 158, 229
  John, 128, 163
  Jonathan, 84, 215
  Judith, 110
  Lydia, 178
  Martha, 14
  Mary, 156, 189
  Mehitable, 271
  Persis, 305
  Phebe, 190
  Polly, 149
  Priscilla, 103, 215
  Rhoda, 140
  Roxa, 25
  Ruth, 95
  Samuel, 103
  Sarah, 163, 266
  Sibilla, 8
  Sophronia W., 165
  William, 127, 266, 361
  William (Jr.), 125
  Zachariah, 110
Shearman, Mary, 115
  Peace, 261
Sheburne, Dorothy, 102
  Sarah, 99
Sheldon, George, 262
  Isaac, 137
  Sally, 217
Shepard, Mary, 151
  Phebe, 246
  Susan B., 39
Shepardson, Zebediah, 118
Shepherd, Ruth, 278
Shepunghs, Philip Marion,
  137
Sherman, Aaron, 153
  Abigail, 153
  Bathsheba, 153
  Betty Doty, 5, 155, 358
  Caleb, 191
  Daniel, 137
  Desire (Doty), 275
  Ebenezer, 153
  Elisha, 153
  Elizabeth, 153
  Experience, 153, 278, 342
  Hannah, 153, 158, 191, 262,
    342
  Huldah, 294
  Jane, 338
  John, 53
  Margaret, 153, 348
  Mary, 36
  Mercy, 298
  Patience, 153
  Prudence, 29

Sherman (cont-d)
  Rachel, 153
  Rebecca, 337
  Robert, 154, 346
  Samuel, 282
  Sarah, 153
  Susanna, 220, 334
  Thankful, 154
  Thomas, 137
  William, 153, 272, 292,
    293, 342
  Zerviah, 22
Shileber, Jonathan, 26
Shippy, Letitia, 63
Short, Anna, 128
  Elizabeth, 171
  Judith, 233
  Lydia, 65
Shove, Yetmercy, 226, 228
Shreve, Mary, 214
Shurtlef, Susanna, 24
Shurtleff, Benjamin, 24
  Elizabeth (Lettice), 116
  Hannah, 118
  Joseph, 320
  Nathaniel, 282
Shurtliff, Sarah, 131
Shute, Richard, 27
  Richard (Jr.), 30
Sibley, Joseph, 221
  Sarah Smith, 159
Silley, Benjamin, 125
Silvester, Abner, 312, 358
  Chloe, 63
  Content, 312
  Elisha, 63
  Elizabeth, 312
  Eunice, 63
  Grace, 70
  Hannah, 63
  Israel, 69, 70
  Jacob, 63
  James, 63
  Joseph, 311, 312, 316, 353
  Lemuel, 65
  Lillis, 63
  Luke, 63
  Lurana, 63, 65
  Martha, 63
  Mary, 311, 324, 352
  Mercy, 269
  Nathaniel, 63
  Olive, 63
  Ruth, 118, 190, 250, 251,
    343, 345, 352
  Sarah, 312
  Solomon, 312
  Susanna, 312
  Thomas, 63, 93
  Thankful, 324, 352
  Warren, 63
  Zebulon, 63
Simmons, Aaron, 5, 92, 270
  Benjamin, 5, 277, 353
  Benoni, 6
  Consider, 6, 268, 358
  Edward, 6
  Elizabeth, 71, 256
  Hannah, 5
  Ichabod, 6, 353
  Isaac, 4
  Jedidiah, 4, 353
  Jehiel, 4
  John, 4, 5, 6, 71
  Jonathan, 6
  Joseph, 4, 6, 264, 358
  Joshua, 63, 277, 346
  Lemuel, 6

Simmons (cont-d)
  Levi, 4
  Lydia, 6, 67
  Martha, 4, 270
  Mary, 11, 153
  Mercy, 4, 353
  Moses, 4, 130, 346
  Nathaniel, 4, 6, 353
  Noah, 6, 71
  Philippi, 58
  Rebecca, 4, 5, 263, 271,
    345, 346
  William, 6, 346
  Zachariah, 6
Simms, Deborah, 261
Simonds, Hattie H., 49
Simonson, Miriam, 44
Simonton, Matthew, 155
Simpson, Mary (Mrs.), 99
Sims, John, 97, 98
  Phebe Adeline, 203
Sinclair, F.P., 33
Sisson, Content, 140
  James, 142, 303
  Lydia, 262
  Richard, 262
  Sarah, 142
Skeffe, Stephen, 283
Skiff, Deborah, 283
  Joseph, 222
  Mary, 221
  Nathan, 222
  Stephen, 283
Skiffe, Abigail, 283
  James, 207
  John, 206
  Lydia, 329, 343
  Sarah Crandall, 111, 207
Skinner, Abigail, 31
  Esther, 248
  Mary, 44
  Rachel, 228
  Sarah, 248
  Thomas, 31
Slack, Mary, 216
Slade, Esther, 151
  Ruth, 139
  Ruth H. (Macomber), 291
  Sarah, 272
Slate, Mehitable, 48
Slater, Peter, 37
Slew, Mary, 78
Slocum, Benjamin, 140
  Christopher, 137
  Mary, 262
Smale, John, 319
Small, Francis, 180
  Isaac, 319
  Julia A.F., 245
  Thankful, 184
  Zachariah, 183, 200
Smalledge, Elizabeth, 5
Smalley, Benjamin, 176
  Francis (Jr.), 180
  Francis (3d), 180
  Joshua, 197
  Mary, 174
Smith, Abiel, 288
  Abigail, 51, 143, 197, 202
  Abigail ( ), 218
  Agnes, 77
  Andrew, 111
  Anna, 64, 199, 232
  Annie, 233
  Archelans, 196, 197, 201
  Aznbah, 183
  Barnabas, 175
  Barney, 288

404

Washburn (cont-d)
Anna, 11, 355
Asa, 129
Barnabas, 35
Barnebas, 125
Benjamin, 36, 122, 123, 124, 127, 131, 359
Betsey P., 25
Betty, 127
Bezaleel, 124
Charles F., 124
Content, 126, 351
Cyrus, 123, 129
Daniel, 123, 127
Deliverance, 124, 125, 127, 132
Deliverance (Orcutt), 132
Ebenezer, 35, 123, 124, 129
Edward, 123, 125, 354
Edward (Jr.), 123
Eleazer, 123, 124, 131, 359, 361
Eliab, 125
Elisha, 36
Elizabeth, 124, 125, 127
Elizabeth (Shaw), 110, 116
Ephraim, 36, 71, 127, 354
Eunice, 125, 131
Ezekiel, 125, 127
Ezra, 128
Ezra (Jr.), 123
George B., 124
Gideon, 126
Hannah, 94, 122, 124, 131, 352
Harriet, 317
Hephzibah, 127, 132
Hiram, 124
Huldah, 127, 270, 359
Ichabod, 36
Isaac, 123, 125
Isaiah, 123
Israel, 124, 131
Jabez, 36, 120, 354
James, 125, 126
Jane, 124, 126, 131, 149, 354
Japhet, 127
Jemimah, 124
Jeremiah, 125
Joanna, 124
John, 35, 36, 113, 122, 124, 126, 359
John (Jr.), 251
Jonah, 126
Jonah (Jr.), 123
Jonathan, 123, 124, 125, 127, 129, 354
Joseph, 107, 126, 127, 129, 347
Joshua, 131
Josiah, 123, 125, 126, 127, 354
Kezia, 128
Leonard, 124
Lettice, 126
Lettis, 126
Levi, 125
Linus, 123, 124
Linus (Capt.), 124
Lois, 307
Luther, 123
Lydia, 124, 125, 127
Marsena, 131
Martha, 125, 352
Mary, 25, 96, 108, 113, 114, 122, 129, 346, 360, 361

Washburn (cont-d)
Mercy, 29, 35, 172, 250, 344, 349, 352
Moses, 126, 355
Nathan, 123
Nathaniel, 123, 126, 359
Nehemiah, 123, 131
Olive, 124
Oliver, 125
Peter, 126
Phebe, 127
Phoebe, 124
Polly, 118
Rebecca, 122, 124, 126
Renel, 124
Robert, 124
Salmon, 123
Sampson, 131, 362
Samson, 123
Samuel, 122, 131, 132
Sarah, 124, 126, 131, 132, 328
Seth, 36, 125, 128, 129
Seth (Jr.), 124
Silence, 131
Solomon, 124, 125, 132
Stephen, 124
Susanna, 11, 124, 128
Tabitha, 124
Thankful, 36, 127
Thomas, 132, 355
Wealthy, 128
William, 126, 127, 271
Zenas, 127, 131
Zerviah, 125
Zilpha, 125
Washburne, Jane, 145
Waterman, Abiah, 284
Abigail, 283
Ann, 233
Anna, 223
Anthony, 10, 22, 105, 283, 347, 359
Benjamin, 23, 46
Bethiah, 284
Deborah, 284
Elizabeth, 114, 283, 306, 343
Freeman, 149, 359
Ichabod, 26, 246, 359
Isaac, 22, 279, 359
James, 22
John, 22, 24, 355
Jonathan, 23
Joseph, 282, 283, 284, 347
Josiah, 26
Jotham (Rev.), 284
Lucy, 23
Lucy (Sampson), 266
Lydia, 92, 284, 355
Mary, 71, 350
Mary (West), 314
Nathaniel, 286
Orphan, 282, 346, 349
Perez, 23
Priscilla, 26
Rebecca, 26, 71, 350
Robert, 23, 26, 355
Samuel, 26, 144, 158, 355
Sarah, 284
Seth, 26
Thomas, 26, 35, 283, 355, 359
Waters, Asa, 39
Chloe, 39
Hannah, 31
Hezekiah, 289
Isaiah (Rev.), 289

Waters (cont-d)
Luther, 289
William, 31
Zebulon, 39
Watrons, Mehitable, 238
Watson, Elkanah, 340
John, 233
Mary, 83, 85
Matthew, 233
Mercy, 82
Mercy (Hedge), 82
Phebe, 85
Wautier, Alexandre, 113
Wayt, Ezra, 27
Weaver, Jonathan, 52
Mary (Evans), 52
Weaving, Margaret Agnes, 78
Webb, Christopher, 18
Darius, 44, 58
Ebenezer, 44
Jerusha, 19
Joshua, 44
Lucretia, 325
Margaret, 309
Mary, 306
Peter, 19
Priscilla, 19
Samuel, 44
Sarah, 18
Thomas S., 194
Thomas Smith, 194
Webber, Mary, 269
Webster, John, 48
Lois, 241
Noah, 49
Taylor, 156
William, 156
Weeks, Lydia, 147
Nathaniel, 69
Welch, James, 36
Weld, Edward, 297
Sarah, 14
Wells, Meriah, 302
Wendall, Lucretia, 213
Wendell, John Hunt, 290
Wensley, Sarah, 97, 340
Wentworth, Edward, 135
Polly, 289
Wesson, Caroline S., 362
Caroline Stevens, 85
West, Abigal, 251
Anne, 142
Bartholomew, 139
Benjamin, 273
Bethiah, 285
Betty, 114, 285, 359
Charles, 273
Elizabeth, 273
Esther, 250
Francis, 273
Hannah, 139, 142, 350
Huldah, 274
Jean, 324
John, 273
Josiah, 285
Judah, 285
Luna, 215
Lydia, 169, 285, 350
Martha, 273
Mary, 283, 314
Parnel, 329
Pelatiah, 10
Rebecca, 285
Rebecca (Wetherhead), 320
Samuel, 4, 124, 127, 139, 274, 285
Samuel (Elder), 274
Sarah, 150, 273

412

West (cont-d)
Stephen, 139
Susanna, 273
Thomas, 274, 283, 298, 329
Thomas (Elder), 273
Thomas (Rev.), 2
William, 273
Westgate, Earl, 137
Elizabeth ( ), 137, 233
George, 137
John, 137
Rebecca, 137
Weston, Abigail, 123
Abigail A., 165
Abner, 270, 279, 359
Benjamin, 270, 274, 276
Daniel (Capt.), 287
David, 266
Edmund, 270, 355
Elnathan, 5
Esther, 259
Ezra, 104
Hannah, 163
Harvey, 270, 361
Ichabod, 267
Isaac, 271
James, 271
John, 271, 274
John Granger, 271
Judith, 43
Lewis, 270, 359
Marcia, 117
Mary, 4, 123, 190, 270,
355
Mehitable, 271
Nathan, 271, 275, 347
Patty, 312
Rebecca, 12, 271
Rhoda, 72
Samuel, 5
Sarah, 277
Susanna, 328
Thomas, 5, 132, 231
William, 270, 355, 359
Zachariah, 271
Wetherel, William, 174
Wetherell, Daniel, 61
Elizabeth (Lothrop), 314
Hannah, 61, 70, 345
Hannah ( ), 320
Mary, 61
Mercy, 208
Wetherhead, Rebecca, 320
Remembrance, 323
Thomas, 328
Wheat, Hannah, 44
Solomon (Dr.), 43
Wheatley, Sarah, 193
Wheaton, Christian, 169
Wheelding, Joseph, 208
Wheeler, Catharine S., 1
Emma, 1
Isaac, 1
Mary, 148
Mary Ann, 1
Obadiah, 337
Rebecca S., 1
Robert, 1
Samuel, 321
Williard (Capt.), 1
Wheelock, Jerome, 103
Ralph, 280
Welden, Joseph, 329
Wheldon, Katherine, 191
Whetstone, Hannah ( ), 327
Whippe, Jane, 9
Whipple, Abigail, 298
Dorothy, 134

Whipple (cont-d)
Hope, 308
Peter, 308
William, 308
Whippo, James, 326
Whiston, Sarah, 225
Whitcomb, Candace, 299
Jonathan, 299
White, Abigail, 141, 166,
332, 333, 336
Abijah, 287, 334, 355
Abner, 140, 332
Alvan, 337
Andrew, 140
Anna, 279, 332, 334, 337,
339
Anne, 18, 335
Benjamin, 154, 332, 333,
336
Caleb, 337
Catharine, 154
Christiana, 334
Christopher, 140
Christopher T., 140
Cornelius, 333
Daniel, 333, 334
David, 338
David D., 140
Deborah, 337, 338
Dorcas, 335
Ebenezer, 334
Ebenezer (Rev.), 184
Eleazer, 334
Elijah, 204
Elisabeth, 291, 336
Eliza A., (Mrs.), 338
Elizabeth, 140, 332, 337
Endoxa, 178
Esther, 335
Experience, 336
Ezra S., 337
George, 140, 320, 332, 333,
337
Gideon, 334, 355
Hannah, 12, 19, 139, 140,
332, 333, 336, 354
Hnnah Ruggles, 335
Harriet A., 140
Haturah, 336
Holder, 336
Hope, 338
Humphry, 333
Israel, 140, 332
James, 337
Jane, 338
Jedidah, 58, 71
Jedidiah, 337
Jerathunael, 336
Joanna, 334, 340, 355
Job, 275, 276
John, 334, 337, 338, 339,
347
John (2d), 275
Jonathan, 332, 334, 335
Joseph, 334, 335
Josiah, 337
Judith, 339
Justice, 337
Justus, 337, 338
Kate, 334
Katharine, 338
Keziah ( ), 129
Keziah (Hall), 132
Lemuel, 334
Lizzie F., 338
Love, 332, 336, 338
Lucy A., 299
Lusanna, 335, 355

White (cont-d)
Lydia, 87
Malatiah, 339
Margaret, 339
Margret, 332
Martha, 337
Mary, 261, 263, 332, 335,
336, 337, 338, 354
Mary A. (Almy), 140
Mehitable, 267
Melatiah, 337
Melletiah, 337
Merchant, 338
Mercy, 153, 333, 338, 342
Micah, 96
Minerva, 338
Molly, 333
Nathan (Jr.), 20
Nathaniel, 337
Nathaniel (Dr.), 242
Noah, 140
Obadiah, 334
Obed, 332, 336
Oliver, 141
Paul, 334
Peleg, 140, 332, 336
Penelope, 332, 339
Pennelabe, 338
Peregrine, 140, 333, 337
Phineas, 338
Priscilla, 338
Rachel, 20
Rebecca, 332
Resolved, 336, 337, 338
Resolved (Capt)., 337
Rhoda, 332
Roger, 140, 141, 332, 336
Rufus, 337
Ruth, 123, 141, 332, 336
Ruth D., 140
Sally, 336
Samuel, 332, 333, 336, 337
Samuel (Jr.), 335
Sarah, 140, 141, 238, 289,
334, 335
Seth, 339
Silvanus, 338
Silvenus, 332
Susanna, 337
Susanna ( ), 340
Sylvanus, 337
Tabitha, 338
Thankful, 184, 334, 358
Theophilus, 332
Theophis, 336
Thomas, 140, 141, 332, 334,
336, 337, 338, 339
Timothy, 337
Urania, 334
William, 140, 332, 338,
339, 347, 359
William (Jr.), 332, 336
William S., 337
William (2d), 332
William (3d), 336
Whitfield, Rebecca, 147
Whitford, Mary, 27
Samuel, 32
Whiting, Ann, 39
Charles, 49
Elizabeth, 40
Elizabeth Bartlett, 41
Ephraim, 40
John, 40
Samuel, 40
Samuel (Rev.), 39
Sarah Cornelia, 40
Sybil, 39